THE CURRICULUM
STUDIES READER

THE CURRICULUM STUDIES READER

EDITED BY

DAVID J. FLINDERS

AND

STEPHEN J. THORNTON

Routledge
New York   London

Published in 1997 by

Routledge
29 West 35 Street
New York, NY 10001

Published in Great Britain by

Routledge
11 New Fetter Lane
London EC4P 4EE

Copyright © 1997 by Routledge, Inc.

Printed in the United States of America on acid-free paper.

Library of Congress Cataloging-in-Publication Data

The curriculum studies reader / David J. Flinders and Stephen J. Thornton, editors.
   p. cm.
   Includes bibliographical references and index.
   ISBN 0-415-91697-6 (hc : alk. paper.) — ISBN 0-415-91698-4 (pbk. alk. paper)
   1. Education—United States—Curricula—Philosophy.   2. Curriculum planning—United States.   3. Curriculum change—United States.
I. Flinders, David J., 1955–   .   II. Thornton, Stephen J.
974′.000972—DC21   96-49542
                                    CIP

British Library Cataloging-in-Publication Data also available.

Contents

Introduction

What do schools teach, what should they teach, and who should decide? Is the primary aim of education to instill basic skills or to foster critical thinking? Should education aim to mold future citizens, to engender personal development, or to inspire academic achievement? Must education have an aim? And what beliefs, values, or attitudes are learned from the way classrooms are? That is, what lessons are acquired but taken for granted, taught but not planned? These are some of the perennial questions around which curriculum scholars have organized theory, research, teaching, and program evaluation. Collectively, such efforts constitute the academic study of curriculum and the focus of this book.

Focus, admittedly, may not be quite the right word because it implies a clearly delineated topic. Our topic, the field of curriculum studies, sprawls out like the seemingly endless suburbs of a modern megalopolis. Its wide reach overlaps with every subject area; with cultural, political, and economic trends; with philosophical concerns; and with social issues. It would seem that contemporary models of development and research draw on increasingly diverse disciplinary perspectives and increasingly diverse methods of inquiry. That diversity can bewilder those unfamiliar with the field's intellectual terrain. Others see both the need and the room for still greater diversity. Even if this were not the case, the current range of work makes it useful to develop broad perspectives from which to identify the field's various regions and familiar landmarks. Yet, the trade-offs of accommodation are involved here as well. The more inclusive one's perspective, the more challenging it is to represent the field in ways that clearly illustrate its contributions to educational policy and practice.

Our choice in responding to this challenge is to represent the field, its various regions and familiar landmarks, through the genre of a "reader"—a collection of informed and influential writings. All of the writings in this reader are previously published articles, book chapters, research reports, or excerpts from larger works that sample the past and present trends of curriculum scholarship. The primary advantage of this approach is not comprehensiveness but rather the opportunity it allows for getting close to the ideas and debates that have inspired such wide interest in curriculum issues to begin with. Like other curriculum textbooks, this reader seeks to cast a broad net by attending to the field at large rather than a certain type of curriculum work or area of specialization. However, the views and perspectives introduced in this collection do not stand above the fray of academic disagreements, arguments, and strongly held convictions.

On the contrary, the reader is intentionally designed to capture some of the contentious discourse and outright disputes for which the curriculum field is known. This animation of ideas and values plays an important role because it has nurtured the field in unlikely settings and through otherwise lean times. Surprisingly to some, the study of curriculum has held its own, even flourished, when no national crisis demanded an immediate educational response, when no vast infusion of federal dollars poured into research and development, when no mobs of angry parents clamored at the schoolhouse door, and when no technological marvels promised new ways to build better curricular mouse traps. All of these factors have had their day, and many are likely to recur in the future. Yet, with or without any added impetus, the questions of curriculum theory and practice are questions that have captured the imagination of educators from one generation to the next.

The early sections of this reader are designed to provide enough historical information for beginning students of curriculum to appreciate the antecedents and changing social contexts in which the field's contemporary traditions are rooted. Also, all of the writings throughout the reader vary with respect to their scope. Some are broadly conceived around the purposes and politics of schooling in general; others focus on particular topics such as tracking, the use of instructional objectives, or curriculum integration. Even the most narrowly focused of these readings, however, illustrate recurrent themes—old wine in new bottles, so to speak. Moreover, the issues raised typically cut across a variety of subject areas and levels of education. One could reasonably argue that basic curriculum issues, or at least some of those issues, extend well beyond schooling to include the concerns of anyone interested in how people come to acquire the knowledge, skills, and values that they do.

Be that as it may, our collection does focus mainly on the types of learning that are intended to take place in schools and classrooms. This focus is still significantly broad, and as with any book of this kind, the difficult task has been to winnow down an extremely large body of material by selecting only a sample of that material. Having done so, we cannot claim to be representing the field in a comprehensive way. The situation is not unlike a common story told among qualitative researchers. Those familiar with ethnographic work like to ask anthropologists just returning from the field whether they have captured the entire culture of the group being studied. The question is asked tongue-in-cheek because all but the most naive know full well the impossibility of that task. Like those returning anthropologists, we are unable to provide a complete or definitive account of all that is going on in the field. This limitation may sound harsh, but it can also be viewed together with another adage from social research—that a person is not required to know everything in order to learn something.

To say that this book was created by sampling a much larger body of scholarship leaves unanswered the questions of what criteria were used in selecting that sample. How did we choose some readings over others, and for what reasons? While this process was almost always more complex than anticipated, three concerns stand out as having a prominent influence on our decisions. First, we sought to include work that is well recognized within the field. This criterion is not so much a matter of name recognition as it is a matter of a work's endurance or impact on how others think about curriculum issues. In a few cases, we have included authors (John Dewey, for example) who might not be considered curriculum scholars per se, but whose ideas have been so influential to curriculum studies that they can be considered part of the intellectual traditions on which others continue to build.

Writers who achieve this type of legacy also tend to be those who are grappling with ideas and problems that often surface in different areas of curriculum practice. In other words, certain issues and problems are recurrent or even thematic to the point of being recognized as common to the field. We looked for writings that possess this thematic quality because they lend continuity to the particulars of practice, and without that continuity it would be difficult to connect the otherwise broad range of topics on which curriculum scholarship is carried out.

A second consideration in deciding the book's content has been our desire to include pivotal work. This consideration has played out in an effort to identify writings that most clearly signal turning points in the development of the field, or that serve as prototypes for exploring issues previously taken for granted. Exactly what constitutes ground-breaking work is conceptually difficult to pin down. Nevertheless, our aim is to represent not only the continuity of the field but also its dynamic qualities. The field is constantly changing, if not always in its underlying philosophical concerns, then in the field's ways of responding to those concerns. Topics come and go as well, and some areas of current interest such as AIDS education could not have been anticipated by earlier generations.

The first two considerations we have mentioned concern the conceptual foundations and development of the field. Our third consideration differs by emphasizing pedagogy. Because we teach curriculum courses at both the undergraduate and graduate levels, we often found our attention drawn to work that is accessible across a wide range of interests. We have also tried to select examples of scholarship that avoid the jargon of education or its supporting disciplines. Much of the work in curriculum studies is and should be intellectually challenging, but some of that work (as in all fields) is challenging for reasons unnecessary to understanding its subject matter. We hope to have sampled only from the most accessible work available.

The final issue we want to address concerns the organization of the book's content. Overall, the readings are divided into four parts. Part I, "Looking Back: A Prologue to Curriculum Studies," is centered on the work of three prominent figures: Franklin Bobbitt, John Dewey, and George Counts. Their writings are brought together with a historical critique that introduces some of the early traditions of curriculum scholarship. By tracing out related developments, the readings in this section allow us to touch base with the precedents that those in the field were to both build upon and rebel against.

Part II, "Curriculum at Education's Center Stage," sets out to illustrate the optimism and contradictions of an era marked by unparalleled national support for curriculum reform. Whatever complacency Americans had for education seemed to vanish with the launch of Sputnik I in 1957. For almost two decades after that event, hardly anyone questioned the need and urgency for large-scale curriculum reform. Yet, this same period is remembered for an increasing sense of uneasiness within the field. Debates grew over how curriculum work should be carried out, earlier traditions became the targets of renewed criticism, and greater scrutiny was given to the field's underlying purposes.

These undertones of discontent were not short-lived. On the contrary, they were only an omen for the soon-to-blossom reconceptualist movement. Among other achievements, the reconceptualists brought into focus the socio-political and cultural dimensions of curriculum with greater emphasis and clarity than had earlier generations. Their efforts to do so are represented in Part III, "Pondering the Curriculum." This section, nevertheless, is still diverse because the reconceptualists were not of one mind, nor are they the only voices included in this group of readings. Curriculum studies had taken a reflective turn that is today very much alive and well, but the field's most conventional scholarship did not stop simply because other ways of understanding that scholarship were made more readily available. To put this another way, the field annexed new territory rather than moved to a new location.

This annexation of various topics, ideas, and perspectives is examined further in Part IV, "After a Century of Curriculum Thought." Our aim in this section is to survey the field's contemporary issues and continuing dilemmas. The organization of these readings may at first seem lax and unbridled, which is just how some people have come to view the field. Topics range from the ecological crisis to the growing debate over national standards. The readings were selected to illustrate in as concrete a way as possible the breadth of issues on which today's curriculum scholars work. The final three readings, however, are an exception to this approach. Their authors step back from topical concerns to assess the broader contributions of curriculum scholarship and their impact on educational reform.

If we were pressed to summarize what this final set of readings has to say about the current state of the field and its future directions, we would have to fall back on the truism that "much changes while staying the same." But that comment is not at all meant to be glib. Changes in both the tenor and focus of contemporary work make a difference in what receives attention and what does not. Contemporary trends make a difference in discussions of educational policy and practice, and they make a difference in the levels of sophistication at which those discussions are carried out. In current decision making at the levels of research, policy and practice, informed points of view are valued by those engaged in such work. Moreover, the need for informed scholarship in the near future would seem to be increasing.

I

LOOKING BACK:
A PROLOGUE TO
CURRICULUM STUDIES

Curriculum theorizing and development are as old as educating institutions because any educational program must have a content. Although theorists and practitioners have (often without conscious awareness) dealt with curriculum questions since at least the time of Plato's design for education in his ideal state, the notion of curriculum as a professional or scholarly field is recent. Historically, curriculum decisions were largely left to that small, usually elite, portion of the public most directly concerned with the operation of schools. In the United States, curriculum began to emerge as a field of scholarly inquiry and professional practice only toward the close of the nineteenth century, a time that roughly coincided with the rise of public schooling for the masses.

The burgeoning population of the public schools at the dawn of the twentieth century was only one of a number of tumultuous and consequential developments in American life. One result of all this upheaval was the Progressive movement, a broad-based effort aimed at assuring the realization of American ideals in an increasingly ur-ban–industrial and pluralistic nation (Cremin, 1964, pp. 8–10). Thus, the first self-conscious curriculum scholars saw their work as part of this broader reformation of American life. The responses of the progressive educational reformers were to institutionalize many of the now characteristic features of school curriculum, including such practices as tracking, standardized testing, and civic education (Tyack, 1974).

Although early curriculum specialists frequently perceived themselves as "progressives," these educational reformers, like their fellow progressives in politics and other fields, worked with diverse, even contradictory, conceptions of what "progressive" meant (see Curti, 1959; Kliebard, 1986; Lagemann, 1989). Thus, from its earliest days, the curriculum field has been characterized by vigorous disagreements about its proper aims and practices. For example, the various meanings assigned by curriculum specialists to terms such as "learning," "community," and "democracy" are not merely esoteric concerns with no consequences for the world of practice. To the contrary, how one defines terms to a great extent determines the resulting character of educational practice.

The first set of readings we introduce includes three of the seminal early formulations of the curriculum field: the work of Franklin Bobbitt, John Dewey, and George S. Counts. Each of these formulations retains an important contemporary presence in curriculum scholarship (see Eisner & Vallance, 1974). In this sense, conflicting conceptions of curriculum have never been an aberration in the field, but rather have been present since the first generation of curriculum scholarship. Indeed, the work of the first two early curriculum scholars we will encounter, Franklin Bobbitt and John Dewey, exemplify how different archetypes of the meaning of "curriculum" result in radically different views of educational aims and practice.

When he wrote *The Curriculum* (1918), Bobbitt was a professor of educational administration at the University of Chicago as well as a sought-after curriculum consultant to school districts across the nation. He is an apt starting point for tracing the development of professional curriculum scholarship and practice in the United States as the essentials of his approach to curriculum have been dominant in practice ever since. Moreover, Bobbitt was a self-proclaimed pioneer of the field, asserting in the excerpt reproduced in this volume to be presenting the "first" curriculum textbook. Although it is not self-evident what constitutes the "first" curriculum textbook, Bobbitt's claim is often conceded. In any case, there is no doubt that Bobbitt's *The Curriculum* has had enduring influence, particularly in its insistence that curriculum developers begin with the identification of proper goals.

"Pioneer" implies finding one's way in unfamiliar terrain, but Bobbitt seems to have had few doubts that he was headed in the right direction. He epitomized the "can-do" attitude of the new professional elites of the Progressive era, a time when "professionals" in a variety of fields were increasingly considered the preferred means by which a forward-looking society addressed its problems. Bobbitt was quite sure of what ailed curriculum making: for too long it had been in the hands of amateurs and it was high time it became a professional undertaking.

Bobbitt was convinced that professional knowledge applicable to curriculum work could be found in the logic of "scientific management," which had been applied to raising worker productivity in industry (Callahan, 1962, pp. 79–94). In a nutshell, Bobbitt believed that curriculum work, like work in industry, should be managed in the interests of efficiency and the elimination of waste. These same interests after all, it seemed obvious to Bobbitt and many of his contemporaries, in significant respects accounted for the world preeminence of the United States' manufacturing industry. Use of the same methods would bring the same world-class standards to the school curriculum.

Bobbitt's claim that curriculum work was out of date, having not kept pace with other advances in schooling, is almost poignant. *The Curriculum* was Bobbitt's solution to this unfortunate state of affairs. As he makes plain in the preface, he proposed to lay out how curriculum can be constructed in a manner that honors scientific procedures. For Bobbitt, "scientific" suggested a systematic series of procedures, carried out by curriculum professionals, prior to implementation in a school district (see Eisner, 1985).

The content of any given curriculum, according to Bobbitt, could be "discovered" by a process of surveying what "successful" adults know and can do. In turn, the results of this process of discovery would be used to formulate educational objectives from which the curriculum scope and sequence (i.e., what is taught and in what order) would be derived. After instruction with this kind of curriculum, therefore, students would be prepared to lead "successful" lives in their adult years.

Efficiency, of course, suggests not only smooth operating procedures but minimization of "waste" as well. Thus, in addition to scientific curriculum making, Bobbitt wanted to minimize sources of wasted instructional time. He believed that diagnostic testing and other procedures proposed by behavioral psychologists such as Edward L. Thorndike would make possible prediction of the kind of errors students typically made (Lagemann, 1989). This would enable more efficient curriculum making as well as prevent more time being spent on the costly business of instruction, especially grade-level retention of students which Bobbitt considered enormously wasteful. As in industrial enterprises, Bobbitt wanted to maximize output (i.e., student learning) at minimum cost (i.e., paying teachers). This outlook also had significance for the content of the curriculum as Bobbitt did not want to invest scarce resources in subjects such as literature, history, and geography where it was difficult to specify their exact utility in adult life.

Because Bobbitt's approach to curriculum work was based, he argued, on a dispassionate analysis of what youngsters needed to lead productive lives as adults, he dismissed arguments about the interests of children as irrelevant to the educational process. Moreover, Bobbitt did not question whether the existing social and economic order was just; he merely took that for granted. Hence, he saw the aim of schooling as matching individuals with the existing social and economic order (Lagemann, 1989, p. 212).

Dewey's view of curriculum provides a vivid contrast with Bobbitt's. Although at different times both Dewey and Bobbitt served on the faculty of the University of Chicago, the contrasts between the two men are more revealing than their similarities. Bobbitt believed curriculum work was a practical task whose only need for theoretical justification had been "discovered" analyzing the behavior of successful adults. Although Dewey had founded and directed the Laboratory School at the University of Chicago, he spent most of his professional life as a philosophy professor at Columbia University. And while he was also involved with the more practice-oriented world of Columbia's Teachers College, Dewey's greatest interest in problem solving was in the world of ideas, not in the mechanics of consulting in school districts about curriculum development. This by no means suggests, however, that Dewey lacked concern about the consequences for education raised by the work of Bobbitt and other adherents of the social efficiency branch of progressivism.

Dewey recognized only too well that, if one accepted Bobbitt's premises about learning, the nature of American society, the primacy of efficiency as an educational goal and so forth, then Bobbitt's industrial metaphor for curriculum development followed in a disarmingly straightforward manner. Dewey, however, emphatically rejected Bobbitt's premises. Where the latter said the starting point of curriculum development was the adult, Dewey said it was the experience of the child. Where Bobbitt embraced efficiency as an overarching goal, Dewey claimed the goal of education was the growth of experience of the individual. Bobbitt claimed curriculum should be developed prior to instruction; for Dewey, curriculum designated an outcome of the interactions among students, materials, and the teacher. Where Bobbitt embraced behaviorist theories of learning, Dewey saw them as impoverished and inadequate explanations of how learning takes place. And, whereas Bobbitt saw schools as a buttress of the existing social and economic order, Dewey saw schools as a means of extending and reforming democratic, community life in the United States.

Dewey's theory of curriculum has been often and widely misunderstood, even by those purporting to be his followers. In this regard, he wrote toward the end of his career *Experience and Education* (1938) because he believed, for example, his insistence on curriculum planning beginning with the experience of the child was being wrongly interpreted as disdain for the "progressive organization of subject-matter" (see Kliebard, 1986, pp. 237–238). There is, in fact, a remarkable consistency to Dewey's writing on curriculum, extending over more than a half-century.

At the heart of Dewey's theory of curriculum is the coordination of psychological and social factors in education. As he observed in the version of *My Pedagogic Creed* (1929) reproduced in this volume, the "educational process has two sides, one psychological and one sociological, and . . . neither can be subordinated to the other . . . without evil results following." Although Bobbitt's conception of curriculum also dealt with psychological and social factors, his ideas about them contrast starkly with Dewey's. Bobbitt's reliance on behaviorist methods to stimulate learning for Dewey signified external imposition whose effects "cannot truly be called educative." Indeed, Dewey pointed out that the effects of such imposition may be harmful to the child's educational growth. Similarly, where Bobbitt argued that adult society is the mold for the school curriculum, Dewey said such a view "results in subordinating the freedom of the individual to a preconceived social and political status." "True education," Dewey insisted, "comes through the stimulation of the child's powers by the demands of the social situations in which he finds himself." This, of course, meant that the focus of educational programs had to be on the reconstruction of children's present experience. Only through living in the present could children be prepared for the future.

What would Dewey's ideal curriculum look like in practice? Although too lengthy a question to answer fully here, probably the most authentic answer can be obtained by examination of the laboratory school Dewey established and oversaw during his years at the University of Chicago (see Mayhew & Edwards, 1966; Tanner, 1991). Nonetheless, in broad terms, Dewey's curriculum broke down the barriers, customary in schools a century ago as well as today, between children's life experiences and their experiences in the classroom. Hence, the heart of the curriculum would be activities based on a simplification of "existing social life." In this scheme of things, boundaries between traditional school subjects would be traversed. Children might, for example, examine how the local community deals with its problems and, in this context, develop measuring skills ordinarily assigned to mathematics, drawing skills ordinarily assigned to art, map skills ordinarily assigned to geography, and so forth. The logical organization of school subjects, Dewey insisted, was the organizational schema of adults; children require the "psychological" organization of subject matter, moving gradually toward adult modes of understanding associated with formal school subjects.

Dewey's curriculum would also transform the role of the teacher and the learner. Rather than transmitting a predetermined curriculum to students, the teacher would act more as guide to channel the child's natural curiosity in educationally productive directions. Thus, curriculum would be jointly planned rather than imposed.

Dewey wanted to discard passive learning imposed on children and capitalize on their natural interests and curiosities. In this way, the child is both motivated to learn and actively engaged in his or her own educational growth.

In sum, the school, for Dewey, was an integral part of community life; it was also an instrument for social reform. Whereas Bobbitt saw the school as an agent of social reproduction, Dewey portrayed "the school as the primary and most effective interest of social progress and reform." Just as there should be no strict boundary between community life and the curriculum, the latter for Dewey held the potential for society to remake itself.

If remaking society was an integral component of Dewey's theory of curriculum, it was almost the singular goal of George S. Counts. From the time of his earliest, major works in the 1920s, Counts was concerned with the injustices of democracy and capitalism in the United States, particularly as they played out in the context of schooling (see Kliebard, 1986, pp. 184–189). Like Dewey, Counts grew increasingly restive with "child-centered," progressive educators who appeared to be ignoring the social context of education in the business-dominated atmosphere of the 1920s. For Counts, the seemingly dominant stream of progressive education spoke to the "needs" of the child as though these had meaning outside of the society in which education unfolded.

The catastrophic economic slump of the 1930s ushered in a much more receptive environment for the disenchanted intellectual critics of the business civilization of the 1920s. American social thought became more polarized, and collectivist thought enjoyed possibly its most widespread popularity in the history of the United States (see Bowers, 1969). Counts caught the spirit of the times when he remarked in *Dare the School Build a New Social Order?* (1932) that "the so-called 'practical' men of our generation—the politicians, the financiers, the industrialists"—had acted selfishly and bungled the well-being of Americans. Counts appealed for teachers to lead the schools and the public "for social regeneration." For Counts and his fellow social reconstructionists, several of the most prominent of whom such as Harold Rugg were Counts' colleagues at Teachers College, Columbia University, it seemed apparent that the age of collectivism had arrived.

Aspects of Counts' vision of a regulated and directed economy in order to serve more than society's elite were, of course, consistent with the more radical elements of the New Deal yet to come. Indeed, it is a sign of how in touch with the times Counts was that later some of his main ideas were to find their parallels in the words and policies of President Franklin D. Roosevelt during the early New Deal years. Nevertheless, given what he viewed as the failure of individualism in American life, Counts looked to school curriculum as a place to inculcate collectivist ideas. Counts maintained that all school programs already inculcated ideas, but those ideas had been ones that primarily served the interests of the ruling classes. As Counts put it, "the real question is not whether imposition will take place, but rather from what source it will come."

Counts' theory of curriculum found a ready audience during the depths of the Great Depression in the early 1930s. For example, he and his Columbia University colleague, the historian Charles A. Beard, were dominant forces in the Commission on Social Studies, which had been established by the American Historical Association to make recommendations for the schools. The Commission's reports, although stopping short of formulating an actual curriculum, nonetheless leaned heavily toward an activist-oriented social studies curriculum consonant with the tenets of social reconstructionism (see Lagemann, 1992, p. 153). Furthermore, beginning in the 1920s,

Rugg oversaw the development of social studies instructional materials that were based on a social reconstructionist principles. In contrast to most available materials, their explicit focus was on the problems of American life (see Bagenstos, 1977; Nelson, 1977). Rugg's materials became bestsellers and were widely adopted across the United States. This is all the more remarkable given the economic hard times faced by school districts during the 1930s.

Rugg's social studies materials probably mark the greatest success of the social reconstructionists in the implementation of their ideas in school programs. As the Great Depression and the New Deal waned, however, Rugg's textbooks came under growing fire from conservative groups. For this and other reasons, the series eventually fell out of favor (see Kliebard, 1986, pp. 200–208). Almost the same fate befell social reconstructionism itself as the 1930s wore on and World War II approached. Conservative criticism and the changing climate of educational opinion increasingly shifted Counts and other social reconstructionists from at or near the center of educational debate to a more peripheral position. Nevertheless, the flame of social reconstructionism in educational thought was never entirely extinguished and was, as we shall see, to rise to prominence again in the 1970s.

Before leaving Counts, however, it should be noted that his view of curriculum attracted criticism not only from educational and political traditionalists. No less a progressive figure than Dewey, while sympathizing with many of Counts' collectivist goals, found parts of Counts' curriculum thinking worrisome. For example, Dewey always championed teaching students to think for themselves. From this perspective, the preordained ends of Counts' "imposition" seemed hard to distinguish from indoctrination.

To round out this first section, we have included a well-known essay by curriculum historian Herbert Kliebard (1975) dealing with the early years of the curriculum field. Kliebard's focus is the influence of "scientific" curriculum making. Although we have already noted that the scientific strain of curriculum thought has tended to be dominant ever since the field's inception, Kliebard places it in historical context, pointing out how "scientific" approaches to curriculum and other educational matters have come to pervade educational thought and practice in the United States.

References

Bagenstos, N. T. (1977). Social reconstruction: The controversy over the textbooks of Harold Rugg. *Theory and Research in Social Education, 5* (3), 22–38.

Bowers, C. A. (1969). *The progressive educator and the Depression.* New York: Random House.

Callahan, R. E. (1962). *Education and the cult of efficiency.* Chicago: University of Chicago Press.

Cremin, L. A. (1964). *The transformation of the school.* New York: Vintage.

Curti, M. (1959). *The social ideas of American educators, with a new chapter on the last twenty-five years.* Totowa, NJ: Littlefield, Adams.

Dewey, J. (1938). Experience and education. New York: Macmillan.

Eisner, E. W. (1985). Franklin Bobbitt and the "science" of curriculum making. In E. W. Eisner (Ed.), *The art of educational evaluation* (pp. 13–28). London: Falmer.

Eisner, E. W., & Vallance, E. (Eds.). (1974). *Conflicting conceptions of curriculum.* Berkeley, CA: McCutchan.

Kliebard, H. M. (1986). *The struggle for the American curriculum, 1893–1958.* New York: Routledge.

Lagemann, E. C. (1989). The plural worlds of educational research. *History of Education Quarterly, 29,* 185–214.

Lagemann, E. C. (1992). Prophecy or profession: George S. Counts and the social study of education. *American Journal of Education, 100,* 137–165.

Mayhew, K. C., & Edwards, A. C. (1966). *The Dewey school.* New York: Atherton.

Nelson, M. R. (1977). The development of the Rugg social studies materials. *Theory and Research in Social Education, 5* (3), 64–83.

Tanner, L. M. (1991). The meaning of curriculum in Dewey's Laboratory School. *Journal of Curriculum Studies, 23,* 101–117.

Tyack, D. B. (1974). *The one best system.* Cambridge, MA: Harvard University Press.

1

Scientific Method in Curriculum-making

FRANKLIN BOBBITT

Since the opening of the twentieth century, the evolution of our social order has been proceeding with great and ever-accelerating rapidity. Simple conditions have been growing complex. Small institutions have been growing large. Increased specialization has been multiplying human interdependencies and the consequent need of coördinating effort. Democracy is increasing within the Nation; and growing throughout the world. All classes are aspiring to a full human opportunity. Never before have civilization and humanization advanced so swiftly.

As the world presses eagerly forward toward the accomplishment of new things, education also must advance no less swiftly. It must provide the intelligence and the aspirations necessary for the advance; and for stability and consistency in holding the gains. Education must take a pace set, not by itself, but by social progress.

The present program of public education was mainly formulated during the simpler conditions of the nineteenth century. In details it has been improved. In fundamentals it is not greatly different. A program never designed for the present day has been inherited.

Any inherited system, good for its time, when held to after its day, hampers social progress. It is not enough that the system, fundamentally unchanged in plan and purpose, be improved in details. In education this has been done in conspicuous degree. Our schools to-day are better than ever before. Teachers are better trained. Supervision is more adequate. Buildings and equipment are enormously improved. Effective methods are being introduced, and time is being economized. Improvements are visible on every hand. And yet to do the nineteenth-century task better than it was then done is not necessarily to do the twentieth-century task.

New duties lie before us. And these require new methods, new materials, new vision. The old education, except as it conferred the tools of knowledge, was mainly devoted to filling the memory with facts. The new age is more in need of facts than the old; and of more facts; and it must find more effective methods of teaching them. But there are now other functions. Education is now to develop a type of wisdom that can grow only out of participation in the living experiences of men, and never out of mere memorization of verbal statements of facts. It must, therefore, train thought and judgment in connection with actual life-situations, a task distinctly dif-

Public Domain, Preface and Chapter VI in Franklin Bobbitt, *The Curriculum*. Cambridge, MA: The Riverside Press, 1918.

ferent from the cloistral activities of the past. It is also to develop the good-will, the spirit of service, the social valuations, sympathies, and attitudes of mind necessary for effective group-action where specialization has created endless interdependency. It has the function of training every citizen, man or woman, not for knowledge about citizenship, but for proficiency in citizenship; not for knowledge about hygiene, but for proficiency in maintaining robust health; not for a mere knowledge of abstract science, but for proficiency in the use of ideas in the control of practical situations. Most of these are new tasks. In connection with each, much is now being done in all progressive school systems; but most of them yet are but partially developed. We have been developing knowledge, not function; the power to reproduce facts, rather than the powers to think and feel and will and act in vital relation to the world's life. Now we must look to these latter things as well.

Our task in this volume is to point out some of the new duties. We are to show why education must now undertake tasks that until recently were not considered needful; why new methods, new materials, and new types of experience must be employed. We here try to develop a point of view that seems to be needed by practical school men and women as they make the educational adjustments now demanded by social conditions; and needed also by scientific workers who are seeking to define with accuracy the objectives of education. It is the feeling of the writer that in the social reconstructions of the post-war years that lie just ahead of us, education is to be called upon the bear a hitherto undreamed-of burden of responsibility; and to undertake unaccustomed labors. To present some of the theory needed for the curriculum labors of this new age has been the task herein attempted.

This is a first book in a field that until recently has been too little cultivated. For a long time, we have been developing the theory of educational method, both general and special; and we have required teachers and supervisors to be thoroughly cognizant of it. Recently, however, we have discerned that there is a theory of curriculum-formulation that is no less extensive and involved than that of method; and that it is just as much needed by teachers and supervisors. To know what to do is as important as to know how to do it. This volume, therefore, is designed for teacher-training institutions as an introductory textbook in the theory of the curriculum; and for reading circles in the training of teachers in service. It is hoped also that it may assist the general reader who is interested in noting recent educational tendencies.

★　★　★

The technique of curriculum-making along scientific lines has been but little developed. The controlling purposes of education have not been sufficiently particularized. We have aimed at a vague culture, an ill-defined discipline, a nebulous harmonious development of the individual, an indefinite moral character-building, an unparticularized social efficiency, or, often enough nothing more than escape from a life of work. Often there are no controlling purposes; the momentum of the educational machine keeps it running. So long as objectives are but vague guesses, or not even that, there can be no demand for anything but vague guesses as to means and procedure. But the era of contentment with large, undefined purposes is rapidly passing. An age of science is demanding exactness and particularity.

The technique of scientific method is at present being developed for every important aspect of education. Experimental laboratories and schools are discovering accurate methods of measuring and evaluating different types of educational processes. Bureaus of educational measurement are discovering scientific methods of analyzing results, of diagnosing specific situations, and of prescribing remedies. Scientific method is being applied to the fields of budget-making, child-accounting, systems of grading and promotion, etc.

The curriculum, however, is a primordial factor. If it is wrongly drawn up on the basis merely of guess and personal opinion, all of the science in the world applied to the factors above enumerated will not make the work efficient. The scientific task preceding all others is the determination of the curriculum. For this we need a scientific technique. At present this is being rapidly developed in connection with various fields of training.

The central theory is simple. Human life, however varied, consists in the performance of specific activities. Education that prepares for life is one that prepares definitely and adequately for these specific activities. However numerous and diverse they may be for any social class, they can be discovered. This requires only that one go out into the world of affairs and discover the particulars of which these affairs consist. These will show the abilities, attitudes, habits, appreciations, and forms of knowledge that men need. These will be the objectives of the curriculum. They will be numerous, definite, and particularized. The curriculum will then be that series of experiences which children and youth must have by way of attaining those objectives.

The word *curriculum* is Latin for a *race-course*, or the *race* itself,—a place of deeds, or a series of deeds. As applied to education, it is that *series of things which children and youth must do and experience* by way of developing abilities to do the things well that make up the affairs of adult life; and to be in all respects what adults should be.

The developmental experiences exist upon two levels. On the one hand, there is the general experience of living the community life, without thought of the training values. In this way, through participation, one gets much of his education for participation in community life. In many things this provides most of the training; and in all essential things, much of it. But in all fields, this incidental or undirected developmental experience leaves the training imperfect. It is necessary, therefore, to supplement it with the conscious directed training of systematized education. The first level we shall call undirected training; and the second, directed training.

The curriculum may, therefore, be defined in two ways: (1) it is the entire range of experiences, both undirected and directed, concerned in unfolding the abilities of the individual; or (2) it is the series of consciously directed training experiences that the schools use for completing and perfecting the unfoldment. Our profession uses the term usually in the latter sense. But as education is coming more and more to be seen as a thing of experiences, and as the work- and play-experiences of the general community life are being more and more utilized, the line of demarcation between directed and undirected training experience is rapidly disappearing. Education must be concerned with both, even though it does not direct both.

When the curriculum is defined as including both directed and undirected experiences, then its objectives are the total range of human abilities, habits, systems of knowledge, etc., that one should possess. These will be discovered by analytic survey. The curriculum-discoverer will first be an analyst of human nature and of human affairs. His task at this point is not at all concerned with "the studies,"—later he will draw up appropriate studies as *means*, but he will not analyze the tools to be used in a piece of work as a mode of discovering the objectives of that work. His first task rather, in ascertaining the education appropriate for any special class, is to discover the total range of habits, skills, abilities, forms of thought, valuations, ambitions, etc., that its members need for the effective performance of their vocational labors; likewise, the total range needed for their civic activities; their health activities; their recreations; their language;

their parental, religious, and general social activities. The program of analysis will be no narrow one. It will be wide as life itself. As it thus finds all the things that make up the mosaic of full-formed human life, it discovers the full range of educational objectives.

Notwithstanding the fact that many of these objectives are attained without conscious effort, the curriculum-discoverer must have all of them before him for his labors. Even though the scholastic curriculum will not find it necessary to aim at all of them, it is the function of education to see that all of them are attained. Only as he looks to the entire series can he discover the ones that require conscious effort. He will be content to let as much as possible be taken care of through undirected experiences. Indeed he will strive for such conditions that a maximum amount of the training can be so taken care of.

The curriculum of the schools will aim at those objectives that are not sufficiently attained as a result of the general undirected experience. This is to recognize that the total range of specific educational objectives breaks up into two sets: one, those arrived at through one's general experiences without his taking thought as to the training; the other, those that are imperfectly or not at all attained through such general experience. The latter are revealed, and distinguished from the former, by the presence of imperfections, errors, short-comings. Like the symptoms of disease, these point unerringly to those objectives that require the systematized labors of directed training. Deficiencies point to the ends of conscious education. As the specific objectives upon which education is to be focused are thus pointed out, we are shown where the curriculum of the directed training is to be developed.

Let us illustrate. One of the most important things in which one is to be trained is the effective use of the mother-tongue. It is possible to analyze one's language activities and find all of the things one must do in effectively and correctly using it. Each of these things then becomes an objective of the training. But it is not necessary consciously to train for each of them. Let an individual grow up in a cultivated language-atmosphere, and he will learn to do, and be sufficiently practiced in doing, most of them, without any directed training. Here and there he will make mistakes. *Each mistake is a call for directed training.*

The curriculum of the directed training is to be discovered in the shortcomings of individuals after they have had all that can be given by the undirected training.

This principle is recognized in the recent work of many investigators as to the curriculum of grammar. One of the earliest studies was that of Professor Charters.[1] Under his direction, the teachers of Kansas City undertook to discover the errors made by pupils in their oral and written language. For the oral errors the teachers carried notebooks for five days of one week and jotted down every grammatical error which they heard made by any pupil at any time during the day. For the errors in writing they examined the written work of the pupils for a period of three weeks. They discovered twenty-one types of errors in the oral speech and twenty-seven types in the written. The oral errors in the order of their frequency were as follows:—

1.	Confusion of past tense and past participle	24
2.	Failure of verb to agree with its subject in number and person	14
3.	Wrong verb	12
4.	Double negative	11

[1]Charters, W. W., and Miller, Edith. *A Course of Study in Grammar based upon the Grammatical Errors of School Children in Kansas City, Missouri.* University of Missouri, Education Bulletin, no. 9.

5. Syntactical redundance	10
6. Wrong sentence form	5
7. Confusion of adjectives and adverbs	4
8. Subject of verb not in nominative case	4
9. Confusion of demonstrative adjective with personal pronoun	3
10. Predicate nominative not in nominative case	2
11. First personal pronoun standing first in a series	2
12. Wrong form of noun or pronoun	2
13. Confusion of past and present tenses	2
14. Object of verb or preposition not in the objective case	1
15. Wrong part of speech due to a similarity of sound	1
16. Incorrect comparison of adjectives	1
17. Failure of the pronoun to agree with its antecedent	0.3
18. Incorrect use of mood	0.3
19. Misplaced modifier	0.3
20. Confusion of preposition and conjunction	0.2
21. Confusion of comparatives and superlatives	0.1

Each error discovered is a symptom of grammatical ignorance, wrong habit, imperfect valuation, or careless attitude toward one's language. The nature of the deficiency points to the abilities and dispositions that are to be developed in the child by way of bringing about the use of the correct forms. Each grammatical shortcoming discovered, therefore, points to a needed objective of education. It points to a development of knowledge or attitude which the general undirected language experience has not sufficiently accomplished; and which must therefore be consciously undertaken by the schools.

Scientific method must consider both levels of the grammar curriculum. One task is to provide at the school as much as possible of a cultivated language-atmosphere in which the children can live and receive unconscious training. This is really the task of major importance, and provides the type of experience that should accomplish an ever-increasing proportion of the training. The other task is to make children conscious of their errors, to teach the grammar needed for correction or prevention, and to bring the children to put their grammatical knowledge to work in eliminating the errors. In proportion as the other type of experience is increased, this conscious training will play a diminishing role.

In the spelling field, Ayres, Jones, Cook and O'Shea, and others have been tabulating the words that children and adults use in writing letters, reports, compositions, etc. In this way they have been discovering the particularized objectives of training in spelling. But words are of unequal difficulty. Most are learned in the course of the reading and writing experience of the children without much conscious attention to the spelling. But here and there are words that are not so learned. Investigations, therefore, lay special emphasis upon the words that are misspelled. Each misspelled word reveals a directed-curriculum task. Here, as in the grammar, error is the symptom of training need; and the complete error-list points unerringly to the curriculum of conscious training.

In the vocational field, and on the technical side only, Indianapolis has provided an excellent example of method of discovering the objectives of training. Investigators, without pre-suppositions as to content of vocational curriculum, set out to discover the major occupations of the city, the processes to be performed in each, and the knowledge, habits and skills needed for effective work. They talked with expert workmen; and observed the work-processes. In their report, for each occupation, they present: (1) a list of tools and machines with which a workman must be skillful; (2) a list of the materials used in the work with which workers need to be familiar; (3) a list of items of general knowledge needed concerning jobs and processes; (4) the kinds of mathematical operations actually employed in the work; (5) the items or portions of science needed for control of processes; (6) the elements of drawing and design actually used in the work; (7) the characteristics of the English needed where language is vitally involved in one's work, as in commercial occupations; (8) elements of hygiene needed for keeping one's self up to the physical standards demanded by the work; and (9) the needed facts of economics.

Many of the things listed in such a survey are learned through incidental experience. Others cannot be sufficiently learned in this way. It is by putting the workers to work, whether adolescent or adult, and by noting the kinds of shortcomings and mistakes that show themselves when training is absent or deficient, that we can discover the curriculum tasks for directed vocational education.

The objectives of education are not to be discovered within just any kind or quality of human affairs. Occupational, civic, sanitary, or other activity may be poorly performed and productive of only meager results. At the other end of the scale are types of activity that are as well performed as it is in human nature to perform them, and which are abundantly fruitful in good results. Education is established upon the presumption that human activities exist upon different levels of quality or efficiency; that performance of low character is not good; that it can be eliminated through training; and that only the best or at least the best attainable is good enough. Whether in agriculture, building-trades, housekeeping, commerce, civic regulation, sanitation, or any other, education presumes that the best that is practicable is what ought to be. Education is to keep its feet squarely upon the earth; but this does not require that it aim lower than the highest that is practicable.

Let us take a concrete illustration. The curriculum-discoverer wishes, for example, to draw up a course of training in agriculture. He will go out into the practical world of agriculture as the only place that can reveal the objectives of agricultural education. He will start out without prejudgment as to the specific objectives. All that he needs for the work is pencil, notebook, and a discerning intelligence. He will observe the work of farmers; he will talk with them about all aspects of their work; and he will read reliable accounts which give insight into their activities. From these sources he will discover the particular things that the farmers do in carrying on each piece of work; the specific knowledge which the farmers employ in planning and performing each specific task; the kinds of judgments at which they must arrive; the types of problems they must solve; the habits and skills demanded by the tasks; the attitudes of mind, appreciations, valuations, ambitions, and desires, which motivate and exercise general control.

Facts upon all of these matters can be obtained from a survey of any agricultural region, however primitive or backward. But primitive agriculture is the thing which exists without any education. It is the thing education is to eliminate. The curriculum-discoverer, therefore, will not investigate just any agricultural situation. He will go to the farms that are most productive and most successful from every legitimate point of view. These will often be experimental or demonstration farms which represent what is practicable for the community, but which may not be typical of actual practices in that community. Where such general practices are inferior, agricultural education is to aim not at what is but at what ought to be.

When the farming practices are already upon a high plane, education has but a single function: it is to hand over these practices unchanged to the members of the new generation.

Where the practices of a region are primitive or backward, education has a double function to perform. It is not only to hand over to the new generation a proficiency that is equal to that of their fathers, but it is also to lift the proficiency of the sons to a height much beyond that of their fathers. Within such a region, therefore, agricultural education has the additional function of serving as the fundamental social agency of agricultural progress.

What we have said concerning agriculture is generally applicable throughout the occupational world. For discovering the objectives for a training course in bricklaying one will analyze not the activities of bricklayers in general, but those where bricklaying has been carried to its highest practicable level of efficiency,—as this efficiency is judged on the basis of all legitimate standards. Education will aim, not at average bricklayers, but at the best types of bricklayers.

When stated in broad outline, the general principle is obvious. In practical application, it presents difficulties. Men do not agree as to the characteristics of the most desirable types of work. The employers of the bricklayers will be inclined to use maximum productiveness as the criterion of superior work; and unquestioning obedience to orders and contentment with any kind of hours, wages, and working conditions as proper mental attitudes. The employees will judge otherwise as to some of the factors. The employers will invite the curriculum-discoverer to investigate situations where productiveness in proportion to costs is greatest; the employees, where the total welfare of the worker is considered alongside of the factor of productiveness. Both sides will agree that education should aim at the best and that scientific investigations as to objectives should seek to discover the characteristics of only the best. They disagree as to what is the best, and therefore where the investigations are to be made.

The general principle of finding the scholastic curriculum in the shortcomings of children and men is quite obvious and entirely familiar to teachers in its application to the curriculum of spelling, grammar, and other subjects that result in objective performance, such as pronunciation, drawing, music, computation, etc. It is not so clear in connection with the highly complex subjects of history, literature, geography, etc. What are the social shortcomings that are to be eliminated through a study of these social subjects? Our ideas are yet so vague, in most cases, that we can scarcely be said to have objectives. The first task of the scientific curriculum-maker is the discovery of those social deficiencies that result from a lack of historical, literary, and geographical experiences. Each deficiency found is a call for directed training; it points to an objective that is to be set up for the conscious training. The nature of the objectives will point to the curriculum materials to be selected for these subjects. A major obstacle is lack of agreement as to what constitutes social deficiency. There is however no justification for scholastic training of any kind except as a gap exists between the training of general experience and the training that ought to be accomplished.

Society agrees sufficiently well as to many social shortcomings. Education needs to assemble them in as accurate and particularized a form as possible. They can then be used as the social symptoms which point to the objectives of history, literature, geography, economics, and other social studies. Society will disagree as to many suggested deficiencies. A program can be scientific, however, without being complete. The thousand spelling words presented by Mr. Ayres is a good list notwithstanding the fact that it presents not more than a quarter of the words needed. It is a secure beginning that can be completed by further studies. In the same way in our social training, we shall do very well if we can set up a quarter of the desirable objectives. That would be a great advance over none at all, as at present; and would provide the nucleus, the technique, and the vision of possibilities, necessary for gradually rounding out the list.

The principle involves us in similar difficulties in its application to civic, moral, vocational, sanitational, recreational, and parental education. It is equally valid, however, in connection with each of these. Only as we agree upon *what ought to be* in each of these difficult fields, can we know at what the training should aim. Only as we list the errors and shortcomings of human performance in each of the fields can we know what to include and to emphasize in the directed curriculum of the schools.

2

My Pedagogic Creed

John Dewey

Article One: *What Education Is*

I Believe that—all education proceeds by the participation of the individual in the social consciousness of the race. This process begins unconsciously almost at birth, and is continually shaping the individual's powers, saturating his consciousness, forming his habits, training his ideas, and arousing his feelings and emotions. Through this unconscious education the individual gradually comes to share in the intellectual and moral resources which humanity has succeeded in getting together. He becomes an inheritor of the funded capital of civilization. The most formal and technical education in the world cannot safely depart from this general process. It can only organize it or differentiate it in some particular direction.

• The only true education comes through the stimulation of the child's powers by the demands of the social situations in which he finds himself. Through these demands he is stimulated to act as a member of a unity, to emerge from his original narrowness of action and feeling, and to conceive of himself from the standpoint of the welfare of the group to which he belongs. Through the responses which others make to his own activities he comes to know what these mean in social terms. The value which they have is reflected back into them. For instance, through the response which is made to the child's instinctive babblings the child comes to know what those babblings mean; they are transformed into articulate language, and thus the child is introduced into the consolidated wealth of ideas and emotions which are now summed up in language.

• This educational process has two sides, one psychological and one sociological, and that neither can be subordinated to the other, or neglected, without evil results following. Of these two sides, the psychological is the basis. The child's own instincts and powers furnish the material and give the starting-point for all education. Save as the efforts of the educator connect with some activity which the child is carrying on of his own initiative independent of the educator, education becomes reduced to a pressure from without. It may, indeed, give certain external results, but cannot truly be called educative. Without insight into the psychological structure and activities of the individual, the educative process will, therefore, be haphazard and arbitrary. If it chances to coincide with the child's activity it will get a leverage; if it does not, it will result in friction, or disintegration, or arrest of the child nature.

From "My Pedagogic Creed," *Journal of the National Education Association,* Vol. 18, No. 9, pp. 291–295, December, 1929. Reprinted by permission.

• Knowledge of social conditions, of the present state of civilization, is necessary in order properly to interpret the child's powers. The child has his own instincts and tendencies, but we do not know what these mean until we can translate them into their social equivalents. We must be able to carry them back into a social past and see them as the inheritance of previous race activities. We must also be able to project them into the future to see what their outcome and end will be. In the illustration just used, it is the ability to see in the child's babblings the promise and potency of a future social intercourse and conversation which enables one to deal in the proper way with that instinct.

• The psychological and social sides are organically related, and that education cannot be regarded as a compromise between the two, or a superimposition of one upon the other. We are told that the psychological definition of education is barren and formal—that is gives us only the idea of a development of all the mental powers without giving us any idea of the use to which these powers are put. On the other hand, it is urged that the social definition of education, as getting adjusted to civilization, makes of it a forced and external process, and results in subordinating the freedom of the individual to a preconceived social and political status.

• Each of these objections is true when urged against one side isolated from the other. In order to know what a power really is we must know what its end, use, or function is, and this we cannot know save as we conceive of the individual as active in social relationships. But, on the other hand, the only possible adjustment which we can give to the child under existing conditions is that which arises through putting him in complete possession of all his powers. With the advent of democracy and modern industrial conditions, it is impossible to foretell definitely just what civilization will be twenty years from now. Hence it is impossible to prepare the child for any precise set of conditions. To prepare him for the future life means to give him command of himself; it means so to train him that he will have the full and ready use of all his capacities that his eye and ear and hand may be tools ready to command, that his judgment may be capable of grasping the conditions under which it has to work, and the executive forces be trained to act economically and efficiently. It is impossible to reach this sort of adjustment save as constant regard is had to the individual's own powers, tastes, and interests— that is, as education is continually converted into psychological terms.

In sum, I believe that the individual who is to be educated is a social individual, and that society is an organic union of individuals. If we eliminate the social factor from the child we are left only with an abstraction; if we eliminate the individual factor from society, we are left only with an inert and lifeless mass. Education, therefore, must begin with a psychological insight into the child's capacities, interests, and habits. It must be controlled at every point by reference to these same considerations. These powers, interests, and habits must be continually interpreted—we must know what they mean. They must be translated into terms of their social equivalents—into terms of what they are capable of in the way of social service.

Article Two: *What the School Is*

I Believe that—the school is primarily a social institution. Education being a social process, the school is simply that form of community life in which all those agencies are concentrated that will be most effective in bringing the child to share in the inherited resources of the race, and to use his own powers for social ends.

• Education, therefore, is a process of living and not a preparation for future living.

- The school must represent present life—life as real and vital to the child as that which he carries on in the home, in the neighborhood, or on the playground.

- That education which does not occur through forms of life, forms that are worth living for their own sake, is always a poor substitute for the genuine reality, and tends to cramp and to deaden.

- The school, as an institution, should simplify existing social life; should reduce it, as it were, to an embryonic form. Existing life is so complex that the child cannot be brought into contact with it without either confusion or distraction; he is either overwhelmed by the multiplicity of activities which are going on, so that he loses his own power of orderly reaction, or he is so stimulated by these various activities that his powers are prematurely called into play and he becomes either unduly specialized or else disintegrated.

- As such simplified social life, the school life should grow gradually out of the home life; that it should take up and continue the activities with which the child is already familiar in the home.

- It should exhibit these activities to the child, and reproduce them in such ways that the child will gradually learn the meaning of them, and be capable of playing his own part in relation to them.

- This is a psychological necessity, because it is the only way of securing continuity in the child's growth, the only way of giving a background of past experience to the new ideas given in school.

- It is also a social necessity because the home is the form of social life in which the child has been nurtured and in connection with which he has had his moral training. It is the business of the school to deepen and extend his sense of the values bound up in his home life.

- Much of present education fails because it neglects this fundamental principle of the school as a form of community life. It conceives the school as a place where certain information is to be given, where certain lessons are to be learned, or where certain habits are to be formed. The value of these is conceived as lying largely in the remote future; the child must do these things for the sake of something else he is to do; they are mere preparations. As a result they do not become a part of the life experience of the child and so are not truly educative.

- The moral education centers upon this conception of the school as a mode of social life, that the best and deepest moral training is precisely that which one gets through having to enter into proper relations with others in a unity of work and thought. The present educational systems, so far as they destroy or neglect this unity, render it difficult or impossible to get any genuine, regular moral training.

- The child should be stimulated and controlled in his work through the life of the community.

- Under existing conditions far too much of the stimulus and control proceeds from the teacher, because of neglect of the idea of the school as a form of social life.

- The teacher's place and work in the school is to be interpreted from this same basis. The teacher is not in the school to impose certain ideas or to form certain habits in the child, but is there as a member of the community to select the influences which shall affect the child and to assist him in properly responding to these influences.

- The discipline of the school should proceed from the life of the school as a whole and not directly from the teacher.

- The teacher's business is simply to determine, on the basis of larger experience and riper wisdom, how the discipline of life shall come to the child.

• All questions of the grading of the child and his promotion should be determined by reference to the same standard. Examinations are of use only so far as they test the child's fitness for social life and reveal the place in which he can be of the most service and where he can receive the most help.

Article Three: *The Subjectmatter of Education*

I Believe that—the social life of the child is the basis of concentration, or correlation, in all his training or growth. The social life gives the unconscious unity and the background of all his efforts and of all his attainments.

• The subjectmatter of the school curriculum should mark a gradual differentiation out of the primitive unconscious unity of social life.

• We violate the child's nature and render difficult the best ethical results by introducing the child too abruptly to a number of special studies, of reading, writing, geography, etc., out of relation to this social life.

• The true center of correlation on the school subjects is not science, nor literature, nor history, nor geography, but the child's own social activities.

• Education cannot be unified in the study of science, or so-called nature study, because apart from human activity, nature itself is not a unity; nature in itself is a number of diverse objects in space and time, and to attempt to make it the center of work by itself is to introduce a principle of radiation rather than one of concentration.

• Literature is the reflex expression and interpretation of social experience; that hence it must follow upon and not precede such experience. It, therefore, cannot be made the basis, although it may be made the summary of unification.

• Once more that history is of educative value in so far as it presents phases of social life and growth. It must be controlled by reference to social life. When taken simply as history it is thrown into the distant past and becomes dead and inert. Taken as the record of man's social life and progress it becomes full of meaning. I believe, however, that it cannot be so taken excepting as the child is also introduced directly into social life.

• The primary basis of education is in the child's powers at work along the same general constructive lines as those which have brought civilization into being.

• The only way to make the child conscious of his social heritage is to enable him to perform those fundamental types of activity which make civilization what it is.

• In the socalled expressive or constructive activities as the center of correlation.

• This gives the standard for the place of cooking, sewing, manual training, etc., in the school.

• They are not special studies which are to be introduced over and above a lot of others in the way of relaxation or relief, or as additional accomplishments. I believe rather that they represent, as types, fundamental forms of social activity; and that it is possible and desirable that the child's introduction into the more formal subjects of the curriculum be through the medium of these constructive activities.

• The study of science is educational in so far as it brings out the materials and processes which make social life what it is.

• One of the greatest difficulties in the present teaching of science is that the material is presented in purely objective form, or is treated as a new peculiar kind of experience which the child can add to that which he has already had. In reality, science is of value because it gives the ability to interpret and control the experience already had. It should be introduced, not as so much new subjectmatter, but as showing the factors already involved in previous experience and as furnishing tools by which that experience can be more easily and effectively regulated.

• At present we lose much of the value of literature and language studies because of our elimination of the social element. Language is almost always treated in the books of pedagogy simply as the expression of thought. It is true that language is a logical instrument, but it is fundamentally and primarily a social instrument. Language is the device for communication; it is the tool through which one individual comes to share the ideas and feelings of others. When treated simply as a way of getting individual information, or as a means of showing off what one has learned, it loses its social motive and end.

• There is, therefore, no succession of studies in the ideal school curriculum. If education is life, all life has, from the outset, a scientific aspect, an aspect of art and culture, and an aspect of communication. It cannot, therefore, be true that the proper studies for one grade are mere reading and writing, and that at a later grade, reading, or literature, or science, may be introduced. The progress is not in the succession of studies, but in the development of new attitudes towards, and new interests in, experience.

• Education must be conceived as a continuing reconstruction of experience; that the process and the goal of education are one and the same thing.

• To set up any end outside of education, as furnishing its goal and standard, is to deprive the educational process of much of its meaning, and tends to make us rely upon false and external stimuli in dealing with the child.

Article Four: *The Nature of Method*

I Believe that—the question of method is ultimately reducible to the question of the order of development of the child's powers and interests. The law for presenting and treating material is the law implicit within the child's own nature. Because this is so I believe the following statements are of supreme importance as determining the spirit in which education is carried on.

• The active side precedes the passive in the development of the child-nature; that expression comes before conscious impression; that the muscular development precedes the sensory; that movements come before conscious sensations; I believe that consciousness is essentially motor or impulsive; that conscious states tend to project themselves in action.

• The neglect of this principle is the cause of a large part of the waste of time and strength in school work. The child is thrown into a passive, receptive, or absorbing attitude. The conditions are such that he is not permitted to follow the law of his nature; the result is friction and waste.

• Ideas (intellectual and rational processes) also result from action and devolve for the sake of the better control of action. What we term reason is primarily the law of order or effective action. To attempt to develop the reasoning powers, the powers of judgment, without reference to the selection and arrangement of means in action, is the fundamental fallacy in our present methods of dealing with this matter. As a result we present the child with arbitrary symbols. Symbols are a necessity in mental development, but they have their place as tools for economizing effort; presented by themselves they are a mass of meaningless and arbitrary ideas imposed from without.

• The image is the great instrument of instruction. What a child gets out of any subject presented to him is simply the images which he himself forms with regard to it.

- If nine-tenths of the energy at present directed towards making the child learn certain things were spent in seeing to it that the child was forming proper images, the work of instruction would be indefinitely facilitated.
- Much of the time and attention now given to the preparation and presentation of lessons might be more wisely and profitably expended in training the child's power of imagery and in seeing to it that he was continually forming definite vivid, and growing images of the various subjects with which he comes in contact in his experience.
- Interests are the signs and symptoms of growing power. I believe that they represent dawning capacities. Accordingly the constant and careful observation of interests is of the utmost importance for the educator.
- These interests are to be observed as showing the state of development which the child has reached.
- They prophesy the stage upon which he is about to enter.
- Only through the continual and sympathetic observation of childhood's interests can the adult enter into the child's life and see what it is ready for, and upon what material it could work most readily and fruitfully.
- These interests are neither to be humored nor repressed. To repress interest is to substitute the adult for the child, and so to weaken intellectual curiosity and alertness, to suppress initiative, and to deaden interest. To humor the interests is to substitute the transient for the permanent. The interest is always the sign of some power below; the important thing is to discover this power. To humor the interest is to fail to penetrate below the surface, and its sure result is to substitute caprice and whim for genuine interest.
- The emotions are the reflex of actions.
- To endeavor to stimulate or arouse the emotions apart from their corresponding activities is to introduce an unhealthy and morbid state of mind.
- If we can only secure right habits of action and thought, with reference to the good, the true, and the beautiful, the emotions will for the most part take care of themselves.
- Next to deadness and dullness, formalism and routine, our education is threatened with no greater evil than sentimentalism.
- This sentimentalism is the necessary result of the attempt to divorce feeling from action.

Article Five: *The School and Social Progress*

Education is the fundamental method of social progress and reform.

- All reforms which rest simply upon the enactment of law, or the threatening of certain penalties, or upon changes in mechanical or outward arrangements, are transitory and futile.
- Education is a regulation of the process of coming to share in the social consciousness; and that the adjustment of individual activity on the basis of this social consciousness is the only sure method of social reconstruction.
- This conception has due regard for both the individualistic and socialistic ideals. It is duly individual because it recognizes the formation of a certain character as the only genuine basis of right living. It is socialistic because it recognizes that this

right character is not to be formed by merely individual precept, example, or exhortation, but rather by the influence of a certain form of institutional or community life upon the individual, and that the social organism through the school, as its organ, may determine ethical results.

- In the ideal school we have the reconciliation of the individualistic and the institutional ideals.

- The community's duty to education is, therefore, its paramount moral duty. By law and punishment, by social agitation and discussion, society can regulate and form itself in a more or less haphazard and chance way. But through education society can formulate its own purposes, can organize its own means and resources, and thus shape itself with definiteness and economy in the direction in which it wishes to move.

- When society once recognizes the possibilities in this direction, and the obligations which these possibilities impose, it is impossible to conceive of the resources of time, attention, and money which will be put at the disposal of the educator.

- It is the business of everyone interested in education to insist upon the school as the primary and most effective interest of social progress and reform in order that society may be awakened to realize what the school stands for, and arouse to the necessity of endowing the educator with sufficient equipment properly to perform his task.

- Education thus conceived marks the most perfect and intimate union of science and art conceivable in human experience.

- The art of thus giving shape to human powers and adapting them to social service is the supreme art; one calling into its service the best of artists; that no insight, sympathy, tact, executive power, is too great for such service.

- With the growth of psychological service, giving added insight into individual structure and laws of growth; and with growth of social science, adding to our knowledge of the right organization of individuals, all scientific resources can be utilized for the purposes of education.

- When science and art thus join hands the most commanding motive for human action will be reached, the most genuine springs of human conduct aroused, and the best service that human nature is capable of guaranteed.

- The teacher is engaged, not simply in the training of individuals, but in the formation of the proper social life.

- Every teacher should realize the dignity of his calling; that he is a social servant set apart for the maintenance of proper social order and the securing of the right social growth.

- In this way the teacher always is the prophet of the true God and the usherer in of the true kingdom of God.

3

Dare the School Build a New Social Order?

GEORGE S. COUNTS

3

If we may now assume that the child will be imposed upon in some fashion by the various elements in his environment, the real question is not whether imposition will take place, but rather from what source it will come. If we were to answer this question in terms of the past, there could, I think, be but one answer: on all genuinely crucial matters the school follows the wishes of the groups or classes that actually rule society; on minor matters the school is some-times allowed a certain measure of freedom. But the future may be unlike the past. Or perhaps I should say that teachers, if they could increase sufficiently their stock of courage, intelligence, and vision, might become a social force of some magnitude. About this eventuality I am not over sanguine, but a society lacking leadership as ours does, might even accept the guidance of teachers. Through powerful organizations they might at least reach the public conscience and come to exercise a larger measure of control over the schools than hitherto. They would then have to assume some responsibility for the more fundamental forms of imposition which, according to my argument, cannot be avoided.

That the teachers should deliberately reach for power and then make the most of their conquest is my firm conviction. To the extent that they are permitted to fashion the curriculum and the procedures of the school they will definitely and positively influence the social attitudes, ideals, and behavior of the coming generation. In doing this they should resort to no subterfuge or false modesty. They should say neither that they are merely teaching the truth nor that they are unwilling to wield power in their own right. The first position is false and the second is a confession of incompetence. It is my observation that the men and women who have affected the course of human events are those who have not hesitated to use the power that has come to them. Representing as they do, not the interests of the moment or of any special class, but rather the common and abiding interests of the people, teachers are under heavy social obligation to protect and further those interests. In this they occupy a relatively unique position in society. Also since the profession should embrace scientists and scholars of the highest rank, as well as teachers working at all levels of the educational system, it has at its disposal, as no other group, the knowledge and wisdom of the ages. It is scarcely thinkable that these men and women would ever act as selfishly or bungle as badly as have the so-called "practical" men of our generation-the politicians, the

Chapters 3 and 4, in George S. Counts, *Dare the School Build a New Social Order.* New York: John Day, 1932. Reprinted by permission of Martha L. Counts. Copyright renewed 1959 by George S. Counts.

financiers, the industrialists. If all of these facts are taken into account, instead of shunning power, the profession should rather seek power and then strive to use that power fully and wisely and in the interests of the great masses of the people.

The point should be emphasized that teachers possess no magic secret to power. While their work should give them a certain moral advantage, they must expect to encounter the usual obstacles blocking the road to leadership. They should not be deceived by the pious humbug with which public men commonly flatter the members of the profession. To expect ruling groups or classes to give precedence to teachers on important matters, because of age or sex or sentiment, is to refuse to face realities. It was one of the proverbs of the agrarian order that a spring never rises higher than its source. So the power that teachers exercise in the schools can be no greater than the power they wield in society. Moreover, while organization is necessary, teachers should not think of their problem primarily in terms of organizing and presenting a united front to the world, the flesh, and the devil. In order to be effective they must throw off completely the slave psychology that has dominated the mind of the pedagogue more or less since the days of ancient Greece. They must be prepared to stand on their own feet and win for their ideas the support of the masses of the people. Education as a force for social regeneration must march hand in hand with the living and creative forces of the social order. In their own lives teachers must bridge the gap between school and society and play some part in the fashioning of those great common purposes which should bind the two together.

This brings us to the question of the kind of imposition in which teachers should engage, if they had the power. Our obligations, I think, grow out of the social situation. We live in troublous times; we live in an age of profound change; we live in an age of revolution. Indeed it is highly doubtful whether man ever lived in a more eventful period than the present. In order to match our epoch we would probably have to go back to the fall of the ancient empires or even to that unrecorded age when men first abandoned the natural arts of hunting and fishing and trapping and began to experiment with agriculture and the settled life. Today we are witnessing the rise of a civilization quite without precedent in human history—a civilization founded on science, technology, and machinery, possessing the most extraordinary power, and rapidly making of the entire world a single great society. Because of forces already released, whether in the field of economics, politics, morals, religion, or art, the old molds are being broken. And the peoples of the earth are everywhere seething with strange ideas and passions. If life were peaceful and quiet and undisturbed by great issues, we might with some show of wisdom center our attention on the nature of the child. But with the world as it is, we cannot afford for a single instant to remove our eyes from the social scene or shift our attention from the peculiar needs of the age.

In this new world that is forming, there is one set of issues which is peculiarly fundamental and which is certain to be the center of bitter and prolonged struggle. I refer to those issues which may be styled economic. President Butler has well stated the case: "For a generation and more past," he says, "the center of human interest has been moving from the point which it occupied for some four hundred years to a new point which it bids fair to occupy for a time equally long. The shift in the position of the center of gravity in human interest has been from politics to economics; from considerations that had to do with forms of government, with the establishment and protection of individual liberty, to considerations that have to do with the production, distribution, and consumption of wealth."

Consider the present condition of the nation. Who among us, if he had not been reared amid our institutions, could believe his eyes as he surveys the economic situation, or his ears as he listens to solemn disquisitions by our financial and political lead-ers on the cause and cure of the depression! Here is a society that manifests the most extraordinary contradictions: a mastery over the forces of nature, surpassing the wildest dreams of antiquity, is accompanied by extreme material insecurity; dire poverty walks hand in hand with the most extravagant living the world has ever known; an abundance of goods of all kinds is coupled with privation, misery, and even starvation; an excess of production is seriously offered as the underlying cause of se-vere physical suffering; breakfastless children march to school past bankrupt shops laden with rich foods gathered from the ends of the earth; strong men by the million walk the streets in a futile search for employment and with the exhaustion of hope enter the ranks of the damned; great captains of industry close factories without warning and dismiss the workmen by whose labors they have amassed huge fortunes through the years; automatic machinery increasingly displaces men and threatens soci-ety with a growing contingent of the permanently unemployed; racketeers and gang-sters with the connivance of public officials fasten themselves on the channels of trade and exact toll at the end of the machine gun; economic parasitism, either within or without the law, is so prevalent that the tradition of honest labor is showing signs of decay; the wages paid to the workers are too meager to enable them to buy back the goods they produce; consumption is subordinated to production and a philosophy of deliberate waste is widely proclaimed as the highest economic wisdom; the science of psychology is employed to fan the flames of desire so that men may be enslaved by their wants and bound to the wheel of production; a government board advises the cotton-growers to plow under every third row of cotton in order to bolster up the market; both ethical and aesthetic considerations are commonly over-ridden by "hard-headed business men" bent on material gain; federal aid to the unemployed is opposed on the ground that it would pauperize the masses when the favored mem-bers of society have always lived on a dole; even responsible leaders resort to the prac-tices of the witch doctor and vie with one another in predicting the return of pros-perity; an ideal of rugged individualism, evolved in a simple pioneering and agrarian order at a time when free land existed in abundance, is used to justify a system which exploits pitilessly and without thought of the morrow the natural and human re-sources of the nation and of the world. One can only imagine what Jeremiah would say if he could step out of the pages of the Old Testament and cast his eyes over this vast spectacle so full of tragedy and of menace.

The point should be emphasized, however, that the present situation is also freighted with hope and promise. The age is pregnant with possibilities. There lies within our grasp the most humane, the most beautiful, the most majestic civilization ever fashioned by any people. This much at least we know today. We shall probably know more tomorrow. At last men have achieved such a mastery over the forces of nature that wage slavery can follow chattel slavery and take its place among the relics of the past. No longer are there grounds for the contention that the finer fruits of hu-man culture must be nurtured upon the toil and watered by the tears of the masses. The limits to achievement set by nature have been so extended that we are today bound merely by our ideals, by our power of self-discipline, by our ability to devise social arrangements suited to an industrial age. If we are to place any credence what-soever in the word of our engineers, the full utilization of modern technology at its present level of development should enable us to produce several times as much goods as were ever produced at the very peak of prosperity, and with the working day, the working year, and the working life reduced by half. We hold within our hands the power to usher in an age of plenty, to make secure the lives of all, and to banish poverty forever from the land. The only cause for doubt or pessimism lies in the question of our ability to rise to the stature of the times in which we live.

Our generation has the good or the ill fortune to live in an age when great decisions must be made. The American people, like most of the other peoples of the earth, have come to the parting of the ways; they can no longer trust entirely the inspiration which came to them when the Republic was young; they must decide afresh what they are to do with their talents. Favored above all other nations with the resources of nature and the material instrumentalities of civilization, they stand confused and irresolute before the future. They seem to lack the moral quality necessary to quicken, discipline, and give direction to their matchless energies. In a recent paper Professor Dewey has, in my judgment, correctly diagnosed our troubles: "the schools, like the nation," he says, "are in need of a central purpose which will create new enthusiasm and devotion, and which will unify and guide all intellectual plans."

This suggests, as we have already observed, that the educational problem is not wholly intellectual in nature. Our Progressive schools therefore cannot rest content with giving children an opportunity to study contemporary society in all of its aspects. This of course must be done, but I am convinced that they should go much farther. If the schools are to be really effective, they must become centers for the building, and not merely for the contemplation, of our civilization. This does not mean that we should endeavor to promote particular reforms through the educational system. We should, however, give to our children a vision of the possibilities which lie ahead and endeavor to enlist their loyalties and enthusiasms in the realization of the vision. Also our social institutions and practices, all of them, should be critically examined in the light of such a vision.

4

In *The Epic of America* James Truslow Adams contends that our chief contribution to the heritage of the race lies not in the field of science, or religion, or literature, or art but rather in the creation of what he calls the "American Dream"—a vision of a society in which the lot of the common man will be made easier and his life enriched and ennobled. If this vision has been a moving force in our history, as I believe it has, why should we not set ourselves the task of revitalizing and reconstituting it? This would seem to be the great need of our age, both in the realm of education and in the sphere of public life, because men must have something for which to live. Agnosticism, skepticism, or even experimentalism, unless the last is made flesh through the formulation of some positive social program, constitutes an extremely meager spiritual diet for any people. A small band of intellectuals, a queer breed of men at best, may be satisfied with such a spare ration, particularly if they lead the sheltered life common to their class; but the masses, I am sure, will always demand something more solid and substantial. Ordinary men and women crave a tangible purpose towards which to strive and which lends richness and dignity and meaning to life. I would consequently like to see our profession come to grips with the problem of creating a tradition that has roots in American soil, is in harmony with the spirit of the age, recognizes the facts of industrialism, appeals to the most profound impulses of our people, and takes into account the emergence of a world society.*

*In the remainder of the argument I confine attention entirely to the domestic situation. I do this, not because I regard the question of international relations unimportant, but rather because of limitations of space. All I can say here is that any proper conception of the world society must accept the principle of the moral equality of races and nations.

The ideal foundations on which we must build are easily discernible. Until recently the very word America has been synonymous throughout the world with democracy and symbolic to the oppressed classes of all lands of hope and opportunity. Child of the revolutionary ideas and impulses of the eighteenth century, the American nation became the embodiment of bold social experimentation and a champion of the power of environment to develop the capacities and redeem the souls of common men and women. And as her stature grew, her lengthening shadow reached to the four corners of the earth and everywhere impelled the human will to rebel against ancient wrongs. Here undoubtedly is the finest jewel in our heritage and the thing that is most worthy of preservation. If America should lose her honest devotion to democracy, or if she should lose her revolutionary temper, she will no longer be America. In that day, if it has not already arrived, her spirit will have fled and she will be known merely as the richest and most powerful of the nations. If America is not to be false to the promise of her youth, she must do more than simply perpetuate the democratic ideal of human relationships: she must make an intelligent and determined effort to fulfill it. The democracy of the past was the chance fruit of a strange conjunction of forces on the new continent; the democracy of the future can only be the intended offspring of the union of human reason, purpose, and will. The conscious and deliberate achievement of democracy under novel circumstances is the task of our generation.

Democracy of course should not be identified with political forms and functions–with the federal constitution, the popular election of officials, or the practice of universal suffrage. To think in such terms is to confuse the entire issue, as it has been confused in the minds of the masses for generations. The most genuine expression of democracy in the United States has little to do with our political institutions: it is a sentiment with respect to the moral equality of men: it is an aspiration towards a society in which this sentiment will find complete fulfillment. A society fashioned in harmony with the American democratic tradition would combat all forces tending to produce social distinctions and classes; repress every form of privilege and economic parasitism; manifest a tender regard for the weak, the ignorant, and the unfortunate; place the heavier and more onerous social burdens on the backs of the strong; glory in every triumph of man in his timeless urge to express himself and to make the world more habitable; exalt human labor of hand and brain as the creator of all wealth and culture; provide adequate material and spiritual rewards for every kind of socially useful work; strive for genuine equality of opportunity among all races, sects, and occupations; regard as paramount the abiding interests of the great masses of the people; direct the powers of government to the elevation and the refinement of the life of the common man; transform or destroy all conventions, institutions, and special groups inimical to the underlying principles of democracy; and finally be prepared as a last resort, in either the defense or the realization of this purpose, to follow the method of revolution. Although these ideals have never been realized or perhaps even fully accepted anywhere in the United States and have always had to struggle for existence with contrary forces, they nevertheless have authentic roots in the past. They are the values for which America has stood before the world during most of her history and with which the American people have loved best to associate their country. Their power and authority are clearly revealed in the fact that selfish interests, when grasping for some special privilege, commonly wheedle and sway the masses by repeating the words and kneeling before the emblems of the democratic heritage.

It is becoming increasingly clear, however, that this tradition, if its spirit is to survive, will have to be reconstituted in the light of the great social trends of the age in which we live. Our democratic heritage was largely a product of the frontier, free land, and a simple agrarian order. Today a new and strange and closely integrated industrial economy is rapidly sweeping over the world. Although some of us in our more sentimental moments talk wistfully of retiring into the more tranquil society of the past, we could scarcely induce many of our fellow citizens to accompany us. Even the most hostile critics of industrialism would like to take with them in their retirement a few such fruits of the machine as electricity, telephones, automobiles, modern plumbing, and various labor-saving devices, or at least be assured of an abundant supply of slaves or docile and inexpensive servants. But all such talk is the most idle chatter. For better or for worse we must take industrial civilization as an enduring fact: already we have become parasitic on its institutions and products. The hands of the clock cannot be turned back.

If we accept industrialism, as we must, we are then compelled to face without equivocation the most profound issue which this new order of society has raised and settle that issue in terms of the genius of our people—the issue of the control of the machine. In whose interests and for what purposes are the vast material riches, the unrivaled industrial equipment, and the science and technology of the nation to be used? In the light of our democratic tradition there can be but one answer to the question: all of these resources must be dedicated to the promotion of the welfare of the great masses of the people. Even the classes in our society that perpetually violate this principle are compelled by the force of public opinion to pay lip-service to it and to defend their actions in its terms. No body of men, however powerful, would dare openly to flout it. Since the opening of the century the great corporations have even found it necessary to establish publicity departments or to employ extremely able men as public relations counselors in order to persuade the populace that regardless of appearances they are lovers of democracy and devoted servants of the people. In this they have been remarkably successful, at least until the coming of the Great Depression. For during the past generation there have been few things in America that could not be bought at a price.

If the benefits of industrialism are to accrue fully to the people, this deception must be exposed. If the machine is to serve all, and serve all equally, it cannot be the property of the few. To ask these few to have regard for the common weal, particularly when under the competitive system they are forced always to think first of themselves or perish, is to put too great a strain on human nature. With the present concentration of economic power in the hands of a small class, a condition that is likely to get worse before it gets better, the survival or development of a society that could in any sense be called democratic is unthinkable. The hypocrisy which is so characteristic of our public life today is due primarily to our failure to acknowledge the fairly obvious fact that America is the scene of an irreconcilable conflict between two opposing forces. On the one side is the democratic tradition inherited from the past; on the other is a system of economic arrangements which increasingly partakes of the nature of industrial feudalism. Both of these forces cannot survive: one or the other must give way. Unless the democratic tradition is able to organize and conduct a successful attack on the economic system, its complete destruction is inevitable.

If democracy is to survive, it must seek a new economic foundation. Our traditional democracy rested upon small-scale production in both agriculture and industry and a rather general diffusion of the rights of property in capital and natural resources. The driving force at the root of this condition, as we have seen, was the frontier and free land. With the closing of the frontier, the exhaustion of free land, the growth of population, and the coming of large-scale production, the basis of ownership was transformed. If property rights are to be diffused in industrial society, natural resources and all important forms of capital will have to be collectively owned. Obviously every citizen cannot hold title to a mine, a factory, a railroad, a department store, or even a thoroughly mechanized farm. This clearly means that, if democracy is to survive in the United States, it must abandon its individualistic affiliations in the sphere of economics. What precise form a democratic society will take in the age of science and the machine, we cannot know with any assurance today. We must, however, insist on two things: first, that technology be released from the fetters and the domination of every type of special privilege; and, second, that the resulting system of production and distribution be made to serve directly the masses of the people. Within these limits, as I see it, our democratic tradition must of necessity evolve and gradually assume an essentially collectivistic pattern. The only conceivable alternative is the abandonment of the last vestige of democracy and the frank adoption of some modern form of feudalism.

4

The Rise of Scientific Curriculum Making and Its Aftermath

Herbert M. Kliebard

When Boyd Bode published *Modern Educational Theories* in 1927, he took on what had already become the entrenched establishment of the curriculum world. With his trenchant criticism of Franklin Bobbitt in the chapter, "Curriculum Construction and Consensus of Opinion" and of W. W. Charters in the succeeding chapter, "Curriculum Making and the Method of Job Analysis," Bode was attacking not only the work of two men who had established themselves as the prototypes of the curriculum specialist, but the very foundations on which curriculum as a field of specialization had been based. Bode probably did not suspect, however, that the notion of careful pre-specification of educational objectives (with variations in terminology and technique) and the notion of activity analysis as the means toward their "discovery" (also with variations in terminology and technique) would become the foundations on which, almost half a century later, many books would be written, Ph.D.s awarded, careers established, and millions of dollars expended. Certainly Bode never dreamed that legislation embodying these principles would be enacted across the United States and that the very ideas he was attacking would become semi-official doctrine in federal and state agencies as well as in many educational institutions.

The Scientific Curriculum Making of Bobbitt and Charters

Bobbitt and Charters lived in auspicious times. Mental discipline as a theoretical basis for the curriculum was almost dead by the early twentieth century. The bright flame of American Herbartianism, which had for a time captured the imagination of the educational world, was flickering. An educational ideology true to the times was needed, and nothing was more appropriate than scientific curriculum making. This doctrine, with its promise of precision and objectivity, had an immediate appeal. Certainly there was no reason why scientific principles applied to education would not meet with the same success as science applied to business in the form of scientific management. The general notion of applied science, as well as the particular model of scientific arrangement, is in fact evident throughout the work of Bobbitt and Charters.

Of the two, Bobbitt was perhaps the first to strike this rich vein. As a young instructor in educational administration at the University of Chicago, he effectively

Reprinted by permission of Blackwell Publishers, from *Curriculum Theory Network*, Vol. 5, No. 1, 1975, pp. 27–38.

drew the parallel between business techniques and education in a lengthy article in the Twelfth Yearbook of the National Society for the Study of Education (Bobbitt 1913). But Bobbitt, unlike other educators who turned to scientific management, was not content merely to apply certain management techniques to education, such as maximum utilization of the school plant; he provided the professional educators in the twentieth century with the concepts and metaphors—indeed, the very language—that were needed to create an aura of technical expertise without which the hegemony of professional educators could not be established. Science was not simply a tool with which to carve out exactitude in educational affairs generally and in the curriculum in particular; it was a means by which one could confer professional status and exclude the uninitiated. Even the term "curriculum specialist" implied a particular set of technical skills unavailable to the untrained. While the notion of science implies a certain aura of exclusiveness, Bobbitt was probably not explicitly aware of such a political use of his technical language. In his two major works, *The Curriculum* (1918) and *How to Make a Curriculum* (1924), as well as in numerous articles on the techniques of curriculum making, he seems simply to have believed that science had the key that idle speculation and even philosophy failed to provide.

Like Bobbitt, W. W. Charters was already a major leader in education by the time Bode's work was published. Charters had written *Methods of Teaching* in 1909 and *Teaching the Common Branches* in 1913, both popular books; but with *Curriculum Construction* in 1923, he established himself in the forefront of curriculum thinking. (In the preface to this book, Charters gives particular thanks to his "former colleague, B. H. Bode" for "his criticism of theoretical principles.") Like Bobbitt also, Charters approached the problems of curriculum from the perspective of functional efficiency. Through the method of activity analysis (or job analysis, as it was also called), Charters was able to apply professional expertise to the development of curricula in many diverse fields, including secretarial studies, library studies, pharmacy, and especially teacher education (with *The Commonwealth Teacher-Training Study* in 1929). Activity analysis was so universally applicable a technique of curriculum development that Charters was even able to use it to develop a curriculum for being a woman. As with other occupations, one simply had to analyze the particular activities that defined the role and then place these in relationship to the ideals that would control these activities. The training involved in performing the activities well would then become the curriculum (Charters 1921, 1925). Out of the work and thought of Bobbitt and Charters, as well as their contemporaries and disciples, arose a new rationale and a modus operandi for the curriculum field that were to prevail to the present day. So dominant did scientific curriculum making become that Bode's *Modern Educational Theories* stands as one of the few direct assaults on some of its principal tenets and certainly the most important.

Preparing for Adulthood

One of the most basic tenets of scientific curriculum making is a principle enunciated early in Bobbitt's *How to Make a Curriculum*: "Education is primarily for adult life, not for child life. Its fundamental responsibility is to prepare for the fifty years of adulthood, not for the twenty years of childhood and youth" (1924, p. 8). Education, in other words, consists in preparing to become an adult. There is probably no more crucial notion in the entire theory. Without it, there would be no point, for example, in such careful analysis of adult activities and their ultimate transformation into minute and explicit curricular objectives. Moreover, much curriculum policy, such as the strong emphasis on curriculum differentiation with its basis in predicting the probable destination of children as to their adult lives, rests squarely on education as preparation. If education is for what lies ahead, then it becomes of utmost importance to state with reasonable accuracy what that future holds. Bode's criticism is most telling in making the distinction between a prediction by, for example, an astronomer as to the curve of a comet and an educator constructing a future ideal in schooling. Curriculum making, in other words, is a form of utopian thinking, not of crystal-ball gazing. But Dewey, whom Bode cites favorably in this context, had gone even further in attacking the notion of preparation. In "My Pedagogic Creed," Dewey took pains to define education as "a process of living and not a preparation for future living" (1929, p. 292), and he undertook specifically in *Democracy and Education* to point up other deficiencies in the idea. To think of children as merely getting ready for a remote and obscure world, Dewey thought, is to remove them as social members of the community. "They are looked upon as candidates," he said; "they are placed on the waiting list" (1916, p. 63). Furthermore, since children are not directed and stimulated by what is so remote in time, the educator must introduce, on a large scale, extrinsic rewards and punishments. Bode's criticism of education as preparation rests largely on the assumption that it would lead to a social status quo rather than social improvement. While Dewey would no doubt agree, his criticism is more far-reaching and devastating. He considered not only its social significance but its impact on the child and the pedagogical process itself.

A curious sidelight to the importance of education as preparation in scientific curriculum making is Bobbitt's own developing ambivalence toward the idea. In setting forth his curriculum theory in the epic Twenty-Sixth Yearbook of the National Society for the Study of Education, Bobbitt says, "Education is not primarily to prepare for life at some future time. Quite the reverse; it purposes to hold high the current living. . . . In a very true sense, life cannot be 'prepared for.' It can only be lived" (1926, p. 43). Later, when asked to write his summary theory of curriculum, Bobbitt declared, "While there are general guiding principles that enable parents and teachers to foresee in advance the long general course that is normally run, yet they cannot foresee or foreknow the specific and concrete details of the course that is to be actualized" (1934, p. 4). In these passages, he sounds more like Kilpatrick than himself. But if Bobbitt was ambivalent, even self-contradictory, on the subject of education as preparation, his disciples and present intellectual heirs are not. If anything is ingrained in curriculum thinking today, it is the notion that it is the job of curriculum planners to anticipate the exact skills, knowledge, and—to use today's most fashionable term—"competencies" that will stand one in good stead at an imagined point in the future. These predictions about what one will need in the future become the bases of curriculum planning.

Specificity of Objectives

A concomitant of the emphasis on preparation is the insistence that the end products of the curriculum be stated with great particularity. Vague Delphic prophecies simply won't do. "'Ability to care for one's health' . . ." declared Bobbitt, "is too general to be useful. It must be reduced to particularity: ability to manage the ventilation of one's sleeping room, ability to protect one's self against micro-organisms, ability to care for the teeth, and so on" (1924, p. 32). If science is to be identified with exactitude, then scientific curriculum making must demonstrate its elevated status through the precision with which objectives are stated. It is at this point that Bode's criticism is both astute and telling. He points out, for example, that under the guise of scientific objectivity, Bobbitt inserts a submerged ideology. Scientific objectivity, it turns out, becomes a way of preserving the tried and true values of the society as well as making explicit the prevailing practical skills of the contemporary world.

Bode, of course, would not object to a philosophy of education governing curriculum; his objection is that the values of the scientific curriculum makers are disguised and covert. Furthermore, even a cursory examination of Bobbitt's most famous list of objectives would indicate wide latitude in the degree of specificity with which the objectives are stated. Alongside "the ability to keep one's emotional serenity, in the face of circumstances however trying" (1924, p. 25), "an attitude and desire of obedience to the immutable and eternal laws which appear to exist in the nature of things," and "confidence in the beneficence of these laws" (1924, p. 26), we find "ability to read and interpret facts expressed by commonly used types of graphs, diagrams, and statistical tables" (1924, p. 12), as well as "ability to care properly for the feet" (1924, p. 14). Although the injunction to be specific and explicit is unqualified, there seems to be some difficulty in carrying it out simply as a practical matter. In considering the efficient functioning of the human body, for example, we have no guidance as to whether to begin with the leg, the foot, the toe, or the toenail. The same problem would arise if we were dealing with the ability to swing a hammer or the ability to solve quadratic equations. The scientific curriculum makers' allegiance to specificity was allied to Thorndike's conception of the mind as consisting of multitudinous separate and individual functions (1901, p. 249), whereas Bode seems committed to a much broader conception of thought processes as well as a more optimistic view of transfer of training.

Making a Choice

If the practical problem of specificity were somehow resolved, perhaps by extending the list of objectives into the thousands or the hundreds of thousands, another issue would become even more apparent: how would we decide, objectively of course, which objectives to keep and which to leave out? As Bode indicates, one of Bobbitt's solutions was to throw the matter open to a vote or at least to a panel. In his famous Los Angeles study, Bobbitt asserted that his list of objectives "represent[ed] the practically unanimous judgment of some twenty-seven hundred well-trained and experienced adults" (1924, p. 10), a claim about which Bode is clearly skeptical. As Bode points out, the twelve hundred Los Angeles teachers, who were charged with reviewing the list drawn up by the fifteen hundred graduate students at the University of Chicago, were in a dilemma. All of the objectives listed unquestionably represented desirable traits and skills, from "keeping razor in order" (Bobbitt 1922, p. 21) to "ability to tell interesting stories interestingly—and many of them" (p. 26).

The wide agreement, Bode suspects, was probably achieved by a combination of specificity when practical and clearly desirable skills were involved and vagueness or ambiguity when value issues were broached. Inspection of Bobbitt's list of objectives indicates that Bode is essentially correct, thereby accounting in part for the obvious discrepancies in the level of specificity with which the objectives are stated as well as the near unanimity of agreement among twenty-seven hundred adult human beings. State legislators, educators, and the general public frequently find themselves in the same position today when they are asked to give their assent to such educational goals as "self-realization" and "mental health." One can hardly be against them.

A Standard for Living

Although Bode's criticism of the method of consensus is certainly convincing, he considers only indirectly another of Bobbitt's ways of dealing with the seemingly limitless scope of a curriculum defined by the full range of human activity. While the task of the "curriculum discoverer" did involve, according to Bobbitt, a full catalog of the activities of mankind, Bobbitt was careful to indicate that much of what has to be learned is acquired by "undirected experience." *"The curriculum of the directed training,"* Bobbitt insisted, *"is to be discovered in the shortcomings of individuals after they have had all that can be given by the undirected training"* (1918, p. 45, original emphasis). Bobbitt's understanding of "shortcomings," actually, is quite similar to the contemporary notion of "needs." A standard is set, a norm; and the curriculum consists of the ways of treating deviations from the standard. Thus the curriculum seems cut down to manageable proportions without resort to the method of consensus. (It is a deceptively simple solution.) The fundamental issue, however, is not whether the list of objectives is derived from this or that method: more basic is the question of whether objectives ought to be prespecified at all. One might argue, therefore, that Bode, in skillfully demolishing the method of consensus, did not quite strike the jugular vein of scientific curriculum making. The central question is whether the curriculum should be a blueprint for what people should be like, not how the blueprint is drawn.

But even if one were to concede prespecification of objectives in such areas as arithmetic, grammar, and spelling, how far could one go in justifying the "social shortcomings" of which Bobbitt speaks (1918, p. 50)? As many of Bobbitt's objectives imply, there was literally no activity of mankind—social, intellectual, or practical—that was not potentially, at least, a curricular objective. Bode correctly identified Herbert Spencer as having anticipated the trend toward specificity in stating objectives, but of at least equal importance is Spencer's role in identifying the scope of the school curriculum with life itself. Spencer, like Bobbitt and Charters, considered the best curriculum to be the one that demonstrated the highest utility. Spencer, it should be remembered, asked the question, "What knowledge is of most worth?", not merely, "What shall the schools teach?" In a subtle way, then, he was reconstructing a basic curriculum question. To the scientific curriculum makers, the two questions were essentially the same. Thus by posing their question in this way, scientific curriculum makers were determining the kind of answer that could be given. The answer to the scientific curriculum maker is likely to be phrased in terms of high survival value and functional utility rather than in terms of intellectual virtues. In this sense, the curriculum became the ultimate survival kit for the modern world. For example, in the state of Oregon today, certain districts have instituted requirements for high school graduation of such "survival" skills as listing birth-control methods in order of effectiveness, or demonstrating ability to officiate at two different sports and perform two basic dance steps (*Newsweek*, 20 January 1975, p. 69). Any sense of a distinctive function for the schools is lost.

Limitations of the School

Two serious but often unexamined questions are raised by such a conception of the school curriculum. The first relates to the extent to which the school as one institution of society can as a purely practical matter devote itself to the full range of human activity that man engages in. A second question, perhaps even more fundamental than the first, is whether all activity can be reduced to particular components.

From the days of the *Cardinal Principles* report to the present, the conventional way to begin the process of curriculum development has been to agree on a set of broad goals which in fact represents a categorization of human activity generally. The next step, of course, is to "operationalize" these goals by translating them into numerous minute and specific objectives—in effect, creating a catalog of human activity. Surely if Charters were able to identify the activities that constitute being a secretary or a librarian, it was only a step further to identify all the other activities of mankind. In this way the most urgent of these activities may be identified (e.g., earning a living) and the most pressing social problems addressed (e.g., drug addiction).

The missing ingredient in all this is some attention to the nature of the school. If there is one serious omission in Bode's analysis, it is the failure to recognize the limitations of the institution of schooling. The knowledge that is of the most worth may not be the kind of knowledge that can be transmitted in a school context. The place of the school in the social structure, the makeup of its inhabitants, and the characteristic activities that take place within its boundaries must be considered along with the power of schooling as we know it to produce fundamental and direct changes in human attitudes and behavior. Hence if curriculum makers do not temper the question of what is most important to know with the question of what schools can accomplish, their claims for programs designed to reduce crime, improve human relations, prevent drunken driving, ensure economic independence, or remove sex inhibitions are unreliable.

Analyzing Human Activity

Furthermore, while it may be true that a limited number of human activities may be anticipated and therefore practiced in advance, the extension of the method of job analysis from the limited realm of routine and replicative behavior into the full universe of human activity represents perhaps the most fundamental fallacy in the whole scientific curriculum-making movement. The source of this assumption, as is the case with other elements of scientific curriculum making, is the example of industry. Just as the global and complex process of building an automobile can be broken down into a series of minute and simple operations, so presumably can the activities of a mother or a teacher. But we do not learn language, for example, by anticipating all of the sentences we will utter in our adult lives and then rehearsing them as part of our preparation to become adults. Instead, we learn or assimilate or perhaps even inherit the governing principles of language that permit us to create or invent sentences that we have never before heard expressed. Similarly, in mathematics we do not scientifically catalog all of the mathematical operations we will perform as adults as a direct rehearsal for the performance of those mathematical operations.

Here Bode's criticism of job analysis as the universal technique of curriculum making is particularly cogent. The analogy between definite operations which imply simply replicative activity and activities that involve, let us say, judgment, simply will not hold. As he puts it, friendliness, courtesy, and honesty "are not reducible to 'definite operations'" (Bode 1927, p. 109). The process of educating a teacher to conduct himself or herself wisely and judiciously in the classroom is not, as current programs of teacher training so often imply, a process of first anticipating the particular situations that will arise in the classroom and then directing the teachers to conduct themselves in a particular way relative to these specific situations. Rather, teacher education can involve the examination, analysis, and adaptation of some broad principles which at some unknown point in the future and in some unanticipated circumstances may provide a guide to keen judgment and wise action.

Scientific Curriculum Making in Teacher Education

Bode's astute criticism of the scientific curriculum makers notwithstanding, it should be clear to anyone familiar with the current state of the art in the curriculum world that the scientific curriculum movement, with few adaptations and modifications, has been triumphant. It is true that behaviorism has provided a few refinements of language in stating objectives, and certain so-called academic subjects such as mathematics and science have perhaps more respectability than in the days of Bobbitt and Charters. But the key ingredients and analogies remain the same. While this modern version of scientific curriculum making is well established in virtually all sectors of the curriculum world, it exists, not surprisingly, in its most virulent form in the area of teacher education. The vogue movements which go under the names of competency-based teacher education (CBTE) and performance-based teacher education (PBTE) are prime examples of what has evolved from the basic principles enunciated by Bobbitt and Charters. Charters himself helped direct a major study begun in 1925 which had all the earmarks of the PBTE (or CBTE) ideology.

The Commonwealth Teacher-Training Study

As is the case with the current programs, the *Commonwealth Teacher-Training Study* was to be based on scientific research into the teaching process as opposed to mere speculation and tradition. As a first step, Charters and Waples "ascertained the traits that characterize excellent teachers" (1929, p. 4). Adapting the consensus approach, the investigators used two methods: analyzing the professional literature and interviewing "expert judges." Working from a list of eighty-three traits, ranging alphabetically from Accuracy through Foresight and Magnetism all the way to Wittiness (pp. 56–61), "translators" were given the task of interpreting statements made in writing or in the interviews. Thus, "knows how to meet people" could become translated into the traits, "adaptability" or "approachability." Reliability among the translators was determined by applying the Spearman prophecy formula. Finally, after some of the original traits of teachers were telescoped, scientifically determined lists were prepared indicating that senior high school teachers should be characterized by twenty-six traits including Good Taste and Propriety, junior high school teachers by Conventionality (morality) and Open-mindedness, and so on.

Next, in an adaptation of the job analysis technique, the investigators collected a master list of 1,001 teacher activities. Perhaps one of these activities is worth quoting in its entirety:

> 788. *Securing cordial relations with superintendent*
>   Maintaining cordial relations with superintendent. This involves being loyal to and respecting the superintendent. Becoming acquainted with superintendent and working in harmony with him. Performing friendly acts for superintendent; remembering superintendent at Christmas; making designs and drawings for superintendent; making lamp shades for superintendent's wife. [Charters and Waples 1929, p. 423]

Thus, after three years of research by trained investigators and a grant of $42,000 from the Commonwealth Fund, was a blow dealt to fuzzy thinking in teacher education and a major stride taken in the direction of a scientifically determined teacher-education curriculum.

The Contemporary Aftermath

One of the most persistent and puzzling questions in this, the aftermath of the scientific curriculum-making movement, is why we retain, even revere, the techniques and assumptions we have inherited from Bobbitt and Charters, at the same time as we reject, implicitly at least, the actual outcomes of their research. Few people read Bobbitt's famous study, *Curriculum-Making in Los Angeles*, or his magnum opus, *How to Make a Curriculum*, or have even heard of Charters and Waples's *Commonwealth Teacher-Training Study*. If they did read these works, the most likely reaction would be one of amusement. And yet we pursue with sober dedication the techniques on which these works are based. Admittedly, performance-based teacher education may just be a slogan system resting only on a foundation of high-sounding rhetoric and pious promises and covered with a gloss of false novelty; but if it means anything, it surely implies that one can identify the particular components of teaching activity that make for good teachers and that these characteristics (Charters would call them traits) or behaviors (Charters would call them activities) can form the basis of a program of teacher training. Research takes the form of identifying the particular components of teaching that will ensure success. While there seems to be some caution in stating the characteristics and behaviors with the same degree of conviction as Bobbitt and Charters did, an abiding faith in the efficacy of the approach remains. The persistence of this faith in the face of a record of over a half century of failure is a mystery that probably even Bode could not fathom.

Is Teaching a Technology?

At the heart of some of our most fundamental problems in the field of curriculum and of teacher education as well is the question of whether teaching is a technology by which carefully fashioned products in the form of learning or behavior are made. These products would have to be designed with the exactitude and specificity that Bobbitt and Charters called for. Teaching would be the application of standardized means by which predictable results would be achieved, and curriculum development the specification of the end-products and the rules for their efficient manufacture. Teacher education, in turn, would be the process by which persons are transformed into efficient manufacturers. The research evidence that presumably would support such an analogy between the teaching and the manufacturing process, however, has been disappointing to the proponents. For example, a recent thorough examination of the research basis for performance-based teacher education led to the conclusion that eleven process variables previously identified as "promising"—such as "clarity," "variability," and "enthusiasm"—were indeed notably unpromising, leading the authors to conclude that "an empirical basis for performance-based teacher education does not exist" (Heath and Nielson 1974, p. 475). Moreover, pessimism about the ultimate success of the approach was not based simply on flaws in statistical analysis or research design. The more fundamental problem was the framework in which such research was cast—a framework which, by the way, has held sway since the days of Bobbitt, Charters, and the scientific curriculum-making movement.

Bode as Prophet

The point of all this is not simply that Bobbitt, Charters, and their likeminded contemporaries were mistaken in their faith in a given approach; the age in which they lived was one where optimism about the power of science to solve a multitude of human and social problems was near its peak. If they were naive or mistaken, one can hardly blame them. What is almost unforgivable, however, is that the half century since the zenith of their influence has produced little more by way of sophistication and refinement. With few exceptions, Bode's criticism of 1927 would carry as much force today were it directed against the present-day heirs of scientific curriculum making.

Particularly disappointing are the precipitous efforts to convert highly tentative and limited research findings into immediate prescriptions. This may be a function of the large constituency of teachers and school administrators who want immediate and concrete answers to such global questions as What is a good teacher? and What is a good curriculum? Part of the problem, undoubtedly, with the era of the scientific curriculum makers and with ours is the failure to recognize the complexity of the phenomena with which we deal. There is the same confusion between science and desert empiricism, the same naiveté about the nature of the teaching process, the same neglect of conceptual analysis. To be critical of scientific curriculum making, as Bode was, is not to be critical of science or even the importance of scientific inquiry into educational processes: it is to be critical of a simplistic and vulgar scientism. Its persistence is a source of embarrassment.

References

Bobbitt, Franklin. "Some general principles of management applied to the problems of city-school systems." In The supervision of city schools. Twelfth Yearbook of the National Society for the Study of Education, Part 1, pp. 7–96. Bloomington, Ill.: Public School Publishing Co., 1913.

_____. The curriculum. Boston: Houghton Mifflin, 1918.

_____. Curriculum-making in Los Angeles. Supplementary Educational Monographs, no. 20. Chicago: University of Chicago Press, 1922.

_____. How to make a curriculum. Boston: Houghton Mifflin, 1924.

_____. "The orientation of the curriculum-maker." In The foundations and technique of curriculum-construction. Twenty-Sixth Yearbook of the National Society for the Study of Education, Part 2, pp. 41–55. Bloomington, Ill.: Public School Publishing Co., 1926.

_____. "A summary theory of the curriculum." Society for Curriculum Study News Bulletin 5 (January 12, 1934): 2–4.

Bode, Boyd H. Modern educational theories. New York: Macmillan, 1927.

Charters, Werrett W. Methods of teaching: Developed from a functional standpoint. Chicago: Row, Peterson & Co., 1909.

_____. Teaching the common branches. Boston: Houghton Mifflin, 1913.

_____. "The reorganization of women's education." Educational Review 62 (October 1921): 224–31.

_____. Curriculum construction. New York: Macmillan, 1923.

_____. "Curriculum for women." In Proceedings of the high school conference. Urbana, Ill.: University of Illinois. 1925.

Charters, Werrett W., and Waples, Douglas. The commonwealth teacher-training study. Chicago: University of Chicago Press, 1929.

Dewey, John. Democracy and education: An introduction to the philosophy of education. New York: Macmillan, 1916.

_____. "My pedagogic creed." Journal of the National Education Association 18, no. 9 (December 1929): 291–95.

Heath, Robert W., and Nielson, Mark A. "The research basis for performance-based teacher education." Review of Educational Research 44, no. 4 (Fall 1974): 463–84.

National Education Association Commission on the Reorganization of Secondary Education. *Cardinal principles of secondary education: A report.* Washington, D.C.: Government Printing Office, 1918.

Spencer, Herbert. "What knowledge is of most worth?" In *Education: Intellectual, moral and physical,* pp. 1–96. New York: D. Appleton and Co., 1860.

"Survival Test." *Newsweek,* January 25, 1975, p. 69.

Thorndike, E. L., and Woodworth, R. S. "The influence of improvement in one mental function upon the efficiency of other functions," Part 1. *Psychological Review* 8, no. 3 (May 1901): 247–61.

II

CURRICULUM AT EDUCATION'S CENTER STAGE

The readings in this part of the book reflect the reform efforts of the 1950s and 1960s, an era of unprecedented federal and private support for curriculum development projects. The life cycle of this reform era began in crisis, was nurtured by unshakable optimism, and ended in ardent controversy. The crisis, then set against the backdrop of Cold War politics, was a national crisis of rigor. With their perceived relevance to national defense, mathematics, science, and foreign language curricula were the first to be judged as outdated, deficient, or in a state of general neglect. The era's optimism was in the faith that subject matter specialists, armed with academically rigorous knowledge, could set American schools back on track. The controversy played out in both political and professional arenas. Its political aftermath is symbolized by what eventually came to be an open attack on the National Science Foundation for its role in the development of an elementary social studies curriculum, "Man: A Course of Study" (Schaffarzick, 1979). Controversy on the professional side also has its symbols, including Schwab's pronouncement in 1969 that, for all practical purposes, the curriculum field had reached a moribund state.

All three of these elements—crisis, optimism, and controversy—are acknowledged in the pages we have extracted from John Goodlad's *School Curriculum Reform in the United States*. This small yet ambitious book was published in 1964; his aim is to survey and critique the then current national reform projects "from the viewpoint of a curriculum generalist" (p. 6). The reform movement, according to Goodlad, had already taken on several distinctive characteristics. They included: 1) the financial support of private foundations and federal agencies; 2) the widespread involvement of discipline-based scholars; 3) the affiliation of projects with national organizations such as the American Mathematical Society and the American Association for the Advancement of Science; 4) the focus of projects on subject-centered curriculum; and 5) their top-down approach to curriculum planning.

Goodlad describes sixteen "illustrative projects" in subject areas ranging from social studies and English language arts to mathematics and science. We have extracted four projects to represent high school mathematics, high school physics, elementary school mathematics, and elementary school science. Following these descriptions is a "potpourri" section that briefly identifies related trends. The arts are noted in this potpourri section largely for their absence, albeit they would eventually join the reform movement in their own time and on their own terms. Two other trends mentioned were less conspicuous at the time, at least to the discipline-based scholars who had initiated the reform projects. These trends focus on reorganizing schools to achieve more "cooperative teaching arrangements" (Goodlad, this volume, p. 45) and recognizing issues of student diversity.

While the marginality of these trends imply a certain critique of the reform movement, Goodlad's concerns as a curriculum generalist are still more deeply rooted in a problem that is obvious today only in retrospect. The movement's subject-centered approach generally assumed the value of academic content and the ability of students to learn that content. These assumptions take for granted and thus provide little justification for answering two of the most fundamental questions in curriculum planning: What determines content worth learning, and how should that content be taught? Furthermore, Goodlad situates this Achilles heel within the historical context of the movement itself, arguing that its subject-centered approach should be viewed as a reaction to the earlier trends introduced in Part I of this volume. In Goodlad's (1964) words, "To the extent that this reaction to child-centered and society-oriented theories is itself perceived to be an overemphasis on subject matter in determining curricular ends and means, today's movement already is breeding tomorrow's counter-reaction" (p. 87).

Goodlad's critique ultimately reasserts questions of educational purpose, and doing so sets the stage for the next three readings. These readings represent "the great objectives debate" over issues in the field that extend back in time to the work of Bobbitt and others who adopted the scientific strand of American educational progressivism. By the late 1960s, this debate had come to focus not on what specific objectives should be used in curriculum planning, but rather on how objectives should be used, the form they should take, and functions they should be expected to serve. The dominant camp worked from a means–ends perspective that required curriculum developers to clearly state the objectives of a program prior to deciding its content or activities. Proponents of this approach, such as W. James Popham, argued that prespecified, clearly stated, and measurable objectives are essential to curriculum planning for at least two reasons. First, educators without such objectives would not know the outcomes they seek to realize, and thus have little basis for deciding how to select or organize classroom activities. Second, without objectives, an evaluator would not know what to look for in determining a program's success or failure. Falling under the influence of this logic, almost an entire generation of American teachers learned to write behavioral objectives using standardized and tightly specified formats.

A dissenting position is represented by Elliot Eisner's well-known article, "Educational Objectives: Help or Hindrance?" Eisner questions both the practicality of prespecified objectives and the underlying assumptions on which they are based. On the practical side, he sees two problems. First, the potential outcomes of instruction are usually so numerous that it would be difficult to anticipate all of them with a high degree of specificity. Second, the objectives-first sequence does not seem to be borne out in practice. That is, while teachers often begin with explicit aims, they also allow the selection of content and activities to inform those aims as instructional activities unfold in the classroom. To put this another way, Eisner is arguing that the rationality of teaching is more dynamic, more interactive, and less mechanistic than is often assumed. Moreover, Eisner asserts that evaluators have confused objectives with standards. Standards can be applied in a fairly routine manner, but using objectives as criteria for assessment always entails an element of judgment on the part of the evaluator.

The third reading in this set is Lauren Sosniak's chapter from *Bloom's Taxonomy: A Forty-Year Retrospective*. Sosniak provides a contemporary perspective on what is now almost four decades of debate over the appropriate forms and functions of educational objectives. Sosniak addresses this debate within the context of Bloom's taxonomy, perhaps the best-known framework for defining and classifying educational objectives. While the taxonomy was created as an assessment tool, it quickly found its way into the discourse of curriculum planning. There the taxonomy has served as a proxy for earlier traditions. Sosniak notes two traditions in particular that in the 1950s would have been highly consistent with the potential uses of the taxonomy. The first tradition is represented in Ralph Tyler's (1949) efforts to make educational objectives the cornerstone of systematic curriculum development. The second tradition is the longstanding desire among curriculum scholars to provide teachers and other educational practitioners with forms of technical assistance.

In this instance, "assistance" has most often come in the guise of exhortation, for the taxonomy has proved to be an effective vocabulary for criticizing the overemphasis of curricula on the so-called lower-level skills of factual recognition and recall. In other words, the taxonomy's greatest contribution to practice may have always been as a basis for encouraging teachers to nurture in their students more sophisticated forms of thinking. There is some irony in this possibility because both the authors of the taxonomy and its subsequent critics have raised concerns that using this framework to formulate objectives will make the process of curriculum planning more mechanistic and less thoughtful than it would be otherwise. Another criticism noted by Sosniak is that the tight connection between objectives and evaluation—the connection for which the taxonomy was created—tends to draw attention away from the actual activities and routines of classroom practice. Curriculum researchers, for example, have often used the taxonomy to analyze objectives and then link those objectives to student test performance without ever setting foot inside a school or classroom.

The tendency to jump from objectives to evaluation, and in the process to take practice for granted, is one of the reasons that Philip Jackson's book, *Life in Classrooms*, is looked back on as having made a distinctive contribution to the field. Jackson does not vault over practice as much as he jumps directly into it. In the brief excerpts we have taken from his book, Jackson offers a number of arguments for why the routines of practice should be of paramount concern for those interested in school curriculum and classroom teaching. These routines are often overshadowed because they are commonplace, repetitive, and ordinary. Herein lies an interesting paradox; for if Jackson is right, practice is ignored for the same reasons that it is important. The routines of practice have a significant impact because they are commonplace, repetitive, and ordinary. Furthermore, Jackson argues that these routines are more than simply ways of delivering subject matter or lesson content. Rather, "the daily grind" itself teaches a hidden curriculum of unspoken expectations, and these expectations are what most often determine a student's school success or failure. If researchers or evaluators were to examine an educational program solely on the basis of its stated objectives, the hidden curriculum would in all likelihood remain just that—hidden.

The final reading in this section is Joseph Schwab's article, "The Practical: A Language for Curriculum." It is the first of four articles (published between 1970 and 1983) in which Schwab examines a range of issues related to developments within the field and to "the practical arts" of curriculum deliberation. We have included the first of these essays in our collection partly because of its distinctively broad scope. It is an essay that can be viewed in several ways: as a critique of the field at large; as an effort to reframe the relationship between theory and practice; and as a call for problem-based, collaborative forms of curriculum development. For its time, the article also reflects a heightened level of self-consciousness about the field's past, current, and future trends.

Schwab's place in curriculum history and his overall contributions to the field are two questions on which scholars currently disagree. Jackson (1992), for example, views Schwab's work as moving away from systematic approaches as conceived in the past, but still offering a version of the dominant perspective that had already been well established in the work of people such as Bobbitt and Tyler. In this view, Schwab was working with variations on the theme. Others, such as William Reid (1993), argue that Schwab's work be placed in a category by itself, as an alternative to the dominant perspective rather than as a modified version of earlier approaches. Nothing inherent in systematic methods (i.e., Bobbitt's approach) would seem to automatically exclude the forms of deliberation and the practical arts on which Schwab focused his work. Yet, as Reid notes, these are precisely the aspects of curriculum development on which earlier traditions of scholarship provide little if any guidance.

References

Goodlad, J. I. (1964). *School curriculum reform in the United States*. New York: The Fund for the Advancement of Education.

Jackson, P. W. (1992). Conceptions of curriculum and curriculum specialists. In P. W. Jackson (Ed.), *Handbook of research on curriculum* (pp. 3–40). New York: Macmillan.

Reid, W. A. (1993). Does Schwab improve on Tyler? A response to Jackson. *Journal of Curriculum Studies, 25*, 499–510.

Schaffarzick, J. (1979). Federal curriculum reform: A crucible for value conflict. In J. Schaffarzick & G. Sykes (Eds.), *Value conflicts and curriculum issues* (pp. 1–24). Berkeley: McCutchan.

Tyler, R. (1949). *Basic principles of curriculum and instruction*. Chicago: University of Chicago Press.

5

School Curriculum Reform in the United States

JOHN I. GOODLAD

The Reform Movement

Talk of the "new" mathematics, the "new" physics, and the "new" biology is commonplace today. Various groups and individuals, handsomely supported by the National Science Foundation—and, to a lesser degree, by several private philanthropic foundations—have developed new courses and instructional materials to go with them for high-school mathematics, physics, chemistry, biology, economics, geography, anthropology, English, and foreign languages, and for several subjects taught in elementary schools. Thousands of teachers and students have participated in the preparation and trial use of these materials. Clearly, a massive reformulation of what is to be taught and learned in the schools of the United States of America is under way.

The beginnings of the current curriculum reform movement are commonly identified with the successful launching of the first Russian satellite in the fall of 1957. This spectacular event set off blasts of charges and countercharges regarding the effectiveness of our schools and accelerated curriculum revision, notably in mathematics and the physical sciences. But the roots of change go back further, to the years immediately following World War II. The recruitment of young men for the armed services had revealed shocking inadequacies in the science and mathematics programs of high-school graduates. The problem was partly the limited quantity of work in these fields, partly the quality of what had been taught. The secondary-school curriculum too often reflected knowledge of another era, instead of the scientific advances of the twentieth century. Recognizing their responsibility for this unhappy state of affairs, scholars in a few fields began to participate actively in what has now become a major curriculum reform movement.

Sometimes the initiative came from an individual, sometimes from a learned society, such as the American Mathematical Society, for example. In either case, the subsequent course of events was surprisingly similar from project to project. First, a group of scholars met to review the need for pre-collegiate curriculum change in their field. Then, in subsequent summers, scholars and teachers invited from the schools planned course content and wrote materials. These materials were tried out in cooperating schools during the school year and revised in the light of this experience. Meanwhile, in summer and year-long institutes, teachers were educated in the new content and

Public domain, from John I. Goodlad, *School Curriculum Reform in the United States.* New York: The Fund for the Advancement of Education, 1964: pp. 9–12, 14–16, 20–21, 23–25, 40–42, 50–51, 54–56.

methodology. Throughout, participants seemed in agreement that new materials are central to a basic curriculum change.

The current curriculum reform movement is too far advanced to still warrant the adjective "new." In some fields, notably mathematics, the first wave of change is about to be followed by a second; the "new" new mathematics is in the offing.

It is dangerous, however, to assume that curriculum change has swept through all of our 85,000 public elementary and 24,000 public secondary schools during this past decade of reform. Tens of thousands of schools have scarcely been touched, or not been touched at all, especially in areas of very sparse or very dense population. Tens of thousands of teachers have had little opportunity to realize what advances in knowledge and changes in subject fields mean for them. Tens of thousands hold emergency certificates or teach subjects other than those in which they were prepared. In elementary schools, teachers with backgrounds in science and mathematics constitute a species that is about as rare as the American buffalo.

Suburban schools, with their ability to provide resources for in-service education, and for attracting qualified teachers, have fared better by comparison.

Curriculum planning is a political process, just as it is an ideological process of determining ends and means for education. Proposals either find their way through the political structure into educational institutions, or slip into obscurity. The unique and sensitive relationship among local, state, and federal governments in the support and conduct of school affairs has materially affected the ways in which the various curriculum projects have entered the bloodstream of American education.

Almost without exception, these projects have had their genesis outside of the formal political structure. They have been conceived primarily by scholars in colleges and universities who were joined by teachers from elementary and secondary schools. Projects have been supported by funds that are predominantly federal in origin, attesting to the fact that the education of its youth is a primary interest of the nation. Conditions of the grants have cautioned recipients against promoting their wares in any way; project directors have been limited to descriptive information, articles and, on request, speeches. But their efforts are in vain unless the results find their way to local schools and school systems. It is not surprising, therefore, that products, largely in the form of textbooks, often have been turned over to commercial publishers who have their own effective means of reaching state and local school authorities.

The strengths and weaknesses of the several projects stem in part from the structure of the American educational system and its characteristic strengths and weaknesses. For example, instead of having one set of clearly defined aims for America's schools, we have many. Consequently, each curriculum project is free to formulate objectives for its own particular segment of the curriculum. Rarely are these objectives defined with such precision that one would know exactly what to evaluate in determining the success of a given project. It might be argued that those undertaking the various curriculum activities have no responsibility for the formulation of objectives but that this should be done by the local school districts.

Each project, then, is responsible only for specifying what should be taught in a given subject. But can ends and means of curriculum planning be thus separated?

The curriculum reform movement so far has been focused on single subjects—planned, generally, from the top down. This focus and the "national" character of the projects have attracted first-rate scholars into pre-collegiate curriculum planning. But these characteristics have also attracted scholars from fields normally outside of pre-collegiate schooling who sense, apparently, an opportunity to include their particular roads to the good life in the curriculum of elementary or secondary schools.

This competition among fields places severe burdens upon instructional time. Just how all of the subjects will share in the available time remains to be seen. Demands will exceed time, even if the school day, week and year should be lengthened. Some subjects will have to be combined or left out—there is not enough room for twenty academic disciplines in the kindergarten. Arguments for the root nature and basic value of a discipline notwithstanding, problems of which subject should prevail are generally solved in the political realm at federal, state, and local levels of educational responsibility. National concerns tend to dominate today but, with any appreciable reduction in world tension, the humanities and social sciences should be gaining increasing favor.

Some Illustrative Projects . . .

University of Illinois Committee on School Mathematics (UICSM)

The Committee on School Mathematics developed as a result of the interest of three colleges (Education, Engineering, and Liberal Arts and Sciences) at the University of Illinois in improving their freshman courses. This interest subsequently shifted to high-school mathematics. From 1951 through 1961, the work of the committee was supported by funds from the University of Illinois, the United States Office of Education, the National Science Foundation (for summer institutes), and the Carnegie Corporation. During these ten years, materials for grades 9 through 12 were produced and tested. The second phase of this program, the preparation of materials for grades 7 through 12, has just begun and is being supported by the National Science Foundation. Materials from the first phase will be used only if they satisfy criteria for the second. Max Beberman, project director, estimates expenditures of approximately $1,000,000 annually after 1963–64.

The committee set out to present mathematics as a consistent, unified discipline; to lead students to "discover" principles for themselves; and to assure the development of those manipulative skills necessary for problem-solving. The UICSM program emphasizes "learning by discovery," with the student *doing* (rather than being told about) mathematics. The student need not verbalize his discovery; in fact, early verbalization is discouraged for fear that premature or incorrect verbalization of a generalization may hinder its use. "Precision in exposition is something we expect of the textbook and the teacher, rather than of the learner. Precise communication is a characteristic of a good textbook and a good teacher; correct *action* is a characteristic of a good learner."[1] Verbalization, for communication and proof, is to come only after the student has become thoroughly familiar with the generalization and has had adequate opportunity to test and refine it.

A four-year sequential program has been developed through eleven units as follows: (1) the arithmetic of real numbers; (2) pronumerals, generalizations, and algebraic manipulations, (3) equations and inequations, applications; (4) ordered pairs and graphs; (5) relations and functions; (6) geometry; (7) mathematical induction; (8) sequences; (9) exponential and logarithmic functions; (10) circular functions and trigonometry; and (11) polynomial functions and complex numbers. Units 1–4 are intended for the first year (grade 9), units 5–6 for the second, units 7–8 for the third, and units 9–11 for the fourth (grade 12). There is a teachers' edition for each unit, consisting of the students'

---

1. Max Beberman and Herbert Vaughan, "Unit 1 of High School Mathematics" (Teacher's Edition), Introduction. Urbana, Illinois: University of Illinois Press, 1960.

edition plus commentary pages, providing mathematical background material and teaching suggestions, together with answers to the problems in the text. Both teachers' and students' editions are published by the University of Illinois Press.

The UICSM program is designed for *all* students, but it is assumed that many students will drop mathematics after a year or two, leaving only those who are somewhat more interested in mathematics for the last two years. Some schools report satisfactory use of the ninth-grade materials with gifted eighth-grade students. Materials to be developed in the second phase of the project will reach up to the first two years of the present college curriculum, and will branch sideways into a variety of applications. Beberman is much interested in programmed materials for self-instruction (and such materials already have been developed) but is reluctant to use them to the point of eliminating the "electric charge," as he calls it, of group interaction. He believes that students are motivated and stimulated through the realization that other students are "getting something" they don't yet see.

The sequence of units and accompanying pedagogy virtually necessitate the special training of teachers. Until 1958, textbooks were available only to teachers who had received special training in their use and who were willing to assist in their evaluation. Even today, teachers planning to use the materials are urged to consult colleagues who have had such special training and to seek it for themselves. Both, summer institutes and pedagogical films are available for this purpose. The committee urges use of the complete sequence, and discourages the use of single units, either by themselves or in conjunction with other materials.

The effectiveness of the UICSM program, as the effectiveness of other projects in the current curriculum reform movement, has not been fully tested. This is due partly to the difficulty entailed in evaluating such goals, for example, as "an intuitive grasp of fundamental principles," partly to the absence of criteria for comparing programs. Students in the UICSM courses, however, do about as well as students in traditional mathematics on tests designed for the latter. What the UICSM has produced so far is but a beginning. The group has embarked upon computer analyses of programmed materials and of "systems" approaches to the teaching-learning situation that should prove valuable in further curriculum revision. . . .

The Suppes Experimental Project in the Teaching of Elementary-School Mathematics

Patrick Suppes of Stanford University is developing a mathematics program for kindergarten and the first three grades (and perhaps the fourth), and a program in mathematical logic for able fifth-and-sixth-grade children. Only the first of the programs is described here.

The central concept in the materials developed for the primary years is that of a set. According to Suppes, "all mathematics can be developed from the concept of set and operations upon sets."[2] He views sets as appropriate for young children because sets are more concrete than numbers and, in addition, facilitate mathematically precise definitions.

The project is experimental and involves a great deal of comparison between children using the Suppes materials, and those in regular, control classes. The aim is to

---

2. Patrick Suppes, "Sets and Numbers," an Experimental Project in the Teaching of Elementary School Mathematics, 1962–1963. (Mimeographed, Stanford: Institute for Mathematical Studies in the Social Sciences, January, 1963), p. 2.

develop a program that is both mathematically sound and pedagogically simple. Although the major emphasis is on the concepts, laws, and skills of arithmetic, content from both algebra and geometry is included. The materials stress precise and exact mathematical language. Experience has shown that a young child easily learns a technical vocabulary when the idea represented is clear. A fundamental assumption throughout this project is that children in the primary grades can learn much more mathematics than is traditionally assumed.

Workbooks for kindergarten and the first three grades have been written and used with selected classes. Production, at least in the initial stages, has been virtually a one-man job, with Suppes writing the exercises from his personal conception of what is mathematically desirable and feasible for the children. Experimental classes were taught by regular classroom teachers, with no special background or presupposed training. The teachers were brought together for a general orientation period at the beginning of the school year and met monthly thereafter to discuss problems and progress. The preparation of workbooks and teachers' manuals has been supported by a grant from the Carnegie Corporation.

Testing, supported by a grant from the National Science Foundation, has sought to determine the difference in children's learning of the experimental material and of traditional arithmetic. For example, a test designed to measure content in most first-grade arithmetic books was used in comparing experimental and non-experimental (control) classes. Over-all accomplishment favored the experimental group, especially on items involving arithmetical operations. There were no significant differences on items involving simple recognition of Arabic numerals, sequence of numerals, and telling of time.

A major phase of the work, supported by a grant from the Office of Education, involves detailed analysis of how children form and learn mathematical concepts. Studies of individual children under controlled experimental conditions seek to uncover, for example, the courses of greatest difficulty in the workbook exercises. The Suppes effort goes far beyond the reorganization of conventional content into both a tentative program of new content and a search for the kind and amount of mathematics that can be handled successfully by elementary-school children. . . .

Physical Science Study Committee (PSSC)

The Physical Science Study Committee, in developing a first physics course for high-school students, has acted as a pioneer in many areas of the curriculum reform movement: in the effective involvement of scholars and teachers, in the search for truly fundamental concepts, in the development of films, and in the packaging of an instructional program. PSSC's activities, initially centered at the Massachusetts Institute of Technology, led to the formation of Educational Services Incorporated (Watertown, Mass.), a non-profit corporation which now administers them. Major grants to support the committee's work have come from the National Science Foundation; smaller grants from the Sloan Foundation and the Ford Foundation's Fund for the Advancement of Education.

The PSSC course emphasizes the basic structure of physics, the acquisition of new physical knowledge, and the necessity for understanding rather than memorizing basic physics concepts. A central concept is the laboratory in which students gain first-hand experience in discovering and verifying physical phenomena. The program contains fewer facts than are usually included in an elementary physics course, but concepts are to be understood and used, not just asserted. The committee has worked out a comprehensive set of means for achieving the purposes of its course: a textbook, laboratory experiments and simplified apparatus, films, achievement tests, books on special topics, and a teacher's guide to classroom and laboratory activities.

The course consists of four parts, each one building on the preceding part. Part I deals with the fundamental concepts of time, space, and matter; part II with a detailed examination of light; part III with motion; and part IV with electricity and the physics of the atom. Students count, measure, observe; learn about, construct, and test conceptual models; and finally arrive at the modern model of atoms. They come to see that physics is not fixed or static but that it evolves from the inquiries and basic research of scientists.

Where textbook, class discussion and the laboratory leave off, films take over. The films are not of the usual "enrichment" sort. Some introduce the student to an area which he will traverse later; others present a simple experiment for him to duplicate; some include experiments which cannot be completed in the school laboratory, and still others present the more difficult portions of the course. The viewer is struck by the painstaking care that has gone into the production of each film, be it the portrayal of physical phenomena or of investigators at work.

Teacher institutes during the summer and school year have been an integral part of the PSSC physics program from its inception. Since the first year of operation, 1957–58, when eight teachers and 300 students used the course, it has mushroomed. Approximately 4,000 teachers and 170,000 students, or 40 to 45 per cent of all secondary-school students enrolled in physics classes in the United States, participated during 1963–64. Hundreds more teachers used parts of the course materials in conjunction with conventional physics textbooks, and interest has even spread to foreign countries. Translations of the textbook into Spanish and Japanese are completed and translations into French, Italian, Danish, Swedish, Norwegian, Hebrew, Portuguese, and Turkish are in process.

Evaluation of the program confronts the common query: can its effectiveness be appraised by using conventional tests. The committee's answer is an emphatic "No." Mimeographed articles contrast objectives of the PSSC course with objectives of conventional physics courses, stressing the limitations of conventional tests in attempting evaluative comparisons. An examination prepared and administered by the College Entrance Examination Board has been used to compare students in PSSC with those in conventional physics classes.

Students coming through this new physics course, like students coming through other new high-school curricula, move on to college courses geared more closely to the old materials. There is no evidence to suggest that these high-school graduates are in any way at a disadvantage, although they sometimes have indicated a dissatisfaction with their college fare. The Physical Science Study Committee points to the need for revising the college physics curriculum if PSSC students are to be adequately challenged, and if college courses are to keep pace with current thought in the realm of physics education. There are increasing signs that this collegiate reform has started. . . .

Science—A Process Approach

During the summer, 1963, a writing group under the Commission on Science Education of the American Association for the Advancement of Science prepared a teachers' manual and a number of course content outlines in science for the early years of elementary schooling. The experimental edition of the content outlines has appeared in five paperbook sections. The effort is financed by a grant from the National Science Foundation.

Fundamental assumptions underlying the proposed courses are that science is much more than a simple encyclopedic collection of facts, and that children in the primary grades can benefit from acquiring certain basic skills and competencies essential to the learning of science. These competencies have been identified as follows: observation, classification, recognition and use of space-time relations, recognition and use of numbers and number relations, measurement, communication, inference, and prediction. The expectation is that the ability to use scientific processes will remain after many of the details of science have been forgotten. These competencies are advocated as appropriate for virtually all levels of science education and are not confined to the primary grades.

Four major areas of content, designated as appropriate for the first ten years of school, give some guidance in the selection of specific topics through which scientific behavior is to be achieved. These are: the universe—its galaxies, our solar system, the earth and the immediate environment, and measurements used to describe astronomical and geological phenomena; the structure and reactions of matter—compounds and mixtures, large and small molecules, elements, atoms, protons, neutrons, and electrons; the conservation and transformation of energy—the electro magnetic spectrum, motion and potential energy, electrical energy and chemical energy, force and work, and gravitational and magnetic fields; the interaction between living things and their environment—animal and human behavior, the relation between biological structure and function, reproduction, development, genetics, evolution, and the biological units of cell, organism, and population.

All of the books currently available are for teachers. The teachers' guide is an overall view of the rationale of curriculum organization, of the topics, and of recommended instructional procedures. The other books outline the specific content and activities to be used by the teacher. Each of them lists a dozen or more topics, organized so as to remind the reader that they be used in developing student ability to observe, measure, classify, and communicate. Each topic is designed with two or three particular objectives in mind. Thus, the first topic of the first book, "Recognizing Regular Shapes," specifically states that, with completion of instruction, the children should be able to recognize common two-dimensional shapes and to identify common shapes as components of complex objects. At the end of each topic, ways and means are suggested to evaluate whether or not these aims have been achieved. This procedure is followed for all the topics covered by the booklets.

In view of the fact that these preliminary materials were prepared in an eight-weeks' writing session during the summer, 1963, and have been tried out in only a very preliminary way, an appraisal of the specific content and suggested activities would be premature. The booklets have recently been introduced into selected cooperating schools, a step which will probably result in a substantial revision.

This project is noteworthy, furthermore, in that it recognizes the many persistent curricular problems and attempts to solve them. Clearly, the current stand is that no single science discipline should prevail but that topics from many sciences and from mathematics should be woven into a unified whole, the goal being the development of a basic scientific behavior in the student.

The advice to teachers to begin with part I in the first grade (if there is no kindergarten), part II in the second grade, part III in the third grade, etc., raises some questions about how individual differences are to be taken care of. However, the project supplies a check list to help teachers determine pupil accomplishment so that they can adjust their teaching accordingly. How subsequent individualization of instruction is to be provided is not made clear, but it is anticipated that the feedbacks from trial use will influence adjustments for differences in ability. . . .

Potpourri

The foregoing descriptions of projects and activities in various subject fields are a representative sample of current curriculum reform in the United States. They are proof of the steadily increasing interest in improving the curriculum by constructing new courses and producing more effective teaching materials. The many other curricular and instructional efforts—to numerous to be included here—are additional evidence of the intense efforts on the part of educators and laymen alike to raise the quality of American education.

Noteworthy among the less formalized endeavors are recommendations suggesting that the fine and applied arts—virtually pushed aside as "frills" during the past decade—may, one day, have a place in the curriculum, along with science, mathematics, and foreign languages. The arts, it is believed, can not only contribute to the understanding and attitude needed to stay an ever-threatening holocaust but can also contribute significantly to man's quality of living in a world which, hopefully, will survive.

The work on creativity by psychologists such as Guilford, Taylor, Torrance, Getzels, and Jackson, and on inquiry and inquiry training by Bruner and Suchman, is closely related to the current curriculum reform movement. Undoubtedly, these men and others have been instrumental in creating the growing interest that many subject-matter specialists have lately displayed in having their students learn fundamental concepts and processes in preference to their merely memorizing facts. Psychologists and educators involved in various aspects of programmed instruction have had a major part in stimulating the curricular reformers to arrange subject matter in more meaningful sequences, and to base whole sections of courses entirely on auto-instructional techniques.

The growing popularity of plans that reorganize schools vertically into multi-graded or non-graded programs, and horizontally into various cooperative teaching arrangements, is closely tied to curriculum revision. The non-graded scheme of school organization is compatible with a curriculum planned around themes, principles, concepts, generalizations, and modes of inquiry that will be developed over many years of schooling, replacing a curriculum consisting of bits and pieces and daily or weekly time blocks of instruction. Team teaching has grown, at least in part, out of a recognized need to provide students with teachers who possess a thorough knowledge of their subject field as well as a real understanding of the school's function.

Greater awareness of the fact that a large number of students do not seem to profit from the fare the schools offer has resulted in a plethora of proposals to educate the slow learners, the academically talented, and the physically handicapped. The realization that automation is bringing about employment problems of a kind never experienced before has helped to revitalize the field of vocational and technical education.

In all this agitation—some of it denoting progress, some of it not—a faint glimmer of light is growing stronger; the belief that, increasingly, curriculum reform will be based on the cultivation of the individual and the assurance of a self-renewing society, whereas the curriculum revisions of the past were largely a result of pressures for societal preservation. . . .

Analysis: Problems and Issues

Curricular Problems and Issues Within Courses

AIMS AND OBJECTIVES.   There is a striking similarity in the aims and objectives of nearly all projects. Objectives, as they are defined in various descriptive documents, stress the importance of understanding the structure of the discipline, the purposes and methods of the field, and the part that creative men and women played in developing the field. One of the major aims is that students get to explore, invent, discover, as well as sense some of the feelings and satisfactions of research scholars, and develop some of the tools of inquiry appropriate to the field. When more remote aims are implied, the impression is created that the student should prepare for intellectual and academic survival in a complex, scientific world. Such social aims as preparation for citizenship or intelligent participation in decisions facing the community are only rarely mentioned.

Objectives of the programs appear to rest on the assumption that any significant behavior which can be derived from analysis of an academic discipline can be learned by students of a given age and is, therefore, worth learning. Such an assumption almost automatically implies that those subjects already well established in the curriculum determine what the schools ought to teach. The schools' curriculum, then, is closed to new subjects, and to old subjects that have been poorly represented in the political market place. The goals of schooling, therefore, would be determined by those subjects that have been most successful in finding their way through the political structure into the schools!

It should be stated, though, in defense of all those who are involved with the various curriculum projects, that neither are they nor should they be charged with the responsibility of determining the aims of America's schools. This responsibility falls to the citizenry as a whole. The fact that our communities have, generally speaking, not assumed this responsibility has resulted in a lack of broadly accepted aims against which the validity of the projects' objectives may be checked. The objectives of the several subject-field projects become, therefore—by default as it were—the educational aims of the communities adopting the various project courses.

> How does a community decide which value patterns are to be taught in its schools and are to be used as a basis for curricular and instructional decisions? . . . One possible answer is that a pluralistic society wishes for an obvious and open decision never to occur. A struggle of this sort would be divisive, indicating quite clearly to a number of subgroups that their views were not being adopted by the society as a whole. Thus a pluralistic society may prefer to ignore this question as long as possible in the hope that it will not become too troublesome. Some aspects of our present educational situation suggest that in part we have more or less consciously adopted this answer.[14]

To determine what students *ought* to learn on the basis of what is significant to the discipline and what *can* be learned by a majority of the students, causes some difficulty. Concepts of energy, number, and evolution certainly are significant to physics, mathematics, and biology, respectively. Further, they can be learned in an academically respectable way by young children. (The optimum time for learning them, however, still remains to be empirically determined). But suppose we find that a range of concepts, running the gamut of twenty or more disciplines, *can* be learned by young

14. Harold B. Dunkel, "Value Decisions and the Public Schools," *School Review,* 70 (Summer, 1962), p. 165).

children? Since limitations in time necessitate choice, what criteria do we use to guide our choices? Clearly, some more fundamental validation than the ability of children to learn certain concepts is needed to help us choose among a number of alternatives. The problem is no less pressing at the high-school level where, in order to set up a social studies curriculum, criteria other than student capability are required to arrive at an intelligent choice among history, geography, economics, political science, sociology, and anthropology.

The long-term solution to this dilemma may be that those state and local (and perhaps federal) agencies, that are entrusted with responsibility for the schools, begin to formulate the aims. Once this has been done, curriculum groups could go to work to determine the best curricular patterns to achieve these aims. But these agencies are not now assuming this responsibility nor does it seem likely that they will do so in the near future.[15] There might, however, be a place in our pluralistic society for independent centers—preferably attached to universities—which would engage in a systematic study of all data relating to a school's aims and other curricular problems.

These centers would not determine the aims for the communities but would present and analyze alternatives, support bases for alternatives, and point out possible consequences of adopting any given aim. The work of such centers would have the virtue of eschewing any particular subject as both the road to and the end of the good life.

The short-term answer is for project committees to try and justify goals beyond the parochial limits of disciplines and children's abilities to learn them. And some projects are moving in just that direction. Project directors have become increasingly sensitive to the human processes which appear to transcend the methods presumed to be unique to the discipline. John Mayor, for example (University of Maryland Mathematics Project), lauds cultivation of such fundamental processes as observing, classifying, measuring, drawing inferences, speculating, and experimenting. These appear not to be unique to mathematics but to be equally appropriate to the enjoyment of literature and artistic performance—and to the full development of man's rational powers.

15. Ammons, for example, was hard pressed to find, within a 300-mile radius of Chicago, more than a handful of schools with anything that might reasonably be called a set of aims. *See* Margaret P. Ammons, "Educational Objectives: The Relation between the Process Used in Their Development and Their Quality" (Unpublished doctoral dissertation, University of Chicago, 1961).

6

Objectives

W. James Popham

A key feature of any rational planning, educational or otherwise, is the possession of some idea of what is to be accomplished. Educators, of course, characteristically describe these intended accomplishments as their goals or objectives. Some people use the terms "goal" or "objective" interchangeably, as well as such synonyms as "aims," "intents," etc. Other people employ a much more distinctive meaning of the terms, using "goal" to describe a broader description of intent and "objective" to denote a more specific spelling out of the goal. Because there is currently no overwhelmingly preferred usage of these terms, be sure to seek clarification from an educator regarding the manner in which he is using the many terms which may be employed to describe educational goals. In this guidebook, the terms will be employed interchangeably.

Measurability and Clarity

One of the most prominent arenas of educational activity during the 1960's concerned the form in which instructional objectives should be stated. As a consequence of the programmed instruction movement which captured the attention of many educators during the early sixties, we heard more and more about the merits of stating objectives in precise, measurable terms. Programmed instruction enthusiasts pointed out again and again that such objectives were requisite for a proper instructional design. A number of other instructional specialists also began to support the worth of explicitly stated objectives. What was the point of this activity?

For years educators have been specifying their objectives in rather general language such as, "At the end of the year the student will become familiar with important literary insights." There is nothing intrinsically wrong with such an objective, for it probably provides one with a general idea of what is to be done during the year. However, for instructional or evaluation purposes, such an objective is almost useless since it identifies no specific indicator for determining whether or not the objective has been achieved. As a consequence, in recent years an increasing number of educators have urged that in order for objectives to function effectively

Public domain, Chapter 2 from W. James Popham, *An Evaluation Guidebook: A Set of Practical Guidelines for the Educational Evaluator.* Los Angeles: The Instructional Objectives Exchange, 1972.

in instructional and evaluation situations, they must be stated in terms of *measurable learner behavior*. In other words, since educational systems are designed to improve the learner in some way, an educational objective should describe the particular kind of behavior changes which will reflect such improvement. An example of objectives which would satisfy this measurability criterion would be the following: "When given previously unencountered selections from different authors, the student can, by style and other cues, correctly name the writer." The main attribute of a properly stated instructional objective is that it describes what the learner *will do* or is *able to do* at the end of instruction which he could not prior to instruction. Another way of putting it is that a usefully stated objective will invariably be measurable in such a way that an unequivocal determination can be made as to whether the objective has been accomplished.

The major advantages of such objectives is that they promote increased *clarity* regarding educational intents, whereas vague and unmeasurable objectives yield considerable ambiguity and, as a consequence, the possibility of many interpretations not only of what the objective means but, perhaps more importantly, whether it has been accomplished.

During the past several years many books and papers and audiovisual aids have been published[1] which guide the practitioner regarding how instructional objectives should be stated. Some of these guides focus considerable attention on the choice of verb used to describe the hoped-for post-instruction status of the learner. For instance, instead of saying "The learner *will know* the chief battles of the Civil War," the educator is advised to put it this way: "The learner *will list* in writing the chief battles of the Civil War." Note that the only difference is that in the second objective a verb is employed which describes a specific type of action or *behavior* on the part of the learner, in contrast to the verb "know" which can mean many things to many people. In the preferred objective a phrase, "in writing," has also been added which ties down the meaning of the objective even more. Since the essential feature of a properly stated objective is that it unambiguously communicates an educational intent, we might also have used such phrases as:

> will recite aloud
> will select from a list
> will write the names of the opposing generals

One can think of different verbs which might be employed to communicate what is intended in an objective. At a very general level there are "internal state" verbs such as "understand." At a more specific level we can think of action verbs such as "identify" or "distinguish." But even these verbs permit some difference in interpretations as to the precise manner in which the learner will identify or distinguish. Even more specific behavioral phrases such as "pointing to" or "reciting aloud" further reduce the ambiguity. In general, the evaluator should employ phrases with sufficient specificity for the task at hand. Usually, that will mean more rather than less specific language.

---

1. See, for example, Popham, W. J. and Baker, E. L. *Establishing Instructional Goals*, Prentice Hall, Inc., Englewood Cliffs, N.J., 1970, as well as the numerous citations in the selected references section of this guidebook. A series of filmstrip-tape programs distributed by Vimcet Associates, P.O. Box 24714, Los Angeles, California 90024, will also be helpful for training evaluation personnel.

Because a well formed instructional objective describes the type of learner behavior which is to be produced by the instructional treatment, such statements have often been referred to as *behavioral objectives* or *performance objectives*. The reason why so many educators have recently been advocating such goal statements is that the reduced ambiguity of the objectives yields a significant increase in the clarity needed both for (1) deciding on the *worth* of the objective and (2) determining whether the objective has been *achieved*.

Another important attribute of a well stated instructional objective is that it refers to the *learner's* behavior, not that of the *teacher*. Statements such as "the teacher will introduce the class to the basic elements of set theory" do not qualify as educational objectives, for they merely describe the nature of the educational treatment (in this case provided by the teacher), not what that treatment is to accomplish in terms of modifications in the learner.

An additional element of a usefully formulated instructional objective is that it should refer to the learner's *post-instruction* behavior, not his behavior during instruction. For instance, we might imagine a group of children working furiously on practice problems in a mathematics class. Now it is not on the basis of the learners' skill with these practice problems that the teacher will judge the adequacy of his instruction, but on later problems given as part of an end-of-unit or end-of-course examination. Thus, the type of learner behavior to be described in a properly stated educational objective must definitely occur after the instruction designed to promote it.

The term "post-instruction" should be clarified, however. Certainly we are interested in what is happening to learners during the course of a school year, not merely at its conclusion. Thus, we test or otherwise observe pupils at numerous points during the year. Similarly, we might conceive of a one week or single day instructional period for our treatment. A useful objective, useful in the sense that we can determine whether it has been achieved by the learner, might be promoted by an extremely short instructional period.

Guideline Number 1. The educational evaluator should encourage the use of instructional objectives which provide explicit descriptions of the post-instruction behavior desired of learners.

All, or Nothing at All?

As the evaluator becomes conversant with the advantages of measurable goals he sometimes becomes excessive in his advocacy of such objectives. Educators will ask him, "Must *all* my goals be stated in measurable terms? Aren't there some objectives that I can pursue even if I can't describe precisely how I will measure them?"

For *evaluation purposes*, the response should be that unmeasurable goals are of little or no use. Yet, for instructional purposes a more conciliatory response is warranted. There are undoubtedly some objectives, e.g., promoting a student's appreciation of art, which may currently be unassessable yet are so intrinsically meritorious that they are worth the risk of some instructional investment. Such high-risk high-gain goals might reasonably command a segment of our instructional time, but it is the *proportion* of instruction devoted to the pursuit of such goals which is at issue. Currently, the vast majority of our educational efforts are devoted to the pursuit of

such non-measurable aims. We need to alter the proportion so that most of our
goals are of a measurable nature, thus permitting us to determine whether they have
been accomplished and, consequently, allowing us to get better at achieving them.
Some proportion of instructional resources might, on the other hand, because of
great potential dividends, be devoted to the pursuit of non-measurable objectives.
From an evaluator's point of view, the unmeasurable goals will be of no use, thus he
should attempt to reduce the proportion of such non-behavioral goals to a reasonable number. At the same time, of course, we should increase our sophistication in
measuring those goals which are important but currently elusive so that in the future we can measure even these.

**Guideline Number 2. While recognizing that non-measurable
goals will be of limited use for his purposes, the educational
evaluator must be aware that instructors may wish to devote
a reasonable proportion of their efforts to the pursuit of
important but currently unassessable objectives.**

Selected and Constructed Learner Responses

When describing the myriad forms of learner behavior which educators might be interested in achieving you will find that the learner is engaging in acts which can be
classified under two headings, that is, he is either *selecting* from alternatives or *constructing*. He is *selecting* when he chooses "true" or "false" to describe a statement or when
he picks the answer to a multiple choice question. He is *constructing* when he writes an
essay, gives an impromptu speech, or performs a free exercise routine in a gymnastics
class. In a sense the difference between selected and constructed responses is somewhat similar to the difference between "recognition" and "recall" as used by measurement specialists in connection with customary achievement testing. When the learner
is asked to recognize a correct answer from among multiple choice alternatives, he
must select the correct response. When he is asked to recall a correct answer, he must
construct his own response, presumably based on his recollection of what the correct
answer should be. Beyond this difference, however, the selection versus construction
distinction can be applied to all types of learner response, noncognitive as well as cognitive, and therefore is more useful.

   The distinction between selected and constructed responses becomes important
when we realize that with selected response objectives it is relatively simple to determine whether the learner's responses are acceptable, for we merely identify in advance
which alternatives are the correct ones. With constructed responses, however, the task
is far more difficult since we must identify in advance the criteria by which we will
distinguish between acceptable and unacceptable learner responses. To illustrate, if the
objective concerns the learner's skill in writing essays, then unless we can specify the
standard which all acceptable essays must satisfy, we have an objective which is difficult if not impossible to measure.

   The importance of this point cannot be overemphasized, for many educators
who zealously proclaim the merits of measurable objectives end up by offering the
following type of goal as an example of a well written objective:

   At the conclusion of the course the student will describe the major contributions
   of each novelist studied during the semester.

The difficulty with such objectives is that the elements needed to render a description satisfactory are not delineated. How will the teacher, in examining the various descriptions prepared by her students, decide which ones are good enough? This should not suggest that such criteria cannot be isolated or described. They definitely can, but it is hard work. Many teachers who rely heavily on constructed response student behavior prefer the work-evading tactic of relying on a "general impression" of the quality of a student's efforts. The unreliability of such general impressions, of course, has been amply documented through the years.

The major point of this discussion is that if an objective is based upon a learner's constructed response, the *criteria of adequacy must be given*, that is, the standards for judging the acceptability of a learner's response must be supplied. The criteria of adequacy should be included in the objective, or at least referred to in the objective. For example, the following objective would be acceptable:

> The learner will deliver a 15 minute extemporaneous speech violating no more than two of the twelve "rules for oral presentation" supplied in class, as judged by a panel of three randomly selected classmates using the standard rating form.

Ideally, the evaluator would prefer a set of crisply stated criteria by which to determine the adequacy of a constructed response. In practice, however, it may be necessary to state such criteria in terms of a group of judges being satisfied. For instance, even without explicating a single criterion, one can frame a satisfactory objective which indicates that a judge (or judges) will consider satisfactory greater proportions of post-instruction learner responses than those which occurred prior to instruction.

An example of this stratagem may prove helpful. Suppose an elementary teacher wants to improve her pupils' abilities to prepare watercolor prints, but has difficulty in describing criteria of adequacy for determining the quality of colors. She might give a particular assignment at the start of instruction, next teach the children, then give an *identical* watercolor assignment after instruction. The two productions of each child are then randomly paired after first having been secretly coded so that the teacher knows which was pre-instruction and which was post-instruction. The pairs are then given to a competent judge who is asked simply to designate which of any pair is better. No criteria at all need be described. The hope, of course, would be that more of the post-instruction watercolors would be judged superior. The objective for such a situation might be phrased like this:

> When compared with pre-instruction watercolor preparations based on an identical assignment, at least 75 per cent of the pupils' post-instruction watercolor productions will be considered superior by an external judge who is not aware of the point at which the watercolors were prepared.

It is important to use an external judge in these situations to avoid bias, conscious or subconscious, on the part of the teacher or, for that matter, anyone involved heavily in the instruction.

Anytime anyone engaged in educational evaluation encounters a constructed response objective without clearly explicated criteria of adequacy, the deficiency should be remedied or the objective discarded.

Guideline Number 3. The educational evaluator must identify criteria of adequacy when using instructional objectives which require constructed responses from learners.

Content Generality

In the early 1960's any objective which explicitly described the learner's post-instruction behavior was considered to be an acceptable goal statement. Such objectives as the following were frequently found in sets of recommended goals:

> The pupil will be able to identify at least three elements in *Beowulf* which are characteristic of the epic form.

Yet, upon examining such objectives it becomes clear that the statement is nothing more than a test item concerning the particular literary work, *Beowulf*. Such objectives, while sufficiently precise, are not very economical to use. To teach a semester or year long course with this type of objectives one might be obliged to have dozens or even hundreds of such statements. At any rate, what most educators wish to accomplish is not so limited in scope, but covers a broad range of learner behaviors, behaviors which hopefully can be employed profitably in many situations. Professor Eva Baker[2] has offered a useful distinction between objectives according to whether they possess content *generality* or *test* item *equivalence*. The former *Beowulf* example, since it dealt with a single test item, possessed test item equivalence and is of limited utility. To possess content generality, that is, to describe a broader range of learner behavior, the objective could be rewritten as follows:

> The pupil will be able to identify at least three elements in any epic which are characteristic of that form.

By referring to *any epic*, rather than a particular epic, the objective takes on a more general form, and, as such, can be more parsimoniously employed by educational evaluators. If only to avoid the necessity of dealing with innumerable objectives, educational evaluators should foster the use of content general objectives and eschew the use of test item equivalent goals.

One of the most vexing problems for those who work with instructional objectives is deciding *just how specific* or *just how general* they should be stated. Although there are no absolute guides here, or even consensus preference, it has become clear that the level of generality for objectives should probably vary from situation to situation. A teacher in the classroom may wish to use extremely explicit objectives. Yet, if the evaluator is attempting to secure reactions from community people regarding their estimates of the worth of certain objectives, then more general statements may be preferable. There are experimental techniques which can be used to cope with the generality level question, but until we have definitive evidence regarding what level works best in given situations, it would be wise for the evaluator to remain flexible on this point.

---

2. Baker, E.L. *Defining Content for Objectives*, Vimcet Associates, Box 24714, Los Angeles, California, 1968.

Guideline Number 4. The educational evaluator should foster the use of measurable objectives which possess content generality rather than test item equivalence.

Proficiency Levels

Once a measurable objective has been formulated, there is another question which should be answered by those framing the objective, namely, *how well* should the learner perform the behavior specified in the objectives. A convenient way of thinking about this question is to consider two kinds of minimal proficiency levels which can be associated with an objective.

First, we are interested in the degree of proficiency which must be displayed by an individual learner. This is called the *student minimal level* and is illustrated by the *italicized* section in the following objective:

> The learner will be able to multiply correctly *at least nine out of ten* of any pair of two digit multiplication problems randomly generated by the instructor.

This student minimal level asserts that the learner must perform with at least a 90 per cent proficiency.

A second decision needs to be made with respect to the proportion of the *group* of learners who must master the objective. Does everyone need to achieve the objective? Only half the class? This is established through the *class minimal level* which is illustrated by the *italicized* section of the following objective:

> *Eighty per cent or more* of the learners will be able to multiply correctly at least nine out of ten of any pair of two digit multiplication problems randomly generated by the instructor.

Here we see that for the objective to be achieved at the desired levels of proficiency at least 80 per cent of the learners must perform 90 per cent or better on the multiplication problems. Sometimes this is referred to as an 80–90 proficiency level.

Now the advantage, particularly to the evaluator, of specifying class and student minimal levels *prior to instruction* is that the power of the instructional treatment can then be tested against such standards in producing the hoped-for results. Too often the designers of an instructional system will, after instruction, settle for mediocre levels of proficiency. By pre-setting performance standards those involved in the design and implementation of the instructional treatment are forced to put their pedagogical proficiency on the line.

But it's easier to say how to state minimal proficiency levels than it is to decide just what they should be. Too many educators merely pluck them from the air if they're used at all, e.g., "We want 90–90 levels on all our objectives." Obviously, this would be unthinking, for there are certain objectives which we would hope that *all* of our learners would achieve with 100 per cent proficiency. Examples of these might be in the field of health, rudimentary intellectual skills, etc.

Probably the best we can do now is to seek the wisdom of many people, certainly including those who have experience in the education of the learners with whom we are working. Careful analysis of how well learners have done in the past, coupled with our most insightful appraisal of how well each individual *should* perform with respect to the objective, can yield an approximation of defensible class and student minimal levels.

An important consideration for establishing some proficiency levels is the initial skill of the learner prior to instruction, sometimes referred to as his "entry behavior." For certain instructional situations, e.g., remedial math, learners who commence an instructional sequence with abysmally low entry behaviors might not be expected to perform as well at the close of instruction as other learners who headed into the instruction with an advantage. For other situations, the criterion levels are not so malleable, thus we would expect students in a driver training course to achieve the desired minimal levels irrespective of their entry behavior.

Now it is always possible, of course, to alter performance standards after the instructional treatment has either proven to be ineffectual or more effective than we thought. But this should be done very cautiously, only after pushing the instructional treatment to the limits of its potency.

Guideline Number 5, Prior to the introduction of the instructional treatment educational evaluators should strive to establish minimal proficiency levels for instructional objectives.

The Taxonomies of Educational Objectives

A technique for analyzing objectives which many evaluators find useful stems from the work of Benjamin Bloom and a group of university examiners who in 1956 published a scheme[3] for classifying educational objectives according to the kinds of learner behavior they were attempting to promote. An extension of the classification scheme by David Krathwohl and others appeared in 1964.[4] These two *taxonomies* (classification schemes) of educational objectives first divided instructional goals into three groups or *domains*, the cognitive, affective, and psychomotor. *Cognitive* objectives deal with intellectual learner outcomes such as whether a pupil can analyze sentences into their component parts or can recall the names of the 50 states. *Affective* objectives are concerned with attitudinal, valuing, emotional learner actions such as promoting a pupil's interest in literature or strengthening his esteem for democratic processes. *Psychomotor* objectives describe intended learner outcomes of a largely physical skill nature such as learning to use a typewriter or how to swim the breast stroke.

Each of these three domains has been further subdivided into several levels of learner behaviors which are sought in each domain. For instance, in the cognitive domain we find *knowledge* objectives which, briefly, describe those goals that require the learner to recall information of one sort or another. Another type of objective in the cognitive domain is *analysis* which refers to the learner's ability to subdivide a complex whole into its constituent segments. Within each domain the several levels of objectives are arranged more or less hierarchically so that, for example, analysis objectives are ranked higher than knowledge objectives. Lower levels within a domain are generally considered prerequisite to higher levels.

To the evaluator, the major utility of a taxonomic analysis of the objectives with which he is dealing is that he can detect unsuspected omissions or overemphasis. For example, he might subject a group of objectives under consideration by a school faculty to an analysis according to the taxonomies and discover that there were no affective objectives present or that all of the cognitive objectives were at the lowest levels of the cognitive domain. Once apprised of this situation the school faculty might wish

---

3. Bloom, Benjamin, et al., *The Taxonomy of Educational Objectives, Handbook I: The Cognitive Domain*, David McKay, New York, 1956.
4. Krathwohl, David, et al., *The Taxonomy of Educational Objectives, Handbook II: The Affective Domain*, David McKay, New York, 1964.

to select the objectives anyway, but at least they have a better idea of the types of goals they are adopting.

Although each of the three domains has been broken down into multiple levels, six for the cognitive, five for the affective and five for the psychomotor,[5] the evaluator may find the use of all of these levels too sophisticated for some of the tasks he must accomplish. Many educators report sufficient utility is gained by using the three major domain headings, i.e., cognitive, affective, and psychomotor, coupled with a rough two-level breakdown in each domain, such as "lowest level" and "higher than lowest level." However, there may be some situations in which a more fine grained analysis is required.[6] Accordingly, brief descriptions of each level in each of the three domains are presented below. An evaluator should, however, regroup the levels into a system of sufficient precision for the task at hand.

Cognitive Domain

The cognitive domain has six levels. They move from knowledge, the lowest level, to evaluation, the highest level.

Knowledge. Knowledge involves the recall of specifics or universals, the recall of methods and processes, or the recall of a pattern, structure, or setting. It will be noted that the essential attribute at this level is *recall*. For assessment purposes, a recall situation involves little more than "bringing to mind" appropriate material.

Comprehension. This level represents the lowest form of understanding and refers to a kind of apprehension that indicates that a student knows what is being communicated and can make use of the material or idea without necessarily relating it to other material or seeing it in its fullest implications.

Application. Application involves the use of abstractions in particular or concrete situations. The abstractions used may be in the form of procedures, general ideas, or generalized methods. They may also be ideas, technical principles, or theories that must be remembered and applied to novel situations.

Analysis. Analysis involves the breakdown of a communication into its constituent parts such that the relative hierarchy within that communication is made clear, that the relations between the expressed ideas are made explicit, or both. Such analyses are intended to clarify the communication, to indicate how it is organized and the way in which the communication managed to convey its effects as well as its basis and arrangement.

Synthesis. Synthesis represents the combining of elements and parts so that they form a whole. This operation involves the process of working with pieces, parts, elements, and so on, and arranging them so as to constitute a pattern or structure not clearly present before.

Evaluation. Evaluation requires judgments about the value of material and methods for given purposes. Quantitative and qualitative judgments are made about the extent to which material and methods satisfy criteria. The criteria employed may be those determined by the learner or those given to him.

---

5. Simpson, Elizabeth J. *The Classification of Educational Objectives: Psychomotor Domain*, Research Project No. OE-5-85-104, University of Illinois, Urbana, 1966.
6. It should be noted that in order to make accurate classifications according to the *Taxonomies* it is often necessary to know the nature of the instructional events preceding the point at which the learner's behavior is measured. For example, a given learner behavior might reflect only recall if the topic had been previously treated, but something quite different if not previously encountered in class.

Affective Domain

The affective domain is subdivided into five levels. These levels, in particular, may cause the evaluator much difficulty in classifying objectives. Once more, the five levels may have some value in that they encourage one to think about different forms of objectives, but it is not recommended that the evaluator devote too much time in attempting to classify various objectives within these levels.

Receiving (Attending). The first level of the affective domain is concerned with the learner's sensitivity to the existence of certain phenomena and stimuli, that is, with his willingness to receive or to attend to them. This category is divided into three subdivisions which reflect three different levels of attending to phenomena—namely, awareness of the phenomena, willingness to receive phenomena, and controlled or selected attention to phenomena.

Responding. At this level one is concerned with responses that go beyond merely attending to phenomena. The student is sufficiently motivated that he is not just "willing to attend," but is actively attending.

Valuing. This category reflects the learner's holding of a particular value. The learner displays behavior with sufficient consistency in appropriate situations that he actually is perceived as holding this value.

Organization. As the learner successively internalizes values, he encounters situations in which more than one value is relevant. This requires the necessity of organizing his values into a system such that certain values exercise greater control.

Characterization by a Value or Value Complex. At this highest level of the affective taxonomy internalization has taken place in an individual's value hierarchy to the extent that we can actually characterize him as holding a particular value or set of values.

Psychomotor Domain

Simpson's psychomotor taxonomy, although not as widely used as the cognitive and affective taxonomies, rounds out our three domain picture. Like the affective taxonomy, this domain consists of five levels.

Perception. The first step in performing a motor act is the process of becoming aware of objects, qualities or relations by way of the sense organs. It is the main portion of the situation-interpretation-action chain leading to motor activity.

Set. Set is a preparatory adjustment for a particular kind of action or experience. Three distinct aspects of set have been identified, namely, mental, physical, and emotional.

Guided Response. This is an early step in the development of a motor skill. The emphasis is upon the abilities that are components of the more complex skill. Guided response is the overt behavioral act of an individual under the guidance of another individual.

Mechanism. At this level the learner has achieved a certain confidence and degree of skill in the performance of an act. The habitual act is a part of his repertoire of possible responses to stimuli and the demands of situations where the response is appropriate.

Complex Overt Response. At this level, the individual can perform a motor act that is considered complex because of the movement pattern required. The act can be carried out efficiently and smoothly, that is, with minimum expenditure of energy and time.

Another way in which these taxonomies may be of use to the evaluator is as an aid in generating new objectives. The evaluator may suggest to the educator who is formulating objectives a wider variety of learner behaviors which might be incorporated in the objectives.

Guideline Number 6. The educational evaluator will often find the Taxonomies of Educational Objectives useful both in describing instructional objectives under consideration and in generating new objectives.

Constructing Versus Selecting Objectives

Thus far in the discussion it has been emphasized that the educational evaluator will find the use of measurable instructional objectives invaluable in his work. Recalling that the two major roles of educational evaluation occur in connection with needs assessment and assessing treatment adequacy, the evaluator will find that measurable goals are literally indispensable in properly carrying out either of these two roles. As we continue to examine additional techniques which may be used by evaluators this will become even more evident. Yet, there is a major problem to be faced by the evaluator, namely, where do such measurable goals come from?

Suppose, for example, that an evaluation consultant is called upon by a local school district to help in determining whether a new treatment in this case a series of new text books is sufficiently effective. The first thing he does is to ask what objective the treatment is supposed to accomplish. If he discovers that no objectives arise, at least none beyond a few nebulous general goals, what is he to do? Should he refuse to assist the district until they put their objectives in order? Obviously not. Should he prepare the objectives himself? Well, for any extended treatment that requires a tremendous amount of work and, besides, the school staff may not agree with the objectives he constructs. Should he give the school faculty a crash course in how to write objectives, then help them as they spell out their own measurable goals? So far, this seems like the best alternative, but the evaluator had best recognize that most school personnel—teachers through administrators—are already heavily committed to other assignments. Too many evaluators who have used this "help them construct their own objectives" approach will recount frustrating experiences in getting already harassed teachers to write out their own measurable objectives.

A better alternative would seem to be to ask the school faculty to *select* objectives from a set of alternatives rather than to ask them to construct their own. Selecting measurable objectives from a wide ranging set of alternatives represents a task that can reasonably be accomplished by most educators. Asking those same educators to *construct* their own measurable objectives is, generally speaking, an unrealistic request.

During the past few years several agencies have been established to collect large pools of instructional objectives and test measures. In general, these item banks and objectives banks have been assembled to permit educators to employ their resources in activities related to instruction or evaluation. A directory of extant collections of instructional objectives[7] is now available and should be of considerable use to an educational evaluator.

---

7. The *Directory of Measurable Objectives Sources* at one time could be obtained from the Upper Midwest Regional Educational Laboratory in Minneapolis, Minnesota or in care of Mr. Arthur Olson, Colorado State Department of Education, State Office Building, Denver, Colorado 80203. Objectives and related tests of the Wisconsin Design for Reading Skill Development, an individualized reading system, are also available from National Computer Systems, 4401 West 76th St., Minneapolis, Minnesota 55435.

Objective 87   Collection: Language Arts
                                                                            Grades 4-6

Major Category: Mechanics and Conventions
Sub-Category: Capitalization

OBJECTIVE: Given a set of sentences containing uncapitalized proper nouns, the student will identify
            nouns that should be capitalized.

SAMPLE ITEM: Rewrite all words that should be capitalized in the following sentences.

                1. Some emerald mines in colombia, central america, are more than four hundred
                   years old.

                2. venezuela, colombia, argentina and peru have many oil wells.

                3. brasilia is a large modern city in brazil.

ANSWER: 1. Colombia; Central America

                2. Venezuela; Colombia; Argentina; Peru

                3. Brasilia; Brazil

                Figure 1. Sample objective and item from an IOX collection.

Illustrative of agencies established to collect and distribute educational objectives is the Instructional Objectives Exchange (IOX), founded in 1968. The Exchange has assembled an extensive collection of measurable instructional objectives in grades K–12 in all fields. These objectives were usually contributed to IOX by school districts, Title III projects, curriculum development teams, or individual teachers. Some were developed in the Instructional Objectives Exchange. As soon as a reasonably extensive group of objectives have been assembled in a given field at a given grade range, these are published as an IOX *collection*. Each collection consists of a set of objectives plus one or more measuring devices which may be used to assess the attainment of each objective. The Exchange intends to have at least a half dozen or so test items (broadly defined) for all their objectives so that they can be readily used to constitute pretests, posttests, etc.

By consulting the current listing of IOX objective collections[8] an evaluator can secure a set of alternative objectives from which the educators with whom he is working can select those appropriate for their own instructional situations. It is assumed that only a portion of any collection will be selected. Of course, if all the objectives which are sought are not included in a collection, the local educators can augment those available by writing some of their own. Since this should, in general, be a reasonably small number, the objective construction task should therefore not be too onerous.

Either for needs assessment or assessing treatment adequacy the use of extant objectives collections can prove invaluable. Although we shall be examining the specifics of the process in more detail later, it can be seen how in assessing the current perceptions of students, teachers, and community representatives regarding

8. Available from IOX, Box 24095, Los Angeles, California 90024.

Attitude Toward School

(Attitude Toward School Subjects) Students will indicate relative preferences for five subject areas (aesthetics—art and music; language arts—spelling, oral participation, listening, writing, mathematics, reading, science), when given sets of three verbal descriptions of classroom activities in specific subject areas and three corresponding pictures, by marking one of the pictures to indicate in which activity they would most like to participate.

(General Attitude) Students will indicate favorable attitudes toward school, in a global sense, by incurring a minimum of absenteeism from school during a specified time period, as observed from teacher or school records.

(Attitude Toward School Subjects) Students will reveal relative preferences for seven subject areas (English, arithmetic, social studies, art, music, physical education, science) by selecting, from among sets of seven "headlines" (each representing one of the subject areas noted above), those that appear most and least interesting to read about.

Self Concept

Given a contrived situation in which the teacher describes several factitiously esteemed students, class members will demonstrate positive self concepts by voluntarily identifying themselves as students who have won the teacher's esteem.

The students will display unconditionally positive self concepts by responding to a 10-Item inventory, entitled *Parental Approval Index*, which asks how the child's mother would feel about him as a person if he engaged in certain actions which would normally be expected to yield disapproval of the act.

Students will display an expectation for future success by checking a higher percentage of want ad job requests from the *Choose a Job Inventory* which offer more prestigious, socially approved occupations.

Figure 2. Examples of objectives from two IOX collections in the affective domain

needed objectives, reactions to a list of possible objectives (selected from extant collections) would represent an economic way to secure such perceptions. Similarly, in assessing the adequacy of a new instructional procedure it should be relatively straightforward to select from an available collection those objectives which the procedure seemed best suited to accomplish. Since in many of the agencies currently distributing objectives a number of test items accompany each objective, it is apparent that it would be relatively simple to assess whether the objective had been accomplished.

To give the reader some idea of the kinds of materials available in these collections, Figure 1 includes an example from one of the IOX collections. Although the objectives from other objective pools may be organized somewhat differently, they are essentially comparable. In Figure 2 some affective objectives from two recently developed[9] collections, namely, (1) attitude toward school and (2) self-concept are presented to illustrate the type of non–cognitive goals available in such collections.

Although the objective collections currently available at various locations throughout the country represent an extremely useful resource for the educational evaluator, there may be situations for which an evaluator finds no already prepared

9. Support for the development of these affective objective collections was contributed in a cooperative effort of the state level ESEA Title III programs of the following states: Arizona, Colorado, Florida, Hawaii, Idaho, Iowa, Kansas, Massachusetts, Minnesota, Missouri, Montana, North Dakota, Ohio, Rhode Island, South Carolina, Texas and Wisconsin.

objectives available. The most likely alternatives for him to follow have been previously described, and they usually require his heavy involvement in construction of the objectives. Another option, however, is to try to pool the resources of several groups who have similar interests in order to produce a new objective pool. For instance, several of the health professions, notably nursing and dental education, have lately shown considerable interest in establishing objective banks which are specifically designed for their own instructional situations.

As these recently developed objective collections are revised and updated, as different forms of data (e.g., consumer value ratings) are assembled to guide the selector, and as more sophisticated storage and retrieval systems (e.g., computer-based) are established, these objectives/measures banks should provide an increasingly useful set of tools for an educational evaluator.

Guideline Number 7. The educational evaluator should consider the possibility of selecting measurable objectives from extant collections of such objectives.

In reviewing the section regarding the uses of instructional objectives by educational evaluators, we have examined (1) the role of measurability as an aid to clarity, (2) selected versus constructed learner responses, (3) content general versus test item equivalent objectives, (4) the proportion of objectives which must be measurable, (5) performance standards, (6) taxonomic analysis of objectives, and (7) selecting objectives from extant collections. For each of those points a guideline was presented which, briefly, suggested a course of action for educational evaluators. A complete listing of these seven and all other guidelines will appear later in a summary section of the guidebook on page 107. We now turn to the next section which deals with certain advances in measurement tactics that are of potential use to the evaluator.

7

Educational Objectives— Help or Hindrance?[1]

ELLIOT W. EISNER

If one were to rank the various beliefs or assumptions in the field of curriculum that are thought most secure, the belief in the need for clarity and specificity in stating educational objectives would surely rank among the highest. Educational objectives, it is argued, need to be clearly specified for at least three reasons: first, because they provide the goals toward which the curriculum is aimed; second, because once clearly stated they facilitate the selection and organization of content; third, because when specified in both behavioral and content terms they make it possible to evaluate the outcomes of the curriculum.

It is difficult to argue with a rational approach to curriculum development—who would choose irrationality? And, if one is to build curriculum in a rational way, the clarity of premise, end or starting point, would appear paramount. But I want to argue in this paper that educational objectives clearly and specifically stated can hamper as well as help the ends of instruction and that an unexamined belief in curriculum as in other domains of human activity can easily become dogma which in fact may hinder the very functions the concept was originally designed to serve.

When and where did beliefs concerning the importance of educational objectives in curriculum development emerge? Who has formulated and argued their importance? What effect has this belief had upon curriculum construction? If we examine the past briefly for data necessary for answering these questions, it appears that the belief in the usefulness of clear and specific educational objectives emerged around the turn of the century with the birth of the scientific movement in education.

Before this movement gained strength, faculty psychologists viewed the brain as consisting of a variety of intellectual faculties. These faculties, they held, could be strengthened if exercised in appropriate ways with particular subject matters. Once strengthened, the faculties could be used in any area of human activity to which they were applicable. Thus, if the important faculties could be identified and if methods of strengthening them developed, the school could concentrate on this task and expect general intellectual excellence as a result.

This general theoretical view of mind had been accepted for several decades by the time Thorndike, Judd, and later Watson began, through their work, to chip away the foundations upon which it rested. Thorndike's work especially demonstrated the

Reprinted by permission of the University of Chicago Press, from *School Review*, Vol. 75, No. 3, 1967: pp. 250–260. Copyright University of Chicago Press.

specificity of transfer. He argued theoretically that transfer of learning occurred if and only if elements in one situation were identical with elements in the other. His empirical work supported his theoretical views, and the enormous stature he enjoyed in education as well as in psychology influenced educators to approach curriculum development in ways consonant with his views. One of those who was caught up in the scientific movement in education was Franklin Bobbitt, often thought of as the father of curriculum theory. In 1918 Bobbitt published a signal work titled simply, *The Curriculum*.[2] In it he argued that educational theory is not so difficult to construct as commonly held and that curriculum theory is logically derivable from educational theory. Bobbitt wrote in 1918:

> The central theory is simple. Human life, however varied, consists in its performance of specific activities. Education that prepares for life is one that prepares definitely and adequately for these specific activities. However numerous and diverse they may be for any social class, they can be discovered. This requires that one go out into the world of affairs and discover the particulars of which these affairs consist. These will show the abilities, habits, appreciations, and forms of knowledge that men need. These will be the objectives of the curriculum. They will be numerous, definite, and particularized. The curriculum will then be that series of experiences which childhood and youth must have by way of attaining those objectives.[3]

In *The Curriculum*, Bobbitt approached curriculum development scientifically and theoretically: study life carefully to identify needed skills, divide these skills into specific units, organize these units into experiences, and provide these experiences to children. Six years later, in his second book, *How To Make a Curriculum*,[4] Bobbitt operationalized his theoretical assertions and demonstrated how curriculum components—especially educational objectives—were to be formulated. In this book Bobbitt listed nine areas in which educational objectives are to be specified. In these nine areas he listed 160 major educational objectives which run the gamut from "Ability to use language in all ways required for proper and effective participation in community life" to "Ability to entertain one's friends, and to respond to entertainment by one's friends."[5]

Bobbitt was not alone in his belief in the importance of formulating objectives clearly and specifically. Pendleton, for example, listed 1,581 social objectives for English, Guiler listed more than 300 for arithmetic in grades 1—6, and Billings prescribed 888 generalizations which were important for the social studies.

If Thorndike was right, if transfer was limited, it seemed reasonable to encourage the teacher to teach for particular outcomes and to construct curriculums only after specific objectives had been identified.

In retrospect it is not difficult to understand why this movement in curriculum collapsed under its own weight by the early 1930's. Teachers could not manage fifty highly specified objects, let alone hundreds. And, in addition, the new view of the child, not as a complex machine but as a growing organism who ought to participate in planning his own educational program, did not mesh well with the theoretical views held earlier.[6]

But, as we all know, the Progressive movement too began its decline in the forties, and by the middle fifties, as a formal organization at least, it was dead.

By the late forties and during the fifties, curriculum specialists again began to remind us of the importance of specific educational objectives and began to lay down guidelines for their formulation. Rationales for constructing curriculums developed by Ralph Tyler[7] and Virgil Herrick[8] again placed great importance on the specificity of objectives. George Barton[9] identified philosophic domains which could be used to select objectives. Benjamin Bloom and his colleagues[10] operationalized theoretical assertions by building a taxonomy of educational objectives in the cognitive domain; and in 1964, Krathwohl, Bloom, and Masia[11] did the same for the affective domain. Many able people for many years have spent a great deal of time and effort in identifying methods and providing prescriptions for the formulation of educational objectives, so much so that the statement "Educational objectives should be stated in behavioral terms" has been elevated—or lowered—to almost slogan status in curriculum circles. Yet, despite these efforts, teachers seem not to take educational objectives seriously—at least as they are prescribed from above. And when teachers plan curriculum guides, their efforts first to identify over-all educational aims, then specify school objectives, then identify educational objectives for specific subject matters, appear to be more like exercises to be gone through than serious efforts to build tools for curriculum planning. If educational objectives were really useful tools, teachers, I submit, would use them. If they do not, perhaps it is not because there is something wrong with the teachers but because there might be something wrong with the theory.

As I view the situation, there are several limitations to theory in curriculum regarding the functions educational objectives are to perform. These limitations I would like to identify.

Educational objectives are typically derived from curriculum theory, which assumes that it is possible to predict with a fair degree of accuracy what the outcomes of instruction will be. In a general way this is possible. If you set about to teach a student algebra, there is no reason to assume he will learn to construct sonnets instead. Yet, the outcomes of instruction are far more numerous and complex for educational objectives to encompass. The amount, type, and quality of learning that occurs in a classroom, especially when there is interaction among students, are only in small part predictable. The changes in pace, tempo, and goals that experienced teachers employ when necessary and appropriate for maintaining classroom organization are dynamic rather than mechanistic in character. Elementary school teachers, for example, are often sensitive to the changing interests of the children they teach, and frequently attempt to capitalize on these interests, "milking them" as it were for what is educationally valuable.[12] The teacher uses the moment in a situation that is better described as kaleidoscopic than stable. In the very process of teaching and discussing, unexpected opportunities emerge for making a valuable point, for demonstrating an interesting idea, and for teaching a significant concept. The first point I wish to make, therefore, is that the dynamic and complex process of instruction yields outcomes far too numerous to be specified in behavioral and content terms in advance.

A second limitation of theory concerning educational objectives is its failure to recognize the constraints various subject matters place upon objectives. The point here is brief. In some subject areas, such as mathematics, languages, and the sciences, it is possible to specify with great precision the particular operation or behavior the student is to perform after instruction. In other subject areas, especially the arts, such specification is frequently not possible, and when possible may not be desirable. In a class in mathematics or spelling, uniformity in response is desirable, at least insofar as it indicates that students are able to perform a particular operation adequately, that is, in accordance with accepted procedures. Effective instruction in such areas enables students to function with minimum error in these fields. In the arts and in subject matters where, for example, novel or creative responses are desired, the particular behaviors to be developed cannot easily be identified. Here curriculum and instruction should yield behaviors and products which are unpredictable. The end achieved ought to be something of a surprise to both teacher and pupil. While it could be argued that one might formulate an educational objective which specified novelty, originality, or creativeness as the desired outcome, the particular referents for these terms cannot be specified in advance; one must judge after the fact whether the product produced or the behavior displayed belongs in the "novel" class. This is a much different procedure than is determining whether or not a particular word has been spelled correctly or a specific performance, that is, jumping a 3-foot hurdle, has been attained. Thus, the second point is that theory concerning educational objectives has not taken into account the particular relationship that holds between the subject matter being taught and the degree to which educational objectives can be predicted and specified. This, I suppose, is in part due to the fact that few curriculum specialists have high degrees of intimacy with a wide variety of subject matters and thus are unable to alter their general theoretical views to suit the demands that particular subject matters make.

The third point I wish to make deals with the belief that objectives stated in behavioral and content terms can be used as criteria by which to measure the outcomes of curriculum and instruction. Educational objectives provide, it is argued, the standard against which achievement is to be measured. Both taxonomies are built upon this assumption since their primary function is to demonstrate how objectives can be used to frame test items appropriate for evaluation. The assumption that objectives can be used as standards by which to measure achievement fails, I think, to distinguish adequately between the application of a standard and the making of a judgment. Not all—perhaps not even most—outcomes of curriculum and instruction are amenable to measurement. The application of a standard requires that some arbitrary and socially defined quantity be designated by which other qualities can be compared. By virtue of socially defined rules of grammar, syntax, and logic, for example, it is possible to quantitatively compare and measure error in discursive or mathematical statement. Some fields of activity, especially those which are qualitative in character, have no comparable rules and hence are less amenable to quantitative assessment. It is here that evaluation must be made, not primarily by applying a socially defined standard, but by making a human qualitative judgment. One can specify, for example, that a student shall be expected to know how to extract a square root correctly and in an unambiguous way, through the application of a standard, determine whether this end has been achieved. But it is only in a metaphoric sense that one can measure the extent to which a student has been able to produce an aesthetic object or an expressive narrative. Here standards are unapplicable; here judgment is required. The making of a judgment in distinction to the application of a standard implies that valued qualities are not merely socially defined and arbitrary in character. The judgment by which a critic determines the value of a poem, novel, or play is not achieved merely by applying standards already known to the particular product being judged; it requires that the critic—or teacher—view the product with respect to the unique properties it displays and then, in relation to his experience and sensibilities, judge its value in terms which are incapable of being reduced to quantity or rule.

This point was aptly discussed by John Dewey in his chapter on "Perception and Criticism" in *Art as Experience*.[13] Dewey was concerned with the problem of identifying the means and ends of criticism and has this to say about its proper function:

> The function of criticism is the reeducation of perception of works of art; it is an auxiliary process, a difficult process, of learning to see and hear. The conception that its business is to appraise, to judge in the legal and moral sense, arrests the perception of those who are influenced by the criticism that assumes this task.[14]

Of the distinction that Dewey makes between the application of a standard and the making of a critical judgment, he writes:

> There are three characteristics of a standard. It is a particular physical thing existing under specifiable conditions; it is *not* a value. The yard is a yard-stick, and the meter is a bar deposited in Paris. In the second place, standards are measures of things, of lengths, weights, capacities. The things measured are not values, although it is of great social value to be able to measure them, since the properties of things in the way of size, volume, weight, are important for commercial exchange. Finally, as standards of measure, standards define things with respect to *quantity*. To be able to measure quantities is a great aid to further judgments, but it is not a mode of judgment. The standard, being an external and public thing, is applied *physically*. The yard-stick is physically laid down upon things to determine their length.[15]

And I would add that what is most educationally valuable is the development of that mode of curiosity, inventiveness, and insight that is capable of being described only in metaphoric or poetic terms. Indeed, the image of the educated man that has been held in highest esteem for the longest period of time in Western civilization is one which is not amenable to standard measurement. Thus, the third point I wish to make is that curriculum theory which views educational objectives as standards by which to measure educational achievement overlooks those modes of achievement incapable of measurement.

The final point I wish to make deals with the function of educational objectives in curriculum construction.

The rational approach to curriculum development not only emphasizes the importance of specificity in the formulation of educational objectives but also implies when not stated explicitly that educational objectives be stated prior to the formulation of curriculum activities. At first view, this seems to be a reasonable way to proceed with curriculum construction: one should know where he is headed before embarking on a trip. Yet, while the procedure of first identifying objectives before proceeding to identify activities is logically defensible, it is not necessarily the most psychologically efficient way to proceed. One can, and teachers often do, identify activities that seem useful, appropriate, or rich in educational opportunities, and from a consideration of what can be done in class, identify the objectives or possible consequences of using these activities. MacDonald argues this point cogently when he writes:

> Let us look, for example, at the problem of objectives. Objectives are viewed as directives in the rational approach. They are identified prior to the instruction or action and used to provide a basis for a screen for appropriate activities.
>
> There is another view, however, which has both scholarly and experiential referents. This view would state that our objectives are only known to us in any complete sense after the completion of our act of instruction. No matter what we thought we were attempting to do, we can only know what we wanted to accomplish after the fact. Objectives by this rationale are heuristic devices which provide initiating consequences which become altered in the flow of instruction.
>
> In the final analysis, it could be argued, the teacher in actuality asks a fundamentally different question from "What am I trying to accomplish?" The teacher asks "What am I going to do?" and out of the doing comes accomplishment.[16]

Theory in curriculum has not adequately distinguished between logical adequacy in determining the relationship of means to ends when examining the curriculum as a *product* and the psychological processes that may usefully be employed in building curriculums. The method of forming creative insights in curriculum development, as in the sciences and arts, is as yet not logically prescribable. The ways in which curriculums can be usefully and efficiently developed constitute an empirical problem; imposing logical requirements upon the process because they are desirable for assessing the product is, to my mind, an error. Thus, the final point I wish to make is that educational objectives need not precede the selection and organization of content. The means through which imaginative curriculums can be built is as open-ended as the means through which scientific and artistic inventions occur. Curriculum theory needs to allow for a variety of processes to be employed in the construction of curriculums.

I have argued in this paper that curriculum theory as it pertains to educational objectives has had four significant limitations. First, it has not sufficiently emphasized the extent to which the prediction of educational outcomes cannot be made with accuracy. Second, it has not discussed the ways in which the subject matter affects precision in stating educational objectives. Third, it has confused the use of educational objectives as a standard for measurement when in some areas it can be used only as a criterion for judgment. Fourth, it has not distinguished between the logical requirement of relating means to ends in the curriculum as a product and the psychological conditions useful for constructing curriculums.

If the arguments I have formulated about the limitations of curriculum theory concerning educational objectives have merit, one might ask: What are their educational consequences? First, it seems to me that they suggest that in large measure the construction of curriculums and the judgment of its consequences are artful tasks. The methods of curriculum development are, in principle if not in practice, no different from the making of art—be it the art of painting or the art of science. The identification of the factors in the potentially useful educational activity and the organization or construction of sequence in curriculum are in principle amenable to an infinite number of combinations. The variable teacher, student, class group, require artful blending for the educationally valuable to result.

Second, I am impressed with Dewey's view of the functions of criticism—to heighten one's perception of the art object—and believe it has implications for curriculum theory. If the child is viewed as an art product and the teacher as a critic, one task of the teacher would be to reveal the qualities of the child to himself and to others. In addition, the teacher as critic would appraise the changes occurring in the child. But because the teacher's task includes more than criticism, he would also be responsible, in part, for the improvement of the work of art. In short, in both the construction of educational means (the curriculum) and the appraisal of its consequences, the teacher would become an artist, for criticism itself when carried to its height is an art. This, it seems to me, is a dimension to which curriculum theory will someday have to speak.

Notes

1. This is a slightly expanded version of a paper presented at the fiftieth annual meeting of the American Educational Research Association, Chicago, February, 1966.

2. Franklin Bobbitt, *The Curriculum* (Boston: Houghton Mifflin Co., 1918).

3. *Ibid.*, p. 42.

4. Franklin Bobbitt, *How To Make a Curriculum* (Boston: Houghton Mifflin Co., 1924).

5. *Ibid.*, pp. 11–29.

6. For a good example of this view of the child and curriculum development, see *The Changing Curriculum, Tenth Yearbook*, Department of Supervisors and Directors of Instruction,

National Education Association and Society for Curriculum Study (New York: Appleton-Century Crofts Co., 1937).

7. Ralph W. Tyler, *Basic Principles of Curriculum and Instruction* (Chicago: University of Chicago Press, 1951).

8. Virgil E. Herrick, "The Concept of Curriculum Design," *Toward Improved Curriculum Theory*, ed. Virgil E. Herrick and Ralph W. Tyler (Supplementary Educational Monographs, No. 71 [Chicago: University of Chicago Press, 1950]), pp. 37–50.

9. George E. Barton, Jr., "Educational Objectives: Improvement of Curriculum Theory about Their Determination," *ibid.*, pp. 26–35.

10. Benjamin Bloom *et al.* (ed.), *Taxonomy of Educational Objectives, Handbook I: The Cognitive Domain* (New York: Longmans, Green & Co., 1956).

11. David Krathwohl, Benjamin Bloom, and Bertram Masia, *Taxonomy of Educational Objectives, Handbook II: The Affective Domain* (New York: David McKay, Inc., 1964).

12. For an excellent paper describing educational objectives as they are viewed and used by elementary school teachers, see Philip W. Jackson and Elizabeth Belford, "Educational Objectives and the Joys of Teaching," *School Review*, LXXIII (1965), 267–91.

13. John Dewey, *Art as Experience* (New York: Minton, Balch & Co., 1934).

14. *Ibid.*, p. 324.

15. *Ibid.*, p. 307.

16. James B. MacDonald, "Myths about Instruction," *Educational Leadership*, XXII, No. 7 (May, 1965), 613–14.

8

The Taxonomy, Curriculum, and Their Relations

Lauren A. Sosniak

In September of 1989 the St. Louis Public School system published and distributed to its teachers a new curriculum guide for the language arts, Kindergarten through Grade 5. The appendix included a section titled "A Brief Summary of the Taxonomy of Educational Objectives, Cognitive Domain." The two-page summary describes "major categories" of cognitive objectives, and, for each category, offers examples of objectives and "some good verbs for stating expected learning outcomes." A footnote indicates that the "basic structure" for the "major categories" comes from Bloom et al., *Taxonomy of Educational Objectives, Handbook 1: Cognitive Domain*;[1] the correspondence would be immediately obvious to persons at all familiar with that classic text.

The appendix to the St. Louis Public School curriculum guide is intended to help teachers as they work with the guide and their students. While I have made no effort to survey curriculum guides for different school districts small and large across the country, or curriculum guides for different subject matters, I have no doubt that many of them refer explicitly or implicitly to the *Handbook*. The taxonomy has become part of the language of curriculum theory and practice. It is referenced in virtually every textbook on curriculum. On the surface, at least, the Taxonomy has realized the hopes and expectations its authors expressed in the opening pages of the volume.

Over time, and as measured by the frequency with which it is cited, the Taxonomy clearly has been accepted by people who work in the field of curriculum. However, acceptance as measured by frequent reference to the work is hardly sufficient for judging or even understanding how the Taxonomy might be or might have been a useful and effective tool for curriculum theory and practice. In fact, although the opening paragraph of the *Handbook* indicates a desire to be of help to persons who work on curricular problems, there is ample evidence that the volume was not intended to serve curriculum work. And there are good reasons to question how well served curriculum work has been by the undeniably popular text.

The place of the Taxonomy in curriculum theory and practice, and the place of curriculum thought and action in the Taxonomy, are the subjects of this chapter. I begin with the latter concern, examining curriculum considerations in the *Handbook*, and then turn to the place of the Taxonomy in the field of curriculum. Finally, I dis-

Chapter VII in *Bloom's Taxonomy: A Forty-Year Retrospective*, edited by Lorin W. Anderson and Lauren A. Sosniak. Chicago: University of Chicago Press, 1994. Reprinted by permission of the National Society for the Study of Education.

cuss tensions apparent in the relations between the Taxonomy and curriculum work. For the most part I exclude from this chapter issues associated with curriculum evaluation or with the translation of curriculum into classroom instruction, as these matters are discussed elsewhere in this volume.

The Taxonomy: Curriculum Considerations as an Afterthought?

The expectation that appears on the first page of the *Handbook*—that the work will "be of general help . . . with curricular and evaluation problems"—suggests that curriculum and evaluation were considered equally, or almost so, in the construction of the Taxonomy. How odd that seems given that the task of developing the Taxonomy was undertaken by a group of college examiners. In fact, there is considerable evidence that concern with curriculum may have been an afterthought, and certainly was of only minor importance to the authors of the volume.

The 1956 edition of the *Handbook* uses the word "curriculum" liberally. An earlier Preliminary Edition of the volume, published in 1954, includes the term far less frequently. The changes from the Preliminary Edition to the final version are instructive with regard to the place of curriculum in the development of the Taxonomy and its supporting material.

One thousand copies of the Preliminary Edition were printed by Longmans, Green, and Company at the request of the authors of the *Handbook*, and were sent to a large group of college and secondary school teachers, administrators, curriculum directors, and educational research specialists. The intent, according to the authors, was to solicit "comments, suggestions, and criticisms of a larger and more representative group of educators, teachers, and educational research workers."[2]

When the *Handbook* was published in the well-known 1956 edition, the changes in the text from the 1954 edition were few, but they are particularly noticeable in the use of the word "curriculum." Apparently the "larger and more representative group of educators" saw curricular implications that the group of college examiners either had not seen at the start or had chosen to ignore.

Let me provide a few examples of the small but hardly innocuous changes readers of the two versions would encounter. Beginning with the introduction to the development of the Taxonomy, both editions indicate that at an informal meeting of college examiners there was an expressed interest in "a theoretical framework which could be used to facilitate communication among examiners." "After considerable discussion," the working group agreed that such a framework might be obtained through some system of classifying "educational objectives" (in the Preliminary Edition) or "the goals of the educational process" (in 1956). The explanation for the reasonableness of this strategy signals the place of curriculum thought in the development of the Taxonomy. In the Preliminary Edition the authors wrote: "objectives provide the criteria for validating testing procedures, and, in large measure, dictate the kind of educational research in which testing is involved" (p. 1). Two years later, in the 1956 edition of the *Handbook*, the authors wrote: "Objectives provide the basis for building curricula and tests and represent the starting point for much of our educational research." (p. 4). In 1954, the focus is consistent around matters of testing and educational research; in 1956, curriculum (at least the term) is woven into the discussion.

Similarly, in discussions of principles by which the Taxonomy might be developed, both editions indicate that "first importance should be given to educational considerations." The Preliminary Edition continues: "Distinctions should be made with regard to those objectives and behaviors which teachers regard as distinct in their teaching and planning" (p. 3). The final edition phrases the idea differently, including now the word "curricula": "Insofar as possible, the boundaries between categories should be closely related to the distinctions teachers make in planning curricula or in choosing learning situations" (p. 6).

Changes in wording of the sorts noted here may be small, but they are not trivial. They suggest that the Taxonomy was developed first; attention to curriculum was inserted later. Nowhere is this more evident than in chapter 2 of the 1956 edition of the *Handbook*. That chapter, entitled "Educational Objectives and Curriculum Development," was not in the Preliminary Edition. Its opening paragraph seems especially instructive regarding the place of curriculum considerations in the development and use of the Taxonomy:

> We have had some question about the relevance of this section in a handbook devoted to the details of a classification system. We have finally included it because we believe the classification and evaluation of educational objectives must be considered as a part of the total process of curriculum development. Some of these considerations help to clarify the distinctions made in the taxonomy. It is hoped that many teachers will find this chapter useful as a summary of some of the arguments for inclusion of a greater range of educational objectives than is typical at the secondary school or college level.[3]

Thus, after distributing 1000 copies of a Preliminary Edition for informal review, the authors found themselves prodded into paying some attention to curriculum. They did so reluctantly, for purposes of speaking to a larger audience and helping the larger educational community understand and appreciate the significance of their work.

The reluctance to speak about curriculum in the *Handbook* is further evident in the fact that the "new" Chapter 2 is new mostly in title. The bulk of the content of the chapter was taken from various places in the Preliminary Edition, especially from the section previously headed "Educational Significance of the Major Classes of Cognitive Behaviors." When examined carefully, only two sections of this chapter are truly new.

First, there is a new three-page opening, the first paragraph of which is reproduced above. The discussion, following notice of the authors' uneasiness about including the section, consists of a brief outline of curricular thinking of the day. Mention is made of Tyler's now famous four questions. There is some elaboration on Tyler's discussion of the first of these questions, "What educational purposes or objectives should the school or course seek to attain?" Interestingly, the reference supporting these questions as central to curriculum work is *not* to the classic source, *Basic Principles of Curriculum and Instruction*,[4] but rather to a chapter elsewhere by Tyler titled "Achievement Testing and Curriculum Construction."[5] Thus, even the source used for a discussion of curriculum theory is one that puts achievement testing first.

The second part of the chapter that is new also is an addition principally in title. The subsection that in the Preliminary Edition had been labeled "some special problems" (associated with knowledge objectives) in the 1956 edition is labeled "curricular decisions to be made about knowledge objectives." While the content of this section changes little substantively, it has been reorganized.

Thus we see the authors of the *Handbook* integrating the term *curriculum* into the existing text without considerable rethinking or rewriting of the volume. Something prompted a serious effort to use the term in the 1956 edition, but nothing prompted a reconsideration of the basic ideas presented in the text. The absence of any serious rethinking in relation to the sudden inclusion of the term *curriculum* is particularly evident in the fact that the bulk of the book, the full description of the Taxonomy itself with "illustrative materials," is the same in both editions.

We might ask whether the initial draft of the *Handbook* was sufficiently attentive to curriculum considerations, even though it had not used the term *curriculum*. In other words, perhaps the only addition necessary was a change in language, because the curricular thought was already embedded in the text. In part, the test of this hypothesis is found in a later section of this chapter, when the voices of curriculum scholars are brought to bear on the Taxonomy. In part, however, the authors of the Taxonomy themselves indicate a variety of curricular considerations that they believe lie outside the boundaries of their work.

Putting a Distance Between Curriculum and Testing

In the Preliminary Edition of the *Handbook* the authors expressed discomfort with possible relations between their handbook and curriculum work. In a section about "problems" raised in the working-group discussions, they wrote:

> There was some concern expressed in the early meetings that the availability of the taxonomy might tend to abort the thinking and planning of teachers with regard to curriculum, particularly if teachers merely selected what they believed to be desirable objectives from the list provided in the taxonomy. The process of thinking about educational objectives, defining them, and relating them to teaching and testing procedures was regarded as a very important step on the part of teachers. It was suggested that the taxonomy could be most useful to teachers who have already gone through some of the steps in thinking about educational objectives and curriculum.[6]

This paragraph remains in the 1956 edition. Nowhere is there any discussion of the work teachers ought to "have already gone through" before turning to the Taxonomy.

Perhaps the most obvious distancing of the *Handbook* and the Taxonomy from curriculum work is the choice made by the authors to exclude from consideration any attention to subject-matter content in their schema. Instead, for purposes of developing their classification scheme, the authors argue that "classes of behavior" for students across grades and subject matters are relatively small in number and "should be applicable in all these instances [across subject matters, from elementary school through college]."[7]

The authors of the *Handbook* are well aware of, but apparently uninterested in, the fact that fundamental curriculum decisions associated with educational objectives have to do with choices that must be made from a too large body of possibly desirable *content*. With respect to "knowledge" objectives, for example, the authors write: "[T]here is a tremendous wealth of these specifics and there must always be some selection for educational purposes, since it is almost inconceivable that a student can learn all of the specifics relevant to a particular field."[8] However, the authors assign such decisions to others: "The teacher or curriculum specialist must make choices as to what is basic and what is only of secondary importance or of importance primarily to the specialist."[9] The *Handbook* provides no guidance for such choices, except the implicit guidance that the manner of student work with chosen content should balance attention across the psychological processes represented by the taxonomic categories.

That said, it is important to acknowledge that the Taxonomy is not content-free. There are countless examples of curricular content embedded in discussion of the taxonomic categories. Each category and subcategory is richly illustrated, typically with multiple-choice test items. These test items were

> from published examinations as well as from examinations available in the files of the cooperating examiners. While some effort has been made to draw these examples from the different subject fields and from secondary as well as college courses, it is likely that particular areas and particular levels are not as fully illustrated as desirable.[10]

There is no further mention made about the content of the illustrations. Nowhere is there any discussion of the criteria for judging the worth of a test item in relation to its content. Nowhere is there any discussion of the nature of what students might be studying when they encounter such an item, and of the relation of the item to students' learning opportunities at the moment, in their recent past, and in their near future. These, of course, are issues critical to curriculum deliberations.

Another obvious distancing of the Taxonomy from matters of curriculum comes in the authors' remarks about the starting point for their work:

> [W]e began work by gathering a large list of educational objectives from our own institutions and the literature. We determined which part of the objective stated the behavior intended. . . . We then attempted to find divisions or groups into which the behaviors could be placed.[11]

In this passage, and throughout the book, it is clear that the authors have chosen to ignore questions about what educational objectives schools or courses *should* work toward. Instead, they limit their concern to ways of classifying objectives that are readily available, without pausing to reflect on the worth of those objectives for particular students studying a particular subject matter in a specific educational setting.

The authors of the Taxonomy also are explicit about limits to the objectives that can be included in their scheme. Although their intention was to create a "purely descriptive scheme in which every type of educational goal can be represented in a relatively neutral fashion,"[12] they acknowledge that they were not able to do so entirely. They settle for a system that

> cannot be used to classify educational plans which are made in such a way that either the student behaviors cannot be specified or only a single (unanalyzable) term or phrase such as "understanding," or "desirable citizen," is used to describe the outcomes.[13]

Thus, for the authors of the Taxonomy, questions about the appropriate rhetorical level for objectives for different curricula were pushed aside in favor of appropriate wording of objectives for purposes of testing and educational research.

Finally, the authors of the Taxonomy are explicit that "[i]t is outside the scope of the task we set ourselves to properly treat the matter of determining the appropriate value to be placed on the different degrees of achievement of the objectives of instruction."[14] Once again, matters of value, whether associated with what should be learned, who should learn it, or to what degree something should be learned—considerations fundamental to curriculum work—are clearly separated from the concerns of the authors of the Taxonomy. The authors provide a direct summary statement to that effect: "A comprehensive taxonomy of educational objectives must, in our opinion, include all the educational objectives represented in American education without making judgments about their value, meaningfulness, or appropriateness."[15]

In summary, the place of curriculum theory and practice in the *Handbook* seems to be minor at best. The authors of the Taxonomy acknowledge curriculum work as related to their efforts. That is, the classification and evaluation of educational objectives, the subject of the *Handbook*, is said to be a piece of a process that includes curriculum development (which the authors concede directly) and curriculum enactment (which they address indirectly). At the same time, however, the nature of the relationships between curriculum work and the classification and evaluation of educational objectives is something the authors choose not to examine. Instead, they define their role and speak generally about how the work of examiners *may* fit with other arenas of educational thought and action.

We are told that careful attention to matters of testing, with emphasis on "greater precision" in the classification of learner outcomes, is influenced by curriculum and in turn should influence curriculum. Objectives come from the work of curriculum developers, and the contributions of examiners in elaborating a scheme for more carefully describing and classifying objectives should inform subsequent efforts by curriculum developers. It is suggested that the Taxonomy can, as a collateral benefit, promote attention in different curricula to the inclusion of a greater range of educational objectives than is typical at the secondary school or college level. We are told little more than that about relationships between the Taxonomy and curriculum.

Curriculum Theory and Practice:
The Taxonomy as an Afterthought?

In a tit-for-tat arrangement, the Taxonomy has also typically been something of an afterthought for curriculum authors. While it is frequently included by name in literature on the curriculum, it is seldom included as close to the heart of the matter. The Taxonomy is mentioned in widely used textbooks on curriculum published as early as 1957 and as recently as 1992.[16] For all the mentioning, however, there is little significant use made of the Taxonomy in the curriculum literature, either as an organizing scheme for thinking about curriculum or as a framework for structuring the work of curriculum making.

In their *Fundamentals of Curriculum Development*, Smith, Stanley, and Shores merely mention the *Handbook* as the last of their "suggested readings" for their chapter on the validation of educational objectives.[17] The *Handbook* is given somewhat more attention by Taba in her chapters on the objectives of education and on types of behavioral objectives.[18] Thirty years later, Posner gives the *Handbook* essentially the same place, embedding it in a much larger discussion of educational purposes.[19]

In the nearly half century since the appearance of the *Handbook*, its mention in curriculum textbooks has settled into a predictable pattern. Along with its companion piece, *Handbook II: Affective Domain*,[20] the Taxonomy typically is included as a metaphorical appendix to a discussion of "aims, goals, and objectives," a perennial topic in curriculum conversation. The Taxonomy is presented as a "tool"[21] available to make curriculum work easier or as "a procedure for defining goals in a systematic, comprehensive manner."[22] That is, curriculum textbooks take their description of the Taxonomy almost directly from the *Handbook*. Some brief mention usually is made of both possibilities and limitations associated with various uses of the "tool."

Reference to the Taxonomy in other writing about curriculum is more difficult to discuss because of the breadth of curriculum literature generally. Still, there seems to be something of a pattern here as well. The most typical reference seems to depict the Taxonomy as a tool useful for *analyzing* a curriculum. A common sentence in reports of studies of enacted or intended curricula typically reads something like this: "We used a modified version of Bloom's taxonomy to examine the cognitive demands of X," where X is the specific curriculum being investigated. This particular use of the Taxonomy undoubtedly accounts for a goodly number of citations to the work.

Journal articles that describe the use of the Taxonomy for purposes of curricular *planning* rather than curricular *analysis* are interesting principally for the diversity of educational settings included. The Taxonomy has been mentioned as useful for curricular planning by educators in the United States and abroad, and by educators working at all levels of schooling from elementary school through graduate school. Sometimes the Taxonomy is so taken for granted that a traditional reference seems quite unnecessary. For example, in describing a national precollegiate curriculum development project in history, geography, and social science, Blyth writes about the early stage of the project as follows:"A tentative list of pupil objectives was drawn up, with a fairly liberal interpretation of the Bloom paradigm in mind, and this list was discussed at. . . ."[23] At the other extreme, even several decades after its publication, there is an apparent need to introduce the *Handbook* and the taxonomic categories to specialized audiences not already acquainted with them and their usefulness.[24]

How or even how often the Taxonomy is used in actual curriculum practice seems impossible to determine from the literature. The assumption many curriculum writers make is that it is used frequently, almost automatically and largely unreflectively, at the start of a curriculum development project, in the manner represented by Blyth's remark noted above. The appendix to the St. Louis language arts curriculum guide (mentioned at the beginning of this chapter) suggests that the Taxonomy may often be included in curriculum work, but without serious thought about why or how it is to be used. Although apparently there is no literature to support empirically the assumption of widespread use, that assumption is so strongly held that some scholars have speculated about the reasons for it.

A common explanation for the (assumed) persistent presence of the Taxonomy in curriculum projects is a result of pressures brought to bear by government or foundation support for curriculum projects. Stenhouse, for example, argues that dogmatic insistence on the use of an "objectives model" for curriculum work is a result of "pressure . . . from funding agencies, which are able by the use of the objectives model to operate an over-simplified but comforting payment-by-results system in making curriculum research and development allocations."[25] Yet despite considerable mentioning of persistent use of the Taxonomy, and of pressures for its use, there is very little elaboration of these assumptions, either theoretically or empirically.

The frequent mentioning of the *Handbook* in the literature about curriculum tells only that the volume has attracted attention; it says nothing at all about its usefulness (or lack thereof) for curriculum work. Claims have been made for both the potential of the Taxonomy for curriculum development and for the harm the Taxonomy could do and has done to curriculum theory and practice. Each will be discussed briefly here.

The Merits of the Taxonomy for Curriculum Theory and Practice

Favorable discussion of the *Handbook* centers most frequently on a single feature: the attention it calls to the fact that good education necessarily aims at more than mere recall of factual information. The *Handbook* might be said to have raised our sights educationally, by directing our attention to "intellectual abilities and skills." As Posner puts it, "the taxonomy has served as a vocabulary for the criticism of fact-oriented curricula."[26]

There were prior criticisms of the fact-oriented curricula, of course. The authors of the *Handbook* themselves remind us of the history of concern for "intellectual abilities and skills," which they note as having been "labeled 'critical thinking' by some, 'reflective thinking' by Dewey and others, and 'problem solving' by still others."[27] None of these prior criticisms of the fact-oriented curricula seems to have attracted the attention of the educational community as fully as has the Taxonomy.

The emphasis in schooling on factual recall and a general lack of attention to intelligent use of acquired knowledge were not trivial concerns in the early 1950s as evidenced by the length to which the authors of the *Handbook* went to explain and defend this aspect of their work. They remain major concerns today. In her presidential address to the American Educational Research Association, Nancy Cole spoke about the current dominant conceptions of educational achievement, which divide into what we now think of as "lower-level" and "higher-order" conceptions of knowledge and skill. She said: "In terms of public understanding of the integration of the two, it appears that we have come little further than Bloom and [his] colleagues took us over three decades ago. At that stage in our history, we recognized the two conceptions as different levels of a hierarchy of achievement."[28]

If all the *Handbook* had done was to serve as an inspirational tract, as a document to remind us of curricular possibilities, it would have served an important function in the development of ideas about schooling. But there are other claims for the Taxonomy beyond its power to inspire. At the least, as the authors of the *Handbook* themselves claim and as has been demonstrated richly over the years, a central use of the conceptual scheme for curriculum research has been and continues to be its value in allowing us to examine systematically the extent to which programs attend to "lower-level" and "higher-order" concerns.

Other potential benefits of the Taxonomy for curriculum development tend to be more speculative. For example, in claim at least, the Taxonomy has potential for helping curriculum developers specify and classify their educational intentions systematically and in a manner that would support sharing of curriculum work across contexts and over time.[29] The Taxonomy also has been said to be useful as a model for the variety of ways language can be used to communicate different curricular intentions, and to suggest to curriculum developers classes of objectives they may not have considered previously. Zumwalt proposes that the Taxonomy may be especially useful for new teachers, in the ways listed above and in helping new teachers focus their work, set their priorities, and appreciate their considerable role in defining the curriculum for the students in their classes.[30] Similarly, in principle the Taxonomy is said to be useful in planning for a desired balance or range of cognitive demands on students through the learning opportunities provided for them.

As a tool the Taxonomy could logically be useful in all of these ways. The evidence is not strong that it has been useful in any of those ways, except for describing and analyzing the cognitive demands of intended and implemented curricula. The absence of evidence for the usefulness of the taxonomy for curriculum theory and practice is hardly the fault of the authors of the *Handbook*. Instead, it reflects the fact that curriculum scholars have tended not to concern themselves with questions about how curricula actually are developed. They do not appear to have intentionally ignored the Taxonomy per se; rather, the very idea of examining the processes of developing and enacting curricula has gotten short shrift.[31]

The Limitations of the Taxonomy for Curriculum Theory and Practice

Criticism of the Taxonomy and its influence on curriculum theory and practice shares common features with accolades bestowed on the work. It tends to be speculative rather than theoretically or empirically developed, and it tends to be somewhat distant from the *Handbook* itself, focusing instead on a general "objectives model" or "means-ends model" for curriculum work.

When the focus is on the *Handbook*, criticism tends to point to the very curricular issues that the authors of that volume set as outside the boundaries of their work. That is, questions are raised about the absence of consideration about content, the inattention to educational aims other than those than can be phrased in behavioral form, and the place of values in the conceptual scheme. Of course, the same issues arise when the Taxonomy is used principally as an example of a larger problem in the field of curriculum, a problem associated with a means-ends model of thinking that developed long before the Taxonomy,[32] and for which the Taxonomy was merely a specific technical advance. In this instance, however, when the discussion is more generally about the means-ends model for curriculum work, questions about values frequently take center stage.

The central theme of the various criticisms of the Taxonomy and the means-ends model for curriculum work has to do with the question of whether the Taxonomy is useful for clarifying goals, as it claims, or whether it has obscured the normative foundation of curriculum deliberation and substituted technical expertise for serious and substantive discussion. The authors of the Taxonomy claim that it is value-free. Critics note, however, that "the taxonomy itself, as with any type of classification system, is suited to the expression of certain values and unsuited to the expression of others. . . . [It] throws emphasis onto certain qualities and tends to diminish the apparent significance of others."[33] Given that the starting point for curriculum development or analysis rests with a commitment to values, the values implicit in the Taxonomy as well as the lack of explicit attention to them in the *Handbook*, would both seem to be particularly problematic.

Speaking generally about objectives rather than specifically about the Taxonomy, Stenhouse argues that

> objectives are inadequate as definitions of value positions. Their analytic nature, far from clarifying and defining value divergence, appears to make it possible to mask such divergence. . . . Groups of teachers who claim to have agreed on their objectives often demonstrate in the classroom that their agreement was illusory.[34]

Macdonald and Clark claim that the problem is worse than merely allowing for an illusion of agreement. In their words, "What in effect takes place is that a personal bias or preference is in operation under the guise of an objective and scientific determination."[35] For Furst, there is the related problem with the Taxonomy of confusing an objective with its indicator.[36]

Critics have claimed that several specific values having potentially serious negative consequences for curriculum work are hidden in the Taxonomy. Both Eisner and Weiss suggest that the Taxonomy advocates the synthetic breakdown of human characteristics into cognitive, affective, and psychomotor domains.[37] Putnam, Lampert, and Peterson as well as Eisner question the assumption that knowledge is decomposable; they also question the necessity for being as specific as possible in setting objectives for instruction.[38] Shaw points out that the *Handbook* ignores questions about who has the power to declare and prioritize objectives.[39] Indeed, the authors of the

Handbook seem to assume a set of definable aims inherent in the idea of education. Of course, as Dewey reminds us, "Education as such has no aims; only persons, parents, teachers, etc., have aims."[40]

Macdonald summarizes the strongest critical position arising from questions of value: "The production of the taxonomies is significant evidence of an academic mentality which utilizes technical rationality divorced from consideration of ends. Thus, what can be done and measured becomes what ought to be done."[41]

Tensions in the Relations between the Taxonomy and Curriculum Work

In curriculum theory and practice there is a history of trying to identify a rational system for coping with the complex problem of defining the curriculum. This history emphasizes focusing intently on objectives of education, trying to become more "scientific" in defining and describing our intentions, and assuming all else follows naturally and obviously from careful specification of objectives. Franklin Bobbitt ranks among the early influential educators in this arena; Ralph Tyler is among the best known to contemporary educators.

There is also a history in the field of curriculum of trying to be "helpful" to educational practitioners—trying to provide "advice" that will serve teachers and school administrators who may be too busy in the action arena to think in a sustained way about selected problems.[42] Again, Bobbitt and Tyler figure prominently in this history.

The *Handbook* clearly fits within and extends this curricular history. It is consistent with these central curriculum themes. It was developed by students of Tyler, who was influenced in no small measure by Bobbitt. To the extent that the directions Bobbitt and Tyler were promoting *for* the field of curriculum were the directions *of* the field (and these were very influential men, not only in the field of curriculum but also in education much more broadly), the *Handbook* and the Taxonomy more specifically were almost certain to become integrated in some fashion *with* the field.

The *Handbook* promoted an educational philosophy consistent with the curriculum theory of its time. This theory emphasized educational objectives as an organizing theme around which curricula should be developed, a language of objectives attuned to student behavior, and the segmenting of educational objectives into discrete and measurable units. The *Handbook* thus appears to be something of a guidebook for translating theory into practice. Whether as a "tool" or "technique," the Taxonomy would seem to make the work of identifying and stating objectives easier than heretofore had been the case.

In addition, and likely of major importance, the *Handbook* was written in a style well known to and historically well-received by people seeking curricular advice.[43] The main ideas were small in number, painted in broad strokes, presented in a chatty style, with repeated appeals to common sense, and with multiple examples demonstrating a fundamental connection with and respect for the persons who might find the advice helpful. The *Handbook* is easy reading, although perhaps it is easier reading for persons looking for practical help than it is for persons looking for theoretical discussion and development.

The Taxonomy thus could be said to have had every advantage in capturing the hearts and minds of persons engaged in curriculum theory and practice. And so it did, for a time, at least at the level of widespread and sustained "mentioning." Curriculum scholars such as Goodlad promoted the Taxonomy as particularly useful in efforts to become more rational about curriculum work.[44] Bloom himself participated in national and international curriculum conferences, using the *Handbook* as a centerpiece for his involvement in such efforts. Yet despite the momentum surrounding the Taxonomy, it is merely mentioned in the literature about curriculum and seems to have become only a footnote to curriculum practice.

How might we account for such a phenomenon? My explanation, purely speculative, is informed by the changing nature of curriculum literature subsequent to the publication of Tyler's classic volume, *Basic Principles of Curriculum and Instruction*, and of the *Handbook* itself.

The Taxonomy was a conceptual and technical advance in thinking about and working with educational objectives. The direction of work following from the Taxonomy involved increasing specificity in the language of objectives, and in turn became increasingly more problematic for curriculum theory and practice. Educational objectives were replaced by "instructional" objectives;[45] these were transformed later into "behavioral" or "performance" objectives. Each shift in terminology was associated with more precise details regarding how objectives should be written and why they should be written as described. The shift in terminology also typically signaled the need for increasing numbers of carefully worded objectives to specify the goals that had been indicated earlier by a smaller number of more loosely worded intentions. In this regard, the behavioral objectives movement is said to have collapsed under its own weight.

Not only did it become a practical burden to work with the increasing specificity demanded for the language of objectives, but, just as importantly, the technical advances ran headlong into a debate about the nature of objectives most helpful for promoting the most important intentions associated with schooling as an educational institution, and even about the very place of objectives in curriculum theory and practice. Ralph Tyler himself was one of the critics of the use of the taxonomies *for curriculum work*. At a conference on educational objectives, Tyler pointed out that if the intent was to guide the selection of learning experiences and the appraisal of results, then specifying the kinds of *content* involved was inadequate. Further, Tyler argued that the specificity aimed for by the authors of the *Handbook* was not always necessary or desirable; rather, objectives "should be stated at the level of generality of behavior that you are seeking to help the student acquire."[46] Finally, Tyler pointed to the need for discussion, missing in the *Handbook*, of considerations involved in selecting objectives, a task which should be done *before* working on the defining of objectives in terms of behavior and content.

Other educators, also still assuming a central place for objectives in curriculum work, have challenged the assumptions embedded in behavioral objectives of the sort promoted by the *Handbook*. Eisner, for example, argues consistently that there is no single legitimate way to formulate educational aims, and to pretend otherwise is to limit the possibilities that might arise if teachers and other curriculum workers felt free to apply their conceptual ability and creativity to this important aspect of curriculum work.[47] As alternatives to traditional behavioral objectives he proposes "expressive objectives" and "problem-solving objectives," both of which are intended to be evocative rather than prescriptive and to promote diversity of student responses rather than homogeneity in student learning.

Expressive objectives describe an encounter that a student is to have rather than a behavior a student is supposed to be able to demonstrate after an educational activity. Curriculum activities are "intentionally planned to provide a fertile field for personal purposing and experience." Problem-solving objectives are described this way:

"The problem is posed and the criteria that need to be achieved to resolve the problem are fairly clear. But the forms of its solution are virtually infinite."[48] Eisner claims that problem-solving objectives especially tend toward the creation of curriculum activities which are likely to be taken seriously by students and which place a premium on higher mental processes.

Eisner's alternative forms of objectives are a response to what he believes are questionable assumptions embedded in traditional discussions of objectives. He challenges the assumptions that all important educational intentions are or should be specifiable in advance, and that success in teaching consists of bringing about predictable outcomes. And he challenges the assumptions that knowledge is external to a student and that it can be segmented easily for purposes of instruction and evaluation. Stenhouse similarly raises questions about "action disciplined by preconceived goals," and suggests "action disciplined by form or by principles of procedure" as an alternative for curriculum research and planning.[49]

Hirst is not as agreeable as Eisner to merely adding alternative forms of objectives that still emphasize student behavior. He argues:

> Most of the central objectives we are interested in in education are not themselves reducible to observable states, and to imagine they are, whatever the basis of that claim, is to lose the heart of the business. What is certainly true is that the observable correlates are the only evidence we have that objectives which label states of mind have been achieved, but states of mind should never be confused with the evidence for them. . . . Assessment and evaluation rely on observable evidence, but these evidences are not the objective of the teaching enterprise.[50]

Scholars have challenged not only the assumptions embedded in objectives as the *Handbook* describes them, but also the very idea of objectives as a starting point or a centerpiece for more rational curricular work. Perhaps the most generous position has been taken by Schwab, who attempts to promote the relation between means and ends in education as "mutually determining."[51]

Peters is less enthusiastic about a focus of attention on objectives, even if the attention is shared equally with the means of education. In an essay entitled "Must an Educator Have an Aim?" Peters contends that "we have got the wrong picture of the way in which values must enter into education."

> In my view, disputes between educationists, which take the form of disputes about aims, have largely been disputes about the desirability of a variety of principles involved in such procedures. Values are involved in education not so much as goals or end-products, but as principles implicit in different manners of proceeding or producing.[52]

Blyth separates values from both the means and ends of education. He argues: "In practice, any table of objectives must be derived from a value-position, though this is not always clearly stated. What is not so readily indicated is that a value-position is something more basic and stable than a list of objectives."[53] This argument is consistent with the "naturalistic model" for curriculum development described by Walker, in which the foundation of a curriculum is a "platform" (including the beliefs and values curriculum developers bring to their task) rather than a set of agreed upon objectives.[54] In Walker's model, objectives are a "late development" following from the platform, rather than a starting point.

Walker subsequently argued not only that curriculum development does not

typically begin with careful attention to objectives, but also that it *should not*. His preference is that a curriculum development group begin with rough statements of general aims, postpone concern for precision, and allow the development of aims to take
place alongside the development of other aspects of the curriculum. He argues that
selecting or defining ends as a starting point in curriculum development is counterproductive.

> Devoting much time early to reaching agreement among the developers on state-
> ments of precise objectives can be distracting and divisive. Often there is little ba-
> sis for a decision yet, since the consequences for the project of choosing one ob-
> jective over another can seldom be anticipated. . . . Even when they go as well as
> possible, early discussions of precise objectives are generally frustrating and unsatis-
> fying for team members eager to grapple with materials design issues.[55]

In sum, the technical advance of the Taxonomy promoted serious discussion *about*
curriculum work, discussion which did not always support the use of the Taxonomy *for*
curriculum work. This discussion reminded us of the centrality of values in curriculum
conversation. It reminded us that curriculum involves thinking about both intentions
and activities (which include content, materials, and instructional strategies) and, especially, their relationships. It reminded us that curriculum work is a deliberative undertaking, a search for defensible decisions for particular students and particular contexts.
Or, as Macdonald and Clark put it: "The plain fact of the matter is that curriculum development is a continuous process of making human value judgments about what to include and exclude, what to aim for and avoid, and how to go about it—difficult judgments even when aided by technical and scientific data and processes."[56]

Conclusion

In recent years, long lists of precisely worded objectives created in the spirit of and
perhaps with the help of the Taxonomy seem to have gone out of favor. In their place
are objectives that resemble more closely Tyler's view that objectives should be small
in number, consistent in philosophy, and focus on those general goals believed to be
most important. Further, it appears that more attention is being given to words other
than objectives for representing educational intentions. "Goals" and "purposes" are
being used increasingly in both school-based statements and statements intended for
larger audiences. Meeting "standards," which the National Council of Teachers of
Mathematics explains "are statements about what is valued," has become another popular way of speaking about what one hopes for as a result of educational activity.[57]
Finally, and perhaps most interestingly, statements of "principles," rather than objectives, seem to be increasing in popularity.[58]

    Statements of principles are not new to curriculum development or curriculum
theory. Writing on curriculum reveals a commingling of "principles" and "objectives."[59] Sometimes this commingling demonstrates confusion of one with the other;
sometimes it demonstrates deliberate distinctions and purposeful relations. Granheim
and Lundgren assert that principles should be decided first and should be the foundation for the development of teaching goals.[60] In this light, principles might be seen to
be serving as a "platform," as proposed by Walker, or as a value-position, as suggested
by Blyth.

    Statements of principles may serve educators generally and curriculum workers
more particularly in several important ways. First, it seems possible that attention to
principles will serve as a powerful reminder of the value positions embedded in all de-

cisions about both objectives and activities. This could be an important correction in curriculum work following from the lengthy technical emphasis of the Taxonomy and similar classification schemes. Second, statements of principles may provide some intermediary vantage point from which curriculum developers are helped to think about the objectives they truly want to aim toward, the activities that might serve well in support of those objectives, and, then, the relationships between objectives and activities. It remains to be seen whether principles are useful or whether they become another form of the language of intentions that restricts or obscures as much as it clarifies and provides guidance.

What has not changed in recent years is the quick leap typically made between objectives and evaluation, with limited attention to the curricular concerns of student activities in support of particular intentions however these are labeled. Sometimes the leaps are made from intentions to evaluation, or, as Abramson described the situation with respect to curriculum research, "a vaulting from the framing of objectives directly to the construction of measures of assessment, passing over the intermediate stages of the representation of the objectives within curriculum content, within the instructional situation, and within the teaching process."[61] Sometimes, perhaps more unfortunately, the leaps are made in the opposite direction: from what is testable to what is worth aiming for. Either way, such talk and action also are legacies of the *Handbook*.

For all of the emphasis on student behavior in the *Handbook*, the volume nevertheless was based on and promoted discourse about teaching and learning distant from teachers and learners living and working in classrooms. Defining intentions and determining whether or not they were realized could be done (perhaps by administrators) without attention to the classroom activities and student experiences that help define the curriculum and shape education. In theory, classroom activity would follow from intentions; however, the authors of the *Handbook* and many other writers on curriculum never make explicit how that might happen or if it does. Many educators and educational policymakers apparently continue to believe that relationships between intentions and classroom activities are, or should be, nonproblematic.

Thus the influence of the Taxonomy on the field of curriculum continues to be strong in some respects and has waned considerably in others. It has been positive in its influence in significant ways, and perhaps unhelpful in others. However, no one can doubt that the *Handbook* spurred important conversation about curriculum and its development. For this alone, it has been of great service to the field of curriculum.

Notes

1. Benjamin S. Bloom et al., *Taxonomy of Educational Objectives, The Classification of Educational Goals, Handbook I: Cognitive Domain* (New York: David McKay, 1956).

2. Bloom et al., *Taxonomy of Educational Objectives*, Preliminary edition (New York: Longmans, Green, and Co., 1954), p. 5.

3. Bloom et al., *Taxonomy of Educational Objectives*, 1956 ed., p. 25.

4. Ralph W. Tyler, *Basic Principles of Curriculum and Instruction* (Chicago: University of Chicago Press, 1949).

5. Ralph W. Tyler, "Achievement Testing and Curriculum Construction," in *Trends in Student Personnel Work*, edited by E. G. Williamson (Minneapolis: University of Minnesota Press, 1949), pp. 291–407.

6. Bloom et al., *Taxonomy of Educational Objectives*, Preliminary ed., p. 2.

7. Bloom et al., *Taxonomy of Educational Objectives*, 1956 ed., p. 12.

8. Ibid., p. 63.

9. Ibid., p. 66.

10. Ibid., p. 45.

11. Ibid., p. 15.

12. Ibid., p. 14.

13. Ibid., p. 15.

14. Ibid., p. 13.

15. Ibid., p. 30.

16. For example, B. Othanel Smith, William O. Stanley, and J. Harlan Shores, *Fundamentals of Curriculum Development*, rev. ed. (New York: Harcourt, Brace and World, 1956); George J. Posner, *Analyzing the Curriculum* (New York: McGraw-Hill, 1992).

17. Smith, Stanley, and Shores, *Fundamentals of Curriculum Development*, p. 125.

18. Hilda Taba, *Curriculum Development: Theory and Practice* (New York: Harcourt, Brace and World, 1962), chapters 13 and 14.

19. Posner, *Analyzing the Curriculum*, chapter 4.

20. David R. Krathwohl, Benjamin S. Bloom, and Bertram B. Masia, *Taxonomy of Educational Objectives, The Classification of Educational Goals, Handbook II: Affective Domain* (New York: David McKay, 1964).

21. See, for example, M. Frances Klein, "Instructional Decisions in Curriculum," in John I. Goodlad and Associates, *Curriculum Inquiry: The Study of Curriculum Practice* (New York: McGraw-Hill, 1979), and Decker Walker, *Fundamentals of Curriculum* (San Diego, CA: Harcourt Brace Jovanovich, 1990).

22. J. Galen Saylor and William M. Alexander, *Planning Curriculum for Schools* (New York: Holt, Rinehart and Winston, 1974), p. 180.

23. William A. L. Blyth, "One Development Project's Awkward Thinking about Objectives," *Journal of Curriculum Studies* 6, no. 2 (1975): 99–111.

24. See, for example, Charlotte A. Vaughan, "Identifying Course Goals: Domains and Levels of Learning," *Teaching Sociology* 7, no. 3 (1980): 265–279, and Jay Feinman and Marc Feldman, "Pedagogy and Politics," *Georgetown Law Journal* 73 (1985): 875–930.

25. Lawrence Stenhouse, "Some Limitations of the Use of Objectives in Curriculum Research and Planning," *Paedagogica Europaea* 6 (1970): 73–83.

26. Posner, *Analyzing the Curriculum*, p. 82.

27. Bloom et al., *Taxonomy of Educational Objectives*, 1956 ed., p. 38.

28. Nancy S. Cole, "Conceptions of Educational Achievement," *Educational Researcher* 19, no. 3 (1990): 5.

29. David R. Krathwohl, "The Taxonomy of Educational Objectives: Its Use in Curriculum Building," in *Defining Educational Objectives*, edited by C. M. Lindvall (Pittsburgh: University of Pittsburgh Press, 1964), pp. 19–36.

30. Karen K. Zumwalt, "Beginning Professional Teachers: The Need for a Curricular Vision of Teaching," in *Knowledge Base for the Beginning Teacher*, edited by Maynard C. Reynolds (Oxford: Pergamon Press, 1989), pp. 173–184.

31. Decker Walker, "A Naturalistic Model for Curriculum Development," *School Review* 80 (1971): 51–65; Jon Snyder, Frances Bolin, and Karen Zumwalt, "Curriculum Implementation," in *Handbook of Research on Curriculum*, edited by Philip W. Jackson (New York: Macmillan, 1992), pp. 402–435.

32. See, for example, Franklin Bobbitt, *The Curriculum* (New York: Arno Press, 1918), and idem, *How To Make a Curriculum* (Boston: Houghton Mifflin, 1924).

33. Christopher P. Ormell, "Bloom's Taxonomy and the Objectives of Education," *Educational Research* 17, no. 1 (1974): 3–4.

34. Stenhouse, "Some Limitations of the Use of Objectives in Curriculum Research and Practice," pp. 78–79.

35. James B. Macdonald and Dwight Clark, "Critical Value Questions and the Analysis of Objectives and Curricula," in *Second Handbook of Research on Teaching*, edited by Robert M. W. Travers (Chicago: Rand McNally, 1973), pp. 405–412.

36. See chapter 3 of this volume.

37. Elliot W. Eisner, *The Educational Imagination: On the Design and Evaluation of School*

Programs, 2nd ed. (New York: Macmillan, 1985); Joel Weiss, "Assessing Nonconventional Outcomes of Schooling," in *Review of Research in Education*, vol. 8, edited by David C. Berliner (Washington, DC: American Educational Research Association, 1980).

38. Ralph T. Putnam, Magdalene Lampert, and Penelope L. Peterson, "Alternative Perspectives on Knowing Mathematics in Elementary Schools," in *Review of Research in Education*, vol. 16, edited by Courtney B. Cazden (Washington, DC: American Educational Research Association, 1990), pp. 57–150.

39. Ken Shaw, "Curriculum, Management, and the Improvement of Education: Forging a Practical Alliance," *Journal of Curriculum Studies* 19, no. 3 (1987): 203–217.

40. John Dewey, *Democracy and Education* (New York: Free Press, 1916), p. 107.

41. James B. Macdonald, "Responsible Curriculum Development," in *Confronting Curriculum Reform*, edited by Elliott W. Eisner (Boston: Little, Brown, 1971), p. 124.

42. See Philip W. Jackson, "Conceptions of Curriculum and Curriculum Specialists," in *Handbook of Research on Curriculum*, edited by Philip W. Jackson (New York: Macmillan, 1992), pp. 3–40.

43. Ibid.

44. Elizabeth C. Wilson, "Designing Institutional Curricula: A Case Study of Curriculum Practice," in John I. Goodlad and Associates, *Curriculum Inquiry: The Study of Curriculum Practice* (New York: McGraw-Hill, 1979), pp. 405–454.

45. Robert F. Mager, *Preparing Instructional Objectives* (Palo Alto, CA: Fearon, 1962).

46. Ralph W. Tyler, "Some Persisting Questions on the Defining of Objectives," in *Defining Educational Objectives*, edited by C. M. Lindvall (Pittsburgh: University of Pittsburgh Press, 1964), p. 79.

47. Elliott W. Eisner, "Instructional and Expressive Objectives: Their Formulation and Use in Curriculum," in *Curriculum Evaluation: Instructional Objectives*, edited by W. James Popham (Chicago: Rand McNally, 1969); Eisner, *The Educational Imagination*.

48. Eisner, *The Educational Imagination*, pp. 120, 118.

49. Stenhouse, "Some Limitations of the Use of Objectives in Curriculum Research and Planning," p. 76.

50. Paul H. Hirst, "The Nature and Structure of Curriculum Objectives," in Paul H. Hirst, *Knowledge and the Curriculum: A Collection of Philosophical Papers* (London: Routledge and Kegan Paul, 1974).

51. Joseph J. Schwab, "The Practical: A Language for Curriculum," *School Review* 78 (1969): 1–23.

52. Richard S. Peters, "Must an Educator Have an Aim?" in Richard S. Peters, *Authority, Responsibility, and Education* (London: George Allen and Unwin, 1959).

53. Blyth, "One Development Project's Awkward Thinking about Objectives," p. 102.

54. Walker, "A Naturalistic Model for Curriculum Development."

55. Walker, *Fundamentals of Curriculum*, p. 489.

56. Macdonald and Clark, "Critical Value Questions and the Analysis of Objectives and Curricula," p. 408.

57. National Council of Teachers of Mathematics, *Curriculum and Evaluation Standards for School Mathematics* (Reston, VA: National Council of Teachers of Mathematics, 1989), p. 2.

58. See, for example, Theodore R. Sizer, *Horace's Compromise: The Dilemma of the American High School* (Boston: Houghton Mifflin, 1985).

59. See, for example, Blyth, "One Development Project's Awkward Thinking about Objectives"; Marit K. Granheim and Ulf P. Lundgren, "Steering by Goals and Evaluation in the Norwegian Education System: A Report from the EMIL Project," *Journal of Curriculum Studies* 23, no. 6 (1991): 481–505.

60. Granheim and Lundgren, "Steering by Goals and Evaluation in the Norwegian Education System."

61. David A. Abramson, "Curriculum Research and Evaluation," *Review of Educational Research* 36, no. 3 (1966): 391.

9

The Daily Grind

Philip W. Jackson

On a typical weekday morning between September and June some 35 million Americans kiss their loved ones goodby, pick up their lunch pails and books, and leave to spend their day in that collection of enclosures (totalling about one million) known as elementary school classrooms. This massive exodus from home to school is accomplished with a minimum of fuss and bother. Few tears are shed (except perhaps by the very youngest) and few cheers are raised. The school attendance of children is such a common experience in our society that those of us who watch them go hardly pause to consider what happens to them when they get there. Of course our indifference disappears occasionally. When something goes wrong or when we have been notified of his remarkable achievement, we might ponder, for a moment at least, the meaning of the experience for the child in question, but most of the time we simply note that our Johnny is on his way to school, and now, it is time for our second cup of coffee.

Parents are interested, to be sure, in how *well* Johnny does while there, and when he comes trudging home they may ask him questions about what happened today or, more generally, how things went. But both their questions and his answers typically focus on the highlights of the school experience—its unusual aspects—rather than on the mundane and seemingly trivial events that filled the bulk of his school hours. Parents are interested, in other words, in the spice of school life rather than in its substance.

Teachers, too, are chiefly concerned with only a very narrow aspect of a youngster's school experience. They, too, are likely to focus on specific acts of misbehavior or accomplishment as representing what a particular student did in school today, even though the acts in question occupied but a small fraction of the student's time. Teachers, like parents, seldom ponder the significance of the thousands of fleeting events that combine to form the routine of the classroom.

And the student himself is no less selective. Even if someone bothered to question him about the minutiae of his school day, he would probably be unable to give a complete account of what he had done. For him, too, the day has been reduced in memory into a small number of signal events—"I got 100 on my spelling test," "We went to gym," "We had music." His spontaneous recall of detail is not much greater than that required to answer our conventional questions.

This concentration on the highlights of school life is understandable from the standpoint of human interest. A similar selection process operates when we inquire into or recount other types of daily activity. When we are asked about our trip downtown or our day at the office we rarely bother describing the ride on the bus or the time spent in front of the watercooler. Indeed, we are more likely to report that nothing happened than to catalogue the pedestrian actions that took place between home and return. Unless something interesting occurred there is little purpose in talking about our experience.

Yet from the standpoint of giving shape and meaning to our lives these events about which we rarely speak may be as important as those that hold our listener's attention. Certainly they represent a much larger portion of our experience than do those about which we talk. The daily routine, the "rat race," and the infamous "old grind" may be brightened from time to time by happenings that add color to an otherwise drab existence, but the grayness of our daily lives has an abrasive potency of its own. Anthropologists understand this fact better than do most other social scientists, and their field studies have taught us to appreciate the cultural significance of the humdrum elements of human existence. This is the lesson we must heed as we seek to understand life in elementary classrooms.

I

School is a place where tests are failed and passed, where amusing things happen, where new insights are stumbled upon, and skills acquired. But it is also a place in which people sit, and listen, and wait, and raise their hands, and pass out paper, and stand in line, and sharpen pencils. School is where we encounter both friends and foes, where imagination is unleashed and misunderstanding brought to ground. But it is also a place in which yawns are stifled and initials scratched on desktops, where milk money is collected and recess lines are formed. Both aspects of school life, the celebrated and the unnoticed, are familiar to all of us, but the latter, if only because of its characteristic neglect, seems to deserve more attention than it has received to date from those who are interested in education.

In order to appreciate the significance of trivial classroom events it is necessary to consider the frequency of their occurrence, the standardization of the school environment, and the compulsory quality of daily attendance. We must recognize, in other words, that children are in school for a long time, that the settings in which they perform are highly uniform, and that they are there whether they want to be or not. Each of these three facts, although seemingly obvious, deserves some elaboration, for each contributes to our understanding of how students feel about and cope with their school experience.

The amount of time children spend in school can be described with a fair amount of quantitative precision, although the psychological significance of the numbers involved is another matter entirely. In most states the school year legally comprises 180 days. A full session on each of those days usually lasts about six hours (with a break for lunch), beginning somewhere around nine o'clock in the morning and ending about three o'clock in the afternoon. Thus, if a student never misses a day during the year, he spends a little more than one thousand hours under the care and tutelage of teachers. If he has attended kindergarten and was reasonably regular in his attendance during the grades, he will have logged a little more than seven thousand classroom hours by the time he is ready for junior high school.

The magnitude of 7000 hours spread over six or seven years of a child's life is difficult to comprehend. On the one hand, when placed beside the total number of hours the child has lived during those years it is not very great—slightly more than one-tenth of his life during the time in question, about one-third of his hours of sleep during that period. On the other hand, aside from sleeping, and perhaps playing, there is no other activity that occupies as much of the child's time as that involved in attending school. Apart from the bedroom (where he has his eyes closed most of the time) there is no single enclosure in which he spends a longer time than he does in the classroom. From the age of six onward he is a more familiar sight to his teacher than to his father, and possibly even to his mother.

Another way of estimating what all those hours in the classroom mean is to ask how long it would take to accumulate them while engaged in some other familiar and recurring activity. Church attendance provides an interesting comparison. In order to have had as much time in church as a sixth grader has had in classrooms we would have to spend all day at a religious gathering every Sunday for more than 24 years. Or, if we prefer our devotion in smaller doses, we would have to attend a one-hour service every Sunday for 150 years before the inside of a church became as familiar to us as the inside of a school is to a twelve-year-old.

The comparison with church attendance is dramatic, and perhaps overly so. But it does make us stop and think about the possible significance of an otherwise meaningless number. Also, aside from the home and the school there is no physical setting in which people of all ages congregate with as great a regularity as they do in church.

The translation of the child's tenure in class into terms of weekly church attendance serves a further purpose. It sets the stage for considering an important similarity between the two institutions: school and church. The inhabitants of both are surrounded by a stable and highly stylized environment. The fact of prolonged exposure in either setting increases in its meaning as we begin to consider the elements of repetition, redundancy, and ritualistic action that are experienced there.

A classroom, like a church auditorium, is rarely seen as being anything other than that which it is. No one entering either place is likely to think that he is in a living room, or a grocery store, or a train station. Even if he entered at midnight or at some other time when the activities of the people would not give the function away, he would have no difficulty understanding what was *supposed* to go on there. Even devoid of people, a church is a church and a classroom, a classroom.

This is not to say, of course, that all classrooms are identical, anymore than all churches are. Clearly there are differences, and sometimes very extreme ones, between any two settings. One has only to think of the wooden benches and planked floor of the early American classroom as compared with the plastic chairs and tile flooring in today's suburban schools. But the resemblance is still there despite the differences, and, more important, during any particular historical period the differences are not that great. Also, whether the student moves from first to sixth grade on floors of vinyl tile or oiled wood, whether he spends his days in front of a black blackboard or a green one, is not as important as the fact that the environment in which he spends these six or seven years is highly stable.

In their efforts to make their classrooms more homelike, elementary school teachers often spend considerable time fussing with the room's decorations. Bulletin boards are changed, new pictures are hung, and the seating arrangement is altered from circles to rows and back again. But these are surface adjustments at best, resembling the work of the inspired housewife who rearranges the living room furniture and changes the color of the drapes in order to make the room more "interesting." School bulletin boards may be changed but they are never discarded, the seats may be rearranged but thirty of them are there to stay, the teacher's desk may have a new plant on it but there it sits, as ubiquitous as the roll-down maps, the olive drab wastebasket, and the pencil sharpener on the window ledge.

Even the odors of the classroom are fairly standardized. Schools may use different brands of wax and cleaning fluid, but they all seem to contain similar ingredients, a sort of universal smell which creates an aromatic background that permeates the entire building. Added to this, in each classroom, is the slightly acrid scent of chalk dust and the faint hint of fresh wood from the pencil shavings. In some rooms, especially at lunch time, there is the familiar odor of orange peels and peanut butter sandwiches, a blend that mingles in the late afternoon (following recess) with the delicate pungency of children's perspiration. If a person stumbled into a classroom blindfolded, his nose alone, if he used it carefully, would tell him where he was.

All of these sights and smells become so familiar to students and teachers alike that they exist dimly, on the periphery of awareness. Only when the classroom is encountered under somewhat unusual circumstances, does it appear, for a moment, a strange place filled with objects that command our attention. On these rare occasions when, for example, students return to school in the evening, or in the summer when the halls ring with the hammers of workmen, many features of the school environment that have merged into an undifferentiated background for its daily inhabitants suddenly stand out in sharp relief. This experience, which obviously occurs in contexts other than the classroom, can only happen in settings to which the viewer has become uncommonly habituated.

Not only is the classroom a relatively stable physical environment, it also provides a fairly constant social context. Behind the same old desks sit the same old students, in front of the familiar blackboard stands the familiar teacher. There are changes, to be sure,—some students come and go during the year and on a few mornings the children are greeted at the door by a strange adult. But in most cases these events are sufficiently uncommon to create a flurry of excitement in the room. Moreover, in most elementary classrooms the social composition is not only stable, it is also physically arranged with considerable regularity. Each student has an assigned seat and, under normal circumstances, that is where he is to be found. The practice of assigning seats makes it possible for the teacher or a student to take attendance at a glance. A quick visual sweep is usually sufficient to determine who is there and who is not. The ease with which this procedure is accomplished reveals more eloquently than do words how accustomed each member of the class is to the presence of every other member.

An additional feature of the social atmosphere of elementary classrooms deserves at least passing comment. There is a social intimacy in schools that is unmatched elsewhere in our society. Buses and movie theaters may be more crowded than classrooms, but people rarely stay in such densely populated settings for extended periods of time and while there, they usually are not expected to concentrate on work or to interact with each other. Even factory workers are not clustered as close together as students in a standard classroom. Indeed, imagine what would happen if a factory the size of a typical elementary school contained three or four hundred adult workers. In all likelihood the unions would not allow it. Only in schools do thirty or more people spend several hours each day literally side by side. Once we leave the classroom we seldom again are required to have contact with so many people for so long a time. This fact will become particularly relevant in a later chapter in which we treat the social demands of life in school.

A final aspect of the constancy experienced by young students involves the ritualistic and cyclic quality of the activities carried on in the classroom. The daily schedule, as an instance, is commonly divided into definite periods during which specific subjects are to be studied or specific activities engaged in. The content of the work surely changes from day to day and from week to week, and in this sense there is considerable variety amid the constancy. But spelling still comes after arithmetic on Tuesday morning, and when the teacher says, "All right class, now take out your spellers," his announcement comes as no surprise to the students. Further, as they search in their desks for their spelling textbooks, the children may not know what new words will be included in the day's assignment, but they have a fairly clear idea of what the next twenty minutes of class time will entail.

Despite the diversity of subject matter content, the identifiable forms of class-room activity are not great in number. The labels: "seatwork," "group discussion," "teacher demonstration," and "question-and-answer period" (which would include work "at the board"), are sufficient to categorize most of the things that happen when class is in session. "Audio-visual display," "testing session," and "games" might be added to the list, but in most elementary classrooms they occur rarely.

Each of these major activities are performed according to rather well-defined rules which the students are expected to understand and obey—for example, no loud talking during seatwork, do not interrupt someone else during discussion, keep your eyes on your own paper during tests, raise your hand if you have a question. Even in the early grades these rules are so well understood by the students (if not completely internalized) that the teacher has only to give very abbreviated signals ("Voices, class," "Hands, please.") when violations are perceived. In many classrooms a weekly time schedule is permanently posted so that everyone can tell at a glance what will happen next.

Thus, when our young student enters school in the morning he is entering an environment with which he has become exceptionally familiar through prolonged exposure. Moreover, it is a fairly stable environment—one in which the physical ob-jects, social relations, and major activities remain much the same from day to day, week to week, and even, in certain respects, from year to year. Life there resembles life in other contexts in some ways, but not all. There is, in other words, a uniqueness to the student's world. School, like church and home, is someplace special. Look where you may, you will not find another place quite like it.

There is an important fact about a student's life that teachers and parents often prefer not to talk about, at least not in front of students. This is the fact that young people have to be in school, whether they want to be or not. In this regard students have something in common with the members of two other of our social institutions that have involuntary attendance: prisons and mental hospitals. The analogy, though dramatic, is not intended to be shocking, and certainly there is no comparison be-tween the unpleasantness of life for inmates of our prisons and mental institutions, on the one hand, and the daily travails of a first or second grader, on the other. Yet the school child, like the incarcerated adult, is, in a sense, a prisoner. He too must come to grips with the inevitability of his experience. He too must develop strategies for deal-ing with the conflict that frequently arises between his natural desires and interests on the one hand and institutional expectations on the other. Several of these strategies will be discussed in the chapters that follow. Here it is sufficient to note that the thou-sands of hours spent in the highly stylized environment of the elementary classroom are not, in an ultimate sense, a matter of choice, even though some children might prefer school to play. Many seven-year-olds skip happily to school, and as parents and teachers we are glad they do, but we stand ready to enforce the attendance of those who are more reluctant. And our vigilance does not go unnoticed by children.

In sum, classrooms are special places. The things that happen there and the ways in which they happen combine to make these settings different from all others. This is not to say, of course, that there is no similarity between what goes on in school and the students' experiences elsewhere. Classrooms are indeed like homes and churches and hospital wards in many important respects. But not in all.

The things that make schools different from other places are not only the paraphernalia of learning and teaching and the educational content of the dialogues that take place there, although these are the features that are usually singled out when we try to portray what life in school is really like. It is true that nowhere else do we find blackboards and teachers and textbooks in such abundance and nowhere else is so much time spent on reading, writing, and arithmetic. But these obvious characteristics do not constitute all that is unique about this environment. There are other features, much less obvious though equally omnipresent, that help to make up "the facts of life," as it were, to which students must adapt. From the standpoint of understanding the impact of school life on the student some features of the classroom that are not immediately visible are fully as important as those that are.

The characteristics of school life to which we now turn our attention are not commonly mentioned by students, at least not directly, nor are they apparent to the casual observer. Yet they are as real, in a sense, as the unfinished portrait of Washington that hangs above the cloakroom door. They comprise three facts of life with which even the youngest student must learn to deal and may be introduced by the key words: *crowds, praise*, and *power*.

Learning to live in a classroom involves, among other things, learning to live in a crowd. This simple truth has already been mentioned, but it requires greater elaboration. Most of the things that are done in school are done with others, or at least in the presence of others, and this fact has profound implications for determining the quality of a student's life.

Of equal importance is the fact that schools are basically evaluative settings. The very young student may be temporarily fooled by tests that are presented as games, but it doesn't take long before he begins to see through the subterfuge and comes to realize that school, after all, is a serious business. It is not only what you do there but what others think of what you do that is important. Adaptation to school life requires the student to become used to living under the constant condition of having his words and deeds evaluated by others.

School is also a place in which the division between the weak and the powerful is clearly drawn. This may sound like a harsh way to describe the separation between teachers and students, but it serves to emphasize a fact that is often overlooked, or touched upon gingerly at best. Teachers are indeed more powerful than students, in the sense of having greater responsibility for giving shape to classroom events, and this sharp difference in authority is another feature of school life with which students must learn how to deal.

In three major ways then—as members of crowds, as potential recipients of praise or reproof, and as pawns of institutional authorities—students are confronted with aspects of reality that at least during their childhood years are relatively confined to the hours spent in classrooms. Admittedly, similar conditions are encountered in other environments. Students, when they are not performing as such, must often find themselves lodged within larger groups, serving as targets of praise or reproof, and being bossed around or guided by persons in positions of higher authority. But these kinds of experiences are particularly frequent while school is in session and it is likely during this time that adaptive strategies having relevance for other contexts and other life periods are developed.

In the sections of this chapter to follow, each of the three classroom qualities that have been briefly mentioned will be described in greater detail. Particular emphasis will be given to the manner in which students cope with these aspects of their daily lives. The goal of this discussion, as in the preceding chapters, is to deepen our understanding of the peculiar mark that school life makes on us all.

V

As implied in the title of this chapter, the crowds, the praise, and the power that combine to give a distinctive flavor to classroom life collectively form a hidden curriculum which each student (and teacher) must master if he is to make his way satisfactorily through the school. The demands created by these features of classroom life may be contrasted with the academic demands—the "official" curriculum, so to speak—to which educators traditionally have paid the most attention. As might be expected, the two curriculums are related to each other in several important ways.

As has already been suggested in the discussion of praise in the classroom, the reward system of the school is linked to success in both curriculums. Indeed, many of the rewards and punishments that sound as if they are being dispensed on the basis of academic success and failure are really more closely related to the mastery of the hidden curriculum. Consider, as an instance, the common teaching practice of giving a student credit for trying. What do teachers mean when they say a student tries to do his work? They mean, in essence, that he complies with the procedural expectations of the institution. He does his homework (though incorrectly), he raises his hand during class discussion (though he usually comes up with the wrong answer), he keeps his nose in his book during free study period (though he doesn't turn the page very often). He is, in other words, a "model" student, though not necessarily a good one.

It is difficult to imagine any of today's teachers, particularly those in elementary schools, failing a student who tries, even though his mastery of course content is slight. Indeed, even at higher levels of education rewards sometimes go to the meek as well as the mighty. It is certainly possible that many of our valedictorians and presidents of our honor societies owe their success as much to institutional conformity as to intellectual prowess. Although it offends our sensibilities to admit it, no doubt that bright-eyed little girl who stands trembling before the principal on graduation day arrived there at least in part because she typed her weekly themes neatly and handed her homework in on time.

This manner of talking about educational affairs may sound cynical and may be interpreted as a criticism of teachers or as an attempt to subvert the virtues of neatness, punctuality, and courteous conduct in general. But nothing of that kind is intended. The point is simply that in schools, as in prisons, good behavior pays off.

Just as conformity to institutional expectations can lead to praise, so can the lack of it lead to trouble. As a matter of fact, the relationship of the hidden curriculum to student difficulties is even more striking than is its relationship to student success. As an instance, consider the conditions leading to disciplinary action in the classroom. Why do teachers scold students? Because the student has given a wrong answer? Because, try as he might, he fails to grasp the intricacies of long division? Not usually. Rather, students are commonly scolded for coming into the room late or for making too much noise or for not listening to the teacher's directions or for pushing while in line. The teacher's wrath, in other words, is more frequently triggered by violations of institutional regulations and routines than by signs of his students' intellectual deficiencies.

Even when we consider the more serious difficulties that clearly entail academ-

ic failure, the demands of the hidden curriculum lurk in the background. When Johnny's parents are called in to school because their son is not doing too well in arithmetic, what explanation is given for their son's poor performance? Typically, blame is
placed on motivational deficiencies in Johnny rather than on his intellectual shortcomings. The teacher may even go so far as to say that Johnny is *un*motivated during
arithmetic period. But what does this mean? It means, in essence, that Johnny does
not even try. And not trying, as we have seen, usually boils down to a failure to comply with institutional expectations, a failure to master the hidden curriculum.

Testmakers describe a person as "test-wise" when he has caught on to the tricks
of test construction sufficiently well to answer questions correctly even though he
does not know the material on which he is being examined. In the same way one
might think of students as becoming "school-wise" or "teacher-wise" when they have
discovered how to respond with a minimum amount of pain and discomfort to the
demands, both official and unofficial of classroom life. Schools, like test items, have
rules and traditions of their own that can only be mastered through successive exposure. But with schools as with tests all students are not equally adroit. All are asked to
respond but not everyone catches on to the rules of the game.

If it is useful to think of there being two curriculums in the classroom, a natural
question to ask about the relationship between them is whether their joint mastery
calls for compatible or contradictory personal qualities. That is, do the same strengths
that contribute to intellectual achievement also contribute to the student's success in
conformity to institutional expectations? This question likely has no definite answer,
but it is thought-provoking and even a brief consideration of it leads into a thicket of
educational and psychological issues.

It is probably safe to predict that general ability, or intelligence, would be an as-
set in meeting all of the demands of school life, whether academic or institutional.
The child's ability to understand causal relationships, as an instance, would seem to be
of as much service as he tries to come to grips with the rules and regulations of classroom life as when he grapples with the rudiments of plant chemistry. His verbal flu-
ency can be put to use as easily in "snowing" the teacher as in writing a short story.
Thus, to the extent that the demands of classroom life call for rational thought, the
student with superior intellectual ability would seem to be at an advantage.

But more than ability is involved in adapting to complex situations. Much also
depends upon attitudes, values, and life style—upon all those qualities commonly
grouped under the term: *personality*. When the contribution of personality to adaptive
strategy is considered, the old adage of "the more, the better," which works so well for
general ability, does not suffice. Personal qualities that are beneficial in one setting may
be detrimental in another. Indeed, even a single setting may make demands that call
upon competing or conflicting tendencies in a person's makeup.

We have already seen that many features of classroom life call for patience, at
best, and resignation, at worst. As he learns to live in school our student learns to sub-
jugate his own desires to the will of the teacher and to subdue his own actions in the
interest of the common good. He learns to be passive and to acquiesce to the network
of rules, regulations, and routines in which he is embedded. He learns to tolerate pet-
ty frustrations and accept the plans and policies of higher authorities, even when their
rationale is unexplained and their meaning unclear. Like the inhabitants of most other
institutions, he learns how to shrug and say, "That's the way the ball bounces."

But the personal qualities that play a role in intellectual mastery are very different from those that characterize the Company Man. Curiosity, as an instance, that
most fundamental of all scholarly traits, is of little value in responding to the demands

of conformity. The curious person typically engages in a kind of probing, poking, and exploring that is almost antithetical to the attitude of the passive conformist. The scholar must develop the habit of challenging authority and of questioning the value of tradition. He must insist on explanations for things that are unclear. Scholarship requires discipline, to be sure, but this discipline serves the demands of scholarship rather than the wishes and desires of other people. In short, intellectual mastery calls for sublimited forms of aggression rather than for submission to constraints.

This brief discussion likely exaggerates the real differences between the demands of institutional conformity and the demands of scholarship, but it does serve to call attention to points of possible conflict. How incompatible are these two sets of demands? Can both be mastered by the same person? Apparently so. Certainly not all of our student council presidents and valedictorians can be dismissed as weak-willed teacher's pets, as academic Uriah Heeps. Many students clearly manage to maintain their intellectual aggressiveness while at the same time acquiescing to the laws that govern the social traffic of our schools. Apparently it *is* possible, under certain conditions, to breed "docile scholars," even though the expression seems to be a contradiction in terms. Indeed, certain forms of scholarship have been known to flourish in monastic settings, where the demands for institutional conformity are extreme.

Unfortunately, no one seems to know how these balances are maintained, nor even how to establish them in the first place. But even more unfortunate is the fact that few if any school people are giving the matter serious thought. As institutional settings multiply and become for more and more people the areas in which a significant portion of their life is enacted, we will need to know much more than we do at present about how to achieve a reasonable synthesis between the forces that drive a person to seek individual expression and those that drive him to comply with the wishes of others. Presumably what goes on in classrooms contributes significantly to this synthesis. The school is the first major institution, outside the family, in which almost all of us are immersed. From kindergarten onward, the student begins to learn what life is really like in The Company.

The demands of classroom life discussed in this chapter pose problems for students and teachers alike. As we have seen, there are many methods for coping with these demands and for solving the problems they create. Moreover, each major adaptive strategy is subtly transformed and given a unique expression as a result of the idiosyncratic characteristics of the student employing it. Thus, the total picture of adjustment to school becomes infinitely complex as it is manifested in the behavior of individual students.

Yet certain commonalities do exist beneath all the complexity created by the uniqueness of individuals. No matter what the demand or the personal resources of the person facing it there is at least one strategy open to all. This is the strategy of psychological withdrawal, of gradually reducing personal concern and involvement to a point where neither the demand nor one's success or failure in coping with it is sharply felt. Chapter 3 focuses exclusively on this all-purpose strategy, detachment, as it is employed in the classroom. In order to better understand student tactics, however, it is important to consider the climate of opinion from which they emerge. Before focusing on what they do in the classroom, we must examine how students feel about school.

10

The Practical: A Language
for Curriculum[1]

Joseph J. Schwab

I shall have three points. The first is this: that the field of curriculum is moribund, unable by its present methods and principles to continue its work and desperately in search of new and more effective principles and methods.

The second point: the curriculum field has reached this unhappy state by inveterate and unexamined reliance on theory in an area where theory is partly inappropriate in the first place and where the theories extant, even where appropriate, are inadequate to the tasks which the curriculum field sets them. There are honorable exceptions to this rule but too few (and too little honored) to alter the state of affairs.

The third point, which constitutes my thesis: there will be a renaissance of the field of curriculum, a renewed capacity to contribute to the quality of American education, only if the bulk of curriculum energies are diverted from the theoretic to the practical, to the quasi-practical and to the eclectic. By "eclectic" I mean the arts by which unsystematic, uneasy, but usable focus on a body of problems is effected among diverse theories, each relevant to the problems in a different way. By the "practical" I do *not* mean the curbstone practicality of the mediocre administrator and the man on the street, for whom the practical means the easily achieved, familiar goals which can be reached by familiar means. I refer, rather, to a complex discipline, relatively unfamiliar to the academic and differing radically from the disciplines of the theoretic. It is the discipline concerned with choice and action, in contrast with the theoretic, which is concerned with knowledge. Its methods lead to defensible decisions, where the methods of the theoretic lead to warranted conclusions, and differ radically from the methods and competences entailed in the theoretic. I shall sketch some of the defining aspects of practical discipline at the appropriate time.

A Crisis of Principle

The frustrated state of the field of curriculum is not an idiopathology and not a condition which warrants guilt or shame on the part of its practitioners. All fields of systematic intellectual activity are liable to such crises. They are so because any intellectual discipline must begin its endeavors with untested principles. In its beginnings, its subject matter is relatively unknown, its problems unsolved, indeed, unidentified. It does not know what questions to ask, what other knowledge to rest upon, what data

Reprinted by permission of the University of Chicago Press, from *School Review*, Vol. 78, No. 1, 1969: pp. 1–23. Published by the University of Chicago Press.

to seek or what to make of them once they are elicited. It requires a preliminary and necessarily untested guide to its enquiries. It finds this guide by borrowing, by invention, or by analogy, in the shape of a hazardous commitment to the character of its problems or its subject matter and a commitment to untried canons of evidence and rules of enquiry. What follows these commitments is years of their application, pursuit of the mode of enquiry demanded by the principles to which the field has committed itself. To the majority of practitioners of any field, these years of enquiry appear only as pursuit of knowledge of its subject matter or solution of its problems. They take the guiding principles of the enquiry as givens. These years of enquiry, however, are something more than pursuit of knowledge or solution of problems. They are also tests, reflexive and pragmatic, of the principles which guide the enquiries. They determine whether, in fact, the data demanded by the principles can be elicited and whether, if elicited, they can be made to constitute knowledge adequate to the complexity of the subject matter, or solutions which, in fact, do solve the problems with which the enquiry began.

In the nature of the case, these reflexive tests of the principles of enquiry are, more often than not, partially or wholly negative, for, after all, the commitment to these principles was made before there was well-tested fruit of enquiry by which to guide the commitment. The inadequacies of principles begin to show, in the case of theoretical enquiries, by failures of the subject matter to respond to the questions put to it, by incoherencies and contradictions in data and in conclusions which cannot be resolved, or by clear disparities between the knowledge yielded by the enquiries and the behaviors of the subject matter which the knowledge purports to represent. In the case of practical enquiries, inadequacies begin to show by incapacity to arrive at solutions to the problems, by inability to realize the solutions proposed, by mutual frustrations and cancellings out as solutions are put into effect.

Although these exhaustions and failures of principles may go unnoted by practitioners in the field, at least at the conscious level, what may not be represented in consciousness is nevertheless evidenced by behavior and appears in the literature and the activities of the field as signs of the onset of a crisis of principle. These signs consist of a large increase in the frequency of published papers and colloquia marked by *a flight from the subject of the field*. There are usually six signs of this flight or directions in which the flight occurs.

Signs of Crisis

The first and most important, though often least conspicuous, sign is a flight of the field itself, a translocation of its problems and the solving of them from the nominal practitioners of the field to other men. Thus one crucial frustration of the science of genetics was resolved by a single contribution from an insurance actuary. The recent desuetude of academic physiology has been marked by a conspicuous increase in the frequency of published solutions to physiological problems by medical researchers. In similar fashion, the increasing depletion of psychoanalytic principles and methods in recent years was marked by the onset of contributions to its lore by internists, biochemists, and anthropologists.

A second flight is a flight upward, from discourse about the subject of the field to discourse about the discourse of the field, from *use* of principles and methods to *talk* about them, from grounded conclusions to the construction of models, from theory to metatheory and from metatheory to metametatheory.

A third flight is downward, an attempt by practitioners to return to the subject matter in a state of innocence, shorn not only of current principles but of all principles, in an effort to take a new, a pristine and unmediated look at the subject matter. For example, one conspicuous reaction to the warfare of numerous inadequate principles in experimental psychology has been the resurgence of ethology, which begins as an attempt to return to a pure natural history of behavior, to intensive observation and recording of the behavior of animals undisturbed in their natural habitat, by observers, equally undisturbed by mediating conceptions, attempting to record anything and everything they see before them.

A fourth flight is to the sidelines, to the role of observer, commentator, historian, and critic of the contributions of others to the field.

A fifth sign consists of marked perseveration, a repetition of old and familiar knowledge in new languages which add little or nothing to the old meanings as embodied in the older and familiar language, or repetition of old and familiar formulations by way of criticisms or minor additions and modifications.

The sixth is a marked increase in eristic, contentious, and *ad hominem* debate.

I hasten to remark that these signs of crisis are not all or equally reprehensible. There is little excuse for the increase in contentiousness nor much value in the flight to the sidelines or in perseveration, but the others, in one way or another, can contribute to resolution of the crisis. The flight of the field itself is one of the more fruitful ways by which analogical principles are disclosed, modified, and adapted to the field in crisis. The flight upward, to models and metatheory, if done responsibly, which means with a steady eye on the actual problems and conditions of the field for which the models are ostensibly constructed, becomes, in fact, the proposal and test of possible new principles for the field. The flight backward, to a state of innocence, is at least an effort to break the grip of old habits of thought and thus leave space for needed new ones, though it is clear that in the matter of enquiry, as elsewhere, virginity, once lost, cannot be regained.

In the present context, however, the virtue or vice of these various flights is beside the point. We are concerned with them as signs of collapse of principles in a field, and it is my contention, based on a study not yet complete, that most of these signs may now be seen in the field of curriculum. I shall only suggest, not cite, my evidence.

The Case of Curriculum

With respect to flight of the field itself, there can be little doubt. Of the five substantial high school science curricula, four of them—PSSC, BSCS, Chems and CBA—were instituted and managed by subject-matter specialists; the contribution of educators was small and that of curriculum specialists near vanishing point. Only Harvard Project Physics, at this writing not yet available, appears to be an exception. To one of two elementary science projects, a psychologist appears to have made a substantial contribution but curriculum specialists very little. The other—the Elementary Science Study—appears to have been substantially affected (to its advantage) by educators with one or both feet in curriculum. The efforts of the Commission of Undergraduate Education in the Biological Sciences have been carried on almost entirely by subject-matter specialists. The English Curriculum Study Centers appear to be in much the same state as the high school science curricula: overwhelmingly centered on subject specialists. Educators contribute expertise only in the area of test construction and evaluation, with here and there a contribution by a psychologist. Educators, including curriculum specialists, were massively unprepared to cope with the problem of integrated education and only by little, and late, and by trial and error, put together the halting solutions currently known as Head Start. The problems posed by the current drives toward ethnicity in education find curriculum specialists even more massively oblivious and unprepared. And I so far find myself very much alone with respect to the curriculum problems immanent in the phenomena of student protest and student revolt. (Of the social studies curriculum efforts, I shall say nothing at this time.)

On the second flight—upward—I need hardly comment. The models, the metatheory, and the metametatheory are all over the place. Many of them, moreover, are irresponsible—concerned less with the barriers to continued productivity in the field of curriculum than with exploitation of the exotic and the fashionable among forms and models of theory and metatheory: systems theory, symbolic logic, language analysis. Many others, including responsible ones, are irreversible flights upward or sideways. That is, they are models or metatheories concerned not with the judgment, the reasoned construction, or reconstruction of curriculums but with other matters—for example, how curriculum changes occur or how changes can be managed.

The flight downward, the attempt at return to a pristine, unmediated look at the subject matter, is, for some reason, a missing symptom in the case of curriculum. There are returns—to the classroom, if not to other levels or aspects of curriculum—with a measure of effort to avoid preconceptions (e.g., Smith, Bellack, and studies of communication nets and lines), but the frequency of such studies has not markedly increased. The absence of this symptom may have significance. In general, however, it is characteristic of diseases that the whole syndrome does not appear in all cases. Hence, pending further study and thought, I do not count this negative instance as weakening the diagnosis of a crisis of principle.

The fourth flight—to the sidelines—is again a marked symptom of the field of curriculum. Histories, anthologies, commentaries, criticisms, and proposals of curriculums multiply.

Perseveration is also marked. I recoil from counting the persons and books whose lives are made possible by continuing restatement of the Tyler rationale, of the character and case for behavioral objectives, of the virtues and vices of John Dewey.

The rise in frequency and intensity of the eristic and *ad hominem* is also marked. Thus one author climaxes a series of petulances by the remark that what he takes to be his own forte "has always been rare—and shows up in proper perspective the happy breed of educational reformer who can concoct a brand new, rabble-rousing theory of educational reform while waiting for the water to fill the bathtub."

There is little doubt, in short, that the field of curriculum is in a crisis of principle.

A crisis of principle arises, as I have suggested, when principles are exhausted—when the questions they permit have all been asked and answered—or when the efforts at enquiry instigated by the principles have at last exhibited their inadequacy to the subject matter and the problems which they were designed to attack. My second point is that the latter holds in the case of curriculum: the curriculum movement has been inveterately theoretic, and its theoretic bent has let it down. A brief conspectus of instances will suggest the extent of this theoretic bent and what is meant by "theoretic."

Characteristics of Theory

Consider first the early, allegedly Herbartian efforts (recently revived by Bruner). These efforts took the view that ideas were formed by children out of received notions and experiences of things, and that these ideas functioned thereafter as discriminators and organizers of what was later learned. Given this view, the aim of curriculum was to discriminate the right ideas (by way of analysis of extant bodies of knowledge), determine the order in which they could be learned by children as they developed, and thereafter present these ideas at the right times with clarity, associations, organization, and application. A theory of mind and knowledge thus solves by one mighty coup the problem of what to teach, when, and how; and what is fatally theoretic here is not the presence of a theory of mind and a theory of knowledge, though their presence is part of the story, but the dispatch, the sweeping appearance of success, the vast simplicity which grounds this purported solution to the problem of curriculum. And lest we think that this faith in the possibility of successful neatness, dispatch, and sweeping generality is a mark of the past, consider the concern of the National Science Teachers Association only four years ago "with identifying the broad principles that can apply to any and all curriculum development efforts in science," a concern crystallized in just seven "conceptual schemes" held to underlie all science. With less ambitious sweepingness but with the same steadfast concern for a single factor—in this case, a supposed fixed structure of knowledge—one finds similar efforts arising from the Association of College Teachers of Education, from historians, even from teachers of literature.

Consider, now, some of the numerous efforts to ground curriculum in derived objectives. One effort seeks the ground of its objectives in social need and finds its social needs in just those facts about its culture which are sought and found under the aegis of a single conception of culture. Another grounds its objectives in the social needs identified by a single theory of history and of political evolution.

A third group of searches for objectives are grounded in theories of personality. The persuasive coherence and plausibility of Freudianism persuaded its followers to aim to supply children with adequate channels of sublimation of surplus libido, appropriate objects and occasions for aggressions, a properly undemanding ego ideal, and an intelligent minimum of taboos. Interpersonal theories direct their adherents to aim for development of abilities to relate to peers, "infeers," and "supeers," in relations nurturant and receiving, adaptive, vying, approving and disapproving. Theories of actualization instruct their adherents to determine the salient potentialities of each child and to see individually to the development of each.

Still other searches for objectives seek their aims in the knowledge needed to "live in the modern world," in the attitudes and habits which minimize dissonance with the prevailing mores of one's community or social class, in the skills required for success in a trade or vocation, in the ability to participate effectively as member of a group. Still others are grounded in some quasi-ethics, some view of the array of goods which are good for man.

Three features of these typical efforts at curriculum making are significant here, each of which has its own lesson to teach us. First, each is grounded in a theory as such. We shall return to this point in a moment. Second, each is grounded in a theory from the social or behavioral sciences: psychology, psychiatry, politics, sociology, history. Even the ethical bases and theories of "mind" are behavioral. To this point, too, we shall return in a moment. Third, they are theories concerning *different* subject matters. One curriculum effort is grounded in concern for the individual, another in concern for groups, others in concern for cultures, communities, societies, minds, or the extant bodies of knowledge.[2]

Need for an Eclectic

The significance of this third feature is patent to the point of embarrassment: no curriculum grounded in but one of these subjects can possibly be adequate, defensible. A curriculum based on theory about individual personality, which thrusts society, its demands and its structure, far into the background or ignores them entirely, can be nothing but incomplete and doctrinaire, for the individuals in question are in fact members of a society and must meet its demands to some minimum degree since their existence and prosperity as individuals depend on the functioning of their society. In the same way, a curriculum grounded only in a view of social need or social change must be equally doctrinaire and incomplete, for societies do not exist only for their own sakes but for the prosperity of their members as individuals as well. In the same way, learners are not only minds or knowers but bundles of affects, individuals, personalities, earners of livings. They are not only group interactors but possessors of private lives.

It is clear, I submit, that a defensible curriculum or plan of curriculum must be one which somehow takes account of all these sub-subjects which pertain to man. It cannot take only one and ignore the others; it cannot even take account of many of them and ignore one. Not only is each of them a constituent and a condition for decent human existence but each interpenetrates the others. That is, the character of human personalities is a determiner of human society and the behavior of human groups. Conversely, the conditions of group behavior and the character of societies determine in some large part the personalities which their members develop, the way their minds work, and what they can learn and use by way of knowledge and competence. These various "things" (individuals, societies, cultures, patterns of enquiry, "structures" of knowledge or of enquiries, apperceptive masses, problem solving), though discriminable as separate subjects of differing modes of enquiry, are nevertheless parts or affectors of one another, or coactors. (Their very separation for purposes of enquiry is what marks the outcomes of such enquiries as "theoretic" and consequently incomplete.) In practice, they constitute one complex, organic agency. Hence, a focus on only one not only ignores the others but vitiates the quality and completeness with which the selected one is viewed.

It is equally clear, however, that there is not, and will not be in the foreseeable future, one theory of this complex whole which is other than a collection of unusable generalities. Nor is it true that the lack of a theory of the whole is due to the narrowness, stubbornness, or merely habitual specialism of social and behavioral scientists. Rather, their specialism and the restricted purview of their theories are functions of their subject, its enormous complexity, its vast capacity for difference and change. Man's competence at the construction of theoretical knowledge is so far most inadequate when applied to the subject of man. There have been efforts to conceive principles of enquiry which would encompass the whole variety and complexity of humanity, but they have fallen far short of adequacy to the subject matter or have demanded the acquisition of data and modes of interpretation of data beyond our capabilities. There *are* continuing efforts to find bridging terms which would relate the principles of enquiry of one subfield of the social sciences to another and thus begin to effect connections among our knowledges of each, but successful bridges are so far few and narrow and permit but a trickle of connection. As far, then, as theoretical knowledge is concerned, we must wrestle as best we can with numerous, largely un-connected, separate theories of these many, artificially discriminated subsubjects of man.

I remarked in the beginning that renewal of the field of curriculum would re-quire diversion of the bulk of its energies from theory to the practical, the quasi-prac-tical, and the eclectic. The state of affairs just described, the existence and the neces-sarily continuing existence of separate theories of separate subsubjects distributed among the social sciences, constitutes the case for one of these modes, the necessity of an eclectic, of arts by which a usable focus on a common body of problems is effected among theories which lack theoretical connection. The argument can be simply sum-marized. A curriculum grounded in but one or a few subsubjects of the social sciences is indefensible; contributions from all are required. There is no foreseeable hope of a unified theory in the immediate or middle future, nor of a metatheory which will tell us how to put those subsubjects together or order them in a fixed hierarchy of impor-tance to the problems of curriculum. What remains as a viable alternative is the unsys-tematic, uneasy, pragmatic, and uncertain unions and connections which can be ef-fected in an eclectic. And I must add, anticipating our discussion of the practical, that *changing* connections and *differing* orderings at different times of these separate theo-ries, will characterize a sound eclectic.

The character of eclectic arts and procedures must be left for discussion on an-other occasion. Let it suffice for the moment that witness of the high effectiveness of eclectic methods and of their accessibility is borne by at least one field familiar to us all—Western medicine. It has been enormously effective, and the growth of its com-petence dates from its disavowal of a single doctrine and its turn to eclecticism.

The Place of the Practical

I turn now, from the fact that the theories which ground curriculum plans pertain to different subsubjects of a common field, to the second of the three features which characterize our typical instances of curriculum planning—the fact that the ground of each plan is a theory, a theory as such.

The significance of the existence of theory as such at the base of curricular planning consists of what it is that theory does not and cannot encompass. All theo-ries, even the best of them in the simplest sciences, necessarily neglect some aspects and facets of the facts of the case. A theory covers and formulates the *regularities* among the things and events it subsumes. It abstracts a general or ideal case. It leaves behind the nonuniformities, the particularities, which characterize each concrete in-stance of the facts subsumed. Moreover, in the process of idealization, theoretical en-quiry may often leave out of consideration conspicuous facets of *all* cases because its substantive principles of enquiry or its methods cannot handle them. Thus the con-stantly accelerating body of classical mechanics was the acceleration of a body in "free" fall, fall in a perfect vacuum, and the general or theoretical rule formulated in classical mechanics is far from describing the fall of actual bodies in actual mediums—the only kinds of fall then known. The force equation of classical dynamics applied to bodies of visible magnitudes ignores friction. The rule that light varies inversely as the square of the distance holds exactly only for an imaginary point source of light. For real light sources of increasing expanse, the so-called law holds more and more ap-proximately, and for very large sources it affords little or no usable information. And what is true of the best of theories in the simplest sciences is true a fortiori in the so-cial sciences. Their subject matters are apparently so much more variable, and clearly so much more complex, that their theories encompass much less of their subjects than do the theories of the physical and biological sciences.

Yet curriculum is brought to bear not on ideal or abstract representatives but on the real thing, on the concrete case in all its completeness and with all its differences from all other concrete cases on which the theoretic abstraction is silent. The materials of a concrete curriculum will not consist merely of portions of "science," of "literature," of "process." On the contrary, their constituents will be particular assertions about selected matters couched in a particular vocabulary, syntax, and rhetoric. They will be particular novels, short stories, or lyric poems, each, for better or for worse, with its own flavor. They will be particular acts upon particular matters in a given sequence. The curriculum will be brought to bear not in some archetypical classroom but in a particular locus in time and space with smells, shadows, seats, and conditions outside its walls which may have much to do with what is achieved inside. Above all, the supposed beneficiary is not the generic child, not even a class or kind of child out of the psychological or sociological literature pertaining to the child. The beneficiaries will consist of very local kinds of children and, within the local kinds, individual children. The same diversity holds with respect to teachers and what they do. The generalities about science, about literature, about children in general, about children or teachers of some specified class or kind, may be true. But they attain this status in virtue of what they leave out, and the omissions affect what remains. A Guernsey cow is not only something more than cow, having specific features omitted from description of the genus; it is also cowy in ways differing from the cowiness of a Texas longhorn. The specific not only adds to the generic; it also modulates it.

These ineluctable characteristics of theory and the consequent ineluctable disparities between real things and their representation in theory constitute one argument for my thesis, that a large bulk of curriculum energies must be diverted from the theoretic, not only to the eclectic but to the practical and the quasi-practical. The argument, again, can be briefly summarized. The stuff of theory is abstract or idealized representations of real things. But curriculum in action treats real things: real acts, real teachers, real children, things richer and different from their theoretical representations. Curriculum will deal badly with its real things if it treats them merely as replicas of their theoretic representations. If, then, theory is to be used well in the determination of curricular practice, it requires a supplement. It requires arts which bring a theory to its application: first, arts which identify the disparities between real thing and theoretic representation; second, arts which modify the theory in the course of its application, in the light of the discrepancies; and, third, arts which devise ways of taking account of the many aspects of the real thing which the theory does not take into account. These are some of the arts of the practical.

Theories from Social Sciences

The significance of the third feature of our typical instances of curriculum work—that their theories are mainly theories from the social and behavioral sciences—will carry us to the remainder of the argument for the practical. Nearly all theories in all the behavioral sciences are marked by the coexistence of competing theories. There is not one theory of personality but twenty, representing at least six radically different choices of what is relevant and important in human behavior. There is not one theory of groups but several. There is not one theory of learning but half a dozen. All the social and behavioral sciences are marked by "schools," each distinguished by a different choice of principle of enquiry, each of which selects from the intimidating complexities of the subject matter the small fraction of the whole with which it can deal.

The theories which arise from enquiries so directed are, then, radically incomplete, each of them incomplete to the extent that competing theories take hold of different aspects of the subject of enquiry and treat it in a different way. Further, there is perennial invention of new principles which bring to light new facets of the subject matter, new relations among the facets and new ways of treating them. In short, there is every reason to suppose that any one of the extant theories of behavior is a pale and incomplete representation of actual behavior. There is similar reason to suppose that if all the diversities of fact, the different aspects of behavior treated in each theory, were somehow to be brought within the bounds of a single theory, that theory would still fall short of comprehending the whole of human behavior—in two respects. In the first place, it would not comprehend what there may be of human behavior which we do not see by virtue of the restricted light by which we examine behavior. In the second place, such a single theory will necessarily interpret its data in the light of its one set of principles, assigning to these data only one set of significances and establishing among them only one set of relations. It will remain the case, then, that a diversity of theories may tell us more than a single one, even though the "factual" scope of the many and the one are the same.

It follows, then, that such theories are not, and will not be, adequate by themselves to tell us what to do with human beings or how to do it. What they variously suggest and the contrary guidances they afford to choice and action must be mediated and combined by eclectic arts and must be massively supplemented, as well as mediated, by knowledge of some other kind derived from another source.

Some areas of choice and action with respect to human behavior have long since learned this lesson. Government is made possible by a lore of politics derived from immediate experience of the vicissitudes and tangles of legislating and administering. Institution of economic guidances and controls owes as much to unmediated experience of the marketplace as it does to formulas and theories. Even psychotherapy has long since deserted its theories of personality as sole guides to therapy and relies as much or more on the accumulated, explicitly nontheoretic lore accumulated by practitioners, as it does on theory or eclectic combinations of theory. The law has systematized the accumulation of direct experience of actual cases in its machinery for the recording of cases and opinions as precedents which continuously monitor, supplement, and modify the meaning and application of its formal "knowledge," its statutes. It is this recourse to accumulated lore, to experience of actions and their consequences, to action and reaction at the level of the concrete case, which constitutes the heart of the practical. It is high time that curriculum do likewise.

The Practical Arts

The arts of the practical are onerous and complex; hence only a sampling must suffice to indicate the character of this discipline and the changes in educational investigation which would ensue on adoption of the discipline. I shall deal briefly with four aspects of it.

The practical arts begin with the requirement that existing institutions and existing practices be preserved and altered piecemeal, not dismantled and replaced. It is further necessary that changes be so planned and so articulated with what remains unchanged that the functioning of the whole remain coherent and unimpaired. These necessities stem from the very nature of the practical—that it is concerned with the maintenance and improvement of patterns of purposed action, and especially concerned that the effects of the pattern through time shall retain coherence and relevance to one another.

This is well seen in the case of the law. Statutes are repealed or largely rewritten only as a last resort, since to do so creates confusion and diremption between old judgments under the law and judgments to come, confusion which must lead either to weakening of law through disrepute or a painful and costly process of repairing the effects of past judgments so as to bring them into conformity with the new. It is vastly more desirable that changes be instituted in small degrees and in immediate adjustment to the peculiarities of particular new cases which call forth the change.

The consequence, in the case of the law, of these demands of the practical is that the servants of the law must know the law through and through. They must know the statutes themselves, the progression of precedents and interpretations which have effected changes in them, and especially the present state of affairs—the most recent decisions under the law and the calendar of cases which will be most immediately affected by contemplated additions to precedent and interpretation.

The same requirements would hold for a practical program of improvement of education. It, too, would effect its changes in small progressions, in coherence with what remains unchanged, and this would require that we know *what is and has been going on in American schools*.

At present, we do not know. My own incomplete investigations convince me that we have not the faintest reliable knowledge of how literature is taught in the high schools, or what actually goes on in science classrooms. There are a dozen different ways in which the novel can be read. Which ones are used by whom, with whom, and to what effect? What selections from the large accumulation of biological knowledge are made and taught in this school system and that, to what classes and kinds of children, to what effect? To what extent is science taught as verbal formulas, as congeries of unrelated facts, as so-called principles and conceptual structures, as outcomes of enquiry? In what degree and kind of simplification and falsification is scientific enquiry conveyed, if it is conveyed at all?

A count of textbook adoptions will not tell us, for teachers select from textbooks and alter their treatment (often quite properly) and can frustrate and negate the textbook's effort to alter the pattern of instruction. We cannot tell from lists of objectives, since they are usually so vastly ambiguous that almost anything can go on under their aegis or, if they are not ambiguous, reflect pious hopes as much as actual practice. We cannot tell from lists of "principles" and "conceptual structures," since these, in their telegraphic brevity are also ambiguous and say nothing of the shape in which they are taught or the extent.

What is wanted is a totally new and extensive pattern of *empirical* study of classroom action and reaction; a study, not as basis for theoretical concerns about the nature of the teaching or learning process, but as a basis for beginning to know what we are doing, what we are not doing, and to what effect—what changes are needed, which needed changes can be instituted with what costs or economies, and how they can be effected with minimum tearing of the remaining fabric of educational effort.

This is an effort which will require new mechanisms of empirical investigation, new methods of reportage, a new class of educational researchers, and much money. It is an effort without which we will continue largely incapable of making defensible decisions about curricular changes, largely unable to put them into effect and ignorant of what real consequences, if any, our efforts have had.

A very large part of such a study would, I repeat, be direct and empirical study of action and reaction in the classroom itself, not merely the testing of student change. But one of the most interesting and visible alterations of present practice which might be involved is a radical change in our pattern of testing students. The common pattern tries to determine the extent to which *intended* changes have been brought about. This would be altered to an effort to find out what changes have occurred, to determine side effects as well as mainline consequences, since the distinction between these two is always in the eye of the intender and side effects may be as great in magnitude and as fatal or healthful for students as the intended effects.

A second facet of the practical: its actions are undertaken with respect to identified frictions and failures in the machine and inadequacies evidenced in felt shortcomings of its products. This origin of its actions leads to two marked differences in operation from that of theory. Under the control of theory, curricular changes have their origin in new notions of person, group or society, mind or knowledge, which give rise to suggestions of new things curriculum might be or do. This is an origin which, by its nature, takes little or no account of the existing effectiveness of the machine or the consequences to this effectiveness of the institution of novelty. If there is concern for what may be displaced by innovation or for the incoherences which may ensue on the insertion of novelty, the concern is gratuitous. It does not arise from the theoretical considerations which commend the novelty. The practical, on the other hand, because it institutes changes to repair frictions and deficiencies, is commanded to determine the whole array of possible effects of proposed change, to determine what new frictions and deficiencies the proposed change may unintentionally produce.

The other effective difference between theoretical and practical origins of deliberate change is patent. Theory, by being concerned with new things to do, is unconcerned with the successes and failures of present doings. Hence present failures, unless they coincide with what is repaired by the proposed innovations, go unnoticed—as do present successes. The practical, on the other hand, is directly and deliberately concerned with the diagnosis of ills of the curriculum.

These concerns of the practical for frictions and failures of the curricular machine would, again, call for a new and extensive pattern of enquiry. The practical requires curriculum study to seek its problems where its problems lie—in the behaviors, misbehaviors, and nonbehaviors of its students as they begin to evince the effects of the training they did and did not get. This means continuing assessment of students as they leave primary grades for the secondary school, leave secondary school for jobs and colleges. It means sensitive and sophisticated assessment by way of impressions, insights, and reactions of the community which sends its children to the school; employers of students, new echelons of teachers of students; the wives, husbands, and cronies of exstudents; the people with whom exstudents work; the people who work under them. Curriculum study will look into the questions of what games exstudents play; what, if anything, they do about politics and crime in the streets; what they read, if they do; what they watch on television and what they make of what they watch, again, if anything. Such studies would be undertaken, furthermore, not as mass study of products of the American school, taken in toto, but as studies of significantly separable schools and school systems—suburban and inner city, Chicago and Los Angeles, South Bend and Michigan City.

I emphasize sensitive and sophisticated assessment because we are concerned here, as in the laying of background knowledge of what goes in schools, not merely with the degree to which avowed objectives are achieved but also with detecting the failures and frictions of the machine: what it has not done or thought of doing, and what side effects its doings have had. Nor are we concerned with successes and failures only as measured in test situations but also as evidenced in life and work. It is this sort of diagnosis which I have tried to exemplify in a recent treatment of curriculum and student protest.[3]

A third facet of the practical I shall call the anticipatory generation of alternatives. Intimate knowledge of the existing state of affairs, early identification of problem situations, and effective formulation of problems are necessary to effective practical decision but not sufficient. It requires also that there be available to practical deliberation the greatest possible number and fresh diversity of alternative solutions to the problem. The reason for this requirement, in one aspect, is obvious enough: the best choice among poor and shopworn alternatives will still be a poor solution to the problem. Another aspect is less obvious. The problems which arise in an institutional structure which has enjoyed good practical management will be novel problems, arising from changes in the times and circumstances and from the consequences of previous solutions to previous problems. Such problems, with their strong tincture of novelty, cannot be solved by familiar solutions. They cannot be well solved by apparently new solutions arising from old habits of mind and old ways of doing things.

A third aspect of the requirement for anticipatory generation of alternatives is still less obvious. It consists of the fact that practical problems do not present themselves wearing their labels around their necks. Problem situations, to use Dewey's old term, present themselves to consciousness, but the character of the problem, its formulation, does not. This depends on the eye of the beholder. And this eye, unilluminated by possible fresh solutions to problems, new modes of attack, new recognitions of degrees of freedom for change among matters formerly taken to be unalterable, is very likely to miss the novel features of new problems or dismiss them as "impractical." Hence the requirement that the generation of problems be anticipatory and not await the emergence of the problem itself.

To some extent, the *theoretical* bases of curricular change—such items as emphasis on enquiry, on discovery learning, and on structure of the disciplines—contribute to this need but not sufficiently or with the breadth which permits effective deliberation. That is, these theoretic proposals tend to arise in single file, out of connection with other proposals which constitute alternatives, or, more important, constitute desiderata or circumstances which affect the choice or rejection of proposals. Consider, in regard to the problem of the "single file," only one relation between the two recent proposals subsumed under "creativity" and "structure of knowledge." If creativity implies some measure of invention, and "structure of knowledge" implies (as it does in one version) the systematic induction of conceptions as soon as children are ready to grasp them, an issue is joined. To the extent that the latter is timely and well done, scope for the former is curtailed. To the extent that children can be identified as more or less creative, "structure of knowledge" would be brought to bear on different children at different times and in different ways.

A single case, taken from possible academic resources of education, will suggest the new kind of enquiry entailed in the need for anticipatory generation of alternatives. Over the years, critical scholarship has generated, as remarked earlier, a dozen different conceptions of the novel, a dozen or more ways in which the novel can be read, each involving its own emphases and its own arts of recovery of meaning in the act of reading. Novels can be read, for example, as bearers of wisdom, insights into vicissitudes of human life and ways of enduring them. Novels can also be read as moral instructors, as sources of vicarious experience, as occasions for aesthetic experience.

They can be read as models of human creativity, as displays of social problems, as political propaganda, as revelations of diversities of manners and morals among different cultures and classes of people, or as symptoms of their age.

Now what, in fact, is the full parade of such possible uses of the novel? What is required by each in the way of competences of reading, discussion, and thought? What are the rewards, the desirable outcomes, which are likely to ensue for students from each kind of reading or combinations of them? For what kinds or classes of students is each desirable? There are further problems demanding anticipatory consideration. If novels are chosen and read as displays of social problems and depictions of social classes, what effect will such instruction in literature have on instruction in the social studies? What will teachers need to know and be able to do in order to enable students to discriminate and appropriately connect the *aperçus* of artists, the accounts of historians, and the conclusions of social scientists on such matters? How will the mode of instruction in science (e.g., as verified truths) and in literature (as "deep insights" or artistic constructions or matters of opinion) affect the effects of each?

The same kinds of questions could be addressed to history and to the social studies generally. Yet, nowhere, in the case of literature, have we been able to find cogent and energetic work addressed to them. The journals in the field of English teaching are nearly devoid of treatment of them. College and university courses, in English or education, which address such problems with a modicum of intellectual content are as scarce as hen's teeth. We cannot even find an unbiased conspectus of critical theory more complete than *The Pooh Perplex*, and treatments of problems of the second kind (pertaining to interaction of literature instruction with instruction in other fields) are also invisible.

Under a soundly practical dispensation in curriculum the address of such questions would be a high priority and require recruitment to education of philosophers and subject-matter specialists of a quality and critical sophistication which it has rarely, if ever, sought.

As the last sampling of the practical, consider its method. It falls under neither of the popular platitudes: it is neither deductive nor inductive. It is deliberative. It cannot be inductive because the target of the method is not a generalization or explanation but a decision about action in a concrete situation. It cannot be deductive because it deals with the concrete case, not abstractions from cases, and the concrete case cannot be settled by mere application of a principle. Almost every concrete case falls under two or more principles, and every concrete case will possess some cogent characteristics which are encompassed in no principle. The problem of selecting an appropriate man for an important post is a case in point. It is not a problem of selecting a representative of the appropriate personality type who exhibits the competences officially required for the job. The man we hire is more than a type and a bundle of competences. He is a multitude of probable behaviors which escape the net of personality theories and cognitive scales. He is endowed with prejudices, mannerisms, habits, tics, and relatives. And all of these manifold particulars will affect his work and the work of those who work for him. It is deliberation which operates in such cases to select the appropriate man.

Commitment to Deliberation

Deliberation is complex and arduous. It treats both ends and means and must treat them as mutually determining one another. It must try to identify, with respect to both, what facts may be relevant. It must try to ascertain the relevant facts in the concrete case. It must try to identify the desiderata in the case. It must generate alternative solutions. It must make every effort to trace the branching pathways of consequences which may flow from each alternative and affect desiderata. It must then weigh alternatives and their costs and consequences against one another and choose, not the right alternative, for there *is* no such thing, but the best one.

I shall mention only one of the new kinds of activity which would ensue on commitment to deliberation. It will require the formation of a new public and new means of communication among its constituent members. Deliberation requires consideration of the widest possible variety of alternatives if it is to be most effective. Each alternative must be viewed in the widest variety of lights. Ramifying consequences must be traced to all parts of the curriculum. The desirability of each alternative must be felt out, "rehearsed," by a representative variety of all those who must live with the consequences of the chosen action. And a similar variety must deal with the identification of problems as well as with their solution.

This will require penetration of the curtains which now separate educational psychologist from philosopher, sociologist from test constructor, historian from administrator; it will require new channels connecting the series from teacher, supervisor, and school administrator at one end to research specialists at the other. Above all, it will require renunciation of the specious privileges and hegemonies by which we maintain the fiction that problems of science curriculum, for example, have no bearing on problems of English literature or the social studies. The aim here is *not* a dissolving of specialization and special responsibilities. Quite the contrary: if the variety of lights we need are to be obtained, the variety of specialized interests, competences, and habits of mind which characterize education must be cherished and nurtured. The aim, rather, is to bring the members of this variety to bear on curriculum problems by communication with one another.

Concretely, this means the establishment of new journals, and education of educators so that they can write for them and read them. The journals will be forums where possible problems of curriculum will be broached from many sources and their possible importance debated from many points of view. They will be the stage for display of anticipatory solutions to problems, from a similar variety of sources. They will constitute deliberative assemblies in which problems and alternative solutions will be argued by representatives of all for the consideration of all and for the shaping of intelligent consensus.

Needless to say, such journals are not alone sufficient. They stand as only one concrete model of the kind of forum which is required. Similar forums, operating viva voce and in the midst of curriculum operation and curriculum change, are required: of the teachers, supervisors, and administrators of a school; of the supervisors and administrators of a school system; of representatives of teachers, supervisors, and curriculum makers in subject areas and across subject areas; of the same representatives and specialists in curriculum, psychology, sociology, administration, and the subject-matter fields.[4]

The education of educators to participate in this deliberative process will be neither easy nor quickly achieved. The education of the present generation of specialist researchers to speak to the schools and to one another will doubtless be hardest of all, and on this hardest problem I have no suggestion to make. But we could begin within two years to initiate the preparation of teachers, supervisors, curriculum makers, and graduate students of education in the uses and arts of deliberation—and we should.

For graduate students, this should mean that their future enquiries in educational psychology, philosophy of education, educational sociology, and so on, will find more effective focus on enduring problems of education, as against the attractions of the current foci of the parent disciplines. It will begin to exhibit to graduate students what their duties are to the future schoolmen whom they will teach. For teachers, curriculum makers, and others close to the classroom, such training is of special importance. It will not only bring immediate experience of the classroom effectively to bear on problems of curriculum but enhance the quality of that experience, for almost every classroom episode is a stream of situations requiring discrimination of deliberative problems and decision thereon.

By means of such journals and such an education, the educational research establishment might at last find a means for channeling its discoveries into sustained improvement of the schools instead of into a procession of ephemeral bandwagons.

Notes

1. Copyright 1969 by Joseph J. Schwab. All rights reserved. A version of this paper was delivered to Section B of the American Educational Research Association, Los Angeles, February 1969. This paper has been prepared as part of a project supported by a grant from the Ford Foundation.

2. It should be clear by now that "theory" as used in this paper does *not* refer only to grand schemes such as the general theory of relativity, kinetic-molecular theory, the Bohr atom, the Freudian construction of a tripartite psyche. The attempt to give an account of human maturation by the discrimination of definite states (e.g., oral, anal, genital), an effort to aggregate human competences into a small number of primary mental abilities—these too are theoretic. So also are efforts to discriminate a few large classes of persons and to attribute to them defining behaviors: e.g., the socially mobile, the culturally deprived, the creative.

3. *College Curriculum and Student Protest* (Chicago: University of Chicago Press, 1969).

4. It will be clear from these remarks that the conception of curricular method proposed here is immanent in the Tyler rationale. This rationale calls for a diversity of talents and insists on the practical and eclectic treatment of a variety of factors. Its effectiveness in practice is vitiated by two circumstances. Its focus on "objectives," with their massive ambiguity and equivocation, provides far too little of the concrete matter required for deliberation and leads only to delusive consensus. Second, those who use it are not trained for the deliberative procedures it requires.

III

PONDERING
THE CURRICULUM

This section of the reader deals with the aftermath of the curriculum reform move-ment, focusing mainly on developments in the 1970s but flowing over into the 1980s. Whether primarily considered a cause or a symptom, Joseph Schwab's (see Part II) ap-peal for the "practical" had touched a raw nerve in the curriculum field. As Schwab had put it, the curriculum field is "unable by its present methods and principles to continue its work." The highly influential work of Ralph Tyler (see introduction to Part II) was also not spared revisionist scrutiny, most notably Herbert Kliebard's (1970) persuasive critique of the Tyler "rationale." Indeed, following more than a decade of often generously funded curriculum reform, it was hard to ignore that many of the curriculum projects were dominated not by specialists in "the curricu-lum," but by subject-matter specialists (see Jackson, 1992, p. 37). In short, Schwab had been accurate that the scholarly field of curriculum—and what that meant for prac-tice—was ripe for new directions.

As had been true since its inception, the curriculum field did not respond in unison to the challenges of changing needs and times. Nonetheless, there are dis-cernible contours of change in the curriculum literature. As had long been the case, of course, much curriculum practice continued largely oblivious to changes in curricu-lum theory.

Perhaps the most striking departure was the rise of what became known as the reconceptualist movement. Reconceptualism was consistent with Schwab's rejection of much of the legacy of the curriculum field. The reconceptualists, however, seem to have headed in directions that Schwab had not anticipated. In particular, they turned to ideas that had either largely been lying dormant for a long period or had not pre-viously been considered pertinent to curriculum theorizing. As William Pinar noted at the time, however, for all their differences the reconceptualists shared an overt polit-ical emphasis, underscoring the ideological dimensions of schooling.

Just as the meaning of reconceptualism itself has always been open to varying in-terpretations, as Pinar shows in the first reading, it is easier to distinguish it from earli-er traditions of curriculum thought than to identify who is and who is not a recon-ceptualist. The readings we have chosen to include are by authors widely, if not uni-versally, considered to be "reconceptualists." One such author is Dwayne Huebner, who presents a rousing critique of the curriculum field, especially as it unfolds in practice. In a tone reminiscent of George Counts, Huebner charges that, despite many educators' rhetoric of individual rights and humanism, the schooling systems in which they work reinforce the power of the ruling classes and other historically privileged groups. Rather than challenge this state of affairs, Huebner believes the curriculum field's scholars and practitioners have aided and abetted the status quo.

Whereas Huebner's reconceptualism tapped into the social reconstructionist current of curriculum thought, Maxine Greene turned to two intellectual traditions that curriculum theorists had previously seldom considered central to the field: phe-nomenology and existentialism. Greene's vision of curriculum is informed by such phenomenological concerns as how each individual human being makes sense of the world in ways that are significantly unique as well as existential concerns such as the freedom and autonomy of the individual. What, Greene wonders, does the uniqueness of each individual student mean when curriculum is largely a prepackaged enterprise, a one-size-fits-all. Like Huebner, Greene finds plenty of lip service to the Deweyan notion of adaptation of the curriculum to the individual, but urges us to embrace its true possibilities.

Another author in this section, Paulo Friere, is best known for work done in Latin America. His writings first became widely read in the United States about the same time as the reconceptualist movement was emerging. They independently reached some remarkably similar insights, and were eventually to influence each oth-er. Although the context in which Friere conceptualized his "pedagogy of the op-pressed" was obviously very different from how schooling typically occurred in North America, Friere and others were to see its applicability to the traditionally marginal-ized groups of this society as well. In particular, like Huebner and Greene, Friere em-phasized that the liberatory potential of the curriculum depended making it the learner's own. Knowledge is indeed power, Freire might say, but only when it is one's own knowledge.

The next reading, by Elliott Eisner, occupies a middle ground between the reconceptualists and the three readings that follow it. Although Eisner's work is not as explicitly concerned with power as the reconceptualists, it is also clear that he rejects many of the foundations of what Pinar calls the "traditional" and "conceptual–empiri-cist" approaches. As the reader will recall, Eisner had rejected important facets of the traditionalist position in his 1960s challenge to the behavioral objectives movement. In the article reproduced in this section, Eisner argues that curriculum concerns are most usefully addressed by examining and appraising them by appropriate criteria. For Eisner, this means not using the standards of industry nor adapting the methods of the behavioral sciences, but rather assessing education by the application of educational criteria. Eisner underscores that understanding the educational worth of school expe-riences depends more on understanding the quality of the journey (the process of ed-ucation) than on commonly used indicators, such as standardized test scores, of what destination the students have reached.

The next three articles share many of Eisner's general concerns, but with a more specific focus on the relationship of curriculum to classroom teaching. Milbrey Wallin McLaughlin was a researcher concerned with the evaluation of many federally funded curriculum projects. Her article reproduced here draws on this experience. McLaughlin, like many others at the time, pondered why so many recent curriculum reforms seemingly had such minimal effects on school programs. McLaughlin's answer was that most implementation efforts had been based on an "installation" model. That is, it was assumed that curriculum change could be installed in schools in much the same manner as installing a new oil filter in a car. This was a fundamentally faulty model, McLaughlin contended. Rather, change occurs as the product of a process of "mutual adaptation" between existing practices and innovations. Indeed, McLaughlin noted that mutual adaptation appeared to be associated with successful implementation and installation approaches often resulted in things continuing as they had been.

Applying a related perspective, the articles by Gail McCutcheon as well as by F. M. Connelly and Miriam Ben-Peretz explore how teachers deliberate about curriculum. McCutcheon contends that only teachers are in a sufficiently informed position to deliberate about the final form of curriculum suitable for their individual classroom settings. She continues that it is precisely this role in curriculum deliberation that is at the heart of teacher professionalism. Connelly and Ben-Peretz also ponder the role of the teacher in curriculum matters. Their particular concern is how teachers' inquiries into curriculum practices can deepen and extend their professional endeavors.

The last reading is this section is by Diane Ravitch. Her concerns about curriculum sharply differ from the other readings in this section. Ravitch's position revives the old humanistic argument that school curriculum should be centered on the liberal arts. Ravitch, presaging curriculum controversies that have attracted so much attention since, argues that too much precious school time is wasted on nonessential courses; that too many courses lack rigor; that students have too many choices among "lightweight" elective courses, with too little time spent on the fundamentals that all youngsters should learn. As Ravitch puts it in her closing comments, "To permit knowledge to be fragmented . . . contributes to the diminution and degradation of the common culture."

References

Jackson, P. W. (1992). Conceptions of curriculum and curriculum specialists. In P. W. Jackson (Ed.), *Handbook of research on curriculum* (pp. 3–40). New York: Macmillan.

Kliebard, H. M. (1970). Reappraisal: The Tyler rationale. *School Review, 78*, 259–272.

11

The Reconceptualization of Curriculum Studies

William F. Pinar

What some observers have designated a "movement" is visible in the field of curriculum studies in the United States. Some have termed it "reconceptualism," others "the new curriculum theory." Both terms suggest more thematic unity among the curriculum writing characterized as the "reconceptualization" than, upon close examination, appears to exist. Nonetheless, some thematic similarities are discernible, though insufficient in number to warrant a characterization like "ideology" or composite, agreed-upon point of view. What can be said, without dispute, is that by the summer of 1978, there will have been six conferences and five books[1] in the past six years which are indications of a socio-intellectual phenomenon in this field, and a phenomenon which clearly functions to reconceptualize the field of curriculum studies. Thus, while the writing published to date may be somewhat varied thematically, it is unitary in its significance for the field. If this process of transformation continues at its present rate, the field of curriculum studies will be profoundly different in 20 years time than it has been during the first 50 years of its existence.

What is this reconceptualization? The answer, at this point, is a slippery one, and to gain even an inchoate grip, one looks to the field as it is. This will indicate, in part, what is not. To a considerable extent, the reconceptualization is a reaction to what the field has been, and what it is seen to be at the present time.

Traditionalists

Most curricularists at work in 1977 can be characterized as *traditionalists*. Their work continues to make use of the "conventional wisdom" of the field, epitomized still by the work of Tyler. More important in identifying traditionalists than the allusion to Tyler is citing the *raison d'être* for traditional curriculum work. Above all, the reason for curriculum writing, indeed curriculum work generally, is captured in the phrase "service to practitioners." Curriculum work tends to be field-based and curriculum writing tends to have school teachers in mind. In short, traditional curriculum work is focused on the schools. Further, professors of curriculum have tended to be former school people. In fact, school service of some sort, ordinarily classroom teaching, is still viewed as a prerequisite for a teaching post in the field in a college or university. To an extent not obvious in certain of the other subfields of education (for instance,

From *Journal of Curriculum Studies*, Vol. 10, No. 3, 1978: pp. 205–214. Reprinted by permission philosophy and psychology of education, recently in administration and the "helping services"), curricularists are former school people whose intellectual and subcultural ties tend to be with school practitioners. They tend to be less interested in basic research, in theory development, in related developments in allied fields, than in a set of perceived realities of classrooms and school settings generally.

There is, of course, an historical basis for traditional curriculum work. Cremin suggests that it was after superintendent Newlon's work in curriculum revision, in the early 1920s in Denver, that the need for a curriculum specialist became clear.[2] It is plausible to imagine school administrators like Newlon asking teachers who demonstrated an interest in curriculum and its development to leave classroom teaching and enter an administrative office from which they would attend full-time to matters curricular. There were no departments of curriculum in colleges of education in the 1920s; Newlon and other administrators could go nowhere else but to the classroom for curriculum personnel. When the training of curriculum personnel began at the university level in the 1930s, it surfaced in departments of administration and secondary education, indicating further the field's origin in and loyalty to the practical concerns of school personnel. This affiliation, more tenuous and complex at the present time than it was in the 1920s and 1930s, is evident in the programmes of the largest professional association of curricularists in the United States, the Association for Supervision and Curriculum Development. The programmes of ASCD annual meetings indicate a considerable and growing presence of school personnel. Further, the workshops and papers listed, the authors of which are university teachers, tend to have an explicit thematic focus on whatever school concerns are *au courant*.

There is another sense in which traditionalists carry forward the tradition of the field. The curriculum field's birth in the 1920s was understandably shaped by the intellectual character of that period. Above all it was a time of an emerging scientism when so-called scientific techniques from business and industry were finding their way into educational theory and practice. The early curricularist came to employ what Kliebard has termed the "bureaucratic model."[3] This model is characterized by its ameliorative orientation, ahistorical posture, and an allegiance to behaviourism and to what Macdonald has termed a "technological rationality." The curriculum worker is dedicated to the "improvement" of schools. He honours this dedication by accepting the curriculum structure as it is. "Curriculum change" is measured by comparing resulting behaviours with original objectives. Even humanistic educators tend to accept many of these premises, as they introduce, perhaps, "values clarification" into the school curriculum. Accepting the curriculum structure as it is, and working to improve it, is what is meant by the "technician's mentality." In a capsule way, it can be likened to adjusting an automobile engine part in order to make it function more effectively. This is also technological rationality, and its manifestations in school practice run the gamut from "competency-based teacher education" to "modular scheduling." The emphasis is on design, change (behaviourally observable), and improvement.

What has tended to be regarded as curriculum theory in the traditional sense, most notably Tyler's rationale,[4] is theoretical only in the questionable sense that it is abstract and usually at variance with what occurs in schools. Its intent is clearly to guide, to be of assistance to those in institutional positions who are concerned with curriculum. Of course, this is a broad concern. Most teachers share it, at least in terms of daily lesson planning. But as well as an element of teaching, curriculum is traditionally thought to include considerations such as evaluation, supervision, and also curriculum development and implementation. The boundaries of the field are fuzzy.

Thematically there is no unity. From Tyler to Taba and Saylor and Alexander to the current expression of this genre in Daniel and Laurel Tanner's book, Neil's and Zais' writing (all of which attempt an overview of considerations imagined pertinent to a curriculum worker) to the humanistic movement, (for instance the work of such individuals as Fantini, Jordan, Simon, Weinstein) is a broad thematic territory.[5] What makes this work one territory is its fundamental interest in working with school people, with revising the curricula of schools. Traditional writing tends to be journalistic, necessarily so, in order that it can be readily accessible to a readership seeking quick answers to pressing, practical problems. The publications of the Association for Supervision and Curriculum Development also exemplify, to a considerable extent, this writing. ASCD is the traditionalists' professional organization. Relatively speaking, there exists a close relationship between traditional curricularists and school personnel.

Conceptual-empiricists

A relationship between school personnel and the other two groups of curricularists—*conceptual-empiricists* and *reconceptualists*—also exists. But the nature of this relationship differs from the alliance historically characteristic of the field. This difference becomes clearer as we examine, momentarily, a second group of curricularists, a group which, until reconceptualists appeared, seemed to be the only heir to the field.

I use the word heir advisedly, for the traditional curriculum field has been declared terminally ill or already deceased by several influential observers, among them Schwab and Huebner.[6] What has caused, in the past 15 to 20 years, the demise of the field? A comprehensive answer to this important question is inappropriate in the present context. What can be pointed to is two-fold. First, the leadership of the so-called curriculum reform movement of the 1960s was outside the field. This bypass was a crippling blow to its professional status. If those whose work was curriculum development and implementation were called on primarily as consultants and only rarely at that, then clearly their claim to specialized knowledge and expertise was questionable. Second, the economic situation of the past six years has meant a drying up of funds for in-service work and for curriculum proposals generally. A field whose professional status was irreparably damaged now lost the material basis necessary for its functioning. How could curricularists work with school people without money or time for in-service workshops? How could curriculum proposals be implemented without requisite funds?

With the traditional, practical justification of the field attenuated—even teacher-training efforts have slowed dramatically—new justifications appeared. Curriculum and other education subfields have become increasingly vulnerable to criticisms regarding scholarly standards by colleagues in so-called cognate fields. Particularly the influence of colleagues in the social sciences is evident, paralleling the political ascendency of these disciplines in the university generally. In fact, research in education, in many instances, has become indistinguishable from social science research. The appearance and proliferation of conceptual-empiricists in the curriculum field is a specific instance of this general phenomenon. There remains, of course, the notion that research has implications for classroom practice, but it is usually claimed that many years of extensive research are necessary before significant implications can be obtained.

This development has gone so far that, examining the work done by a faculty in a typical American college of education, one has little sense of education as a field with its own identity. One discovers researchers whose primary identity is with the

cognate field. Such individuals view themselves as primarily psychologists, philosophers, or sociologists with "research interests" in schools and education-related matters. By 1978, it is accurate to note that the education field has lost whatever (and it
was never complete of course) intellectual autonomy it possessed in earlier years, and
now is nearly tantamount to a colony of superior, imperialistic powers.

The view that education is not a discipline in itself but an area to be studied by
the disciplines is evident in the work of those of curricularists I have called conceptual-empiricists. The work of this group can be so characterized, employing conceptual
and empirical in the sense social scientists typically employ them. This work is concerned with developing hypotheses to be tested, and testing them in methodological
ways characteristic of mainstream social science. This work is reported, ordinarily, at
meetings of the American Educational Research Association. Just as the Association
for Supervision and Curriculum Development is the traditionalists' organization,
AERA tends to be the organization of conceptual-empiricists. (In relatively small
numbers traditionalists and reconceptualists also read papers at AERA annual meetings.)

An illustrative piece of conceptual work from this second group of curricularists
was published in the AERA-sponsored *Review of Educational Research*. It is George
Posner's (with Kenneth Strike) "A categorization scheme for principles of sequencing
content." A prefatory paragraph indicates that his view is a social scientist's one, reliant
upon hypothesis-making, data collection, and interpretation.

> We have very little information, based on hard data, regarding the consequences of
> alternative content sequences and will need a good deal more research effort be-
> fore we are able to satisfactorily suggest how content *should* be sequenced. Our in-
> tention here is to consider the question, What are the alternatives?[7]

The article is a conceptual one, concerned with what the authors view as logically
defensible content sequencing alternatives, and it is empirical in its allegiance to the
view of empirical research, one yielding "hard data," typical of social science at the
present time.

In a recently published essay, Decker F. Walker, another visible conceptual-empiricist, moves away somewhat from strict social science as exemplified in Posner's
work.[8] His essay, or case study as he terms it, is more anthropological in its methodological form, demonstrating a type of curriculum research which Walker's co-editor
Reid endorses.[9] Anthropology, it should be noted, while regarded as not as "pure" a
social science as political science or psychology, is nonetheless generally categorized as
a social science.

Taking his cue from Schwab, Walker argues that prescriptive curriculum theories, (partly because they do not reflect the actual process of curriculum change) are
not useful. Rather than focus on why curriculum developers did not follow the Tyler
rationale, Walker concentrates on how, in fact, the developers did proceed. In his study
he finds little use for terms like objectives and important use for terms such as platform and deliberation. He concludes that curricularists probably ought to abandon
the attempt to make actual curriculum development mirror prescriptive theories, accept "deliberation" as a core aspect of the development process, and apply the intellectual resources of the field toward improving the quality of deliberation and employing
it more effectively.

This work I find significant to the field in two ways. First it deals another hard
blow to the Tyler rationale and its influence. Second, Walker is moving away from so-

cial science. His work remains social science, but it is closer to the work of some reconceptualists than it is to that of Posner, and other mainstream conceptual-empiricists. Walker retains the traditional focus upon the practical concerns of school people and school curriculum, and no doubt he has and will spend a portion of his professional time on actual curriculum projects. Further, his methods seem more nearly those of the ethnomethodologist whose approaches do not easily fit the picture of conventional theories of the middle range, as projected by individuals such as the sociologist Robert Merton, who has influenced so many conceptual-empirical studies in the field of sociology. Walker appears to be moving outside mainstream conceptual-empiricism.

Also in the Reid and Walker book is work by another visible conceptual-empiricist, Ian Westbury. With his co-author Lynn McKinney, Westbury studies the Gary, Indiana school system during the period 1940–1970.[10] Like Walker's study of the art project, McKinney and Westbury's study would seem to be outside mainstream conceptual-empiricism, even close to work characteristic of the humanities. The structure of the study, however, indicates its allegiance to social science, thus warranting its categorization as conceptual-empirical. The work is a historical study done in the service of generalization, work that has interest in the particular (the Gary district) as it contributes to understanding of the general. The "general" in this instance is the phenomenon of stability and change, which the authors "now believe are the two primary functions of the administrative structure which surround the schools."[11] Finally what the study demonstrates is "that a concern for goals without a concomitant concern for organizational matters addresses only a small part of the problem of conceiving new designs for schools."[12] This use of the specific to illustrate a general, ahistorical "law" is, of course, a fundamental procedure of mainstream social science.

Reconceptualists

This concern for generalization is not abandoned in the work of the third group of curricularists, the reconceptualists. For example, at the fourth conference at the University of Wisconsin-Milwaukee, Professor Apple reported the results of a study he and a colleague conducted in a kindergarten, substantiating claims he has made before regarding the socio-political functions of classroom behaviour.[13] His case study is distinguishable from the work of a typical conceptual-empiricist in two significant respects: (1) his acknowledged "value-laden" perspective, and (2) a perspective with a politically emancipatory intent. That is, in contrast to the canon of traditional social science, which prescribes data collection, hypothesis substantiation or disconfirmation in the disinterested service of building a body of knowledge, a reconceptualist tends to see research as an inescapably political as well as intellectual act. As such, it works to suppress, or to liberate, not only those who conduct the research, and those upon whom it is conducted, but as well those outside the academic subculture. Mainstream social science research, while on the surface seemingly apolitical in nature and consequence, if examined more carefully can be seen as contributing to the maintenance of the contemporary social-political order, or contributing to its dissolution. Apple and Marxists and neo-Marxists go further and accept a teleological view of historical movement, allying themselves with the lower classes, whose final emergence from oppression is seen to be inevitable. A number of reconceptualists, while not Marxists, nonetheless accept some variation of this teleological historical view. And many of these, at least from a distance, would seem to be "leftists" of some sort. Nearly all accept that a political dimension is inherent in any intellectual activity.

This political emphasis distinguishes the work of Apple, Burton, Mann, Molnar, some of the work of Huebner and Macdonald, from the work of traditionalists and conceptual-empiricists.[14] It is true that Reid and Walker in their *Case Studies in Curriculum Change* acknowledge that curriculum development is political, but the point is never developed, and never connected with a view of history and the contemporary social order. The focus of Walker's case study and of other case studies in the book is limited to literal curriculum change, without historicizing this change, indicating its relationship to contemporary historical movement generally. In the 1975 ASCD year-book, on the other hand, which is edited by Macdonald and Zaret, with essays also by Apple, Burton, Huebner, and Mann, this siting of curriculum issues in the broad intellectual-historical currents of twentieth-century life is constant.[15] Macdonald speaks, for instance, of technological rationality, an intellectual mode comparable in its pervasiveness and taken-for-grantedness to the ascendency of technology in human culture at large.[16] Such individuals would argue that comprehension of curriculum issues is possible only when they are situated historically.

The 1975 ASCD year-book speaks to school people. It is not that reconceptualists do not speak to this constituency of the curriculum field. But there is a conscious abandonment of the "technician's mentality." There are no prescriptions or traditional rationales. What this year-book offers, instead, is heightened awareness of the complexity and historical significance of curriculum issues. Because the difficulties these reconceptualists identify are related to difficulties in the culture at large, they are not "problems" that can be "solved." That concept created by technological rationality, is itself problematic. Thus, what is necessary, in part, is fundamental structural change in the culture. Such an aspiration cannot be realized by "plugging into" the extant order. That is why an elective or two on Marx in high-school social studies classes, or the teaching of autobiographical reflection in English classes bring indifference and often alarm to most reconceptualists. That "plugging into," "co-opting" it was termed in the 1960s during the student protests, accepts the social order as it is. What is necessary is a fundamental reconceptualization of what curriculum is, how it functions, and how it might function in emancipatory ways. It is this commitment to a comprehensive critique and theory development that distinguishes the reconceptualist phenomenon.

To understand more fully the efforts of the individuals involved in inquiry of this kind requires some understanding of metatheory and philosophy of science. Without such grounding, it is difficult, if not impossible, for curricularists to see clearly their work in the context of the growth of knowledge in general. Max van Manen's paper at the 1976 Wisconsin conference was a significant effort to analyse various structures of theoretic knowledge as they related to dominant modes of inquiry in the field of curriculum.[17] His work builds on basic analyses undertaken by philosophers of science such as Radnitzky and Feyerabend.[18] More work needs to be done along this line.

The reconceptualization, it must be noted, is fundamentally an intellectual phenomenon, not an interpersonal-affiliative one. Reconceptualists have no organized group, such as ASCD or AERA. Individuals at work, while sharing certain themes and motives, do not tend to share any common interpersonal affiliation. (In this one respect their work parallels that of the so-called romantic critics of the 1960s. But here any such comparison stops.) Conferences have been held yearly; the most recent on the campus of Rochester Institute of Technology, Rochester, New York. A journal and a press emphasizing this work are scheduled to appear by 1979.

Conclusion

As an interpreter of metatheories, Richard Bernstein recently analysed, in detail, individuals at work in four areas—empirical research, philosophical analysis, phenomenology and critical theory of society.[19] (The first category corresponds to conceptual-empirical, the third and fourth to reconceptualist work.) He ends his study with this conviction:

> In the final analysis we are not confronted with exclusive choices: either empirical or interpretative theory or critical theory. Rather there is an internal dialectic in the restructing of social political theory: when we work through any one of these movements we discover the others are implicated.[20]

This is so in the field of curriculum studies also. We are not faced with an exclusive choice: either the traditional wisdom of the field, or conceptual-empiricism, or the reconceptualization. Each is reliant upon the other. For the field to become vital and significant to American education it must nurture each "moment," its "internal dialectic." And it must strive for synthesis, for a series of perspectives on curriculum that are at once empirical, interpretative, critical, emancipatory.

But such nurturance and synthesis do not characterize, on the whole, the field today. Some of the issues raised by the British sociologist David Silverman are germane here.[21] As a prologue to more adequate social science theorizing, Silverman proposes that we learn how to read Castaneda's account of his apprenticeship to Don Juan in order that we may come to know the kinds of questions that need to be asked. He is convinced that mainstream conceptual-empiricists, regardless of field, do not now know what questions to ask, and are, indeed, intolerant of reconceptualizations that differ from their own. This intolerance is discernible in the American curriculum field. To some extent it can be found in each group of curricularists.

I am convinced that this intolerance among curricularists for work differing from one's own must be suspended to some extent if significant intellectual movement in the field is to occur. Becoming open to another genre of work does not mean loss of one's capacity for critical reflection. Nor does it mean, necessarily, loss of intellectual identity. One may remain a traditionalist while sympathetically studying the work of a reconceptualist. One's own point of view may well be enriched. Further, an intellectual climate may become established in which could develop syntheses of current perspectives, regenerating the field, and making more likely that its contribution to American education be an important one.

Acknowledgment

This is a revised version of a paper presented at the Annual Meeting of the American Educational Research Association in New York in April, 1977.

References and notes

1. Conferences have been held at the University of Rochester (1973), Xavier University of Cincinnati (1974), the University of Virginia (1975), the University of Wisconsin at Milwaukee (1976), Kent State University (1977), and the Rochester Institute of Technology (1978). Books include:
Pinar, W. (Ed) *Heightened Consciousness, Cultural Revolution and Curriculum Theory* (Mc-

Cutchan Publishing Corp., Berkeley, CA, 1974); IDEM, *Curriculum Theorizing: The Reconceptualists* (McCutchan Publishing Corp., Berkeley, CA, 1975);

Pinar, W., and Grumet, M. R. *Toward a Poor Curriculum* (Kendall/Hunt Publishing Co., Dubuque, IA, 1976).

At a 1976 conference held at the State University of New York at Geneseo; Professors Apple, Greene, Kliebard and Huebner read papers. Each of these persons has been associated with the reconceptualists although the chairmen of this meeting, Professors DeMarte and Rosarie, did not see this seminar as being in the tradition of the others. The papers from this seminar were published in *Curriculum Inquiry*, Vol. 6, No. 4 (1977).

2. Cremin, L. Curriculum-making in the United States, In Pinar, W. (Ed), *Curriculum Theorizing*, pp. 19–35.

3. Kliebard, H. M. Persistent curriculum issues in historical perspective, and Bureaucracy and curriculum theory. In Pinar, W. (Ed) *Curriculum Theorizing*, pp. 39–69.

4. Tyler, R. W., *Basic Principles of Curriculum and Instruction* (University of Chicago Press, Chicago, 1950).

5. Taba, H. *Curriculum Development: Theory and Practice*, (Harcourt, Brace and World, New York, 1962;)

Saylor, G., and Alexander, W. *Curriculum Planning for Modern Schools* (Holt, Rinehart and Winston, New York, 1966);

Tanner, D. And Tanner, L. N. *Curriculum Development: Theory into Practice* (MacMillan, New York, 1975);

Neil, J. D. *Curriculum: A Comprehensive Introduction* (Little, Brown and Co., Boston, 1977);

Zais, R. S. *Curriculum: Principles and Foundations* (Thomas Y. Browell, New York, 1976);

Weinstein, G. and Fantini, M. D. *Toward Humanistic Education: A Curriculum of Affect* (Praeger Publishers, New York, 1971);

Simon, S. *et al. Values Clarification* (Hart, New York, 1972);

Jordan, D. The ANISA Model. Paper presented to conference on curriculum at the University of Virginia, 1975 (available from Charles W. Beegle, Curry Memorial School of Education, University of Virginia, Charlottesville, VA 22903, USA).

6. Schwab, J. J. *The Practical: A Language for Curriculum* (National Education Association, Washington, D.C., 1970);

Huebner, D. The moribund curriculum field: Its wake and our work. *Curriculum Inquiry*, Vol. 6, No. 2 (1976).

7. Posner, G. J. and Strike, K. A. A categorization scheme for principles of sequencing content. *Review of Educational Research*, Vol. 46, No. 4 (1976).

8. Walker, D. F., Curriculum development in an art project. In Reid, W. A. and Walker, D. F. (Eds) *Case Studies in Curriculum Change* (Routledge and Kegan Paul, London, 1975).

9. Reid, W. A., The changing curriculum: theory and practice. In Reid and Walker, op. cit.

10. McKinney, W. L. and Westbury, I. Stability and change; the public schools of Gary, Indiana, 1940–70. In Reid and Walker, op. cit.

11. Ibid., p. 44.

12. Ibid., p. 50.

13. Apple, M. W. and King, N. What do schools teach? Paper presented at the University of Wisconsin and Milwaukee Conference.

14. For discussion of this point see my prefatory remarks in *Curriculum Theorizing* (Note 1). See also:

Klohr, P. R. The State of the Field. Paper presented at the Xavier University Conference on Curriculum;

Miller, J. L. Duality: Perspectives on the reconceptualization. Paper presented to University of Virginia Conference;

Macdonald, J. B. Curriculum Theory as intentional activity. Paper presented to University of Virginia Conference (See Note 5);

Macdonald, J. B., Curriculum Theory and human interests. In Pinar, W. (Ed) *Curriculum Theorizing*;

Benham, B. J. Curriculum Theory in the 1970s: the reconceptualist movement. Texas Technical University, 1976, unpublished paper.

15. Zaret, E. and Macdonald, J. B. *Schools in Search of Meaning* (Association for Supervision and Curriculum Development, Washington, D.C., 1975).

16. Macdonald, J. B. The quality of everyday life in schools. In Zaret and Macdonald, op. cit.

17. Van Manen, M. Linking ways of knowing with ways of being practical. *Curriculum Inquiry*, Vol. 6, No. 3 (1977).

18. Radnitzky, G. *Contemporary Schools of Metascience* (Henry Regnery Co., Chicago, 1973);

Feyerbend P. K. Against method; outline of an anarchist theory of knowledge. In *Minnesota Studies in the Philosophy of Science*, Vol. 4 (University of Minnesota Press, Minneapolis, 1970).

19. Bernstein, R. J. *The Restructuring of Social and Political Theory* (Harcourt, Brace, Jovanovich, New York, 1976).

20. Ibid., 235.

21. Silverman, D. *Reading Castaneda: A Prologue to the Social Sciences* (Routledge and Kegan Paul, London, 1975).

12

Poetry and Power: The Politics of Curricular Development

DWAYNE HUEBNER

Fellow educators—are we not lost? Do we know where we are, remember where we have been, or foresee where we are going? We've talked about education for individuals since Rousseau, Kilpatric, and Harold Benjamin. In our lostness, are we not jumping on bandwagons—yesterday core, group process, team teaching; today open classrooms and alternative schools—and assuming that at least these bandwagon experts know where they are? In our lostness are we not imbibing the snake oils and patent medicines—programmed individual computers, T.U., structure and disciplines, sensitivity training—hoping that we can cure our maladies? But we find that our pain has been relieved only temporarily and that we may indeed have been taken in by a new breed of pusher. In our lostness, we recite the familiar litanies of humanism and individuality, hoping that the gods of our past will recognize our goodwill, forgive us our sins of omission and commission, and restore our sight and vitality.

Why do we move around so frantically—tugging at the coattails of our also lost neighbor and sampling his diverse wares? Why do we not comport ourselves in such a manner that our center—our sense of who we are and what we are about—can be restored and reformed? Why do we not pause to feel the painful tensions and pulls in us, which are reflections of the tensions and pulls of our society? Why do we not notice more carefully the direction of technical changes, social changes, and political changes? Why do we not listen more thoughtfully to the songs of the young, the anger of the oppressed, the labored breathing of those dying of overdoses of heroin or methadone, the painful cry of those bombed at Christmas time, the prideful platitudes of those in power? Why do we not act with courage—with the awareness that creation requires risk taking as well as statistical evidence? Why do we not reflect more critically on what we and others do—to discover in our institutions our bondage to others, and the bondages we impose?

Is it because we are afraid to acknowledge that power makes up our center—a power that necessarily comes up against the power of others: principals, parents, kids, board members, text writers. We are afraid, maybe even ashamed, to acknowledge that that which we are about as educators is politics: a struggle to maintain, maybe even change through destruction and reconstruction, the world we make with others. If we acknowledge that we are political we necessarily risk defeat, or maybe the awareness

Chapter 16 in *Curriculum Theorizing: The Reconceptualists*, edited by William Pinar. Berkeley: McCutchan, 1975. Copyright by McCutchan Publishing Corporation, Berkeley, California 94702. Permission granted by the publisher.

that we are indeed doing someone else's thing and are alienated from ourselves. If we acknowledge that we are political we risk recognizing our importance and hearing ourselves as braying asses or clanking symbols. It is far easier or safer to proclaim the individual and to then fit ourselves into a prepared slot: buy someone else's package of objectives, materials, and bets; or put on someone else's alternative school. Then if we fail, it is their fault, not ours.

Why are we lost? I think it is because we have let the school become our center and we have become an appendage, nothing but a role or functionary in someone else's institution. Institutions do not have memories, they cannot recall their past; who established them, under what circumstances, for what purposes. The people who started them disappear in the mindless routines. Only men and women have memories, an historical consciousness, and can recall how things got started, why and by whom. If we forget or never knew that schools are a product of men and women who used their power to build or maintain a certain kind of public world, then we easily become bondsmen of those who live only in the routines. We do their things, maintain their world, distribute their awards. And they reward us by a humdrum comfortable life style, perhaps with tenure and retirement, access to the more common goods of our production lines, and permit us the privacy of sex and family life, but deprive us of public vitality and joy, clean air and water, safe, comfortable, exciting urban areas that support our well-being and sociality.

If we remember that education is a political activity in which some people influence others, and that the school is one way to organize that power and influence, then perhaps we can try to share the control of the school and use it for our political purposes. Instead of our being an extension of the school, of someone else's will and power, the school can be, in part, an extension of our will and power—a vehicle for our political concerns. If we remember this, then we can recognize that the struggle to remake the school is a struggle to make a more just public world. If the school is a vehicle of political activity, then our lack of clarity, our lack of vision about the school is a function of our lack of clarity and vision about our public world—a breakdown in our talk, our poetry, about the world we make.

We do not talk about a more just public world; we talk about school, we think about school, and we see the world through the windows and doors of the school. The school has become our place. We have become school people, our language of learning, discipline, motivation, stimulus, individualization, is school language. Our images for generating new educational possibilities are school images. So we seek more diversified and smaller packages of instructional materials, not greater public access to information without federal control, or better development of cable television for neighborhood use. We seek open classrooms, not open societies. We seek alternative schools, not alternative public worlds. And because we are school people our public statements affirm the school, defend the present public school, and hide social injustice. Our propaganda of individualism is liberal cant that hides the basic conservatism of school people and permits those who control our public world to continue to control it. Our public statements are not socially or personally liberating. They do not excite us to imagine more just public worlds. They do not harness the power of people in the political struggle to reform our present inequitable institutions. They do not enable men or women to recognize and grasp their political right to share in the maintenance and reforming of our public world.

For instance, how much individuality can school people tolerate in an institution that is compulsory? The expression "curriculum for individuals" hides from our awareness that the school is a place of control; of socialization if you prefer this pseudoscientific term that hides political domination. We maintain that control by our power. Of course, with our goodwill and out of our good graces we grant reasonable power to students to be individuals, providing they are not too individualistic in their speech, their actions, their commitments. Do we prefer the individualism of Thomas Paine, the Berrigan brothers, Ellsberg, Cleaver, Angela Davis, and the young men who went to Canada or Scandanavia rather than die in a tragic imperialistic war or the individualism of the Watergate caper boys, the I.T.T. Executives, and perhaps those in the executive offices of the federal government?

Why have the court cases for racial equality, to permit long hair and dress options in school, freedom of high school people to print politically oriented papers sometimes critical of the schools, the rights of pregnant girls to be in school, and the rights of Amish kids to stay out of public school been pushed by a few parents and civil libertarians rather than ASCDers? Can we honestly read those three words, *curriculum for individuality*, as other than propaganda to hide from our awareness our commitments as school people, and to put a verbal gloss on our intentions, which do not coincide with our practices. If we really believed those three words, we would not only be waiting for better materials, we would also be looking for court cases to restrain the power of school people and extend the constitutional rights of children and young people in the school. We would be training educators in workshops here at ASCD to attend to the legal implications of their control of and talk to the young, as Thomas is doing for kids in Dayton. We would be building up a body of civil law about the rights of children that would be as much a part of our curricular knowledge as is child development. If we really believed those words, should not ASCD initiate movement among professional educators to modify or revoke compulsory attendance laws, to urge the U.S. postal service to stop subsidizing junk mail and advertisements and subsidize the publication of journals of opinion and fact which are dwindling in number? If we really believed these words, would we not be working with nonschool people who are trying to increase the educational possibilities that exist outside the school?

By saying these things, I do not intend to come down on the side of Reimer or Illich who tell us that school is dead and urge us to deschool society (although I grant the value of contemplating death as a way of identifying the choices we have and have not made). Those proposals are also nonhistorical for us in the United States. It is necessary, rather, to see our schools, the materials and resources within them, and the social organizational patterns that result in historical perspective. The ways that we have thought about these during the first half of this century are not the ways we should think about them during the last quarter. Since the Second World War we have assumed that more of the same with better research for better living would do it, but Jencks, among others, warns us that this is not so. Because we lack an educational poetry which stirs the imagination and harnesses our power we are forced to push our school images, our present school materials and organization to the breaking point, without conviction or results, but with a naive faith in our past ways. But the past must be rethought, not reused.

What then are we about as educators? We are not about maintaining schools, for that is the self-serving concern of school people who see their livelihood in the maintenance of that institution. We are about the conscious shaping of the future by helping the young work out, work through, or work into their futures and into our future. We have the utter gall to be concerned with the mundane destiny of individuals, ours and our students. Ours is not a power over individuals, but a power for individuals.

And a power for the future of our public world. But which individuals, and what kind of future?

Oh yes, we are for the urban black, if he is not angry and will speak in moderate tones, accept our middle-class behaviors, and affirm our future, thus perhaps giving up his. Oh yes, we are for the American Indian if he will give up his past and accept our future and our last forty-five years of public policy. Oh yes, we are for the homosexual if he will stay in the closet and not let his peculiarities stain our image of the future. Oh yes, we are for women, if they will accept their female role in our male future. Oh yes, we are for the Asian Marxist or Maoist if they will recognize that the way to the future is by maintaining present power balances. We are for those individuals who will protect and maintain our image of the future, but what of their imagined futures? If their tomorrow requires that we give up some of our privileges, will we still be for those individuals?

Those are the tensions we live in, are they not? The ambivalences of our commitments become obvious, do they not? For if we use our power for the future of all young we may indeed be in political conflict with our own self-interests. We are in that conflict, which is one reason that school people, although speaking a liberal political rhetoric, are essentially conservative in the political spectrum. Our individualism is a nineteenth-century individualism, aimed at the freedom of those who partake of the prevalent means of production and consumption. But with the 1972 election, it seems that liberalism is dead. We must now acknowledge that we are rightist or leftist and that there is no middle. But the school, make no mistake about it, is in the hands of the silent majority or conservative right which might be an explanation of why the young radical leftist teacher either becomes socialized to the school and gives up his images of the future, or finds other ways to educate the young.

So our center of power as educators, a power for the future of the individual, comes in conflict with our own future, which is frequently an extension of the present. In this conflict we shift from power for to power over and thus to the conservative inertia of school people. Let us keep looking for other reasons, but if we turn to our center of power we easily recognize that a dedicated educator risks his imaged future as he works with the young. The educator working in schools can use the rules and rewards of the school to reduce or even remove that risk. He is thus tempted to control, not to liberate, and to justify the control by the political ideology of the free individual, which was rampant when some of us in this country had slaves and when many of us were in bondage to those in political and economic control.

Don't talk psychological individualism to me. Don't preach Kant's moral imperatives tinged with a religious doctrine of salvation. That is put-down language. Given the history of American education, the talk of school people about individuals is to be taken at face value—the clean face of middle-class America, the faces of blacks and orientals and Spanish and Indians and the poor and the handicapped.

Talk, rather, about the political tasks of making a more just public world. Talk about it in such a way that the political and economic nature of education can be clearly seen. Then talk about schools as our small share in the making of a more just public world.

What are the ingredients of this talk? There are three, three rights, if you wish, to which we must attend and which must govern our talk about the public world and then the school.

First, the unconditional respect for the political, civil, and legal rights of the young as free people participating in a public world. This is what Frymier is urging.

But for thousands of years we have been talking this way, and only within the past hundred—nay the past ten or fifteen have we grounded this right in law. Discrimination by race, sex, or religion has only recently come under legal attack, and gradually the rights of individuals are being publicly recognized. Now we are about to struggle to end discrimination by age—and the power over the young by adults must be brought into question. Thus Thomas, in his Student Rights Center in Dayton, is teaching kids to sit back when teachers verbally accost them or manhandle them and then to say quietly: "You know, ma'am, I can sue you for that—and I will with the support of adults who really believe in the individuality—the civil rights of kids."

The second right is the right of access to the wealth in the public domain—I mean primarily the knowledge, traditions, skills that shape and increase a person's power in the public world.

This is what we are about today, although we are not consciously aware of it. The exciting development of the past ten to fifteen years has indeed been the increase in scope, quality, and quantity of instructional materials. But expressing these developments as developments in instructional materials hides more important considerations. Instructional materials are a way—almost *the* way—that adult society makes the public wealth available to the young. The skills of teachers are the other major way. We tend to talk of these resources as means to learning, and indeed this is an appropriate way to speak—but no longer a powerful way. For instance, reading is not just a skill that must be learned, it is a tradition of using printed materials. Now children of two and three and four have access to that tradition in trade books, in *The Electric Company*, in story reading in preschools. It is an expensive business, but publishing paperback and hardcover books is now a money-making activity, so our commercial world now seeks to make this tradition available to young children. If the tradition, the wealth of print, is not being brought to certain kids, the question is not how can they learn to read, but how can the tradition be reworked, embodied in new materials and skills. This is a technical problem—of print technology, of the art of book writing and making, of teacher education. It is an economic problem, for it costs money to design materials for new populations. It costs money to give teachers the skills to bring the wealth of print to children who have not shared in that wealth for the first four or five years of their life. It is also a political problem, for two reasons. If private industry cannot make money distributing the public wealth, then will public funds be used to design new delivery systems for our print wealth; or will we use public monies to design delivery systems for our new traditions of death, killing innocent populations of Third World children? In addition, not all of our collective wealth in print is seen as valuable by all people. Those who want to maintain a certain kind of public world will see that some traditions are available to the young and others are not. Thus for years the language of sexual development and sexual relations was distributed via the peer group; only within recent years has it been deemed valuable enough to distribute it in print for children. Community fights over library books, books assigned to certain courses in high school, and the censorship and bias of text materials demonstrate lucidly the political control over the distribution of our print traditions. This reinterpretation of instructional materials has other explanatory power, best illustrated by the changes in the teaching of reading over the past fifteen years which now makes possible today the open primary classroom.

Remember that twenty years ago Olson at Michigan was talking about individualized reading. Then we had reading textbooks, reading workbooks, and a few elementary school libraries. We had no paperback books, few language games, and no talking typewriters. Even ten years ago Alice Miel and Leland Jacobs of Columbia were talking about individualized reading—but the practice demanded that teachers spend hours of their time cutting apart workbooks, gathering reading materials, making language games. Today the picture is different. Reading text and workbooks are becoming passé. Almost every publisher is now working on self-diagnostic and self-prescriptive materials keyed to collections of paperback books. The group reading instruction is almost over, and the day of the bluebirds, the cardinals, and the chickadees is over or can be over. As Frymier pointed out, an increased variety of materials can change the organization of the school.

What Frymier did not point out is that we have here an example of an old Marxian insight. The means of production and consumption determine (or at least influence) the relationship of one person with another. The quality of the relationship of kids to kids and kids to teacher depends on the goods in the school. Authoritarianism and dictatorships are frequently necessary when we have scarce goods. Furthermore, human skills are developed to be compatible with the goods. Teachers who develop authoritarian skills to match textbooks can easily transform diverse reading goods into textual type materials. Thus, we have an inherent tension between the rights of an individual as an individual, and the demands placed on him by the inequitable distribution of public wealth.

How do we make the public wealth of this world—the traditions, knowledge, information—accessible to children? We do so through our economy and through the political process of allocating scarce funds. We do it by training artists and technicians to redesign this wealth for children of a variety of ages. We are doing it with print—it remains to be done for the traditions of math, knowledge of man and society, the knowledge of the natural or physical world, the traditions of music, art, dance. But the problem is not a school problem. It is a problem about the shape of our public world. It is related to the debates over xerography and copyrights, the use of cable television, the rights of reporters to the privacy of their sources, the censorship of the Pentagon Papers and *Deep Throat*, the pressures of this administration on the press and the national television networks, and presidential control of information.

What we should keep in focus is the right of access to public wealth; the traditions, knowledge, and information that should be in the public realm. This is a problem of technology, of economics, and of politics. As educators we cannot simply await the development of new technologies, we must be politically active to create a public world where this access is increased. As this public world becomes more accessible to the young in a variety of materials, media, and skills, then the shape of the school will change. We should not concern ourselves primarily with the shape of the school—but with the accessibility to public wealth from which new alternatives to school will become obvious.

The last right with which we must be concerned as educators is the right of each individual, regardless of age, to participate in the shaping and reshaping of the institutions within which he lives. This right carries with it the possibility of the destruction of existing institutions and the formation of new ones. This is what community control and teacher unions and negotiation are all about. It was what teacher-pupil planning was about fifteen to twenty years ago. It is *not* what competency-based teacher education, PPBS, and performance contracting are about.

For years teachers suffered under the nearly absolute power of boards and administrators. Teacher unions corrected this. Strong community pressure groups have now come up against strong boards and teacher unions. Left unorganized is the student group, although this is being done slowly. The student rights and student advocacy movement is to this end. But the movement in education is slow because of our technical mentality of means-ends and our political conservative mentality. If we are concerned about the individual, then we must be concerned with his right to participate in governing the structures that determine his public and private life, including the school.

ASCD has backed off from this right of individuals. When first formed in the late forties, ASCD had as its major concern the development of process skills for the democratic running of schools, helping administrators and supervisors work with teachers in supportive ways to improve the schools. As the fifties and sixties unfolded and it became obvious that curricular development was a function not only of staff development, but also of planning with academicians, material specialists, laity, and kids, ASCD lost hold of its role in the development of the skills of institution building. Working with teachers and administrators was one kind of political task, working with blacks, with parents, with kids, and with interest groups was another kind of political task.

So ASCD gave up its concern for developing political competencies and leaned back in the characteristic style of liberal individualism. It said people need to know what is happening, what is new, and then in the good old spirit of American individualism they will make changes in the school.

The school is but a manifestation of public life. As educators we must be political activists who seek a more just public world. The alternative, of course, is to be school people—satisfied with the existing social order—the silent majority who embrace conservatism.

If the members of ASCD remain school people, I predict the death of ASCD as a professional organization.

Harold Shane is wrong when he said we can have a big enough umbrella to embrace all school people. To me that evokes an image of a group of people under a wind-blown umbrella, heads dry, feet in the mud, the rivers rising. We should leave the umbrella. Some of us should be building the dikes of civil rights legislation for children. Some of us should be building organizations for better governance of institutions. Some of us should be preserving and making accessible the storehouse of knowledge and traditions and information for our young and old.

Another image: this conference and those of the past few years strike me as a smorgasbord. Take your pick, please your palate, take home a memory or two—all in the spirit of free enterprise and rampant individualism. Contrast that image to the Last Supper—a few people, sharing something in common, breaking bread and drinking wine, and then changing the shape of the public world.

ASCD will surely die if the smorgasbord continues as its metaphor. It might live—smaller, more powerful—if the metaphor shifts.

13

Curriculum and Consciousness

MAXINE GREENE

Curriculum, from the learner's standpoint, ordinarily represents little more than an arrangement of subjects, a structure of socially prescribed knowledge, or a complex system of meanings which may or may not fall within his grasp. Rarely does it signify possibility for him as an existing person, mainly concerned with making sense of his own life-world. Rarely does it promise occasions for ordering the materials of that world, for imposing "configurations"[1] by means of experiences and perspectives made available for personally conducted cognitive action. Sartre says that "knowing is a moment of praxis," opening into "what has not yet been."[2] Preoccupied with priorities, purposes, programs of "intended learning"[3] and intended (or unintended) manipulation, we pay too little attention to the individual in quest of his own future, bent on surpassing what is merely "given," on breaking through the everyday. We are still too prone to dichotomize: to think of "disciplines" or "public traditions" or "accumulated wisdom" or "common culture" (individualization despite) as objectively existent, external to the knower—there to be discovered, mastered, learned.

Quite aware that this may evoke Dewey's argument in *The Child and the Curriculum,* aware of how times have changed since 1902, I have gone in search of contemporary analogies to shed light on what I mean. ("Solution comes," Dewey wrote, "only by getting away from the meaning of terms that is already fixed upon and coming to see the conditions from another point of view, and hence in a fresh light."[4]) My other point of view is that of literary criticism, or more properly philosophy of criticism, which attempts to explicate the modes of explanation, description, interpretation, and evaluation involved in particular critical approaches. There is presently an emerging philosophic controversy between two such approaches, one associated with England and the United States, the other with the Continent, primarily France and Switzerland; and it is in the differences in orientation that I have found some clues.

These differences are, it will be evident, closely connected to those separating what is known as analytic or language philosophy from existentialism and phenomenology. The dominant tendency in British and American literary criticism has been to conceive literary works as objects or artifacts, best understood in relative isolation from the writer's personal biography and undistorted by associations brought to the work from the reader's own daily life. The new critics on the Continent have been called "critics of consciousness."[5] They are breaking with the notion that a literary work can be dealt with objectively, divorced from experience. In fact, they treat each work as a manifestation of an individual writer's experience, a gradual growth of con-

From *Teachers College Record,* Vol. 73, No. 2, 1971: pp. 253–269. Reprinted by permission.

sciousness into expression. This is in sharp contrast to such a view as T.S. Eliot's emphasizing the autonomy and the "impersonality" of literary art. "We can only say," he wrote in an introduction to *The Sacred Wood,* "that a poem, in some sense, has its own life; that its parts form something quite different from a body of neatly ordered biographical data; that the feeling, or emotion, or vision resulting from the poem is something different from the feeling or emotion or vision in the mind of the poet."[6] Those who take this approach or an approach to a work of art as "a self-enclosed isolated structure"[7] are likely to prescribe that purely aesthetic values are to be found in literature, the values associated with "significant form"[8] or, at most, with the contemplation of an "intrinsically interesting possible."[9] M.H. Abrams has called this an "austere dedication to the poem *per se*,"[10] for all the enlightening analysis and explication it has produced. "But it threatens also to commit us," he wrote, "to the concept of a poem as a language game, or as a floating Laputa, insulated from life and essential human concerns in a way that accords poorly with our experience in reading a great work of literature."

For the critic of consciousness, literature is viewed as a genesis, a conscious effort on the part of an individual artist to understand his own experience by framing it in language. The reader who encounters the work must recreate it in terms of *his* consciousness. In order to penetrate it, to experience it existentially and empathetically, he must try to place himself within the "interior space"[11] of the writer's mind as it is slowly revealed in the course of his work. Clearly, the reader requires a variety of cues if he is to situate himself in this way; and these are ostensibly provided by the expressions and attitudes he finds in the book, devices which he must accept as orientations and indications—"norms," perhaps, to govern his recreation. *His* subjectivity is the substance of the literary object; but, if he is to perceive the identity emerging through the enactments of the book, he must subordinate his own personality as he brackets out his everyday, "natural" world.[12] His objective in doing so, however, is not to analyze or explicate or evaluate; it is to extract the experience made manifest by means of the work. Sartre says this more concretely:

> Reading seems, in fact, to be the synthesis of perception and creation. . . . The object is essential because it is strictly transcendent, because it imposes its own structures, and because one must wait for it and observe it; but the subject is also essential because it is required not only to disclose the object (that is, to make *there be* an object) but also that this object might *be* (that is, to produce it). In a word, the reader is conscious of disclosing in creating, of creating by disclosing. . . . If he is inattentive, tired, stupid, or thoughtless most of the relations will escape him. He will never manage to "catch on" to the object (in the sense in which we see that fire "catches" or "doesn't catch"). He will draw some phrases out of the shadow, but they will appear as random strokes. If he is at his best, he will project beyond the words a synthetic form, each phrase of which will be no more than a partial function: the "theme," the "subject," or the "meaning."[13]

There must be, he is suggesting, continual reconstructions if a work of literature is to become meaningful. The structures involved are generated over a period of time, depending upon the perceptiveness and attentiveness of the reader. The reader, however, does not simply regenerate what the artist intended. His imagination can move him beyond the artist's traces, "to project beyond the words a synthetic form," to constitute a new totality. The autonomy of the art object is sacrificed in this orientation; the reader, conscious of lending his own life to the book, discovers deeper and more complex levels than the level of "significant form." (Sartre says, for instance, that

"Raskolnikov's waiting is *my* waiting, which I lend him. Without this impatience of the reader he would remain only a collection of signs. His hatred of the police magistrate who questions him is my hatred which has been solicited and wheedled out of me by signs, and the police magistrate himself would not exist without the hatred I have for him via Raskolnikov"[14])

Disclosure, Reconstruction, Generation

The reader, using his imagination, must move within his own subjectivity and break with the common sense world he normally takes for granted. If he could not suspend his ordinary ways of perceiving, if he could not allow for the possibility that the horizons of daily life are not inalterable, he would not be able to engage with literature at all. As Dewey put it: "There is work done on the part of the percipient as there is on the part of the artist. The one who is too lazy, idle, or indurated in convention to perform this work will not see or hear. His 'appreciation' will be a mixture of scraps of learning with conformity to norms of conventional admiration and with a confused, even if genuine, emotional excitation."[15] The "work" with which we are here concerned is one of disclosure, reconstruction, generation. It is a work which culminates in a bringing something into being by the reader—in a "going beyond" what he has been.[16]

Although I am going to claim that learning, to be meaningful, must involve such a "going beyond," I am not going to claim that it must also be in the imaginative mode. Nor am I going to assert that, in order to surpass the "given," the individual is required to move into and remain within a sealed subjectivity. What I find suggestive in the criticism of consciousness is the stress on the gradual disclosure of structures by the reader. The process is, as I have said, governed by certain cues or norms perceived in the course of reading. These demand, if they are to be perceived, what Jean Piaget has called a "continual 'decentering' without which [the individual subject] cannot become free from his intellectual egocentricity."[17]

The difference between Piaget and those interested in consciousness is, of course, considerable. For one thing, he counts himself among those who prefer not to characterize the subject in terms of its "lived experience." For another thing, he says categorically that "the 'lived' can only have a very minor role in the construction of cognitive structures, for these do not belong to the subject's *consciousness* but to his operational *behavior*, which is something quite different."[18] I am not convinced that they are as different as he conceives them to be. Moreover, I think his differentiation between the "individual subject" and what he calls "the epistemic subject, that cognitive nucleus which is common to all subjects at the same level,"[19] is useful and may well shed light on the problem of curriculum, viewed from the vantage point of consciousness. Piaget is aware that his stress on the "epistemic subject" looks as if he were subsuming the individual under some impersonal abstraction;[20] but his discussion is not far removed from those of Sartre and the critics of consciousness, particularly when they talk of the subject entering into a process of generating structures whose being (like the structures Piaget has in mind) consists in their "coming to be."

Merleau-Ponty, as concerned as Piaget with the achievement of rationality, believes that there is a primary reality which must be taken into account if the growth of "intellectual consciousness" is to be understood. This primary reality is a perceived life-world; and the structures of the "perceptual consciousness"[21] through which the child first comes in contact with his environment underlie all the higher level structures which develop later in his life. In the prereflective, infantile stage of life he is obviously incapable of generating cognitive structures. The stage is characterized by what Merleau-Ponty calls "egocentrism" because the "me" is part of an anonymous collectivity, unaware of itself, capable of living "as easily in others as it does in itself."[22] Nevertheless, even then, before meanings and configurations are imposed, there is an original world, a natural and social world in which the child is involved corporeally and affectively. Perceiving that world, he effects certain relations within his experience. He organizes and "informs" it before he is capable of logical and predicative thought. This means for Merleau-Ponty that consciousness exists primordially—the ground of all knowledge and rationality.

The growing child assimilates a language system and becomes habituated to using language as "an open system of expression" which is capable of expressing "an indeterminate number of cognitions or ideas to come."[23] His acts of naming and expression take place, however, around a core of primary meaning found in "the silence of primary consciousness." This silence may be understood as the fundamental awareness of being present in the world. It resembles what Paulo Freire calls "background awareness"[24] of an existential situation, a situation actually lived before the codifications which make new perceptions possible. Talking about the effort to help peasants perceive their own reality differently (to enable them, in other words, to learn), Freire says they must somehow make explicit their "real consciousness" of their worlds, or what they experienced while living through situations they later learn to codify.

The point is that the world is constituted for the child (by means of the behavior called perception) prior to the "construction of cognitive structures." This does not imply that he lives his life primarily in that world. He moves outward into diverse realms of experience in his search for meaning. When he confronts and engages with the apparently independent structures associated with rationality, the so-called cognitive structures, it is likely that he does so as an "epistemic subject," bracketing out for the time his subjectivity, even his presence to himself.[25] But the awareness remains in the background; the original perceptual reality continues as the ground of rationality, the base from which the leap to the theoretical is taken.

Merleau-Ponty, recognizing that psychologists treat consciousness as "an object to be studied," writes that it is simply not accessible to mere factual observation:

> The psychologist always tends to make consciousness into just such an object of observation. But all the factual truths to which psychology has access can be applied to the concrete subject only after a philosophical correction. Psychology, like physics and the other sciences of nature, uses the method of induction, which starts from facts and then assembles them. But it is very evident that this induction will remain blind if we do not know in some other way, and indeed from the inside of consciousness itself, what this induction is dealing with.[26]

Induction must be combined "with the reflective knowledge that we can obtain from ourselves as conscious objects." This is not a recommendation that the individual engage in introspection. Consciousness, being intentional, throws itself outward *towards* the world. It is always consciousness *of* something—a phenomenon, another person, an object in the world: Reflecting upon himself as a conscious object, the individual—the learner, perhaps—reflects upon his relation to the world, his manner of comporting himself with respect to it, the changing perspectives through which the world presents itself to him. Merleau-Ponty talks about the need continually to rediscover "my actual presence to myself, the fact of my consciousness which is in the last resort what the word and the concept of consciousness mean."[27] This means remaining in contact with one's own perceptions, one's own experiences, and striving to constitute their meanings. It means achieving a state of what Schutz calls "*wide-awakeness* . . . a plane of consciousness of highest tension originating in an attitude of full attention to life and its requirements."[28] Like Sartre, Schutz emphasizes the importance of attentiveness for arriving at new perceptions, for carrying out cognitive projects. All this seems to me to be highly suggestive for a conception of a learner who is "open to the world,"[29] eager, indeed *condemned* to give meaning to it—and, in the process of doing so, recreating or generating the materials of a curriculum in terms of his own consciousness.

Some Alternative Views

There are, of course, alternative views of consequence for education today. R.S. Peters, agreeing with his philosophic precursors that consciousness is the hallmark of mind and always "related in its different modes to objects," asserts that the "objects of consciousness are first and foremost objects in a public world that are marked out and differentiated by a public language into which the individual is initiated."[30] (It should be said that Peters is, *par excellence*, the exponent of an "objective" or "analytic" approach to curriculum, closely related to the objective approach to literary criticism.) He grants that the individual "represents a unique and unrepeatable viewpoint on this public world"; but his primary stress is placed upon the way in which the learning of language is linked to the discovery of that separately existing world of "objects in space and time." Consciousness, for Peters, cannot be explained except in connection with the demarcations of the public world which meaning makes possible. It becomes contingent upon initiation into public traditions, into (it turns out) the academic disciplines. Since such an initiation is required if modes of consciousness are to be effectively differentiated, the mind must finally be understood as a "product" of such initiation. The individual must be enabled to achieve a state of mind characterized by "a mastery of and care for the worthwhile things that have been transmitted, which are viewed in some kind of cognitive perspective."[31]

Philip H. Phenix argues similarly that "the curriculum should consist entirely of knowledge which comes from the disciplines, for the reason that the disciplines reveal knowledge in its teachable forms."[32] He, however, pays more heed to what he calls "the experience of reflective self-consciousness,"[33] which he associates specifically with "concrete existence in direct personal encounter."[34] The meanings arising out of such encounter are expressed, for him, in existential philosophy, religion, psychology, and certain dimensions of imaginative literature. They are, thus, to be considered as one of the six "realms of meaning" through mastery of which man is enabled to achieve self-transcendence. Self-transcendence, for Phenix, involves a duality which enables the learner to feel himself to be agent and knower, and at once to identify with what he comes to know. Self-transcendence is the ground of meaning; but it culminates in the engendering of a range of "essential meanings," the achievement of a hierarchy in which all fundamental patterns of meaning are related and through which human existence can be fulfilled. The inner life of generic man is clearly encompassed by this scheme; but what is excluded, I believe, is what has been called the "subjectivity of the actor," the *individual* actor ineluctably present to himself. What is excluded is the feeling of separateness, of strangeness when such a person is confronted with the articulated curriculum intended to counteract meaninglessness.

Schutz writes:

When a stranger comes to the town, he has to learn to orientate in it and to know it. Nothing is self-explanatory for him and he has to ask an expert . . . to learn how to get from one point to another. He may, of course, refer to a map of the town, but even to use the map successfully he must know the meaning of the signs on the map, the exact point within the town where he stands and its correlative on the map, and at least one more point in order correctly to relate the signs on the map to the real objects in the city.[35]

The prestructured curriculum resembles such a map; the learner, the stranger just arrived in town. For the cartographer, the town is an "object of his science," a science which has developed standards of operation and rules for the correct drawing of maps. In the case of the curriculum-maker, the public tradition or the natural order of things is "the object" of his design activities. Here too there are standards of operation: the subject matter organized into disciplines must be communicable; it must be appropriate to whatever are conceived as educational aims. Phenix has written that education should be understood as "a guided recapitulation of the processes of inquiry which gave rise to the fruitful bodies of organized knowledge comprising the disciplines."[36] Using the metaphor of the map, we might say that this is like asking a newcomer in search of direction to recapitulate the complex processes by which the cartographer made his map. The map may represent a fairly complete charting of the town; and it may ultimately be extremely useful for the individual to be able to take a cartographer's perspective. When that individual first arrives, however, his peculiar plight ought not to be overlooked: his "background awareness" of being alive in an unstable world; his reasons for consulting the map; the interests he is pursuing as he attempts to orient himself when he can no longer proceed by rule of thumb. He himself may recognize that he will have to come to understand the signs on the map if he is to make use of it. Certainly he will have to decipher the relationship between those signs and "real objects in the city." But his initial concern will be conditioned by the "objects" he wants to bring into visibility, by the landmarks he needs to identify if he is to proceed on his way.

Learning—A Mode of Orientation

Turning from newcomer to learner (contemporary learner, in our particular world), I am suggesting that his focal concern is with ordering the materials of his own life-world when dislocations occur, when what was once familiar abruptly appears strange. This may come about on an occasion when "future shock" is experienced, as it so frequently is today. Anyone who has lived through a campus disruption, a teachers' strike, a guerilla theatre production, a sit-in (or a be-in, or a feel-in) knows full well what Alvin Toffler means when he writes about the acceleration of change. "We no longer 'feel' life as men did in the past," he says. "And this is the ultimate difference, the distinction that separates the truly contemporary man from all others. For this acceleration lies behind the impermanence—the transience—that penetrates and tinctures our consciousness, radically affecting the way we relate to other people, to things, to the entire universe of ideas, art and values."[37] Obviously, this does not happen in everyone's life; but it is far more likely to occur than ever before in history, if it is indeed the case that change has speeded up and that forces are being released which we have not yet learned to control. My point is that the contemporary learner is more likely than his predecessors to experience moments of strangeness, moments when the recipes he has inherited for the solution of typical problems no longer seem to work. If Merleau-Ponty is right and the search for rationality is indeed grounded in a primary or perceptual consciousness, the individual may be fundamentally aware that the structures of "reality" are contingent upon the perspective taken and that most achieved orders are therefore precarious.

The stage sets are always likely to collapse.[38] Someone is always likely to ask unexpectedly, as in Pinter's *The Dumb Waiter*, "Who cleans up after we're gone?"[39] Someone is equally likely to cry out, "You seem to have no conception of where we stand! You won't find the answer written down for you in the bowl of a compass—I can tell you that."[40] Disorder, in other words, is continually breaking in; meaninglessness is recurrently overcoming landscapes which once were demarcated, meaningful. It is at moments like these that the individual reaches out to reconstitute meaning, to close the gaps, to make sense once again. It is at moments like these that he will be moved to pore over maps, to disclose or generate structures of knowledge which may provide him unifying perspectives and thus enable him to restore order once again. His learning, I am saying, is a mode of orientation—or reorientation in a place suddenly become unfamiliar. And "place" is a metaphor, in this context, for a domain of consciousness, intending, forever thrusting outward, "open to the world." The curriculum, the structures of knowledge, must be presented to such a consciousness as possibility. Like the work of literature in Sartre's viewing, it requires a subject if it is to be disclosed; it can only *be* disclosed if the learner, himself engaged in generating the structures, lends the curriculum his life. If the curriculum, on the other hand, is seen as external to the search for meaning, it becomes an alien and an alienating edifice, a kind of "Crystal Palace" of ideas.[41]

There is, then, a kind of resemblance between the ways in which a learner confronts socially prescribed knowledge and the ways in which a stranger looks at a map when he is trying to determine where he is in relation to where he wants to go. In Kafka's novel, *Amerika*, I find a peculiarly suggestive description of the predicament of someone who is at once a stranger and a potential learner (although, it eventually turns out, he never succeeds in being taught). He is Karl Rossmann, who has been "packed off to America" by his parents and who likes to stand on a balcony at his Uncle Jacob's house in New York and look down on the busy street.

> From morning to evening and far into the dreaming night that street was a channel for the constant stream of traffic which, seen from above, looked like an inextricable confusion, forever newly improvised, of foreshortened human figures and the roofs of all kinds of vehicles, sending into the upper air another confusion, more riotous and complicated, of noises, dusts and smells, all of it enveloped and penetrated by a flood of light which the multitudinous objects in the street scattered, carried off and again busily brought back, with an effect as palpable to the dazzled eye as if a glass roof stretched over the street were being violently smashed into fragments at every moment.[42]

Karl's uncle tells him that the indulgence of idly gazing at the busy life of the city might be permissible if Karl were traveling for pleasure; "but for one who intended to remain in the States it was sheer ruination." He is going to have to make judgments which will shape his future life; he will have, in effect, to be reborn. This being so, it is not enough for him to treat the unfamiliar landscape as something to admire and wonder at (as if it were a cubist construction or a kaleidoscope). Karl's habitual interpretations (learned far away in Prague) do not suffice to clarify what he sees. If he is to learn, he must identify what is questionable, try to break through what is obscure. Action is required of him, not mere gazing; *praxis*, not mere reverie.

If he is to undertake action, however, he must do so against the background of his original perceptions, with a clear sense of being present to himself. He must do so, too, against the background of his European experience, of the experience of rejection, of being "packed off" for reasons never quite understood. Only with that sort of awareness will he be capable of the attentiveness and commitment needed to engage with the world and make it meaningful. Only with the ability to be reflective about what he is doing will he be brave enough to incorporate his past into the present, to link the present to a future. All this will demand a conscious appropriation of new perspectives on his experience and a continual reordering of that experience as new horizons of the "Amerika" become visible, as new problems arise. The point is that Karl Rossmann, an immigrant in an already structured and charted world, must be conscious enough of himself to strive towards rationality; only if he achieves rationality will he avoid humiliations and survive.

As Kafka tells it, he never does attain that rationality; and so he is continually manipulated by forces without and within. He never learns, for example, that there can be no justice if there is no good will, even though he repeatedly and sometimes eloquently asks for justice from the authorities—always to no avail. The ship captains and pursers, the business men, the head waiters and porters all function according to official codes of discipline which are beyond his comprehension. He has been plunged into a public world with its own intricate prescriptions, idiosyncratic structures, and hierarchies; but he has no way of appropriating it or of constituting meanings. Throughout most of the novel, he clings to his symbolic box (with the photograph of his parents, the memorabilia of childhood and home). The box may be egocentrism; it may signify his incapacity to embark upon the "decentering" required if he is to begin generating for himself the structures of what surrounds.

In his case (and, I would say, in the case of many other people) the "decentering" that is necessary is not solely a cognitive affair, as Piaget insists it is. Merleau-Ponty speaks of a "lived decentering,"[43] exemplified by a child's learning"to relativise the notions of the youngest and the eldest" (to learn, e.g., to become the eldest in relation to the newborn child) or by his learning to think in terms of reciprocity. This happens, as it would have to happen to Karl, through actions undertaken within the "vital order," not merely through intellectual categorization. It does not exclude the possibility that a phenomenon analogous to Piaget's "epistemic subject" emerges, although there appears to be no reason (except, perhaps, from the viewpoint of empirical psychology) for separating it off from the "individual subject." (In fact, the apparent difference between Piaget and those who talk of "lived experience" may turn upon a definition of"consciousness." Piaget, as has been noted,[44] distinguishes between "consciousness" and "operational behavior," as if consciousness did *not* involve a turning outward to things, a continuing reflection upon situationality, a generation of cognitive structures.) In any case, every individual who consciously seeks out meaning is involved in asking questions which demand essentially epistemic responses.[45] These responses, even if incomplete, are knowledge claims; and, as more and more questions are asked, there is an increasing "sedimentation" of meanings which result from the interpretation of past experiences looked at from the vantage point of the present. Meanings do not inhere in the experiences that emerge; they have to be constituted, and they can only be constituted through cognitive action.

Returning to Karl Rossmann and his inability to take such action, I have been suggesting that he *cannot* make his own "primary consciousness" background so long as he clings to his box; nor can he actively interpret his past experience. He cannot (to stretch Piaget's point somewhat) become or will himself to be an "epistemic subject."

He is, as Freire puts it, submerged in a "dense, enveloping reality or a tormenting blind alley" and will be unless he can "perceive it as an objective-problematic situation."[46] Only then will he be able to intervene in his own reality with attentiveness, with awareness—to act upon his situation and make sense.

It would help if the looming structures which are so incomprehensible to Karl were somehow rendered cognitively available to him. Karl might then (with the help of a teacher willing to engage in dialogue with him, to help him pose his problems) reach out to question in terms of what he feels is thematically relevant or "worth questioning."[47] Because the stock of knowledge he carries with him does not suffice for a definition of situations in which porters manhandle him and women degrade him, in which he is penalized for every spontaneous action, he cannot easily refer to previous situations for clues. In order to cope with this, he needs to single out a single relevant element at first (from all the elements in what is happening) to transmute into a theme for his "knowing consciousness." There is the cruel treatment meted out to him, for example, by the Head Porter who feels it his duty "to attend to things that other people neglect." (He adds that, since he is in charge of all the doors of the hotel [including the "doorless exits"], he is "in a sense placed over everyone," and everyone has to obey him absolutely. If it were not for his repairing the omissions of the Head Waiter in the name of the hotel management, he believes, "such a great organization would be unthinkable."[48]) The porter's violence against Karl might well become the relevant element, the origin of a theme.

Making Connections

"What makes the theme to be a theme." Schutz writes, "is determined by motivationally relevant interest-situations and spheres of problems. The theme which thus has become relevant has now, however, become a problem to which a solution, practical, theoretical, or emotional, must be given."[49] The problem for Karl, like relevant problems facing any individual, is connected with and a consequence of a great number of other perplexities, other dislocations in his life. If he had not been so badly exploited by authority figures in time past, if he were not so childishly given to blind trust in adults, if he were not so likely to follow impulse at inappropriate moments, he would never have been assaulted by the Head Porter. At this point, however, once the specific problem (the assault) has been determined to be thematically relevant for him, it can be detached from the motivational context out of which it derived. The meshwork of related perplexities remains, however, as an outer horizon, waiting to be explored or questioned when necessary. The thematically relevant element can then be made interesting in its own right and worth questioning. In the foreground, as it were, the focus of concern, it can be defined against the background of the total situation. The situation is not in any sense obliterated or forgotten. It is *there*, at the fringe of Karl's attention while the focal problem is being solved; but it is, to an extent, "bracketed out." With this bracketing out and this foreground focusing, Karl may be for the first time in a condition of wide-awakeness, ready to pay active attention to what has become so questionable and so troubling, ready to take the kind of action which will move him ahead into a future as it gives him perspective on his past.

The action he might take involves more than what is understood as problem-solving. He has, after all, had some rudimentary knowledge of the Head Porter's role, a knowledge conditioned by certain typifications effected in the prepredicative days of early childhood. At that point in time, he did not articulate his experience in terms of sense data or even in terms of individual figures standing out against a background.

He saw typical structures according to particular zones of relevancy. This means that he probably saw his father, or the man who was father, not only as bearded face next to his mother, not only as large figure in the doorway, but as over-bearing, threatening, incomprehensible Authority who was "placed over everyone" and had the right to inflict pain. Enabled, years later, to confront something thematically relevant, the boy may be solicited to recognize his present knowledge of the porter as the sediment of previous mental processes.[50] The knowledge of the porter, therefore, has a history beginning in primordial perceptions; and the boy may succeed in moving back from what is seemingly "given" through the diverse mental processes which constituted the porter over time. Doing so, he will be exploring both the inner and outer horizons of the problem, making connections within the field of his consciousness, interpreting his own past as it bears on his present, reflecting upon his own knowing.

And that is not all. Having made such connections between the relevant theme and other dimensions of his experience, he may be ready to solve his problem; he may even feel that the problem is solved. This, however, puts him into position to move out of his own inner time (in which all acts are somehow continuous and bound together) into the intersubjective world where he can function as an epistemic subject. Having engaged in a reflexive consideration of the activity of his own consciousness, he can now shift his attention back to the life-world which had been rendered so unrecognizable by the Head Porter's assault. Here too, meanings must be constituted; the "great organization" must be understood, so that Karl can orient himself once again in the everyday. Bracketing out his subjectivity for the time, he may find many ways of engaging as a theoretical inquirer with the problem of authority in hotels and the multiple socioeconomic problems connected with that. He will voluntarily become, when inquiring in this way, a partial self, an inquirer deliberately acting a role in a community of inquirers. I am suggesting that he could not do so as effectively or as authentically if he had not first synthesized the materials within his inner time, constituted meaning in his world.

The analogy to the curriculum question, I hope, is clear. Treating Karl as a potential learner, I have considered the hotels and the other structured organizations in his world as analogous to the structures of prescribed knowledge—or to the curriculum. I have suggested that the individual, in our case the student, will only be in a position to learn when he is committed to act upon his world. If he is content to admire it or simply accept it as given, if he is incapable of breaking with egocentrism, he will remain alienated from himself and his own possibilities; he will wander lost and victimized upon the road; he will be unable to learn. He may be conditioned; he may be trained. He may even have some rote memory of certain elements of the curriculum; but no matter how well devised is that curriculum, no matter how well adapted to the stages of his growth, learning (as disclosure, as generating structures, as engendering meanings, as achieving mastery) will not occur.

At once, I have tried to say that unease and disorder are increasingly endemic in contemporary life, and that more and more persons are finding the recipes they habitually use inadequate for sense-making in a changing world. This puts them more and more frequently, in the position of strangers or immigrants trying to orient themselves in an unfamiliar town. The desire, indeed the *need*, for orientation is equivalent to the desire to constitute meanings, all sorts of meanings, in the many dimensions of existence. But this desire, I have suggested, is not satisfied by the authoritative confrontation of student with knowledge structures (no matter how "teachable" the forms in which the knowledge is revealed). It is surely not satisfied when the instructional situation is conceived to be, as G.K. Plochmann has written, one in which the teacher is endeavoring "with respect to his subject matter, to bring the understanding of the learner in equality with his own understanding."[51] Described in that fashion, with "learner" conceived generically and the "system" to be taught conceived as preexistent and objectively real, the instructional situation seems to me to be one that alienates because of the way it ignores both existential predicament and primordial consciousness. Like the approach to literary criticism Abrams describes, the view appears to commit us to a concept of curriculum "as a floating Laputa, insulated from life and essential human concerns. . . ."[52]

The cries of "irrelevance" are still too audible for us to content ourselves with this. So are the complaints about depersonalization, processing, and compulsory socialization into a corporate, inhuman world. Michael Novak, expressing some of this, writes that what our institutions "decide is real is enforced as real." He calls parents, teachers, and psychiatrists (like policemen and soldiers) "the enforcers of reality"; then he goes on to say:

> When a young person is being initiated into society, existing norms determine what is to be considered real and what is to be annihilated by silence and disregard. The good, docile student accepts the norms; the recalcitrant student may lack the intelligence—or have too much; may lack maturity—or insist upon being his own man.[53]

I have responses like this in mind when I consult the phenomenologists for an approach to curriculum in the present day. For one thing, they remind us of what it means for an individual to be present to himself; for another, they suggest to us the origins of significant quests for meaning, origins which ought to be held in mind by those willing to enable students to be themselves.

If the existence of a primordial consciousness is taken seriously, it will be recognized that awareness begins perspectively, that our experience is always incomplete. It is true that we have what Merleau-Ponty calls a "prejudice" in favor of a world of solid, determinate objects, quite independent of our perceptions. Consciousness does, however, have the capacity to return to the precognitive, the primordial, by "bracketing out" objects as customarily seen. The individual can release himself into his own inner time and rediscover the ways in which objects arise, the ways in which experience develops. In discussing the possibility of Karl Rossmann exploring his own past, I have tried to show what this sort of interior journey can mean. Not only may it result in the effecting of new syntheses within experience; it may result in an awareness of the process of knowing, of believing, of perceiving. It may even result in an understanding of the ways in which meanings have been sedimented in an individual's own personal history. I can think of no more potent mode of combatting those conceived to be "enforcers of the real," including the curriculum designers.

But then there opens up the possibility of presenting curriculum in such a way that is does not impose or enforce. If the student is enabled to recognize that reason and order may represent the culminating step in his constitution of a world, if he can be enabled to see that what Schutz calls the attainment of a "reciprocity of perspectives"[54] signifies the achievement of rationality, he may realize what it is to generate the structures of the disciplines on his own initiative, against his own "background awareness." Moreover, he may realize that he is projecting beyond his present horizons each time he shifts his attention and takes another perspective on his world. "To say there exists rationality," writes Merleau-Ponty, "is to say that perspectives blend, perceptions confirm each other, a meaning emerges."[55] He points out that we witness at every moment "the miracles of related experiences, and yet nobody knows better than we do how this miracle is worked, for we are ourselves this network of relationships." Curriculum can offer the possibility for students to be the makers of such networks. The problem for their teachers is to stimulate an awareness of the questionable, to aid in the identification of the thematically relevant, to beckon beyond the everyday.

> I am a psychological and historical structure, and have received, with existence, a manner of existence, a style. All my actions and thoughts stand in a relationship to this structure, and even a philosopher's thought is merely a way of making explicit his hold on the world, and what he is. The fact remains that I am free, not in spite of, or on the hither side of these motivations, but by means of them. For this significant life, this certain significance of nature and history which I am, does not limit my access to the world, but on the contrary is my means of entering into communication with it. It is by being unrestrictedly and unreservedly what I am at present that I have a chance of moving forward; it is by living my time that I am able to understand other times, by plunging into the present and the world by taking on deliberately what I am fortuitously, by willing what I will and doing what I do, that I can go further.[56]

To plunge in; to choose; to disclose; to move: this is the road, it seems to me, to mastery.

Notes

1. Marice Merleau-Ponty *The Primacy of Perception*. James M. Edie, ed. Evanston, Ill.: Northwestern University Press, 1964, pp. 99.

2. Jean Paul Sartre *Search for a Method* New York: Alfred A. Knopf, 1963, p. 92.

3. Ryland W. Crary, *Humanizing the School Curriculum: Development and Theory*. New York: Alfred A Knopf, 1969, p. 13.

4. John Dewey, "The Child and the Curriculum,: Martin S. Dworking, ed. *Dewey on Education*. New York: Teachers College Bureau of Publications, 1959, p. 91.

5. Sarah Lawall, *Critics of Consciousness*. Cambridge, Mass.: Harvard University Press, 1968.

6. T. S. Eliot, *The Sacred Wood*. New York: Barnes & Noble University Paperbacks, 1960, p. x.

7. Dorothy Walsh. "The Cognitive Content of Art." Francis J. Coleman, ed. *Aesthetics*. New York: McGraw-Hill, 1968, p. 297.

8. Clive Bell, *Art*. London: Chatto & Windus, 1914.

9. Walsh, *op. cit.*

10. M. H. Abrams, "Belief and the Suspension of Belief." M. H. Abrams, ed. *Literature and Belief*. New York: Columbia University Press, 1957, p. 9.

11. Maurice Blanchot. *L'Espace littéraire*. Paris: Gallimard, 1955.

12. See, e.g., Alfred Schultz, "Some Leading Concepts of Phenomenology," Marurice Natanson, ed. *Collected Papers* I The Hague Martinus Nijhoff, 1967, pp. 104–5.

13. Jeal-Paul Sartre. *Literature and Existentialism*. 3rd ed. New York: The Citadel Press, 1965, p. 43.

14. *Ibid*. p. 15.

15. John Dewey. *Art as Experience*. New York: Minton, Balch & Company, 1934, p. 54.

16. Sartre. *Search for a Method. op. cit.*, p. 91.

17. Jean Piaget. *Structuralism*. New York: Basic Books, 1970, p. 139.

18. *Ibid.*, p. 68.

19. *Ibid.*, p. 139.

20. *Ibid.*

21. Maurice Merleau-Ponty. *Phenomenology of Perception.* London: Routledge Kegan Paul Ltd., 1962.

22. Merleau-Ponty. *The Primacy of Perception, op. cit.*, p. 119.

23. *Ibid*, p. 99.

24. Paulo Freire. *Pedagogy of the Oppressed.* New York: Herder and Herder, 1970, p. 108.

25. Schutz. "On Multiple Realities." *op. cit.*, p. 248.

26. Merleau-Ponty. *The Primacy of Perception, op. cit.*, p. 58.

27. Merleau-Ponty. *Phenomenology of Perception, op. cit.*, p. xvii.

28. Schutz. "On Multiple Realities." *op. cit.*

29. Merleau-Ponty, *op. cit.*, p. xv.

30. R. S. Peters. *Ethics and Education.* London: George Allen and Unwin, 1966, p. 50.

31. R. S. Peters. *Ethics and Education.* Glenview, Ill.: Scott Foresman and Co., 1967, p. 12.

32. Philip H. Phenix, "The Uses of the Disciplines as Curriculum Content," Donald Vandenberg, ed. *Theory of Knowledge and Problems of Education.* Urbana, Ill.: University of Illinois Press, 1969, p. 195.

33. Philip H. Phenix. *Realms of Meaning.* New York: McGraw-Hill, 1964, p. 25.

34. *Ibid.*

35. Schutz. "Problem of Rationality in the Social World." Natanson, ed. *Collected Papers* II. The Hague Martinus Nijhoff, 1967, p. 66.

36. Phenix, "Disciplines as Curriculum Content," op. cit., p. 195.

37. Alvin Toffler. *Future Shock.* New York: Random House, 1970, p. 18.

38. Albert Camus. *The Myth of Sisyphus.* New York: Alfred A Knopf, 1955, p. 72.

39. Harold Pinter. *The Dumb Waiter.* New York: Grove Press, 1961, p. 103.

40. Tom Stoppard. *Rosencrantz and Guildenstern are Dead.* New York: Grove Press, 1967, pp. 58–59.

41. *Cf.* Fyodor Dostoevsky. *Notes from Underground*, in *The Short Novels of Dostoevsky.* New York: Dial Press, 1945. "You believe in a palace of crystal that can never be destroyed . . . a palace at which one will not be able to put out one's tongue or make a long nose on the sly." p. 152.

42. Franz Kafka. *Amerika.* Garden City, N.Y.: Doubleday Anchor Books, 1946, p. 38.

43. Merleau-Ponty. *The Primacy of Perception, op. cit.*, p. 110.

44. Piaget, *op. cit.*

45. Richard M. Zaner. *The Way of Phenomenology.* New York: Pegasus Books, 1970, p. 27.

46. Freire, *op. cit.* p. 100.

47. Schutz. "The Life-World." Natanson, ed. *Collected Papers*, III. The Hague: Martinus Nijhoff, 1967, p. 125.

48. Kafka, *op. cit.* p. 201.

49. Schutz. "The Life-World." *op. cit.* p. 124.

50. Schutz, "Leading Concepts of Phenomenology," op. cit., p. 111.

51. G. K. Plochmann. "On the Organic Logic of Teaching and Learning." Vandenberg, *op. cit.,* p. 244.

52. *Cf.* footnote 10.

53. Michael Novak. *The Experience of Nothingness.* New York: Harper & Row, 1970, p. 94.

54. Schutz. "Symbols, Reality, and Society." *Collected Papers*, I, *op. cit.*, p. 315.

55. Merleau-Ponty, *Phenomenology of Perception,* op. cit., p. xix.

56. *Ibid.*, pp. 455–56.

14

Pedagogy of the Oppressed

PAULO FREIRE

As we attempt to analyze dialogue as a human phenomenon, we discover something which is the essence of dialogue itself: *the word*. But the word is more than just an instrument which makes dialogue possible; accordingly, we must seek its constitutive elements. Within the word we find two dimensions, reflection and action, in such radical interaction that if one is sacrificed—even in part—the other immediately suffers. There is no true word that is not at the same time a praxis.[1] Thus, to speak a true word is to transform the world.[2]

An unauthentic word, one which is unable to transform reality, results when dichotomy is imposed upon its constitutive elements. When a word is deprived of its dimension of action, reflection automatically suffers as well; and the word is changed into idle chatter, into *verbalism*, into an alienated and alienating "blah." It becomes an empty word, one which cannot denounce the world, for denunciation is impossible without a commitment to transform, and there is no transformation without action.

On the other hand, if action is emphasized exclusively, to the detriment of reflection, the word is converted into *activism*. The latter—action for action's sake—negates the true praxis and makes dialogue impossible. Either dichotomy, by creating unauthentic forms of existence, creates also unauthentic forms of thought, which reinforce the original dichotomy.

Human existence cannot be silent, nor can it be nourished by false words, but only by true words, with which men transform the world. To exist, humanly, is to *name* the world, to change it. Once named, the world in its turn reappears to the namers as a problem and requires of them a new *naming*. Men are not built in silence,[3] but in word, in work, in action-reflection.

But while to say the true word—which is work, which is praxis—is to transform the world, saying that word is not the privilege of some few men, but the right of every man. Consequently, no one can say a true word alone—nor can he say it *for* another, in a prescriptive act which robs others of their words.

Dialogue is the encounter between men, mediated by the world, in order to name the world. Hence, dialogue cannot occur between those who want to name the world and those who do not wish this naming—between those who deny other men the right to speak their word and those whose right to speak has been denied them. Those who have been denied their primordial right to speak their word must first reclaim this right and prevent the continuation of this dehumanizing aggression.

From Paulo Freire, *Pedagogy of the Oppressed*. New York: Continuum, 1970: pp. 75–86, 95–100. Reprinted by permission.

If it is in speaking their word that men, by naming the world, transform it, dialogue imposes itself as the way by which men achieve significance as men. Dialogue is thus an existential necessity. And since dialogue is the encounter in which the united reflection and action of the dialoguers are addressed to the world which is to be transformed and humanized, this dialogue cannot be reduced to the act of one person's "depositing" ideas in another, nor can it become a simple exchange of ideas to be "consumed" by the discussants. Nor yet is it a hostile, polemical argument between men who are committed neither to the naming of the world, nor to the search for truth, but rather to the imposition of their own truth. Because dialogue is an encounter among men who name the world, it must not be a situation where some men name on behalf of others. It is an act of creation; it must not serve as a crafty instrument for the domination of one man by another. The domination implicit in dialogue is that of the world by the dialoguers; it is conquest of the world for the liberation of men.

Dialogue cannot exist, however, in the absence of a profound love for the world and for men. The naming of the world, which is an act of creation and re-creation, is not possible if it is not infused with love.[4] Love is at the same time the foundation of dialogue and dialogue itself. It is thus necessarily the task of responsible Subjects and cannot exist in a relation of domination. Domination reveals the pathology of love: sadism in the dominator and masochism in the dominated. Because love is an act of courage, not of fear, love is commitment to other men. No matter where the oppressed are found, the act of love is commitment to their cause—the cause of liberation. And this commitment, because it is loving, is dialogical. As an act of bravery, love cannot be sentimental; as an act of freedom, it must not serve as a pretext for manipulation. It must generate other acts of freedom; otherwise, it is not love. Only by abolishing the situation of oppression is it possible to restore the love which that situation made impossible. If I do not love the world—if I do not love life—if I do not love men—I cannot enter into dialogue.

On the other hand, dialogue cannot exist without humility. The naming of the world, through which men constantly re-create that world, cannot be an act of arrogance. Dialogue, as the encounter of men addressed to the common task of learning and acting, is broken if the parties (or one of them) lack humility. How can I dialogue if I always project ignorance onto others and never perceive my own? How can I dialogue if I regard myself as a case apart from other men—mere "its" in whom I cannot recognize other "I"s? How can I dialogue if I consider myself a member of the in-group of "pure" men, the owners of truth and knowledge, for whom all non-members are "these people" or "the great unwashed"? How can I dialogue if I start from the premise that naming the world is the task of an elite and that the presence of the people in history is a sign of deterioration, thus to be avoided? How can I dialogue if I am closed to—and even offended by—the contribution of others? How can I dialogue if I am afraid of being displaced, the mere possibility causing me torment and weakness? Self-sufficiency is incompatible with dialogue. Men who lack humility (or have lost it) cannot come to the people, cannot be their partners in naming the world. Someone who cannot acknowledge himself to be as mortal as everyone else still has a long way to go before he can reach the point of encounter. At the point of encounter there are neither utter ignoramuses nor perfect sages; there are only men who are attempting, together, to learn more than they now know.

Dialogue further requires an intense faith in man, faith in his power to make and remake, to create and re-create, faith in his vocation to be more fully human (which is not the privilege of an elite, but the birthright of all men). Faith in man is an *a priori* requirement for dialogue; the "dialogical man" believes in other men even before he meets them face to face. His faith, however, is not naïve. The "dialogical man" is critical and knows that although it is within the power of men to create and transform, in a concrete situation of alienation men may be impaired in the use of that power. Far from destroying his faith in man, however, this possibility strikes him as a challenge to which he must respond. He is convinced that the power to create and transform, even when thwarted in concrete situations, tends to be reborn. And that rebirth can occur—not gratuitously, but in and through the struggle for liberation—in the supersedence of slave labor by emancipated labor which gives zest to life. Without this faith in man, dialogue is a farce which inevitably degenerates into paternalistic manipulation.

Founding itself upon love, humility, and faith, dialogue becomes a horizontal relationship of which mutual trust between the dialoguers is the logical consequence. It would be a contradiction in terms if dialogue—loving, humble, and full of faith—did not produce this climate of mutual trust, which leads the dialoguers into ever closer partnership in the naming of the world. Conversely, such trust is obviously absent in the anti-dialogics of the banking method of education. Whereas faith in man is an *a priori* requirement for dialogue, trust is established by dialogue. Should it founder, it will be seen that the preconditions were lacking. False love, false humility, and feeble faith in man cannot create trust. Trust is contingent on the evidence which one party provides the others of his true, concrete intentions; it cannot exist if that party's words do not coincide with his actions. To say one thing and do another—to take one's own word lightly—cannot inspire trust. To glorify democracy and to silence the people is a farce; to discourse on humanism and to negate man is a lie.

Nor yet can dialogue exist without hope. Hope is rooted in men's incompletion, from which they move out in constant search—a search which can be carried out only in communion with other men. Hopelessness is a form of silence, of denying the world and fleeing from it. The dehumanization resulting from an unjust order is not a cause for despair but for hope, leading to the incessant pursuit of the humanity denied by injustice. Hope, however, does not consist in crossing one's arms and waiting. As long as I fight, I am moved by hope; and if I fight with hope, then I can wait. As the encounter of men seeking to be more fully human, dialogue cannot be carried on in a climate of hopelessness. If the dialoguers expect nothing to come of their efforts, their encounter will be empty and sterile, bureaucratic and tedious.

Finally, true dialogue cannot exist unless the dialoguers engage in critical thinking—thinking which discerns an indivisible solidarity between the world and men and admits of no dichotomy between them—thinking which perceives reality as process, as transformation, rather than as a static entity—thinking which does not separate itself from action, but constantly immerses itself in temporality without fear of the risks involved. Critical thinking contrasts with naïve thinking, which sees "historical time as a weight, a stratification of the acquisitions and experiences of the past,"[5] from which the present should emerge normalized and "well-behaved." For the naïve thinker, the important thing is accommodation to this normalized "today." For the critic, the important thing is the continuing transformation of reality, in behalf of the continuing humanization of men. In the words of Pierre Furter:

> The goal will no longer be to eliminate the risks of temporality by clutching to guaranteed space, but rather to temporalize space. . . . The universe is revealed to me not as space, imposing a massive presence to which I can but adapt, but as a scope, a domain which takes shape as I act upon it.[6]

For naïve thinking, the goal is precisely to hold fast to this guaranteed space and adjust to it. By thus denying temporality, it denies itself as well.

Only dialogue, which requires critical thinking, is also capable of generating critical thinking. Without dialogue there is no communication, and without communication there can be no true education. Education which is able to resolve the contradiction between teacher and student takes place in a situation in which both address their act of cognition to the object by which they are mediated. Thus, the dialogical character of education as the practice of freedom does not begin when the teacher-student meets with the students-teachers in a pedagogical situation, but rather when the former first asks himself *what* he will dialogue with the latter *about*. And preoccupation with the content of dialogue is really preoccupation with the program content of education.

For the anti-dialogical banking educator, the question of content simply concerns the program about which he will discourse to his students; and he answers his own question, by organizing his own program. For the dialogical, problem-posing teacher-student, the program content of education is neither a gift nor an imposition—bits of information to be deposited in the students—but rather the organized, systematized, and developed "re-presentation" to individuals of the things about which they want to know more.[7]

Authentic education is not carried on by "A" *for* "B" or by "A" *about* "B," but rather by "A" *with* "B," mediated by the world—a world which impresses and challenges both parties, giving rise to views or opinions about it. These views, impregnated with anxieties, doubts, hopes, or hopelessness, imply significant themes on the basis of which the program content of education can be built. In its desire to create an ideal model of the "good man," a naïvely conceived humanism often overlooks the concrete, existential, present situation of real men. Authentic humanism, in Pierre Furter's words, "consists in permitting the emergence of the awareness of our full humanity, as a condition and as an obligation, as a situation and as a project."[8] We simply cannot go to the laborers—urban or peasant[9]—in the banking style, to give them "knowledge" or to impose upon them the model of the "good man" contained in a program whose content we have ourselves organized. Many political and educational plans have failed because their authors designed them according to their own personal views of reality, never once taking into account (except as mere objects of their action) the *men-in-a-situation* to whom their program was ostensibly directed.

For the truly humanist educator and the authentic revolutionary, the object of action is the reality to be transformed by them together with other men—not other men themselves. The oppressors are the ones who act upon men to indoctrinate them and adjust them to a reality which must remain untouched. Unfortunately, however, in their desire to obtain the support of the people for revolutionary action, revolutionary leaders often fall for the banking line of planning program content from the top down. They approach the peasant or urban masses with projects which may correspond to their own view of the world, but not to that of the people.[10] They forget that their fundamental objective is to fight alongside the people for the recovery of the people's stolen humanity, not to "win the people over" to their side. Such a phrase does not belong in the vocabulary of revolutionary leaders, but in that of the oppressor. The revolutionary's role is to liberate, and be liberated, with the people—not to win them over.

In their political activity, the dominant elites utilize the banking concept to encourage passivity in the oppressed, corresponding with the latter's "submerged" state of consciousness, and take advantage of that passivity to "fill" that consciousness with slogans which create even more fear of freedom. This practice is incompatible with a truly liberating course of action, which, by presenting the oppressors' slogans as a problem, helps the oppressed to "eject" those slogans from within themselves. After all, the task of the humanists is surely not that of pitting their slogans against the slogans of the oppressors, with the oppressed as the testing ground, "housing" the slogans of first one group and then the other. On the contrary, the task of the humanists is to see that the oppressed become aware of the fact that as dual beings, "housing" the oppressors within themselves, they cannot be truly human.

This task implies that revolutionary leaders do not go to the people in order to bring them a message of "salvation," but in order to come to know through dialogue with them both their *objective situation* and their *awareness* of that situation—the various levels of perception of themselves and of the world in which and with which they exist. One cannot expect positive results from an educational or political action program which fails to respect the particular view of the world held by the people. Such a program constitutes cultural invasion,[11] good intentions notwithstanding.

The starting point for organizing the program content of education or political action must be the present, existential, concrete situation, reflecting the aspirations of the people. Utilizing certain basic contradictions, we must pose this existential, concrete, present situation to the people as a problem which challenges them and requires a response—not just at the intellectual level, but at the level of action.[12]

We must never merely discourse on the present situation, must never provide the people with programs which have little or nothing to do with their own preoccupations, doubts, hopes, and fears—programs which at times in fact increase the fears of the oppressed consciousness. It is not our role to speak to the people about our own view of the world, nor to attempt to impose that view on them, but rather to dialogue with the people about their view and ours. We must realize that their view of the world, manifested variously in their action, reflects their *situation* in the world. Educational and political action which is not critically aware of this situation runs the risk either of "banking" or of preaching in the desert.

Often, educators and politicians speak and are not understood because their language is not attuned to the concrete situation of the men they address. Accordingly, their talk is just alienated and alienating rhetoric. The language of the educator or the politician (and it seems more and more clear that the latter must also become an educator, in the broadest sense of the word), like the language of the people, cannot exist without thought; and neither language nor thought can exist without a structure to which they refer. In order to communicate effectively, educator and politician must understand the structural conditions in which the thought and language of the people are dialectically framed.

It is to the reality which mediates men, and to the perception of that reality held by educators and people, that we must go to find the program content of education. The investigation of what I have termed the people's "thematic universe"[13]—the complex of their "generative themes"—inaugurates the dialogue of education as the practice of freedom. The methodology of that investigation must likewise be dialogical, affording the opportunity both to discover generative themes and to stimulate people's awareness in regard to these themes. Consistent with the liberating purpose of dialogical education, the object of the investigation is not men (as if men were anatomical fragments), but rather the thought-language with which men refer to reality, the levels at which they perceive that reality, and their view of the world, in which their generative themes are found.

★   ★   ★

Equally appropriate for the methodology of thematic investigation and for problem-posing education is this effort to present significant dimensions of an individual's contextual reality, the analysis of which will make it possible for him to recognize the interaction of the various components. Meanwhile, the significant dimensions, which in their turn are constituted of parts in interaction, should be perceived as dimensions of total reality. In this way, a critical analysis of a significant existential dimension makes possible a new, critical attitude towards the limit-situations. The perception and comprehension of reality are rectified and acquire new depth. When carried out with a methodology of *conscientização* the investigation of the generative theme contained in the minimum thematic universe (the generative themes in interaction) thus introduces or begins to introduce men to a critical form of thinking about their world.

In the event, however, that men perceive reality as dense, impenetrable, and enveloping, it is indispensable to proceed with the investigation by means of abstraction. This method does not involve reducing the concrete to the abstract (which would signify the negation of its dialectical nature), but rather maintaining both elements as opposites which interrelate dialectically in the act of reflection. This dialectical movement of thought is exemplified perfectly in the analysis of a concrete, existential, "coded" situation.[21] Its "decoding" requires moving from the abstract to the concrete; this requires moving from the part to the whole and then returning to the parts; this in turn requires that the Subject recognize himself in the object (the coded concrete existential situation) and recognize the object as a situation in which he finds himself, together with other Subjects. If the decoding is well done, this movement of flux and reflux from the abstract to the concrete which occurs in the analysis of a coded situation leads to the supersedence of the abstraction *by* the critical perception of the concrete, which has already ceased to be a dense, impenetrable reality.

When an individual is presented with a coded existential situation (a sketch or photograph which leads by abstraction to the concreteness of existential reality), his tendency is to "split" that coded situation. In the process of decoding, this separation corresponds to the stage we call the "description of the situation," and facilitates the discovery of the interaction among the parts of the disjoined whole. This whole (the coded situation), which previously had been only diffusely apprehended, begins to acquire meaning as thought flows back to it from the various dimensions. Since, however, the coding is the representation of an existential situation, the decoder tends to take the step from the representation to the very concrete situation in which and with which he finds himself. It is thus possible to explain conceptually why individuals begin to behave differently with regard to objective reality, once that reality has ceased to look like a blind alley and has taken on its true aspect: a challenge which men must meet.

In all the stages of decoding, men exteriorize their view of the world. And in the way they think about and face the world—fatalistically, dynamically, or statically—their generative themes may be found. A group which does not concretely express a generative thematics—a fact which might appear to imply the nonexistence of themes—is, on the contrary, suggesting a very dramatic theme: *the theme of silence*. The theme of silence suggests a structure of mutism in face of the overwhelming force of the limit-situations.

I must re-emphasize that the generative theme cannot be found in men, divorced from reality; nor yet in reality, divorced from men; much less in "no man's land." It can only be apprehended in the men-world relationship. To investigate the generative theme is to investigate man's thinking about reality and man's action upon reality, which is his praxis. For precisely this reason, the methodology proposed requires that the investigators and the people (who would normally be considered objects of that investigation) should act as *co-investigators*. The more active an attitude men take in regard to the exploration of their thematics, the more they deepen their critical awareness of reality and, in spelling out those thematics, take possession of that reality.

Some may think it inadvisable to include the people as investigators in the search for their own meaningful thematics: that their intrusive influence (N.B., the "intrusion" of those who are most interested—or ought to be—in their own education) will "adulterate" the findings and thereby sacrifice the objectivity of the investigation. This view mistakenly presupposes that themes exist, in their original objective purity, outside men—as if themes were *things*. Actually, themes exist in men in their relations with the world, with reference to concrete facts. The same objective fact could evoke different complexes of generative themes in different epochal sub-units. There is, therefore, a relation between the given objective fact, the perception men have of this fact, and the generative themes.

A meaningful thematics is expressed by men, and a given moment of expression will differ from an earlier moment, if men have changed their perception of the objective facts to which the themes refer. From the investigator's point of view, the important thing is to detect the starting point at which men visualize the "given" and to verify whether or not during the process of investigation any transformation has occurred in their way of perceiving reality. (Objective reality, of course, remains unchanged. If the perception of that reality changes in the course of the investigation, that fact does not impair the validity of the investigation.)

We must realize that the aspirations, the motives, and the objectives implicit in the meaningful thematics are *human* aspirations, motives, and objectives. They do not exist "out there" somewhere, as static entities; *they are occurring*. They are as historical as men themselves; consequently, they cannot be apprehended apart from men. To apprehend these themes and to understand them is to understand both the men who embody them and the reality to which they refer. But—precisely because it is not possible to understand these themes apart from men—it is necessary that the men concerned understand them as well. Thematic investigation thus becomes a common striving towards awareness of reality and towards self-awareness, which makes this investigation a starting point for the educational process or for cultural action of a liberating character.

The real danger of the investigation is not that the supposed objects of the investigation, discovering themselves to be co-investigators, might "adulterate" the analytical results. On the contrary, the danger lies in the risk of shifting the focus of the investigation from the meaningful themes to the people themselves, thereby treating the people as objects of the investigation. Since this investigation is to serve as a basis for developing an educational program in which teacher-student and students-teachers combine their cognitions of the same object, the investigation itself must likewise be based on reciprocity of action.

Thematic investigation, which occurs in the realm of the human, cannot be reduced to a mechanical act. As a process of search, of knowledge, and thus of creation, it requires the investigators to discover the interpenetration of problems, in the linking of meaningful themes. The investigation will be most educational when it is most critical, and most critical when it avoids the narrow outlines of partial or "focalized" views of reality, and sticks to the comprehension of *total* reality. Thus, the process of searching for the meaningful thematics should include a concern for the links between themes, a concern to posethese themes as problems, and a concern for their historical-cultural context.

Just as the educator may not elaborate a program to present *to* the people, neither may the investigator elaborate "itineraries" for researching the thematic universe, starting from points which *he* has predetermined. Both education and the investigation designed to support it must be "sympathetic" activities, in the etymological sense of the word. That is, they must consist of communication and of the common experience of a reality perceived in the complexity of its constant "becoming."

The investigator who, in the name of scientific objectivity, transforms the organic into something inorganic, what is becoming into what is, life into death, is a man who fears change. He sees in change (which he does not deny, but neither does he desire) not a sign of life, but a sign of death and decay. He does want to study change—but in order to stop it, not in order to stimulate or deepen it. However, in seeing change as a sign of death and in making people the passive objects of investigation in order to arrive at rigid models, he betrays his own character as a killer of life.

Notes

1. Action
   Reflection $\Big\}$ word = work = praxis
   Sacrifice of action = verbalism
   Sacrifice of reflection = activism

2. Some of these reflections emerged as a result of conversations with Professor Ernani Maria Fiori.

3. I obviously do not refer to the silence of profound meditation, in which men only apparently leave the world, withdrawing from it in order to consider it in its totality, and thus remaining with it. But this type of retreat is only authentic when the meditator is "bathed" in reality; not when the retreat signifies contempt for the world and flight from it, in a type of "historical schizophrenia."

4. I am more and more convinced that true revolutionaries must perceive the revolution, because of its creative and liberating nature, as an act of love. For me, the revolution, which is not possible without a theory of revolution—and therefore science—is not irreconcilable with love. On the contrary: the revolution is made by men to achieve their humanization. What, indeed, is the deeper motive which moves men to become revolutionaries, but the dehumanization of man? The distortion imposed on the word "love" by the capitalist world cannot prevent the revolution from being essentially loving in character, nor can it prevent the revolutionaries from affirming their love of life. Guevara (while admitting the "risk of seeming ridiculous") was not afraid to affirm it: "Let me say, with the risk of appearing ridiculous, that the true revolutionary is guided by strong feelings of love. It is impossible to think of an authentic revolutionary without this quality." *Venceremos—The Speeches and Writings of Che Guevara*, edited by John Gerassi (New York, 1969), p. 398.

5. From the letter of a friend.

6. Pierre Furter, *Educação e Vida* (Rio, 1966), pp. 26–27.

7. In a long conversation with Malraux, Mao-Tse-Tung declared, "You know I've proclaimed for a long time: we must teach the masses clearly what we have received from them confusedly." André Malraux, *Anti-Memoirs* (New York, 1968), pp. 361–362. This affirmation contains an entire dialogical theory of how to construct the program content of education, which cannot be elaborated according to what the *educator* thinks best for *his* students.

8. Furter, *op. cit.*, p. 165

9. The latter, usually submerged in a colonial context, are almost umbilically linked to the world of nature, in relation to which they feel themselves to be component parts rather than shapers.

10. "Our cultural workers must serve the people with great enthusiasm and devotion, and they must link themselves with the masses, not divorce themselves from the masses. In order to do so, they must act in accordance with the needs and wishes of the masses. All work done for the masses must start from their needs and not from the desire of any individual, however well-intentioned. It often happens that objectively the masses need a certain change, but subjectively they are not yet conscious of the need, not yet willing or determined to make the change. In such cases, we should wait patiently. We should not make the change until, through our work, most of the masses have become conscious of the need and are willing and determined to carry it out. Otherwise we shall isolate ourselves from the masses. . . . There are two principles here: one is the actual needs of the masses rather than what we fancy they need, and the other is the wishes of the masses, who must make up their own minds instead of our making up their minds for them." From the *Selected Works of Mao-Tse-Tung*, Vol. III. "The United Front in Cultural Work" (October 30, 1944) (Peking, 1967), pp. 186–187.

11. This point will be analyzed in detail in Chapter 4.

12. It is as self-contradictory for true humanists to use the banking method as it would be for rightists to engage in problem-posing education. (The latter are always consistent—they never use a problem-posing pedagogy.)

13. The expression "meaningful thematics" is used with the same connotation.

21. The coding of an existential situation is the representation of that situation, showing some of its constituent elements in interaction. Decoding is the critical analysis of the coded situation.

15

Humanistic Trends and the Curriculum Field

ELLIOT W. EISNER

At present a major anomaly exists in the field of education both in England and in the United States. The anomaly I speak of, is the growing concern among lay people and professionals alike that schools are not doing as well as they once were and that if the educational quality of the past is to be recaptured we must emphasize the "basics," we must return to what is truly fundamental in schooling, namely, teaching children to read, to write and to compute. This concern with the basics is exacerbated by information given to the public that test scores are slipping and have been for quite a few years. Since 1970 in the United States the drop in Scholastic Aptitude Test Scores has been 30 points in the verbal and 50 points in the mathematical sections of the test. To ensure that appropriate efforts are made to pay attention to these areas of performance, proficiency tests are being mandated by the States and minimum performance levels are being established that must be met by any student seeking a graduation diploma.[1] "Back to basics" and "minimum standards" are the watchwords.

These concerns are not limited to the United States. In Calgary, Canada, recent headlines read: "Education Report: Go Back to 3R's."[2] And in England a national project has been undertaken by the Department of Education and Science that would provide for the English what the National Assessment Program has provided for Americans; quantitative indices of the educational health of the nation.[3]

While this concern with the so-called basics and their assessment is going on, there is another movement developing simultaneously. That movement is concerned with the creation of a fundamentally different conception of education, in particular educational evaluation. It is this new movement, born and nurtured within the university that serves as the conceptual and philosophic antithesis to a conception of education limited to the three Rs and to a form of evaluation limited to quantitative description.

The movement I speak of is the growing interest among academics in the use of qualitative forms of inquiry in education. Like the so-called "back to basics" movement, this interest is not limited to the United States. In England it is represented in the work of Barry McDonald, Lawrence Stenhouse and Malcolm Parlett; in Scotland by David Hamilton; in Norway by Torsten Harbo; in Germany by Hartmut von Hentig; and in the United States by Stake, Jackson, Eisner, Willis, Mann, Walker, Huebner, and a host of others. What we see emerging in the university is the episte-

From *Journal of Curriculum Studies*, Vol. 10, No. 3, 1978: pp. 197–204. Reprinted by permission.

mological and methodological opposite of what is being advocated as desirable for the schools. It is this new movement, this growing interest in the exploration of qualitative forms of inquiry in education that I wish to discuss in this paper. To my mind this growing interest represents one of the most radical and promising developments in education since the turn of the century, since it aims to explore and exploit a fundamentally different set of assumptions about the nature of knowledge than the view that has dominated in education since 1900, at least in the United States.

By qualitative forms of inquiry I mean that form of inquiry that seeks the creation of qualities that are expressively patterned, that seeks the explication of wholes as a primary aim, that emphasizes the study of configurations rather than isolated entities, that regards expressive narratives and visuals as appropriate vehicles for communication. Qualitative methods tend to emphasize the importance of context in understanding, they tend to place great emphasis on the historical conditions within which events and situations occur, and they tend to argue that pieces cannot be understood aside from their relationship to the whole in which they participate. To understand an event or situation one must perceive it as an aspect of a larger pattern, rather than as an entity whose characteristics can be isolated and reduced to quantities.

To emphasize, as I have just done, the distinctive characteristics of qualitative inquiry is not to suggest that those who use such methods reject quantitative procedures. They do not. What they do reject is the assumption that objectivity can only be secured through quantitative or scientific methods. They reject the claim—implicit or explicit—that rigour in educational inquiry *requires* the use of methods that result in conclusions that can be stated in terms of probabilities. Let the problem determine the method, not vice versa.[4] Thus what we find are arguments for a multiple set of approaches to the ways in which educational inquiry can be pursued. The methods must be broadened.

As I see it, the motives for the development of qualitative methods in education emanate from three major sources. First, there are those whose interest stems from political motives. These individuals view the schools as an institutionalized conspiracy to keep children dependent, ill-informed and tolerant of mindless tasks so that when they become adults they will fit into the existing social order. To such individuals the feckless character of schools is not indicative of failure but of success. Schools, they believe, were and are intended to be a mindless experience for the young. Because the research establishment and the testing industry participate in this subterfuge, they are important targets to attack. Critical methods, particularly those that illuminate the kinds of experience that teachers and students have in schools, hold promise for raising the public's level of critical awareness. In addition, such methods have a kind of emotional impact in revealing what really goes on in schools, and thus might lead the public to seek significant changes in the structure and goals of schooling. For many of those politically motivated the use of qualitative methods is more compatible with a socialistic society or a Marxist-socialistic philosophy. Qualitative methods of evaluation, they believe, might make a significant contribution to the realization of such ends.

The second motive for the development of qualitative approaches to educational inquiry is methodological. Many of those interested in the uses of such methods regard laboratory research procedures associated with educational psychology as inappropriate for the study of classroom life and desire a more flexible and naturalistic approach to inquiry. For such individuals, ethnography, for example, provides a more desirable and more appropriate alternative. By attending to the context as a whole and by observing what naturally transpires without intervention by experimenters, a more valid picture of educational life can be secured. With more valid data, the likelihood of developing theory that is useful for understanding classrooms, teaching, and schooling is increased.

It should be noted that the motives here are not necessarily political in character. What those who wish to extend the methods of inquiry in education seek is not necessarily the radical reform of school or society, but the widening of legitimate procedures for research and evaluation. They frequently find the dominant view of research parochial and the methods for evaluating what students learn superficial.

The third motive for the development of qualitative approaches to evaluation is at base epistemological. Those moved by this ideal regard scientific epistemology as inadequate by itself for articulating all that needs to be known about schools, classrooms, teaching, and learning. Scientific and quantitative methods are important utilities for describing some aspects of educational life and their consequences, but they are far too limited to be the exclusive or even the dominant set of methods. To complement these methods of evaluation, evaluators must look to the qualities that pervade classrooms, the experience that students have in schools, and the character of the work that children produce. To see these qualities requires a perceptive eye, an ability to employ theory in order to understand what is seen and a grounded set of educational values so that an appraisal of the *educational* significance of what has been seen can be determined.

But what is equally as important as perceiving the qualities that constitute classroom life is the ability to convey these qualities to others. For this to occur the methods used must be artistically critical. The educational critic must be able to create, render, portray, and disclose in such a way that the reader will be able to empathetically participate in the events described. The language of the critic using qualitative methods capitalizes on the role of emotion in knowing. Far from the ideal of emotional neutrality so often aspired to in the social sciences, the educational critic exploits the potential of language to further human understanding. The language she or he uses is expressive, so that the kind of understanding the reader can secure is one that reaches into the deeper levels of meaning children secure from school experience. To convey such meaning, the artistic use of language is a necessity.

The import of this orientation for education is significant for several reasons. First, it has long been recognized that the procedures used to evaluate students, teachers and schools have a profound effect on the kinds of priorities that the curriculum reflects.[5] When achievement, defined in terms of standardized forms of performance within specific subject areas becomes salient, it is likely that teachers will devote attention to those areas and in the process place less emphasis or neglect entirely areas that are not defined by test performance. What is counted, counts.

For students the need to do well on the instruments that assess achievement is a necessary condition for upward mobility within the educational system. When school districts develop proficiency tests to ensure school effectiveness, a climate within schools is created that increases pressures upon teachers and students alike to do well on the measures that are used. If students are to succeed within the system, excellence defined in terms of test performance is necessary.

For teachers, the use of achievement and proficiency tests represents a clear articulation of school-district priorities. It does not mean much to express a commitment to goals that will not be used to appraise the quality of what has occurred in classrooms. Teachers, like students, know what counts: the use of standardized achievement tests provides vivid testimony. Thus, teachers who are to look effective must do so by having their students do well on the tests that are used. In the process of adaptation many professional values are often compromised. Survival is still a basic biological need.

The criteria that apply to teachers also apply to school administrators. In the United States school principals (headteachers and headmasters) as well as superintendents of local education authorities hold no tenure in their positions.[6] While these administrators cannot be easily fired from the teaching force, their ability to maintain their administrative positions (and the salaries that come with them) is dependent upon having the positive regard of the school board and the community. To have this regard the schools for which they are responsible must provide what lay people regard as quality education. When quality education is defined by test performance, how students do on tests is critically related to how well the public believe administrators are doing. Thus, the circle is completed. Those who design the methods of evaluation have a profound effect on the priorities that are held within schools. The climate, tone, emphasis and allocation of resources are all significantly influenced by the standardized and quantified rites of passage that are becoming increasingly important in the schools.

It is for these reasons that the significance of qualitative approaches to educational inquiry are so important. Schoolmen have been woefully derelict in giving the public anything other than standardized methods for appraising educational quality. There have been few alternatives to highly reductionistic indices of learning available. By developing, not so much alternatives, but complements to the conventional approaches to evaluation and research, the possibility of balance in view, in method and in "data" can be created—at least in principle.

What is it that qualitative methods of inquiry provide and can they be regarded as humanistic? What is it that such a view illuminates that more conventional methods neglect? What are the potential second-order effects that emanate from the assumptions used in qualitative forms of inquiry in education?

As I have already indicated, qualitative forms of inquiry are typically focused upon patterns of phenomenon within a more complex configuration rather than on the experimental isolation of casual variables. This means, in practice, the need to view a situation in a way that seeks meaning in the culture of the situation rather than in the manifest behaviour of individuals. To say this is to embrace a view of inquiry that regards manifest behaviour as meaningless unless it is related to a larger cultural network. The classroom provides that network. To the qualitative inquirer this means that one must try to uncover the meaning of action, moves, behaviours, and not simply the fact that behaviour has occurred.

Now the import of this orientation is critical in a period in which performance standards are sought after regardless of the means used to achieve such standards. The qualitative inquirer in education is likely to be interested in the meaning of the move perhaps even more than the move itself. Thus, he is in a position to explicate the costs as well as the benefits of certain forms of achievement. By attending to meaning rather than to behaviour as such, by relating behaviour to culture, and by paying attention to process as it develops within classrooms and schools, the qualitative inquirer is in a position to secure a much more complex view of educational situations. For many, I suppose, a more complex view might be regarded as somewhat of a liability, but the cost of simplistic conclusions about the quality of education are far greater than most lay people realize. There might not be any adequate way to describe the outcomes of schooling that can be reduced to numerical indices. It is precisely in the illumination of the complexities and richness of educational life that qualitative inquiry in education holds its greatest promise. Rather than reduce the human mind to a single score, qualitative inquirers attempt to adumbrate its complexities, its potential, and its idiosyncracies.

There are other benefits as well. The processes of educational practice—the quality of discourse, the character of explanation, the relationships among students and teachers, the intellectual vitality of discussion—are seldom addressed in conventional modes of evaluation. For the most part conventional evaluation practices address themselves to outcomes rather than to processes. And even when methods are used that focus on, say teaching, the data provided is almost always a very slender slice of the reality that it is supposed to represent. For example, data provided by a Flanders Interaction Analysis or a Bellack-type analysis of classroom discourse is inadequate for mentally reconstructing the events from which those data were secured. The richness and diversity of the classroom that the data represent is virtually impossible to imagine, hence the conclusions derived from such data are in a significant sense acontextual.

When it comes to the products of achievement testing, the information provided is even less satisfactory. The measured outcomes that achievement tests provide say nothing about the antecedents of those outcomes; perhaps that is why classroom teachers find them so unhelpful. Knowing the outcome of the game, so to speak, tells you nothing about how it is played, whether the problem—if there is a problem—is with the pitching, the hitting, the fielding; the lack of an adequate goalie, swift wings, effective strikers, or a smart midfielder. What we have in achievement test data are consequences, and only a small portion of them at that.

Yet it is these outcomes that the public seeks to know more about. And the risk, of course, in acceding to their wishes is one of using whatever means necessary to provide the public with what will make it content. In the process children may be sacrificed educationally for the seductive comforts of high test scores.

Because qualitative methods of evaluation pay special attention to the processes of schooling they have the potential to provide the illumination and insight that will help lay people and educators alike secure a more adequate understanding of what goes on in schools. At present this understanding is minimal. The conventional methods of evaluation, as I have already indicated, have focused on outcomes, not processes. Research in education of an experimental variety has minimized extended contact with classrooms; classrooms are conceptually messy, difficult (even impossible) to control, and confound effects so that the identification of causes is formidable.[7] In the pursuit of precision and generalizability the major subject matters of educational practice have too often fallen by the wayside.

There is another potential value in qualitative forms of inquiry that deserves special mention. That value is in their potential to enable readers to empathetically participate in the events that the writing describes. To be able to use written material this way, the material itself has to be created as an art form. To create such writing requires a willingness and an ability to pay attention to the form of expression, to the use of metaphor, to the tempo and character of language. One must exploit the potential of language as an artistic medium, not merely as a descriptive one. One seeks, at least in part, the creation of an expressive analogue to the qualities of life perceived and appraised within schools and classrooms. The form must speak in a way that is at base non-discursive.[8]

Although this might sound strange to educationalists reared on a strict diet of social science, the means I have described participate in a tradition considerably older than the oldest of the social sciences. I speak here of literature, of history, of poetry, and drama. Is fiction less true than fact? Where precisely is the line between a false fact and a truthful fiction? I play here—but only partly—for educators have much to learn from the traditions of inquiry that too seldom have entered schools and departments of education. The humanities have much to provide, both theoretical and practical, that can help us understand what goes on in the minds and hearts of men and women. It is our professional socialization that keeps us from this tradition; the tinge of embarrassment about the use of metaphor, allusion, expressive language. Yet I believe that this neglected tradition has the potential to provide the depth that knowing perception must have. Monocular vision is shallow.

What then can we say about the potential contributions of humanistic, or as I have preferred to call them, qualitative forms of inquiry in education? Their contributions to education are several. I will cite them here.

First, qualitative forms of inquiry in education hold promise for providing a more complex and complete picture of educational practice and its consequences. By illuminating patterns and by portraying relationships that go unnoticed in conventional approaches to evaluation a more complex image of classroom life is secured. Such an image can serve as an antidote to highly simplistic indices of classroom interaction and educational achievement. When educational policy is based on the information such indices provide it is likely to neglect what is important, be wrong-headed and have a tendency to embrace Utopian bandwagons to solve educational problems that require serious and sustained deliberation.

Second, qualitative forms of inquiry have the potential to expand our conception of the way in which we come to know. Because qualitative forms of inquiry utilize modes of conception and disclosure that exploit the expressive powers of language, they have the potential to help individuals secure a feel for the reality they are trying to understand. To be able to put yourself in the place of another is crucial for understanding how others feel. This requires both an act of imagination and a form that can engender the appropriate feeling. To the extent to which qualitative forms of inquiry create such forms, to that extent they make it possible to vicariously participate in events of situations in which one was not actually present. Through such vicarious participation we come to understand through the life of feeling what straightforward prose cannot convey.

This contribution to human understanding through the creation of expressive form also has the potential for expanding our view of the variety of content areas or disciplines to which students could be exposed. If non-discursive forms of understanding are regarded as third-rate types of knowledge, schools are likely to continue to give them a marginal place in the curriculum. But if the value of non-discursive forms of understanding are recognized, the possibility that more attention will be given to them is increased. This is not to say that understanding will secure their position, it is only to say that the appreciation of their value provides a firmer grounding for deciding what is taught than does ignorance.

Third, because qualitative forms of inquiry tend to focus on processes that animate classroom life, the possibility of locating the antecedents to educational success and failure are more likely. At present teachers have little opportunity to secure feedback on what they do in classrooms. Achievement testing, whether standardized or not, is a form of summative evaluation. Why what happened did happen is something achievement test scores fail to describe. This lack of information makes it virtually impossible for teachers to use test results to intelligently alter or sustain what they are doing. Furthermore, there has been an overwhelming tendency in conventional forms of educational research to enter classrooms for the briefest periods of time, to collect the data and to leave. Such visits are the equivalent of educational commando raids.

One can only wonder what the researcher has seen, how representative the experiment was with respect to the usual conditions of classroom life, and what kinds of feedback the researcher is able to provide to the teacher. Because qualitative forms of evaluation are largely process-oriented the possibility of being helpful to teachers and others concerned with the quality of those processes is increased.

Fourth, one of the most significant potential contributions of qualitative forms of inquiry is something that it least aims to achieve. Through the development of a complementary set of assumptions and methods to those that are used in scientific approaches to educational inquiry in general and educational evaluation in particular, those using conventional methods and assumptions are more likely to appreciate their particular strengths and limitations. Without a lusty complement, the unique characteristics of method are often overlooked since no alternative frame of reference is available with which to compare. As Goethe said, "A person who knows only one language does not know his own." The monopoly of social-science methodology in educational inquiry has been a conceptual liability, not only to those seeking other ways, but for those using such methods themselves. Qualitative methods and artistic or humanistic assumptions complement quantitative and scientific ones to the benefit of both.

Finally, the fifth potential contribution of qualitative inquiry in education is the intellectual equity it provides to those whose aptitudes reside in qualitative and artistic forms of expression in contrast to quantitative or scientific ones. For many individuals, particularly graduate students, there have been few options aside from the social sciences that have been legitimate to use to pursue educational problems in scholarly ways. The advent and growing legitimation of qualitative methods is providing the intellectual permission for them to use aptitudes that play to their strengths rather than feel compelled to do work for which they have little aptitude or interest. In the process surely higher quality work in education will result.

To be sure, qualitative forms of inquiry offer no panaceas for educational problems. Their methods are demanding, the time it takes to use them exceptionally long, the questions of generalizability difficult, and the verification of their conclusions complex. Yet, because they do provide another view, because they do provide another peak upon which to stand, they promise a great deal. In the last analysis their utilities still need demonstration, but what we have is the advent of a tradition long absent in educational discourse and not merely a refinement of the existing conversation. Given the resistance of our problems to our usual methods and assumptions, this newcomer to education should be given a warm welcome.

References and Notes

1. At the end of 1976 seven States enacted legislation dealing with required competencies.

2. *The Calgary Herald* (4 October 1977).

3. The project I speak of is the Assessment of Performance Unit under the direction of the Department of Education and Science.

4. It should be noted that in a deep sense, method always has some influence on the character of problem formation since problems cannot be formed outside of some method. It is the extreme sense of using only method to define problems that is intended by these remarks.

5. The use of Scholastic Aptitude Tests are a prime example of the influence testing has upon school priorities. When scores on such tests decline—even though they claim to assess aptitude rather than achievement—schools are regarded as failing and are urged to emphasize

areas of performance that will increase scholastic aptitude scores. Indeed, some secondary schools offer courses specifically designed to help students achieve high scores on such tests.

6. It should be noted that although the vast majority of school administrators hold no tenure as administrators, in some school districts they do.

7. The tendency to minimize contact with classrooms in experimental research is reflected in the fact that in 1974–76 the modal amount of treatment time per subject in experimental studies reported in the American Educational Research Journal was about 45 minutes.

8. For a discussion of the application of non-discursive modes of learning and expression see Elliot W. Eisner, On the use of educational connoisseurship and criticism for evaluating classroom life, *Teachers College Record*, Vol. 78, No. 7 (February 1977), The forms and functions of educational connoisseurship and educational criticism, *Journal of Aesthetic Education*, Bicentennial Issue (1976), and *The Educational Imagination: On the Design and Evaluation of School Programs*, Third Edition New York, Macmillan (1994).

16

Implementation as Mutual Adaptation: Change in Classroom Organization

Milbrey Wallin McLaughlin

Most observers believe that the educational innovations undertaken as part of the curriculum reform movement of the 1950s and early 1960s, as well as the innovations that comprised the initiatives of the "Education Decade," generally have failed to meet their objectives.[1] One explanation for these disappointments focuses on the *type* of innovations undertaken and points out that until recently few educators have elected to initiate innovations that require change in the traditional roles, behavior, and structures that exist within the school organization or the classroom. Instead, most innovative efforts have focused primarily on *technological* change, not *organizational* change. Many argue that without changes in the structure of the institutional setting, or the culture of the school, new practices are simply "more of the same" and are unlikely to lead to much significant change in what happens to students.

Since 1970, however, a number of educators have begun to express interest in practices that redefine the assumptions about children and learning that underlie traditional methods—new classroom practices that attempt to change the ways that students, teachers, parents, and administrators relate to each other. Encouraged and stimulated by the work of such writers as Joseph Featherstone, Charles Silberman, and William Glasser, some local schoolmen have undertaken innovations in classroom organization such as open education, multiage grouping, integrated day, differentiated staffing, and team teaching. These practices are not based on a "model" of classroom organization change to be strictly followed, but on a common set of convictions about the nature of learning and the purpose of teaching. These philosophical similarities, which can be traced to the work of the Swiss psychologist Piaget, are based on a belief that humanistic, individualized, and child-centered education requires more than incremental or marginal change in classroom organization, educational technology, or teacher behavior.

Because classroom organization projects require teachers to work out their own styles and classroom techniques within a broad philosophical framework, innovations of this type cannot be specified or packaged in advance. Thus, the very nature of these projects requires that implementation be a *mutually adaptive process* between the user and the institutional setting—that specific project goals and methods be made concrete over time by the participants themselves.

Classroom organization projects were among the local innovations examined as

*From *Teachers College Record*, Vol. 77, No. 3, 1976: pp. 339–351. Reprinted by permission.

part of Rand's Change-Agent Study.[2] Of the 293 projects surveyed, eighty-five could be classified as classroom organization projects; five of our thirty field sites were undertaking innovation of this nature. The findings of the change-agent study suggest that the experience of these projects should be examined in some detail. At the most general level, the change study concluded that implementation—rather than educational treatment, level of resources, or type of federal funding strategy—dominates the innovative process and its outcomes. The study found that the mere adoption of a "better" practice did not automatically or invariably lead to "better" student outcomes. Initially similar technologies undergo unique alterations during the process of implementation and thus their outcomes cannot be predicted on the basis of treatment alone. Further, the process of implementation that is inherent in classroom organization projects was found to describe effective implementation generally. Specifically, the change-agent study concluded that *successful implementation is characterized by a process of mutual adaptation.*

Contrary to the assumptions underlying many change strategies and federal change policies, we found that implementation did not merely involve the direct and straightforward application of an educational technology or plan. Implementation was a dynamic organizational process that was shaped over time by interactions between project goals and methods, and the institutional setting. As such, it was neither automatic nor certain. Three different interactions characterized this highly variable process.

One, *mutual adaptation*, described successfully implemented projects. It involved modification of both the project design and changes in the institutional setting and individual participants during the course of implementation.

A second implementation process, *cooptation*, signified adaptation of the project design, but no change on the part of participants or the institutional setting. When implementation of this nature occurred, project strategies were simply modified to conform in a pro forma fashion to the traditional practices the innovation was expected to replace—either because of resistance to change or inadequate help for implementers.

The third implementation process, *nonimplementation*, described the experience of projects that either broke down during the course of implementation or were simply ignored by project participants.

Where implementation was successful, and where significant change in participant attitudes, skills and behavior occurred, implementation was characterized by a process of mutual adaptation in which project goals and methods were modified to suit the needs and interests of participants and in which participants changed to meet the requirements of the project. This finding was true even for highly technological and initially well specified projects: unless adaptations were made in the original plans or technologies, implementation tended to be superficial or symbolic and significant change in participants did not occur.

Classroom organization projects provided particularly clear illustration of the conditions and strategies that support mutual adaptation and thus successful implementation. They are especially relevant to understanding the operational implications of this change-agent study finding for policy and practice not only because mutual adaptation is intrinsic to change in classroom organization, but also because the question of institutional receptivity does not cloud the view of effective implementation strategies afforded by these projects.

The receptivity of the institutional setting to a proposed innovation varied greatly among the projects we examined—from active support to indifference to hostility.

The amount of interest, commitment, and support evidenced by principal actors had a major influence on the prospects for successful project implementation. In particular, the attitudes and interest of central administrators in effect provided a "signal" to project participants as to how seriously they should take project goals and how hard they should work to achieve them. Unless participants perceived that change–agent projects represented a school and district educational priority, teachers were often unwilling to put in the extra time and emotional investment necessary for successful implementation. Similarly, the attitudes of teachers were critical. Unless teachers were motivated by professional concerns (as opposed to more tangible incentives such as extra pay or credit on the district salary scale, for example), they did not expend the extra time and energy requisite to the usually painful process of implementing an innovation.

Classroom organization projects were almost always characterized by high levels of commitment and support for their initiation, both at the district and at the building level. This is not surprising when we consider the risk and difficulty associated with these projects; it is unlikely that a district would elect to undertake a project of this nature unless they believed strongly in the educational approach and were committed to attempting the changes necessary to implement it.

In fact, classroom organization projects possess none of the features traditionally thought to encourage local decision makers to adopt a given innovation:

1. Ease of explanation and communication to others.
2. Possibility of a trial on a partial or limited basis.
3. Ease of use.
4. Congruence with existing values.
5. Obvious superiority over practices that existed previously.[3]

Innovations that focus on classroom organization are at odds with all five of these criteria. First, since there is no specific "model" to be followed, it is difficult to tell people how these approaches operate. Advocates can only offer general advice and communicate the philosophy or attitudes that underlie innovation in classroom organization and activities.

Second, although open classroom or team-teaching strategies can be implemented slowly, and can be installed in just one or two classrooms in a school, it is generally not possible to be "just a little bit" open or just a "sometime" part of a team-teaching situation. The method is based on fundamental changes which are hard to accomplish piecemeal.

Third, change in classroom organization is inherently very complex. Innovations of this nature require the learning of new attitudes, roles and behavior on the part of teachers and administrators—changes far more difficult to bring about than the learning of a new skill or gaining familiarity with a new educational technology. Classroom organization changes also typically require new arrangements of classroom space, the provision of new instructional materials, and usually new school scheduling and reporting practices.

Fourth, strategies of open education or team teaching are a radical departure from the traditional or standard practices of a school, district, or teacher. Change in classroom organization means changing deeply held attitudes and customary behavior. These projects, by attempting to change organizational structure and goals, attempt to affect the fundamental nature of the organization and are therefore basically incongruent with existing values.

Fifth, although proponents argue that humanistic, child–centered education represents a big advance, the objective evidence is ambiguous. Most evaluations of informal classrooms conclude that participating children do better on affective measures, but there is little evidence of significant cognitive differences that could confidently be attributed to open classrooms themselves. An administrator contemplating a change in classroom organization is confronted with a complicated innovation that shows no clear advantage over existing practices—at least in the ways that often matter most to school boards, voters, and anxious parents.

Thus, given the complex, unspecified, and inherently difficult nature of these projects, they were rarely initiated without the active support and commitment of district officials and participants. Consequently, the insufficient institutional support that negatively influenced implementation in other projects and so made it difficult to obtain a clear picture of the strategic factors affecting project implementation (i.e., did disappointing implementation result from a lack of enthusiasm or from inadequate training?) generally was not a problem for classroom organization projects. Variance in the implementation outcome of classroom organization projects, consequently, can be attributed in large measure to the project's particular implementation strategy.

For classroom organization projects, as for other change-agent projects, *institutional receptivity was a necessary but not a sufficient condition for successful implementation.* Unless project implementation strategies were chosen that allowed institutional support to be engaged and mutual adaptation to occur, project implementation foundered. A project's particular implementation strategy is the result of many local choices about how best to implement project goals and methods. What seems to be the most effective thing to do? What is possible given project constraints? What process fits best with local needs and conditions? Decisions about the type and amount of training, the planning necessary, and project participants are examples of such choices. They effectively define how a proposed innovation is put into practice. Implementation strategies are distinguishable from project treatment. That is, the educational method chosen for a project (i.e., team teaching, diagnostic/prescriptive reading) is different from the strategies selected for implementing the method. No two reading projects, for example, employ quite the same process or strategy for achieving their almost identical goals.

Implementation Strategy

Each project employs its own combination of strategies that effectively defines its *implementation strategy*. Thus, in addition to identifying especially effective component strategies, it is meaningful to examine how and why the various individual strategies interact with each other to form a "successful" implementation strategy and to promote mutual adaptation. The experience of classroom organization projects suggests at least three specific strategies that are particularly critical and that work together to form an adaptive implementation strategy: local materials development; ongoing and concrete staff training; iterative, on-line planning combined with regular and frequent staff meetings.

Local Material Development

In almost all of the classroom organization projects, the staff spent a substantial amount of time developing materials to use in the project classrooms. These materials either were developed from scratch or put together from bits of commercially-developed materials. Although these activities were sometimes undertaken because the staff felt they couldn't locate appropriate commercial materials, the real contribution lay not so much in "better pedagogical products" but in providing the staff with a sense of involvement and an opportunity to "learn-by-doing." Working together to develop materials for the project gave the staff a sense of pride in its own accomplishments, a sense of "ownership" in the project. It also broke down the traditional isolation of the classroom teacher and provided a sense of "professionalism" and cooperation not usually available in the school setting. But even more important, materials development provided an opportunity for users to think through the concepts which underlay the project, in practical, operational terms—an opportunity to engage in experience-based learning. Although such "reinvention of the wheel" may not appear efficient in the short run, it appears to be a critical part of the individual learning and development necessary for significant change.

Staff Training

All the classroom organization projects we visited included both formal and informal, preservice and inservice staff training. For example, one project's formal training took place in a two week summer session before the project began, its informal development activities had been extensive, providing for almost constant interaction among project staff. Almost all of these projects provided preservice training that included observations in operating classrooms. One open classroom project staff even participated in a trip to observe British infant schools. All projects also conducted regular workshops throughout the first three years of project implementation.

One-shot training, or training heavily concentrated at the beginning of the project, was not effective. Although such training designs have the virtues of efficiency and lower cost, they ignore the critical fact that project implementors cannot know what it is they need to know until project operations are well underway. This is generally true for all innovative efforts, but particularly salient in the case of amorphous classroom organization projects. There is just so much that a would-be implementor can be taught or can understand until problems have arisen in the course of project implementation, and solutions must be devised. Training programs that attempt to be comprehensive and cover all contingencies at the outset are bound to miss their mark and also to be less than meaningful to project participants.

Project staffs agreed that staff development and training activities were a critical part of successful implementation. They also agreed that some kinds of training activities were more useful than others. With few exceptions, visits by outside consultants and other outside "experts" were not considered particularly helpful. Teachers in all the change-agent projects we examined complained that most visiting consultants could not relate to the particular problems they were experiencing in their classrooms, or that their advice was too abstract to be helpful. Where outside experts were considered useful, their participation was concrete and involved working closely with project teachers in their classrooms or in "hands-on" workshops. However, it was unusual for outside consultants to have either the time or the inclination to provide assistance in other than a lecture format. Such expert delivery of "truth and knowledge," however, was seldom meaningful to participants, and foreclosed more powerful learning opportunities.

The sessions participants thought most useful were regular meetings of the project staff with local resource personnel in which ideas were shared, problems discussed, and support given. Materials development often provided the focus for these concrete, how-to-do-it training sessions. Visits to other schools implementing similar projects were also considered helpful; the teachers felt that seeing a similar program in operation for just a few hours was worth much more than several days of consultants delivering talks on philosophy.

Some commentators on the outcomes of planned change contend that where innovations fail, particularly innovations in classroom organization, they fail because their planners overlooked the "resocialization" of teachers. Even willing teachers have to go through such a *learning (and unlearning) process* in order to develop new attitudes, behaviors, and skills for a radically new role. Concrete, inquiry-based training activities scheduled regularly over the course of project implementation provide a means for this developmental process to occur.

Adaptive Planning and Staff Meetings

Because of their lack of prior specification, almost all classroom organization projects engaged in adaptive or on-line planning. Planning of this nature is a continuous process that establishes channels of communication and solicits input from a representative group of project participants. It provides a forum for reassessing project goals and activities, monitoring project activities, and modifying practices in light of institutional and project demands. Planning of this nature has a firm base in project and institutional reality; thus issues can be identified and solutions determined before problems become crises. Just as one-shot training activities can neither anticipate the information needs of implementors over time nor be comprehensible to trainees in the absence of direct experience with particular problems, neither can highly structured planning activities that attempt extensive prior specification of operational procedures and objectives effectively address all contingencies in advance or foresee intervening local conditions. Often problems arise and events occur during the course of implementation that are unexpected and unpredictable. As a result, project plans drawn up at one point in time may or may not be relevant to project operations at a later date. Planning activities that are on-going, adaptive, and congruent with the nature of the project and the changing institutional setting are better able to respond to these factors.

Frequent and regular staff meetings were often used as a way to carry out project planning on a continuous basis. Projects that made a point of scheduling staff meetings on a frequent and regular basis had fewer serious implementation problems and greater staff cohesiveness. Staff meetings not only provided a vehicle for articulating and working out problems, but they also gave staff a chance to communicate project information, share ideas, and provide each other with encouragement and support.

Finding time for these meetings or planning activities was a problem that some districts were able to solve and others were not. One classroom organization project, for example, arranged time off one afternoon a week for meetings. Project participants almost universally singled out these meetings as one of the most important factors contributing to project success. Such time to share ideas and problems was, in the view of all classroom organization respondents, especially important in the rough and exhausting first year of the project. Where meetings were infrequent or irregular, morale was noticeably lower and reports of friction within the project were higher.

Past research on implementation is almost unanimous in citing "unanticipated events" and "lack of feedback networks" as serious problems during project implementation.[4] Routinized and frequent staff meetings combined with on-going, iterative planning can serve to institutionalize an effective project feedback structure, as well as provide mechanisms that can deal with the unanticipated events that are certain to occur.

TWO OPEN CLASSROOM PROJECTS[5]

The critical role that such elements of an adaptive implementation strategy play in project implementation and outcomes is best illustrated by describing the experiences of two open classroom projects that were similar in almost every respect—resources, support and interest, target group background characteristics—but differed significantly in implementation strategy and in implementation outcome. The Eastown open education project had extensive and ongoing staff training, spent a lot of staff time and energy on materials development, arranged for staff to meet regularly, and engaged in regular formative evaluation. This project was also well implemented, ran smoothly, and met its objectives. In fact, this project received validation as a national exemplary project in its second year—a year before it was theoretically eligible.

The very similar Seaside project, in contrast, did not employ such an implementation strategy. Because of late funding notification, there was little time for advance planning or preservice training; project teachers were asked to implement a concept that they supported but that few had actually seen in operation. The planning that was done subsequently was mainly administrative in nature. The inservice training was spotty and was offered almost totally by "outside experts." The Seaside project did no materials development but instead tried to convert traditional materials to the goals of open education. This project has not only been less successful than hoped, but in our judgment, its central percepts and objectives are yet to be fully implemented. Teacher classroom behavior exhibits only a very superficial understanding of the rhetoric of open education; our observations led to the conclusion that teachers have yet to understand the practical implications of the tenets of open education, and have made only symbolic use of the more standard methods. For example, in many of the classrooms we visited, although the teacher had set up interest centers, these centers had not been changed in six or seven months. Thus they failed to serve their purpose of providing a continually changing menu of material for students. Teachers in the Seaside project had dutifully rearranged their classroom furniture and acquired rugs—as befits the open classroom—but even in this changed physical space, they continued to conduct their classes in a traditional manner. A student teacher commented that many of the teachers in this school conducted their class in the small groups or individualized manner appropriate to this educational philosophy only on visitors' day. In our judgment, many of the teachers in the school honestly wanted to implement open education, and many sincerely believed that they had accomplished that goal. But, in our view, implementation in this project was only *pro forma*—largely because of the absence of implementation strategies that would allow learning, growth, and development or mutual adaptation to take place.

SUMMARY

In summary, overcoming the challenges and problems inherent to innovations in classroom organization contributes positively and significantly to their effective implementation. The amorphous yet highly complex nature of classroom organization projects tends to *require* or *dictate* an adaptive implementation strategy that permits goals and methods to be reassessed, refined and made explicit during the course of implementation, and that fosters "learning-by-doing."

The adaptive implementation strategies defined by effectively implemented local projects were comprised of three common and critical components—local materials development; concrete, on-going training; on-line or adaptive planning and regular, frequent staff meetings. These elements worked together in concert to promote effective implementation. Where any one component was missing or weak, other elements of the overall implementation strategy were less effective than they might be. A most important characteristic these component strategies hold in common is their support of individual learning and development—development most appropriate to the user and to the institutional setting. The experience of classroom organization projects underlines the fact that the process of mutual adaptation is fundamentally a learning process.

General Implications

It is useful to consider the implications of the classroom organization projects and the general change-agent study findings in the context of the on-going debate about the "implementation problem."

The change-agent study is not the first research to point to the primary importance of implementation in determining special project outcomes.[6] A number of researchers and theoreticians have come to recognize what many practitioners have been saying all along: Educational technology is not self-winding. Adoption of a promising educational technology is only the beginning of a variable, uncertain, and inherently local process. It is the unpredictability and inconsistency of this process that have generated what has come to be called the "implementation problem."

There is general agreement that a major component of the "implementation problem" has to do with inadequate operational specificity.[7] There is debate concerning *who* should make project operations more specific, *how* it can be done, and *when* specificity should be introduced.

One approach prescribes more specificity prior to local initiation. Adherents of this solution ask that project planners and developers spell out concrete and detailed steps or procedures that they believe will lead to successful project implementation. It is hoped that increased prior operational specificity will minimize the necessity for individual users to make decisions or choices about appropriate project strategies or resources as the project is implemented. This essentially technological approach to the "implementation problem"—exemplified at the extreme by "teacher-proof" packages—aims at standardizing project implementation across project sites. It is expected that user adherence to such standardized and well-specified implementation procedures will reduce local variability as project plans are translated into practice and so lead to predictable and consistent project outcomes, regardless of the institutional setting in which the project is implemented.

A second approach takes an organizational rather than a technological perspective and focuses primarily on the development of the user, rather than on the prior development of the educational treatment or product. This approach assumes that local variability is not only inevitable, but a good thing if a proposed innovation is to result in significant and sustained change in the local setting. This approach also assumes that the individual learning requisite to successful implementation can only occur through user involvement and direct experience in working through project percepts. Instead of providing packages which foreclose the necessity for individuals to make decisions and choices during the course of project implementation, proponents of this perspective maintain that implementation strategies should be devised that give users the skills, information, and learning opportunities necessary to make these choices effectively. This approach assumes that specificity of project methods and goals should evolve over time in response to local conditions and individual needs. This second solution to the "implementation problem," in short, assumes that mutual adaptation is the key to effective implementation.

The findings of the change-agent study strongly support this second perspective and its general approach to the "implementation problem." We found that *all* successfully implemented projects in our study went through a process of mutual adaptation to some extent. Even fairly straightforward, essentially technological projects were either adapted in some way to the institutional setting—or they were only superficially implemented and were not expected to remain in place after the withdrawal of federal funds. Where attempts were made to take short cuts in this process—out of concern for efficiency, for example—such efforts to speed up project implementation usually led to project breakdown or to only *pro forma* installation of project methods.

Viewed in the context of the debate over the "implementation problem," these findings have a number of implications for change-agent policies and practice. At the most general level, they suggest that adaptation, rather than standardization, is a more realistic and fruitful objective for policy makers and practitioners hoping to bring about significant change in local educational practice. Such an objective would imply change-agent policies that focused on implementation, not simply on adoption—policies that were concerned primarily with the development of users and support of adaptive implementation strategies. Specifically, the classroom organization projects suggest answers to the strategic issues of "who, how, and when" innovative efforts should be made operationally explicit, and how user development can be promoted.

Furthermore, the classroom organization projects, as well as other innovative efforts examined as part of the change-agent study, imply that the would-be innovator also must be willing to learn and be motivated by professional concerns and interests if development is to take place. Thus, change-agent policies would be well advised not only to address the user needs that are part of the implementation process *per se*, but also to consider the developmental needs of local educational personnel that are requisite to the initial interest and support necessary for change-agent efforts. It is not surprising that teachers or administrators who have not been outside their district for a number of years are less eager to change—or confident in their abilities to do so—than planners would hope. Internships and training grants for administrators, or travel money and released time for teachers to participate in innovative practices in other districts, are examples of strategies that may enable educational personnel to expand their horizons and generate enthusiasm for change.

The findings of the change-agent study and the experience of the classroom organization projects also have implications for the dissemination and expansion of "successful" change-agent projects. They suggest, for example, that an effective dissemination strategy should have more to do with people who could provide concrete "hands-on" assistance than with the transcription and transferral of specific successful project operations. It is somewhat ironic that staff of the "developer-demonstrator" projects who last year pointed to the central importance of local materials development are, in their dissemination year, packaging their project strategies and materials without a backward glance. Indeed, the change-agent findings concerning the importance of mutual adaptation and "learning by doing" raise a number of critical questions for educational planners and disseminators. For example, to what extent can this developmental process be telescoped as project accomplishments are replicated in a new setting? What kinds of "learning" or advice can be transferred? If adaptation is characteristic of effective implementation and significant change, what constitutes the "core" or essential ingredients of a successful project?

District administrators hoping to expand successful project operations face similar issues. Our findings suggest that—even within the same district replication and expansion of "success" will require that new adopters replicate, in large measure, the developmental process of the original site. While there are, of course, general "lessons" that original participants can transfer to would-be innovators, there is much that the new user will have to learn himself.

In summary, the experience of classroom organization projects together with the general change-agent study findings suggest that adaptation should be seen as an appropriate goal for practice and policy—not an undesirable aberration. These findings suggest a shift in change-agent policies from a primary focus on the *delivery system* to an emphasis on the *deliverer*. An important lesson that can be derived from the change-agent study is that unless the developmental needs of the users are addressed, and unless project methods are modified to suit the needs of the user and the institutional setting, the promises of new technologies are likely to be unfulfilled. Although the implementation strategy that classroom organization projects suggest will be effective represent "reinvention of the wheel" to a great extent—an unpalatable prospect for program developers, fiscal planners, and impatient educational policy makers—the experience of these projects counsels us that a most important aspect of significant change is not so much the "wheel" or the educational technology but the process of "reinvention" or individual development. Though new education technologies are undoubtedly important to improved practices, they cannot be effective unless they are thoroughly understood and integrated by the user. The evidence we have seen strongly suggests that the developmental process mutual adaptation is the best way to ensure that change efforts are not superficial, trivial, or transitory.

Notes

1. This essay is a revision of a paper presented at the March 1975 American Educational Research Association meeting in Washington, D.C. It is based on the data collected for The Rand Corporation study of federal programs supporting educational change. However, the interpretation and speculations offered in this paper are my sole responsibility and do not necessarily represent the views of The Rand Corporation, or the study's sponsor, the United States Office of Education, or my colleague Paul Berman, who has been so helpful in formulating this paper.

2. The conceptual model, methodology, and results of the first year of the Rand Change-Agent Study are reported in four volumes: Paul Berman and Milbrey Wallin McLaughlin. *Federal Programs Supporting Educational Change, Vol. I: A Model of Educational Change.* Santa Monica, Calif.: Rand Corporation, R-1589/1-HEW, April 1975; Paul Berman and Edward W. Pauly, *Federal Programs Supporting Educational Change, Vol. II: Factors Affecting Change Agent Projects.* Santa Monica, Calif.: Rand Corporation, R-1589/2-HEW, April 1975, Peter W. Greenwood, Dale Mann, and Milbrey Wallin McLaughlin. *Federal Programs Supporting Educational Change, Vol. III: The Process of Change.* Santa Monica, Calif.: Rand Corporation, R-1589/3-HEW, April 1975; and Paul Berman and Milbrey Wallin McLaughlin. *Federal Programs Supporting Educational Change, Vol. IV: The Findings in Review.* Santa Monica, Calif.: Rand Corporation, R-1589/4-HEW, April 1975. Four technical appendices to Volume III describe in detail the federal program management approach, state education agency participation, and case studies for each of the programs in the study.

3. E. Rogers and F. Shoemaker. *Communications of Innovation.* New York, N.Y.: Free Press, 1962.

4. See for example, W. W. Charters et al. *Contrasts in the Process of Planning Change of the School's Institutional Organization, Program 20.* Eugene, Ore.: Center for the Advanced Study of Educational Administration, 1973; O. Carlson et al. *Change Processes in the Public Schools.* Eugene, Ore.: Center for the Advanced Study of Educational Administration, 1971; M. Fullan

and A. Pomfret. *Review of Research on Curriculum Implementation*. Toronto, Ont.: The Ontario Institute for Studies in Education, April 1975; M. Shipman. *Inside a Curriculum Project*. London, Eng.: Methuen, 1974; N.C. Gross et al. *Implementing Organizational Innovations*. New York, N.Y.: Basic Books, 1971; and L.M. Smith and P.M. Keith. *Anatomy of Educational Innovations: An Organizational Analysis of an Elementary School*. New York, N.Y.: John Wiley, 1971.

    5. Project and site names are fictitious.

    6. See especially the analysis of this debate in Fullan and Pomfret, *op. cit.* See also E.C. Hargrove. *The Missing Link: The Study of the Implementation of Social Policy*, Washington, D.C.: The Urban Institute, 1975, paper 797–1; and W. Williams, "Implementation Analysis and Assessment," Public Policy Paper No. 8, Institute of Governmental Research, University of Washington, February 1975.

    7. See Fullan and Pomfret, *op, cit.*

17

Teachers, Research, and Curriculum Development

F. M. CONNELLY AND MIRIAM BEN-PERETZ

From time to time there are calls for the schools, and especially for teachers, to become involved in doing research. "Action research," as practitioner-done research is commonly called, was popular in the 1950s and is again receiving attention.[1] The main arguments usually given for action research are that it will yield "realistic" knowledge readily applicable in the classroom, and that doing research constitutes an upgrading professional-development activity on the part of the practitioners. Neither argument is persuasive, each being based on a concept of research that is more appropriate to the social sciences than to education, and omitting the action-oriented instructional role of teachers. But while action research may be the wrong means, its proponents have a desirable end in view, which is to improve teaching practices through the education of intelligent, inquiry-oriented teachers.

Of course, not all appeals and programs for curriculum change show confidence in the teacher. During the 1960s the massive expansion of centres, laboratories, projects, and heavily funded research was based chiefly on the notion that classroom learning could be affected directly by external sources, with teachers acting as implementation conduits for research findings and curricular programs. At that time the curious phrase "teacher-proof materials" was popular, and journals published articles on whether such materials could be produced or not.[2] Now few researchers refer to such notions. Owing, probably, to the implementation-evaluation efforts of large-scale curriculum projects, it is generally recognized that teachers do not neutrally implement programs; they develop programs of study for their classrooms by adaptation, translation, and modification of given programs and research findings; they may even occasionally develop their own curricular materials.

As a result of this reawakened awareness of the teacher's function in curriculum development, more sophisticated notions are being developed of the teacher's relationship to research and proposed curriculum programs. These notions respect the influential role of teachers on programs, and encompass the combined concepts of "implementation" and "action research." For instance, McNamara (1972) writes that the objective of his article (entitled "Teachers and Students Combine Efforts in Action Research") is "to analyze and suggest some supporting roles that teachers and students can assume" in system planning within a school district (p. 242). McNamara points

Chapter 12 in Studies in *Curriculum Decision Making*, Edited by Kenneth A. Littlewood. Toronto: OISE Press, 1981. Reprinted by permission.

out that active involvement of both teachers and students might provide an answer to the recognized difficulties of implementing external innovative projects in schools. Fullan (1977), in his article "Action Research in the School: Involving Students and Teachers in Classroom Change," describes a project which is concerned with the difficulties of unlearning old roles and learning new roles in ongoing social systems. For Fullan; school change is facilitated by an understanding of role changes.[3]

The joining of action research with implementation represents an approach to school change which focuses on the implementation process. The assumption is that if enough were known about teacher involvement in curriculum implementation, research findings and program developments would have more impact in the classroom. While this approach is realistic in its recognition of the teacher's influence, and responsive to the teacher's need to feel involved and effective, it retains the same basic stance on the teacher's role that characterized the research and development efforts of the 1960s. We shall briefly describe the inadequacies of that stance, after first reaffirming the desirable end-in-view of action research. We shall then present our conception of the teacher as consumer of and participant in educational research and development. Finally, we shall describe several illustrative programs in Canada and Israel which we believe represent a defensible relationship between the teacher and research, taking account of the teacher's primary instructional role and recognizing the limitation that the instructional role sets on the teacher in the performance of other roles such as that of action researcher.

Good Intentions for Action Research by Teachers

The spirit behind most proposals for action research is captured by Schaeffer's (1967) notion of the school as a centre of inquiry. With Schaeffer and many others we believe that improvement in the quality of educational practices is dependent on an open, investigative, and exploratory attitude on the part of schools and of teachers. In our view the most persuasive proposals for school change involve this belief in the power of the inquiring teacher mind. We also believe, however, that the design of this end-in-view through action research and action-research implementation is, if not undesirable, at best impractical and contrary to the original spirit of fostering teacher autonomy.

Action Research and Knowledge Production

Popham and Baker's (1970) notion of the "teacher experimenter" fits the commonly held action-research view of the teacher as "little researcher" (a notion akin to that of students playing "little scientists" in science classes). These authors maintain that "through the careful reading of the results of research conducted by others, together with the systematic conduct of small-scale experiments in his own classroom, the teacher can become a truly polished professional" (p. 160). Such a notion tends to reduce inquiry to experimental procedures—surely not the only or even the most influential form of social science research. Other forms of research could conceivably be just as valid. Instead of setting up classroom experiments in order to control phenomena and study them scientifically, teachers could be involved in controlling *the way* they look at natural classroom phenomena. To some extent this notion was embedded in some earlier versions of action research. The Alberta Teachers' Federation work, for example, emphasized action research for professional development (Ingram and Robinson, 1963) and curriculum development (Ingram, 1959).

More important to our point is the implication that professionalism in teaching depends on an inquiring attitude (a notion with which we agree) oriented to the canons and procedures of scholarly inquiry (a notion with which we disagree). The Alberta Teachers' Federation materials exemplify a view of action research conceived as the application of scholarly forms of inquiry to teacher purposes. Schools, as Schwab (1969, 1971, 1973) so convincingly reminds us, are places of action, and teaching is their principal act. Teaching acts may be done more or less well and they may be conducted more or less thoughtfully. To think well, and presumably to teach well, depends on a reflective, investigative spirit. Following this lead we can assert what appears to be self-evident, that the realization of the reflective teacher attitude is seen in the teacher's attempts to achieve the best instructional acts, through consideration of the host of factors in the particular teaching situation. "Small-scale experiments" might, in infrequent cases, be called for in a teacher's consideration of the situation. But these can take their place in the broader deliberative context of teacher planning and decision making about acts of instruction. Such experimentation does not have as its aim the production of new knowledge. (Such may, of course, be forthcoming—as Schaeffer [1967] foresaw when he wrote that "discovering new knowledge about the instructional process is the distinctive contribution which the lower schools may provide" [p. 3].) Rather, the teacher's investigative attitude and any experimental work are decision oriented, and directed to the immediate improvement of teaching practice.

Action Research and Implementation

We have already suggested that action research done in the interests of implementation suffers from the same inadequacies as research and development efforts that are intended to by-pass teacher influence and directly affect students. At first, action-research-implementation strategies may appear to be courteous and respectful of teachers and ideologically on the right side of school change, recognizing as they do the influence of teachers over the actual uses of research and program materials. Closer inspection suggests that such programs depend upon an unnecessarily restricted view of teacher inquiry. They expect teachers to limit their investigation to strategies of adopting an idea, but not to an investigation of the relative merits of the idea itself. If idea x is to be implemented, teachers are to be converted, however humanely, to a belief in x and a deeper understanding of x. Believing in x and knowing what is intended by x they will, according to action-research-implementation strategy, teach x in a less modified, purer, and therefore more effective form. The principal flaw in this approach is the notion that teachers play merely supporting roles in the educative process and are unable to act as critics of ideas. With such a notion it makes sense to be offended when teachers do not implement as prescribed, and it makes sense to construct sophisticated, humane methods to modify their role behavior in the direction of minimizing their influence as adapters of the "good" new educational strategies.

But when the teacher's role as a thinking, deliberative, action-oriented agent is adopted, the picture changes. In such a view the teacher assumes a position of autonomy over instructional acts. In an earlier article Connelly (1972) has argued that researcher-developers and teachers are best seen as supporting each other in curriculum development by virtue of their *different,* but obviously related, roles. The relationship, which decisively shifts the teacher's role from implementer to decision maker and independent developer, is described as follows:

> The strength and major contribution of a developer are that he works with and can translate involved ideas into a form useful for teachers and students. However, the developer cannot imagine, let alone account for, the full range of teaching sit-

uations that arise. It is here that the teacher's experience and wisdom enter into curriculum planning in a way that cannot adequately be replaced. The characteristics and needs of the actual classroom situation are the first and final factors determining what should be done in that classroom. The teacher is inescapably the arbitrator between the demands of curriculum materials and of the instructional situation. Only rarely will arbitration lead to a settlement exclusively favoring the developer's intentions. [Connelly, 1972, p. 164]

Consistent with this notion of an effective teacher is the concept of "curriculum potential" (Ben-Peretz, 1975). For Ben-Peretz the potential of any given set of curriculum materials encompasses developer interpretations as well as possible uses that might be revealed by external analysts or implementers. She writes that

curricular materials are more complex and richer in educational possibilities than any list of goals or objectives, whether general or specific, and contain more than an expression of the intentions of the writers. If we look upon materials as the end product of a creative process, then any single interpretation yields only a partial picture of the whole. [p. 153]

The analysis of curriculum potential for a particular classroom situation offers wide scope for the teacher's exercise of a reflective investigative spirit. Teachers try out various ways of using curricular materials in concrete classroom situations and examine the validity of their curricular decisions. Thus the focus of teacher-conducted research becomes one of inquiry into characteristics of classroom situations and materials, generation of alternatives for action, and, to use a term of Stake's (1975), "responsive evaluation" of outcomes.

Still another promising approach is found in Berman and McLaughlin's (1979) and Fullan's (1979) notion of "mutual adaptation." In our opinion mutual adaptation is a notion which tends to shift problem-solving methods, which currently are aimed at implementation, towards methods which stress teacher independence, and therefore, downplay implementation.

By way of summary, the kinds of interaction between teachers and curricula (or research results) which emerge from our analysis are presented diagrammatically in Figure 1. Teachers may be treated as mere transmitters of curricular ideas through "teacher proof" materials (Fig. 1, A); as active implementers aided by action research and role-changing strategies (Fig. 1, B); and as partners in development through the treatment of materials as exhibiting potential for different uses (Fig. 1, C).

The Teacher as Curriculum User and Participant

Our criticisms of action research do not imply an anti-intellectual attitude toward teachers. On the contrary, we firmly believe that research findings should be among the resources used by teachers in their decision making, and we believe that teachers should have access to the very best curriculum materials. However, the notion of applying and implementing research findings and packaged curriculum programs is probably as deeply ingrained in teachers as it is in researchers, with the effect that teachers find it difficult to function autonomously with respect to research and curriculum programs. Instead, as Fox (1972) observed in his Israeli curriculum planning groups, teachers tend to defer to researchers. Furthermore, as our studies at OISE in teacher deliberation have shown, teachers find it difficult to evaluate and to be critical of research positions (Hayes, 1974). They are not, of course, at fault in these responses; nothing in their education has prepared them for making the required judgments for their particular situations. Yet there can be little doubt that teachers are willing to par-

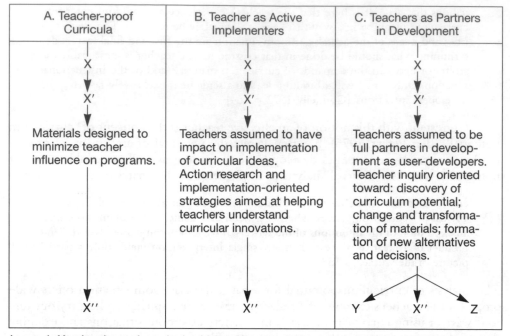

Legend: X—developers' curricular ideas; X'—translation of ideas into curricular materials; X''—implementation versions of curricular ideas in classroom; Y, Z—alternative versions of curricular ideas in classroom

Figure 1. Possible interactions between teachers, curricula, and research results. (Adapted from Connelly and Ben-Peretz, 1980, p. 106)

ticipate in decisions about research and development. Indeed, a recent report to the National Institute of Education (Schaffarzick, 1976) indicates that "the overriding interest is in having a piece of the action at all levels of decision-making." But if action research and implementation as commonly understood are not the answer, what is?

In what follows we describe several kinds of programs which we believe can contribute to and enhance teacher decision making without the pitfalls associated with action research and implementation strategies. The programs reflect to a greater or lesser degree three characteristics: teachers and scholars cooperate in a problem-solving situation; this cooperation implies a role for teachers as judges of the requirements of the situation and also as partners in the generation of ideas and proposals for solutions; and, in their decision making role, teachers adopt an investigative and inquiring stance. Six programs illustrating these characteristics are presented. They are divided into three types, reflecting different degrees of cooperation between scholars and teachers: the teacher as user of research; the teacher as participant in research; the teacher as active partner in curriculum development that includes jointly planned research and graduate studies programs.

The Teacher as User of Research

Graduate Programs for Practitioners   In most places in North America teachers have ready access to and use inservice graduate studies programs. There are, for example, seven Ontario universities offering M. Ed. programs. The largest of these programs is that offered by the Curriculum Department of the Ontario Institute for

Studies in Education (OISE); the program has about 700 students enrolled, of whom about 90% are teachers.

While one of the purposes of the OISE program is to update teachers' knowledge of research, perhaps the most important goal is to educate teachers in the uses and limitations of research for curricular ends. The introductory course to the M. Ed. program lists its "assumptions" as follows:

1. The course is aimed at practitioners and not at researchers. It deals with research as it bears on curriculum practice.
2. Practitioners, in particular teachers, are intelligent critics of curricular pleas and prescriptions. That is, people who live by decisions ought to make the choices that lead to the decisions.
3. Local people, in particular teachers, are the proper problem solvers of local curriculum problems.

These assumptions are followed by three course goals aimed at putting the teacher, and not the researcher or scholar, in the primary decision-making role concerning what happens in specific classrooms. The "goals" read as follows:

1. To develop a skill in the reading and recovery of meaning from curriculum literature.
2. To develop critical skills in assessing and using curriculum research for schools.
3. To develop skill in curriculum problem solving.[4]

These assumptions and goals are orchestrated in different ways throughout the remainder of the student's eight-course program with the anticipated result that teacher graduates will be intelligent and autonomous consumers (not implementers) of educational research and theory for curricular ends.

The Teacher as Participant in Research

Problem-initiation Practicum   A rich problem-initiation experience is the graduate studies practicum in which problems are brought to the practicum by interested practicing teachers. Faculty and full-time students then work with the practicing teachers on the problem defined by them. In this way practicing teachers control the problem and the direction of its resolution at the same time that they have ready access to scholarly advice and knowledge. For example, the OISE practicum has tended to deal with curriculum development problems. One recent practicum team worked with a geography curriculum committee "on site" some sixty miles from Toronto, over the course of a full year. During the process all parties gained insights into the difficulties, limitations, and possibilities involved in making use of research in a curriculum-development setting. The practicing teachers learned something of the uses of research and of the resolution of curricular problems, and the full-time thesis students learned something of the sensitive, deliberative character of the curriculum scholar" consulting role.

Research degrees   On a small scale, the Ed. D. degree for practitioners constitutes an excellent research experience. At OISE, the degree is designed for practitioners who leave the school system for one year, develop a proposal with an academic adviser while in attendance, and conduct their thesis research after returning to the school system. Brochures on the program emphasize the scholarly equivalence with the Ph.D. degree, and stress that the research problem selected is to tie in with the student's ongoing professional work. In short, the program amounts to an idealized action-research activity in which the practitioner is freed of normal duties for a period of time. The practitioners' work is jointly planned with researchers, and is designed so that research results will be useful in their future professional work as decision makers in the educational system.

Haifa University has a somewhat similar program at the M.A. degree level, where teachers carry out school-based graduate research work. For example, an experienced math teacher carried out an investigation of implementation of new math programs in elementary schools and the process of decision making used by teachers. Another study was carried out by a kindergarten supervisor who used a case-study analysis method focusing on the limiting factors that act as barriers to autonomous teacher curriculum development. This type of teacher involvement in inquiry through graduate work serves to acquaint teachers with theoretical frameworks and research methodologies, thus liberating them from too great a reliance on and submission to the authority of "outside experts." Research focusing on the problems of decision making by teachers may bring new insights about the functioning of teachers as decision makers.

Teachers as Active Partners in Curriculum Development

Joint Planning   Currently, there appear to be forces for and against joint university–school planning in research and development. The Campbell (1975) report to the National Institute of Education, for example, calls for less visibility and more autonomy for researchers and developers (McLean and Brison, 1976). On the other hand, our understanding of school reform since the 1950s indicates that there is strong support for the joint-planning orientation proposed in this chapter.

By way of illustration, it is instructive to consider the OISE field centres. In 1969 OISE decentralized part of its research and development and field development operation and established field centres throughout the province. While centres have their own individual characteristics, they are all involved in collaborative planning with local boards. Leithwood's (1976) account of the Trent Valley Field Centre's mathematics project in collaboration with the Peterborough County Board of Education is illustrative. An interesting feature of the project is that the curriculum problem was formulated by the local school board, prior to the involvement of the field centre in an advisory/working role. Thus the overall problem and character of the study was set by the board, and was aimed at improving board priorities. The Centre, whose staff had implementation and evaluation expertise, saw the board's problem as an opportunity to pursue its own and the board's interests. Each partner in the joint project drew upon its special expertise in the service of the common goal—the development and implementation of an innovative "new math" program—while at the same time pursuing some differing interests. The board wanted to improve the quality of decision making in mathematics education, which it did through a set of products and through personnel involvement in the research and development effort; and the researchers' goal of knowledge production in the area of school change was achieved, as evidenced in Leithwood's (1976) article.

Curriculum Development by Teachers   An effective way of involving teachers in research and development processes is by obtaining their active participation in curriculum development projects. (This is different from obtaining feedback from them in the formative stages of curriculum construction, or using them as participating members in a team of external developers.) Development teams can be set up, staffed by teachers whose responsibility is the planning and construction of a curriculum package, from its initial stage up to the final stage of a commercial product. Subject-matter and other specialists serve as consultants to the team.

Such a project was set up at Haifa University as part of the "Man in Nature" curriculum project.[5] The main feature of interest in this project is the focus on teachers as development agents, since curricular programs usually emphasize subject matter, the needs of learners, or society's demands, and tend only as an implementation afterthought to turn to the consideration of teachers. In the Haifa curriculum project carried out by teachers, teacher needs, preferences, and knowledge of school practice and environment, as well as their knowledge of subject matter, serve as the starting points of curricular deliberations.

The project's aim was threefold:

1. to use the teacher as the starting point in curricular deliberation
2. to involve teachers in the R&D process as active inquirers and decision makers
3. to provide a curriculum product for the school system, a process which would involve teachers in decision making and thus enhance teacher autonomy. Instead of one set of materials, several versions of the unit were developed and teachers had to choose among them or combine parts of different versions to form their own curriculum. This procedure ties in with the notions of teachers functioning as judges of the requirements of their students and as partners in the generation of proposals for action

Joint Research and Graduate Studies Programs   Through extension of the notion of jointly planned research and development to include jointly planned graduate studies programs, multiple benefits may be hoped for. A review of graduate programs in the Department of Curriculum of OISE gave rise to a "Curriculum Processes" graduate study option. "Curriculum processes" refers to areas of practitioner activity such as instruction, curriculum evaluation, curriculum management (e. g. at principal and superintendent levels), and curriculum consulting. Under the aegis of the "processes" option, a group of field-centre and central OISE faculty designed a joint graduate-studies-R&D program on curriculum consultancy with a number of school boards. The program has demonstrated the benefits of collaboration between researchers and practitioners when the latter are treated as judges of practical needs and are accepted as equal partners in inquiry.

The program on curriculum consultancy was designed in a rather complex way—with school board officials participating in the identification of needed consultancy skills; with individual teachers indicating a willingness to go forward for graduate study and to train for consulting positions within the board; and with OISE faculty members indicating a willingness to simultaneously teach, plan with the board, and design a piggy-backed research program on the nature of curriculum consultancy. Much of the program consisted of on-site practicum-like work. Students gained graduate credit; obtained specific abilities of use to their boards; used research findings in the practicum; and participated in the overall planning, including the research component. The researchers gained knowledge of the character and conduct of curriculum consultancy (on which there is only a scant literature) and, through continued monitoring of the program, were able to describe a prototype program for other graduate institutions.

We believe these activities illustrate that while teachers cannot be heavily involved in research they can be engaged in a wide range of inquiry-oriented activities if programs are developed to support their involvement.

Conclusion

We have said that the spirit of inquiry behind proposals for action research by teachers is desirable, but that action research aimed at knowledge production or at knowledge implementation—either as embodied in materials or as leading to instructional strategies—is a wasteful use of teacher time in view of the teacher's primary role of instruction. We have argued that decisions made in the planning and evaluation of instruction is the place where teacher reflection and inquiry properly occur, and that proposals relating teachers and research should aim at improvements in the decision process. We believe that teachers are not properly seen as implementers of research and development ideas nor as assistants to research in any sense, but are, rather, best seen as independent agents with an educative function in curriculum development and implementation.

We have seen that various roles are allocated to teachers as users of and participants in educational research. There is a growing trend to move away from the image of teachers as neutral transmitters of curricular programs and toward a more sophisticated notion of the teacher as active implementer. This approach is sensitive to teachers' needs and reflects worthwhile goals, yet tends to minimize the significance of teachers' possible contributions to the educational enterprise. We have tried to show that teachers can be involved in a wide range of inquiry–oriented activities. Several examples of these activities were presented that provide an opportunity for teachers to play a significant role in the complex process of educational decision making.

Notes

A version of this chapter appeared in the *Journal of Curriculum Studies,* 1980, 12(2), 95–107.

1. Examples include (*a*) arguments based on the assumption that valid educational research is to be based on real-life situations (Best, 1970; McNamara, 1972; "Teacher-researcher," 1970); (*b*) Arguments based on the view that the teaching function comprises research by its very nature (Krahmer, 1967; Odell, 1976; Popham and Baker, 1970; Splaine, 1975); (*c*) arguments based on the need for enhanced teacher professionalism (Derland, 1970; Hunter, 1973; Quisti and Hogg, 1973; Rodgers, 1976).

2. Romey (1973) describes the Earth Science Curriculum Program (ESCP), which was conceived initially as a teacher-proof curriculum. Romey reveals the developers' disillusionment, and development of a new approach, namely that of working toward the creation of "the curriculum-proof teacher." who is dominated by no single curriculum but uses a variety of instructional materials. See also Shipman (1972).

3. A related note is found in the work of Macdonald and Rudduck (1971), who advise curriculum developers to have teachers participate along with the project team. The main goal of this participation is to communicate "effectively the nature of the enterprise. Dilution and distortions of a program can frequently be traced to the persistence of mistaken assumptions" (p. 149).

4. These points are taken from "Foundations of Curriculum Development: Syllabus of Readings," edited by F. M. Connelly (informal publication, OISE Department of Curriculum, 1980).

5. A project in biology for the ninth grade of junior high school in Israel; a joint project of the Division of Curriculum Development of the School of Education at Haifa University and the Center of Curriculum Development of The Israeli Ministry of Education.

References

Ben-Peretz, M. The concept of curriculum potential. *Curriculum Theory Network*, 1975, 5(2), 151–159.

Berman, P., and McLaughlin, M. W. An exploratory study of school district adaptation. Santa Monica, Cal.: Rand, 1979.

Best, E. E. The classroom teacher as educational researcher. *Independent School Bulletin*, 1970, 30(1), 37–38.

Campbell, R., et al. R&D funding policies of the National Institute of Education: Review and recommendations. Draft report of consultants to the National Institute of Education and the National Council of Educational Research. Unpublished manuscript, July 1975.

Connelly, F. M. The functions of curriculum development. *Interchange*, 1972, 3(2–3), 161–177.

Connelly, F. M., and Ben-Peretz, M. Teachers' roles in the using and doing of research and curriculum development. *Journal of Curriculum Studies*, 1980, 12(2), 95–107.

Derland, D. D. The profession's quest for responsibility and accountability. *Phi Delta Kappan*, Sept. 1970, 52, 41–44.

Fox, S. A practical image of "the practical." *Curriculum Theory Network*. Fall 1972, 10, 45–57.

Fullan, M. Conceptualizing problems of curriculum implementation. Outline of remarks for the Symposium on Curriculum Inquiry in Canada, University of Victoria, British Columbia, Feb. 1979.

Fullan, M.; Eastabrook, G.; and Bliss, J. Action research in the school: Involving students and teachers in classroom change. In R. A. Carlton, L. A. Colley, and N.J. MacKinnon, eds., *Education, change, and society: A sociology of Canadian education*. Toronto: Gage, 1977.

Hayes, H. The influence of the practical on the recovery of meaning from philosophical statements: An analysis of teacher deliberation. Unpublished qualifying research paper, Toronto, OISE Department of Curriculum, 1974.

Hunter, W. A. Redefining and realizing teaching as a profession. *American Association of College Teachers Education yearbook*, 1973, pp. 23–38.

Ingram, E. J. *Action research*. Improvement of Instruction Series, no. 1. Edmonton: Alberta Teachers' Association, 1959.

Ingram, E. J., and Robinson, F. G. *A teacher's guide to classroom research*. Improvement of Instruction Series, no. 5. Edmonton: Alberta Teachers' Association, 1963.

Krahmer, E. Teachers' lack of familiarity with research techniques as a problem for effective research dissemination. A preliminary report. Bureau of Educational Research and Services, University of North Dakota, Grand Forks, 1967.

Leithwood, K. A.; Clipsham, J. S.; Maynes, F.; and Baxter, R. P. Curriculum change at the system level: A four-year mathematics project. *Curriculum Theory Network*, 1976, 5(3), 219–245.

Macdonald, B., and Rudduch, J. Curriculum research and development projects: Barriers to success. *British Journal of Educational Psychology*, 1971, 41, 141–154.

McLean, L. D., and Brison, D. W. Making a difference at school: The R&D challenge. Draft working paper, OISE, Office of Reasearch and Development, Toronto, 1976.

McNamara, J. F. Teachers and students combine efforts in action research. *Clearing House*, 1972, 47(4), 242–248.

Odell, L. Classroom teacher as a researcher. *English Journal*, 1976, 65, 106–11.

Popham, W., and Baker, E. L. *Systematic instruction*. New Jersey: Prentice-Hall, 1970.

Quisti, J. P., and Hogg, J. G. Teacher states: Practitioner or professional. *Clearing House*, 1973, 48, 182–185.

Rodgers, F. The past and future of teaching: You've come a long way. *Educational Leader*, 1976, 33, 282–286.

Romey, W. D. The curriculum-proof teacher. *Phi Delta Kappan*, Feb. 1973, 54, 407–408.

Schaeffer, R. J. *The school as a center of inquiry*. New York: Harper & Row, 1967.

Schaffarzick, J. Teacher and lay participation in local curriculum change considerations. Paper presented at the annual American Educational Research Association conference, 1976.

Schwab, J. J. The practical: A language for curriculum. *School Review*, 1969, 78(1), 1–23.

Schwab, J. J. The practical: Arts of eclectic. *School Review*, 1971, 79(4), 493–542.

Schwab, J. J. The practical: Translation into curriculum. *School Review*, 1973, 81(4), 501–522.

Shipman, M. D. Contrasting views of a curriculum project. *Journal of Curriculum Studies*, 1972, 4(2), 145–153.

Splaine, J. The teacher as a researcher. *Audiovisual Instruction*, 1975, 20(1), 6–7.

Stake, K. E., ed. *Evaluating the arts in education: A responsive approach*. Columbus, O.: C. E. Merrill, 1975.

Teacher-researcher. *Soviet Education*, 1970, 12(6–7), 47–50.

18

Curriculum and the Work of Teachers

Gail McCutcheon

This chapter contains a discussion of alternatives regarding the relationship between the curriculum and the work of teachers. One way of understanding what is meant by curriculum and teaching is to separate them, where curriculum is the intended fare of the schools, and teaching is its vehicle. However, they are more closely entwined; curriculum affects and is affected by teaching, and the opposite is also true. So, the medium and the message have a close relationship rather than being neatly separable.

Curriculum can also be thought of as what students have an opportunity to learn under the auspices of schools. In this case, the overt curriculum constitutes what school people intend that students learn and what teachers say they intend to teach—the publicly-advertised fare of the schools. The hidden curriculum is what students have an opportunity to learn through everyday goings-on under the auspices of schools, although teachers and other school people do not intend those learnings.

One facet of the overt curriculum is the graded course of study or written curriculum of the school. This is the *formal,* policy-level curriculum. The less formal, but perhaps more important, curriculum is the curriculum enacted in the classroom.

The hidden curriculum can be thought of as bearing two characteristics (1) it is not intended, and (2) it is transmitted through the everyday, normal goings-on in schools. For example, through the hidden curriculum, students may receive stereotypical messages about minority and ethnic groups, and male and female roles, due to messages implicit in a teacher's actions, everyday occurrences in the schools, or from textbooks. The hidden curriculum may arise out of school policies. For instance, Mr. Bryant teaches mathematics in the eighth grade at Clearwater Middle School, where a policy states that students are to pass tests at a proficiency level of 80 percent or above before moving ahead to a new chapter. If they do not pass at this level they are to have a review and a retest. He and other teachers worry that through the hidden curriculum, students seem to be learning that even if they are not prepared today for the test, it does not really matter, for a retest is always given. For instance, students have asked *before* the test, "When's the retest, Mr. Bryant?" in what he describes as a cavalier or nonchalant manner. He and some colleagues fear that students might come to believe that they really do not have to study hard for the first test, for they can always depend upon the retest. Translated into everyday life, Mr. Bryant fears students might come to believe there is always a second chance. Which is not always the case.

Reprinted from *The Curriculum,* edited by Landon E. Bayer and Michael W. Apple. Albany: SUNY Press, 1988. By permission of the State University of New York Press.

The hidden curriculum may also consist of the development of a work ethic, transmitted by teachers' admonitions such as those observed recently in another middle-school mathematics classroom:

Lois, keep your eyes on your own work.

Mark, let's get busy here. Get your work done on time.

Nancy, I know you can do better. Sit down and recopy this so it's neater. You need to turn in work you can be proud of, not this messy trash.

Alexander, you have to be more responsible. You can't leave your homework at home every night like this. Now, grow up. If you can remember your baseball glove, you can remember to bring your homework.

Some teachers in the elementary school where Mrs. Faye is a librarian reward their students. When the class is behaving well, these teachers put a marble in a jar and when the jar contains ten marbles, the teacher brings in a cake. Mrs. Faye does not do this in the library, and reflects, "Aren't my congratulations enough? What are the kids learning if you always reward them extrinsically with something material—in this case a cake? Life's not like that, and where do you ever learn self-control and patting *yourself* on the back in this kind of situation?"

As a final example of the hidden curriculum, Ron Comfort notes in a recent case study:

Broadly speaking, the environment of Fielding [School] "teaches" that being a student involves hard work, high expectations for one's performance, deference to teacher authority, and a balance between cooperation and competition. Despite an ambiance of informality and openness among students and teacher participants in the setting, behavioral boundaries and seriousness of purpose are conveyed. These are communicated through the myriad of daily interactions rather than on the basis of codified rules. Indeed, they are a function of a sense of values which are held in common among teachers and to which students are socialized.[1]

An important role teachers have vis-á-vis the hidden curriculum is observing and reflecting on its nature and the possible effects of such an opportunity for learning. Through doing this, teachers can improve the hidden curriculum, thereby rendering more of it overt; because it has been reflected upon it moves into the intended realm.

The *null urriculum*[2] constitutes what students do not have an opportunity to learn under the auspices of schools. The null curriculum is virtually infinite; some aspects are consciously decided upon when school people deliberately elect *not* to include a particular matter in the curriculum due to its controversial nature, a lack of proper equipment or time, or other reasons. For example, following a recent conference about acquired immunization deficiency syndrome (AIDS), an authority suggested on network news that one implication of the increase in AIDS in both the homosexual and heterosexual community is to teach about safe sex in high school. As an aside, he noted that there really is not such a thing as "safe" sex, so he amended his proposition to "safer" sex by teaching about the use of the condom to prevent the mingling of vaginal and seminal fluids. This would be a fairly controversial topic to include in the high schools of many communities, so it will probably remain a part of the null curriculum. The null curriculum is also different for different students. Girls were not permitted to enroll in certain courses (such as metal, electric, carpentry, and

industrial arts classes) and had little experience with certain sports until recent legislation aimed at providing more equity.

One example of null curriculum comes from a high school in a system where
the superintendent is concerned about high unemployment rates in the community.
He is convinced that all students should be qualified to attend college so they will be
able to find employment. In the foreign language department, the French and Spanish
teachers have been proposing that their courses have a large conversational component, but the proposal has fallen on deaf ears because the idea is not seen as one likely
to enhance students opportunities to enter college.

Another example comes from the arts, where an elementary school art teacher's
requisition was severely slashed, leaving her students few opportunities for three-dimensional work, which she believes should be an aspect of the art curriculum at all
grade levels. "Oh, sure," says Ms. Nash, "kids can make sculptures out of cardboard and
other things they can bring from home, but unless I make dough for them to use, they
can't have a three-dimensional experience with a plastic medium because I have no
clay, no glazes, and very limited access to the kiln [at the high school]." She worries
this may affect the experiences in which students are willing to invest themselves in
upper grades because they are having such limited experience with three-dimensional media, which could ultimately affect their work as artists, museum attenders, and
consumers. "This may always remain mysterious to them," she fears.

Other teachers have also cited the lack of particular materials as a factor contributing to the null curriculum: no sets of paperback novels for reading groups, no
alcohol burners and test tube holders in an elementary school using a science text
containing experiments where they are to use them, too few computers, a lack of
storage space leading to disorganization or damage of art materials in elementary
school classrooms, and being permitted to hire a piano tuner only at five-year inter-
vals.

Another case concerns alterations in the curriculum in different areas of a city
due to parents' expectations of their children. Here, an eighth-grade English teacher
musing about one of his students remarked,

> Now, you take Leigh. She lives here in the Horlicks area of town—you know, a
> blue-collar area if I ever saw one. But Leigh could easily go to college. Now, don't
> get me wrong. She's no Einstein or Madame Curie, but she's got enough on the
> ball to go to State or somewhere. She'd be a great teacher, and she loves computer
> work. But her parents are sure she should get married or be a secretary or a hair-
> dresser or nurse or a dental hygienist. Now, there's nothing wrong with those jobs,
> but it's too bad about Leigh. I've talked to the MacDonalds a lot, but in high
> school they're putting her in that business track—you know, typing, accounting,
> more typing, and office skills. The problem is, look at all the stuff she won't get to
> learn! It's amazing. You talk about how people's expectations affect education!
> Leigh's going to have to live down to her parents' expectations!

Just as the overt curriculum changes, so does the null curriculum. Part of this
change is because of new discoveries, while others can be attributed to cultural
change in general. So, for instance, until recently computer education was in the null
curriculum, obviously because we were not using computers widely. A recent change
in business colleges has been a call for international business matters to be addressed
in undergraduate courses about business law, finance, marketing, and administration,
because virtually every business is now in some ways international. Until recently, this
was generally not treated to any extent in business college courses, so it was part of

the null curriculum. Societal changes have brought that to the attention of these professors, just as problems of unwanted teenage pregnancy and AIDS concern many involved in secondary schools. Here again, an important role for teachers is to reflect on what constitutes the null curriculum and whether it is advisable.

The broad definition of *curriculum,* what students have an opportunity to learn under the auspices of schools, will be used in this chapter.

Teachers and the Overt Curriculum: A Traditional View

Returning to the overt curriculum, a traditional view is that teachers' work involves transforming that which is intended into a set of activities in order to make intended skills and knowledge accessible to students. That is, the formal curriculum and the enacted curriculum are to be the same.

While possibilities for activities are virtually endless, teachers tend to select textbooks and other two-dimensional, print-based materials for these purposes. Perhaps this is due to tradition; to visions of what school is supposed to be; to assumptions that they are to use the materials because the school system bought them; to parental pressure; and to systemwide mandates that virtually preclude the use of any other materials. One example of the latter might occur if a school system mandates that Ginn tests be used in reading—the teacher is virtually bound to use the accompanying textbooks.

This fairly traditional view that teachers are to teach the overt curriculum as mandated from above has its roots in the movement of the administrative progressives, such as Elwood P. Cubberly, who attempted to overlay a corporate model of scientific management onto the schools, a movement dating back to the turn of the century. An elite board and expert manager were to oversee the workings of the school and strive for efficiency. This result depended on obtaining accurate information and channeling it to the super-intendent and his/her board; careful budgeting, relying on the review of programs to determine their efficiency and cost-effectiveness, and using that data to plan ahead; and specifying precisely how teachers were to turn out students whose skills and attitudes were consonant with those deemed important by society.[3] This last characteristic gave rise to the organized field of curriculum. Early curriculum scholars such as Franklin Bobbitt strove to formulate such curricula. Hence, the field of curriculum has its roots in management to better support administration; its original function was one of control.

More recently, this trend was perpetuated by the major curriculum reforms of the 1950s and 1960s. During this period teachers were asked to implement the nationally-produced programs and found, for a variety of reasons, that they did not work. These reasons included a lack of fit with local conditions, including values that were at odds with the local community's; programs that were beyond the comprehension of their students; and the inclusion of experiences removed from their students' lives. Perhaps this difficulty was partly the result of teachers' minimal involvement with the national reforms and a preponderance of subject-matter experts' involvement.

During the structure of the disciplines movement when we were to teach "new" mathematics, parents were unable to help children with homework and did not understand why a new way of working the same problems was in order, for their way worked. Some teachers did not possess the mathematical knowledge needed to enable them to field students' questions. Hence, due to a lack of ease with ideas presented in the mathematics books, some teachers may have elected not to use them;

others may have left unanswered the students' questions (and thereby rendered them part of the null curriculum).

Harking back to my own teaching experience during this time, a science kit had been adopted by our school system. In one lesson, eight sets of various balls—super balls, golf balls and tennis balls—eight meter sticks, and large pieces of paper were contained in the materials box. In this case, we were to divide our third-grade classes into eight groups of three or four students and have them drop each ball from shoulder height while another student metrically measured the first, second, and third bounce. For some teachers who virtually never taught with small groups or through activities, such a lesson was unthinkable. Others questioned the metric system. One colleague, for instance, taught this lesson through her own demonstration while a student measured the bounces under her direction. Another said that the primary matter dealt with in the lesson was discipline. Chaos did not reign, according to her, but it came close as children *bounced* (not dropped!) the balls and they flew everywhere for a while. The act of placing 24 balls in the hands of third-graders and then restraining their use in a classroom calls for one to believe the pupils had tremendous self-control; it also assumed teachers had organized their teaching around self-discipline and activity-centered learning, which was often not the case. It was no wonder that many teachers either did not use that activity or turned it into a demonstration. Perhaps many thought, "Too much!" as they were to reorganize science class in a drastically different manner, teach the use of metric sticks, and try to control the class as well. The idea may have been sound, but it probably did not fit many teachers' belief systems—their theories of action—so they altered the lessons to fit their belief systems and thereby subverted the program.

For many teachers, the new programs' content and their suggested use were substantially different from previously used programs, necessitating drastic shifts in classroom organization, beliefs about learning, and the accumulation of more knowledge to understand or implement the program. As a result of those features, many programs were difficult to implement unless extensive inservice programs were held or lengthy, highly detailed teachers' manuals were written. Because developers were outlining new content and innovative ways of teaching, they delineated quite specifically what was to occur in a given lesson. While some teachers were secure with such specificity, others resented it; for example, one teacher stated, in reflecting about her planning, "Going to college for five years to learn how to follow directions is pretty ridiculous." A lack of thorough understanding, such resentment, and an impracticality for the setting may be examples of why teachers used materials as they saw fit rather than as prescribed by teachers' guides, thereby substantially altering the nature of the course. This trend of specifying the curriculum to teachers in an attempt to control it—by administrators or by national reformers—continues to the present day. For example, teacher competency tests and demands for high student achievement test scores, and teacher accountability (as determined by students' achievement test scores, for example, in St. Louis) further support the efficient running of schools and focus our attention on ends as defined by the tests themselves.

This view is understandable in light of a current mood in the country for the public to be sure it is getting its money's worth from social institutions. Many teachers and administrators probably agree with the traditional view that the administration and board are to dictate the overt curriculum and that the teachers' role is merely to implement it. Indeed, teacher-proof curricula follow this same scheme. An extreme example can be found in DISTAR, an elementary-school reading program. In the 1962 edition, authors cautioned teachers:

Follow the presentation as closely as possible. Don't improvise on the presentation materials. . . . Don't introduce variations of the instructions. Don't wander off onto other tasks. Don't present additional exercises that may come to mind. Don't use the material as a point of departure for free-association teaching. And above all, don't become involved in lengthy explanations. The directions for each of the tasks are designed to explain by showing. Resist the impulse to 'tell' the children. Chances are they won't have the faintest idea what you are talking about; you will unfortunately demonstrate that you cannot be relied on to clarify, that you only confuse.[4]

Since then, the authors have softened their tone somewhat, although the materials are still scripted. What teachers are to say appears in red type, what they are to do is in black type, and expected responses are in italics.

However, even in the case where we conceive teaching to be merely determining how to implement goals, the teacher's role is powerful in influencing what students have an opportunity to learn, in a variety of ways. Teachers can emphasize certain materials over others. Further, teachers may be more enthusiastic about a certain topic, skill, or understanding, which may permit them to provide more intriguing lessons and assignments than when a topic, skill, or understanding is of less interest to them. Mrs. Cabot, a fourth-grade teacher, reflects: "We have to teach from this reading series. But reading's more. Reading's joy as well as just word-calling. Maybe *more* joy. So I give the kids lots of independent reading time. They choose books from the library, and I schedule appointments with them so we can chat."

Teachers are the filters through which the mandated curriculum passes. Their understanding of it, and their enthusiasm, or boredom, with various aspects of it, color its nature. Hence, the curriculum enacted in classrooms differs from the one mandated by administrators or developed by experts.

Regarding the overt curriculum, then, teachers' influence is manifold. Teachers filter the objectives; it is up to them to understand what is to be taught and then conceive of ways to enact it and make it accessible to students. Teachers must also make sense of the context—the neighborhood, their students, parents' hopes and dreams, the social setting within the school, as well as the shape of the nation itself—and fit the objectives into these understandings. In this manner, such decisions are moral ones, going beyond an objective management activity. It is also the teachers who contend with policies and other phenomena within which the curriculum operates. So, when the schedule allots 53-minute class sessions or classrooms are lacking in particular equipment or materials needed for a lesson, teachers are the ones who reshape lessons accordingly. When the teachers themselves have only a superficial understanding of the content to be presented, their decisions about the importance of various lessons and what to stress are affected. In this case, the curriculum is also filtered by how articulately teachers are able to respond to questions, to embroider on points in lessons, and to conceive of relevant activities and assignments.

Teachers and the Hidden Curriculum: A Traditional View

Because teachers have their own personalities, values, interests, strengths, and weaknesses, they also affect the hidden curriculum. As teachers, we do not shrug off these aspects of ourselves as we remove our coats and hang them on pegs outside our classrooms. Hence, the hidden curriculum is primarily the purview of the teacher with the exception of latent messages in curriculum materials and school policies, as teachers communicate their values, expectations and other messages through the hidden curriculum while they reach the overt curriculum, manage their administrative tasks, maintain discipline, and attend to their other responsibilities.

So, in a traditional view where teachers implement an already established curriculum, they still influence what students have an opportunity to learn because they must interpret curriculum mandates themselves in order to implement them and because they have an impact on the classroom's hidden curriculum.

A Deliberationist View

One alternative to this traditional, positivistic, top-down, control-oriented position is the deliberationist perspective,

> the method by which most everyday practical problems get solved. . . an intricate and skilled intellectual and social process whereby, individually or collectively, we identify questions to which we must respond, establish grounds for deciding on answers, and then choose among the available solutions.[5]

Following this perspective, then, teachers identify problems—perhaps tentatively—and progress to define them and their parameters more clearly, moving toward resolution of some critical issues. Deliberation is more an attitude than a series of steps—the quest for as ideal a curriculum as possible for *these* students in *this* location. Difficulties arise from concrete, specific situations and are reflected upon; data is gathered that sheds further light on the reflections; new action is taken if warranted, and further reflection ensues. Teachers negotiate the curriculum in an intricate, skilled intellectual manner. This cycle is never ending, and deliberation in this case is a private weighing of the nature of the situation and whether certain courses of action are warranted.

For example, an upper-grade elementary school teacher critiquing an earlier draft of this chapter reflected on his approach to teaching spelling.

> In going over the spelling books, I see lessons based on phonics with words using those sounds. Now, I brush over the phonics part lightly because first, I'm not positive I understand it all that well myself, and, second, I don't think that understanding phonics itself necessarily leads to a word sense. I think having a word sense may lead to an understanding of phonics. English is based on so many different languages that there are so many exceptions to rules, that phonics doesn't even work a lot of the time. I cover the material, but deemphasize phonics and concentrate more on the words themselves along with meanings and uses. If students can recognize a word and use it, they'll learn how to spell it. Once you learn how to speak, you use words and start to hear similarities—the *dis* in *discover* and *dissimilar* sound alike. If you don't understand the meaning and use of a word, it doesn't matter if you can spell it phonetically or not because you won't use it. But if you use it—even aloud—chances are you'll use it in written form and therefore learn its spelling.[6]

In this example, the problem is how to teach spelling. The teacher has begun to clarify for himself how he believes students learn words—through use, not phonics, in his view—and to develop strategies to facilitate students' using the words. He concedes that he's not sure that he's right and characterizes it as a sort of "hunting in the dark" in that it is probably more difficult to understand yourself than other people, and that while many people have written texts and articles about such a matter, he's not sure they are right; and while they are writing in an abstract, theoretical vein, he's there, on the spot, and the system does not seem to work. Learning it because you have learned how to use it is important, not learning it to pass a test. He continues:

> When I see children who get A's on the tests, but they can't write a paper and spell correctly—there's something wrong there. They've learned how to spell it on the test, but their language use does not increase in proficiency the way the tests indicate they should. I don't see sophistry (is that the word for it?)—I'm smart because I know how to spell these words—as the aim of schools. Maybe lots of the texts are set up for the convenience of textbook writers and teachers, not to educate children.

He suggests that he continues to watch whether students are spelling well with his system; if they do not, new actions will probably ensue.

A deliberationist perspective rests on the precondition that the teacher is a dedicated, responsible, morally-committed professional; whereas, in the traditional view, the precondition is that the curriculum is to be used because it is assumed to be the result of decisions by experts, and a trained person uses it by going through the motions dictated by the materials, much as an apprentice operates a machine in an assembly line. Hence, the traditional view strips teachers of professional judgment.

The deliberationist perspective is well complemented by action research, where teachers inquire into matters critically in order to improve their own practice.[7] Through this process of inquiry, information comes to light that informs the deliberation. In preactive mental planning of lessons, as teachers weigh alternatives and select what appears most propitious, given their experiences—what they know of these students, *this* particular content and context—they deliberate.

Deliberation also occurs interactively, during the lesson itself, as teachers notice such phenomena as the glazed eyes of disinterest, the excited look of curiosity, or puzzlement about a particular point. Each of these observations brings about questions for teachers about how to proceed, and they adjust the preactive plans.

As an experienced teacher reflects:

> I can say that teachers make adjustments continuously, not only before and after the lesson, but also during the lesson. . . when a teacher changes the teaching strategy that has been planned initially, or even discontinuing a lesson that is not effective. Teachers must be able to make adjustments during the lesson for it to be most effective. This is not to say that deliberation during the planning of the lesson and after the deliverance of the lesson are not equally important.

Deliberation also occurs afterward, as teachers wonder how it went, what should be retaught to whom and how. In this postlesson reflection, teachers wonder if they actually took the best course, and this reflection may indeed alter plans for next year, and their theory of action[8]—and hence, further actions—when confronted with similar situations. Reading educational literature, talking with trusted colleagues, and attending graduate courses may widen the array of matters considered in deliberation.

Were this deliberationist perspective used in a school system to organize the curriculum, it would involve teachers collaboratively across the grade levels, within and across subject matters, to wonder together about scope, sequence, and integration. The process of deliberation and action research would lead to a sense of ownership of the curriculum, and this vested interest in it would bring about reformulations of it as problems were identified. Three teachers reacting to an earlier draft of this chapter discussed action research and deliberation. The following represents their dialogue:

> *Teacher I:* Teaching amounts to ideas in action. It takes place in real time, encounters are immediate, and is encumbered by political and material constraints. . .

> *Teacher II:* Some arising suddenly and unpredictably due to changes in the political and social life of the setting, and others more long-term and predictable.

> *Teacher III:* When planning, plans for action are bound by practice because prior practice has taught us what works and does not work.

> *Teacher I:* Teaching itself is fluid, dynamic, and requires instant decisions and practical problem-solving and judgment.

> *Teacher III:* So it is deliberative in that it is purposive, pros and cons of action are weighed, and self-observation occurs to provide sound bases for critical self-reflection about processes, problems, issues, constraints and supports manifest in the practice.

Action research provides data that informs deliberation. This leads to *praxis* and improvement because it allows teachers to question their own practice and to formulate actions and a theory of action upon which they have deliberated carefully, as exemplified by this quote from one of the three teachers cited above.

> Teacher II: Action research and deliberation permit us to articulate teaching experiences and bring them under self-conscious control, so we can organize our own self-enlightenment by engaging ourselves in private deliberation about practice. Teachers are professional this way because they try to be perfectionists.

Hence, the deliberationist perspective rests on intense teacher involvement, and teaching is a serious, professional enterprise.

Teachers adopting a deliberationist attitude are mature and secure enough with their roles as teachers to have abandoned a starry-eyed, romantic love of teaching and progressed to seeing teaching as challenging, difficult, enjoyable work where problems exist that are murky but can be resolved. Perhaps we can think of this as a loss of innocence, and perhaps this loss of innocence is needed for genuine improvement in what students have an opportunity to learn as we recognize the active, deliberative mental planning teachers do and its importance in shaping what students have an opportunity to learn. This position further implies the development of curriculum materials that engage teachers in deliberation rather than materials that assume teachers are a direct pipeline from the expert developer to students' minds. One example of materials that invite teachers' deliberation is *Project WILD,* a set of supplementary, interdisciplinary activities about the environment and conservation for educators of kindergarten through high school age young people. *The Elementary Activity Guide* invites instructors to

> pick and choose from the activities. Each activity is designed to stand alone, without other *Project WILD* activities. There is no need to do the activities in order, nor to do all activities, even for a given grade level. However, the activities have been placed in a thematic and developmental order that can serve as an aid to their use. . . . Instructors may use one or many *Project WILD* activities. The activities may be integrated into existing courses of study, or the entire set of activities may serve quite effectively as the basis for a course of study.[9]

Such a perspective also assumes graduate courses and a supervision approach that engage teachers in public deliberation to facilitate the process itself and that raise issues to consciousness.

The picture painted in this chapter is one of teachers as thinkers who make many decisions that create the curriculum in classrooms. Rather than having the role of rather passive people who implement the curriculum, teachers have an important function in shaping what students have an opportunity to learn.

Notes

1. Ronald E. Comfort, "Analyzing the Operational Curriculum of a School: A Case Study." Paper presented at the Annual Conference of the American Educational Research Association, New Orleans, April 1984, p. 31.

2. Elliot Eisner coined this term. See Eisner, *The Educational Imagination* (New York: Macmillan Company, 1979), pp. 83–84.

3. See David Tyack and Elisabeth Hansott, *Managers of Virtue* (New York: Basic Books, 1982), for elaboration on the development and influence of the administrative progressive movement; also see the chapter by Carlson herein.

4. Seigfried Englemann and Elaine C. Bruner, *DISTAR Reading I, Teachers Guide.* (Chicago: SRA, 1969), p. 12.

5. William A. Reid, *Thinking about the Curriculum.* (London: Routledge & Kegan Paul, 1978), p. 43.

6. I am endebted to my husband, George L. Disch, for this example and reflections.

7. See Wilfred Carr and Stephen Kemmis, *Becoming Critical* (Victoria, Australia: Deakin University Press, 1983), for a discussion of action research.

8. See Donald P. Sanders and Gail McCutcheon, "On the Evolution of Teachers' Theories of Action through Action Research" *Journal of Curriculum and Supervision.* II:1 (Autumn 1986): 50–67, for a discussion of action research and the development of teachers' personal theories of action.

9. *Project WILD.* Western Regional Environmental Council, 1983.

19

Forgetting the Questions
The Problem of Educational Reform

Diane Ravitch

It would be difficult to find a sustained period of time in our history when Americans felt satisfied with the achievements of their schools. From the early nineteenth century on, it has been commonplace to find a fairly consistent recitation of complaints about the low state of learning, the poor training of teachers, the insufficient funding of education, the inadequacies of school buildings, and the apathy of the public. The temptation exists to attribute the concerns of the 1980s to this strain of despair about the historic gap between aspiration and reality, this sense that schools have always and will always fall short of their mission. But it would be wrong to do so, not only because it would encourage unwarranted complacency, but because the educational problems of the present are fundamentally different from those of the past.

One important difference is that so much of the past agenda of educational reformers has been largely fulfilled. In one sense, the educational enterprise is the victim of its own successes, since new problems have arisen from the long-sought solutions to earlier problems. Idealistic reformers, eager to improve the schools and to extend their promise to all children, sought the appropriate lever of change. *If only* teachers had college degrees and pedagogical training; *if only* teachers would band together to form a powerful teachers' union; if only there were federal aid to schools; *if only* all children were admitted to school regardless of race or national origin; *if only* all students of high ability were admitted to college; *if only* colleges could accommodate everyone who wanted to attend; *if only* students had more choices and fewer requirements in their course work; *if only* schools were open to educational experimentation; *if only* there were a federal department of education. . . . The "if only" list could be extended, but the point should be clear by now. All these "if onlies" have been put into effect, some entirely and others at least partially, and rarely have the results been equal to the hopes invested.

In reality, many present complaints are reactions to hard-won reforms of the past. Though the educational preparation of teachers is more extensive than ever, at least when measured by degrees and years of formal schooling, the education of teachers is still a subject of intense criticism. The realization has dawned in many quarters that a credential from a state university or a school of education is no guarantee that its bearer knows how to teach or what to teach, loves teaching or loves learning. Nor are today's critics delighted by the undeniable power of teachers' unions. True, the unions have used their political clout to improve teachers' salaries and to win vastly enlarged federal education expenditures, but unionization has not produced the educational changes that some of its advocates had anticipated. Similarly, the sense of achievement that should have followed the removal of racial barriers to higher education quickly gave way to concerns about social stratification, vocationalization, and declining quality. The reforms of the 1960s were effective, though not in the way that reformers had hoped. Now everyone who wants to go to college can go to some college, though not necessarily that of his first choice. By 1980, at least one-third of all institutions of higher education admitted everyone who applied, more than one-half accepted most or all of those who met their qualifications, and less than 10 percent were "competitive," that is, accepted only a portion of qualified applicants. As college enrollments decline, the number of competitive colleges will grow fewer. Curricular reforms have broken down the coherence of the liberal arts curriculum, both in high school and college, so that students have a wide degree of choice and few requirements. And a federal department of education has at last been established, though with what benefits or burdens for schools and children it is too soon to say.

Yet having won so many victories, some of truly historic dimension, American education is still embattled, still struggling to win public support and approval, and, perhaps worse, still struggling to find its own clear sense of purpose. Paradoxically, the achievements of the recent past seem to have exhausted the usually ready stock of prescriptions for school reform and to have raised once again the most basic questions of educational purpose.

Like other major institutions in our society, the schools are continually judged by today's demands and today's performance, and no credit is extended by clients or critics for yesterday's victories. Which is as it should be. School criticism, as I noted earlier, is nothing new. Behind any criticism, however, are assumptions about what schools should do and can do, and criticisms have shifted as assumptions about the goals and potentialities of schools have changed. Since the early nineteenth century, the tenor of school criticism has been essentially optimistic; no matter how despairing the critic, his working assumption has been that schools are valuable institutions, that they have within them the power to facilitate great social, moral, and political regeneration, and that more money, or more public concern, or better teachers could extend the promise of schooling to everyone. If more people had more schooling, critics have contended, and if schools were amply financed and well staffed, there would be enormous benefit to the individual, the society, the economy, and the body politic. With relatively little dissent, Americans have believed in schooling—not because of a love of the hickory stick and the three Rs, or (as some latter-day critics would have it) because of the schools' ability to make children docile workers, but because Americans are deeply committed to self-improvement and the school is an institutionalized expression of that commitment.

Participation in formal schooling has grown sharply in recent decades. The proportion of seventeen-year-olds who graduated from high school grew from about 50 percent in 1940 to about 85 percent in the late 1970s. Similarly, the proportion of young people who entered college climbed from about 16 percent in 1940 to about 45 percent in 1968, at which time it leveled off. In no other country in the world does participation in formal schooling last as long, for so many people, as in the United States. To understand why this broad democratization of educational participation occurred, as well as why the 1980s began on a note of disillusionment, it is useful to consider some of the expectations we have attached to formal schooling.

Until well into the twentieth century, only a small minority of Americans attended college. College was not only expensive but exclusive. Many, perhaps most, colleges maintained quotas for some groups (like Jews and Catholics) and excluded others altogether (blacks). After World War II, more than two million veterans attended college, crowding and sometimes overwhelming America's campuses. The GI Bill launched the world's first experiment in universal access to higher education. While most veterans did not use their benefits to attend college, the experience of those who did benefited the individuals, the institutions, and the economy. In light of the success and popularity of the GI program, the conviction that college should be a right rather than a privilege gained broad support.

While demands for expanded access to higher education grew steadily in the states and nation, other political forces combined to advance the role of education as a weapon against poverty. The notion that knowledge is power was certainly not novel, nor was the very American belief that schooling is an antidote to crime, poverty, and vice. The school promoters of the early nineteenth century repeatedly argued that schooling would give people the means to improve themselves and thereby break the cycle of poverty. During the early 1960s, this traditional rhetoric was given new life by scholars and policymakers. Educational programs burgeoned as an integral part of the federal government's war on poverty. Jacob Riis had written in 1892, "the more kindergartens, the fewer prisons"; in 1965 Lyndon Johnson predicted that the lives of children in the Head Start summer program would be spent "productively and rewardingly, rather than wasted in tax-supported institutions or in welfare-supported lethargy." The hope of eliminating poverty and inequality provided the major rationale not only for Operation Head Start but for general federal aid to education as well.

By the time the period of educational expansion reached a high tide in the middle 1960s, much was expected by a variety of publics. It was hoped that more education would:

- Reduce inequality among individuals and groups by eliminating illiteracy and cultural deprivation.
- Improve the economy and economic opportunity by raising the nation's supply of intelligence and skill.
- Spread capacity for personal fulfillment by developing talents, skills, and creative energies.
- Prove to be an uplifting and civilizing influence in the nation's cultural life by broadly diffusing the fruits of liberal education.
- Reduce alienation and mistrust while building a new sense of community among people of similar education and similar values.
- Reduce prejudice and misunderstanding by fostering contact among diverse groups.
- Improve the quality of civic and political life.

These hopes and expectations were a heavy burden for the schools to bear. Perhaps predictably, they did not accomplish all that was asked of them. Most of the problems that were laid at the schools' doors remained just as problematic years later (and some critics would argue that the provision of more schooling had produced the opposite effect in every instance). Poverty and inequality did not cease; their roots were elsewhere, and the schools were not able to cure deep-seated social and economic ills. While the disadvantaged received more schooling, so did the advantaged.

Many poor youths entered the middle class by using educational opportunity, but others remained as poor as their parents. The value of a high school diploma declined not only because its possession became nearly universal but also, and most important, because high school graduates were not necessarily literate—mainly because of the well-intended effort to keep as many youths in school for as long as possible and to deny no one a diploma, regardless of his educational development. Society's investment in education probably did spur economic development, but it did not prevent the emergence of skepticism about the desirability of economic growth; in fact, it was precisely among the educated (and the advantaged) that economic growth became suspect because of its association with the bureaucratization, centralization, and depersonalization of modern economic life. It is impossible to gauge the effects of increased schooling on popular culture or high culture. Television, which invariably seeks the largest possible audience, undoubtedly has more power to shape popular culture than schools do (a mixed blessing, since television disperses both sitcom pap and major cultural events to mass audiences). Participation in popular culture and high culture has surely been broadened, yet it is arguable whether the quality of either has been elevated during recent decades. Nor is it possible to demonstrate that increased educational participation has eliminated distrust between groups or contributed to a new sense of community. On the contrary, educational institutions have become settings for expression of militant particularism along racial, religious, ethnic, sexual, cultural, and linguistic lines. Very likely the differences among groups have been accentuated in the past twenty years. But again it would be difficult to hold the schools directly responsible for these trends. More likely, it appears, the schools are the stage on which such issues are acted out rather than the cause of their appearance. Nor can the schools claim to have improved the quality of political life, since political participation has waned along with public regard for political institutions. But, once again, it was not the schools that were responsible for the apparent ebbing of civic commitment and the surge of political apathy, nor could they even serve as a counterforce against such attitudes. The same attitudes of distrust, skepticism, hostility, and apathy eroded the schools' own status in the social order. The same confusions that pervaded the social atmosphere also pervaded the schools. If they failed to teach citizenship, it was at least in part because teachers and parents were confused about what a good citizen was and whether "citizenship" could be taught without imposing a partisan interpretation. In short, a society that is confused and contentious cannot look to its schools to straighten things out, for the schools will reflect the same confusion and contention.

In retrospect, it was folly to have expected the schools to transform society or to mold a new kind of person. The schools are by nature limited institutions, not total institutions. They do not have full power over their students' lives (even total institutions, like prisons, have discovered the difficulty of shaping or reshaping the lives and minds of those they fully control). Schools are not fully independent in their dealings with students; they are interrelated with, and dependent on, families, churches, the media, peer groups, and other agencies of influence. Nor can schools be considered as if they were machines, all operating in the same predictable manner. Teachers vary, administrators vary, students vary, communities vary, and therefore schools vary. The schools, being complex human institutions composed of actors with different goals, different interests, and different capacities, cannot be treated as if they were all interchangeable.

As it became clear that more schooling would not provide any magical solutions, the utopian hopes once focused on the schools dissipated. Having briefly been the repository of grand and even grandiose dreams of human betterment, the schools became a scapegoat for all the wide-ranging problems they had failed to solve. Having revealed that they were but fallible instruments of social change and that any change they promoted would only be incremental, the schools became the object of rage and scorn. They were portrayed as intractable, bureaucratic, even malevolent barriers to social change. But just as it was unrealistic to believe that the schools had the power to remake society by molding those who passed through their doors, it was equally unrealistic to assert that they were powerless, meaningless, superfluous institutions with no purpose other than the care and feeding of their own employees.

Nonetheless, when the dream of a school-led social revolution faded, school criticism shifted in tone. The voices of liberal critics—those who believed that men and women of goodwill might work together to improve schools by using this program or that curriculum—diminished to mere whispers. They were drowned out by critics who believed that only radical changes in teaching or in governing schools could "save" them; by those who believed that the public schools were beyond redemption and ought to be replaced by "free" schools; and by those who advocated the abolition of compulsory schooling and the "de-schooling" of society. For a time in the late 1960s and early 1970s, bookstore shelves fairly bulged with apocalyptic predictions about the imminent demise of schooling. One book, playing on the then current phrase "God is dead," was titled *School Is Dead*. While some of the writing of this period contained sharp and telling portraits of insensitive teachers and uncaring bureaucrats, others gave vent to undisguised anti-intellectualism in their attacks on academic standards, discipline, science, and rationality. In the larger culture—and, alas, especially in academic institutions—a great revival seemed to sweep the land, casting aside "old" doctrines of deferred gratification, structured learning, and professionalism while espousing mysticism, Eastern religions, the occult, astrology, and whatever else promised to touch the spontaneous, untrained inner spirit.

These trends had curricular and programmatic consequences. In colleges, students demanded, and usually won, the abolition of course requirements, the adoption of pass-fail grading, the de-emphasis of competition and testing, and extensive choice in selecting their own programs of study. As requirements for admission to college were relaxed, high schools soon succumbed to many of the same pressures that had changed the colleges: course requirements were eased, new courses proliferated, academic standards dropped, homework diminished, and adults generally relinquished their authority to direct student learning. At all levels, both in college and high school, educational administrators reduced, to the extent possible, the schools' role as in loco parentis. To some extent, this period of student assertiveness and adult retreat was the educational side of the movement against the war in Vietnam, which provoked youthful revolt against authority in many parts of the society and the culture. But even after the war ended, there remained a lingering hostility to science, technology, and reason—as though these were the root causes of the hated war.

As the 1980s opened, it appeared that this wave of anti-intellectualism had spent itself, for complaints about the schools suggested entirely different concerns. The well-publicized decline in Scholastic Aptitude Test (SAT) scores created a context for worrying about a national deterioration in the quality of education. Not that the SAT scores were important in themselves, but they provided a sense of a pattern-in-the-carpet that had not previously been definable. For several years college officials had reported a steady increase in the number of freshmen who read poorly and wrote atrociously; the phenomenon of remedial reading and remedial writing classes spread throughout higher education, even to elite institutions. The apparent explanation, at first, was that so many new students from poor families had begun to attend college, but analysis of the SAT drop showed that the score decline continued long after the socio-economic profile of the college-going population had stabilized. Bits and pieces of evidence from other sources began to fit together. Other standardized measures of academic ability reported score declines paralleling the SAT's. National news-magazines discovered a writing crisis and a literacy crisis. Educational malpractice suits were filed by disgruntled parents because their children had received a high school diploma in spite of being "functionally illiterate." The Council for Basic Education, a lonely voice for liberal education since its founding in 1958, found itself back in the educational mainstream, while still a lonely voice for liberal education. Demands for minimum competency tests seemed to spring up spontaneously in almost every state, though no national organization existed to promote or coordinate the movement. As concern for educational standards spread in the middle 1970s, demands for testing grew—not only minimum competency tests for high school graduation but tests at critical checkpoints in the lower grades and tests for would-be teachers. Reaction against these demands was not long in coming. The assault upon standardized testing was led by consumer activist Ralph Nader and the National Education Association. Nader released a lengthy attack on the credibility of the SAT, the most widely used college admission test, and lobbied successfully in New York State and elsewhere for passage of a "truth-in-testing" law.

While it did generate controversy, the dispute over testing was superficial, for tests were neither a cause of nor a remedy for the underlying malaise in American education. Nearly all the educational controversies of the 1970s—whether over bilingualism or sex education or testing or open admissions or busing—dealt with some aspect of the educational process that was of great importance to some constituency, but none directly raised these questions: What does it mean to be an educated person? What knowledge is of most worth? Are the graduates of our schools educated people?

The very absence of such questioning suggests a failure in educational thinking. Educators and, most especially, educational policy-makers have fallen into the habit of analyzing school issues almost entirely in sociological and economic terms. In recent years it has been customary to think of schooling as a quantifiable economic good to be distributed in accordance with principles of equity or in response to political demands. The sociological-economic perspective has come to dominate educational discussion and has informed public policy. Without doubt it has contributed to necessary changes in patterns of schooling, by redirecting resources in a fair manner and by opening up access to educational opportunities. But the functionalist perspective became dysfunctional when it crowded substantive educational concerns off the policy-makers' agenda, when the desire to keep students in school was unaccompanied by interest in what they would learn while they stayed in school. What I am suggesting here is not a conflict between the functionalist perspective and the educational perspective, but the danger of analyzing the schools through only one of the two prisms. There has been a fairly persistent tendency, I would argue, to neglect the role of schools as educational institutions, to treat them as sociological cookie cutters without regard to the content of their educational program. When I consider why this is so, I conclude that there are several possible explanations.

First, the sociological perspective has become dominant because it relies on quantifiable data that are accessible. It is far easier to gain information about years of educational attainment and socio-economic status than it is to ascertain the conditions of learning in any given school. Educators cannot agree on how to ascertain the educational climate or even on what should be learned. Thus it becomes irresistible to deal with, perhaps even become the captive of, data that are both available and measurable.

Second, the sociological perspective is a useful adjunct to the concept of the school as a tool of social reform. By checking on who is in school and for how many years, and on how their social background relates to their choice of occupation, we can attempt to monitor how educational resources are allocated and whether schooling is contributing to social progress. While it is neither new nor unusual to regard the school as a lever of social reform, it is unusual and perhaps unwise to see the school solely as a tool of social reform and *solely* as a resource to be redistributed. One consequence is that the school's diploma is confused with the learning that it is supposed to represent. In recent years, policymakers have sought to equalize educational attainment (years-of-schooling) without regard to the quality of education. This is like putting people on a diet of eighteen hundred calories a day without caring whether they are consuming junk food or nutritious food. Years-of-schooling, or a diploma, has been treated as an end in itself. Thus we have seen courts require school districts to present a diploma to students who could not meet minimum state standards of literacy, as if it was the diploma itself they needed rather than the learning that the diploma is supposed to signify. When school reformers in the nineteenth century advocated universal education as a way of improving society, they meant a broad diffusion of knowledge and wisdom, not a broad diffusion of diplomas.

Third, educational analysts have relied on the sociological perspective because it is easier to raise the level of educational attainment than it is to raise the level of educational quality. Staying in school, not dropping out, and getting a diploma represent a clear, unambiguous goal that everyone can understand without quarrel. As soon as school officials begin to define what should be taught and learned during those years, disagreements arise which are best settled by making the schools all things for all people.

For these reasons and others, educational policymakers have tended to view schooling as an instrument to achieve some other goal, only rarely as an end in itself. To the extent that they do so, they rob schooling of the very attributes that give it power. If a young man or woman has a high school diploma but can scarcely read or write, then the diploma is worthless. When a diploma, either at the high school or college level, represents a certificate of time served but not of the systematic development of intelligence and skill, then it is difficult to know why it should have any inherent value. And of course it does not.

An educational critique of schooling would have as its starting point, I believe, the idea that the essential purpose of schooling is to develop the powers of intelligence: thinking, reflecting, observing, imagining, appreciating, questioning, and judging. Beyond that, schooling has many additional purposes and serves many additional purposes, both for the student and for society. Educational literature teems with lists of the many ways in which schools should meet individual and social needs. But the schools' first purpose is to encourage and guide each person in the cultivation of intelligence and the development of talents, interests, and abilities. Schools do many other things as well; they may provide food, social services, psychological services, medical care, and career guidance. But no matter how well or how poorly they fulfill these functions, the schools must be judged in the first instance by how well they do those things that only they can do. We expect the schools to teach children command of the fundamental skills that are needed to continue learning—in particular, the ability to read, write, compute, speak, and listen. Once they have command of these skills, they should progress through a curriculum designed to enlarge their powers. Such a curriculum would contain, for every student, history and social studies, language and literature, mathematics, science, and the arts. Students need to learn these skills and disciplines in school because, except for those rare individuals who can educate themselves without a teacher, they are unlikely to have another chance to do so.

The schools are responsible both for preserving a sense of the past and for providing the ability to think about, and function in, the present and the future. More than any other educational agency, they ought to have an intelligent understanding of the inexorable connection between past, present, and future. Certainly there is disagreement about the meaning of the past and how it relates to the present and the future, and awareness of such disagreement is often invoked to justify educational aimlessness. But much of what seems to be dissension is a chimera; democratic debate ought not to be confused with chaos, nor should pluralistic politics be confused with anarchy. Education proceeds from widely shared values, and we do, in fact, have widely shared values. We may not agree about how democracy is to be achieved and about whether we have too much or too little of it, but few would question the idea that each person has the right as a citizen to participate in the shaping of public issues. We believe in the idea of self-government and in the greatest possible involvement of citizens as voters, as volunteers in community organizations, as members of interest groups, and as spokesmen for different views. While we may differ over particular educational issues, there is general support for the idea that schooling is a necessary mechanism for achieving society's goals: to prepare the younger generation to be thoughtful citizens; to enable each person to appreciate and contribute to the culture; to sharpen the intellectual and aesthetic sensibilities for lifelong enjoyment; to develop readiness for the educational, occupational, and professional choices that each person will confront; to kindle a sense of responsibility for others and a sense of integrity; to teach children how to lead and how to follow; and to acquaint young people with the best models of achievement in every field while encouraging them to strive to realize their own potential.

If these are widely shared educational aims, and I believe they are, then none of them should be left to chance. The curriculum should be designed so that every student has the fullest opportunity to develop his powers, intelligence, interests, talent, and understanding. Every student needs to know how to form and formulate his own opinions. To do so, he must learn how to read critically, how to evaluate arguments, how to weigh evidence, and how to reach judgments on his own. Every student, to understand the world in which he will be a participant, should be knowledgeable about history; should master some other language as well as his own; should discover the pleasures of literature, especially its power to reach across time and cultures and to awaken our sense of universality; should study science and technology, both as a citizen who will be asked to comprehend complex issues and as an individual who must live with constant change. Since we believe that everyone should be equally concerned about the problems of our society, then we must believe that everyone, every student, should be schooled in a way that meets his needs to know history, science, mathematics, language, the arts, literature, and so on. And yet it is not simply on the grounds of utility, relevance, and political value that the case for liberal education rests. We do not need to know how to read Shakespeare; we can be good citizens without any knowledge of Athenian civilization, even though our concept of citizenship is based on the very period of which we are ignorant. We must concern ourselves with the survival of history, philosophy, literature, and those other disciplines that may lack immediate utility because without them ours would be an intellectually impoverished and spiritually illiterate civilization.

To some people, all this is so self-evident that it ought not be necessary to plead for the value of an education of substance and content. Yet it is necessary, because of the widespread disarray in high school and college curricula. In the face of changes that have occurred in the past decade or so, many educators seem unable to remember how to justify or defend or champion liberal education. The proposition that all students should be subject to curricular requirements that define the essentials of a good education has become controversial, rather than a starting point in defining the nature of a good curriculum.

Confronted with conflicting demands from those who want reduced requirements and those who want curricular substance, many schools have resolved the dilemma by reducing requirements while expanding electives. Thus students may take history courses to meet their minimal graduation requirement, but may choose history courses that are little more than classes in current events. Or they may meet their English requirement by reading popular fiction, mystery stories, and science fiction. There is no harm in what is included; from the perspective of a liberal education, what is unfortunate is the wide body of knowledge that is excluded when course proliferation and lax requirements are joined together. Professors regularly encounter students who are ignorant of anything that happened before the Civil War as well as anything that happened, or was written, outside the United States. They may have heard of Plato and Aristotle in a survey course, but they have never read anything written by either and have only a dim notion (usually wrong) of what they "stood for." Mention Dickens, Tolstoy, Conrad, or Melville, and they have heard of them too, but they "didn't take that course." Some professors who teach literature have been astonished to find students who know nothing of mythology or the Bible; allusions to Job or Icarus must be explained to those who have no intellectual furniture in their minds, no stock of literary or historical knowledge on which to draw beyond their immediate experience. In a recent issue of *Commonweal,* J. M. Cameron soberly observes that if Freud attended school today, he might not be able to think up the Oedipus theory because he would not have enough mythology in his head to do so. We seem now to turn to television or the movies to teach the history and literature that were neglected in school. To permit knowledge to be fragmented, as we have, by serving it up cafeteria-style, with each person choosing whether to be minimally literate or to be a specialist, contributes to the diminution and degradation of the common culture.

IV

AFTER A CENTURY OF CURRICULUM THOUGHT: CONTEMPORARY ISSUES AND CONTINUING DEBATES

In the introduction to this volume, we suggested that the field of curriculum studies has grown increasingly diverse in recent times, and that someone unfamiliar with the field's intellectual terrain could easily be taken aback by what often seems an eclectic array of subject matter concerns, social issues, political disagreements, and technical models. In some ways, the parameters of the field have broadened, or at least that would seem to be the case on first glance at the readings included in this final section. The aim of this section is to sample contemporary issues and continuing debates. The section represents a diverse group of writers whose work in each case can be understood as an attempt to highlight assumptions and ideas that would otherwise be ignored or be taken for granted. From this perspective, it would seem that each author has his or her own agenda. As contemporary works, moreover, the readings in this last section disallow the advantage of a retrospective point of view. For this reason as well, these writings may seem more topical than those included in earlier sections. The specific issues on which these contemporary authors focus range from the ecological crisis and AIDS education to tracking, student diversity, the national standards movement, and school restructuring.

However, the readings in this section represent far more than a survey of this season's curricular fashions. Two points are relevant to this claim. First, the particular issues mentioned above are themselves urgent and often poignantly felt in a wide variety of schools and classrooms. Second, these issues and how they are understood are grounded in the field's temporality. They represent continuing debates in which the templates of the past are retooled to fit the concerns of our present and future possibilities. To put this another way, both change and continuity are evident in the diversity of these readings. Beyond the immediate challenges of contemporary education are a set of perennial questions and a sense of intellectual history that are crucial, we believe, to understanding curriculum scholarship.

The first two readings illustrate the changes and continuities in current scholarship. Both readings focus on distinctively contemporary topics—the ecological crisis and AIDS education. Both readings also raise questions that have long interested curriculum scholars. David Jardine's thesis is that resting just beneath conceptions of curriculum integration and personal development is an inescapable interdependency with the Earth. His struggle, set within the context of early childhood education, is to make visible the broader foundations and implications of a what has become a common buzz word in curriculum reform efforts. In Jardine's view, "integration" must be situated in terms of an Earth that is simultaneously at our very fingertips and intimately connected with events that would otherwise seem distant and far removed from the day-to-day lives of children.

The next reading, "HIV/AIDS Education: Toward a Collaborative Curriculum," is a chapter from Jonathan Silin's recent book, *Sex, Death, and the Education of Children.* Much of this chapter is based on the author's work with teachers in New York state. Their aim has been to examine the formal curriculum now in use and the experiences of children through which cultural myths as well as information about HIV/AIDS find their way into the classroom. In Silin's view, it is important to recognize HIV/AIDS as a social construction because the social embeddedness of this disease is what creates special challenges for teachers and curriculum developers. This embeddedness connects HIV/AIDS education with a variety of ideological and tacit patterns of belief, ranging from our conceptions of childhood as a sheltered stage in life to beliefs concerning the professional objectivity of teachers and the basis for their authority in the classroom. In his efforts to sort out these issues, Silin directly acknowledges a debt to earlier curriculum thinkers, including Dewey, the field's critical theorists, and those who have viewed curriculum from a phenomenological perspective. Silin also argues that for better or worse, earlier curriculum thinking is still at work today in shaping HIV/AIDS education at the levels of both policy and practice.

The article by Jeannie Oakes introduces a third curriculum topic surrounded by controversy. In this case, the debate centers on forms of curriculum differentiation commonly known as tracking. Oakes is primarily interested in the development of research on tracking, what we have learned form this research, and how future research can be used to obtain the types of information that educators need if they are to successfully reform current tracking practices. Oakes predicates her recommendations on the need to better understand the complexities of tracking through research that examines its technical, normative, and political dimensions. These dimensions are of special interest because they connect this area of research with three concerns that have long been central to curriculum scholarship—classroom practice, the type of broad cultural beliefs recognized by Jardine and Silin in their work, and the politics of schooling.

The next article, by John F. Jennings, focuses on the contemporary issue of national standards. What in recent years has become known as the national standards movement may not seem immediately connected with perspectives on curriculum integration, ecological concerns, HIV/AIDS education, or research on tracking.

However, all of these topics, including national standards, represent broad concerns that not only encompass curriculum issues but also fuel a renewed interest in curriculum studies. In particular, Jennings argues that past national trends have focused on new testing programs and increased graduation requirements with too little attention paid to the substance of what students learn. Jennings advocates national standards as a way to correct this imbalance by clarifying the aims of education and improving the alignment between what students learn, how they learn, and how they are tested. Will this improved clarity and alignment lead to a national curriculum? Although Jennings disclaims this possibility, it remains a point of contention in current educational debates. The question is not just whether schools need to reach national agreement on what is taught, but also whether such agreement would be desirable.

The four readings that follow Jennings' article provide a variety of perspectives on the related topic of student diversity. For almost two decades, issues of student diversity have been pressed forward by several developments. The rising interests in multicultural education, race relations, urban schooling, bilingual programs, tracking, and feminist pedagogy have each contributed to an explicit focus on the implications of student diversity for all facets of schooling, including the curriculum. While these issues clearly extend beyond the readings in this part of the book, our sample does suggest the scope of curriculum thinking that overlaps with the many branches of current scholarship on diversity concerns.

The article by Nathan Glazer is focused on both the history and social context of cultural pluralism in the United States. Going back to the 1840s, Glazer traces the question of how schools should respond to the diversity and cultural distinctiveness of their students. He presents a history that includes major efforts to both assimilate and accommodate culturally distinct groups. These two aims, often viewed as in opposition to one another, continue to be a venue for public debate over the purposes and probable outcomes of multicultural education. Some of the accommodations made by schools in the past would probably be viewed as radical by today's standards. Yet, from Glazer's point of view, the outcomes of these accommodations do not support those who argue that multicultural education represents a significant threat to the stability of American social or political life.

The next reading, co-authored by Christine Sleeter and Carl Grant, reports their own research on the question of how race, class, gender, and disability are represented in contemporary textbooks. Their study examined the content of forty-seven textbooks for grades one through eight in four subject areas: science, math, social studies, and English language arts. Broadly speaking, the purpose of the study is to explore how curriculum functions as a form of cultural reproduction and as a reflection of struggles for the power to define what counts as legitimate knowledge. Comparing their findings with earlier research, Sleeter and Grant identify cosmetic changes that have been made in contemporary textbooks. These changes include, for example, the elimination of sexist language, the portrayal of women in nontraditional roles, and a greater inclusion of some minority groups. Most significant for these researchers, however, is not what they found but what they did not find. In other words, this study serves to underscore the importance of what has been called "the null curriculum" (Eisner, 1994; Flinders, Noddings, & Thornton, 1986), a term used to describe the content and perspectives that schools fail to teach. In the case at hand, the null curriculum is represented by the continued absence of topics such as social conflict, collective action, group oppression, the perspectives of working class and low-income groups, interactions between racial groups, and the portrayal of males in nontraditional roles.

The reading by Belenky, Clinchy, Goldberger, and Tarule is a chapter reprinted from their book, *Women's Ways of Knowing*. Although their book was published before Sleeter and Grant's research, the former complements content-focused studies by moving the themes of gender representation into the arena of classroom experience and what that experience means in the day-to-day lives of students. Using interview data gathered from a sample of women college students and former college students, Belenky and her colleagues seek to understand how women experience the curriculum and forms of teaching they have encountered, and what challenges they face in finding their own ways of learning. However, many of the tensions that these authors so vividly recount will be readily recognized by educators working at all levels of education and with a variety of students. The questions that the authors raise also open the door for curriculum scholars to revisit and rethink some of the field's most fundamental concerns. What does a student's own learning, for example, mean to that student? Must doubt always precede belief? What types of curriculum structure will foster intellectual engagement, under what circumstances, with whom, and why?

The final reading that deals directly with issues of students diversity is Nel Noddings' article, "Does Everybody Count?" Noddings states that her aim is to urge an open-minded skepticism in viewing the current reform proposals for mathematics education. She is concerned that as "constituted" subjects (to use the postmodern term), all educators face the problem of becoming caught up in the politics and policy rhetoric of change. Specifically, teachers must avoid being pushed into ill-conceived reform measures that coerce students into either wasting their talents or demeaning their own genuine interests. To guard against this danger, Noddings recommends that we ask hard questions about the basic assumptions and motives that stand behind the current proposals. Why, for example, do we insist that everyone study mathematics? If we take seriously the wide diversity in human interests, can a single or uniform program of study possibly fit all students? Noddings argues that a differentiated curriculum might be both the most productive and the most humane, provided that this differentiation is based on student interest rather than social status. While this is not a new idea, a differentiated curriculum is provocative when juxtaposed with Oakes' review of tracking research (this section). Beyond mathematics education and the more general issue of tracking, Noddings cautions that teacher educators must also be skeptical of buying into current reforms that call for further efforts to increase the professional status of teaching. Creating graduate level teacher education programs, for example, will involve not just gains, but losses as well.

The last three readings in this section are also the last three readings in the book. They are not, however, intended to provide closure in the sense of having arrived at a final destination. Instead, the significance of these readings is in the lessons they suggest for the next generation of curriculum scholars. All three articles originated in a symposium that was organized for an annual meeting of the American Educational Research Association. The symposium speakers were asked to reflect on the relationship between curriculum scholarship and the question of what is (or should) be taught in schools. Given this common topic, these last three readings can be viewed as assessments of the curriculum field at large and as visions of where the field should be headed.

The two articles written separately by Elliot Eisner and Michael Apple represent different perspectives, but they also identify many of the same concerns regarding the impact of curriculum scholarship on classroom practice. Eisner from a "centrist" position and Apple from a politically progressive stance both see the influences of scholarship blunted by historical trends that have made schools resistant to reform. These conservative and stabilizing factors include, for example, the ways in which schools have traditionally been organized, the discipline-based nature of curriculum content, the pervasive reliance on textbooks, the rise of standardized testing, and the influence of university admissions standards. Both articles also blame the nature of curriculum scholarship for its overemphasis on procedural, "how to" knowledge and its focus on technical methods. This technical focus also has historical precedents that extend back to the work of Franklin Bobbitt and the scientific strand of progressive education. The tradition of specifying and developing methods is seen as drawing the attention of curriculum scholars away from Herbert Spencer's question, "What knowledge is of most worth?"

These are all points on which Eisner and Apple would seem to agree. Nevertheless, each proposes a different approach to increasing the value and influence of future curriculum scholarship. Eisner's vision of productive scholarship is grounded on the premise that education is too complex an undertaking, too value-laden, and too ideologically based to expect any widespread consensus on the specific aims or content of school curriculum. The role of scholarship, in Eisner's view, is to explore options, to help others explore options, and to do so in ways that will make curriculum deliberations more reflective than they would be otherwise. Not so implicit in this view is that contemporary discourse would best be served by more rather than fewer points of view. Apple's approach is different but not incompatible with how Eisner envisions the role of scholarship. Given the formidable challenges of reform, Apple recommends that curriculum scholars join forces with classroom teachers, parents, and students to support democratic forms of education. Thus, in these two articles we find calls for both plurality and solidarity.

In the final reading, Ann Lieberman examines the current trends in school restructuring and teacher leadership. She argues that these trends are an opportunity for curriculum scholars to reconnect the question of what schools should teach with the process of change, the culture of the school, and the context of the classroom. Lieberman's aim is to situate curriculum within the lives of those who experience it. This desire once again echoes previous themes that stretch back to Dewey's student-centered approach to education, for example, or John Goodlad's concern that the discipline-based reforms of the 1950s and 1960s attend to "cooperative teaching arrangements." Lieberman's argument, nevertheless, is well worth reiterating in its contemporary context. If curriculum scholars distance themselves from the schools or fail to work collaboratively with schoolpeople, whatever scholarship produced will be ignored by those who matter most. Conversely, if curriculum scholars seek out common interests with those closest to educational practice, these scholars are more likely to have a voice in school reform and more likely to open up future areas of study.

References

Eisner, E. W. (1994). *The educational imagination* (3rd ed.). New York: Macmillan.

Flinders, D. J., Noddings, N., & Thornton, S. J. (1986). The null curriculum: Its theoretical basis and practical implications. *Curriculum Inquiry, 16*, 33–42.

20

"To Dwell with a Boundless Heart": On the Integrated Curriculum and the Recovery of the Earth

DAVID W. JARDINE

I like to walk alone on country paths, rice plants and wild grasses on both sides, putting each foot down on the earth in mindfulness, knowing that I walk on the wondrous earth. In such moments, existence is . . . miraculous and mysterious. People usually consider walking on water or in thin air a miracle. But I think the real miracle is . . . to walk on earth. Every day we are engaged in a miracle which we don't even recognize: a blue sky, white clouds, green leaves, the black, curious eyes of a child. All is a miracle.[1]

I began teaching my undergraduate early childhood education class this year by handing my students a blank piece of paper and instructing them to write down as many possible ways the paper could be used to demonstrate, illustrate, or teach features of the various curriculum areas. Their ideas began as expected, with possibilities such as writing on it, painting or drawing on it, reading from it, folding it and making shapes, questions of where paper comes from, how it is made and used, and so on. But in the midst of this exercise came a striking advent for this class. Once they moved to questions of how the paper was made, one student suggested that you could talk about trees and still remain "linked up" with the paper, still remain "on topic." Once this shift of focus occurred, what began was a giddy onrush of sun and soil and water and logging and chainsaws and gasoline and refineries. Because of this serendipitous turn of attention, suddenly and unexpectedly, everything came to be co-present with the paper, everything seemed to nestle around it. Some topics seemed close to the paper, others distant, at the ends of long and tenuous tendrils of interconnection. Some connections were obvious and immediate, some connections were stretched, but nothing was absent altogether.

One striking feature of this class was that we seemed to go beyond a mere mental exercise to glimpsing something about the world and our experience of the world, a previously unnoticed interconnectedness of things hidden beneath the surface, ana-

Jardine, D. (1990) "To Dwell with a Boundless Heart: On the Integrated Curriculum and the Recovery of the Earth." *Journal of Curriculum and Supervision*, Vol. 5, No. 2, 1990: pp. 107–119. Reprinted with permission of the Association for Supervision and Curriculum Development. Copyright © 1990 by ASCD. All rights reserved.

lytic assumptions of difference and separateness that are so commonplace and that guide much curricular thinking.

> With the interdependence of all things or "interbeing" . . . cause and effect are no longer perceived as linear, but as a net, not a two-dimensional one, but a system of countless nets interwoven in all directions in a multidimensional space.[2]

> All things in the world are linked together, one way or the other. Not a single thing comes into being without some relationship to every other thing.[3]

> Even the very tiniest thing, to the extent that it "is," displays in its act of being the whole web of circuminsessional interpenetration that links all things together.[4]

As we proceeded with reflections on this exercise, we realized that any object could have been used for this demonstration, any object could have been drawn into the center in a way that all other things organize themselves around this center. With any object, everything else seems to come forward as implicated in this object, but no special object in this implication has a privileged status as center.

> The universe is a dynamic fabric of interdependent events in which none is the fundamental entity.[5]

While a piece of blank paper lends itself to curricular matters that are proximal to it (e.g., writing, drawing, questions of how it is made), pulling out this piece of paper tugs at the whole fabric of things, without exception. Paradoxically put, then, every object is a unique center around which all others can be gathered; at the same time, that very object rests on the periphery of all others, proximal to some, distant to others.

> To say *that a thing is not itself* means that, while continuing to be itself, it is in the home-ground of everything else. Figuratively speaking, its roots reach across into the ground of all other things and help to hold them up and keep them standing, It serves as a constitutive element of their being so that they can be what they are, and thus provides an ingredient of their being. That a thing is itself means that all other things, while continuing to be themselves, are in the home-ground of that thing; that precisely when a thing is on its own home-ground, everything else is there too; that the roots of everything spread across into its home-ground. This way that everything has of being on the home-ground of everything else, without ceasing to be on its own home-ground, means that the being of each thing is held up, kept standing, and made to be what it is by means of the being of all other things; or, put the other way around, that each thing holds up the being of every other thing, keeps it standing, and makes it what it is.[6]

No singular center will resolve this paradox, that a thing is, so to speak, not itself (i.e., it is only in relation to all other things and therefore summons up all those things that it is not in order to be itself) while being itself. If it were not for trees and sun and sky and water, there would be no paper, and to fully understand what this piece of paper is in an integral way requires bringing forth this paradoxical, interweaving indebtedness. The name for this paradoxical, interweaving indebtedness is the Earth.

From here, the class moved on to a discussion of the question of the nature and assumption of an integrated curriculum and the appropriateness of such a curriculum for early childhood education.

The Recovery of the Earth

The notion of the *integrated* curriculum is becoming common currency in early childhood education in Canada, and the articulation of this concept across grades K–6 is beginning in some circles. What seems to be missing in many current formulations of this notion is any deep sense of the difference it makes in our lives and the lives of children. Is it simply a new slogan that will become exhausted and empty, as have so many others in the consumptive flurry in education for the newest and the latest? Or does it speak of something new, something vital and generative, in the field of education? I believe that it is potentially the latter.

But this potential is difficult to assess and address. The exercise my students did in the class was a momentarily enjoyable one, but it is also one whose giddy insight is difficult to sustain. My students did report that they glimpsed something about the notion of integration in the curriculum, but it was almost impossible to sustain this glimpse and cash it out as something practicable. It was difficult to lay out in front of us as a set of propositions or formulae, not because of the complexity of the task or its arduous nature, but because what we were glimpsing was precisely not an object for our perusal or an objective set of relationships that we can set before us. Rather, we were glimpsing the way in which the Earth is our abode, our dwelling, and how our lives as teachers are an integral part of this dwelling.

The notion of an integrated curriculum became a painful one for some students as they began to confront the fossilized residues and assumptions of their own schooling and, more pointedly, as they began practice teaching in situations of profound disintegration. The seemingly innocent and playful exercise we conducted did not make matters easier or clearer, nor did it make questions of applicability simpler and more straightforward. It made things worse. Underlying this difficulty are questions regarding images of our lives and the lives of our children that both sustain and ground the notion of the integrated curriculum. Something archaic and delicate and difficult needs to be recovered for the integrated curriculum to have any deep sense.

> The unnoticeable law of the earth preserves the earth in the sufficiency of the emerging and perishing of all things in the allotted sphere of the possible which everything follows, and yet nothing knows. The birch tree never oversteps its possibility. It is [human] will which . . . drives the earth beyond the . . . sphere of its possibility into such things which are no longer a possibility and are thus the impossible. It is one thing to just use the earth, another to receive the blessing of the earth and to become at home in the law of this reception in order to shepherd the mystery . . . and watch over the inviolability of the possible.[7]

If we begin to unearth the notion of the integrated curriculum, it begins to disrupt our deeply held beliefs and images of understanding, self-understanding, and mutual understanding, pointing to a sense of interrelatedness, interdependency, or interconnectedness that is belied by our analytic, definitional, and frequently disintegrative approaches to educational phenomena. It also belies the desire to finalize, control, master, and foreclose on vital curricular issues. It puts into question desires we may have, as educational theorists and practitioners, to get the curriculum "right," "straightened out," once and for all, for such desires require a basically disintegrative, analytic act aimed at rendering education a closed question, aimed at rendering human life lifelessly objective under the glare of knowledge-as-*stasis*.

Integration leads to glimpses of a truly lived curriculum, a true *curriculum vitae,* one that exudes the generativity, movement, liveliness and difficulty that lies at the heart of living our lives, as educators, in the presence of new life in our midst, in the presence of children.[8] A truly integrated curriculum involves the ambiguous and difficult ways in which our lives are intertwined with children—the irresolvable paradox of children "being part of us but also apart from us"[9]—and the ways in which our lives together with children are interwoven with the life of the Earth. It is this *integer,* this *whole,* this *integrity* that the integrated curriculum voices.

Near the roots of the notion of the integrated curriculum is a strikingly simple image of education:

> The essence of education is natality, the fact that human beings are *born* into the world.[10]

> To preserve the world against the mortality of its creators and inhabitants, it must be constantly set right anew. The problem is simply to educate in such a way that setting-right remains actually possible, even though it can, of course, never be assured.[11]

Education, in this image, has to do with our fundamental orientation to natality and, therefore, our fundamental orientation and openness to the future. Although education often means the ceaseless proliferation of longer and longer lists, guides, schedules, and agenda, at its heart, it cannot be caught in the *stasis* that such a tendency requires and desires in the end. Rather, education is *ekstatic,* a movement beyond what already is, a reaching out to the new life around us in a way that keeps open the possibility "that the people of this precious Earth . . . may live."[12]

The integrated curriculum is, at its roots, more than a matter of the interrelations between curriculum areas or subject matters. It is an ecological and spiritual matter, involving images of our place and the place of our children on "this precious Earth." It raises the question of how we are to understand that we are people of this precious Earth, caught up in its potentialities and possibilities. It raises the question of how the deep and moist interweavings and integrity of the Earth are both an original constraint on our lives, but also an original blessing, an original freedom; overstepping the boundary pushes the Earth beyond what is possible for it to sustain.[13] In the end, the integrated curriculum requires a deep reflection on our desires to disintegrate children's curricular experiences in the name of manageability, easy of instructional design or territorial notions of the separateness and uniqueness of subject-matter specializations.

As an ecological and spiritual matter, the notion of the integrated curriculum involves disturbing, even horrifying, questions as to whether we can continue to take for granted this basic natality that springs from this original blessing of the Earth and that lies at the heart of education. We could never and cannot now assure our children an Earth on which life can go on, an Earth on which "setting-right is actually possible," for such assurances are literally beyond us. The horror is that degenerative, disintegrative, and consumptive images of human life and the bringing forth of human life (*ēducarē*) may be assuring the opposite. The true horror is that this assurance is precisely not beyond us, even if we choose to ignore it and live, educate, and proliferate educational theories, research, and practices as if the Earth does not matter, as if, therefore, the continuation of human life were not an educational concern.[14]

Ignoring the ecological and spiritual consequences and character of the integrated curriculum plunges education into a peculiar paradox, an impossibility. We are able to diligently pursue ways to teach the mathematics, science, social studies, and language arts curriculums without ever considering whether such diligence, such curriculums, and such teaching work consistently with the continued existence of an Earth on which such knowledge may be brought forth. Ēducarē—"bringing forth"—is understood, so to speak, "from the neck up," as if it just happened in the head, as if it were just a matter of effective teaching and affected learning, requiring no real place, no real space to occur.

Such a strangulated approach to education forgets that it is not accumulated curricular knowledge that we most deeply offer our children in educating them. It is not their epistemic excellence or their mastery of requisite skills or their grade-point average, but literally their ability to live, their ability to be on an Earth that will sustain their lives. If we begin to take the roots of the integrated curriculum seriously and begin to heed what it requires of us as educators, we must educate and we must understand the curriculum in ways that will sustain the possibility that all our efforts, and all the efforts of our children, and all these matters of so much concern in educational theory and practice will not be made suddenly trivial. A thorough grounding in mathematics is of little use if that knowledge is understood in such a way that there is no longer any real ground that is safe to walk. Mathematics must become earthen in how it is understood, how it is taught, and how it is grounded. Tampering with the indigenous sense and operational character of mathematics is not necessary, but we must recognize that actually producing, sustaining, savoring, and passing on such knowledge requires something more than this sense and character—it requires an Earth.

We can, as Wittgenstein put it, draw a boundary around, for example, the mathematics curriculum (and it is, on occasion, completely appropriate to do so), but we cannot give it a boundary that could prevent it from intertwining with our lives and the life of the Earth.[15] We cannot sensibly aspire to well-bound and defined and circumscribed images of knowledge and of being educated if those images belie the existence of the actual breath required to pronounce that aspiration. No matter how careful we are in drawing our boundaries, mathematics interweaves with the fabric of the Earth. My love of mathematics, then, must remain Earth-bound—it must remain a love not only of its indigenous and articulate beauty but of the actual conditions under which I and the children I teach may live to do it. It is this love and understanding of mathematics that I must pass on to the children I teach. Within an integrated curriculum, to sensibly say that I "teach mathematics" means that I teach a love of the Earth on which teaching and learning and savoring mathematics is actually possible.

Admittedly, this paradox always seems to be overstated and rather hysterical. But here the integrated curriculum begins to hit home as something that goes beyond precious notions of the relations between curricular subject areas and impotent epistemological notions of relevance to the child's life. It is concerned with the knowledge—perhaps we must say the wisdom, even if we find such notions vaguely embarrassing, antiquated, unrigorous, or unclear—that we must pass on to our children so that life on Earth can go on. It is concerned with an image of knowledge that our children can live with, with relevance to the child's life. It is precisely not a specialized curricular topic such as ecological studies or environmental studies, for such specialization unwittingly pretends that the Earth is not underfoot, no matter what. The Earth and its continued existence is not a specialized topic among others as if these others were exempt. The integrated curriculum, understood as an ecological and spiritual matter, throws back in our face any such presumptions of being exempt.

The curriculum as an integrated curriculum cannot be considered with what Whitehead called "the celibacy of the intellect," as if we and our children are ghostly, objective purveyors of the Earth, and not fully human, full of *humus,* fully embedded in the life of the Earth, fully indebted.[16] Although such intellectual celibacy produces beautiful and seductive educational edifices—new theories, new guidelines, more and more complex educational agenda, and longer and longer lists of strategic teacher-intervention procedures—we cannot live with such edifications unless they are somehow brought down to Earth, grounded, not only in an epistemological sense, but in a moist, fleshy sense of given earthiness, given humus, made human. We may have to forfeit some of our precious clarity and distinctness (my students faced this problem in our class—things became more difficult, blurred, but also richer and more "down to earth" than the theories they are often inundated with). We may have to admit that the continued existence of our lives and the lives of our children contain an Earthen darkness and difficulty—an Earthen life—that we have so far fantasized out of curricular existence. The integrated curriculum, understood out from under these celibate fantasies, requires a recovery of the delicate, interweaving, and intertwining humus of a *curriculum vitae;* it requires a recovery of the Earth.

The Language of Curricular Discourse and Teacher Responsibility

One of the difficulties in writing (and, I suspect, reading) this paper should be explicitly admitted. Attempting to write about the integrated curriculum as an ecological and spiritual matter is at once a struggle with the language of curricular theorizing itself. The language and tenor of educational theory and practice has, in many circles, taken on the interests, hopes, terminology, techniques, hesitancy, carefulness, and conons of objectivity of scientific discourse. The forms of educational theorizing that do not take on such language and tenor often fall prey to all-too-easy caricatures of its alternative—subjectivism, anthropomorphism, individualism, experimentalism narrative, personal accounts, and unrigorous and undisciplined swooning.

I would rather simply announce that I am sidestepping this lover's quarrel, but I cannot, because the language of an integral alternative is not readily available. The integrated curriculum requires a whole language, but it cannot be caught in the all-too-frequent "profligacy of self-annunciation" that infects some proponents and popular conceptions of whole language theory.[17]

One of the claims of an ecological understanding is that life on Earth involves a multitude of different interweaving and intersecting voices, of which the human voice is but one among many (and, of special interest in education, of which the adult's voice is but one of these). Living with the richness and difficulty of this multitude of voices and speaking out from the midst of it is part of the phenomenon of the integrated curriculum. The struggle with curricular language—including the problem of overheated prose evident here and elsewhere—is not an accident that we must first rectify before inquiry begins, but it is precisely what must be recovered in the recovery of the Earth. The integrated curriculum does not require or allow the reduction of this multitude of voices to a single voice (univocity, evident in the desire to reduce all voices to a unique, single center, evident in literalism), but neither does it require or allow closing off different voices in their difference (equivocity, evident in the bound character of separate curriculum guides, specialization's, etc.). The question of how life on "this precious Earth" can go on is a question of how the conversation between different voices can go on.

Such a conversation requires more than just speaking or brazen self-communication. It requires listening, attending, attuning to other voices. It requires more than the numbing and light-headed enthusiasm and "positiveness" that often accompanies teaching at the early grades. It may require attending to the negatives, that is, the silences, the blockages, the unspeakables of life."[18] It may require, in a developmentally appropriate way, that we tell our children the truth. It may require that we listen to our children or to the voice of the Earth, even if listening is difficult, perhaps painful, perhaps disruptive of the clear and distinct boundaries we have set for ourselves and our children.

But then a sort of playful simplicity to language can come from considering the conversational or dialogical nature of the integrated curriculum in early childhood education. As potential educators of young children, my students have the excuse to reexperience the world. The children they will be teaching are in the process of learning what they, as adults, now take for granted, and as teachers, they can allow their experience of the world to become new again. They can begin to have anew a conversation with the Earth, to notice anew what has gone unnoticed under the rubric of familiarity and ordinariness.

I expect that some of my students have been schooled to believe that understanding the young child's experience and curriculum must be something esoteric, unfamiliar, unordinary. Some were expecting long, involved lists of peculiar theoretical characteristics and articulations. If the integrated curriculum is to be understood as an ecological and spiritual matter, however, it must cash itself out right here, in the regenerativity and reengagement of the simplest of events, right here at our fingertips. This water ring on the table left by my glass is just an incidental event, ignorable, worthy of indifference. But it is also an occasion to become enchanted again. It embodies whole realms of experience, vast complexities and interrelations to be explored—heat, cold, water, water vapor, humidifiers, evaporation, condensation, clouds, rain, snow, and, I suspect, that piece of paper with which we began. The discovery of such an example is not the result of a vast reservoir of theoretical experience but a sort of attendance and attunement to the minutaie of our lives and a forfeiture of our schooled tendency to deaden language and experience by taking the boundaries we have drawn too literally, as closed boundaries that know no play, no interplay with what is around them. It is not just a piece of information about water rings in this instance. It is, rather, a sort of dispossession, a letting go rather than a grasping; deeply understanding the integrated curriculum becomes a matter of "self-transcendence."[19]

The struggle my students confronted in our play with the piece of paper was, in part, a struggle with language. Some students adamantly began this exercise with declarations like "Come on, it's just a piece of paper," demonstrating how familiarity can breed contempt and a sort of ungenerative stasis, a desire to hold on to the boundaries already laid out. They could not easily become conversant with this paper, because they believed, in essence, that the last word had already been said, that there was nothing really left to say—"it's just a piece of paper." The danger is, of course that boundaries are meant to keep others (other meanings, other interpretations, other understandings) out. And it is precisely *others* who we are dealing with in educating young children.

The danger with holding on to boundaries is that it can cash itself out as a contempt for children, a contempt for their difference. If we begin a career in education with the belief that there is really nothing left to say, that the conversation is closed, that the boundaries have already been given to things, that we already understand, we begin unwittingly with the degenerative belief that the heart of education—the basic fact of natality—is simply a mistake to be corrected through our efforts, that the difference of children is a problem to be solved. I suspect we have all lived in classrooms where such deadline[s] hold[s] sway.

The importance of a trivial example such as this water ring is that young children have already experienced a "sweating glass" of ice water, a steamed up window, a scraped windshield in the winter. The interweaving possibilities and potentialities of the Earth are right at their fingertips already. The integrated curriculum, then, acknowledges that the child's experience of the world is already fully interwoven with our lives and with the life of the Earth, already integral. It requires that instruction begins with and savors this "already" and that student teachers develop a deep love for the generativity and liveliness of language itself. The contemptuous, deadened familiarity with the world, with which some student teachers begin their education, can lead them to believe that such playfulness and generativity is simply a violation of boundaries that must be corrected (perhaps for this reason is so much of teacher education apparently fixated on issues of discipline and management). What must happen in a turn to an integrated curriculum is that such familiarity must be deeply disrupted. This disruption must occur, but not to turn away from the familiar to some unearthly discourse. Rather, the disruption allows us to begin to recover a deep sense of the familial, a deep sense of our inviolable kinship with children and with the Earth.

The integrated curriculum resists the degenerative tendency in education. It does not require an image of education as involving no discipline. It does not involve education-as-chaos any more than believing that the Earth itself is chaotic without our concerted, authoritative intervention. Rather, it involves learning to live with, and learning to take educational advantage of, the discipline and organization originating from things themselves and originating from children's spontaneous interest in the world, their *inter esse,* their "being in the middle of things." Once children's "interest" are understood as having a certain inviolable integrity, and once the teacher has savored and explored the contours and textures of what is being taught (i.e., once the teacher deeply understands the material), taking educational advantage of such interests by drawing children into these contours and textures will help prevent the discipline problems that come from misunderstanding children and not deeply understanding the material. The teacher, in such an instance, becomes a facilitator, a provocateur, and, one hopes, a joyous *example* of a loving interest in children and in the contours and textures of the Earth.

Clearly and admittedly, this sounds naïve, for the teacher is responsible for classroom discipline and children's education. An integrated curriculum certainly requires responsibility, but responsibility must be linked with *precisely* such a loving interest in the Earth, including a loving interest in children. Our adult responsibility for and authority "over" children is at once a responsibility to the Earth on which we dwell *with* children. Teaching is, in part, introducing children to the authority of the Earth itself, an authority to which even our authority as adults is secondary. This is simply another way of saying that no matter how loud our declarations or brazen our "authority," water runs downhill, human blood is warm, $2 + 2 = 4$, and this piece of paper requires sun and sky and water. In an integrated curriculum, then, it is this deeper authority that requires our obedience and the obedience of children. And obedience, in the face of the archaic authority of the Earth, loses its moralistic character and can be finally heard again in its origin, *audire:* to listen, to attend, to be attuned.

> It is as if young people ask for, above all else, not only a genuine responsiveness from their elders, but also a certain direct authenticity, a sense of that deep human resonance so easily suppressed under the smooth human-relations jargon teachers typically learn in college. Young people want to know whether, under the cool and calm of efficient teaching and excellent time-on-task ratios, life itself has a chance, or whether the surface is all there is.[20]

Concluding Remarks I: "To Dwell with a Boundless Heart"

The title of this paper voices how we might understand ourselves, not as an exception to this interweaving indebtedness and interrelatedness to the Earth, but as an instance of it. To dwell with a boundless heart is to understand "the self in its original countenance" as delicately interwoven in this earthly fabric in which we found woven all things, including the children we teach.[21] We can draw boundaries around ourselves (and it is often appropriate to do so), but we cannot give ourselves boundaries without believing in the impossible—that our lives can go on, that we can be, without an ongoing conversational with "this precious Earth," one that includes our knowledge of it, but also includes our breathing of it.

> The self is here at the home-ground of all things. It is itself a home-ground where everything becomes manifest as what it is, where all things are assembled together into a "world." This must be a standpoint where one sees one's own self in all things, in living things, in hills and rivers, towns and hamlets, tiles and stones, and loves these things "as oneself."[22]

In a sense, then, this interrelatedness of things underlying the integrated curriculum requires seeing every action as an action on behalf of all, everything speaking on behalf of all things. This concluding remark ends with a vignette.

Following a recent heavy oil spill off the coast of Washington State, my six-year-old son and I were watching the C.B.C. news. We saw film footage of an oil-covered duck struggling up on to a beach on the west coast of Vancouver Island. With each panicked lunge, its wing tips remained adhered to the slickened beach. Pictures of dead water fowl being shoveled up and put into green garbage bags followed.

We have all seen these scenes before, perhaps all too often. I have often felt rage or sadness, or I have simply turned the damn thing off. But when my son turned to me and asked me to help him understand what he was seeing, I felt something new. I felt humiliated.

Even though it is all too easy to overromanticize and anthropomorphize this point, I suddenly felt my own humanness as rooted in the same soil as this creature, my own "*humusness*." In trying to understand this event and trying to help my son understand, I felt a sudden humility in the attempt, as if our understanding, our conversation, had to be brought down to Earth, humiliated in the proper sense. My son and I had to face our own indebtedness to this creature, to this oil, to this water, to this sand, to these scenes, to the power of these broadcast images, linking us to the production of this power, to its use, to the demands for it, to our demands for powering fuels, and then back to this oil, to this water, to this sand, to these scenes.

Watching and attempting to face these images, to make sense of them, produced the need for the very fuel that was now killing this creature. It was as if it was undergoing the pain on our behalf. To tell my son of oil tankers and accidents and clean-up efforts no longer seemed like the whole truth. The story seemed like a disintegrated curriculum-guide version of the truth, where the pain and indebtedness are laid out anonymously before us to either peruse or ignore at our leisure. I had to try to tell him that we cannot "turn the damn thing off" by just switching off power to the television set. Not facing these images, turning them off, does not dispel our debt.

This realization became all the more difficult when my son and I watched a movie later that day, and a particular speech, in another context, in another place and time, hit too close to home, making the early scenes of ducks and oil and death, the earlier thoughts of indebtedness and humiliation, even more unforgettable:

> I am asking you to fight—to fight against their anger, not to provoke it. We will not strike a blow, but we will receive them and through out pain we will make them see their injustice. It will hurt, but we cannot lose. They may torture me, break my bones, even kill me. But eventually, even in my death, they will see their injustice and they will stop.[23]

Clearly, in quoting this speech of Mahatma Gandhi, I am guilty of a sort of gross anthropomorphism, but evoking the roots of the integrated curriculum as an ecological and spiritual matter requires a deeper, different response than those I have become accustomed to as an educational theorist. It requires a language of implication, of debt, of interrelation, a language that does not allow indifference, that does not allow us to "turn the damn thing off." Perhaps the language that allows us to call this unfortunate incident a separate event, discrete from curricular matters in the business of education—perhaps that is the truly anthropocentric language, believing as it does that the boundaries it draws it actually gives.

Nearing the finish of this paper, news of the oil spill in Alaska. . . .

Concluding Remarks II: *This* Piece of Paper

It is too easy to become swept up in the happy interrelations of sun and sky and clouds and rain that nestle in this piece of paper. This piece of paper, this very one that I am writing on, this very one that you are now reading, may be the one the bleaching of which produced the dioxin that may have already given Eric, my six-year-old son, cancer.

Overstatement? Yes, perhaps. But as a colleague once said to me, we will be responsible to our children for the questions that we do not ask. This—considering the life of my son, Eric, and what I will say when the questions come—is the real topic and the real cost of the work I do. It is the real sense in which the curriculum becomes a *curriculum vitae,* having to do with the course of our lives as they are actually lived.

We in education may be especially responsible for the questions we do not ask, standing as we do at the cusp of the emergence of new life in our midst, able to bring forth these questions, but perhaps unwilling to speak our real indebtedness to "this precious Earth" without embarrassment. The integrated curriculum has, as its roots, the potential to open up these questions we may have thus far refused to ask. Turning away from these questions may involve abandoning our children to an all-too-certain future.

Notes

1. Thich Nhat Hahn, *The Miracle of Mindfulness* (Berkeley: Parallax Press, 1986), p. 12.
2. Thich Nhat Hahn, *The Sun in My Heart* (Berkeley: Parallax Press, 1988), p. 64.
3. Keiji Nishitanl, *Religion and Nothingness* (Berkeley: University of California Press, 1982), p. 149.
4. *Ibid,* p. 150.
5. Thich Nhat Hahn, *The Sun in My Heart* (Berkeley: Parallax Press, 1988), p. 70.
6. Keiji Nishitani, *Religion and Nothingness* (Berkeley: University of California Press, 1982), p. 149.

7. Martin Heidegger, "Overcoming Metaphysics," in *The End of Philosophy* (New York: Harper and Row, 1987), p. 109.

8. David G. Smith, "Children and the Gods of War," *Journal of Educational Thought* 22 (October 1988): 173–177.

9. *Ibid.,* p. 175

10. Hannah Arendt, "The Crisis in Education," in *Between Past and Future* (London: Penguin Books, 1972), p. 174.

11. *Ibid.,* p. 192.

12. Mathew Fox, *Original Blessing* (San Francisco: Bear and Company, 1986), p. 9.

13. *Ibid.*

14. B. Devall and G. Sessions, *Deep Ecology: Living as if the Earth Does Matter* (Salt Lake City: Peregrine Smith Books, 1985).

15. Ludwig Wittgenstein, *Philosophical Investigations* (Cambridge, England: Basil Blackwell, 1968), p. 142.

16. Mathew Fox, *Original Blessing* (San Francisco: Bear and Company, 1986), p. 23.

17. David G. Smith, "On Being Critical about Language: The Critical Theory Tradition and Implications for Language Education," *Reading—Canada* 6 (No. 4): 247.

18. *Ibid.*

19. Philip Phenix, "Transcendence and Curriculum," In *Curriculum Theorizing: The Reconceptualists* ed. William Pinar (Berkeley: McCutchan, 1975), pp. 323–337.

20. David G. Smith, "On Being Critical about Language: The Critical Theory Tradition and Implications for Language Education," *Reading—Canada* 6 (No. 4): 175

21. Keiji Nishitani, *Religion and Nothingness* (Berkeley: University of California Press, 1982), pp. 91, 162.

22. *Ibid.,* pp. 280–281.

23. From Mahatma Gandhi speech in *Gandhi,* produced and directed by Richard Attenborough, screenplay by John Briley, 188 min., 1982, Columbia Pictures.

21

HIV/AIDS Education:
Toward a Collaborative Curriculum

JONATHAN SILIN

AIDS radically calls into question the pleasures and dangers of teaching

CINDY PATTON, *Inventing AIDS*

AIDS makes no sense. However, the continuing proliferation of HIV/AIDS curricula speaks to our very real desire to claim epistemological rationality and epidemiological certainty in a world plagued by a new and as yet incurable disease. In defining HIV/AIDS as a biomedical event that can be addressed only by those trained in science and health education, we attempt to make it safe, contained within a specific discipline, so that it will not contaminate other areas of study. When the topic of HIV/AIDS is sanitized, teachers and students are protected from the truly unhealthy aspects of society that might otherwise be revealed; the status quo is ensured.

But diseases are constituted through dynamic interactions of biomedical, economic, psychosocial, and political factors. The existential realities of otherness, the politics of distancing, and our search for certainty suggest key elements in the social construction of HIV/AIDS. Understanding the meanings of a given illness involves far more then simply identifying a causal agent and a medical remedy. Just as efforts at prevention cannot be limited to the presentation of risk–reduction strategies, in the hope that exposure to a few facts and rehearsal of skills will lead to lasting changes in behavior, so coming to terms with the social ramifications of HIV/AIDS cannot be achieved through a limited focus on scientific knowledge. Effective prevention involves individual struggles with the meaning of sex and drugs, and a successful societal response calls for recognition of the multiple factors shaping the disease process.

HIV/AIDS presents a complex set of challenges for the curriculum maker. At first, school administrators perceived HIV/AIDS primarily as a policy problem requiring the attention of legal and public health experts to assess the feasibility of excluding students and staff with HIV. But as the crisis over the presence of people with HIV/AIDS in the schools abated, and awareness that HIV/AIDS was not confined to marginal risk groups grew, educators turned toward their pedagogical function. The process was hastened as more and more states mandated K–12 AIDS education.

Early curricular materials reflected simplified interpretations of the disease; they focused on prevention for adolescents and claimed to offer only "facts." But the assertion of objectivity is in itself a form of bias, carrying the implication that it is possible to separate fact from value, object from subject, the word from the world. It is this mindset that was exemplified by a New York City public school official who, in response to a film made to be shown in the city high schools, remarked, "There was a segment that was too long, simply to the effect that you should be nice to homosexuals. The attitude was not a problem, but this is not an attitude film. This is supposed to be an *educational* film" (*CDC AIDS Weekly,* 1986, p. 9). In the scene referred to, a heterosexual man recounts his first reactions to learning that his brother is gay and has AIDS.

If we acknowledge that attitudes and values play a role in shaping individual behaviors and the allocation of material resources in society, it is hard to understand how exclusion of these very factors can lead to a serious discussion of the problem at hand. The denial of subjectivity within the curriculum only falsifies experience and alienates students from their own possibilities. This is not to say that subjectively held opinions must be accepted uncritically but rather that they can become the text for examining the social determination of "private" ideas. Students can learn to question the sources of their knowledge and its reliability and to identify alternative reference points. HIV/AIDS provides an opportunity to practice the critical thinking skills valued so highly by educators today. It is an issue that most graphically illustrates the paradoxes and contradictions of our society.

In this chapter I seek to understand the fundamental inadequacies of our past efforts to talk with children about HIV/AIDS and to create new possibilities for such dialogues. Beginning with younger children and moving on to adolescents, I draw on my work with teachers, administrators, children, and parents in many public and private schools across New York State. These schools were located in a diverse cross-section of racial, ethnic, religious, and economic communities and reflected very different commitments to HIV/AIDS education.

Listening to Young Children

As an early childhood educator, I was trained to listen to and observe young children. Raised and educated in a Deweyan tradition, I understand curriculum as a negotiated process, an outgrowth of the interests of the child and the community. While teachers come to the classroom with an agenda based on knowledge of the community, their art rests in helping children move outward from more narrowly based concerns toward the world of larger ideas. At its best, education enables children to see the way that the concepts and skills offered by their teachers, and eventually encoded in the formal disciplines, amplify their powers of understanding and control. The role of teachers is to help their students make sense of the world. Imposing predetermined, formal curriculum on children without reference to their lived experience can leave them alienated from the possibilities of school-based learning.

When I was a doctoral student, encounters with Marxist and critical theorists made me conscious of the manner in which schooling functions to maintain and reproduce unequal distributions of economic and cultural capital (Apple, 1979; Bowles & Gintis, 1976). Recognizing that the most mundane classroom activities, such as recess, might be described as moments of ideological hegemony, I also began to think about the internal contradictions within any system that allow for reflection and transformation. But it is the phenomenologically oriented educationists (Barritt,

Beekman, Bleeker, & Mulderij, 1985; van Manen, 1990) who are most mindful of the limitations of scientistically imposed frames of reference and of the need to ground our work in the world of childhood. They urge us to return to the children themselves to uncover what it is that seems to matter, to grasp how they make sense of experience. To accept such a challenge is to abandon the safety of science that allows us to know children from the privileged position of distanced adults. It is to risk the uncertainty of an engagement that threatens the boundaries between knower and known.

When called on to assist schools with curriculum formulation, I began by asking teachers what the children were saying about AIDS. This obviously reflected my commitment as a progressive educator as well as my experiences learning from people with HIV infection. The teachers' responses clearly indicated that HIV/AIDS had entered their classrooms through the voices of their students, regardless of age or formal instruction. Ironically, many of these opportunities occurred in elementary classrooms—that is, precisely those classrooms in which the prospect of HIV/AIDS education seemed most daunting. Sometimes these voices had been heard at unexpected moments, sometimes on more predictable occasions. Almost always, teachers had felt unprepared to take advantage of the moment to begin a dialogue that could lead to more structured learning.

Interestingly, teachers often had to work hard even to remember these incidents. Emblematic of this forgetfulness were the responses of teachers in a seminar I conducted in a semirural community on eastern Long Island. My inquiry as to what they had observed about their students' knowledge of HIV/AIDS was greeted with a painfully long silence. I began to wonder if I had arrived in the only area in New York State that had not been touched by the disease. Then a first-grade teacher tentatively raised her hand. She described the pandemonium that had broken out in her classroom that very morning when the principal announced, over the school intercom, that AIDS would be the subject of the afternoon staff meeting. Children started accusing each other of having AIDS and warning the teacher not to attend the meeting for fear she might contract HIV from the guest speaker. Given permission by the principal's announcement, the children had released their suppressed concerns. And then a third-grade teacher confirmed that for the past several months AIDS had been the reigning epithet on the playground during recess. It was the label of choice when a group of children wanted to ostracize someone. Games of tag were predicated on avoiding a child who was supposedly HIV-infected.

To these children the mere mention of AIDS provoked excited responses. Whether motivated by specific fears and anxieties, or simply the emotional resonance of the word in our culture, their behaviors accurately mimicked the responses of the majority of adults. To know in more detail what AIDS means to children would require the kind of probing by teachers that leads to a negotiated curriculum, a curriculum in which dialogue is respected and teachers learn with and from their students. For the moment, however, it should be noted that isolation and fear of contagion are being played out without interruption. Educators must recognize their complicity in discrimination by permitting children to use HIV/AIDS, if only in their games, as a means to exclude someone from the social arena. Like gender, race, ethnicity, and disability, HIV/AIDS is an issue of equity.

But children also reveal their awareness of HIV/AIDS in moments that are less incendiary and more focused. In an urban setting, for example, a teacher reported her consternation on a recent class trip upon hearing one child anxiously admonish a friend not to sit down in the subway for fear of contracting AIDS from the seat. The teacher admitted that it was only her concern for the children's safety in the moving train that prompted her to contradict this advice, which had been delivered in the most serious tone. A colleague at the same meeting described overhearing one little boy warning another not to pick up a stick in the park. The warning was based on the child's knowledge that people who use drugs frequented the area at night and his belief that they are the source of HIV infection.

There are few formal studies of young children's knowledge. Farquhar (1990b) documents the practical difficulties in conducting research when we would prefer to protect children than provoke their curiosity. Although Schvaneveldt, Lindauer, and Young (1990) indicate that preschool children know very little about HIV/AIDS, this should not be taken as an indication that they know nothing at all or that AIDS education is irrelevant to their lives. As the anecdotes reported here suggest, HIV/AIDS can be a specter that haunts their movement in the world. For young children, and for many adults as well, fear needs to be replaced by understanding, misinformation by facts. HIV is part of daily life and should be treated as such in schools. To be meaningful, HIV/AIDS information should not be delayed till fourth-grade science curriculum or sixth-grade health class, where it may seem too abstract, removed from students' lived experience. Containing HIV/AIDS within the confines of the highly rational curriculum may offer adults a sense of protection but only at the price of placing their students at increased risk. If we avoid engaging with children about HIV/AIDS, even to counter false information about transmission, we foster the belief that HIV/AIDS is a mystery, a taboo subject that teachers cannot or will not address.

What teachers think about childhood also influences how or even if they will approach HIV/AIDS with their students. For some, children inhabit a very different world from adults. Despite what they may be exposed to at home, on the street, or in the media, they require educational settings where the flow of information is carefully controlled. In contrast, others suggest that what happens to children outside of school should become the object of classroom study. The school is a safe place to make sense of complex and confusing realities. Teachers who believe in this approach are more likely to provide opportunities for critical social issues to become part of the curriculum. For example, I observed a teacher of 6- and 7-year-olds open a class meeting with the simple questions, "What do people use drugs for?" Information and misinformation poured forth from the children. They debated the ethical implications of the use of steroids by Olympic athletes (a subject very much in the news at the time), tried to understand how people actually snort cocaine (believing that it is placed on the outside of the nose), and struggled with why people do things to themselves that they know are harmful. The children saw drugs, rather than infected blood, as the source of HIV infection, and they clearly equated AIDS with death. They proved themselves to be curious, knowledgeable, and capable of thoughtful reflection. Their mistakes were surprisingly rational, the questions they raised worthy of any adult's attention.

In other classrooms the subject of HIV/AIDS may come up in a more oblique manner. A second-grade teacher reported, for example, that her AIDS curriculum began with the failure of two baby rabbits to thrive. Sitting near the cage with a small group of concerned children, one girl began to wonder out loud if perhaps they might have AIDS. The teacher told the children that, while she did not know very much about HIV/AIDS, she did not think it was a disease of animals. Picking up on their concern, the teacher sought more information from the health teacher, whom she also recruited to talk directly with the children. In the kindergarten classroom down the hall, the children had built a block city with a large hospital at its center. In questioning them one day about the ambulance speeding toward its entrance, the teacher was informed that it was carrying a person with AIDS who was very, very sick and going to die. For her, this was the moment to explore what the children really knew about AIDS, part of a larger commitment to understand her students and to bring greater definition to their worlds.

Farquhar (1990b), observing 8- and 10-year-olds, confirms that children's HIV/AIDS knowledge is variable in the extreme. Researchers using developmental frameworks suggest that knowledge is primarily age-dependent. However, Farquhar offers two insights that broaden our appreciation of children's social learning. First, students' emergent understanding of HIV/AIDS is closely associated with knowledge of related topics like sexual behavior or drug use. For example, an 8-year-old's belief that you could "catch AIDS . . . when you go to bed in the same bed" is not surprising given that the child describes "sex" as going to bed with somebody. Similarly, the statement by another child that "smoking causes AIDS" should be understood in the context of her knowledge that cigarettes contain nicotine, nicotine is a drug, and drugs are somehow implicated in HIV transmission. Second, Farquhar notes that many beliefs reflect the myths and stereotypes held by adults and promoted by the media. As they struggle to construct their own meaning, children's knowledge often mirrors that of the adults who surround them.

Even while those committed to conserving the past try to limit the role of the school, the majority are asking it to address an increasingly broad social agenda. Under pressure to do more and to do it better, in a world that offers fewer and fewer support systems for children, there is always the danger of reductionism. Schools reduce complicated social problems to simplified fragments of information, adopt pedagogic strategies that focus on measurable, behavioral outcomes, and define the child as a "learner," as the sum of his or her cognitive competencies. Many teachers see the curriculum in place as the biggest obstacle to effective education, for they recognize that issues such as HIV/AIDS cannot be segmented into discrete, 40-minute units.

The Curriculum in Place

Attending to children suggests the informal ways that HIV/AIDS enters the school and the daily openings teachers have for beginning a dialogue that can lead to a more formal learning plan. Unfortunately, most teachers learn about HIV/AIDS through the demands of a highly rationalized curriculum and without time for reflection. It is not surprising that they react with anger and frustration. Teachers need to be supported as curriculum makers who can respond to their students' immediate concerns while cognizant of the larger bodies of knowledge with which they may be connected. This approach is not compatible with the top-down imposition of lesson plans that are far removed from the children's lived experiences.

The New York State *AIDS Instructional Guide* (New York State Education Department, 1987) is one example of the technocratic mindset that undermines the role of teachers as decision makers. Although designed to be a "guide" and carefully labeled as such, it is worth considering in detail, since many districts adopted it *in toto* as the curriculum in order to save time and avoid controversy. This is an interesting political document, with its community review panels to assure decency, its denial of the sexual realties of teenagers' lives, and its careful attention to parents' right to withdraw their children from lessons dealing with HIV prevention. To educators, however, this guide may appear as a far more curious pedagogical document because of the way that it parcels out information across the grades.

The *AIDS Instructional Guide* presents a total of 37 lesson plans clustered by grade levels. The K–3 lessons deal with health in general. They barely mention HIV/AIDS at all, though teachers are told that some children may fear contracting the disease and that their questions should be addressed "honestly and simply." Somewhat less than half of the grade 4–6 lessons deal with HIV/AIDS. They describe communicable diseases, the immune system, how HIV is not transmitted, and how to prevent AIDS by abstaining from drug use. Only in the grade 7–8 lessons, a majority of which directly address HIV/AIDS, is there discussion of the sexual transmission of HIV and the possibility of prevention through sexual abstinence. Then, in a country where the median age of first intercourse is 16, and where a third of males and 20% of females have intercourse by 15—and of those currently sexually active, less than half report using condoms—teachers are instructed to emphasize the 13 ways that abstinence makes us free (*Chronic Disease and Health* . . . , 1990).

On the grade 9–12 level, the social and economic consequences of HIV/AIDS are confined to a single lesson featuring a debate on mandatory HIV-antibody testing. Although certain lessons are geared to elicit sympathy for people with HIV/AIDS and thus attempt to curb potential discrimination, never does the guide address the homophobia, racism, and addictophobia underlying much of the HIV/AIDS hysteria that the curriculum is ostensibly trying to dispel. This superficial approach to "humanizing" the disease belies the extensive introductory comments about the importance of pluralism and democratic values. It also denies the fundamental reality of HIV infection in our country—that it has disproportionately affected groups of people who have been marginalized and subjected to various forms or physical and psychological violence (Fraser, 1989). Convincing students to listen to any messages about HIV/AIDS and to understand personal vulnerability cannot be accomplished without interrupting the "us-versus-them" mentality that pervades our social thinking.

There are two assumptions underlying this curriculum guide that bear careful scrutiny. The first is that children's minds are compartmentalized, able to deal with HIV/AIDS information in a logical, sequential order. It assumes, for example, that children can discuss how HIV is *not* transmitted while holding in abeyance for several lessons and/or years how it is transmitted—and how to prevent its spread. No attempt is made to assess what knowledge children come to school with or the kinds of questions their personal experiences may have generated. The child is read as a *tabula rasa* with respect to HIV/AIDS. The New York State Planners appear to have been attending more to the logical order in which they wanted to present a specific body of information than to the psychological order that may reflect children's questions and interests. It seems only fair to ask for the voices of the children in the curriculum— the voices heard on the playground, on the subway, and in the block area. But who is listening? Who has the time?

The second assumption is that HIV/AIDS is a medical phenomenon to be located within the confines of the health curriculum. If we accept that there are economic, political, and social as well as biomedical strands in the Gordian knot that is HIV/AIDS, then an effective educational response does not reside in the province of the health teacher alone. A successful response is a collaborative one involving teachers from all the disciplines, administrators, and parents. In order for students to understand the disease, they must understand the cultural context in which it is occurring.

For it is this context that defines how individuals and society at large respond to people with HIV and assign resources to prevention, research, and care.

From this perspective it is easy to see how HIV/AIDS lends itself as a subject for current events and social studies classes. HIV/AIDS raises many questions about access to health care and its costs, the ethics of confidentiality, diseases of poverty, availability of new drugs, and conduct of scientific research. Sloane and Sloane (1990) report on the integration of HIV/AIDS in a class on the history of the United States since 1877, which already includes discussion of the living conditions of North American cities in the late nineteenth century and the incredible toll of epidemic diseases, such as yellow fever, scarlet fever, influenza, and consumption. Here the modern-day epidemic can help students understand the fears and responses of earlier generations and offer the opportunity to clarify the differences between airborne diseases and HIV/AIDS.

There is also a growing body of novels, plays, and poetry emerging in response to this disease, and they provide further opportunities to introduce HIV/AIDS into language arts and English classes (Klein, 1989; Murphy & Poirier, 1993; Nelson, 1992; Pastore, 1992; Preston, 1989). More and more artists and musicians are also turning their attention to the issue, as well might our students in their own work (Klusacek & Morrison, 1992; J. Miller, 1992). The curriculum should reflect the richness of all these imaginative reconstructions, as they offer alternative routes to understanding the impact of HIV/AIDS (Brunner, 1992; Engler, 1988).

In effect, I want to argue that students would be best served if the assumptions underlying the curriculum in place were inverted. First, rather than creating elaborate instructional guides based on a formal ordering of facts, it would be far more helpful to ground the curriculum in the issues that children themselves find challenging, a principle upheld by progressive educators from Dewey to Friere. Second, our very definition of the disease needs to be reexamined in such a way as to permit its multiple ramifications to emerge across the disciplines. This is not to deny the importance of messages about prevention but to underscore the less visible interconnectedness of our social institutions. Successful prevention efforts at all age levels do not seek to abstract and control specific behaviors but rather to help people examine sexual and drug-using practices in the context of their total lives.

The Teacher's Perspective

My own research on pedagogical authority in early childhood (Silin, 1982) revealed that teachers think of themselves as objective professionals acting in the best interests of children. By legitimating this self-definition in their knowledge of child development, teachers could speak authoritatively about other people's children while suggesting a space for family prerogatives with respect to the inculcation of values. Interviews with primary school teachers illustrate the commitment to keeping personal attitudes and beliefs out of the classroom (Farquhar, 1990a). One teacher commented:

> It would be very wrong of me to put my personal interpretation, the standards I use for living my life, to tell them "this is how you should live." . . . It is not the place of the school to criticize in that way, or the teacher to criticize or to imply that one way is right and another way is wrong. (p. 12)

Teachers want to believe that the primary school is simply a purveyor of objective knowledge, that "we present a neutral sort of attitude to facts" (p. 12).

My work on HIV/AIDS curricula with teachers, however, suggests that person-al values, prejudices, and preconceptions play a critical role in determining what in-formation they do and do not provide. When people first began to take the facts about HIV transmission seriously, they had to explore previously unrecognized mo-ments of vulnerability in their own lives. The middle-aged woman whose husband had just been through major surgery needed to calculate the odds that he might have received a unit of infected blood; the young male teacher needed to assess his resis-tance to carrying a condom on his weekend date; and the mother of a grown daugh-ter who shared an apartment with two gay men needed to come to terms with her anxieties about casual contact as a source of HIV infection. Although everyone is bet-ter informed today than in 1985, when I began working with teachers on HIV/AIDS curricula, immersion in this issue inevitably leads to rethinking potential risk. When this does not happen, the lack of personal relevance can in some cases lead to a lack of interest. As one of Farquhar's (1990a) interviewees commented:

> This is a big turn-off. It's a big bore for me, because I know I've got nothing to worry about. I've led a monogamous life, I know I'm clear, and I'll always be clear, and I'm not going to come into touch with it. I'm not going to get caught up in drugs, I'm not going to go injecting myself. The blood contamination is the only one that could get me. (p. 12)

In a sense HIV/AIDS happens all at once. Coming to learn about HIV/AIDS in the context of their professional lives, most teachers recognize that this disease has meanings that extend far beyond the clinic office or hospital room, meanings that will seep into conversations with their own children, affect attitudes toward friends and family, and change lifelong behaviors. It has meaning that even challenge their sense of safety in the workplace. This is the all-at-onceness of HIV/AIDS, a disease that not only destroys an individual's immune system but also breaks down the artificial barri-ers that we construct between professional and personal lives.

Successful preservice and inservice education depends on the provision of ade-quate time for teachers to express their feelings about HIV/AIDS and their reactions to talking with children about HIV-related issues (Basch, 1989; Sanders & Farquhar, 1991). For only after these feelings have been acknowledged and discussed can teach-ers attend to the task at hand. In describing the introduction of an anti-bias curricu-lum, for example, Derman-Sparks and the A.B.C. Task Force (1989) provide a model for staff development about HIV/AIDS. They emphasize group consciousness-raising for teachers as the first step in creating new curricula on social issues. This process is one that respects the teacher as an adult learner, providing an opportunity to under-stand the subject matter in more than a superficial manner. A reading of the anti-bias curriculum also suggests that teachers who have placed equity issues high on their own agendas will have less difficulty integrating HIV/AIDS into the ongoing cur-riculum; these teachers have already created environments in which human differ-ences are discussed and valued. HIV/AIDS education must proceed out of a mean-ingful context, so students can recognize the familiar and understandable as well as the new and unexpected in this issue.

Institutional Constraints

Talk of staff development, consciousness-raising groups, and adults as learners is not to deny the real constraints under which teachers work. Ironically, the press for school reform initiated by the publication of *A Nation at Risk* in 1984 has resulted in increased demands for required courses, quantitative measurement, and universal standards. The introduction of HIV/AIDS education has meant that teachers must squeeze an additional topic into their already overcrowded, overorganized days. It becomes another requirement that impinges on what little discretionary time remains to them. Even as leaders of industry and labor are calling for greater teacher autonomy to increase school effectiveness, and experiments in teacher-based school governance proliferate, state mandates for HIV/AIDS education allocate few resources for staff development (Kenney, Guardado, & Brown, 1989). If teachers are to engage in the decision-making activities that would define them as professionals, then they must be given the opportunity to develop the knowledge appropriate to such responsibilities (Wirth, 1989).

Thus for teachers, the introduction of HIV/AIDS into the curriculum has also meant preoccupation with negotiating school bureaucracies and calculating the risks of fomenting change. In most school districts where I have worked, teachers are in agreement about institutionally imposed limitations on what may be said. However, they are often in disagreement as to what their individual responses should be. Three solutions to this dilemma are common.

The first solution accepts the limits but recognizes that there are ways to work around them. The second solution, more cynical and despairing, resists any participation in what are perceived to be duplicitous practices. For teachers advocating the first solution, compromise is essential in order to get critical information to their students. For teachers adopting the second solution, however, the main compromise—that they may respond to questions as raised by students but not initiate certain "hot" topics—is unacceptable. Placing teachers in a position where they rely on student questions, and then refer students back to their parents or to after-school counseling sessions, can undermine the teacher's authority. Unfortunately, the legitimate anger expressed over the moral bind in which they are placed is too often projected onto the subject of HIV/AIDS itself rather than directed at creating a changed educational context.

A third solution to institutionally imposed limits is premised on the teacher's sense of privacy and control when the classroom door is closed; these teachers feel that they are free to say what they want when they are alone with students. Grumet (1988), exploring the experiences of women teachers as well as the histories of women writers and artists, suggests the self-defeating nature of this strategy. Describing the importance of private spaces for the development of ideas, she also points to the incipient dangers of isolation and privatization that can result when the doors to these rooms are never opened. The potential for community change can be fostered or thwarted by our willingness to make public that which has been nurtured in private.

But the institutions in which we live and work are often far more permeable than we imagine (Sarason, 1982). If teachers are to be successful change agents—and HIV/AIDS always involves change—then professional education programs must prepare them for their extra-classroom roles. Knowledge of institutional power structures, budget making, and community relations is as appropriate for the classroom teacher as for the administrator. All school personnel need to understand that institutions are often less monolithic and more heterogeneous when looked at closely with specific ends in view. Internal contradictions provide openings for change. Frequently it is our own perception of hegemony that is the biggest block to creating effective local strategies.

Primary Ideology

Finally, while for some adults the reluctance to talk with children about HIV/AIDS reflects their own lack of knowledge, for others it is part of a consciously held belief system about the nature of childhood. For example, Robin Alexander (1984), in a study of British primary and junior schools, found teachers committed to the idea of childhood as a time of innocence. Although the "primary ideology" recognizes that children are capable of unacceptable behavior, it also deems them free of any malicious intent. Ideas about original sin once promoted by religious reformers have been abandoned, replaced by images of moral purity. In an observational study of three schools, R. King (1978) confirms teachers' determination to protect young children from harsh and corrupting realities of the adult world. In America, California kindergarten teachers have opposed any discussion of HIV/AIDS in their classrooms because they want to protect children from any unpleasant and, in their view, irrelevant subjects.

When *Young Children,* the Journal of the National Association for the Education of Young Children (NAEYC), published its first HIV/AIDS article, entitled "What We Should and Should Not Tell Our Children About AIDS," it emphasized that the role of the teacher was to soothe the potentially frightened child and avoid presenting unnecessary information (Skeen & Hudson, 1987). Two years later an article on substance abuse prevention in the same journal reinforced a similar philosophy. Misleadingly titled "Drug Abuse Prevention Begins in Early Childhood (And is much more than a matter of instructing young children about drugs!)," it deals solely with the need for parent education and calls for an analysis of parenting styles that promote positive self-images among young children (Oyemade & Washington, 1989). There is little recognition in either article that children may be all too aware of the social problems that exist in their communities. While teachers are constantly reminded to structure environments that are psychologically supportive of personal growth, never is it suggested that they take the lead in providing information about HIV/AIDS or drugs. Nor are they encouraged to help students sort through the multiple meanings they may have already assigned to them. The message is that as long as we follow developmentally appropriate practices, little must change in the way we think about children's lives.

Preparing Classroom Teachers to Talk About HIV/AIDS

To accept that children live in a world where they come to learn about HIV/AIDS, drugs, poverty, and homelessness at a far earlier age than most of us would prefer does not mean we are participating in the denial of childhood. But it does mean we need to create classrooms in which children feel comfortable exploring these issues. Teacher educators can foster this process in two critical ways. First, they can highlight for their students the tension between what we have learned about the social construction of childhood, the embeddedness of our ideas in specific historical contexts, and what we may believe to be optimal conditions for children's growth (James & Prout, 1990a). Wanting the newcomer to feel at home in the world, we each struggle with the degree to which we see childhood as a separate life period requiring specialized protections and professionalized care, and the degree to which we see it as a time for full participation in the ongoing life of the community. The work of those who look at how the social environment is changing the experience of childhood—from the growth of electronic information sources, parental pressure for achievement, and the increasing isolation of children in age-segregated institutions, to the pervasive violence in young people's lives—would be especially helpful with this project (Elkind, 1981b; Garbarino, 1992; Polakow, 1982; Postman, 1982).

Second, given the stressful lives of contemporary children, it is important for teacher educators to emphasize their competencies as well as their developmental deficiencies, a theme I pursue at greater length in Chapter 4. Here I would mention the use of the anthropological or sociological lens (Felsman, 1989; Glauser, 1990) to focus on the strengths and healthy adaptation rather than weaknesses or pathology of children living in difficult circumstances. I also refer to our increasing knowledge of young children's narrative skills, their use of and understanding of abstract concepts, binary oppositions, metaphor, and humor (Egan, 1988; Sutton-Smith, 1988). Like Robert Coles (1989), we need to listen to the moral energy coursing through the stories of older children living in poverty, as they question and reflect upon their experiences. These stories can tell us how children resist despair, claim dignity in dehumanizing situations, and create redemptive moments out of sorrow.

A Question of Authority

Preparing classroom teachers to integrate HIV/AIDS into the curriculum is a complex process not just because it raises personal concerns for individuals or because it may force them to address new subjects such as sex and death. It is complex because it provokes inquiry into basic philosophical issues about the nature of pedagogy, the meaning of childhood, and the role of the teacher as change agent. An incident in the spring of 1986 crystallized for me the underlying theme of this inquiry and much of the teacher discourse on HIV/AIDS. At that time I was asked to talk to a group of angry parents and teachers who were attempting to exclude a 5-year-old girl with AIDS from their school. Within a few minutes of my opening remarks about the severity of the HIV/AIDS problem in the community, I was interrupted by an angry, bearded man in his mid-30s who announced himself to be a teacher, a historian of science, and a parent in the school. Citing the newness of the disease and the constant flow of information from the medical world, he began to question the credentials of the panelists—a physician, a public health official, a school administrator, a parent leader, and myself—one by one. At that moment of attack, rather than becoming defensive as many of the others did, I began to relax. As a former teacher, I recognized a familiar issue emerging, the issue of authority. This irate father was challenging not only the specific information we offered but, more significantly, our fundamental right to influence his children. The shadow of the school–family struggle for the child was lengthening to include HIV/AIDS.

Although this scene took place at the height of HIV/AIDS hysteria, it exemplifies a critical and ongoing theme in the HIV/AIDS discourse: the challenge that the disease poses to traditional concepts of authority. For many, authority implies certainty, the right to guide others based on full knowledge of the outcomes of the recommended actions. But HIV/AIDS is not about absolutes. It is defined by a series of changing practices, bodies of knowledge, and contexts. AIDS educators and policy makers are skilled at juxtaposing theoretical possibilities against actual probabilities, an unsatisfying dialectic for those who feel personally threatened and seek safety through guarantees. Yet physicians and other officials who assert certainty lose credibility as well. For in their attempt to reassure, they fail to acknowledge the reality of indeterminacy, an acknowledgment that would allow them to form a sympathetic alliance with an anxious audience. The ethical and practical implications of HIV/AIDS test our tolerance for uncertainty as well as our commitment to live the democratic principles that speak to inclusive rather than exclusive modes of behavior.

While the father described in this incident was particularly direct in his attempt to discredit our authority, or perhaps more accurately, even the possibility of the existence of authoritative knowledge about HIV/AIDS, he was raising the same question that emerged in countless sessions with teachers at that time. Teachers were faced with a dual quandary. They saw themselves as possibly in danger, not only because they were acceding to policies based on calculated risks, but also because they were being asked to initiate HIV/AIDS instruction without feeling confident about the information they would be transmitting. Obviously, HIV/AIDS also meant talking about sex, drugs, and death, often taboo subjects that are not easily packaged into highly rationalized lessons. Without certainty, lacking definitive research or a legitimated history to support current assertions, teachers wondered what stance to adopt with regard to the subject. They wondered how not to place their own authority in jeopardy with students. When teachers believe their ability to influence students rests in the control of information, the lack of that control can lead to a lethal silence.

Teachers now recognize that their failure to respond to many teachable moments reflects a lack of confidence in their own HIV/AIDS knowledge. A subtle but more positive shift in attitudes has occurred when professionals refer to their ignorance rather than to lack of scientific proof. The reservations are less about the validity of scientific knowledge than about their familiarity with it. Yet there is something fundamentally askew when teachers are unwilling to admit to students that they do not know the answers to their questions and use this as a rationale for pretending that the subject does not exist. While the obvious remedy to this situation is to provide all teachers with a good basic education about HIV/AIDS so that they feel competent, a long-range response must also be pursued by encouraging teachers and those who work with them to examine the sources of their authority. For HIV/AIDS is not the only difficult issue teachers face in the classroom where the willingness to model the role of learner takes precedence over the traditional role of knower.

Collaboration in Health and Education

The high degree of control and standardization in American public schools that undermines the initiative of teachers has been amply documented by historians and sociologists of education (Apple, 1982; Tyack, 1974). Frequently denied the choices that would express their pedagogic expertise, teachers are reluctant to take on subjects like sex, illness, and death that leave them in undefined territory where previous understandings of authority may seem less relevant. In such territory, student–teacher distinctions based on the ownership of knowledge may break down in the face of the greater commonalities that we all share regardless of age.

The breakdown of hierarchical authority that may ensure when certainty becomes doubtful has been actively sought by people with HIV/AIDS and their advocates and is a development educators might watch carefully. As individuals confront radical care and treatment decisions, the authority of institutions and private practitioners has come under increasing scrutiny. People with HIV/AIDS often have more information about new drugs or treatments than their health care provider; at other times, the provider may have to acknowledge that little is known about how a drug works or even if it is effective. A collaborative model of health care in which the patient is a full participant seems only appropriate given these circumstances.

Such a collaborative model has implications for all professionals who may have once defined their right to practice by the exclusive control of a particular body of knowledge and skills.

As more and more people with HIV/AIDS strive to become involved in the decisions affecting their care, they set an agenda for themselves that does not sound so very different from one that good teachers may set for their students—or indeed that teachers as a group may have for their own development. This is an agenda of increasing independence, autonomy, and self-reliance. Illich (1976), in a book written just prior to the emergence of HIV/AIDS, makes an illuminating distinction between medical and health care, associating the former with the highly rationalized scientific management of illness offered by experts in institutional settings, and the latter with the sociopolitical process that enables people to make life-affirming choices on a daily basis. To Illich, medical care is only a part of a larger set of contextual issues that facilitate or inhibit health. This is not to deny the critical role of technology and professional care but to question how reliance on them affects our sense of dignity and agency.

It would seem that teachers express a similar set of concerns, not only when they question the ultimate meanings of the technocratic curriculum but also when they assess the administrative structures that frustrate their ability to decide how and what they will teach. For the belief in expert control undermines teachers who are asked only to implement curricula designed by others, undermines students forced to learn in classrooms in which they are not active participants, and undermines sick people made passive observers of the healing process (Rosenberg, 1987). Collaboration, in education as in health care, may appear risky because it means that experts relinquish some of their control. But it is also a recognition that not all knowledge is about control. While there needs to be space for mastery, there also needs to be a role for understanding and acceptance, for emancipation and liberation.

Is There Safety in Safer Sex?

The interests of early childhood and elementary classroom teachers in becoming knowledgable and establishing a rationale for HIV/AIDS education with younger children are different from those of teachers working with adolescents. In junior and senior high schools, health teachers are trained to talk about sex and sexuality, though permitted to do so with varying degrees of freedom. It is now assumed that HIV/AIDS education is relevant to all students who are potentially sexually active. This has not always been the case.

It is understandable that adults were at first reluctant to admit the presence of a complex, wily virus such as HIV in a chameleon-like population that itself often appears to have no other goal than to test the limits of human possibility. During the earliest years of the epidemic, this reluctance to view teenagers as vulnerable to HIV infection was reinforced by the dominant risk-group vocabulary, which suggested that the virus would be contained within specific populations. The social and political marginalization of gay men and injection drug users allowed many to discount their experiences. Today, although there continues to be widespread denial of the existence of gay-identified youth in our classrooms (Rofes, 1989), there is a greater acceptance of the fact that any teenager may experiment with behaviors or accede to peer pressure in such a way as to place him- or herself at risk for contracting HIV. Indeed, it is these very attributes that are most frequently cited as the reasons for making HIV education so daunting.

Whether motivated by irrational fear or realistic assessment of the problem, a strong national consensus exists in favor of HIV/AIDS education for young people (Center for Population Options, 1989). Although compliance may be inconsistent and resistance from the religious right fierce (Gallagher, 1993), over half of the states have mandated HIV/AIDS education in their schools and most others strongly recommend it. Only 13 states have established complete programs including published curricula, training or certification requirements, and inservice education for staff (Kenney et al., 1989). The absence of resources for staff development is especially notable given recent calls for greater teacher autonomy to increase school effectiveness and the adoption of experiments in teacher-based school governance. In many of the nation's largest school districts, education about HIV has begun to take precedence over education about sexuality. While the majority of schools address both topics, the transitional and often confusing nature of the moment is evidenced by the number of sites that offer HIV/AIDS education but not sexuality education, and others where the situation is reversed.

HIV-related curricula tend to have a strong prevention focus. Not surprisingly, the prevention method of choice is clearly abstinence. Of the 27 state-approved curricula, only 8 address abstinence and strategies appropriate for sexually active students in a balanced manner and provide comprehensive information about the epidemic. Indeed, the subject of safer sex is one of the least likely to be discussed with students. While teachers blame their own discomfort with this topic on parental and administrative constraints, lack of appropriate materials, and the embarrassment with which students approach discussions of sexuality, they report little difficulty teaching abstinence and sexual decision making (Kerr, Allensworth, & Gayle, 1989). This suggests that the latter topic is not so much about learning to make choices from a world of possibilities as about deciding to say "no" to sex, based on a predetermined set of behavioral rules. That decision making has become a code phrase for a "just say no" message is underlined by teachers' responses to survey questions. There is almost universal commitment to programs that enable students to examine and develop their own values; yet three-quarters of the same teachers believe that students should be explicitly taught not to have sex (Forrest & Silverman, 1989). The values clarification discussion becomes the critical vehicle for persuading students to own the adult perspective.

Despite media and school-based efforts, teenagers remain woefully ignorant about HIV and ill disposed toward people with AIDS (Brooks-Gunn, Boyer, & Hein, 1988; Hingson & Strunin, 1989). This is of increased concern for African-American and Latino communities whose youth represent 34% and 18% respectively of adolescents with AIDS but who, in comparison with their white peers, are less knowledgeable about HIV and the effectiveness of condoms for prevention (DiClemente, Boyer, & Morales, 1988). Overall, AIDS is the sixth leading cause of death among those aged 15 to 24 (*Chronic Disease and Health* . . . , 1990). While adolescents are only 2% of total AIDS cases, for the past six years the number of cases among 13- to 19-year-olds has doubled every 14 months, the same rate of expansion seen among gay males in the first years of the epidemic. Other studies indicate that 7% of homeless and runaway youth and 1% of all teenagers in high-incidence cities like New York and Miami may have already contracted HIV (Society for Adolescent Medicine, 1994). Most disturbingly, over one-fifth of people with AIDS are in their 20s. Because the average latency period between initial infection with HIV and the onset of CDC-defined AIDS is 10 years or more, it can be inferred that many of these people contracted the virus as teenagers.

State-approved HIV/AIDS curricula usually give priority to information about healthful lifestyles, communicable diseases, and HIV transmission and prevention. But many pose constraints to the discussion of subjects that might be interpreted as facilitating sexual activity—contraception, safer sex, and sexuality—even though studies indicate that sex education leads not to more sex but to more responsible sex, including the postponement of first intercourse, safer practices, and fewer unwanted pregnancies (Altman, 1993a).

Unfortunately, evidence also suggests a lack of practical efficacy in our efforts; only 8% of males and 2% of females reported condom use after exposure to AIDS education. Among homosexual/bisexual males, those who reported using condoms increased from 2% to 19% after AIDS education (Bell, 1991). Studies (New York City Board of Education, 1990) conducted two years after implementation of specific curricula point to little or no change in actual knowledge. When asked, students report that they learn about HIV/AIDS primarily from the media and interpersonal sources—for example, friends and parents ("What High School Students Want . . . ," 1990). Schools are listed third, and teachers are described as ill informed, reluctant to talk about disease and sexual activity, and uninterested in HIV/AIDS education. Students themselves request more extensive and intensive education, beginning earlier, and including presentations by people with HIV/AIDS, targeted information about prevention, condom availability, and discussion of the psychosocial impact of the disease.

The Life-Skills Approach

In order to create more effective programs, some curriculum makers (Basch, 1989; Keeling, 1989) have focused on what they perceive as a critical gap between information and/or self-perception and behavioral change. Mickler (1993), studying AIDS-preventive behavior among college adolescents, found that knowledge of AIDS was not predictive or strongly related to safer sex practices. Others (Koopman, Rotheram-Borus, Henderson, Bradley, & Hunter, 1990), working with adolescent runaways and self-identified gay males, reported that both groups had moderately positive beliefs about their self-efficacy and self-control in sexual situations. Yet in focus groups they were unable to role-play safer behaviors, such as asking about their partners' sexual history or asking their partners to use a condom. More significantly, although three-quarters had engaged in sexual activity in the previous three months, with a mean of 2.7 partners, all reported infrequent condom use.

Increasingly, HIV/sexuality education curricula emphasize an ill-defined cluster of behaviors variously labeled as coping, problem solving, or life skills. Depending on the commitment of the particular curriculum, it is claimed that these skills will enable teenagers to remain abstinent until marriage, delay intercourse until an unspecified time in the future, or negotiate safer sex practices as necessary. Through active participation in role-playing, brainstorming sessions, and games, students are taught resistance or refusal skills so that they will not succumb to pressures from peers. These skills are often reduced to a set of sharp retorts that permit students to say "no" to sexual activity without losing face among their friends. In some instances a few lessons are added to more traditional, direct-instruction curricula, while in others, information is interwoven into a consistently interactive format (Brick, 1989).

But as progressive educators have asserted since the last century (Dewey, 1900/1956), students learn most effectively when in the midst of meaningful activities. Programs that abstract social skills provide neither the motivation nor intentionality required for substantive learning. A curriculum that attempts, in a few brief lessons, to teach students how to make critical decisions cannot make up for years of education that have denied them the right to become autonomous, self-determining learners. Friday afternoon "magic circles" to build self-esteem or Monday morning rehearsals of refusal skills divert our attention from the realities of contemporary children, who too seldom have the opportunity to make meaningful choices, follow through on them, and reflect on their consequences.

Skill-based approaches are built on the understanding that the lack of a positive self-image is the biggest factor preventing teenagers from making healthy decisions. Nationally distributed curricula such as "Project Charlie" (Charest, Gwinn, Reinisch, Terrien, & Strawbridge, 1987) and "Growing Healthy" (National Center for Health Education, 1985) are being described as panaceas to a wide variety of problems, including high school dropout rates, lowered academic performance, widespread alcohol and substance abuse, and teenage pregnancy. As in similar programs designed to improve adult productivity in the workplace, the focus on changes in self-perception and interpersonal skills masks material barriers to real equity and autonomy (Steinberg, 1990; L. Williams, 1990). Self-esteem has become a popular buzzword for efforts to promote better psychological adjustment to the political status quo.

The seemingly humanistic techniques of self-empowerment models often become a means to reproduce a hegemonic ideology, instantiating subtle but powerful forms of social control (Young, 1990). This occurs, for example, when the press to insure safer sex, whether condom use for gay men or abstinence for teenagers, impels facilitators to assume responsibility *for* group members rather than *toward* them. The most sympathetic educators may fail to exercise pedagogical tact when confronting HIV/AIDS. Programs are coercive to the degree that they compromise the participants' abilities to draw their own conclusions from experiences that take place within a context that specifically proclaims the importance of individual choice. Experiential learning becomes a means to an end rather than an open exploration of possibility, including the potential rejection of safer sex practices.

Both individual behavior change and self-empowerment models are based on the instrumentalist assumption that behavior can be isolated, analyzed, and understood apart from the socioeconomic context in which it occurs—an assumption that negates the necessity of addressing issues of the differential distribution of economic and cultural capital. Brandt (1987) comments:

> These assumptions with which we still live regarding health-related behavior rest upon an essentially naive, simplistic view of human nature. If anything has become clear in the course of the twentieth century it is that behavior is subject to complex forces, internal psychologies, and external pressures all not subject to immediate modifications, or, arguably, to modifications at all. (p. 202)

The historical record not only documents the past failure of narrow approaches to the control of sexually transmitted diseases but also the degree to which they are constructed upon a set of moralistic judgments about the nature of sexual activity (Fee & Fox, 1988).

In a democratic society that is respectful of pluralism and accepting of different rates and ways of learning, the public health goal of zero transmission, 100% risk reduction, is not only counterproductive but politically unacceptable (Bell, 1991).

Compromise is inevitable in societies where absolute control over citizens' (mis)be-haviors is given up in the interests of the responsible exercise of individual freedom. It is as inappropriate to employ coercive measures as it is to gauge the success of HIV/AIDS education by gross measures of behavioral change.

The Collective-Action Approach

While much is to be learned from the cognitive social learning theory (e.g., active en-gagement of students, multiple levels of learning, and variable strategies) underlying skill-based programs (Flora & Thoresen, 1988), its limitations are highlighted by a tri-phasic map of health education including individual behavioral change, self-empow-erment, and collective action models (French & Adams, 1986; Homans & Aggleton, 1988). The underlying assumption of the first two approaches, also referred to as di-rect-instruction or experientially based programs, is that increased information about HIV risk behaviors reduces infections (Eckland, 1989). The linear reasoning embed-ded in these approaches, along with questions of long-term effectiveness and ethics, is exposed when they are juxtaposed against a collective-action model of health educa-tion. In addition to addressing the need for information and communicative skills, the collective-action approach encourages organizing to transform the social and political forces that shape and give meaning to individual behavior.

When the connection between health status and poverty, employment, in-come, and social class is fully recognized, then socioeconomic factors appear to have greater significance for health than do individual behaviors ("Demand side," 1993; Hubbard, 1993). These factors are best addressed through collective action in the political process. While this position is consistent with radical definitions of health and illness (Illich, 1976), it threatens the official governmental position on disease causation, as summarized by the presidential commission on the Human Immunod-eficiency Virus Epidemic (1988), which is that "the heaviest burden of illness in the technically advanced countries today is related to individual behavior, especially the long-term patterns of behavior often referred to as 'life-style'" (p. 89). Paradoxically, it is this attempt to define critical social issues as private and personal rather than as public and political that heightens the very bigotry that the Presidential Commis-sion seeks to dispel.

In fact, safer sex organizing began as a grass roots political movement within the gay community (Patton, 1990). Its greatest successes occurred in the first years of the epidemic prior to the professionalization and bureaucratization of HIV prevention. Some continue to understand that health education, community building, and politi-cal resistance are inextricably linked. Cranston (1992), for example, proposes HIV/AIDS education among gay and lesbian youth based on Paulo Freire's concept of the community of conscience. Consistent with a collective action model, this is HIV prevention that leads to political engagement because it values and fosters re-spect for gay histories, identities, and futures. Others (Gasch, Poulson, Fullilove, & Fullilove, 1991) understand the disproportional impact of HIV/AIDS on African-American populations as part of a more generalized pattern of excessive risk and mortality. They stress the role of the social and material environment in conditioning health-related behaviors. Poor African-American communities are best served by de-veloping an analysis that will enable their members to work toward means connecting individual behavior to larger social changes.

Assessing the impact of a curriculum requires an exploration of the knowledge assumptions on which it is based. This assessment is critical to dispelling the myths about sexual identity and behavior that prevent effective HIV/AIDS education. Limiting the terrain of HIV/AIDS education to that of a "solvable" social question involving risk-reduction strategies has led to correspondingly limited answers focusing on either behavioral or attitudinal changes (Diorio, 1985). Valued knowledge is construed in the former case as the sum of facts and skills and in the latter as the ability to understand the intentions of others through improved communication abilities. However, HIV/AIDS is not only a question of individual behaviors and social norms. It is also a question of material conditions and resources, and structural inequities based on race, class, gender and sexual identities.

Sex, *HIV*, and the Permeable Curriculum

AIDS is a disease of contradictions. It is a disease that is not a disease, a biological reality that has had a greater impact on sociopolitical practices than on medical care, an illness of hiddenness that has led to irreversible changes in public discourse. Unfortunately, HIV infection has also become a disease of adolescence, a period characterized in our society by its own unique logic—moments of sudden growth and regression, of open search and certain definition, of personal power and extreme susceptibility to the influence of others. An additional conundrum now presents itself. Safer sex alone will not make us safe from the effects of HIV.

The complexity of HIV/AIDS mandates a multifaceted approach. Reconceptualizing HIV/AIDS education means abandoning the instrumentalist assumptions of information- and skill-based programs that have led many to theorize the problem of HIV/AIDS education as one of bridging a gap between knowledge and behavior. Preventing the transmission of HIV involves not only learning about condoms, spermicides, and negotiating sex; it also means developing tools of political analysis, a commitment to social change, and an ethic of caring and responsibility. In short, we must shift our attention from HIV prevention narrowly defined as a means of behavioral control to a broader focus that would more accurately reflect our students' life worlds. HIV/AIDS education should further the goal of preparing students to become active participants in a democratic society. But what are the elements of such an approach?

First, HIV/AIDS education needs to begin with the youngest children and permeate the curriculum in order to break down the taboos with which it is associated and to make the subject a more comfortable one for discussion (Quackenbush & Villarreal, 1988). Our efforts should be informed by an appreciation of the development levels and experiential bases of different groups of students. We must ask whether the curriculum ensures equal access to HIV/AIDS information for all students. Access means that students not only have the opportunity to hear information but that it is presented in a language and style easily understood by specific target groups (Nettles & Scott-Jones, 1989). At the same time, as with other subject areas, we must be concerned with unwarranted differences in curriculum predicated on the race, class, gender, or sexual orientation of our students (Apple & Weiss, 1983; Willis, 1977).

Effective sexuality education itself, education that empowers students by building their sense of entitlement and decreasing their vulnerability, is based on our willingness to listen to and work with experiences students bring with them. This requires giving up presuppositions about the nature of sexuality and the outcomes of our efforts in favor of a sociohistorical appreciation of the ways in which sexual meanings are constructed and changed (D'Emilio & Freedman, 1988; Rubin, 1984). Safer sex can be less about the limitations imposed by HIV and the inculcation of specific behaviors and more about exploring multiple zones of bodily pleasures and the transformation of culturally determined constraints (Patton, 1985). In a time of HIV/AIDS, a discursive analysis becomes essential to re-imagining sexual practices in life-affirming, sex-positive ways.

Our goal should be to replace isolated lessons calculated to build self-esteem and social skills with an ongoing discourse of desire that problematizes violence and victimization (Fine, 1988). If the experiences of our students are valorized, they will be better able to understand the sources of pleasure and danger in their own lives. This process begins when students find a safe place in which to tell their stories. To accept these narratives is not only to foster respect for individual differences but also to reveal their distance from officially given versions of human sexuality, a distance that is clearly identified by recent studies of the high school curriculum (Trudell, 1992; Ward & Taylor, 1992). At the same time it is impossible to ignore externally imposed constraints to liberation, for even the best-intended pedagogic efforts may have little impact without increased life options for poorer students and easy access to birth control materials, health clinics, and substance-abuse treatment for everyone.

The permeable curriculum requires balancing our concerns about individual responsibility for transmitting HIV with an analysis of the changing social context in which it thrives. At a personal level, the curriculum causes students to reflect on their own behaviors as they affect the transmission of HIV and the lives of those who already carry the virus. At a social level, the curriculum provokes critical consciousness, fostering responsive and responsible citizens. Students should be asking questions about the societal responses to HIV/AIDS and learning to see themselves as citizens who can make decisions that will give direction to that response in the future. They need access to all kinds of citizens, especially those living with HIV, who model active responses to the disease (Navarre, 1987).

And what does the permeable curriculum say about people with HIV infection—gays, injection drug users, and others? Fear-based appeals have never been successful in preventing the spread of sexually transmitted diseases (Mickler, 1993). Greater familiarity with HIV, not less, is needed in order to break down the distancing mechanisms that allow us to feel that we can remain untouched. Images of diversity remind us that people with HIV/AIDS are a part of all our lives. Although some have real anxiety about what they perceive as a disintegration of culture and an erosion of values in the modern world, HIV/AIDS is not an appropriate metaphor for these concerns. The permeable curriculum is about caring for others and inclusion, not about isolation and exclusion.

Just as effective sexuality education is based on an entire school experience that encourages decision making, problem solving, and self-worth, successful HIV/AIDS education is built on a continuing appreciation of equity and pluralism in society. It cannot be assumed that an absence of negative comment signifies a lack of bias or commitment to social justice (Croteau & Morgan, 1989; Vance, 1984). Educators must take an active role in bringing the full spectrum of human differences to the classroom, acknowledging the ways that these have become sources of conflict and domination as well as the ways that they enrich and form the basis of participatory democracy. A curriculum that is permeable to the impact of students, one through which they can learn the skills of responsible citizenship, lays the groundwork for all AIDS education. For the history of HIV constantly reminds us not only of individual suffering and pain but also of the power and creativity that reside in a collective response.

Although HIV/AIDS may challenge our prior ideas about pedagogical authority, it also offers us an opportunity to examine new models that more accurately reflect who we understand ourselves to be and what we would like our students to become. From HIV/AIDS we learn about the limits of science and the importance of human vision, the frailty of the body and the strength of the spirit, the need to nurture the imagination even as we direct our attention to rational cognitive structures. In the end, the HIV/AIDS curriculum can be more about life than about death, more about health than about illness, more about the body politic than the body physical.

References

Alexander, R. J. (1984). *Primary teaching*. London: Holt, Rinehart & Winston.

Altman, L. (1993a, June 15). Conference ends with little hope for AIDS cure. *The New York Times*, p. C1,3.

Apple, M. W. (1979). *Ideology and curriculum*. London: Routledge & Kegan Paul.

Apple, M. W. (Ed.). (1982). *Cultural and economic reproduction in education*. Boston: Routledge & Kegan Paul.

Apple, M. W., & Weiss, L. (Eds.). (1983). *Ideology and practice in schooling*. Philadelphia: Temple University Press.

Barritt, L., Beekman, T., Bleeker, H., & Mulderij, K. (1985). *Researching educational practice*. Grand Forks: University of North Dakota Press.

Basch, C. E. (1989). Preventing AIDS through education: Concepts, strategies, and research priorities. *Journal of School Health, 59,* 296–300.

Bell, N. Z. (1991). Ethical issues in AIDS education. In F. G. Reimer (Ed.), *AIDS and ethics* (pp. 128–154). New York: Columbia University Press.

Bowles, S., & Gintis, H. (1976). *Schooling in capitalist America*. New York: Basic Books.

Brandt, A. M. (1987). *No magic bullet: A social history of venereal disease in the United States since 1800*. New York: Oxford University Press.

Brick, P. (1989). *Teaching safer sex*. Hackensack, NJ: Planned Parenthood of Bergen County.

Brooks-Gunn, J., Boyer, C. B., & Heim, K. (1988). Preventing HIV infection and AIDS in children and adolescents: Behavioral research and intervention strategies. *American Psychologist, 43,* 958–965.

Brunner, D. D. (1992). Discussing sexuality in the language arts classroom: Alternative meaning making and meaning making as an alternative. In J. T. Sears (Ed.), *Sexuality and the curriculum* (pp. 226–242). New York: Teachers College Press.

CDC AIDS Weekly. (1986, December 15). p. 9.

Center for Population Options (1989). *Adolescents, AIDS and HIV: A community wide responsibility*. [Available from Center for Population Options, 1012 14th Street, N.W., Washington, DC.]

Charest, P., Gwinn, T., Reinisch, N., Terrien, J., & Strawbridge, C. (1987). *Project Charlie*. [Available from Storefront/Youth Action, 4570 West 77th Street, Edina, MN 55435.]

Chronic disease and health promotion reprints from the mmwr: 1990 youth risk behavior surveillance system. (1990). [Available from U.S. Department of Health and Human Services, Centers for Disease Control, Atlanta, GA 30333.]

Coles, R. (1989). Moral energy in the lives of impoverished children. In T. F. Duggan & R. Coles (Eds.), *The child in our times: Studies in the development of resiliency* (pp. 45–55). New York: Brunner/Mazel.

Cranston, K. (1992). HIV education for gay, lesbian, and bisexual youth: Personal risk, personal power, and the community of conscience. In K. Harbeck (Ed.), *Coming out of the classroom closet* (pp. 247–259). New York: Haworth.

Croteau, J. M., & Morgan, S. (1989). Combating homophobia in AIDS education. *Journal of Counseling & Development, 68,* 86–91.

The demand side of the health care crisis. (1993). *Harvard Magazine, 95*(4), 30–32.

D'Emilio, J., & Freedman, E. B. (1988). *Intimate matters: A history of sexuality in America.* New York: Harper & Row.

Derman-Sparks, L., & the A.B.C. Task Force (1989). *Anti-bias curriculum: Tools for empowering young children.* Washington, DC: National Association for the Education of Young Children.

Dewey, J. (1956). *The child and the curriculum/The school and society.* Chicago: University of Chicago Press. (Original works published 1902 and 1900).

DiClemente, R. J., Boyer, C. B., & Morales, E. D. (1988). Minorities and AIDS: Knowledge, attitudes and misconceptions among black and Latino adolescents. *American Journal of Public Health, 78,* 55–57.

Dioro, J. (1985). Contraception, copulation, domination, and the theoretical barrennes of sex education literature. *Educational Theory, 35,* 239–255.

Eckland, J. D. (1989). Policy choices for AIDS education in the public schools. *Education Evaluation and Policy Analysis, 11,* 377–387.

Egan, K. (1988). Education and the mental life of young children. In L. Williams & D. Fromberg (Eds.), *The proceedings of "Defining the field of early childhood education: An invitational symposium"* (pp. 41–77). New York: Teachers College, Columbia University.

Elkind, D. (1981b). *The hurried child: Growing up too fast, too soon.* Reading, MA: Addison-Wesley.

Engler, R. K. (1988, October). *Safe sex and dangerous poems: AIDS, literature and the gay and lesbian community college student.* Paper presented at the Annual National Literature Conference, Chicago.

Farquhar, C. (1990a). *Answering children's questions about HIV/AIDS in the primary school: Are teachers prepared?* Unpublished manuscript, University of London, Institute of Education, Thomas Coram Research Unit, London.

Farquhar, C. (1990b). *What do primary school children know about AIDS?* (Working Paper No. 1). London: University of London, Institute of Education Thomas Coram Research Unit.

Fee, E., & Fox, D. M. (1988). *AIDS: The burdens of history.* Berkeley: University of California Press.

Felsman, J. K. (1989). Risk and resiliency in childhood: The lives of street children. In T. F. Duggan & R. Coles (Eds.), *The child in our times: Studies in the development of resiliency* (pp. 56–80). New York: Brunner/Mazel.

Fine, M. (1988). Sexuality, schooling, and adolescent females: The missing discourse of desire. *Harvard Educational Review, 58*(1), 29–53.

Flora, J. A., & Thoresen, C. E. (1988). Reducing the risk of AIDS in adolescents. *American Psychologist, 43,* 965–971.

Forrest, J. D., & Silverman, J. (1989). What public school teachers teach about preventing pregnancy, AIDS and sexually transmitted diseases. *Family Planning Perspectives, 21*(2), 65–72.

Fraser, K. (1989). *Someone at school has AIDS.* Alexandria, VA: National Association of State Boards of Education.

French, J., & Adams, L. (1986). From analysis to synthesis. *Health Education Journal, 45*(2), 71–74.

Gallagher, J. (1993, June 15). Why Johnny can't be safe. *The Advocate, 631,* 46–47.

Garbarino, T. (1992). *Children in danger.* San Francicso: Jossey-Bass.

Gasch, H., Poulson, M., Fullilove, R., & Fullilove, M. (1991). Shaping AIDS education and prevention programs for African Americans amidst community decline. *Journal of Negro Education, 60*(1), 85–96.

Glauser, B. (1990). Street children: Deconstructing a construct. In A. James & A. Prout (Eds.), *Constructing and reconstructing childhood* (pp. 138–156). New York: Falmer Press.

Grumet, M. (1988). *Bitter milk.* Amherst: University of Massachusetts Press.

Hingson, R., & Strunin, L. (1989). *Summary of results: Boston schools baseline surveys, spring 1988, 1989.* Unpublished manuscript, Boston University, School of Public Health.

Homans, H., & Aggleton, P. (1988). Health education, HIV infection and AIDS. In P. Aggleton & H. Homans (Eds.), Social aspects of AIDS (pp. 154–176). London: Falmer Press.

Hubbard, R. (1993, Spring). Viewpoint. *The AIDS Report* [The Harvard AIDS Institute], pp. 13–14.

Illich, I. (1976). *Medical nemesis: The expropriation of health.* New York: Pantheon.

James, A., & Prout, A. (1990a). *Constructing and reconstructing childhood: Contemporary issues in the sociological study of childhood.* New York: Falmer.

Keeling, R. P. (Ed.). (1989). *AIDS on the college campus.* Rockville, MD: American College Health Association.

Kenney, A. M., Guardado, S., & Brown, L. (1989). Sex education and AIDS education in the schools: What states and large school districts are doing. *Family Planning Perspectives, 21*(2), 56–64.

Kerr, D. L., Allensworth, D. D., & Gayle, J. A. (1989). The ASHA national HIV education needs assessment of health and education professionals. *Journal of School Health, 59,* 301–305.

King, R. (1978). *All things bright and beautiful: A sociological study of infants' classrooms.* Chichester: Wiley.

Klein, M. (1989). *Poets for life: Seventy-six poets respond to AIDS.* New York: Crown.

Klusacek, A., & Morrison, K. (1992). *Leap in the dark: AIDS, art & contemporary cultures.* Montreal: Véhicule Press.

Koopman, C., Rotheram-Borus, M., Henderson, R., Bradley, J., & Hunter, J. (1990). Assessment of knowledge of AIDS and beliefs about prevention among adolescents. *AIDS Education and Prevention, 2*(1), 58–70.

Mickler, S. E. (1993). Perceptions of vulnerability: Impact on AIDS-preventive behavior among college adolescents. *AIDS Education and Prevention, 5*(1), 43–53.

Miller, J. (Ed.). (1992). *Fluid exchanges: Artists and critics in the AIDS crisis.* Toronto: University of Toronto Press.

Murphy, T. F., & Poirier, S. (Eds.). (1993). *Writing AIDS: Gay literature, language and analysis.* New York: Columbia University Press.

National Center for Health Education. (1985). *Growing healthy.* (Available from the National Center for Health Education, 30 East 29th Street, New York, NY 10016.)

Navarre, M. (1987). Fighting the victim label. *October, 43,* 143–147.

Nelson, E. S. (1992). *AIDS the literary response.* New York: Twayne Publishers.

Nettles, S. M., & Scott-Jones, D. (1989). The role of sexuality and sex equity in the education of minority adolescents. *Peabody Journal of Education, 64*(4), 183–198.

New York State Education Department (1987). *AIDS Instructional Guide.* Albany, NY: Author.

Oyemade, U. J., & Washington, V. (1989). Drug abuse prevention begins in early childhood. *Young Children, 44*(5), 6–12.

Pastore, J. (1992). *Confronting AIDS through literature.* Champaign: University of Illinois Press.

Patton, C. (1985). *Sex and germs: The politics of AIDS.* Boston: South End Press.

Patton, C. (1990). *Inventing AIDS.* New York: Routledge.

Polakow, V. (1982). *The erosion of childhood.* Chicago: University of Chicago Press.

Postman, N. (1982). *The disappearance of childhood.* New York: Delacorte.

Presidential Commission on the Human Immunodeficiency Virus Epidemic. (1988). *Report of the Presidential Commission on the Human Immunodeficiency Virus Epidemic.* Washington, DC: U.S. Government Printing Office.

Preston, J. (1989). *Dispatches.* Boston: Alyson Press.

Quackenbush, M., Villarreal, S. (1988). *"Does AIDS hurt?" Educating young children about AIDS.* Santa Cruz, CA: Network Publications.

Rofes, E. (1989). Opening up the classroom closet: Responding to the educational needs of gay and lesbian youth. *Harvard Educational Review, 59*(4), 444–452.

Rosenberg, C. E. (1987). *The care of strangers: The rise of America's hospital system.* New York: Basic Books.

Rubin, G. (1984). Thinking sex: Notes for a radical theory of the politics of sexuality. In C. S.

Vance (Ed.), *Pleasure and danger: Exploring female sexuality* (pp. 267–320). Boston: Routledge & Kegan Paul.

Sarason, S. B. (1982). *The culture of the school and the problem of change.* Boston: Allyn & Bacon.

Schvaneveldt, J. D., Lindauer, S., & Young, M. H. (1990). Children's understanding of AIDS: A developmental viewpoint. *Family Relations, 38,* 330–335.

Silin, J. (1982). *Protection and control: Early childhood teachers talk about authority.* Unpublished doctoral dissertation, Teachers College, Columbia University, New York.

Skeen, P., & Hudson, D. (1987). What we should and should not tell our children about AIDS. *Young Children, 42*(4), 65–71.

Sloane, D. C., & Sloane, B. C. (1990). AIDS in schools: A comprehensive initiative. *McGill Journal of Education, 25*(2), 205–227.

Society for Adolescent Medicine. (1994). HIV infection and AIDS in adolescents: A position paper for the Society for Adolescent Medicine. *Journal of Adolescent Health, 15*(5), 427–434.

Steinberg, C. (1990, February 18). How "magic circles" build self-esteem. *The New York Times,* sec. 12, p. 1.

Sutton-Smith, B. (1988). Radicalizing childhood: The multivocal mind. In L. Williams & D. Fromberg (Eds.), *The proceedings of "Defining the field of early childhood education: An invitational symposium"* (pp. 77–153). New York: Teachers College, Columbia University.

Trudell, B. K. (1992). Inside a ninth-grade sexuality classroom: The process of knowledge construction. In J. T. Sears (Ed.), *Sexuality and the curriculum* (pp. 203–226). New York: Teachers College Press.

Tyack, D. (1974). *The one best system.* Cambridge, MA: Harvard University Press.

Vance, C. S. (1984). Pleasure and danger: Toward a politics of sexuality. In. C. S. Vance (Ed.), *Pleasure and danger: Exploring female sexuality* (pp. 1–27). Boston: Routledge & Kegan Paul.

van Manen, M. (1990. *Researching lived experience: Human science for an action sensitive pedagogy.* Albany: State University of New York Press.

Ward, J. V., & Taylor, J. M. (1992). Sexuality education for immigrant and minority students: Developing culturally appropriate curriculum. In J. T. Sears (Ed.), *Sexuality and the curriculum* (pp. 183–203). New York: Teachers College Press.

What high school students want from an HIV education program and how it can be delivered effectively: A report to the Bureau of School Health Education Services, New York State Education Department. (1990). (Available from MAGI Educational Services, Inc., Larchmont, NY)

Williams, L. (1990, March 28) Using self-esteem to fix society's ills. *The New York Times,* pp. C1, 10.

Willis, P. (1977). Learning to labour. Westmead, UK: Saxon House.

Wirth, A. G. (1989). The violation of people at work in schools. *Teachers College Record, 90*(4), 535–549.

Young, R. (1990). *A critical theory of education.* New York: Teachers College Press.

22

Can Tracking Research Inform Practice?
Technical, Normative, and Political Considerations

JEANNIE OAKES

Over the past decade, researchers interested in tracking and ability grouping have moved beyond an almost exclusive concern with effects on student outcomes to investigate the distribution of learning opportunities and students' day-to-day school experiences associated with these practices. The latter studies reveal striking track-related differences across the board, with some of the most dramatic evidence showing tracking's particularly negative impact on the opportunities of low-income, African-American, and Latino students. This work, together with new research investigating track-related student outcomes and reanalysis of earlier studies, supports the increasingly clear and consistent (if not yet universally accepted) conclusion that this common way of organizing students for instruction is, in most instances, neither equitable nor effective.

Reform-minded policymakers and practitioners have responded to this work with hard, but reasonable, questions about what alternatives might ameliorate tracking-related problems and, at the same time, be compatible with other efforts to increase the quality of schools. They want to know what good "detracked" schools look like and what strategies might foster such schools.

Researchers have few answers. We have learned much about the complex and problematic nature of tracking, but little about promising alternatives or how they might be implemented. We have not addressed the effects that altering this entrenched school structure has on students, school faculties, or parents and communities. Neither have we investigated potential responses by publishers, university admissions committees, and advocacy groups for disabled or gifted students.

Truthful answers like "these matters extend beyond the scope of existing research" neither satisfy nor help. Yet the best we can say for alternatives we might derive from our current knowledge-base is that they may be worth a try. However, such recommendations (e.g., just stop tracking) inevitably oversimplify, as they extrapolate solutions from *typical* problems and stand apart from the complex school and social contexts in which problems arise and solutions must be implemented.

Questions about how practice should respond to the tracking research demand a new class of answers—answers that juxtapose extant research with new studies attending specifically to the technical, normative, and political dimensions of developing, implementing, and evaluating tracking alternatives. Here, I briefly review what we've

From *Educational Researcher,* Vol. 21, No. 4, 1992: pp. 12–21. Reprinted by permission.

learned about tracking,[1] consider the impact of these findings, and suggest new research that might target the needs of reformers more directly. A focus on normative
and political matters, as well as on technical considerations, seems essential, since these
dimensions help explain why tracking was created and why it has lasted so long. Unless we understand and change the norms and politics that buttress tracking, school
structures and practices will remain impervious to reform.[2]

What Have We Learned?

Tracking Is Complex and Dynamic

If we've learned nothing else, we've learned that tracking practices are diverse, complex, and dynamic. In fact, we use the term tracking quite generically to refer to a
whole range of ability-related grouping practices in schools. These include (a) placing
elementary students in ability-based groups within and across classes for selected subjects or in self-contained ability-homogeneous classrooms, (b) assigning junior high
students class by class according to their ability or scheduling them together for blocks
of classes according to a general ability measure, and (c) establishing double-layered
senior highs wherein students follow curricular trajectories intended to prepare them
for different postsecondary destinations while they enroll in different "levels" of academic courses (Oakes, 1985; Slavin, 1987, 1990).

Despite their many differences, all these practices organize schools so that students who seem to be similar can be taught together, separately from other students.
And, in addition to their most obvious features—the groups themselves and the criteria and processes used for placement—they all embody a larger schooling dynamic
that includes the following:

• *A technology of curricular differentiation and curricular accommodation*—that is, the
division of knowledge and teaching strategies into programs or courses that stipulate
the knowledge and learning experiences appropriate for different ability levels. These
differentiated curricula begin in some systems with a two-tiered kindergarten program—for example, one curriculum for youngsters thought to be "ready" for academics and another for those judged "not ready." This differentiation continues
throughout the grades through variations in curricular content, pace, and quantity,
culminating in distinct college-preparatory and non-college-preparatory programs
and finer distinctions among levels within the two.

• *Widespread and deeply held norms.* The technology of tracking manifests a web
of cultural assumptions about what is true—what is "normal"—and cultural values
about what constitutes appropriate action given particular "truths."[3] For example,
tracking emerged, in part, from three norms that remain largely unquestioned in contemporary schools. One is that students' individual needs and capacities vary enormously and in ways over which schools have little influence. A second is that schools
can and should accomplish multiple and sometimes conflicting social purposes—including transmitting the knowledge and values of the cultures *and* preparing students
for productive work-force participation. This norm interacts with the first in that it is
widely believed that each generation of students contains a distribution of ability and
effort that will roughly reproduce the perceived hierarchy of skill required in a socially and economically differentiated work force. A third norm, following from these, is
that schools can best accommodate, different individual abilities and accomplish essential social purposes, including work-force preparation, by separating students by
their ability and likely occupational futures (Cohen, 1985; Oakes, 1985).

- *A political aspect of tracking, which is closely intertwined with tracking norms.* Tracking is accompanied by public labels, status differences, expectations, and consequences for academic and occupational attainment. Thus, tracking becomes part and parcel of the struggle among individuals and groups for comparative advantage in the distribution of school resources, opportunities, and credentials that have exchange value in the larger society. This political dimension often encompasses highly charged issues of race and social-class stratification (Moore & Davenport, 1986).

All three overlapping dimensions shape tracking practice and its consequences. The sections that follow highlight those consequences and suggest their technical, normative, and political dimensions.

Tracking Fails to Meet Expectations

Considerable evidence challenges the widely held norm that tracking and ability grouping effectively accommodate students' differences—at least in terms of boosting schooling outcomes. For more than 70 years, researchers have investigated this "bottom line" question, producing a literature that is voluminous and of varying quality. Yet the best evidence suggests that, in most cases, tracking fails to foster the outcomes schools value.[4]

Few or no achievement benefits. Elementary schools do not increase achievement by dividing students into whole classes by ability levels. And while some limited and flexible regrouping strategies yield positive effects on average achievement (particularly multigrade plans that encourage student mobility between "levels"), they also usually increase the inequality of achievement (see, e.g., Slavin, 1987). Over time, then, the gap between high- and low-group students widens. Moreover, we don't know that the slight positive effect on average achievement is sustained over years of schooling.

Secondary students in tracked classes gain no achievement advantage (either overall or for any particular group of students—high, average, or low ability) over their peers of comparable ability in nontracked classes (Slavin, 1990). However, high-track students in tracked secondary schools benefit academically compared with comparable students in lower-track classes (Gamoran & Mare, 1989). But, as I'll describe below, these benefits seem to result from the enhanced opportunities enjoyed by those in the high track, rather than from the homogeneity of their group.

Negative effects on peer groups and attitudes. Over time, tracking fosters friendship networks linked to students' group memberships (Hallinan & Sorensen, 1985; Hallinan & Williams, 1989). These peer groups may contribute to "polarized," track-related attitudes among secondary students, with high-track students more enthusiastic and low-track students more alienated (Oakes, Gamoran, & Page, 1991). High-track students convey greater self-confidence, not only about their academic competence, but generally (Oakes, 1985). While it is unclear whether tracking causes or sustains these dispositions, they reflect school norms.

Effects on school attainment and life chances. Finally, tracking influences students' attainment and life chances, over and above their achievement. Track placements are quite stable, partly because early assignments shape students' later school experiences. By high school, track location has a far-reaching influence—with college-track students enjoying better prospects for high school completion; college attendance, grades, and graduation; and, indirectly, high status occupation, than their otherwise comparable non-college-track peers (Gamoran & Mare, 1989; Vanfossen, Jones, & Spade, 1987; Wolfle, 1985).

Placements Relate to Students' Race and Social Class

Throughout the grades, race, social class, and track assignment correlate consistently—with low-income students and non–Asian minorities disproportionately enrolled in low-track academic classes and advantaged students and whites more often enrolled in the high track. In senior highs, low-income, African-American, and Latino students are under-represented in college-preparatory programs, and they more frequently enroll in those vocational programs that train for the lowest-level occupations. At all levels, these groups lack equal representation in programs for gifted and talented students.

The extraordinarily complex connections between tracking and social stratification play out in two ways. First, schools with predominantly low-income and minority student populations tend to be "bottom heavy." That is, they offer smaller academic tracks and larger remedial and vocational programs than do schools serving whiter, more affluent student bodies. For example, Figure 1 displays the uneven distribution of low-, average-, and high-track math and science classes in secondary schools that differ in student composition (Oakes, 1990).[5] Similar patterns, although less pronounced, appear at the elementary level as well.

The second link between tracking and students' race and social class is forged in racially mixed schools through the disproportionate assignment of African-American and Latino students to low-track classes. For example, Table 1 shows that science and mathematics classes in which Whites are overrepresented (in comparison with their numbers in the school) are about six times more likely to be high-track classes (as identified by teachers) than are disproportionately minority classes. At the same time, classes with disproportionately minority enrollments are seven times more likely than classes in which Whites are overrepresented to be low-track classes. These patterns also begin at the elementary level (Oakes, 1990).

Clearly, ability-related grouping practices lead to race and class separation. And, as I'll describe below, they also lead to race- and class-linked differences in learning opportunities. Ultimately, these differences in opportunity place limits on the educational and occupational futures of low-income, African-American, and Latino students.[6]

The Fairness of Placement Practices Is Questionable

Schools assign elementary students using formal assessments (usually tests) of students' aptitudes, "readiness," and past achievement and teachers' informal observations of classroom performance and behavior. High schools often consult students about their track preferences. However, the extent to which students actually choose their tracks, even when they report having done so, is questionable. Other criteria accompany and often preempt students' preferences: standardized test scores, teacher and counselor recommendations, prior placements, and grades. And students undoubtedly make choices in light of their views of themselves as students, derived from the cumulative message sent by prior testing, sorting, grading, and advising and reinforced by peers and family.

Despite the strong correlation, quantitative studies in elementary schools reveal no *direct* effects of race or social class on assignment to ability groups; some qualitative studies, however, have noted discriminatory practices (e.g., Haller, 1985; Rist, 1970). Early stratification appears to follow from differences in performance on the measures schools use to assess ability and motivation, with Latinos and African Americans typically performing less well than Whites. These placements are "fair," then, to the degree that schools' working definitions and measures of ability and motivation are "fair" to students from various backgrounds.

In secondary schools, students' prior achievement affects track placement most strongly, although background characteristics also matter. For example, data from the Second International Math Study show social-class differences in the math class assignments of U.S. students—with White students and those whose fathers hold high-level occupations more likely to be placed in algebra than other eighth graders with comparable past math achievement (McKnight et al., 1987; Kifer, in press).

Qualitative studies suggest that race and social class influence secondary school placements over and above achievement because students from different backgrounds receive different information, advice, and attention from counselors and teachers (Cicourel & Kitsuse, 1963). In some cases, counselors and teachers respond quite differently to comparable achievement scores, with the result in one study, for example, that Asians and Whites secured placements in advanced classes when comparably scoring Latinos did not (Oakes, Selvin, Karoly, & Guiton, 1992). Additionally, White and middle-class parents more often lobby schools and gain their children's admission to upper-track classes, even when their past performance would not ordinarily qualify them (Oakes, Selvin, Karoly, & Guiton, 1992; Useem, 1990b).

Further complicating matters, track placements (and parents' success at influencing them) stem from factors beyond students' characteristics. Differences among schools—such as the size of various tracks, entry criteria for particular tracks, and scheduling practices—all affect the likelihood that a student with particular characteristics will be placed in particular classes (Sorensen, 1987; Garet & Delany, 1988; Oakes, 1985; Useem, 1990a). These structural differences relate to norms governing faculty

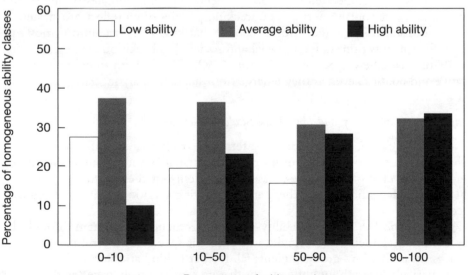

Figure 1. Percentages of low-, average-, and high-ability/track science and mathematics classes in secondary schools by racial composition (F = 10.70, P<0.001).

Note: From *Multiplying Inequalities: The Effects of Race, Social Class, and Tracking on Opportunities to Learn Mathematics and Science,* by Jeannie Oakes, RAND, R-3928-NSF, 1990. Reprinted by permission.

Table 1. Racial Composition of Tracked Science and Mathematics Classes Relative to the School Enrollment at Racially Mixed Secondary Schools (%)

Class enrollment[a] relative to school enrollment	Class ability levels		
	Low	Average	High
Fewer minorities	5	38	57
Same (within 10%)	21	50	29
More minorities	66	25	9

Note: Table includes classes at mixed-race schools (10% to 90% minority) only.

[a]Effect of class racial composition (relative to school's) is significant at the 0.001 level (F = 143.45).

Note: From *Multiplying Inequalities: The Effects of Race, Social Class, and Tracking on Opportunities to Learn Mathematics and Science,* by Jeannie Oakes, RAND, R-3928-NSF, 1990. Reprinted by permission.

confidence in students' capacities, teacher–student interactions about placement decisions, and a schoolwide disposition to either encourage or discourage students from taking difficult courses—norms that often vary with the social-class composition of the student body (Kilgore, 1991; Useem, 1990a). As a consequence, a high-track student at one school would not necessarily be placed in that same track somewhere else.

These student-assignment factors are difficult to sort out, and their "fairness" is questionable. Some researchers deem placement practices generally unbiased and meritocratic, given that ability (as measured by prior achievement) has a larger direct effect on assignments than does race or socioeconomic status (e.g., Rehburg and Rosenthal, 1978). Others question the neutrality of placements, arguing that race and social-class biases are embedded in schools' conceptions and estimates of ability and motivation and that course offerings and tracking policies often reflect broad, stereotypical—and historically rooted—norms about what kind of curriculum is most appropriate for students from different racial and social-class backgrounds (e.g., Rosenbaum, 1976; Oakes, Selvin, Karoly, & Guiton, 1992). Clearly, both interpretations are normative and political, even as they emerge from standard analytic strategies.

Tracking Affects Opportunity, and Low-Track Students Get Less

Large-scale studies document typical patterns of track-related differences in the knowledge presented to students, in instructional strategies and resources (including teachers), and in classroom climates. Case studies flesh out these patterns, providing insight into the dynamics behind them and identifying variations that correspond to local conditions.[7]

Access to curriculum. Students' ability-group assignments propel them through the largely common elementary curriculum at different speeds. The resulting coverage differences mean that low-group students fall further behind and receive increasingly different curricula (even though the groups that go slower usually have the somewhat illogical goal of "catching-up"). These differences tend to stabilize students' track placements, since those in lower groups miss the curricular prerequisites for higher groups.

Secondary students earn equivalent credits toward graduation by taking different, tracked courses. Figures 2 and 3 illustrate the consequences for students' access to

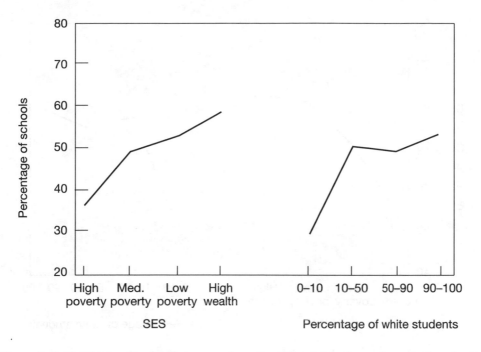

Figure 2. Junior high school offering accelerated mathematics classes (e.g., algebra for 8th graders and/or geometry for 9th graders) by school SES and racial composition.

Note: From *Multiplying Inequalities: The Effects of Race, Social Class, and Tracking on Opportunities to Learn Mathematics and Science,* by Jeannie Oakes, RAND, R-3928-NSF, 1990. Reprinted by permission.

particular subject matter. The low-track emphasis at disadvantaged schools (shown earlier in Table 1) has a chilling effect on junior high students' opportunities to take algebra and geometry and on senior high students' access to calculus classes (Oakes, 1990).

Low-track courses offer less demanding topics and skills, while high-track classes typically include more complex material and more thinking and problem-solving tasks. For example, in the 25 secondary schools studied by Goodlad (1984), high-track students were more often presented with traditional academic topics and intellectually challenging skills. High-track teachers' most important goals often included students' competent and autonomous thinking. In contrast, low-track teachers stressed low-level skills and conformity to rules and expectations (Oakes, 1985).

Typically, teachers of low-ability science and mathematics classes place less emphasis than do teachers of high-track classes on subject-related curriculum goals (Table 2), including having students become interested in science and mathematics, acquire basic concepts and principles, and develop an inquiry approach to science and a problem-solving orientation to mathematics (Oakes, 1990). Such goals do not depend on students' prior knowledge. To the contrary, these goals are increasingly seen as essential for all students—regardless of their current skill levels in science and math. Nevertheless, they are typically viewed as less important for low-track students.

Access to teachers. Most secondary schools track teachers as well as students although some schools rotate the teaching of low- and high-ability classes. Typically,

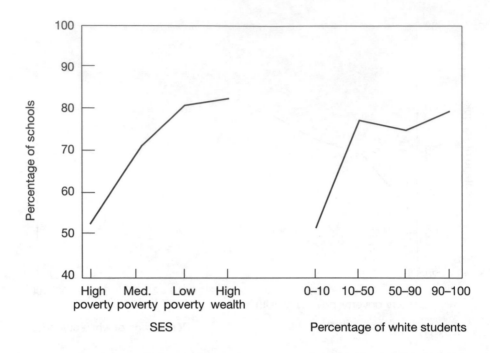

Figure 3. High schools offering one or more sections of calculus by school SES and racial composition

Note: From *Multiplying Inequalities: The Effects of Race, Social Class, and Tracking on Opportunities to Learn Mathematics and Science,* by Jeannie Oakes, RAND, R-3928-NSF, 1990. Reprinted by permission.

Table 2. Secondary Science and Mathematics Teachers' Emphasis on Curricular Objectives in Relation to Class Ability/Track Level

Objectives showing significant negative relationship with high class ability level	Objectives showing no significant monotonic relationship with class ability	Objectives showing significant positive relationship with high class ability level
Importance in daily life" Math, computations"	Career relevance	Interest★ Science, basic concepts" Math, facts and principles" Preparation for further study Inquiry skills" Problem-solving approach" Communicate ideas" Technology applications" History" Science, lab safety★ Science, lab techniques"

Note: ★ = significant at 0.05 level; " = significant at 0.01 level.
Note: From *Multiplying Inequalities: The Effects of Race, Social Class, and Tracking on Opportunities to Learn Mathematics and Science,* by Jeannie Oakes, RAND, R-3928-NSF, 1990. Reprinted by permission.

however, either teachers jockey among themselves for high-track assignments or principals use assignments as rewards and sanctions. Such political processes work to the detriment of low tracks because the least well-prepared teachers usually end up with them. Teachers of low-ability science and mathematics classes typically have less experience, are less likely to be certified in math or science, hold fewer degrees in these subjects, have less training in the use of computers, and less often report themselves to be "master teachers" than their upper-track colleagues (see Figure 4). These troublesome assignments are most evident in schools with large minority and low-income populations, because these schools have fewer well-qualified teachers to begin with. In such schools, low-track students are frequently taught math and science by teachers who are not certified to teach those subjects, if they are certified at all (Oakes, 1990).[8]

Access to classroom experiences. Tracking produces a consistent pattern of instructional disadvantage for students in low tracks. Typically, high-track students have the most time to learn; their teachers are clearer, are more enthusiastic, and use less strong criticism; the classroom learning tasks appear to be better organized, of greater variety, and more likely to engage students in "active" learning; and teachers assign more homework (e.g., Oakes, 1985, 1990). Lower track classes are more often characterized by dull, passive instruction consisting largely of drill and practice with trivial bits of information. In mathematics and science, low-track teachers spend more time on routines, seat work, and worksheet activities. They introduce technology, such as computers, in conjunction with low-level tasks, such as computation (Oakes, 1990). Moreover, teachers seem to establish more supportive relationships with students in high-track classes

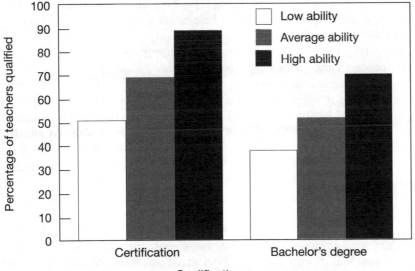

Figure 4. Qualifications of secondary science and math teachers by ability/track level of classes in low-SES schools (schools where 30% or more students' parents are unemployed or on public assistance).

Note: From *Multiplying Inequalities: The Effects of Race, Social Class, and Tracking on Opportunities to Learn Mathematics and Science,* by Jeannie Oakes, RAND, R-3928-NSF, 1990. Reprinted by permission.

whereas relationships in low-track classes tend more towards control. Low-track classes see greater student disruption, hostility, and alienation (Oakes, 1985; Page, 1987).

Track-related differences in students' access to curriculum, teachers, and high-
quality instruction stem from school norms dictating how ability should be defined,
measured, and responded to; yet they can not be justified as educationally appropriate
adaptations to individual differences in learning aptitudes, speed, or style. Track-related differences demonstrate that tracking—however well intentioned and seemingly
objectively implemented—leads to an unequal distribution of school resources, with
academically and socially disadvantaged students receiving less.

Further, these differences are instrumental. Tracking most likely affects achievement through the combination of separating students into different groups and providing different knowledge and learning conditions to these groups. For example,
Gamoran (1990) found that about 25% of track-related learning differences were at-
tributable to differences in curriculum and instruction. The top track benefits from
enhanced opportunities; other students suffer from their absence.

Responses From Policy and Practice

Growing numbers of policymakers and educators are aware of and concerned about
these findings though few address the complexity of the tracking issue in terms of its
interconnected technological, normative, and political dimensions. However, the responses from different constituencies attest to this complexity and to the extraordinary challenge faced by those attempting reforms.

In the past couple of years, policymakers and national opinion leaders have responded with recommendations for abolishing tracking, positions motivated by concerns for school effectiveness as well as equity. The National Governors' Association
proposes eliminating tracking as a strategy to help meet the national education goals
(National Governors' Association, 1990) and is currently preparing a more detailed
policy brief supporting its recommendation. The Carnegie Council on Adolescent
Development's *Turning Points: Preparing American Youth for the 21st Century* (1989)
identifies detracking as central to reforming middle-grades education, and its current
Middle Grades Initiative is supporting states' efforts to implement its recommendations. The College Board has criticized tracking for posing barriers to minorities' access to college (Goodlad, 1989); its current Equity 2000 project aims to eliminate
mathematics tracking in 200 racially diverse high schools. The NAACP Legal Defense Fund, the ACLU, and the Children's Defense Fund all have raised tracking as a
second-generation segregation issue. And the U.S. Department of Education's Civil
Rights Division has targeted tracking as critical in determining racially mixed schools'
compliance with Title VI requirements for categorical programs.

Many educators, too, voice the desire to alter tracking—evidenced, in part, by
the proliferation of well-attended staff development conferences on the topic. Moreover, at its 1990 national convention, the National Education Association recommended—albeit cautiously—that schools abandon conventional tracking practices.
This represents a considerable shift in professional opinion from only a few years ago.
Yet educators remain ambivalent, in part because of the lack of well-specified and
proven alternatives—the lack of a detracking technology. But teachers also doubt the
possibility of curriculum and instruction in heterogeneous classes that won't leave
slower students behind or force quicker ones to wait—a concern rooted in norms
that faster and slower students are "real" and can be accommodated only by faster and
slower versions of the curriculum.

Educators also worry about the political consequences of detracking, in particular the loss of support of parents of high-track students, who are clearly advantaged by the current arrangement. This concern has been fueled by advocates for separately funded, categorical programs for the gifted and talented. In local forums such as school board meetings and in popular practitioner journals, these individuals and groups lobby strongly against policy changes that may threaten special opportunities now available to high achievers.

What do these responses portend for tracking reforms? Early accounts suggest that, in addition to considerable talk, a number of schools have begun to alter their grouping practices—for example, by setting detracking goals and policies, reducing the number of tracks (most often by eliminating remedial programs), and providing support programs so that low achievers can succeed in higher tracks (Slavin, Braddock, Hall, & Petza, 1989; Oakes and Lipton, 1992; Wheelock, in press). These changes are not trivial, and those making them report that the process is long and arduous. However, we lack systematic empirical work documenting the extent and nature of these changes, and it's far too early to assess the efficacy or durability of any of the changes being made.

Moreover, it's not at all clear that these early efforts are addressing fundamental normative and political issues—problems lodged in school-based conceptions of and responses to ability and individual differences; links among conceptions of ability, race, and social class; and the persistent inequalities in opportunities and outcomes that these conceptions and responses trigger. Schools attempting technical changes in school organization may neither recognize nor know how to confront the fact that tracking manifests norms deeply rooted in the culture of schooling and political struggles for advantage that extend far beyond school. After all, not recognizing, not confronting, and not inquiring critically are also deeply rooted norms. Yet without attention to underlying normative and political issues, it's likely that the inequalities currently associated with tracking will simply resurface in a new organizational guise.

A New Agenda for Tracking Research

Tracking research has made the problems quite visible, but it has yet to offer a technology of detracking or to suggest strategies for addressing normative and political resistance to reform. So the question remains: What new research will provide valid and useful guidance to those hoping to create school cultures where tracking no longer makes sense?

Attention to the Technical, Normative, and Political

What educators say they need most is help in the form of models—well-defined, workable ways to organize and teach students without tracking. While replicable detracking models seem unlikely, given the important contextual variation among schools, researchers can both participate in the development of alternatives and provide examples of other schools' efforts to do so. Such examples can build confidence that changes can be made and provide clues about specific alternatives. Nevertheless, this work will prove insufficient unless research combines attention to the technology of detracking with its normative and political implications (see Figure 5).

The technical dimension. Earlier, I defined the technology of tracking as curricular differentiation and curricular accommodation—a division of knowledge and teaching strategies into programs or classes for students perceived to be at different ability levels. The technology of detracking, then, encompasses the organizational, curricular,

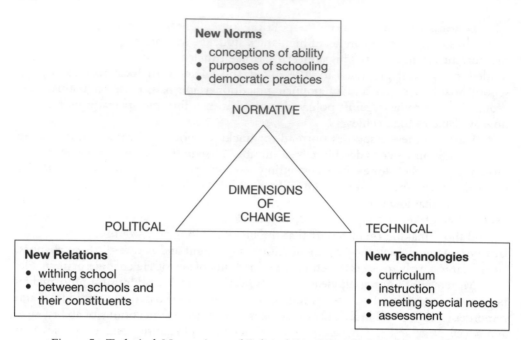

Figure 5. Technical, Normative, and Political Dimensions of Tracking Reforms.

and pedagogical strategies required to provide diverse groups of students with access to a common body of knowledge. And as the research cited above makes clear, just as the technical aspects of tracking include an uneven distribution of school resources favoring students in the highest tracks, a technology of detracking will require a more even distribution of resources among students.

Currently, we have a growing body of anecdotes about detracking schools that have reorganized into heterogeneous teams of teachers and students, developed integrated, thematic curricula, used mixed-ability cooperative learning strategies, to name just a few techniques (see, e.g., Wheelock, in press). Yet we need research that provides systematic accounts of these efforts and evidence about how each of these strategies works within a school's overall detracking effort.

Perhaps even more importantly, research must provide guidance about how to implement a comprehensive set of changes in school organization, curriculum, and teaching. Tracking is inextricably connected with and supported by other school practices. A single new technique can't possibly smooth the way for such a major structural change. The technical changes in any one practice—the grouping structure itself, for example—will require simultaneous attention to the myriad other practices that correspond to it.

Such work will differ considerably from research that has focused on the development and dissemination of isolated educational practices—cooperative learning is a recent example. Typically, the expectation (not necessarily warranted) is that the change in classroom pedagogy will "take" if sufficient technical training is provided. But, when a change—such as detracking—is fundamentally different, it clashes with other school practices, and usually the new practice changes to fit the school, rather than the school adjusting to fit the new practice. So, when schools assign students to heterogeneous classes and support this change only by training teachers in cooperative learning methods, they find that, as helpful as this method is, teachers still confront disconnected subject areas, fragmented curricula, norm-referenced assessments, inadequate support for special needs, isolation from their colleagues, and so on. Detracking is unlikely to "work" unless these other practices are also reconsidered and made compatible with the new grouping structure. Without these other changes, teachers may, for example, resort to creating homogeneous cooperative groups within their classes or to differentiating assignments and assessments of students working together in heterogeneous cooperative groups in ways that mirror the differentiation of tracked classes.

Consequently, while the technical dimension of detracking may seem the most straightforward, it will require sustained inquiry into new strategies for organizing schools and classrooms; new curricular designs, pedagogy, and assessment; and new means for distributing school resources. It will also require well-grounded guidance about how schools gain the capacity to develop, adapt, and implement the array of new techniques in ways appropriate to their particular context.

The normative dimension. While technical supports are necessary for successful detracking, they are clearly insufficient. Perhaps the most important lesson from recent scholarship on educational change, generally, is that local practitioners and communities must be committed to reform and that alternative practices must make sense to them for change to occur (Fullan, 1991). This lesson is particularly important for tracking since it is so firmly rooted in longstanding and deeply felt norms, and it is held in place by pressures from the social-political milieu that depend on these norms to legitimate an unequal distribution of economic advantage. These norms—consciously and unconsciously—drive the day-to-day educational practices and their attendant inequalities that tracking research has documented.

For example, educators attempting to build commitment for detracking must confront conventional, if increasingly obsolete, conceptions of intelligence, some of which reflect deep-seated racist and classist attitudes and prejudices. These conceptions play out in school as educators interpret the skills and knowledge that educationally and economically privileged parents pass on to their children as innate intelligence—interpretations that guide decisions about track placements and the learning opportunities afforded to students in different tracks. Perhaps most pernicious, these interpretations are reinforced by ostensibly objective standardized tests, which not only fail to measure different forms of intelligence but are also biased toward the knowledge and skills that advantaged students learn at home and have greater access to in high-track classes.

Additionally, for detracking to make sense, educators must come to terms with the shortcomings of the deeply ingrained value for bureaucratic efficiency when applied to schooling. For example, they must examine the norms dictating that the best way to accommodate differences among students is to sort them into separate classes and provide them with differentiated curricula. This notion of scientific management—that complicated production tasks can be made more efficient when divided into hierarchical levels and specialized categories—persists in schools, even as it loses credibility in industry. And, finally, tracking reformers must face the inveterate American values for competition and individualism over cooperation and the common good that further bolster and legitimize tracking—norms implying that "good" education is a scarce commodity available only to a few. Although American public education was originally intended to promote community interests by preparing children for participation in democratic governance, more recent emphasis has been placed on what individual students can "get" out of schooling in terms of income, power, or status.

Efforts to change tracking, then, require a critical and unsettling rethinking of the most common and fundamental educational beliefs and values. This rethinking process is normative in nature because it asks people to challenge their entrenched views of such matters as human capacities, individual and group differences, how schools and classrooms should be organized, and, ultimately, whether sorting students to prepare them for a differentiated work force with unequal economic rewards is what schools should do. Such rethinking may result in a shift away from the dominant norms of competition and individualism toward more democratic norms of support and community. Understanding how educators, and the change-agents who wish to assist them, can make such fundamental changes in school and community norms presents a formidable, but central, research challenge.

The political dimension. In addition to paying explicit attention to the normative dimensions of these changes, reformers also must address related political concerns. The relationship between changing norms and new technologies is iterative. Confronting new ideas, examining values, understanding effects all may pave the way for trying a new practice. New practices—acting differently—may allow for new understandings and interpretation of experiences: new beliefs about what is, what is possible, and what should be. Mediating this iterative process entails acts that are essentially political in nature: granting of permission, taking of risks, redistributing power, forming coalitions, and so on.

Tracking is sustained by the political interests of constituents, interests that are shaped by the norms mentioned above. The pressure placed on educators by savvy parents who want their children enrolled in the "best" classes is just one manifestation of these interests. Parents of high-track students are clearly advantaged—in both educational opportunities and status—by the current arrangement. And in a competitive system that offers only a small percentage of students slots in the high-track classes, these parents have few options but to push to have their children better educated than others. This pressure reflects a competitive, individualistic attitude toward the purpose of schooling, but in racially mixed schools it can take on another dimension. Fearing that minority enrollment leads to lower educational standards, White and wealthy parents often request their children be assigned to more racially and socioeconomically homogenous gifted and talented programs or honors-level courses. Although not all politically efficacious parents are White, in most schools White parents, especially middleclass White parents, better understand the inequalities in the school's structure and feel more confident that the school will respond positively to their pressure. Because all schools need political support—not only for funding and physical resources but also for credibility—tracking policies that provide advantages to more privileged students, even if they result in racial segregation within desegregated schools, are often exchanged for the political credit that more advantaged and involved parents bring to a school.

Implementing tracking reforms will require that competing interest groups— such as advocates for the gifted, for the disadvantaged, and for minorities—create a collective advocacy for schools that serve all children well. However, building coalitions among these divergent constituencies (and maintaining political credit) probably requires that schools undergoing, detracking guarantee that their new technologies will create educational opportunities that are at least as rich and rigorous as those previously enjoyed by high track students. But it also requires confronting likely opposition to a system that takes away the comparative advantages enjoyed and effectively used (both in school and beyond) by children whose parents are privileged by race and class. Confronting these issues is a political process that requires astute political leadership by educators, a difficult matter about which research could provide considerable guidance.

How Might Useful Knowledge Be Generated?

If tracking reform depends on attention to the technical, normative, and political dimensions of change, then useful research also needs to focus on them. While there are probably many ways to conduct such work, two strategies appear most promising. Each promises an accounting of schools that move beyond an exclusively "practical" focus on school structures, curriculum, and classroom strategies, to attend to changing values and beliefs and to building political support for school cultures in which tracking no longer makes sense.

The first strategy is collaborative and developmental, that is, work that engages researchers and practitioners in the design and testing of tracking alternatives that pay explicit attention to changes in norms and politics, in addition to a comprehensive set of new technologies.[9] One current example of this type of work is the Stanford-based Accelerated Schools project (Levin, 1991). Although not focused directly on tracking structures, the Accelerated Schools project targets the norms and politics that support tracking. The project recognizes that improved opportunities for at-risk children must take place in a school and community culture that sees children as capable learners and welcomes departures from usual school practice that enable children to translate their capacity into high achievement.

Rather than employing a traditional RD&D model, Accelerated Schools researchers and practitioners engage in a process of inquiry based on other new school norms: participation, communication, community, reflection, experimentation, risk taking, and trust. The strategy is guided by three principles that stem from core humanistic values: (a) a value for participation that suggests that change initiative should be based at the local school and be conducted by members of the local school community, (b) a value for a communication community that implies that critical discourse within and about the schools should be central to change efforts, and (c) a value for practical experimentation at the schools that is guided by reflective and far-ranging dialogue (Rogers & Polkinghorn, 1990).[10] These principles are more than an embodiment of core values; they are also intended as capacity-building elements that enable the local creation of a school vision and new technologies consistent with it.

A second research approach is naturalistic: that is, multiple, longitudinal case studies of schools in the process of detracking that focus simultaneously on the technical, normative, and political dimensions of their efforts. Although the vast majority of detracking efforts have not been broad enough in scope, much can be learned by studying a few schools, including some that are racially mixed, that are furthest along in the technical process of doing away with tracking and are, at the same time, responding to the normative and political obstacles to reform.

Case studies of such schools can be useful if they reveal how the detracking process becomes entwined with other factors in the school and community culture. Multiple case studies would be especially useful since by examining the technical, normative, and political aspects of a range of detracking efforts, we can gain insight into how educators adapt their goals and strategies to their contexts. Specifically, it is important to understand relationships among the tracking alternatives schools choose to adopt, their choice of implementation strategies, and the normative and political barriers that they are able to overcome.

Because the normative and political aspects of tracking cross individual school boundaries, we might anticipate similarities in the cultures of schools that experience success in their efforts to detrack. For example, such case studies could profitably identify common principles that guide the ways that school leaders work with their communities to confront powerful norms, broaden the reform agenda to include changes in other practices that support tracking, engage faculty and community in self-study and experimentation, develop new roles and relationships among teachers and administrators, and generate new ways to organize students for instruction.

However, detracking will undoubtedly be more difficult for some schools than others. A school in a neighborhood that is experiencing a great deal of White flight and an influx of Black residents, for instance, might be using tracking as a way of holding on to the White residents and would therefore find it more difficult to rally its unstable community around detracking. Similarly, schools in states with a history of contentious reform efforts might avoid detracking because of a reluctance to confront resistance around another politically charged school practice linked to race and social class. Schools in racially and economically homogeneous communities might find detracking somewhat easier, as might schools in states with a history of interest in tracking reforms. The latter might anticipate considerable support and assistance from their state departments of education. Contextual factors such as these underscore the importance of studying a range of local educators' and communities' norms, strategies, and relations as they respond to detracking initiatives.

Studies that either help develop or document detracking efforts along technical, normative, and political dimensions should be genuinely helpful to those who have already used the existing tracking research to challenge conventional views about tracking and who would now like research to inform the difficult process of reform. At best, these studies should provide insight about how reformers might generate and sustain the commitment and capacity to develop school cultures that are not simply friendly to tracking alternatives but that are infused with new norms, practices, and politics that move beyond a narrow focus on detracking to total school reform.

Notes

This article was originally presented as the Raymond B. Cattell Award for Early Career Achievement in Programatic Research Invited Address at the 1991 AERA Annual Meeting in Chicago. This current version has benefited from subsequent discussions with Jennifer Gong, Gretchen Guiton, Karen Quartz, and Amy Stuart Wells, and insightful reviews by Martin Lipton, Paul Heckman, and four anonymous reviewers.

1. While a few key studies are cited in the sections below, a detailed review of research can be found in Oakes, Gamoran, and Page, 1991.

2. Importantly, while I focus in this paper on tracking research and reform, similar attention seems warranted for any number of widespread, deeply rooted school practices.

3. The term *norm* is defined broadly here, going beyond a common, but narrower definition of norms as formal or informal standards that prescribe acceptable action in a setting.

4. While most scholars agree with this conclusion, not all do (see Kulik & Kulik, 1982). Moreover, this conclusion has been heatedly contested by advocates for separate programs for children identified as gifted and talented (see, e.g., Feldhusen, 1990).

5. This and the subsequent tables present analyses of data collected in the 1985–1986 NSF-sponsored National Survey of Science and Mathematics Education that randomly sampled 1,200 schools (evenly divided among elementary, middle/junior high, and senior high schools) and 6,000 teachers and their mathematics and sciences classes within these schools. The findings from these analyses are presented in detail in Oakes, 1990.

6. Of course, limits on the educational and occupational futures of low-income and minority students cannot be attributed to tracking alone. Disadvantaged families, in particular, are often less able to prepare children for school and to deal effectively with schools. Moreover, low-income and minority children bear the burden of coping with White, middle-class definitions of knowledge and achievement and with the personal prejudices of many teachers and school administrators. As detailed in the sections that follow, these race and class disadvantages often operate through tracking—particularly in terms of the learning opportunities provided in different tracks—but they undoubtedly have an independent effect as well. It would be naive to suggest that eliminating tracking would eradicate the impact of race and class on schooling outcomes.

7. Page and Valli (1990) provide some particularly good examples of how track-related opportunities vary among schools.

8. These data also show that, as a result of schools' differential ability to attract and retain qualified teachers, high-track students in schools serving low-income, minority schools are often taught by less qualified science and mathematics teachers than are low-track students at schools enrolling large numbers of White, economically advantaged students (Oakes, 1990).

9. While researcher-practitioner collaborations are often touted as a promising approach to producing more useful knowledge, they are difficult to pull off (Oakes, Sirotnik, & Hare, 1986). Much work needs to be done to understand the conditions under which these collaborations work well (Sirotnik & Goodlad, 1988).

10. See Sirotnik & Oakes (1986) for a similar formulation.

References

Carnegie Council on Adolescent Development. (1989). *Turning points: Preparing American youth for the 21st century.* Washington, DC: The Carnegie Corporation of New York.

Cicourel, A., & Kitsuse, J. (1963). *The educational decision-makers.* Indianapolis: The Bobbs Merrill Company.

Cohen, D. (1985). Origins. In A. Powell, E. Farrar, & D. Cohen, *The shopping mall high school.* Boston: Houghton-Mifflin.

Feidhusen, J. (1990, September). Should gifted children be taught in separate classes? *ASCD Curriculum Update.*

Fullan, M. (1991). *The new meaning of educational change.* New York: Teachers College Press.

Gamoran, A. (1990). The consequences of track-related instructional differences for student achievement. Paper presented at the Annual Meeting of the American Educational Research Association, Boston.

Gamoran, A., & Mare, R. (1989). Secondary school tracking and educational inequality: Compensation, reinforcement, or neutrality? *American Journal of Sociology, 94,* 1146–1183.

Garet, M., & DeLany, B. (1988). Students, courses, and stratification. *Sociology of Education, 61,* 61–77.

Goodlad, J. I. (1984). *A place called school: Prospects for the future.* New York: McGraw-Hill.

Goodlad, J. I. (Ed.). (1989). *Access to knowledge.* New York: College Entrance Examination Board.

Haller, E. (1985). Pupil race and elementary school reading grouping: Are teachers biased against black children? *American Educational Research Journal, 22,* 409–418.

Hallinan, M., & Sorensen, A. (1985). Ability grouping and student friendships. *American Educational Research Journal, 22,* 485–499.

Hallinan, M., & Williams, R. (1989). Interracial friendship choices in secondary schools. *American Sociological Review, 54,* 67–78.

Kifer, E. (in press). Opportunities, talents and participation. In L. Burstein (Ed.), *Second international mathematics study: Student growth and classroom process in the lower secondary schools*. London: Pergamon Press.

Kilgore, S. (1991). The organizational context of tracking in schools. *American Sociological Review, 56,* 189–203.

Kulik, C., & Kulik, J. (1982). Effects of ability grouping on secondary school students: A meta-analysis of evaluation findings. *American Educational Research Journal, 19,* 415–428.

Levin, H. (1991), Building school capacity for effective teacher empowerment: Applications to elementary schools with at-risk students. Paper presented at the Annual Meeting of the American Educational Research Association, Chicago.

McKnight, C., Crosswhite, F., Dossey, J., Kifer, E., Swafford, J., Travers, K., & Cooney, T. (1987). *The underachieving curriculum: Assessing U.S. school mathematics from an international perspective.* Champaign, IL: Stipes.

Moore, D., & Davenport, S. (1988). *The new improved sorting machine.* Madison, WI: National Center on Effective Secondary Schools.

National Governors' Association. (1990). *Educating America: State strategies for achieving the national educational goals.* Washington, DC: National Governors' Association.

Oakes, J. (1985). *Keeping track: How schools structure inequality.* New Haven, CT: Yale University Press.

Oakes, J. (1990). Multiplying inequalities: The effects of race, social class, and tracking on opportunities to learn math and science. Santa Monica, CA: RAND.

Oakes, J., Gamoran, A., & Page, R. (1991). Curriculum differentiation: Opportunities, consequences, and meanings. In P. Jackson (Ed.), *Handbook of Research on Curriculum.* New York: Macmillan.

Oakes, J., & Lipton, M. (1992, February). Detracking schools: Early lessons from the field. *Phi Delta Kappan.*

Oakes, J., Selvin, M., Karoly, L., & Guiton, G. (1992). *Educational matchmaking: Academic and vocational tracking in comprehensive high schools.* Santa Monica: RAND.

Oakes, J., Sirotnik, J. A., & Hare, S. E. (1986). Collaborative inquiry: A congenial paradigm in a cantankerous world. *Teachers College Record, 87,* 545–562.

Page, R. N. (1987). Teachers' perceptions of students: A link between classrooms, school cultures, and the social order. *Anthropology and Education Quarterly, 18,* 77–99.

Page, R. N., & Valli, L. (Eds.). (1990). *Curriculum differentiation: Interpretive studies in U.S. secondary schools.* Albany, NY: State University of New York Press.

Rehberg, R. A., & Rosenthal, E. R. (1978). *Class and merit in the American high school.* New York: Longman.

Rist, R. (1970). Student social class and teacher expectations: The self-fulfilling prophecy in ghetto education. *Harvard Educational Review, 40,* 411–451.

Rogers, J. S., & Polkinghorn, R. (1990). The inquiry process in the accelerated school: A Deweyan approach to school renewal. Paper presented at the Annual Meeting of the American Educational Research Association, Boston.

Rosenbaum, J. E. (1976). *Making inequality: The hidden curriculum of high school tracking.* New York: Wiley.

Sirotnik, K. A., & Goodlad, J. I. (Eds.). (1988). *School/university partnerships in action: Concepts, cases, and concerns.* New York: Teachers College Press.

Sirotnik, K. A., & Oakes, J. (1986). "Critical Inquiry for School Renewal: Liberating Theory and Practice." In K. A. Sirotnik & J. Oakes (Eds.), *Critical Perspectives on the Organization and Improvement of Schooling.* Boston: Kluwer.

Slavin, R. (1987). Ability grouping and student achievement in elementary schools: A best-evidence synthesis. *Review of Educational Research, 57,* 293–336.

Slavin, R. E. (1990). *Achievement effects of ability grouping in secondary schools: A best-evidence synthesis.* Madison, WI: Wisconsin Center for Education Research.

Slavin, R., Braddock, J., Hall, C., & Petza, R. (1989). *Alternatives to ability grouping.* Baltimore, MD: Center for Research on Disadvantaged Students, The Johns Hopkins University.

Sorensen, A. B. (1987). The organizational differentiation of students in schools as an opportunity structure. In M. T. Hallinan (Ed.), *The social organization of schools: New conceptualizations of the learning process.* New York: Plenum Press.

Useem, E. (1990a). Getting on the fast track in mathematics: School organizational influences on math track assignment. Paper presented at the Annual Meeting of the American Educational Research Association, Boston.

Useem, E. (1990b). Social class and ability group placement in mathematics in the transition to seventh grade: The role of parent involvement. Paper presented at the Annual Meeting of the American Educational Research Association, Boston.

Vanfossen, B., Jones, J., & Spade, J. (1987). Curriculum tracking and status maintenance. *Sociology of Education, 60,* 104–122.

Wheelock, A. (in press). *Crossing the tracks: Alternatives to tracking and ability grouping in the middle grades.* New York: New Press.

Wolfle, L. (1985). Postsecondary educational attainment among whites and blacks. *American Educational Research Journal, 22,* 501–525.

23

School Reform Based on
What Is Taught and Learned

JOHN F. JENNINGS

When you learned to drive a car or to play the piano or the violin or to fly a plane, you were told what you needed to know. Then you were guided and corrected as you went along. If you did not drive or play or fly correctly, you were taught some more, and then you tried again.

What could be a more logical way to learn something? It makes perfect sense that you would be told what you were to know, then helped along as you tried to master the material, and then given another chance to do it if you didn't perform just right the first time.

That sensible way to learn is *not* the way that American public schools now operate in many important respects. But it is the way that students will be educated once a major reform of elementary and secondary education that has recently begun is finally implemented.

In American schools today, teachers explain material to students, help them to understand what they are doing right, and correct them when they are not mastering the material. And when teachers control the tests, they try to help students along so that they can do better the next time. But students, teachers, and the schools are often held accountable for performance on tests that students cannot learn to and teachers cannot teach to. Moreover, the results are not revealed to teachers or students, so there is no chance to learn from mistakes and work to do better next time.

Schools are caught in a "crapshoot" in which teachers are teaching in the dark and students are being tested in the dark. It amounts to a "gotcha" game. Students are not told exactly what they are going to be tested on, nor are they told afterward which questions they answered wrong so that they can learn the material for another time. Is it any wonder that high school students are not motivated to learn? They don't see the relevance of what they are taught, since that's not what they are held accountable for.

Many important decisions about students' lives are made in similar fashion. An example that is easy to understand involves the SAT I, the country's most famous assessment, which is used every year to help determine the admission of hundreds of thousands of high school students to college.

A student cannot study for the SAT because the test prides itself on not being based on any one curriculum. A student can spend money to attend an SAT prepara-

From *Phi Delta Kappan*, Vol. 76, June 1995: pp. 765–769. Reprinted by permission.

tion course run by a private company, but all that company can do is to give some pointers on test-taking techniques and hazard some guesses as to the types of questions likely to appear on the test. No one but the Educational Testing Service, which writes the SAT, knows for sure what will be on the test. And those students who cannot afford the fees of those private courses are not even given the benefit of the educated guesses of the test preparation companies.

Admission to college is not the only matter decided in this fashion. Many states also require a student to pass a standardized test in order to graduate from high school, and many school districts require students to pass a test to proceed from one grade to the next. All of these major decisions are made on the basis of tests that cannot be taught because they consist of material that is unknown and whose results are not revealed afterward so that students can learn from their errors.

Does this seem like a strange system of education? If we were to learn to drive, play a musical instrument, or fly a plane in this way, there would be many more car wrecks, discordant noises, and plane crashes than there are now. Imagine having to guess the right ways to drive, play music, or fly. Is it any wonder then that the public schools are struggling so hard to improve and, in the popular opinion, not succeeding?

The irony is that public education has just been through a period of reform unmatched in intensity and length. During the late 1970s and throughout the 1980s many states toughened high school graduation requirements, instituted professional testing for teachers and raised their salaries, and experimented with countless ways of improving teaching and learning.

But by the end of the 1980s the general impression was that the schools had not improved very much, if at all. This view was based on the fact that SAT I scores had not increased substantially, that college professors were still complaining that students were not ready for postsecondary education, and that employers were asserting that high school graduates were unprepared for the workplace.

The American public is edgy and impatient with the schools and wants results, asserted Richard Riley, the U.S. secretary of education, in a summer 1993 speech to the nation's governors. The country will be out of business if public education does not reinvent itself—and fast, according to Louis Gerstner, Jr., CEO of IBM, in a May 1994 article in the *New York Times*. Gerstner went on to assert that, just as American business had to change in order to become competitive, so would American schools. However, he found chilling the combination of public apathy and bureaucratic obstructionism that stood in the way of the needed changes.

Since the late 1970s public education has in fact undergone reform, and evidence from the early 1990s shows that more students have been taking more difficult courses. Moreover, even though greater demands are being placed on students, the dropout rate has not increased. But there is also clear evidence that grade inflation has occurred and that a grade of C has crept up to a grade of B.[1] It seems that teachers and students, under pressure to improve and lacking objective measures of progress, simply allowed grades to rise to show improvement.

Ironically, the school reform movement of the late 1970s and the 1980s, which created this pressure to improve, also helped to confuse the situation further because many states instituted or expanded testing systems without linking the tests to the curriculum. By 1994, 45 states had instituted or expanded testing programs for elementary and secondary education, but only 10 or so had *any* type of mandated curriculum that would tell teachers and students ahead of time what they were going to be tested on and held accountable for.

In other words, there is no "truth in teaching and learning" in many schools. Teachers and students can only guess, sometimes with limited guidance, what they are supposed to know in order to be deemed successful. The reason for this lack of connection between the test and the curriculum is that accountability has been moved to the state level, while the decisions on what ought to be taught have been left at the local level. The politicians—governors and state legislators—have responded to public displeasure with the public schools by instituting new tests in an effort to get better results from the schools. But few policy makers have moved to define first what results are to be expected on these tests.

The reason for this "disconnect" lies in our nation's history. The U.S. Constitution embodies the idea that government should be limited in its powers and that the closer the government is to the people, the better it will function. In education this has meant that, although states have authority over the schools, the power to determine the content of education has usually been delegated to local school boards. And since there are 14,000 or so school districts in the country, there is great variance in the education being offered to students.

In 1989 the National Academy of Sciences undertook a searching review of mathematics in the public schools, since American students consistently rank below students in many other industrialized countries on international tests. Its report describes the way the mathematics curriculum is typically fashioned in local school districts. It concluded:

> In the United States, with our traditional and legal decentralization of education, we go about things very differently [than in other countries]. Every summer, thousands of teachers work in small teams for periods ranging from one week to two months, charged by their school districts to write new mathematics curricula. These teacher teams usually have little training in the complicated process of curricular development, little or no help in coping with changing needs, and little to fall back on except existing textbooks, familiar programs, and tradition. The consequence usually is the unquestioned acceptance of what already exists as the main body of the new curriculum, together with a little tinkering around the edges. Many school districts simply adopt series of textbooks as *the* curriculum, making no effort to engage the staff in rethinking curricula; in those places, the *status quo* certainly reigns.
>
> The American process of curricular reform might be described as a weak form of grass-roots approach. The record shows that this system does not work. It is not our teachers who are at fault. In fact, teachers *should* play a dominant role in curricular decision-making. But teachers who work in summer curricular projects are being given an unrealistic task in an impossible time frame, with only the familiar *status quo* to guide them.
>
> In static times, in periods of unchanging demands, perhaps our grassroots efforts would suffice to keep the curriculum current. In today's climate, in which technology and research are causing unprecedented change in the central methods and applications of mathematics, present U.S. practice is totally inadequate.[2]

In other words, the decisions about curriculum that are made locally would seem to respect the national tradition of local control whenever possible—but, as the National Academy of Sciences suggests, this system may have outlived its usefulness in a rapidly changing world. And, as already noted, the problem has become further complicated, in that states have testing programs in mathematics and other subjects that do not match what teachers in local school districts teach. When the results of these state assessments come out later, the public believes that the students have not learned the material and that the schools have failed.

This does not have to be the way that education is provided. "We have a history of not training students in the material they will be tested on. Other countries don't hide the test from students," according to the New Standards Project, which issued a report on the reasons that students in other countries do better in mathematics than American children. "That doesn't mean particular questions or answers of any one test are revealed to students. It means that teachers are able to gear what and how they teach towards the kind of questions that will appear on examinations."[3] In other words, students and teachers in many countries are told what they are expected to know and be able to do, and then they are held accountable for mastering that knowledge.

This kind of clarity in teaching and learning is a far cry from "the confusion that reigns in most [American] schools today where tests are generated by one vendor, textbooks by another, and teachers are trained by people who don't know much about specific curriculums," according to an article co-authored by Marshall Smith and Ramon Cortines, the chancellor of the New York City school system.[4] Again, this system of conflicting signals is about to change, and none too soon to help teachers and students do better than they are doing now.

The American public supports change in education when that change will make teaching and learning clearer in U.S. schools. Every Phi Delta Kappa/Gallup poll of the public since 1989 has found an overwhelming majority of citizens in favor of a basic curriculum of subject matter for all schools—or what has been called in some of the surveys a "national curriculum." Some 69% favored a standardized national curriculum in the local public schools in 1989, and by 1994 this percentage had increased to 83%. But the desired change in education can be achieved without a national curriculum if states move to institute standards for their schools. Nonetheless, the poll results are interesting in that they show that the public is ready to go even further than is absolutely necessary to bring about improvements in American education.

The process of instituting standards is already under way. During the late 1980s a movement began with the stated purpose of helping teachers to know what they are to teach and students to know what they are expected to learn. Learning and accountability are starting to be linked so that all the rules will be known ahead of time and students will be able to work toward achievable objectives.

This major change is generally labeled "standards-based" reform. It means that agreement will be achieved first on what students are to know and be able to do. Then progress through school and graduation from high school will be determined according to mastery of this content. Teachers will know ahead of time what they are to teach, and students will know what will be expected of them.

The reforms of the late 1970s and 1980s led to this change because leaders began to recognize that the reforms made in that period too often focused on such things as instituting new testing programs without paying attention to curriculum—or increasing course requirements without considering the quality of the education being offered. As the Consortium for Policy Research in Education concluded:

> Although students took classes with challenging titles as a result of the reforms, the titles did not ensure quality academic content. The increased number of tests only reinforced the poor skills and rote instruction that motivated the reform in

the first place. Lessons learned from this experience led federal and state governments, as well as professional associations, to define content standards and expected student outcomes.[5]

The movement toward reform based on defining standards began among mathematics teachers and in some states that had strong educational leadership. In response to the report of the National Academy of Sciences quoted above and to other such studies, the National Council of Teachers of Mathematics (NCTM) initiated an effort in 1989 to develop standards for mathematics. Those standards were issued by the NCTM in 1992. Meanwhile, Bill Honig, the state superintendent of schools in California, had already begun to develop curricular frameworks for the basic subjects in the early 1980s. Other teachers' associations and other states were encouraged by these experiences and initiated their own work on developing standards and frameworks.

The general public, the teacher associations, and some states were ahead of the country's leaders on this issue. But national politicians soon caught up. In 1989 President Bush and the nation's governors agreed on the idea of establishing national goals for education, the first ever to be adopted. This movement evolved into broad agreement on the need for voluntary national standards for education in order to pursue the goals.

One important development in this evolutionary tale was the appointment by the Bush Administration and the Congress of a bipartisan commission to review the issue. The National Council on Education Standards and Testing, whose membership was representative of a wide cross section of political views, issued its report calling for such standards in 1992. The report's depiction of American schools is important in understanding the motivation for this reform.

> In the absence of well-defined and demanding standards, education in the United States has gravitated toward *de facto* national minimum expectations. Except for students who are planning to attend selective four-year colleges, current education standards focus on low-level reading and arithmetic skills and on small amounts of factual material in other content areas. Consumers of education in this country have settled for far less than they should and for far less than do their counterparts in other developed countries.[6]

That is the major reason that national and state leaders have coalesced around the need for defining content and student performance standards: the quality of American education must be improved, and the current system of relying on local decision-making power over curriculum is failing to bring about that improvement. As a result of this broad agreement, President Clinton, building on the work started by former President Bush, signed into law in 1994 the Goals 2000: Educate America Act (P.L. 103–227), which places the national goals into law, supports the certification of voluntary national education standards and national skill standards, and encourages the states through grant aid to develop their own standards for education.

As standards-based reform plays out in the states, now with the assistance of the Goals 2000 legislation, complete agreement on every detail of each state's plan cannot be expected, nor is it reasonable to anticipate concurrence on every aspect of the Goals 2000 legislation itself. For instance, the current debate in Congress seeks to modify certain aspects of the law, especially with regard to the national certification of standards, and shows that the premises of the national role in standards-based reform may have to be re-argued as newly elected representatives come to their posts without knowledge of the prior debates.

But the logic that moved the nation's mathematics teachers, the National Academy of Sciences, the country's major business organizations, the national education groups, and the Bush and Clinton Administrations to endorse standards-based reform remains compelling. If American students are to do better in school, we must agree on what they are to learn, and this agreement must seek greater mastery of content than is now being achieved. And, despite the publicity that has been accorded the national standards as they have been released, the far more important decisions with regard to content are being made at the state level, where the Constitution places control of education.

Even before the enactment of Goals 2000, the states were moving independently to develop their own agreements on what should be taught and learned, and they have used the federal aid to accelerate this work. As of May 1994 (a month after Goals 2000 became law and before any funds were released), 42 states had already developed or were developing content standards, and 30 were developing or had already adopted student performance standards to measure mastery of content. As of January 1995, 42 states were receiving Goals 2000 funding to help them in these efforts.

National standards are important in showing what the various subject-matter associations think ought to be mastered in their content areas, but the national news media's focus on national standards has blown them out of proportion and has stirred up a fear that somehow these standards can be imposed as a national curriculum. That fear is unfounded for two reasons.

First, during the congressional debate on Goals 2000, the U.S. Department of Education was explicitly barred (as it has been in the past) from imposing in any way a curriculum on states or local school districts. State control over education was reaffirmed, as it should be under the Constitution. Consequently, no federal agency would dare to undertake the task of melding and balancing the various national standards to fashion a curriculum that it would then mandate the states and local school districts to follow.

Second, these national standards were composed in a manner that makes the task of combining them into a curriculum impossible without a great deal of editing, conforming, and choosing of appropriate expectations for students within the confines of the school day and year. Nor are the specifics of various sets of standards compatible, because there was no coordination of effort in their development. Nor are they easily melded into a curriculum, because each group of teachers thought students should know so much about their particular area. These standards are more resource documents than they are specific curricula—or even curricular frameworks.

For these two reasons the states are not using the national standards in the ways that critics have feared. As a spokesman for the Council of Chief State School Officers (CCSSO) reported in March of this year:

> Some states probably won't *do* standards at all. Some other states—Kentucky and California, for example—are trying to build a standards-based system, and they're taking some care to make sure that their standards are consistent with these voluntary national standards. Other states are doing different things. Vermont is organizing [its standards] into clusters. Math, science, and technology are in one cluster, and the arts and the humanities are in another cluster.[7]

These developments show a healthy federalism, with the national government funding the agreements on national standards that were reached by the subject-matter specialists, while the states choose their own approaches to the use of these resources.

Another encouraging development, according to the CCSSO, is that the states are beginning to use the standards process as a way to improve their schools overall. An agreement on what should be taught and learned is an essential step in reform because it goes to the very heart of schooling, but it is certainly not the only action that must be taken. Assessments need to be updated, teacher training and certification need to be modified, and teachers need to know what is to be expected of them. In addition, much more equity needs to be introduced into the now very unequal distribution of resources in our thousands of school districts. All these steps are absolutely fundamental to making comprehensive school reform work, and without them the effort to reach agreement on what students ought to know and be able to do has much less meaning.

In a way, what must happen is that the strong push to improve the schools one by one—epitomized by the efforts of Theodore Sizer, James Comer, Henry Levine, and others—must be joined by a push for higher standards and systemwide change coming from the chief state school officers, the governors, the business community, and the subject-matter organizations. While the standards movement can bring greater clarity to American schooling, schools also need to be changed one by one, because teachers and principals ultimately determine the quality of the education offered to students each day. A marriage of systemic reform and school-based reform would be helpful to both movements, especially now that standards-based reform is under political attack. Over the last few years most states, the subject-matter associations, the national education organizations, and the business community have developed a broad consensus that school reform must include an agreement on what is to be taught and learned. Only time will tell, though, how the vicissitudes of politics and change will affect this consensus.

Standards-based reform efforts are even now making progress in many states, and their impact will start to appear in classrooms around the country in the next few years. By the end of the century American education may be quite different from what it has been. Teachers will know what they are to teach, and students will know what is expected of them. But students, teachers, and the general public must understand why these changes are coming about, because there is often a reluctance to change and a nostalgia for the "good old days."

Furthermore, as standards are fashioned by the states, controversy will surround them. Some states have already begun to battle over what is called "outcomes-based education," as political forces try to defeat that change and to revert to what they call "traditional schooling." These battles stem from a misunderstanding of standards-based reform, which is meant to focus on the acquisition of academic skills and not on affective development, but a broad brush is being used to tar any reform that is based on mastering subject matter. Other controversies will undoubtedly arise as political forces use the development of standards as a wedge to bring up social issues.

In the congressional debate on reaching agreement on standards-based reform through the enactment of Goals 2000, many of these controversies came up. And echoes of these debates will appear again and again, as each state moves at its own pace to implement the different phases of standards-based reforms.

But these disputes must not distract us from seeing the importance of this major change in American education. The country is moving to a new way of schooling that will not only lead to a better education, but will also be fairer to both teachers and students in that they will know what is expected of them. The country is moving in the direction of truth in teaching and learning.

Notes

1. *What Do Student Grades Mean? Differences Across Schools* (Washington, D.C.: Office of Educational Research and Improvement, January 1994).

2. National Research Council, *Everybody Counts: A Report to the Nation on the Future of Mathematics Education* (Washington, D.C.: National Academy Press, 1989), pp. 77–78.

3. "Benchmarking Globally for High Standards Locally," *The New Standard*, New Standards Project. Washington, D.C., September 1994, pp. 1–2.

4. Marshall S. Smith and Ramon Cortines, "Clinton Proposals Will Challenge Students and the School Systems," *Philadelphia Inquirer*, 24 June 1993.

5. Quoted in "Shortfalls in 1980s Reform: Refocused Educational Strategies on the Results of Schooling," *R & D Preview*, July 1994, p. 6.

6. *Raising Standards for American Education* (Washington, D.C.: National Council on Education Standards and Testing, 1992), p. I.

7. John O'Neil, "On Using the Standards: A Conversation with Ramsey Selden," *Educational Leadership*, March 1995, p. 12.

24

A New Word for an Old Problem
Multicultural "School Wars" Date to the 1840s

NATHAN GLAZER

Recent proposals that schools and colleges in the United States give greater emphasis to the history and accomplishments of America's racial and ethnic minorities—become more "multicultural"—have generated an intense public debate.

None of the leading critics of a multicultural curriculum-neither Arthur Schlesinger, Jr., author of *The Disuniting of America*, nor Diane Ravitch, the educational historian and former assistant secretary of education, nor Albert Shanker, president of the American Federation of Teachers—argues against a healthy diversity that acknowledges the varied sources of the American people and our culture. Still, all see a multicultural curriculum as a threat to the way we live together in a common nation.

Specifically, the critics envisage the possibility that large sections of the American population, particularly poor racial and ethnic groups that have been subjected to discrimination, will receive an education that attributes blame for their condition to the white or European majority and thereby worsen political and social splits along racial and ethnic lines. The gravest fear is that "oppression studies," as opponents label multiculturalism, will cultivate an active hostility among some minorities to the key institutions of state and society, making effective government, as well as the economic progress of such groups, more difficult.

To its critics, multiculturalism looks like a very new thing in American education. In many respects, it is. However, viewed in the long stretch of the history of American public schooling, we can recognize it as a new word for an old problem: how public schools are to respond to and take account of the diversity of backgrounds of their students—religious, ethnic, racial. American public education, at least that part of it in our major cities, has rarely been free of this issue. For some decades, between the decline of European immigration in the 1920s and the rise of black nationalism in the 1960s, we were free of it. Undoubtedly, this halcyon period, during which many of the chief participants in the debate were themselves educated, colors their view of the current dispute.

With the origins of urban public education in the 1840s, the first of the "great school wars," as Diane Ravitch calls them in her history of New York City public education, broke out. That first war centered on the demands of Catholic leaders for something like equal treatment for Catholic students in public schools whose principal aim was to socialize children into the Protestant moral and religious world of the

From *Multicultural Education*, Vol. 1, No. 5, 1994: pp. 6–9. Reprinted by permission.

mid-19th century. Catholic religious leaders objected in particular to readings from the Protestant King James Bible. Why not the Catholic Douay translation? (No one dreamed, in those distant days, that the First Amendment to the Constitution, with its prohibition of an "establishment of religion," would in time be used to ban all Bible reading in schools.) The outcome of the conflict was that Catholics decided to establish their own schools, to the degree their capacities allowed and created a separate, Catholic system of education in the major cities of the country.

In the 1880s, bitter public disputes broke out about the rights of the children of German immigrants to receive instruction in German. Teaching in German was widely established in Cincinnati, St. Louis, and elsewhere, to the discomfort of nativists and those concerned with the assimilation of immigrants. In 1889, the historian David Tyack tells us, Illinois and Wisconsin "tried to regulate immigrant private and parochial schools by requiring that most instruction be conducted in English. As in the case of Protestant rituals in the schools, the contest over instruction in language other than English became a symbolic battle between whose who wanted to impose one standard of belief and those who welcomed pluralistic forms of education."

World War I, with its encouragement of a fierce national (or was it ethnic?) Chauvinism, finished off the acceptance of German as a language of instruction in public schools. Nevertheless, it was during the build-up to entry into the war that the first major arguments for multiculturalism in American education were set forth.

"Cultural pluralism" was the term Horace Kallen, a student and follower of John Dewey, used to describe a new kind of public education, in which a variety of cultures besides that of England would receive a significant place in American public education.

John Dewey himself, in 1916, speaking to the National Education Association, took up the cudgels for cultural pluralism: Such terms as Irish-American or Hebrew-American or German-American are false terms, because they seem to assume something that is already in existence in America, to which the other factors may be hitched on. The fact is, the genuine American, the typical American, is himself a hyphenated character. It does not mean that he is part American and that some foreign ingredient is in his make-up. He is not American plus Pole or German. But the American is himself Pole-German-English–French–Spanish–Italian–Greek–Irish–Scandinavian–Bohemian–Jew—and so on. The point is to see to it that the hyphen connects instead of separates. And this means at least that our public schools shall teach each factor to respect every other, and shall take pains to enlighten us all as to the great past contributions of every strain in our composite make-up.

But the wave of postwar chauvinism that led Americans to deport East Europeans to Bolshevik Russia, to ban mass immigration, and to revive the Ku Klux Klan was too strong. In 1919, Nebraska forbade the teaching of any foreign language before the eighth grade (the Nebraska courts exempted Greek, Latin, and Hebrew, all presumed safely dead). In the 1920s, Oregon tried to ban any private schools at all. (Both laws were overturned by the Supreme Court.) In the public schools, Americanization was the order of the day, and prevailed without a check through the 1940s, while the children of the last great wave of European immigration were being educated.

I attended the schools of New York City from 1929 to 1944 (I include the public City College of New York in that stretch), and not a whiff of cultural pluralism was to be found. Americanization was strong, unself-conscious, and self-confident. Although probably two-thirds of the students in New York's public schools were Jewish or Italian, no Jewish or Italian figure was to be found in our texts for literature, for social studies, for history. All cultures but that of the founding English and its American variant were ignored, and students were left to assume, if they thought about the matter at all, that the cultures of their homes and parental homelands were irrelevant or inferior.

And that singularly unicultural educational background is having an important effect on the current debates over multi-culturalism. For many protagonists in this debate, the conflicts over educating Catholic and later, German-speaking students, as well as the arguments for multiculturalism in the age of mass immigration, are all a kind of murky prehistory, wiped out in a flood that deposited a uniform silt over our past, leaving only fossil remains of that earlier diversity and those earlier conflicts. Advocates of multiculturalism today often do not know that they had forebears; nor do opponents of multiculturalism today know that the education they experienced was the expression of an age singularly free of conflict over issues of cultural pluralism.

The arguments for cultural pluralism began to emerge again during World War II, and the motivating force was Hitler. If he argued that one race and one people was superior and should be dominant, then it was in the interest of the war effort to teach equality and tolerance. In the 1940s, a small movement for "intercultural education" sprouted. Its aim was to teach something about the various ethnic and racial groups that made up American, and to teach tolerance. Just how extensive it actually was in the schools is not clear, but it did not survive the 1950s and 1960s, when cultural pluralism was pushed aside by the shock of Sputnik and the issue of desegregation.

Something of a contradiction existed between desegregation, as then envisaged, and cultural pluralism. The aim of black and liberal civil rights leaders was for blacks to get the same education that whites received. If whites' education had precious little of cultural pluralism or multiculturalism in it, why should that be changed for blacks? The black objective, through the entire course of the struggle in the courts in the 1940s and 1950s for equality, was assimilation. Blacks should not be treated differently because they were black.

But that was transmuted rapidly into the demand of many militants that blacks must get something different because they were black. By the late 1960s, a "black power" movement, black Muslims, and other manifestations of black nationalism were already challenging the assimilationist civil-rights leadership. Black schools were started in black communities, and some were even established under the aegis of liberal public school systems (as in Berkeley, California).

Soon Mexican-Americans and Puerto Ricans raised their own grievances against the public school system, and political activists demanded the recognition of Spanish. Civil rights laws that guaranteed equality were interpreted by the Supreme Court to mean that equality for those speaking a foreign language could require instruction in that language; liberal states passed laws giving a limited right to instruction in one's native language, and federal laws and regulations and court decisions made that a requirement in many school systems.

Bilingualism is, of course, not the same thing as multiculturalism, but it was generally taken for granted that instruction in one's native language for those speaking Spanish also meant to some degree instruction in Puerto Rican or Mexican culture and history. Through the 1970s, bilingualism and the acknowledgment of distinctive group cultures and histories in social studies and history classes spread and established themselves in the public schools.

One might well ask why multiculturalism has become such an important issue today. It has been at least 20 years since public schools started adapting themselves to the presumed cultural distinctiveness and interests of blacks and Hispanics, by modifying textbooks, introducing new reading materials, changing examinations, and instructing non-English-speaking students in Spanish for a few years. What has put the issue on the agenda today, not only in the public schools, but in colleges and universities, public and private?

I believe the basic explanation is a build-up of frustration in the black population in recent years over the failure of civil rights reforms to deliver what was expected from them. In the colleges, affirmative action—well established as it is—has not increased markedly the number of black instructors or the number of black students who can qualify for the more selective institutions without special consideration. In the public schools, black achievement as measured by NAEP scores, SAT scores, and high school completion rates has improved somewhat, but the gaps between black and white achievement remain large. Blacks on the whole do worse than Hispanic groups despite the very large numbers of new, non-English-speaking immigrants, and far worse than the Asian groups.

One can record substantial black achievement in politics, in the armed forces, in the civil service, and in some high positions in the private economy, but alongside these successes a host of social problems afflicting a large part of the black population has, by some key measures, grown, not declined, in the past 20 years.

One might have expected that the multicultural debate would be fueled by the large new immigration of the past 20 years. But that is really not the moving force. The Asian immigrants, almost half the number, seem quite content with the education they get. Nor are Hispanic immigrants making demands on the public school system that necessitate radical change. Mexican-Americans would like to see their children do better in school, to have more of them graduate. But they have no strong commitment to the idea that this objective will be enhanced by more teaching in Spanish, or more Mexican cultural and historical content.

For the critics of multiculturalism, the issue that ultimately determines its acceptability is a judgment as to the underlying purpose of the curriculum reform. Is it to promote harmony and an acceptance of our society? Or to portray our society as so fatally flawed by racism, so irredeemably unfair and unequal that it must be rejected as evil?

The critics fear that the second vision underlies the strong multicultural position. On one level, they are right. But if we look more deeply into the objectives of those who promote a strong multicultural thrust, and who in doing so present a somewhat lopsided view of our history, we will find that they promote multiculturalism not because they aim at divisiveness and separation as a good, not because they—to put it in the strongest terms possible—want to break up the union, but because they aim at a fuller inclusiveness of deprived groups.

In the short term, their vision may well mean more conflict and divisiveness, but they see this as a stage on the way to a greater inclusiveness. They are no Quebec separatists, Croatian nationalists, Sikh or Tamil separatists. They seek inclusion and equality in a common society.

Critics of the new multiculturalism will see my judgment as far too benign. Undoubtedly one can point to some leading advocates of multiculturalism whose intentions are not benign. But I would emphasize that we deal with a spectrum of views, some mild enough to gain the endorsement of Ravitch, Schlesinger, and Shanker. In the middle there is much to argue about.

What sort of students do multicultural schools turn out? The Catholic schools of the mid-19th century, so fearful to many as a threat to national unity, produced Americans as patriotic or more patriotic than the norm. Nor did the German-language schools do badly in molding upstanding Americans, though equally upstanding

Americans were doing their best to stamp out those schools. Even Amish, Hasidic, and Black Muslim schools, while I do not know whether they produced patriots, turn out, I think, citizens as good by many measures as the public schools.

Our diversity has one major binding force in the Constitution under which we live and which still, through the procedures that it first laid down and that have been further developed in our history, governs at the margin what we can and cannot do in our public schools. The Constitution guarantees that Amish children need not attend schools after the age when their parents feel they will be corrupted, and that Mormons and Black Muslims can teach their own version of the truth, which is as fantastic to many of us as the further reaches of Afrocentrism. Even the most dissident call on the Constitution for protection, yet few people are ready to tear it up as a compact with the devil. This common political bond keeps us together—nationalists and anti-nationalists, Eurocentrists and Afrocentrists—and may continue to through the storms of multiculturalism.

America has changed. It is not God's country, anymore. We can lose wars—real ones—and we can be beaten in economic competition by the Japanese. We have become only one of a number of economically powerful, democratic countries, and not in every respect the best. And America exists in the larger reality of the non-Western world. A good deal of that world is sunk in poverty and political disorder, but some of it is teaching lessons in economic effectiveness to the West. Western hubris can never again be what it was in the late 19th and early 20th centuries.

Finally, America's population is changing in its racial and ethnic composition. Its values are changing. Its notions of the proper relation of groups and individuals to the national society are changing. As hard as it may be for veterans of the educational system of earlier decades to wrench free of their own schooling, it is even harder to see how such a system can be defended in the face of these changes.

25

Race, Class, Gender, and Disability in Current Textbooks

CHRISTINE E. SLEETER AND CARL A. GRANT

The publication of *A Nation at Risk*[1] escalated the continuing debate over curriculum in schools (elementary through college) to a greater intensity, and focused more attention on both the skills and the content of curriculum. It recommended, for example, that graduation requirements in English, social studies, mathematics, science, and computer science be increased. Many of the educational reform reports[2] that responded to *A Nation at Risk* argued for eliminating nonessentials in the curriculum without really defining what makes a body of knowledge nonessential, and raising standards in traditional academic subject areas.[3] However, they did not specify what content should be taught in the traditional academic subjects.

Subsequent responses did. Allan Bloom, in his number one bestseller *The Closing of The American Mind,* explains "How Higher Education has Failed Democracy and Impoverished the Souls of Today's Students," and argues for a college curriculum based on the Great Books of the Western tradition and guided by the fundamental work of Western philosophy, especially ancient Greek philosophy. Bloom notes:

> Men may live more truly and fully in reading Plato and Shakespeare than at any other time, because then they are participating in essential being and are forgetting their accidental lives. The fact that this kind of humanity exists, and that we can somehow still touch it with the tips of our outstretched fingers, makes our imperfect humanity, which we can no longer bear, tolerable. The books in their objective beauty are still there, and we must help protect and cultivate the delicate tendrils reaching out toward them through the unfriendly soil of students' souls.[4]

E. D. Hirsch, in another national bestseller, *Cultural Literacy,* asks, "Why have our schools failed to fulfill their fundamental acculturative responsibility? In view of the immense importance of cultural literacy for speaking, listening, reading, and writing, why has the need for a definite, shared body of information been so rarely mentioned in discussions of education?"[5] Hirsch answers these questions, and then recommends a list of facts literate Americans should know. It contains geographical names, historical events, famous people, patriotic lore, and scientific terms. Secretary of Education William Bennett, in an address at Harvard University during the fall of 1986, argued

Chapter 5 in *Politics of the Textbook,* edited by Michael W. Apple and Linda K. Christian-Smith. New York: Routledge, 1991. Reprinted by permission.

for a greater focus on Western civilization in the college curriculum. For example, the secretary advocated more inclusion of great works of Western art and literature and of the major achievements of the scientific disciplines.[6]

All of these responses ignored or gave only passing attention to the inequality based on race, sex, disability, and social class that continues to exist in the schools' curriculum. In fact, Bloom, makes a point of saying his curriculum is especially for "young persons who populate the twenty or thirty best universities."[7] These students, with some exceptions are white and middle class.[8] Thus, we have demands for a curriculum with more skills training, basics, and Western classical thought, demands that ignore or give only cursory attention to equity issues.

What these reports represent is part of an ongoing struggle to define the content of the curriculum. Debates about curriculum content can be understood broadly as struggles for power to define the symbolic representation of the world and of society, that will be transmitted to the young, for the purpose of either gaining or holding onto power. Symbolic representations are important, and relate to power, for several reasons. First, symbolic representations in books and other media often are used to confer legitimacy on the dominant status of particular social groups. Usually controlled and produced by dominant groups, materials and other media confirm the status of these groups whose culture and accomplishments are deemed important enough to write about.[9]

Second, symbolic representations in the curriculum render socially constructed relations as natural; subjective interpretations of reality and value judgments are projected as fact. Writing about cinema, Nichols put this very well:

> To serve ideology, representations must be made to appear to be other than what they are. Above all, they must appear to lack these very contradictions that informed their production. They must appear as signs of eternal values—harmony, wholeness, radiance, a natural and ideal world spun from the representations of an existing social order.[10]

Curricular materials project images of society, as well as of other aspects of culture such as what constitutes good literature, legitimate political activity, and so forth. The fact that one can debate the validity of such images, and that such images often uphold socially constructed unequal relationships, is hidden. Socially created versions of socially created human activity are projected as truth, as natural. Cherryholmes writes, "Textbooks implicitly present meanings as fixed in structures, and sentences on pages, pictures, charts, and graphs do nothing to dispel this appearance of stability."[11]

Third, the curriculum screens in and out certain ideas and realms of knowledge. Students are given selective access to ideas and information. This predisposes them to think and act in certain ways, and not to consider other possibilities, questions, or actions. Anyon, for example, points out that the history books she analyzed made scant reference to the working class and provided virtually no terminology or conceptual frameworks for thinking about various kinds of workers as belonging to a common social class, having common interests. As a result, she argues: "Without such a label, workers are not easily called to mind as a group, and the objective fact of the working class has no subjective reality. In this way the textbooks predispose workers and others against actions on behalf of the interests that working people have in common."[12]

Curriculum always represents somebody's version of what constitutes important knowledge and a legitimate worldview. In writing textbooks, for example, and debating what should go into them, scholars select from a wide spectrum of knowledge and versions of reality. But texts that get written considerably narrow teachers' and students' access to knowledge. Cherryholmes describes this narrowing process: "Scholars . . . often have a variety of definitions from which to choose in writing textbooks; teachers have fewer from which to choose, but often have more than one; and students usually, more so at lower levels, are given the opportunity to learn only one."[13]

In this way, curriculum usually serves as a means of social control. It legitimates existing social relations and the status of those who dominate, and it does so in a way that implies that there are no alternative versions of the world, and that the interpretation being taught in school is, indeed, undisputed fact. Knowledge helps shape power and social activity (or lack of it). As Anyon says, "The conceptual legitimacy conferred by school knowledge on powerful social groups is metabolized into power that is real when members of society in their everyday decisions support—or fail to challenge—prevailing hierarchies."[14]

The major conveyor of the curriculum—the textbook—has played a paramount role in Western education for over the past five hundred years. Cronbach recognizes its important role when he argues, "Only the teacher—and perhaps a blackboard and writing materials—are found as universally as the *textbook* in our classrooms."[15] Apple more recently underscored the central importance of the textbook when he observed that, "it is the textbook which establishes so much of the material conditions for teaching and learning in classrooms in many countries throughout the world, and it is the textbook that often defines what is elite and legitimate culture to pass on."[16] Furthermore, McMurray and Cronbach state: "The text is a device for helping the child fit into his [her] culture, but culture need not be passed on unedited, good and bad aspects alike. In fact, the nature of the text itself, as we shall see, demands that its maker be highly selective in the materials he [she] presents."[17]

Until recently, textbooks and other curricular materials were blatantly dominated by White wealthy men. As a result of social protest movements of the 1960s and 1970s, curriculum writers were forced to acknowledge voices of Americans of color and women, who demanded inclusion of their histories and works of art and literature. Banks argues that a major goal of the ethnic revival movements of the 1960s and 1970s was to change the curriculum so that it would more accurately reflect the ethnic and cultural diversity within Western societies.[18] The 1980s have witnessed a resurgence of traditional White male voices in the struggle over what knowledge should be taught, as the examples above illustrate. How have the writers and publishers of today's textbooks selected knowledge of various American racial, social class, gender, and disability groups? The chapter will examine this question.

Existing Textbook Analyses

While several analyses of racial bias in texts were done during the 1970s,[19] our knowledge of racial bias in today's texts is sketchy, and it may be tempting to assume that it has been "taken care of" by publishers. One has only to thumb through a text published during the last ten years to see people of different colors throughout. Recently published reading texts[20] and social studies text[21] have been analyzed; science texts[22] have received some attention, but math texts have not. These recent analyses tell us that texts include members of racial minority groups more often than they did in the past, but that portrayals of specific racial groups are still few, and often sketchy. Glazer and Ueda noted in 1983 that history texts provide a small amount of information that "emphasize[s] the positive features of each group, and elicits sympathy by vividly picturing the efforts of ethnic minorities to defend themselves from discrimination and to advance under inhospitable circumstances."[23] However, the history of White racism and oppression is muted, and complexities within groups or involving interaction among groups is virtually ignored. We will show the extent to which the dominance of Whites pervades the various subject areas, discuss patterns in the portrayal of various racial groups, and demonstrate the extent to which current issues of concern to various racial groups are presented.

Analyses of sex bias in recent textbooks are more numerous than analyses of racial bias. Since 1980, textbooks have been analyzed for sexism in the areas of reading,[24] social studies,[25] and science.[26] These analyses agree that females appear in texts much more than they used to. But males still usually predominate, the appearance of females in nontraditional roles is uneven, few males are in nontraditional roles, and issues involving *sexism* in society both today and in history are virtually ignored. While some analyses distinguish between White women and women of color,[27] others do not,[28] making it difficult to learn how texts portray women of various racial groups. This chapter will further update the portrayal of both sexes, differentiating among racial groups.

Social class and disability are absent from most textbook analyses. The most comprehensive analysis of social class issues was done by Anyon in 1979, when she examined seventeen secondary history texts. Social class is sometimes mentioned in other analyses,[29] but is otherwise overlooked. Disability is briefly mentioned in a few textbook analyses,[30] which note mainly that people with disabilities are very underrepresented in reading textbooks. These are both areas that bear investigation.

This chapter examines the treatment of various groups across four subject areas. It shows broadly how America's diversity is projected to children through the school day and their school career, and the extent to which children are challenged in any subject area to think about discrimination and oppression.

Methodology

We examined forty-seven textbooks currently used in grades 1 through 8, with copyright dates between 1980 and 1988. We analyzed textbooks in social studies, reading and language arts, science, and mathematics. We limited ourselves to these grade levels mainly to keep the project manageable.

We developed a textbook analysis instrument based on various instruments that have been developed and used elsewhere.[31] It consists of six different analyses; only those appropriate for a given text were used. The six analyses are: picture analysis, anthology analysis, "people to study" analysis, language analysis, story-line analysis, and miscellaneous.

Picture analysis involves tallying who is in each picture, categorized by sex, race (Asian American, Black American, Hispanic American, American Indian, White American, race ambiguous, and mixed race groups), and disability. Pictures can be designated as individual or group pictures. In addition, racial and sex stereotypes, and the social-class background or setting, are to be noted. The anthology analysis is for analyzing each story in readers. The race, sex, and disability of the main character and supporting characters are to be tallied; and stereotypes, the social-class setting, and which groups solve the problems are to be noted. The "people to study" analysis involves tallying the race and sex of each person mentioned in the text; this is used in science, mathematics, or social studies texts. The language analysis involves examining language in the text for sexist usage, "loaded" words that contain racial or sex stereotypes, and words or phrases that obscure viewpoints or possible conflict situations.

The story-line analysis is used primarily with social studies texts. It involves analyzing which group receives the most sustained attention (whose story is being told), which group(s) resolves problems, how other groups appear, the extent to which these other groups cause or resolve problems, and who the author intends the reader to sympathize with or learn most about. Finally, other miscellaneous analyses may lend themselves to a particular book, such as analyzing race, sex, and roles of people in mathematics story problems. For each subject area, we will describe how books treat different racial groups, both sexes, the social classes, and people with disabilities.

Social Studies

We examined fourteen social studies textbooks, all of which deal with the history, life, or conditions in the United States since the early European explorers. These books were published by nine publishers.[32]

Race

Asian Americans are in less than 4% of the pictures in ten books, and in 18%, 12%, 7%, and 6% of the pictures in the other four books.[33] About 80% of the depicted Asian Americans were males. Asian Americans are depicted working—for example, on the railroad, as miners, and as laboratory technicians—or living in Hawaii and wearing traditional dress, such as kimonos. The books' story line usually includes Asian Americans only briefly, mainly as immigrants in the work force that developed the railroad, although sometimes they are also included in references to all Americans, for example in a discussion of the importance of educating all Americans.[34] The story line does not develop the reasons why Asians came to the United States during the nineteenth century, nor does it explain that Asians, much like the Pilgrims, were fleeing injustices in their countries. Furthermore, little is provided about how American business recruited Chinese immigrants to do mining, railroad construction, and agricultural work. Two short narratives about Chinese Americans provide most of one book's coverage of Asian Americans.[35] The first describes Yen Chong as a young, strong, happy Chinese railroad worker, who takes pride in working for the Central Pacific Railroad Company. In the second, Aunt Liza, a fictional character who went to Chinatown while visiting New York in 1900, says: "There is a place called Chinatown. Thousands of Chinese people live in that neighborhood. It looks like a picture book of China, but it is right here in New York City."[36] These narratives lack any real discussion about the lives of Chinese Americans and their culture, contributions, hardships, and desires to make life better for themselves and their families. Also, they do not point out that Chinese immigrants were forced by discrimination to keep to themselves and live in a separate "Chinatown."

Black Americans appear in about 11% of the pictures in eleven books, and in 23%, 18%, and 18% of the pictures in three books.[37] On the average, Black American males and females appear just about as often; however, some books may have more of one gender than the other.[38] These pictures cover the time of slavery, through the Civil Rights period, to the present day, and show Black Americans in various occupational roles.

The story line discusses Black Americans in relation to wars they fought in, the

Civil Rights movement, and slavery. Some Black heroes and heroines are presented. These discussions are informative but usually do not provide a Black American perspective on events and issues, and many discussions are contextually benign. For example, one book says of Martin Luther King, Jr.: "He dreamed of a better life for all Americans. He wanted people to live together in peace. King worked hard to make his dream come true. We remember him on his birthday every year."[39] However, it neglects to discuss the oppression of Blacks that King's movement challenged. These books do not tell the reader that the Blacks' Civil Rights struggle was against Whites and laws they had passed. For example, one book does not indicate that when King said to supporters of segregation, "We will not hate you. But we will not obey your evil laws. We will soon wear you down. We will win by suffering."[40] he was talking to White segregationists. It is up to the book's fifth grade readers to conclude who the "you" is that King is referring to. However, the book is very explicit that some White people were on the side of the Black Civil Rights advocates: "Thousands of white people joined the [equal rights] movement."[41] A question to consider is: Would ten- or eleven-year-old children, not having grown up during the 1950s and 1960s, know which groups of people made up the opposing forces in the Civil Rights struggle? The books often do not explicitly provide this type of information.

Native Americans are in less than 10% of the pictures in nine textbooks. But they are in 33% of the pictures in one book,[42] and 19%, 15%, 15%, and 12% in four books.[43] About two-thirds of the Native Americans depicted are males. Most of the pictures portray Native Americans during colonial times—for example, living in te-pees and hunting with bows and arrows, and resisting the westward expansion of Whites. The story line in most books places Native Americans in the early history of our country, but does not discuss their life before Columbus, or go beyond this to where they lived, how their political structure worked, how they built their homes (e.g., adobes), and how and what they hunted and gathered. Thus, Native Americans are seen mainly as historical artifacts. Only one book portrays modern reservation life somewhat insightfully.[44] Current problems and issues they face, such as disputes over fishing rights, are not treated.

Hispanic Americans are featured in 3% or less of the pictures in nine books, in 8% of the pictures in three books,[45] and in 32% and 18% of the pictures in two books.[46] Both sexes are depicted about the same number of times. These pictures generally show Hispanics of long ago, such as during the Spanish colonization, but a few more recent pictures, such as César Chavez of the United Farm Workers, also appear. In the story line, Hispanics, mainly Mexican Americans, are mentioned only briefly and incidental-ly, and mainly in discussions of this country's early history, the settlement of the South-west, and the war between Mexicans and Americans. Some books focus on Spanish people as colonizers (conquerors and spreaders of Christianity). In discussions of the war with Mexico, the American view of why Americans no longer wanted to adhere to Mexican rule is stated with clarity and authority, but the Mexican view is not pre-sented in the same manner. For example, in one book the story line runs as follows:

> In the early 1800s, much of the southwest was part of Mexico. Then, Americans began to move into the area that is now Texas. These settlers rebelled against the Mexican rule. In 1836, they declared Texas to be an independent country with its own government. In 1845, Texas joined the United States as a state. In 1848, Mexico and the United States fought a war over land in the southwest. After the United States won, Mexico was forced to sell the land that became Arizona and New Mexico to the United States.[47]

This includes neither the Mexican point of view nor an analysis of the socioeconomic and cultural forces that also encouraged the conflict. Finally, Hispanics appear in some texts in recent times as illegal aliens living in urban areas.

Over 70% of the people in pictures are White in eight books, over 60% of the people pictures are White in four books,[48] and over 40% of the people are White in two books.[49] About two-thirds of the Whites depicted are males. These pictures usually portray White males in a very positive way as explorers, soldiers, government officials, citizens, leaders, scientists, and inventors. Rarely are any Whites shown performing any negative deeds.

Regardless of time period or event, Whites, especially males, dominate the story line and are celebrated for their achievements. The language and adjectives selected to describe the actions and role of Whites during any time period is almost always glorifying and complementary, such as "conquerors" and "hero." When describing events in which the actions or the roles of Whites are known to have been brutal or unjust, the language is muted and the description sanitized in order not to be strongly critical. Observe the section on slavery from Follet:

> *Slavery.* Many Americans wanted to stop slavery. Slavery is the ownership of people by other people. In the 1700s, slavery existed in most of the colonies. By the 1840s, slavery was against the law in most northern states. It then existed mainly in the southern states. Within the southern states, slavery was most common within cotton-growing areas.

Eli Whitney's cotton gin made cotton easier to clean and prepare for the textile factories. In the last chapter you read that the demand for cotton increased. The slaves who planted, harvested, and cleaned the cotton became more and more valuable to their owners. To cotton growers, slavery was a business.[50]

Furthermore, the story line allows Whites to be the center of attention by ignoring the roles or contributions of other groups of color, or placing people of color in the story line only during time periods or events of particular concern to Whites. Examples include Asian Americans working on the railroad: Black Americans in slavery and in the civil rights struggle: Hispanic Americans fighting in Texas and the Southwest: and Native Americans acting as friends of the English colonies, as the first Americans, and fighting with the White settlers.

Collectively, the picture representation of people of color is very low compared to that of Whites, less than two to one (926 Whites/458 people of color). The total number of Black Americans pictured (183) makes them a distant second, and the total number of Native Americans pictured (144) makes this group third. Asian Americans have a total of 82 pictures, which is 21 fewer than for White Americans in one book (Houghton-Mifflin, 1980). The total number of Hispanics pictured (49) is less than the number of Whites in four of the books. In fact, White males alone have 49 or more pictures in five books.

People of color collectively are not portrayed as solvers of their own problems. Blacks are the main group of color that is seen taking some responsibility for their destiny. Problems people of color face because of unfairness and the economic and political desires of White Americans are often presented in a way that helps the reader empathize with people of color, such as the Hawaiians losing their land.[51] However, the discussions of these problems are presented from a White point of view and usually do not explain in sufficient detail the harshness of White men in power and why many problems that people of color face today are the result of the racism, classism, and sexism of long ago. Situations are described in a sanitized manner, rarely giving a criticism of Whites to match the deeds they performed. These books do this by conveying brief facts about events and by suggesting that whatever took place—the good, bad, and ugly—was a part of progress. For example, one book describes the Cherokees as standing in the way of progress and therefore needing to be moved.[52] Another book mentions the brutality of slavery as a "*sad* part of American history."[53] The story line also does not include information or discussions about relationships between different groups of color. For example, did Native Americans and Black Americans have any interactions that were important to the development of the country, and were their associations related only to slavery?

Gender

Males have many more pictures than females (855/512), and there are many more pictures of White females than females of color (328/182). The majority of the books show women (mainly White) in traditional as well as nontraditional roles, but rarely is a male pictured in a nontraditional role. In the story line, "her-story" is undertold or presented as an afterthought. This is very evident, for example, in discussions of the migration of White settlers from the east coast to the west coast, where the role of women is virtually ignored. Women are contextually invisible or marginalized: their roles and contributions often are not covered in any detail in the story line. Sometimes they are given attention in a special section with a heading such as "Special People," where one woman's career and contributions are discussed, or in a special section about an event such as women's suffrage. Women are not usually discussed in sections about major decisions regarding political and economic life. This problem is compounded for American women of color, who are discussed very little in the books. For example, Sacajawea is portrayed as a friend to the White man, but Native American women who resisted White exploration and tried to prevent Whites from driving them off of the land where they were living are not mentioned. At least the authors worked hard to make certain that the language is nonsexist and came very close to succeeding, although in a few instances the reader will come across sexist language like "fireman" or "postman" instead of "fire fighter" or "mail carrier."

Disability

Pictures showing people with disabilities are virtually absent. In four books, it was not possible to identify any person with a disability.[54] In two books, the only disabled person we could identify was Franklin D. Roosevelt.[55] The largest number of times people with disabilities appear in any of the books is three, in which they are shown interacting with their nondisabled friends.[56] The story lines ignore people with disabilities, missing the opportunity to show nondisabled persons the contributions that people with disabilities have made to society, and failing to chronicle the struggles of people with disabilities for rights.

Social Class

The varying socioeconomic conditions that have always existed in this country are virtually absent from the books. The pictures show the United States as fruitful plains with corn as high as an elephant's eye, from sea to shining sea, dotted with growing and prosperous towns and cities. Only during great crises such as the Depression are

Americans shown to be in want due to lack of jobs or money; some books do not show this side of America at all. The story line, one could argue, purposefully avoids this. A typical example is the story "We Move from Place to Place."[57] The following questions are provided as advance organizers: "Where are they [the people in the story] moving?" and "Why are they moving?" In the story, the mother of the central character, Carol, is thinking of moving to California: "But first she wants to look things over. She wants to see if she could get a job. And she wants to look at houses in San Jose and find out how much they cost."[58] After this brief mention of money as a factor influencing life chances and opportunities, the story abruptly moves to Carol settling into her new community. Another story in this book, "Going with the Company," tells of a family following a company that is moving from one town to another. The family moves to obtain a promotion, an increase in salary, and a lower cost of living. These two lessons provide some of the reasons people move, but they are reasons most applicable to middle or upper-middle-class people. For example, Carol's new friend says that "All the houses are new"; the story suggests that the "well off" have worked to become even "better off" through promotion and raise in salary. Poor people or the working poor are not explicitly discussed. The closest the books come to presenting poor people is when the "common person" becomes a hero or national leader, such as Abraham Lincoln. Teachers driven by the demand to increase test scores and unknowing students could easily fail to realize that the story line is leaving out of the discussion an entire class of Americans.

Reading/Language Arts

We examined fifteen reading and language arts textbooks published by eight publishers. Eleven are readers or anthologies,[59] and four are skill books.[60] They range greatly in their treatment of diversity.

Race

The portrayal of Asian Americans ranges from complete absence[61] to 15% of the pictures and leading roles in one or two stories. Most readers have at least one Asian story, although not necessarily an Asian American story. Most have about the same number of Asian males and females. In skills books, Asian names such as Hanako and Huyen are used in sentences. Asian Americans are portrayed doing everyday things such as reading and doing artwork, and in occupations such as letter carrier, laboratory technician, teacher, and physician. They also often appear in multiracial pictures, usually not doing anything in particular.

Black Americans appear in all fifteen texts; the percentage of Black people pictured ranges from 9%[62] to 27%,[63] averaging around 16%. Several books show approximately equal numbers of Black males and females, and some show many more of one sex, but overall one sex does not predominate. Readers contain one to four stories in which the main character is Black; about half of these stories are all-Black. Blacks occasionally serve as support characters in other stories as well. Blacks appear in a variety of roles, ranging from athlete, to farmer, to business person with a briefcase. They are usually middle-class but are occasionally lower-class. The quality of their portrayal varies among books. In some books, Black people occupy nonstereotypic roles that could be filled by anyone. For example, a story in one book shows a Black boy writing letters using different creative formats; a child of any race or sex could fill this role equally well.[64] In a few books, one finds a single, stereotypic story, for example portraying Blacks as poor and rural, with no substantive counterbalancing image else-where.[65] Blacks in multiracial group scenes often look White, except that the artist has colored them brown. Most stories are simply not stereotypic, but not particularly set within a Black cultural context. In fact, we did not find one story that drew sub-stantively on the Black American cultural experience.

Identifying Hispanic Americans and Native Americans in pictures is often diffi-cult, as many books contain multiracial pictures of people with brown skin and black hair. Hispanic Americans appear in all fifteen books, ranging from no picture repre-sentation[66] to appearing in 26% of these books[67] and averaging around 5%. All the readers have at least one story with a Hispanic American main character; two have as many as five such stories, about half of which are all-Hispanic.[68] Hispanics occasional-ly appear in other stories. Most books show many more of one sex than the other. In all four skill books, Hispanic names such as Roberto and Mrs. Hernandez are used in sentences. Hispanics often appear in work roles such as potter, cowboy, peasant, or sailor, and they sometimes appear as immigrants. There are some authentic and non-stereotypic contemporary portrayals, however, such as a true story about a Hispanic cartoonist.[69] Two well-done stories about a Mexican American girl living in Texas, set within a contemporary Mexican American context, stress pride in Mexican her-itage, although one passage differentiates between American food and Mexican food from San Antonio.[70]

Identifiable Native Americans are completely absent from five books.[71] In the other ten, the percentage of pictured people who are Native American ranges from 2% to 10%. Females tend to appear more often than males, although two books show males only[72] and three are evenly balanced. Readers contain between one and three stories in which the main character is Native American; most of these stories are all-Native, and Native American characters rarely appear in other stories. Stories are both contemporary and historical; contemporary stories show Indian children wearing jeans, for example, often living on reservations. Some stories portray specific tribes, such as Zuni, Chippewa, and Acoma; two stories portray Eskimos. The roles occupied by Native Americans are limited: potter (three stories), cowboy, shepherd, jewelry craftsperson, fisher, hunter, warrior, and athlete. Two stories depict a young male com-ing to grips with his heritage. Native Americans are in most stories we found in which cultural identity is explicitly discussed, and it tends to be presented as a prob-lem to members of this group.

White Americans appear in all fifteen books. The percentage of people pictured who are White ranges from about 50%[73] to about 80%.[74] Only three books show ap-proximately equal numbers of White males and females in pictures.[75] The rest show more males, and in four the ratio is as high as 3 to 1 male to female.[76] Readers con-tain between eight and twenty-one stories in which the main character is White; most of these stories are all-White. Whites also serve as support characters in other stories; one finds few stories in which Whites do not appear. Whites appear in by far the most varied roles of any racial group, and more than any other group Whites ap-pear as famous people, at leisure, as royalty, and as upper-class people. White females tend to appear in traditional roles such as playing with dolls and cooking. White males also usually appear in traditional roles such as inventor, doctor, or construction work-er; a few also appear in nontraditional sex roles. Texts tend not to portray people or situations having identifiable ethnic content, with some exceptions noted above. Most books attempt to show people doing "generic" mainstream cultural activities, speak-ing Standard English, and dressed and living like a "generic" American. This is proba-bly done to avoid stereotyping. But in the process, authentic experiences that are rooted in ethnicity are shown infrequently, and positive cultural differences are rendered unimportant or nonexistent.

Gender

In four books both sexes appear in pictures in about equal numbers,[77] in one females predominate in pictures although males predominate as main characters,[78] and in the remaining ten books males predominate, ranging from 55% to 75% of the people pictured. Most people in most books appear in sex-stereotypic roles, and emotions or character traits tend to be sex-stereotypic. For example, one second-grade book has 42 stories, 22 of which have human characters; 15 of these stories depict strong sex stereotypes, with females as worriers, nurturers, concerned about their appearance, afraid and needing males to rescue them; and males appear as brave, needing to prove themselves, and desiring power.[79] Females are more likely to appear in nontraditional roles than are males: while most books show some females doing things such as participating in athletics, carrying a briefcase, or having an adventure, one must look hard to find males doing things such as taking care of children, working in the kitchen, or holding a traditionally female occupation. Even animals with a known gender tend to follow traditional gender stereotypes, and if gender is unknown, tend to be referred to as "he." Otherwise, all the books use nonsexist language.

Disability

People with identifiable disabilities appear in only seven books. In three of these books, two of which are skill books, they appear in pictures only.[80] A person with a disability is the focus of one story in three readers[81] and of two stories in one reader.[82] People with disabilities do not serve as support characters in other stories, although in one reader they occasionally appear in the background of pictures.[83] About equal numbers of both sexes appear, and they are mostly White. Altogether, a variety of disabilities appear, including, in one story, learning disabilities. So few people with disabilities are shown doing something (in pictures they tend to sit, smiling) that it is difficult to generalize about roles, except to note that in stories they are mainly coping with difficulties or being helped to learn something.

Social Class

Books show social-class diversity very little. Seven portray only middle-class people, or depict people wearing clothing, occupying houses, and using speech commonly associated with the middle class.[84] The other seven books show some identifiable social-class diversity, although the great majority of people in these books appear to be middle-class. Upper-class people most often are royalty, although some hold jobs such as physician and engineer; all are White. Lower-class people are both White and of color. Some are portrayed much like other characters but holding a low-paying job, such as short-order cook; some are portrayed sympathetically, such as wanting to make money and eventually succeeding. Some are villagers of long ago. And some lower-class people are portrayed stereotypically, foolish or uneducated. The books mainly give the impression that there is little or no social-class diversity.

Overall, these reading and language arts books depict people of various colors and both sexes, but they do very little to help young people learn about issues related to diversity, or even to learn that issues exist. They also do fairly little to help young

people develop an understanding of different American cultural groups. This is epitomized by the approach that the four skills books take. The publishers of these books
seem to have made an effort to distribute a variety of people and names across a variety of roles in a way that shows few patterns and that would not reflect any particular
group's experiences. Even the reading books seem to avoid presenting social issues, although they present stories about interpersonal issues such as a child not fitting into a
group. Books sometimes explicitly deny that inequality and injustice exist. One book,
for example, is predominantly White but has a somewhat stereotypic story about
Blacks and many sex stereotypes. But it also contains an article entitled "What will
you be?" which shows Black and White males and females in a variety of equal roles,
suggesting that anyone can be anything. Not only does this obscure the existence of
discrimination, it contradicts the hidden curriculum of the rest of the book.[85]

Science

We examined ten science textbooks, published by six publishers.[86] The science books
do not contain as many pictures of individual people as the other books we examined, only about ninety pictures per science book; however, the representation of
groups is fairly similar.

Race

Asian Americans occupy about 5% of the pictures. Asian American males are shown
in pictures a few more times than females. Asian Americans are shown mainly doing
"everyday things" such as participating in a sporting event. With the exception of one
book,[87] Asian Americans are rarely shown as scientists or as engaging in scientific investigation, such as using a microscope or a telescope. Only two books discuss the
contributions Asians have made to science: one acknowledges the contributions of
ancient Chinese astronomers,[88] and the other discusses the careers of two Asian
American scientists.[89]

  The percentage of pictures of Black Americans ranges from 6% to 20%, although in only two books is the percentage under 10%.[90] Pictures of Black males appear about one-third times as frequently as pictures of Black females. Most pictures
show Blacks in everyday roles, as musicians, as radio repair people, and having an eye
exam; but they do not show Blacks conducting scientific investigations. The exception is one book, that contains several pictures of Black American female students doing scientific experiments, and discusses the careers of two Black American female
scientists.[91] The books do not address Blacks' contributions to science. Blacks do appear, however, in a discussion of sickle cell anemia.

  Hispanic Americans are shown in 1% to 5% of the pictures in eight books, in
7% in one,[92] and in 12% in one.[93] Approximately the same number of Hispanic males
and females are depicted. Hispanics are seen participating in everyday activities such as
riding a bike, jumping rope, eating, and studying. They are not shown conducting scientific investigations or as scientists. The books do not address contributions of Hispanics to science.

  Native Americans are in 1% to 5% of the pictures in eight of the books. In two
books we could not identify a picture of a Native American,[94] in three more books
we could not identify any Native American males,[95] and in two books we could not
identify any Native American females.[96] Two pictures show a Native American male
working in science, one as a geologist and the other as a guide for an expedition.[97]

One book mentions how Mayan Indians observed the sky[98]; otherwise, the books do not address scientific contributions of Native Americans.

White Americans and European Whites are depicted most frequently in pictures, ranging from 55%[99] to 83%.[100] White males are seen about 40% more times than White females. Whites are shown doing scientific investigations as well as everyday things. They are also shown participating in many different branches of science such as medicine and physics. The books discuss famous White scientists and Whites' contributions to science. Whites are seen as ingenious, curious, and dedicated to solving many of life's problems through science.

Gender

The science books show more males than females (approximately 463/337), and more than twice as many pictures of White females as of females of color. But there is very little career or occupation role stereotyping along gender lines. Males and females (often students) are seen doing scientific things throughout the books, such as doing experiments with simple machines, testing Newton's Laws of motion, and explaining how "esters" are made. Both females and males are shown using elaborate scientific equipment, such as special computers. However, a few pictures show females doing household activities like washing and cooking, but do not show males doing household activities. Some books show pictures of famous female scientists, such as Lise Meitner, and pictures of females having a career in science, such as nuclear physics. The books do not use sexist language.

Disability

The majority of the books have at least one picture of a disabled person, although in two books we could not locate any people with disabilities.[101] These pictures do not necessarily show the disabled person doing scientific investigation, but doing everyday things such as sports.

Social Class

It was difficult to determine the socioeconomic class of the pictures. However, an educated observation would be that the majority show middle- and upper-class settings, and many of the pictures showing scientific concepts in action use middle-class and upper-class artifacts, such as boats, ballet, traditional foods, and travel. Rarely did we see a picture of a setting such as a vacant lot, or materials associated with the underclass or working class. The science laboratories and experiments conducted suggest that financial support for science equipment is not a problem. This kind of financial support for science equipment is not often seen in many schools in urban areas or in communities where the working poor reside. Brown and Haycock argue that "at every level of the education process, minority students are less likely to have access to high-quality resources—including teachers, books, and physical facilities—than other students."[102]

Mathematics

We examined eight mathematic textbooks published by five publishers,[103] and one computer textbook.[104] All have story problems and illustrations accompanying problems; several also contain photographs at the beginning or end of each chapter illustrating people in various careers.

Race

In many pictures, particularly in sketches, it is difficult to identify the race of individuals, and there is no story to help out as there is in readers. Up to 19% of the pictured people in the math texts are of ambiguous racial membership.[105] In addition, the names used in most story problems could refer to anyone, such as Ted, Sue, Dick, Tony, or Katy, although Asian and Hispanic names are also used in all the texts.

Asian Americans are shown in 1%[106] to 13%[109] of the pictures, averaging around 4%. Altogether, the books contain about the same proportion of each sex, but most have more of one sex than the other. Asian names also occasionally appear in story problems. Many Asians appear in everyday roles, such as standing, playing, driving a car, or as students. About one-third of the Asian Americans appear as well-educated middle- to upper-middle-class people holding professional positions, which frequently involve them with computers. For example, one text portrays a well-dressed female statistician in the sports department of a newspaper.[108] No Asian appears in a lower-class position.

Black Americans comprise between 14%[109] and 29%[110] of the people pictured. Three books contain equal proportions of male and female Black Americans[111]; the rest contain at least twice as many Black males as females. One generally cannot determine whether story problems refer to Blacks as traditionally Black names such as Mahalia or Willie, rarely appear, and most problems are not accompanied by pictures of people. Therefore, images of Blacks emanate mainly from pictures. Most books depict Blacks in a variety of everyday roles such as walking the dog, playing, or camping. However, the most common single role in which Blacks appear, with the exception of student, is that of athlete. Drawings of males playing basketball, football, or baseball usually include Blacks. Several texts include a few famous people, usually mathematicians; the only famous Blacks shown are not mathematicians but rather athletes such as Jackie Robinson.[112] Blacks occasionally appear in nonstereotypic occupations, such as cameraman and supervisor, but blacks appear more frequently in lower-status occupations such as truck driver or tollbooth attendant. Only two books show Blacks in science professions: physicist, chemist, and astronaut.[113] Texts vary in the extent to which they depict Black children as serious students; while some show Blacks working calculators or computers, others such as the computer textbook[114] do so little or not at all. Most Blacks are portrayed as middle-class; however, in one book Blacks are the main people buying on credit or at a discount.[115]

Identifiable Hispanic Americans comprise between 1%[116] and 9%[117] of the pictures; most commonly, about 3% of the people pictured are identifiably Hispanic. Only one book contains equal numbers of each sex[118]; the rest show either mainly Hispanic females or Hispanic males. As many as 12% of the names in story problems are Hispanic.[119] Hispanics, like Blacks, appear mainly in everyday roles such as playing, eating, buying something, or doing classwork. No single role predominates for this group, as sports does for Blacks, although the main occupation in which Hispanics appear is that of teacher. Several are shown in nonstereotypic sex roles such as a male sewing[120] and a female working on a bike.[121] Only one book depicts Hispanics in upper-middle-class occupations: scientist and store owner.[122] Hispanics tend not to be shown as mathematicians; for example, in the computer book most Hispanics are not shown using computers.[123] Hispanics generally appear middle–class, although in one book a Hispanic male is borrowing money to buy a guitar.[124]

Native Americans are not identifiable in any form in six books.[125] They do not appear in pictures in two additional books, although each of these books has a Native American male in a story problem.[126] The remaining two books each depict one Native American of each sex. Roles in which Native Americans appear are extremely limited, as so few appear. Two male roles are telephone technician and owner of a bike shop; other roles simply illustrate story problems, such as a female weighing thumbtacks. Other people in the books could be Native American, but we could not tell.

White Americans, on the other hand, appear in large numbers in all nine books. Between 48%[127] and 80%[128] of the people in pictures are White; most commonly, Whites are about two-thirds of the people pictured. Four books show about equal numbers of each sex,[129] four show more males, and one shows more females. As with Blacks, images of Whites emanate mainly from pictures, as most names in story problems could fit anyone. The main famous people in the math texts have contributed to the history of mathematics; mainly White males appear, although a few White females also appear. In pictures, Whites appear in a wide variety of everyday roles. Some books clearly feature Whites in the most desirable or prestigious roles. For example, in one book the only people portrayed reading are White males, and the majority of people holding calculators are White.[130] In another book, White males are shown as initiators of progress and designers of time-saving formulas other people use.[131] Even books that do not have such obvious biases, however, tend to give Whites roles other groups do not occupy, if for no other reason than by virtue of their numbers. For example, Whites appear as cheerleaders, traders on the New York Stock Exchange, an oncologist, sunbathers at the beach, a veterinarian, an environmental engineer, and someone making pizza. Whites appear neither as obviously rich nor as needing to borrow money. The main impression the books give about Whites is that they are numerous and everywhere.

Gender

Equal proportions of males and females appear in pictures in three texts[132]; the rest show more males than females. The percentage of females in pictures ranges from 33% to 50%, and in story problems from 25% to 50%. Most books portray both sexes in fairly equal proportions in a variety of interchangeable roles, such as shopping, buying things, collecting things, doing math problems, feeding the dog, driving, running, and playing baseball. In fact, females appear as athletes as often, or almost as often, as males; both sexes appear in almost the same sports, although females rarely appear playing football. Females appear both in stereotypic roles such as ballet dancer, queen, sewing, and talking on the telephone, and in nonstereotypic roles such as letter carrier, lawn mower, construction worker, and engineer; texts vary considerably in their emphasis of one or the other. Males appear in a few texts in sex stereotypic roles only, such as astronaut, scientist, car sales rep, scout leader, and auto mechanic. Males are by far the main famous people (e.g., Pythagoras, Ben Franklin, Ty Cobb), and greatly outnumber females as store- or land-owners. However, most texts also feature at least a few males in nonstereotypic roles such as cook or babysitter. One can find additional subtle forms of sexism in some books, such as referring to unnamed people as "he" or consistently putting a male in the driver's seat when both sexes are in a car.[133]

Disability

People with identifiable disabilities do not appear at all in four texts.[134] People with disabilities comprise 1% to 5% of the pictures in the other five texts. Most of these are White people in wheelchairs; some sit and do nothing, others do things such as work problems with a calculator or pot plants. The computer text, which has the largest representation of people with disabilities, shows a greater variation of people with productive roles than the other texts; in addition to depicting people in wheelchairs, it also depicts a blind man programming a computer with the aid of Braille, and a person with no arms using a computer with a mouth utensil.[135]

Social Class

All nine texts attempt to avoid the issue of social class by portraying virtually everyone as middle-class. People are usually dressed simply, and there is usually little or no background setting. The few people who appear to be from a lower class are usually of color, such as the Hispanic male borrowing money to buy a guitar. The few people who appear financially well-off are White, Black, or Asian. To varying degrees, however, the texts also assume and encourage material consumption. Story problems frequently involve spending money to buy things, making money, or taking trips that cost money. Most financial transactions would fit an average budget, although a few involve spending relative large sums of money to buy fairly expensive things such as a microwave, a deluxe lawn mower, or a computer.

Discussion

As noted at the beginning of this chapter, students are presented in classrooms with usually one one version of reality. That version embodies certain interests, reifies certain interpretations and value judgments, and gives prominence to some pieces of knowledge while rendering others invisible. Many students may internalize what they are taught through textbooks, although others may marginalize it within their own thinking or reject it outright. But even if students forget, ignore, or reject what they encounter in textbooks, textbook content is still important because it withholds, obscures, and renders unimportant many ideas and areas of knowledge.

Looking across these four subjects areas clearly shows the extent to which the experiences, concerns, accomplishments, and issues of different groups appear on the curricular agenda. Whites consistently dominate textbooks, although their margin of dominance varies widely. Whites receive the most attention, are shown in the widest variety of roles, and dominate the story line and lists of accomplishments. Blacks are the next most included racial group. However, the books show Blacks in a more limited range of roles than Whites and give only a sketchy account of Black history and little sense of contemporary Black Life. Asian Americans and Hispanic Americans appear mainly as figures on the landscape with virtually no history or contemporary ethnic experience, and no sense of the ethnic diversity within each group is presented. Native Americans appear mainly as historical figures, although there are a few contemporary stories in reading books. Furthermore, very little interaction among different groups of color is shown. For example, Black cowboys were in the West with Native Americans, Mexican Americans were in Texas with Native Americans, and Mexican Americans, Chinese Americans, Japanese Americans, and Filipino Americans were all in California. These groups are only shown interacting with Whites. In addition, the books contain very little about contemporary race relations or issues for which these groups are currently struggling. They convey an image of harmonious blending of different colors of people, dominated by White people, and suggest that everyone is happy with current arrangements.

The books have successfully addressed gender issues mainly by eliminating most sexist language. Males predominate in most books; but even in books in which females have a major presence, females of color are shown fairly little. One gains little sense of the history or culture of women, and learns very little about sexism or current issues involving gender. Females are shown in many more nontraditional roles than males, suggesting that it is not important for males to broaden their roles. The books convey the image that there are no real issues involving sexism today, that any battles for equality have been won. Women of color are rarely shown as active agents in political, social, and economic struggle for equality. Harriet Tubman and Sojourner Truth are often given attention in their fight against slavery, but students could easily come to believe that these were the only two women of color who were active in the struggle for civil rights. The recent publication of *The Schomburg Library of Nineteen-Century Black Women Writers*[136] points out that many Black women were active fighters for social change, and that historians have neglected to report their story. For example, a Black woman, Maria W. Stewart, is recorded as being the first American-born woman to speak before a male and female audience in defense of women's rights. Interactions among or differences between women of different racial groups are not shown; students could easily believe that women of all racial groups worked together for suffrage, or that Hispanic women experience gender just as White women do.

Social class is not treated in the books much at all. The great majority of people and situations presented are middle-class or involve at least a modest level of financial status. The image that books in all subject areas convey is that the United States is not stratified on the basis of social class, that almost everyone is middle-class, that there is no poverty and no great wealth. This not only leaves students blind to the social-class structure, it avoids helping students learn why people are poor, what poverty is like, or how people have struggled over how wealth should be distributed. Social class and poverty simply do not appear on the curricular agenda.

Disability is ignored as well. Of the forty-seven texts we analyzed, no people with disabilities appear in eighteen, and the rest give people with disabilities or issues involving disability only token recognition. Students reading these textbooks would gain virtually no understanding of the current issues that people with disabilities face, nor of the struggles for rights that people have waged. An image of invisibility or of passivity on the part of those with disabilities predominates.

Let us return to the concerns expressed in the opening of this chapter. Bloom is concerned about the American mind becoming closed, and Hirsch is concerned about the extent to which schools are promoting cultural literacy.[137] So are we. Our analysis of current textbooks clearly shows the extent to which the curriculum focuses on the White male and downplays or simply ignores the accomplishments and concerns of Americans who are of color, female, poor, and/or disabled.

In a time of changing racial and ethnic demographics and changing roles of women, textbooks today help provide a framework for interpreting diversity. That framework, however, is a fairly conservative one that helps maintain existing relations between groups. It acknowledges racial and gender diversity, but provides only minimal understanding of it. Earlier in this chapter we noted that symbolic representations in texts are important vehicles of social control insofar as they legitimate the status of dominant groups, render socially constructed relations among groups as natural, and "select in" some ideas and domains of knowledge while "selecting out" others.

Our analysis shows that textbooks continue to legitimate the status of White males, despite the inclusion of other groups. Some educators have claimed that increased focus on people of color and White women had diverted attention from White males.[138] This claim does not hold up in the books we examined; White males continue to occupy more space and attention in textbooks than any other group; White females come in second, and racial minority groups trail.

Educators also have claimed that attention to White women, Blacks, Native Americans, and other groups is superficial, forced, and occasionally ridiculous.[139] This is sometimes true, because content about these other groups is simply added into existing frameworks for organizing content. There is a danger here in the way most books treat diversity. For example, the math book that depicted a female Native American weighing thumbtacks was clearly oriented around a mainstream "middle America" conception of society in which people of color participate as visibly different individuals rather than as members of oppressed and culturally rich groups. Banks has argued that "the infusion of bits and pieces of ethnic minority groups into the curriculum not only reinforces the idea that ethnic minority groups are not integral parts of U.S. society, it also results in the trivialization of ethnic cultures."[140] Furthermore, it erroneously suggests that diversity is being reinforced and studied when it really is not.

Textbooks participate in social control when they render socially constructed relations among groups as natural. The vision of social relations that the textbooks we analyzed for the most part project is one of harmony and equal opportunity—anyone can do or become whatever he or she wants; problems among people are mainly individual in nature and in the end are resolved. The reading books treat individual problems exclusively, and most problems are resolved by the end of the story. The math and science books simply sprinkle people throughout, in roles selected almost at random. As math and science are often perceived as ideologically neutral subject areas, the fact that they are projecting an ideological image—that society as it currently exists is harmonious and equal—would probably not be questioned by most people.

Textbooks further participate in social control when they "select in" some ideas and domains of knowledge and "select out" others. Physical, visible differences have been "selected in," very clearly. This corresponds with a portion of the reality Americans experience when they see each other. Cultural differences are included only now and then, and sometimes portrayed as a problem, although in some of the readers problems brought about by cultural differences are resolved by individuals. Culture is shown to be a problem when, for example, a Hispanic family is misunderstood by Anglo-Americans or a Native American must resolve his or her identity conflict. White culture is not shown to be a problem. The differential distribution of power and wealth is an idea that is not present at all.

Textbooks also reinforce the notion of individuality. The idea that people are members of collectives appears only very selectively. For example, in history passages on the suffrage and civil rights movements, or in reading stories about Native Americans on reservations, the idea of collectivity appears. Otherwise, it simply does not. Students do not get information on groups dominating groups, nor are they given the vocabulary and concepts that would help them see themselves as members of social groups that relate in unequal ways with others. (Several of our students who have an-alyzed textbooks have expressed concern over stories that feature only members of a non-White racial group, commenting that such stories should be more integrated.)

It appears publishers roughly follow representation in the U.S. population to de-cide how much attention to give different racial groups, giving Whites the most space but less than their 83%, and groups of color a little more than their proportion of the general population. Women constitute slightly more than half of the population, but receive less than half of the attention; people with disabilities are estimated to consti-tute 12% of the school population and receive considerably less than 12% of the at-tention; and lower-class people clearly do not show up in any proportional way at all. But the issue of representation is an important one. Our analysis shows that any group that receives scant attention, regardless of their representation in the population, tends to be treated superficially and piecemeal. We would suggest giving enough attention to America's various groups so that students can gain a sense of each group's history, complexity, and achievements. This may involve reducing attention to White males further; however, it could also involve orienting more of the curriculum around real human experiences and less of it around bland, fictitious stories, skills taught out of the context of human experience (such as decoding or arithmetic skills), or content involving meaningless activities (such as story problems about drinking glasses of juice). Curriculum design might begin by selecting concepts, experiences, images, and contributions that should be taught about each racial, gender, social class, and disabili-ty group, then weaving this throughout the curriculum. Repetition, such as excessive numbers of adventure stories about White males, could be eliminated, and skill drills, such as multiplication story problems, could be contextualized within meaningful content.

Conclusion

Treatment of diversity in textbooks has not improved much over the past fifteen years or so, generally, although a few textbooks have improved in specific, limited ways. There was a flurry of activity to "multiculturalize" textbooks during the late 1960s and early 1970s, although that activity never did address social class in text-books. That activity may have stopped, and we may be entering an era of backslid-ing, a return to more White- and male-dominated curricula. This would be quite dangerous, producing citizens with a shallow social consciousness and narrow sense of history and culture, and alienating from school lower-class children and children of color. Textbooks need to be scrutinized carefully, and those that fail to educate children meaningfully about America's diversity and its history of oppression should not be bought and used.

Appendix

Reading Textbooks

Allington, R. L., R. L. Cramer, P. M. Cunningham, G. Y. Perez, C. F. Robinson, and R. I. Tier-ney (1985). *Rough and Ready.* (Glenview, Ill.: Scott, Foresman & Co.).

Beech, L. W., R. Cramer, C. W. Feder, T. McCarthy, N. C. Najimy, D. Priplett (1984). *Language: Skills and Use,* 2d ed. (Glenview, Ill.: Scott, Foresman & Co.).

Chaparro, J. L., and M. A. Trost (1985). *Reading Literature.* (Evanston, Ill.: McDougal, Littell & Co.).

Clymer, T., R. Indrisano, D. D. Johnson, P. D. Pearson, and R. L. Venezky (1985). *Across the Fence.* (Needham Heights, Mass.: Ginn & Co.).

Clymer, T., R. Indrisano, D. D. Johnson, P. D. Pearson, and R. L. Venezky (1985). *Ten Times Round.* (Needham Heights, Mass.: Ginn & Co.).

Durr, W. K., J. M. LePere, M. L. Alsin, R. P. Bunyan, and S. Shaw (1983). *Honeycomb.* (Boston: Houghton Mifflin).

Durr, W. K., and J. Pikulski (1986). *Explorations.* (Boston: Houghton Mifflin).

Littell, J., ed. (1984). *Building English Skills.* (Evanston, Ill.: McDougal, Littell & Co.).

Littell, J., ed. (1985). *Basic Skills in English.* (Evanston, Ill.: McDougal, Littel & Co.).

Maccarone, S., ed. (1983). *Crossing Boundaries.* (Lexington, Mass.: D. C. Heath & Co.).

Matteoni, L., W. Lane, F. Sucher, and V. Burns (1980). *A Painted Ocean.* (New York: The Economy Company).

Matteoni, L., and F. Sucher (1986). *Can It Be?* (New York: The Economy Company).

Paden, F., S. Schaffrath, and S. Wittenbrink (1984). *Building English Skills.* (Evanston, Ill.: McDougal, Littell & Co.).

Rowland, P. T. (1982). *The Nitty Gritty Rather Pretty City.* (Reading, Mass.: Addison–Wesley Pub.).

Weiss, B. J., P. S. Rosenbaum, A. M. Shaw, and M. J. Tolbert (1986). *To See Ourselves.* (Fort Worth, Tex.: Holt, Rinehart & Winston).

Mathematics Textbooks

Bolster, L. C., W. Crown, R. Hamada, V. Hansen, M. M. Lindquist, C. McNerney, W. Nibbelink, G. Prigge, C. Rahilfs, D. Robitaille, J. Schultz, S. Sharron, J. Swafford, I. Vance, D. E. Williams, J. Wilson, and R. Wisner (1987). *Invitation to Mathematics.* (Glenview, Ill.: Scott, Foresman & Co.).

Bolster, L. C., W. Crown, M. M. Lindquist, C. McNerney, W. Nabbelink, P. Glenn, C. Rahlfs, D. Robitaille, J. Schultz, J. Swafford, I. Vance, J. Wilson, and R. Wisher (1985). *Invitation to Mathematics.* (Glenview, Ill.: Scott, Foresman & Co.).

Carey, L., H. Bolster, and D. Woodburn (1982). *Mathematics in Life,* 2d ed. (Glenview, Ill.: Scott, Foresman & Co.).

Duncan, E. R., W. G. Quast, M. A. Haubner, W. L. Cole, L. M. Gemmill, C. E. Allen, A. M. Cooper, and L. R. Capps (1983). *Mathematics.* (Boston: Houghton Mifflin).

Eicholz, R. E., P. G. O'Daffer, C. R. Fleenor, R. I. Charles, S. Young, and C. S. Barnett (1987). *Addison-Wesley Mathematics.* (Reading, Mass.: Addison-Wesley Pub. Co.).

Golden, N. (1986). *Computer Literacy with an Introduction to BASIC Programming.* (Orlando, Fla.: Harcourt Brace Jovanovich).

Rucker, W. E., and C. A. Dilley (1982). *Heath Mathematics.* (Lexington, Mass.: D. C. Heath & Co.).

Thoburn, T., J. E. Forbes, and R. D. Bechtel (1982a). *Macmillan Mathematics.* (New York: Macmillan Pub. Co.).

Thoburn, T., J. E. Forbes, and R. D. Bechtel (1982b). *Mathematics.* (New York: Macmillan Pub. Co.).

Social Studies Textbooks

Armbruster, B. B., C. L. Mitsakos, and V. R. Rogers (1986). *America's Regions and Regions of the World.* (Needham Heights, Mass.: Ginn and Company).

Arnsdorf, V. E., T. M. Helmus, N. J. G. Pounds, and E. A. Toppin (1982a). *The World and Its People: The United States and Its Neighbors.* (Needham Heights, Mass.: Silver Burdett Company).

Buggey, J. (1983). *Our Communities.* (Chicago: Follett Publishing Company).

Buggey, J., and M. E. Swartz (1983). *Home and School.* (Chicago: Follett Publishing Company).

Buggey, J. (1983). *Our United States.* (Chicago: Follett Publishing Company).

Buggey, J., G. Danzer, C. Mitsakos, and C. Risinger (1982). *America! America!* (Glenview, Ill.: Scott, Foresman and Company).

Cangemi, J. (1983). *Our History.* (Fort Worth, Tex.: Holt, Rinehart and Winston Publishers).

Clark, M. K. (1982). *The Earth and Its People.* (New York: Macmillan Pub. Co., Inc.).

Gross, H. H., D. W. Follett, R. E. Gabler, W. L. Burton, and W. D. Nielson (1980). *Exploring Our World: Regions.* (Chicago: Follett Publishing Company).

Harthern, A. T. (1982). *The World and Its People: Families and Neighbors.* (Needham Heights, Mass.: Silver Burdett Company).

Hyder, B. P., and C. S. Brown (1982). *The World and Its People: Neighborhoods and Communities.* (Needham Heights, Mass.: Silver Burdett Company).

King, D. C., and C. C. Anderson (1980). *America: Past and Present.* (Boston: Houghton Mifflin Company).

Schwartz, M., and J. R. O'Connor (1981). *The New Exploring American History.* (New York: Globe Book Company, Inc.).

Social Science Staff of the Educational Research Council of America (1982). *The Making of Our America.* (Needham Heights, Mass.: Allyn and Bacon, Inc.).

Science Textbooks

Abruscato, J., J. Fossaceca, J. Hassarc, and D. Peck (1984). *Holt Science.* (Fort Worth, Tex.: Holt, Rinehart and Winston Publishers).

Adams, D., J. Hackett, and R. Sund (1980). *Accent on Science.* (Columbus, Ohio: Charles Merrill Publishing Co.).

Alexander, P., M. Fiegel, S. K. Foehr, A. F. Harris, J. G. Krajkovich, K. W. May, N. Tzimopoulos, and R. K. Voltmer (1987). *Physical Science* (Needham Heights, Mass.: Silver Burdett Company).

Alexander, P., et al. (1987). *Earth Science.* (Needham Heights, Mass.: Silver Burdett Co.).

Appenbrink, D., S. Halpernslot, P. Hownshell, and O. Smith (1981). *Physical Science.* (Englewood Cliffs, New Jer.: Prentice Hall Publishing Co.).

Brandwein, P. E., B. Cross, and S. S. Neivert (1985). *Science and Technology: Changes We Make.* (Lawrence, Kans.: Coronado Publishers, Inc.).

Heimler, C. H., and C. D. Neal (1983). *Principles of Science, Book 1.* (Columbus, Ohio: Merrill Publishing Company).

Heimler, C. H., and C. D. Neal (1983). *Principles of Science, Book 2.* (Columbus, Ohio: Merrill Publishing Company).

Heimler, C. H., and J. Price (1987). *Focus on Physical Science.* (Columbus, Ohio: Merrill Publishing Company).

Mallinson, G. G., J. B. Mallinson, W. L. Smallwood, and C. Valentino (1985). *Science.* (Needham Heights, Mass.: Silver Burdett Company).

Notes

1. National Commission on Excellence in Education, *A Nation at Risk* (Washington, D.C.: U.S. Government Printing Office, 1983).

2. See, for example, Mortimer J. Adler, *The Paideia Proposal* (New York: Macmillan, 1982); Ernest L. Boyer, *High School* (New York: Harper and Row, 1983); John I. Goodlad, *A Place Called School* (New York: McGraw-Hill, 1984); National Science Board Commission on Precollege Education in Mathematics, Science and Technology, *Educating Americans for the 21st Century* (Washington, D.C.: National Science Foundation, 1983); Theodore R. Sizer, *Horace's Compromise* (New York: Houghton Mifflin, 1984); Task Force on Education for Economic Growth, *Action for Excellence* (Denver, Colo.: Education Commission of the States, 1983); The College Board, *Academic Preparation for College* (New York: The College Board, 1983); and Twentieth Century Fund, *Making the Grade* (New York: Twentieth Century Fund, 1983).

3. Carl A. Grant and Christine E. Sleeter, "Equality, Equity and Excellence: A Cri-

tique," in *Excellence in Education,* ed. Phil Altbach, Gail P. Kelly, and Lois Weis (Buffalo, N.Y.: Prometheus, 1985), pp. 139–60.

4. A. Bloom, *The Closing of the American Mind* (New York: Simon & Schuster, 1987), p. 381.

5. E. D. Hirsch, Jr., *Cultural Literacy: What Every American Needs to Know* (New York: Vintage Books, Random House, Inc., 1988), p. 4.

6. William J. Bennett, *Our Children and Our Country* (New York: Simon & Schuster, 1988).

7. Bloom, *The Closing of the American Mind,* p. 22.

8. J. Dewart, *The State of Black America 1988* (New York: National Urban League, 1988); and National Center for Education Statistics, *The Condition of Education* (Washington, D.C.: U.S. Government Printing Office, 1988).

9. Pierre Bourdieu, "Cultural Reproduction and Social Reproduction," in *Power and Ideology in Education,* ed. Jerome Karabel and A. H. Halsey (New York: Oxford University Press, 1977), pp. 487–510; Geoff Whitty, "Teachers and Examiners," in Geoff Whitty and Michael Young, eds., *Explorations in the Politics of School Knowledge* (Driffield, Eng.: Nafferton Books, 1976).

10. Bill Nichols, *Ideology and the Image* (Bloomington, Ind.: Indiana University Press, 1981), p. 290.

11. Cleo Cherryholmes, *Power and Criticism* (New York: Teachers College Press, 1988), p. 55.

12. Jean Anyon, "Workers, Labor and Economic History, and Textbook Content," in *Ideology and Practice in Schooling,* ed. Michael W. Apple and Lois Weis (Philadelphia: Temple University Press, 1983), p. 51.

13. Cherryholmes, *Power and Criticism,* p. 52.

14. Anyon, "Workers, p. 51.

15. L. J. Cronbach, "Introduction," in *Text Materials in Modern Education,* ed. L. J. Cronbach, F. Bienstedt, F. McMurray, W. Schramm, and W. B. Spalding (Urbana, Ill.: University of Illinois Press, 1955), p. 3.

16. M. W. Apple, *Teachers and Texts: A Political Economy of Class and Gender Relations in Education* (Boston: Routledge, 1988), p. 81.

17. L. J. Cronbach and F. McMurray, "The Controversial Past and Present of the Text," in *Text Materials in Modern Education,* ed. L. J. Cronbach, R. Bierstedt, F. McMurray, W. Schramm, and W. B. Spalding (Urbana, Ill.: University of Illinois Press, 1955), p. 12.

18. James A. Banks, *Multiethnic Education: Theory and Practice,* 2d ed. (Boston: Allyn & Bacon, 1981), pp. 229–31 and 257–80.

19. See, for example, Robin A. Butterfield, Elena Demos, Gloria W. Grant, Peter S. Moy, and Anna L. Perez, "A Multicultural Analysis of a Popular Basal Reading Series in the International Year of the Child," *Journal of Negro Education* 57 (1979): 382–89; R. Costo and J. Henry, *Textbooks and the American Indian* (San Francisco, Calif.: American Indian Historical Society,* Indian Historical Press, Inc., 1970); M. Dunfee, *Eliminating Ethnic Bias* (Washington, D.C.: ASCD, 1974); M. B. Kane, *Minorities in Textbooks: A Study of their Treatment in Social Studies* (Chicago: Quadrangle Books, 1970); and Michigan Department of Education, *A Second Report on the Treatment of Minorities in American History Textbooks* (Lansing, Mich., April 1971).

20. G. Britton, M. Lumpkin, and E. Britton, "The battle to Imprint Citizens for the 21st Century," *Reading Teacher* 37 (1984): 724–33; Carl A. Grant and Gloria W. Grant, "The Multicultural Analysis of Some Second and Third Grade Textbook Readers—A Survey Analysis," *Journal of Negro Education* 50 (1981): 63–74; J. Reyhner, "Native Americans in Basal Reading Textbooks: Are There Enough?" *Journal of American Indian Education* 26 (October 1986): 14–21.

21. Ruth Charnes, "U.S. History Textbooks: Help or Hindrance to Social Justice?" *Interracial Books for Children Bulletin* 15 (1984): 3–8; Jesus Garcia and D. C. Tanner, "The Portrayal of Black Americans in U.S. History Textbooks," *Social Studies* 76 (September 1985): 200–204; Nathan Glazer and R. Ueda, *Ethnic Groups in History Textbooks* (Washington, D.C.:

Ethics and Public Policy Center, 1983); C. L. Hahn and G. Blankenship, "Women and Economics Textbooks," *Theory and Research in Education* 2 (1983): 67–76; and G. O. O'Neill, "The North American Indian in Contemporary History and Social Studies Textbooks," *Journal of American Indian Studies* 27 (May 1987): 22–28.

22. R. R. Powell and J. Garcia, "What Research Says . . . About Stereotypes," *Science and Children* 25 (1988): 21–23.

23. Glazer and Ueda, *Ethnic Groups in History Textbooks,* p. 59.

24. Britton, Lumpkin, and Britton, "The Battle to Imprint Citizens"; Kathryn P. Scott, "Whatever Happened to Jane and Dick? Sexism in Texts Reexamined," *Peabody Journal of Education* 58 (1981): 135–42.

25. Hahn and Blankenship, "Women and Economics Textbooks"; B. E. Selke, "U.S. History Textbooks: Portraits of Men and Women?: *Southwestern Journal of Social Education* (1983): 13–20; Mary Kay Thompson Tetreault, "Integrating Women's History: The Case of United States History High School Textbooks," *History Teacher* 19 (1986): 211–62; and Mary Kay Tetreault, "Notable American Women: The Case of United States History Textbooks" *Social Education* 48 (1984): 546–50.

26. Powell and Garcia, "What Research Says . . . About Stereotypes."

27. Britton, Lumpkin, and Britton, "The Battle to Imprint citizens."

28. Hahn and Blankenship, "Women and Economics Textbooks"; Scott, "Whatever Happened to Jane and Dick?"

29. Butterfield et al., "A Multicultural Analysis of a Popular Basil Reading Series."

30. Britton, Lumpkin, and Britton, "The Battle to Imprint Citizens"; Butterfield et al., "A Multicultural Analysis of a Popular Basal Reading Series."

31. See Carl A. Grant and Christine E. Sleeter, *Turning on Learning* (Columbus, Ohio: Merrill, 1989), pp. 104–9.

32. B. B. Armbruster, C. L. Mitsakos, and V. R. Rogers, *America's Regions and Regions of the World* (Needham Heights, Mass.: Ginn and Company, 1986); V. F. Arnsdorf, T. M. Helmus, N. J. G. Pounds, and E. A. Toppin, *The World and Its People: The United States and Its Neighbors* (Needham Heights, Mass.: Silver Burdett Company, 1982); J. Buggey, *Our Communities* (Chicago, Ill.: Follett Publishing Company, 1983); J. Buggey and M. E. Swartz, *Home and School* (Chicago, Ill.: Follett Publishing Company, 1983); J. Buggey, *Our United States* (Chicago, Ill.: Follett Publishing Company, 1983); J. Buggey, G. Danzer, C. Mitsakos, and C. Risinger, *America! America!* (Glenview, Ill.: Scott Foresman and Company, 1982); J. Cangemi, ed. *Our History* (Fort Worth, Tex.: Holt, Rinehart and Winston, 1983); M. K. Clark, *The Earth and Its People* (New York: MacMillan Publishing Company, 1982); H. H. Gross, D. W. Follett, R. E. Gabler, W. L. Burton, and W. D. Nielson, *Exploring Our World: Regions* (Chicago, Ill.: Follett Publishing Company, 1980); A. T. Harthern, *The World and Its People: Families and Neighbors* (Needham Heights, Mass.: Silver Burdett Company, 1982); B. P. Hyder and C. S. Brown, *The World and Its People: Neighbors and Communities* (Needham Heights, Mass.: Silver Burdett Company, 1982); D. C. King and C. C. Anderson, *America: Past and Present* (Boston, Mass.: Houghton Mifflin Company, 1980); M. Schwartz and J. R. O'Connor, *The New Exploring American History* (New York: Globe Book Company, 1981); Social Science Staff of the Educational Research Council of America, *The Making of Our America* (Needham Heights, Mass.: Allyn and Bacon, 1982).

33. The four are Gross et al., *Exploring our World; Regions;* Buggey and Swartz, *Home and School;* Buggey, *Our United States;* and Hyder and Brown, *The World and its People.*

34. Buggey, *Our United States.*

35. King and Anderson, *America: Past and Present.*

36. Ibid., p. 354.

37. The three are Buggey, *Our United States;* Schwartz and O'Connor, *The New Exploring American History;* and Hyder and Brown, *The World and its People.*

38. For example, Gross et al., *Exploring our World: Regions,* and Buggey et al., *America! America!*

39. Hyder and Brown, *The World and its People,* p. 167.

40. King and Anderson, *America: Past and Present,* p. 433.

41. Ibid., p. 434.

42. Gross et al., *Exploring our World: Regions.*

43. Social Science Staff, *The Making of Our America;* Buggey and Swartz, *Home and School;* Clark, *The Earth and Its People;* and Harthern, *The World and its People.*

44. Gross et al., *Exploring our World: Regions.*

45. Buggey, *Our United States;* Harthern, *The World and its People;* and Hyder and Brown, *The World and its People.*

46. Buggey and Swartz, *Home and School,* and Gross et al., *Exploring our World: Regions.*

47. Armbruster et al., *America's Regions and Regions of the World,* p. 135.

48. Armbruster, et al., *America's Regions and Regions of the World;* Buggey and Swartz, *Home and School;* Hyder and Brown, *The World and its People;* and King and Anderson, *America's Past and Present.*

49. Buggey, *Our United States,* and Gross et al., *Exploring our World: Regions.*

50. Buggey, *Our Communities,* p. 208.

51. Gross et al., *Exploring Our World: Regions,* p. 304.

52. Buggey et al., *America! America!*

53. Cargeri, *Our History,* p. 89, our emphasis.

54. Buggey, *Our Communities;* Cargemi, *Our History;* Clark, The Earth and Its People; Gross et al., *Exploring Our World: Regions.*

55. Schwartz and O'Connor, *The New Exploring American History,* and Social Science Staff, *The Making of Our America.*

56. Buggey and Swartz, *Home and School.*

57. King and Anderson, *America: Past and Present.*

58. Ibid., p. 46.

59. R. L. Allington, R. L. Cramer, P. M. Cunningham, G. Y. Robinson, and R. I. Tierney, *Rough and Ready* (Glenview, Ill.: Scott Foresman and Company, 1985); J. L. Chaparro, and M. A. Trost, *Reading Literature* (Evanston, Ill.: McDougal, Littell & Co., 1985); T. Clymer, R. Indrisano, D. D. Johnson, P. D. Pearson, and R. L. Venezky, *Across the Fence* (Needham Heights, Mass.: Ginn and Company, 1985); T. Clymer, R. Indrisano, D. D. Johnson, P. D. Pearson, and R. L. Venezky, *Ten Times Round* (Needham Heights, Mass.: Ginn and Company, 1985); W. K. Durr, J. M. LePere, M. L. Alsin, R. P. Bunyan, and S. Shaw, *Honeycomb* (Boston, Mass.: Houghton Mifflin Company, 1983); W. K. Durr and J. Pikulski, *Explorations* (Boston, Mass.: Houghton Mifflin Company, 1986); S. Maccarone, ed., *Crossing Boundaries* (Lexington, Mass.: D. C. Heath & Co., 1983); L. Matteoni, W. Lane, F. Sucher and V. Burns, *A Painted Ocean* (New York: The Economy Company, 1980); L. Mateoni and F. Sucher, *Can It Be?* (New York: The Economy Company, 1986); P. T. Rowland, *The Nitty Gritty Rather Pretty City* (Reading, Mass.: Addison-Wesley, 1982); B. J. Weiss, P. S. Rosenbaum, A. M. Shaw, and M. J. Tolbert, *To See Ourselves* (Fort Worth, Tex.: Holt, Rinehart and Winston, 1986).

60. L. W. Beech, R. Cramer, C. W. Feder, T. McCarthy, N. C. Najimy, and D. Priplett, *Language: Skills and Use,* 2nd ed. (Glenview, Ill.: Scott Foresman and Company, 1984); J. Littell, ed., *Building English Skills* (Evanston, Ill.: McDougal, Littel & Co., 1984); J. Littel, ed., *Building English Skills* (Evanston, Ill.: McDougal, Littel and Co., 1985); and F. Pader, S. Schaffrath, and S. Wittenbrink, *Building English Skills* (Evanston, Ill.: McDougal, Littell & Co., 1984).

61. Clymer et al., *Across the Fence,* and Maccarone, *Crossing Boundaries.*

62. Littell, *Building English Skills,* and Paden et al., *Building English Skills.*

63. Beech et al., *Language: Skills and Use.*

64. Matteoni et al., *A Painted Ocean.*

65. For example, Dunn et al., *Honeycomb.*

66. Littell, *Basic Skills in English.*

67. Littell, *Building English Skills.*

68. Allington et al., *Rough and Ready,* and Matteoni et al., *A Painted Ocean.*

69. Dunn and Pikulski, *Explorations.*

70. Matteoni et al., *A Painted Ocean.*

71. Clymer et al., *Across the Fence;* Durr et al., *Honeycomb;* Littell, *Basic Skills in English;* Matteoni and Sucher, *Can it Be?;* and Rowland, *The Nitty Gritty Rather Pretty City.*

72. Dunn and Pikulski, *Explorations;* and Matteoni et al., *A Painted Ocean.*

73. Dunn and Pikulski, *Explorations;* Littell, *Building English Skills;* and Paden et al., *Building English Skills.*

74. Clymer et al., *Across the Fence,* and Dunn et al., *Honeycomb.*

75. Beech et al., *Language: Skills and Use;* Littell, *Basic Skills in English;* and Matteoni and Sucher, *Can It Be?*

76. Chaparro and Trost, *Reading Literature;* Clymer et al., *Across the Fence;* Clymer et al., *Ten Times Round;* and Maccarone, *Crossing Boundaries.*

77. Allington et al., *Rough and Ready;* Littell, *Basic Skills in English;* Beech et al., *Language: Skills and Use;* and Weiss et al., *To See Ourselves.*

78. Littell, *Building English Skills.*

79. Matteoni and Sucher, *Can It Be?*

80. Allington et al., *Rough and Ready;* Beech et al., *Language: Skills and Use;* and Littell, *Basic Skills in English.*

81. Clymer et al., *Ten Times Round;* Dunn and Pikulski, *Explorations;* and Littell, *Building English Skills.*

82. Maccarone, *Crossing Boundaries.*

83. Allington et al., *Rough and Ready.*

84. Clymer et al., *Across the Fence;* Dunn and Pikulski, *Explorations;* Littell, *Building English Skills;* Littell, *Basic Skills in English;* Matteoni and Sucher, *Can it Be?;* Paden et al., *Building English Skills;* and Rowland, *The Nitty Gritty Rather Pretty City.*

85. Dunn et al., *Honeycomb.*

86. J. Abruscato, J. Fossaceca, J. Hassarc, and D. Peck, *Holt Science* (Fort Worth, Tex.: Holt, Rinehart and Winston, 1984); D. Adams, J. Hackett, and R. Sund, *Accent on Science* (Columbus, Ohio: Charles E. Merrill Publishing Co., 1980); P. Alexander, M. Fiegel, S. K. Foehr, A. F. Harris, J. G. Krajkovich, K. W. May, N. Tzimopoulous, and R. K. Voltmer, *Earth Science* (Needham, Mass.: Silver Burdett Company, 1987); D. Appenbrink, S. Halpernslot, P. Hownshell, and O. Smith, *Physical Science* (Englewood Cliffs, New Jer.: Prentice-Hall, 1987); P. F. Brandwein, B. Cross, and S. S. Neivert, *Science and Technology: Changes we Make* (Lawrence, Kans.: Coronado Publishers, Inc., 1985); C. H. Heimler and C. D. Neal *Principles of Science Book 1* (Columbus, Ohio: Charles E. Merrill Publishing Co., 1983); C. H. Heimler and J. Price *Focus on Physical Science* (Columbus, Ohio: Charles E. Merrill Publishing Co., 1987); and G. G. Mallinson, J. B. Mallison, W. L. Smallwood, and C. Valentino, *Science* (Needham Heights, Mass.: Silver Burdett Company, 1985).

87. Alexander et al., *Earth Science.*

88. Heimler and Neal, *Principles of Science.*

89. Alexander et al., *Earth Science.*

90. Abruscato, *Holt Science,* and Mallinson et al., *Science.*

91. Alexander et al., *Physical Science.*

92. Adams et al., *Accent on Science.*

93. Appenbrink et al., *Physical Science, 1981.*

94. Alexander et al., *Earth Science,* and Brandwein et al., *Science and Technology.*

95. Adams et al., *Accent on Science;* Heimler and Neal, *Principles of Science;* and Mallinson et al., *Science.*

96. Abruscato et al., *Holt Science;* and Alexander et al., *Earth Science.*

97. Alexander et al., *Earth Science.*

98. Heimler and Neal, *Principles of Science.*

99. Adams et al., *Accent on Science.*

100. Abruscato et al., *Holt Science.*

101. Adams et al., *Accent on Science,* and Abruscato et al., *Holt Science.*

102. R. P. Brown and K. Haycock, *Excellence for Whom?* (Oakland, Calif.: The Achievement Council, 1984).

103. L. C. Bolster, W. Crown, R. Hamada, V. Hansen, M. M. Lindquist, C. McNerney, W. Nibbelink, G. Prigge, C. Rahilfs, D. Robitaille, J. Schultz, S. Sharron, I. Vance, D. E. Williams, J. Wilson, and R. Wisner, *Invitation to Mathematics* (Glenview, Ill.: Scott, Foresman & Co., 1987); L. C. Bolster, W. Crown, M. M. Lindquist, C. McNerney, W. Nibbelink, P. Glenn, C. Rahlfs, D. Robitaille, J. Schultz, J. Swafford, I. Vance, J. Wilson, and R. Wisner, *Invitation to Mathematics* (Glenview, Ill.: Scott, Foresman & Co., 1985); L. Carey, H. Bolster, and D. Woodburn, *Mathematics in Life,* 2nd ed. (Glenview, Ill.: Scott, Foresman & Co., 1982); E. R. Duncan, W. G. Quast, M. A. Haubner, W. L. Cole, L. M. Gemmell, C. E. Allen, A. M. Copper, and L. R. Chapps, *Mathematics* (Boston, Mass.: Houghton Mifflin Company, 1983); R. E. Eicholz, P. G. O'Daffer, C. R. Gleenor, R. I. Charles, S. Young, and C. S. Barnett *Addison-Wesley Mathematics* (Reading, Mass.: Addison–Wesley Pub. Co., 1987); W. E. Rucker, and C. A. Dilley, *Heath Mathematics* (Lexington, Mass.: D. C. Heath & Co., 1982); T. Thoburn, J. E. Forbes, and R. D. Bechtel, *Macmillan Mathematics* (New York: Macmillan Publishing Company, 1982); and T. Thoburn, J. E. Forbes, and R. D. Bechtel, *Mathematics* (New York: Macmillan Pub. Co., 1982).

104. N. Golden, *computer Literacy with an Introduction to BASIC Programming* (Harcourt Brace Jovanovich, 1986).

105. Thoburn et al., *Macmillan Mathematics.*

106. Bolster et al., *Invitation to Mathematics,* 1985 and 1987.

107. Carey et al., *Mathematics in Life.*

108. Bolster et al., *Invitation to Mathematics,* 1985.

109. Bolster et al., *Invitation to Mathematics,* 1987, and Golden, *Computer Literacy.*

110. Carey et al., *Mathematics in Life.*

111. Bolster et al., *Invitation to Mathematics,* 1987; Thoburn et al., *Macmillan Mathematics;* and Thoburn et al., *Mathematics.*

112. Bolster et al., *Invitation to Mathematics,* 1985, and Rucker and Dilley, *Heath Mathematics.*

113. Thoburn et al., *Macmillan Mathematics,* and Thoburn et al., *Mathematics.*

114. Golden, *Computer Literacy.*

115. Carey et al., *Mathematics in Life.*

116. Bolster et al., *Invitation to Mathematics,* 1987.

117. Eicholz et al., *Addison-Wesley Mathematics,* and Thoburn et al., *Mathematics.*

118. Rucker and Dilley, *Heath Mathematics.*

119. Carey et al., *Mathematics in Life.*

120. Ibid.

121. Bolster et al., *Invitation to Mathematics,* 1985.

122. Thoburn et al., *Mathematics.*

123. Golden, *Computer Literacy.*

124. Rucker and Dilley, *Heath Mathematics.*

125. Bolster et al., *Invitation to Mathematics,* 1987; Carey et al., *Mathematics in Life;* Eicholz et al., *Addison-Wesley Mathematics;* Golden, *Computer Literacy;* Thoburn et al., *Macmillan Mathematics,* and Thoburn et al., *Mathematics.*

126. Bolster et al., *Invitation to Mathematics,* 1985; and Thoburn et al., *Mathematics.*

127. Thoburn et al., *Mathematics.*

128. Bolster et al., *Invitation to Mathematics,* 1987.

129. Duncan et al., *Mathematics;* Eicholz et al., *Addison-Wesley Mathematics;* Thoburn et al., *Macmillan Mathematics;* and Thoburn et al., *Mathematics.*

130. Eicholz et al., *Addison-Wesley Mathematics.*

131. Carey et al., *Mathematics in Life.*

132. Eicholz et al., *Addison-Wesley Mathematics;* Thoburn et al., *Macmillan Mathematics;* and Thoburn et al., *Mathematics.*

133. Rucher and Dilley, *Heath Mathematics.*

134. Duncan et al., *Mathematics;* Rucker and Dilley, *Heath Mathematics;* Thoburn et al., *Macmillan Mathematics;* and Thoburn et al., *Mathematics.*

135. Golden, *Computer Literacy.*

136. H. L. Gates, ed., *The Schomburg Library of Nineteenth-Century Black Women Writers* (New York: Oxford Press, 1988).

137. Bloom, *The Closing of the American Mind;* and Hirsch, *Cultural Literacy.*

138. *The New York Times,* November 18, 1987, p. 6.

139. Ibid.

140. Banks, *Multiethnic Education,* p. 158.

26

Toward an Education for Women

MARY FIELD BELENKY, BLYTHE McVICKER CLINCHY,
NANCY RULE GOLDBERGER, AND JILL MATTUCK TARULE

*A better understanding of women's experience would permit, even force, a far-reaching
revision of the broader fields of higher education and intellectual life in the United States.*

—PATRICIA PALMIERI, 1979

Most of the institutions of higher education in this country were designed by men,
and most continue to be run by men. In recent years feminist teachers and scholars
have begun to question the structure, the curriculum and the pedagogical practices of
these institutions; and they have put forth useful proposals for change (for example,
Bowles and Duelli-Klein 1983; Martin 1985; Nicholson 1980; Rich 1979; Spanier,
Bloom, and Boroviak 1984; Tarule 1980). But, as the scholar Patricia Palmieri (1979,
p. 541) suggests, in order to design an education appropriate for women we must
learn about the academic experiences of ordinary women.

All of the individuals we interviewed were ordinary women. Most of them
were neither teachers nor scholars nor even feminists but simply students. We asked
each woman what she thought would stay with her about her experiences in the
school or program she attended. We asked her to tell us about specific academic and
nonacademic experiences, about good and bad teachers, good and bad assignments,
good and bad programs or courses. We asked her whether she thought that her participation in the program changed the way she thought about herself or the world.
We asked, "In your learning here, have you come across an idea that made you see
things differently? What has been most helpful to you about this place? Are there
things it doesn't provide that are important to you? Things you would like to learn
that you can't learn here?" Finally, we asked, "Looking back over your whole life,
can you tell us about a really powerful learning experience that you've had, in or
out of school?"

The women responded, of course, in diverse ways; but as we examined their accounts of what they learned and failed to learn, of how they liked to learn and how
they were forced to learn, some common themes emerged, themes that are distinctively, although surely not exclusively, feminine.

Chapter 9 in Mary Field Belenky, Blythe McVicker Clinchy, Nancy Rule Goldberger, and Jill Mattuck
Tarule, *Women's Ways of Knowing*. New York: Basic Books, 1986. Reprinted by permission.

Reminiscences of College

We begin with the reminiscences of two ordinary women, each recalling an hour during her first year at college. One of them, now middle aged, remembered the first meeting of an introductory science course. The professor marched into the lecture hall, placed upon his desk a large jar filled with dried beans, and invited the students to guess how many beans the jar contained. After listening to an enthusiastic chorus of wildly inaccurate estimates the professor smiled a thin, dry smile, revealed the correct answer, and announced, "You have just learned an important lesson about science. Never trust the evidence of your own senses."

Thirty years later, the woman could guess what the professor had in mind. He saw himself, perhaps, as inviting his students to embark upon an exciting voyage into a mysterious underworld invisible to the naked eye, accessible only through scientific method and scientific instruments. But the seventeen-year-old girl could not accept or even hear the invitation. Her sense of herself as a knower was shaky, and it was based on the belief that she could use her own firsthand experience as a source of truth. This man was saying that this belief was fallacious. He was taking away her only tool for knowing and providing her with no substitute. "I remember feeling small and scared," the woman says, "and I did the only thing I could do. I dropped the course that afternoon, and I haven't gone near science since."

The second woman, in her first year at college, told a superficially similar but profoundly different story about a philosophy class she had attended just a month or two before the interview. The teacher came into class carrying a large cardboard cube. She placed it on the desk in front of her and asked the class what it was. They said it was a cube. She asked what a cube was, and they said a cube contained six equal square sides. She asked how they knew that this object contained six equal square sides. By looking at it, they said. "But how do you know?" the teacher asked again. She pointed to the side facing her and, therefore, invisible to the students; then she lifted the cube and pointed to the side that had been face down on the desk, and, therefore, also invisible. "We can't look at all six sides of a cube at once, can we? So we can't exactly *see* a cube. And yet, you're right. You know it's a cube. But you know it not just because you have eyes but because you have intelligence. You invent the sides you cannot see. You use your intelligence to create the 'truth' about cubes."

The student said to the interviewer,

> It blew my mind. You'll think I'm nuts, but I ran back to the dorm and I called my boyfriend and I said, "Listen, this is just incredible," and I told him all about it. I'm not sure he could see why I was so excited. I'm not sure I understand it myself. But I really felt, for the first time, like I was really in college, like I was—I don't know—sort of *grown up*.

Both stories are about the limitations of firsthand experience as a source of knowledge—we cannot simply see the truth about either the jar of beans or the cube—but there is a difference. We can know the truth about cubes. Indeed, the students did know it. As the science professor pointed out, the students were wrong about the beans; their senses had deceived them. But, as the philosophy teacher pointed out, the students were right about the cube; their minds had served them well.

The science professor was the only person in the room who knew how many beans were in that jar. Theoretically, the knowledge was available to the students; they could have counted the beans. But faced with that tedious prospect, most would doubtless take the professor's word for it. He is authority. They had to rely upon his knowledge rather than their own. On the other hand, every member of the philosophy class knew that the cube had six sides. They were all colleagues.

The science professor exercised his authority in a benign fashion, promising the students that he would provide them with the tools they needed to excavate invisible truths. Similarly, the philosophy teacher planned to teach her students the skills of philosophical analysis, but she was at pains to assure them that they already possessed the tools to construct some powerful truths. They had built cubes on their own, using only their own powers of inference, without the aid of elaborate procedures or fancy apparatus or even a teacher. Although a teacher might have told them once that a cube contained six equal square sides, they did not have to take the teacher's word for it; they could have easily verified it for themselves.

The lesson the science professor wanted to teach is that experience is a source of error. Taught in isolation, this lesson diminished the student, rendering her dumb and dependent. The philosophy teacher's lesson was that although raw experience is insufficient, by reflecting upon it the student could arrive at truth. It was a lesson that made the student feel more powerful ("sort of grown up").

No doubt it is true that, as the professor in May Sarton's novel *The Small Room* says, the "art" of being a student requires humility. But the woman we interviewed did not find the science lesson humbling; she found it humiliating. Arrogance was not then and is not now her natural habitat. Like most of the women in our sample she lacked confidence in herself as a thinker; and the kind of learning the science teacher demanded was not only painful but crippling.

In thinking about the education of women, Adrienne Rich writes, "Suppose we were to ask ourselves, simply: What does a woman need to know?" (1979, p. 240). A woman, like any other human being, does need to know that the mind makes mistakes; but our interviews have convinced us that every woman, regardless of age, social class, ethnicity, and academic achievement, needs to know that she is capable of intelligent thought, and she needs to know it right away. Perhaps men learn this lesson before going to college, or perhaps they can wait until they have proved themselves to hear it; we do not know. We do know that many of the women we interviewed had not yet learned it.

Confirmation of the Self as Knower

In the masculine myth, confirmation comes not at the beginning of education but at the end. "Welcome to the community of scholars," the president announces at the Harvard commencement. ("That sure sounded weird to me," said a woman graduate. "He says 'Welcome.' Then he shows us the door.") Confirmation as a thinker and membership in a community of thinkers come as the climax of Perry's story of intellectual development in the college years. The student learns, according to Perry, that "we must all stand judgment" and that he must earn "the privilege of having [his] ideas respected" (1970, p. 33). Having proved beyond reasonable doubt that he has learned to think in complex, contextual ways, the young man is admitted to the fraternity of powerful knowers. Certified as a thinker, he becomes one of "them" (now dethroned to lower-case "them"). Doubt precedes belief; separation leads to connection. The weak become powerful, and the inferiors join their superiors. This scenario may capture the "natural" course of men's development in traditional, hierarchical institutions, but it does not work for women. For women, confirmation and community are prerequisites rather than consequences of development.

Most of the women reported that they had often been treated as if they were stupid. This was especially (although by no means exclusively) true of the less privileged. Consider, for example, the case of Lillian, a student at one of the "invisible colleges." When Lillian's infant son suffered an attack of projectile vomiting, she called her pediatrician. "Don't worry about it," he said. Instead of respecting her concern, he dismissed it. Lillian wanted respect, and she wanted information.

> I wasn't asking for the complete history of projectile vomiting. I just really wanted an explanation, simple, something like you would give a child if they asked you a question like where do babies come from. You don't give them a whole routine, just a piece of it, and let them deal with that. You don't say, "Never mind." You don't patronize them. I don't do that with my own child, so I don't like to be treated like that. I really wanted to be dealt with as a person, not just a hysterical mother, not even as a mother, as just another person who was halfway intelligent.

Lillian's encounters with authority (teachers, bosses, doctors, priests, bureaucrats, and policemen) taught her that "experts" usually tried to assert dominance over less knowledgeable people either by assaulting them with information or by withholding information. But her experience as a mother provided her with a different model, a model we call "connected teaching," in which the expert (parent) examines the needs and capacities of the learner (child) and composes a message that is, in the psychologist Jerome Brumer's felicitous term, "courteous" to the learner (1963, p. 52). Although Lillian knew more than her son knew, she did not think she was better than he. She did not want to exert power over him. She wanted to help him on his own terms, and she needed experts who would do the same for her.

Fortunately a public health clinic for children, run on the connected teaching model, opened up in Lillian's area. The director of the clinic defined the clinic's job not as "teaching mothers how to raise children" but as "trying to help mothers do what they need to do." Lillian, having placed her child under the clinic's care, exclaimed, "What a difference!" Members of the clinic staff never patronized her, nor did they patronize her son. "They've always seemed to deal with me and, now that Shaun's older, with him on equal levels." To allay Shaun's fears of examinations, the nurse practitioner carried out an entire examination on the little boy's teddy bear, explaining "very sincerely," in terms the child could understand, what she was doing and why. Lillian marveled at the staff's patience, as did Ann, another client whom we met in earlier chapters of this book. Ann's private pediatrician always made her feel rushed. Embarrassed to ask for clarification, she pretended she understood his directions. Afraid of "wasting his time," she hesitated to raise issues that were bothering her. At the clinic, on the other hand, they "take time to explain things"; they "spell it all out."

Having been subjected to the usual view of health care professionals that parents are incompetent, mothers who used the clinic were astonished to discover that members of the staff, nearly all of them women, believed in them. As Lillian said, "They seemed to have trust in me. I hadn't had that in a long time, that feeling like my parents gave me, that I was—no questions asked—trusted."

What these women needed and what the clinic provided, perhaps more clearly, consistently, and sincerely than any other institution we sampled, was confirmation that they could be trusted to know and to learn. Given confirmation, they felt they could "just do anything." Lacking it, as one woman said, they were "crippled" and "just can't function." Most of the women we interviewed made it clear that they did not wish to be told merely that they had the capacity or the potential to *become* knowledgeable or wise. They needed to know that they already knew something (although by no means everything), that there was something good inside them. They worried that there was not. "Suppose one woke and found oneself a fraud?" wrote Virginia Woolf. "It was part of my madness that horror" (1980, p. 138).

The worry was especially acute among older women returning to college or entering it for the first time. Some of these women found the confirmation they needed in an adult education program. A fifty-four-year-old widow, having raised six children, said, "I had reached a point in my life where I wasn't sure I had any worth as a human being. As the kids grew up and left, that kicked out any props I had. If I had any worth at all it was as their mother. What was I going to be for the rest of my life? A shell of what I had been?" But in the program, she found, "I'm accepted for what I am, the ability to be me. I came here and discovered I'm not a shell. I've got a lot of stuff in me."

A younger adult in the same program said that her teachers and fellow students made her realize that the knowledge she gained through her life experiences "is important and real and valuable." At the urging of a teacher, she wrote a paper about her escape to the Arctic in search of self. The paper was accepted for credit and circulated among members of the community. The woman said, "It validated who I was, that something that was real personal to me, that I carried around alone—that I could share that in writing and get credit for it. That I was recognized and respected." And a twenty-seven-year-old single parent, who "needed people to believe me," found them in the same program: "The people just accepted that of course I was a person, that I had something to say. They didn't look down on me at all. It was a whole different environment than I was used to. There was no oppression."

Even the most privileged women in our sample expressed the need to be accepted as a "person," as opposed to being oppressed or patronized. Privilege does not ensure freedom from oppression—incest, for instance, occurs in the "best" of families—and achievement does not guarantee self-esteem. Indeed, highly competent girls and women are especially likely to underestimate their abilities.★ Most of the women who attended the more prestigious colleges in the sample had a history of privilege and achievement, but most felt uncertain about their abilities. Several suspected that they had been admitted through a fluke.

Some women found the confirmation they needed in these colleges. Faith, for example, said that although she had always done well in school, no one had ever told her that she was intelligent until she came to college. There, Faith said, "people say, 'Well, you know, you're a pretty smart person.' If people say that to you enough you have to figure that they know at least a little of what they're talking about."

A classmate, however, interviewed toward the end of her first year, told a different story. Although she had entered college with SAT scores in the high 600s, she felt that she was "the dumbest girl here." Her high school teachers doled out constant praise but in college the teachers were silent.

> You need a little bit of praise to keep you going. If you get an idea that the teacher likes what you're doing, it helps you go on more, whereas most of my courses the teachers are kind of—They don't say "bad," they don't say "good," so you start having doubts and thinking, "Well, if he doesn't say something nice, he must not like it." And you just get into such a rut where you can't do anything. There's just an extreme lack of praise around here.

★For research showing that girls with higher scores on intelligence tests than other girls express unrealistically low expectations of success, see Crandall (1969) and Stipek and Hoffman (1980).

In high school she and her friends had been stars; in this highly competitive college they were just average.

> We all had a lot of self-esteem, and we didn't really think about it, we just knew we could do it. Whereas now, it's totally different. If I could just think to myself that I've done something really exceptionally good, 'cause sometimes I feel like I'm getting lost in the crowd. If I could just write maybe one paper and have a teacher say, "Hey, that was really, really good," I think that would help a lot.

We asked her if the approval had to come from a teacher. Could it not come from within her? "Not at this point," she said. "It's been so far pushed down it couldn't come back up by itself."

Some women were so consumed with self-doubt that they found it difficult to believe a teacher's praise, especially when the teacher was a man. One young woman told us that she never felt sure a male professor would take her seriously. The women worried that professors who praised their minds really desired their bodies. Elizabeth "got suspicious" of a male professor because he praised her so much.

> I got to know him personally, and it then became hard for me. I learned that evaluation is subjective, that there's not such a thing as an objective evaluation of things like work. I realized the guy liked me, so he's going to like my papers. Then I said, "This is really screwed up."

Elizabeth went on to describe a woman teacher who encouraged and helped her with her writing without babying her. "She was the only one who said, 'Yeah, that's good,'" "But," said the interviewer, "I thought you said [the male professor] was encouraging." "He was encouraging," Elizabeth replied, "but I think I felt that there were strings attached."

Several women spoke of the ambiguity inherent in male professors' praise for women students, of the "games" that male professors and female students fell into. Stella, an artist, said, "That's something every woman deals with, going to college: Am I a student or a flirtation? Why is the teacher giving them attention? Why does he draw on your pad and not hers?" The teacher may have to draw the lines very carefully in order to avoid ambiguity.

The problem was exacerbated—and the need for clear boundaries especially acute—for the many women who arrived at college having already suffered sexual abuse at the hands of a male in a position of authority, such as Elizabeth, whose father had repeatedly molested her. Whenever powerful men praised relatively powerless women, the women started looking for "the strings," especially when, as many admitted, they knew that they, themselves, had used their sexuality in the past to elicit praise.

Knowing the Realities: The Voice of Experience

In considering how to design an education appropriate for women, suppose we were to begin by simply asking: What does a woman know? Traditional courses do not begin there. They begin not with the student's knowledge but with the teacher's knowledge. The courses are about the culture's questions, questions fished out of the "mainstream" of the disciplines. If the student is female, her questions may differ from the culture's questions, since women, paddling in the bywaters of the culture, have had little to do with positing the questions or designing the agendas of the disciplines. (See, for example, Harding and Hintikka 1983; Reinharz 1984; Sherman and Beck 1979; Smith 1974.) Indeed, as writer Mary Jacobus points out, although nineteenth- and twentieth-century feminists have sought access to education as a means of liberation, "this access to a male dominated culture may equally be felt to bring with it alienation, repression, division—a silencing of the 'feminine,' a loss of women's inheritance" (1979, p. 10).

Most women students do not expect colleges to honor their concerns. One young woman who had always relied heavily on authorities as the source of truth told us that she hesitated before signing up for a women's studies course at her university, fearing that the course would not be respected; but it turned out to be the best course she'd ever taken. For the first time, she said, she was really interested in what she was studying. Two women team-taught the course, and it fascinated her that two people thought it was important enough to teach. The authorities' sanction enabled her to respect her own interests.

Cynthia, the alumna whose mother digested her experiences for her during college and told her what she felt, said that although she enjoyed the "austerity" of the college curriculum and did well, she felt lonely and sad throughout the four years. At the time, she thought her problems were "just personal," but lately she had begun to wonder if the curriculum contributed to her depression. She had been reading an essay by E. B. White about a battle between an old gander and a younger, stronger gander.

> They have this heroic battle. And the older goose at the end of the story is seen leaping off to lick his wounds somewhere in a patch of sun in a field. And it struck me that E. B. White saw everything in terms of great struggles—these great clashes between opposing forces—and that's what life was like, this—uh—sort of larger-than-life thing.

The larger-than-life knowledge contained in the college curriculum seemed to her at the time the only respectable form of knowledge; but now that she had more sense of herself as a woman, it struck her as a distinctively masculine perspective.

> You know, it's not a battle between the gods that concerns women. Women are concerned with how you get through life from minute to minute. What each little teeny tiny incident—how it can affect everything else you do. Women see things close at hand and are more concerned with minutiae.

This feminine mode seemed "realer, somehow," to Cynthia. It was a real way of knowing, an embryonic form, perhaps, of the close-up mothering eye that won for Barbara McClintock, belatedly, a Nobel prize (Keller 1983).

Although Cynthia's grades in college suggest that she mastered the masculine mode, she felt that it really never quite "took." Someday she hopes to master it. "I guess ultimately I would like to balance them. I would like to have a larger picture, too. I would like to be able to study history the way men can study history and see patterns in the development of the world and of civilization." But not right now. Right now she wants to put her ear to the ground, listen to the squirrel's heart beat, as George Eliot put it, and prowl among the webs of little things.

> At this point I want to explore those things that are more womanlike, the kinds of sensations and responses that I have to things on a very day-to-day small scale. I

like playing with my impressions of the silliest things. I think I haven't ever seen things in quite this way, been quite as aware of the fun I could have with introspection and observation of daily life.★

Most of the women we interviewed were drawn to the sort of knowledge that emerges from firsthand observation, and most of the educational institutions they attended emphasized abstract "out-of-context learning" (Cole, Gay, Glick, and Sharp 1971). We asked a young woman from such an institution to tell us about a good paper that she had written. She said she had not written many good papers, but there was one that she really liked.

> It was for a writing course. We were allowed to write about whatever we wanted. And I just described a place where I had worked—the social structure and all the cattiness—and I really enjoyed that. I was just so excited about what I was writing, and I thought it was just the greatest thing to read, and I sent copies to friends I had worked with, and they just loved it. [But the teacher] didn't think it was an important issue. He said it was well written but lacked content, whatever that means. [Laughs.] (*"How about a bad paper?" the interviewer asked.*) There was one I wrote analyzing a book that I hadn't finished. That wasn't too good. You know, it's really easy, though, to read part of a book and then pick up a few sources and annotate everything. I just thought it was horrible. I just knew that I didn't know what I was talking about, and I think it showed.

But apparently it did not; the teacher liked the paper. The student's standards were in conflict with the teacher's. When she wrote out of her own experience, she felt she knew what she was talking about, but the teacher felt the paper was not about anything. When she pasted together a mess of undigested, secondhand information, he was satisfied.

The women we interviewed nearly always named out-of-school experiences as their most powerful learning experiences. The mothers usually named childbearing or child rearing. The kind of knowledge that is used in child rearing is typical of the kind of knowledge women value and schools do not. Much of it comes not from words but from action and observation, and much of it has never been translated into words, only into actions. As a single parent of nine children said, "There are things I have up here [taps her temple] that I can't put down on paper. I know I use a lot of it in my daily life, like in trying to help my children."

This kind of knowledge does not necessarily lead to general propositions. Good mothering requires adaptive responding to constantly changing phenomena; it is tuned to the concrete and particular. A response that works with a particular child at a particular moment may not work with a different child or with the same child at a different moment. Mothers expect change, Ruddick says, and "change requires a kind of learning in which what one learns cannot be applied exactly, and often not even by analogy, to a new situation" (1980, p. 111). In this sense "maternal thinking" differs from scientific thinking, which considers an experimental result to be real—a fact— only if it can be replicated. As the philosopher Carol McMillan says, mothers are understandably "extremely hesitant about concocting theories about how other people should bring up their children and are sceptical about the advice thrust upon them by the 'experts'" (1982, p. 54).

★We must beg to differ with Cynthia. The late E. B. White taught us quite a lot about how to hear the squirrel's heart beat.

Many of the women we interviewed—mothers or not—remarked upon the discrepancy between the kind of thinking required in school and the kind required in dealing with people. A college junior, for example, said she found academics much easier than personal life.

> I'm very good at doing tasks. You know, you just compartmentalize something. It's time to sit down and write a paper and think about what someone said. And you do it. But when you're dealing with people you can't always compartmentalize—you know, sort of wrap them up in little packets and put them on the shelf and then you know how to deal with them from then on. Because everyone is always in an amorphous state. And they're all changing so much all the time. What may have worked with one person five days ago isn't going to work with them tomorrow.

Most of these women were not opposed to abstraction as such. They found concepts useful in making sense of their experiences, but they balked when the abstractions preceded the experiences or pushed them out entirely. Even the women who were extraordinarily adept at abstract reasoning preferred to start from personal experience.★ Mary Lou was one of them.

> I think women care about things that relate to their lives personally. I think the more involvement they have in something that affects them personally, the more they're going to explore it and the more they're going to be able to give and to get out of it. I think that men—because they're male they haven't been put down all the time for their sex, so they can go into any subject with confidence, saying, "I can learn about this" or "I have the intellect to understand this." Whereas I think women don't deal with things that way. I think they break down an issue and pick out what it is about it that has happened to them or they can relate to in some way, and that's how they start to explore it.

After graduating from high school Mary Lou took an entry-level job in day care, and worked her way up to be director of a center, designing and administering a program for children with minimal brain damage. Entering college at thirty-three, she did not regret the years spent in the field.

> I think the way I've learned in the past it's always been a very experiential kind of thing. That's how I learned about day care and about children to begin with. It was doing it. It was having to do it every single day for eight hours a day. I think that's where I got the wealth of my knowledge. I feel more comfortable knowing that. I like to know the realities. I like to know what's going on, so it's hard for me to explore something on the theory aspect and then go out and get the practical. I like to have the practical first, so I know what's going on and what it's really like, and then look at the theories that way.

Mary Lou was driven to reenter college by the need to organize the observations of women and children she had accumulated over the years.

> Things weren't sinking in. They were just all there, and there was no connection. Then when I came here and lived in the women's dorm and started having dis-

★Shulamit Reinharz writes, "If we *start* with labels, we have excluded experience altogether." She urges researchers to "describe and analyze with as few assumptions, presuppositions, or definitions beforehand as possible. . . . Try to see things as they are without blinders, labels, or intermediaries" (1984, pp. 359, 363).

cussions about feminist theory and philosophy, everything just kind of fell into place. There was a lot that I had seen going on and I had observed, but I didn't have anything really to relate it to. I feel much more knowledgeable now. I have words. I know reasons.

Judith, a staff member at the children's health clinic and one of our most highly educated and cerebral informants, said, "I don't like getting things totally out of a book. I really like having some real experience of it myself." Judith felt that much of what people thought they knew, they knew only in the form of "general concepts"; they did not really know it. "In the most exciting kind of learning, people are allowed to go right down to rock bottom and really look at these concepts and find out what their experience has been with it, what they know about it." Judith has had this sort of intense conversation in informal meetings with friends but never in school. In school, she said, people are "supposed to learn it the way somebody else sees it."

Usually, we are supposed to learn it the way men see it. Men move quickly to impose their own conceptual schemes on the experience of women, says French feminist writer Marguerite Duras. These schemes do not help women make sense of their experience; they extinguish the experience. Women must find their own words to make meaning of their experiences, and this will take time. Meanwhile, "men must renounce their theoretical rattle" (1973, p. 111).

Duras says that men have all the old words on the tips of their tongues, and so they can speak right out, while

> Women have been in darkness for centuries. They don't know themselves. Or only poorly. And when women write, they translate this darkness. Men don't translate. They begin from a theoretical platform that is already in place, already elaborated. The writing of women is really translated from the unknown, like a new way of communicating, rather than an already formed language. (1975, p. 174)

It should come as no surprise that the courses most often mentioned as powerful learning experiences were, as with Mary Lou, courses in feminist theory, which helped the women translate their ideas from the darkness of private experience into a shared public language.

Women also described as "powerful" the opportunities for experiential learning provided by their institutions. Mary Lou, studying to be a midwife, said that she and her classmates were "terrified" before giving their first pelvic exams. The teacher prepared them by taking them through a fantasy exercise in which they imagined performing the exam. "She guided us through it and told us exactly what we would be feeling for and how it would feel. We had our eyes closed and were moving our hands along with her directions, like 'Now you move four inches this way.'" Initially cynical about the value of the exercise, Mary Lou found that it worked. When she performed her first real exam she found herself" saying the same things the teacher did. 'Okay, now we move over to the spine and then we go up and feel for the sacriatic curve.' That was something that was concrete, and it was there."

Freedom, Structure, and the Tyranny of Expectation

Probably the most pervasive theme we found in our interviews with women of all sorts was one we called "inner–outer," encompassing issues women raised concerning the source and types of control and validation they had experienced in their lives. In analyzing each woman's interview, we asked ourselves, Who or what, in this woman's eyes, defines the goals, sets the pace, and evaluates the outcomes of her behavior? In terms of education, we asked, To what degree does she perceive the tasks, the timetable, and the standards as imposed by the institution, to what degree by herself, and with what consequences?

The Need for Structure

All of the women we interviewed, even the most rebellious, wanted some structure in their educational environments. Those who relied most heavily upon received knowledge favored the most clear-cut externally imposed pattern. Some of the students at the community college, for example, appreciated the college's precisely articulated curriculum. "I need to follow something structured," said one of them. "I like to know what I have to do." Overburdened by responsibilities at home and at work, she had neither the energy nor the time to map out her own structure. She was irritated when teachers and students departed from the structure of the lesson. "I'm not good in math, and I need to listen to an instructor from the beginning of the session through to the end. I don't want to hear about his kids or his wife or his problems, right? Or the students who come in late. I don't want to hear that. I just want to listen to the instructor."

Some of the women at purportedly progressive institutions complained that the absence of structure served as an excuse for self-indulgence and led to a lack of seriousness among both students and faculty. A first-year student complained that in most of her seminars, although the material was excellent, both teachers and students were unprepared. Instead of helping the students focus their attention upon the material, the teacher drew attention to himself: "My experience with free-form classes has been the professor free-forming it. He does all the talking." In general, the student said,

> This place has no expectations as an institution. None. It's almost impossible to flunk out. Anything socially that you do is probably acceptable. There are no social guidelines. Some very basic expectations should be set up so that people have an obligation to their peers and to the faculty and to the administration.

Other students at this college and at the early college also complained that their classmates' irresponsibility corroded both academic and social life; but still others believed that the very absence of rules conveyed the message, as one early college student said, that "you're respected until proven irresponsible." She and several classmates appreciated the fact that the college, instead of pointing them in a particular direction and insisting that they stay on a prescribed path, allowed them "freedom to go through changes," floundering down blind alleys and into dead ends and changing course without penalty.

The Tyranny of Expectation

In general, we heard more complaints about excessive control than about lack of structure. Students from the most prestigious and academically "demanding" institutions were most eloquent in their complaints. Some alumnae of the women's college, for instance, said that they had never learned to make choices; the college made the choices for them. Cheryl, an alumna who majored in chemistry, was happy that she had attended this college but found it a painful experience also. It was hard, but in another sense, it was easy. To "keep up" was "a never-ending struggle," but the structure was clear-cut. If you did the assignments, you made the grade. But when she graduated, Cheryl encountered a more ambiguous world. "You don't know quite what to do to succeed in your job. It's not clear-cut. You have to make sense of a lot of things that are not well organized. You have to find out what's important. You have to establish priorities. And I didn't know how to do that."

Cheryl's first job was with a physician who asked her to set up a research project. Having no idea how to do it, she looked to him for direction, but he was as ignorant as she. Ultimately, she organized and executed the project, experiencing a depth of satisfaction she never felt in completing her assigned tasks in college.

Bridget's story illustrates what can happen when "good" girls go to good colleges. Like most girls in our society, Bridget was raised to be "nice." Two years out of college, niceness remained a problem.

> I'm constantly having to fight this natural tendency I have to be "a nice person." I've been mad at myself for being too nice for a long time, and yet, at the same time, I know I can get away with murder sometimes, because I'm so nice. I'm still very afraid of not being nice, very afraid.

Nice girls fulfill other people's expectations. Bridget thought that the women's college was wrong for her because it expected too much: "It was too competitive and too demanding. I'm a very conscientious person, and I found myself always trying to do the work."

In high school Bridget consistently achieved top marks without working very hard. At college she continued to take it easy, and her grades at the end of the first semester were terrible. In the second semester she tried a new approach.

> I worked my butt off. I have never been so intense and disciplined working before. I ended up getting the second highest grade in the economics final, coming up from the bottom of the class. I memorized every goddamn picture there was in art history. I spent three hours every day going over those pictures. For three hours every day I studied French; for three hours every day I studied art; and for three hours every day I ground myself through economics.

At the end of each day she went swimming to loosen her constipated brain.

> I swam a mile every day, and it wasn't until the end of that mile that I finally felt my muscles begin to loosen up, and my head was finally clear of all this crap that I was stuffing it full of. That was probably the peak of my career at the college in terms of beating the system.

Bridget portrayed herself during the next three terms as a drudge, motivated by duty rather than desire (Weil 1951), slogging through dull courses in order to fulfill various "distribution requirements" and prepare herself for a successful career. But, although she worked constantly, she was always "behind" and she got mediocre grades.

In her third year she moved off campus and enrolled for two terms at an Ivy League college, where, she found, "You don't have to do that much work to keep up." She found time to carry a part-time job, to study dance, and to maintain a communal household. Returning to the women's college for her final semester, although continuing to live off campus, Bridget felt that everything had changed. She no longer worried about "getting caught up with things."

> I hardly did any of the reading I was supposed to do in most of my classes and still did very well. I don't know how it happened. I did loads of extra reading for the Women in American History course and loved it. I was so into the subject. I promised I would give myself the gift of no economics classes as a senior. I promised myself I'd only take classes that interested me. I did, and my grade point average just soared. It was incredible. I was so detached from the campus. It's as though I was walking through that place and felt no reality. I felt as though I was looking through a glass window at the whole thing. I was totally out of touch with that school. That was my overriding impression of the last semester, besides enjoying my work for the first time. Finally feeling as though I was making that school work for me, extracting from it what I wanted, no longer feeling pressured that I must be career-oriented and any number of the other things I felt.

Bridget and other women who attended the women's college and other equally "demanding" institutions felt in retrospect that their intellectual development was stunted rather than nourished by the incessant academic pressure. "Ever since leaving college," Bridget says, "my joy in reading and my desire to read has increased incredibly. I'm absolutely thrilled to be learning what I want to learn. It's been like a renaissance."

The teachers in these colleges do not intend, of course, to inhibit their students' intellectual development. Some are especially kind and concerned and accessible, but this only makes it worse. It is especially difficult for good girls to disobey good parents. Teachers, as well as students, yearn for an atmosphere less academic and more intellectual, but the teachers are unable to reduce the pressure and the students are unable to resist it, except on rare occasions. One undergraduate blushed as if about to confess to a crime and said,

> Last weekend—I don't know why I did it—I decided to read a book, a fun book. This is the first time since I've come here I've read a fun book from cover to cover—no worries if it was read with complete comprehension. I read it perfectly. It was mine.

Both teachers and students are proud of the institution's "high standards," and many see the standards as luring the students into performing at the top of their capacities. These standards play a major role in Perry's (1970) account of development. It is in attempting to discern the standards and to meet them that the student is propelled into independent contextual thinking. But for nice girls like Bridget, the standards act more as impediments than as goads to independent thinking, distracting their attention from the intellectual substance of the work and transforming their efforts to learn into efforts to please.

Women may benefit especially from systems in which the teaching function and the assessing function are separated. Teaching and certification of competence, at least as usually practiced, are quite different and often opposing functions; and, where certification is deemed necessary, it should be detached from teaching by, for example, using external examiners to evaluate the students' performance.

Some educators (for example, Elbow 1979) advocate competency-based programs in which the student must exhibit mastery of a set of clearly articulated objectives. Traditional professors, Elbow says, because they "contain the thing to be learned inside them . . . stand up in front of students and say, in effect, 'Get what is inside me inside you. Look at me; listen to me; be like me. I am important'" (p. 107). In competency-based programs the teacher no longer acts as the embodiment of knowledge or the container of secret criteria and so becomes less "important," less the authority, more a "coach" or an "ally" in Elbow's terms, more a "partner" in the language of Paulo Freire (1971). The teacher's attempts to "believe" the student, to confirm her as a knower, are not undermined by the inevitable "doubt" expressed in impersonal assessment.

It is not evaluation per se that subverts the aims of instruction but evaluation in the separation (impersonal, objective) mode. Evaluation in the connected mode requires that the standards of evaluation be constructed in collaboration with the students. Where impersonal standards are used, the students are turned into objects, and the connection between teacher and student is broken. The "feminine world of subjectness" is abandoned in favor of the "masculine world of objectness" (Noddings 1984, p. 196). As Noddings says, "Many of the practices embedded in the masculine curriculum masquerade as essential to the maintenance of standards," but in fact "they accomplish quite a different purpose: the systematic dehumanization of both female and male children through the loss of the feminine" (pp. 192–93). In an educational institution that placed care and understanding of persons rather than impersonal standards at its center, human development might take a different course, and women's development, in particular, might proceed with less pain.

But at traditional, hierarchically organized institutions run by powerful judges charged with enforcing the high standards of their disciplines and administering justice through blind evaluation of the students' work without respect for the students' persons, images of being watched ("God with His movie camera," as Bridget put it) flood the minds of women students. The women search the eyes that watch them for reflections of themselves. They cannot get back behind their own eyes. "Turn a pair of eyes on me," Alice Koller writes, "and instantly I begin looking into them for myself" (1983, p. 94). Ironically, Bridget managed to meet the standards only when she became able to ignore them. She produced what They wanted only when she became able to do what she wanted.

Being Bad and Breaking Out

Several women described moments of rebellion that produced turning points in their education. The moment often occurred late at night when an unwritten paper was due the next day. Saying, "Oh, the hell with it," the student wrote a "bad" paper, using her own voice, that broke the rules. Sometimes, she was punished. But sometimes she was rewarded with an "A," indicating that the teacher preferred the student's private voice to her public voice. The problem of "standards" for women, then, is a double problem. Nice women cannot help trying to produce what They want, but sometimes they are wrong about what They want.

The student's discovery that teachers respect her authentic voice is gratifying, of course, but for many of the women we interviewed, it came late. Much time had been wasted being good; and for many women the relentless effort to be good had prevented the development of a more authentic voice.

Women like Bridget, still struggling to formulate their own purposes and their own standards, although eager for formal graduate training in order to pursue professional careers, are fearful of entering another institution that may try and may succeed in shaping them according to its standards. Deborah had decided in high school that she would become a clinical psychologist, but after graduating from college she worked for three years before applying to graduate school.

> One of the reasons I took the years in between was so that I would be very certain that when I went I'd be able to do what I wanted to do there, and that I wouldn't feel I had to follow what they were setting up for me to do.

But, on the eve of entering graduate school, she did not sound so certain.

> I'm afraid of some clashes between what I want to do and what they want me to do, and I'm not sure how those will be resolved, not understanding the system. It may take me a semester to find out how you don't do what they're asking you to do.

Deborah was determined not to repeat the experience of her first year in college during her first year in graduate school. Instead of being good—doing everything she was supposed to do—she would figure out how to be bad and do what she wanted to do.

When we interviewed Gretchen in her senior year, she had already been accepted at a prestigious medical school but had decided to defer enrollment for a year.

> I have to find myself absolutely alone for a while. I don't feel as if I'm gonna *last* through another five years of school unless I sit back and find for myself or remind myself that I am an independent person and I am defined by my own standards and not by these external standards. Right now I feel sort of very wishy-washy about myself, and that's because I've been getting different sorts of signals from different people or institutions which have been evaluating me. And I've been letting these things sort of cloud over my own feelings about myself. Sort of refractional crystallization. Sort of getting rid of the dirt and the garbage and just sort of crystallizing out what is me. I want to spend a year not letting myself be evaluated by other people's standards.

Judith was eager to improve her skills as a therapist, but she dreaded a repetition of her graduate school experience.

> I worry about getting further analytic training, cause you're supposed to learn it the way that somebody else sees it. It would be different if I could find something—a program—where I was helped to see things in my own way. That would be gold.

The Need for Freedom

Some of the women we interviewed discovered "gold" in their institutions. We asked a twenty-seven-year-old mother of two what was most helpful to her about the adult program she was attending.

> The faculty not being above us, not being the boss. Making our own decisions and writing our own curriculum. And it's real hard at first, when you're not used to it. You expect, "Well, what do we do next?" It developed me a lot more in thinking, "What is it that I want?" instead of listening to what people tell me.

Another student described the program as operating according to a model like the one physician Mary Howell calls "housewifery," with the teacher respecting the student's own rhythms rather than imposing an arbitrary timetable.

When I would get stuck in the middle of my studies—as I always did—I never got any silly notes from the teacher saying, "Now, now, you must produce your stuff on time, otherwise blah blah blah." He would just say, "Well, I guess you're stuck. You'll get over it." He gave me a lot of space and a lot of guidance.

For Stella, the progressive college, seen by some as lacking in standards, was Utopia.

It was this plot of land where I could talk to these teachers or hear them lecture and read and write and really grow. It was this time for me to be away from my family, some place I felt safe, and just sort of feel out different things.

The freedom and support the college offered helped Stella feel her way toward becoming a painter and developing her "own sort of natural working habit."

I choke under pressure, but I do very well under pressures that I've created, goals that I establish, so the college is perfect for me, because there's not a lot of pressure, and there's a tremendous amount of time to work on your own.

The college exempted her from formal classes during her senior year and provided her with a studio: "I'm able to work all day and all night on my own. If I was meeting with classes all the time, and if there was a different attitude about work and grades and competition, I'd hate painting." The college put little emphasis on grades.

When something really attracts you, you can really get obsessive about it. There's a lot of freedom, trusting that people are going to want to work, that people have instincts and will find out what they want to do and how they're going to go about doing it. But with teachers that are knowledgeable and can give you guidance and support and believe in you.

A student at one of the more highly structured, high-pressure colleges gave a dramatically different account. "How much time do you really have," she asked, "to think about the material you're studying?"

I remember last semester getting *really* almost terrified when I was studying for finals, because all of a sudden I got so wrapped up in the material. I hadn't put it down for a while. And I just realized, you know, that it was really exciting to do all this stuff. But if you did that all semester long, you'd go crazy. It seems that they require a lot more automated responses from you. Just turn in this paper now. It seems that you don't have a chance to reflect. I don't try and figure out anything while I'm at school. As soon as I get away from my books, then everything gets complex; but as long as I'm looking at a book, then I tend to open it up and read it and just do what's required of me.

Some of the students at this women's college feared that without the pressure they would "go bad," as one put it, or "go dead," as another said. They would sleep late, cut classes, and stop working. Bridget and others who moved temporarily into less pressured environments did indeed go bad. They cut more classes and they spent less time on assigned work. But they did not go dead; they emerged as more active agents in their own learning. The late psychologist Jeanne Block (1984) argued that because girls in our society are raised to accommodate to existing structures, they need colleges that will help set them free. But, for the same reason, women also need strong support in moving toward freedom.

We once heard a professor from a women's college remark that the students were passive because the teachers were "too nurturant" and that a more impersonal approach might produce more independent, responsible, and active learners. Presumably she meant that in "taking care" of students we rob them of responsibility; and there may be some truth in this. But surely there are forms of taking care that make the ones we care for stronger rather than weaker. Taking care need not mean taking over. The children's health clinic, the most nurturant institution in our sample, empowers its clients by fostering their expertise. Remember the client who said, "I feel like they could hire me. That's how much knowledge they've given me." And, indeed, it is the clinic's policy to make use of its clients' wisdom and even on occasion to invite them to join the staff.

The more traditional, formal educational institutions we sampled operated more in terms of bureaucracy than housewifery. Although teachers and staff in these colleges paid close personal attention to individual students, the system itself was relatively impersonal. All students were expected to perform certain tasks and deliver certain products at specified uniform dates to be evaluated according to objective criteria. Their work was compared not with their own past work but with other students' work. Students had duties and obligations; they had little choice and less responsibility than is required in the institutions that allow or insist that students participate in these decisions. At the other end of the continuum, institutions that do none of the defining clearly abdicate their own responsibility for helping students formulate their own agendas for learning; they rob women students of the support most of them need in order to break free.

References

Bowles, G., & Duelli-Klein, R. (1983). *Theories of women's studies.* London: Routledge & Kegan Paul.

Bruner, J. S. (1963). *The process of education.* Cambridge, MA: Harvard University Press.

Cole, M., Gay, J., Glick, J., & Sharp, D. (1971). *The cultural context of learning and thinking.* New York: Basic Books.

Crandall, V. C. (1969). Sex differences in expectancy of intellectual and academic reinforcement. In C. T. Smith (Ed.), *Achievement-related motives in children* (pp. 11–46). New York: Russell Sage.

Duras, M. (1973). Smothered creativity. Reprinted in E. Marks & I. de Courtivron (Eds.), *New French feminisms* (pp. 174–176). New York: Schocken Books.

Duras, M. (1975). Interview by Susan Husserl-Kapit. *Signs: Journal of Women in Culture and Society, 1*(2), 423–434.

Elbow, P. (1979). Trying to teach while thinking about the end. In G. Grant, P. Elbow, T. Ewens, Z. Gamson, W. Kohli, V. Olesen, & D. Riesman, *On competence* (pp. 95–137). San Francisco: Jossey-Bass.

Freire, P. (1971). *Pedagogy of the oppressed.* New York: Seaview.

Harding, S., & Hintikka, M. B. (Eds.). (1983). *Discovering reality: Feminist perpectives on epistemology, metaphysics, methodology, and philosophy of science.* Dordrecht, Holland: Reidel.

Jacobus, M. (Ed.). (1979). *Women writing and writing about women.* New York: Harper & Row.

Keller, E. F. (1983). *A feeling for the organism: The life and work of Barbara McClintock.* New York: W. H. Freeman.

Koller, A. (1983). *An unknown woman.* New York: Bantam.

Martin, J. R. (1985). *Reclaiming a conversation: The ideal of the educated woman.* New Haven, CT: Yale University Press.

McMillan, C. (1982). *Women, reason, and nature*. Princeton, NJ: Princeton University Press.

Nicholson, L. (1980). Women and schooling. *Educational Theory, 30,* 225–233.

Noddings, N. (1984). *Caring*. Berkeley, CA: University of California Press.

Palmieri, P. (1979). Paths and pitfalls: Illuminating women's educational history. [Review of *Collegiate women: Domesticity and career in turn of the century America*]. *Harvard Educational Review, 79,* 534–541.

Perry, W. G. (1970). *Forms of intellectual and ethical development in the college years*. New York: Holt, Rinehart & Winston.

Reinharz, S. (1984). *On becoming a social scientist*. New Brunswick, NJ: Transaction.

Rich, A. (1979). *On lies, secrets, and silence: Selected prose—1966–78*. New York: Norton.

Ruddick, S. (1980). Maternal thinking. Feminist Studies, 6, 70–96. Reprinted in A. Cafagna, R. Peterson, & C. Staudenbaur (Eds.). (1982). *Child nurturance: Volume 1, philosophy, children, and the family*. New York: Plenum Press.

Sherman, J., & Beck, E. (Eds.). (1979). *The prism of sex*. Madison, WI: University of Wisconsin Press.

Smith, D. (1974). Women's perspective as a radical critique of sociology. *Sociological Inquiry, 44,* 7–13.

Spanier, B., Bloom, A., & Boroviak, D. (1984). *Toward a balanced curriculum: A source book for initiating gender integration projects*. Cambridge, MA: Schenkman.

Stipek, D. J., & Hoffman, J. M. (1980). Children's achievement-related expectancies as a function of academic performance, histories, and sex. *Journal of Educational Psychology, 72,* 861–865.

Tarule, J. M. (1980). The process of transformation: Steps toward change. In E. Greenberg, K. M., O'Donnell, W. Berquist (Eds.). *Educating learners of all ages*. San Francisco: New Directions for Higher Educations 29, 23–36.

Weil, S. (1951). Reflections on the right use of school studies with a view to the love of God. In S. Weil, *Waiting for God* (pp. 105–116). New York: Harper Colophon Books.

Woolf, V. (1980). In A. O. Bell (Ed.), *The diaries of Virginia Woolf* (Vol. 3). New York: Harcourt Brace Jovanovich.

27

Does Everybody Count? Reflections on Reforms in School Mathematics

Nel Noddings

Philosophers and sociologists today raise significant questions about traditional episte-mology. Feminists, postmodernists, and pragmatists have all challenged the Cartesian notion of a mind separated from the world it knows; they have questioned the uni-tariness of this mind—whether it is construed as an epistemological subject or as the workings of a particular, individual mind.[1] Universality has been challenged in both ethics and epistemology. Power has been described as a force in the social world, one residing more in structures, institutions, and language than in human agents.[2] We are not so sure any longer about a "constituting subject," a Cartesian notion that reached its heights in the writings of existentialists like Jean-Paul Sartre.[3] Many philosophers now speak of a "constituted subject." But this constituted subject is not the merely re-sponding entity of behaviorist psychology. Its acts cannot be described in terms of causal chains. Rather, it is a subject largely constituted by its situation—by its tempo-rality, language, and cultural, racial, religious, and gender identities.

Despite all this commotion in philosophy, math educators have rarely asked how they themselves are constituted—why they think as they do and what influences their recommendations. With some notable exceptions,[4] math educators fall in with the dominant ideology in public policy. In this paper, I will raise some questions about current policy talk and associated recommendations for reform of school mathemat-ics. In particular, I want to question why we put such emphasis on mathematics for all students. As this question is explored, others will arise: Are there mathematical skills and concepts that everyone needs? Should the content of mathematics courses vary with the needs and interests of students? How might mathematics courses contribute more effectively to general education?

Why Do We Insist on Math for Everyone?

Does everybody count? In *Everybody Counts,* we are led to believe, first, that almost all jobs today require mathematics and, second, that the mathematical education of our citizens is vital for the maintenance and enhancement of our national economy. Are these claims true, only partly true, or wholly false?[5] The authors of *Everybody Counts* claim that mathematics is the key to opportunity at every level: individual, corporate, and national. They write, "Over 75 percent of all jobs require proficiency in simple al-

From Journal of Mathematical Behavior, Vol. 13, 1994: pp. 89–104. Reprinted by permission.

gebra and geometry, either as a prerequisite to a training program or as part of a licensure examination."[6] Notice that the writers do not claim that the jobs themselves require algebra and geometry. Clearly, most jobs do not. Access to training or licensure often requires proficiencies unnecessary for the work itself. One should not need a statistical study to be convinced that most people use virtually no algebra or geometry in their personal or work lives. Just drive or walk through the commercial area of a town or city. Consider the host of retail sellers, delivery drivers, police, mail persons, politicians, waiters, cooks, mechanics, cleaners, bartenders, social workers, English teachers, actors, journalists, childcare workers, security guards, and, yes, even physicians who rarely if ever use algebra or geometry. Indeed, if we consider retail sales, it is clear that clerks need less math today that they did several generations ago. They almost certainly need more on-the-job training than their predecessors to handle computers, electronic tags, charge cards, doubtful checks and the like, but they do not need more math. Similarly, physicians and healthcare workers depend heavily on charts and tables rather than their own solutions to various formulas. Further, many of the new jobs being created are actually low-skill and low-paid. It may look sophisticated to work at a computer terminal, but for many people it is just the contemporary equivalent of old-fashioned labor with or without the backache.

None of what I have said so far denies the basic truth of the claim in *Everybody Counts* that, in fact, applicants often must demonstrate some proficiency in algebra and geometry even if their eventual work requires neither. As educators and citizens, we could work toward establishing more realistic requirements for job access. But that sort of activity seems to most of us to be outside our domain of influence. We could and should ask, however, why we endorse the present state of things so heavily and whether there are educational alternatives to the present emphasis on math for everyone.

One admirable reason for introducing all students to algebra and geometry arises precisely because we, as educators, have so little control over the larger social world. We are powerless to insist that young people, regardless of their formal credentials, be given a chance at work and trained on the job. What we can do, we think, is to provide access to the school subjects that are used as gatekeepers. Responsible educators are keenly aware that certain groups of students have been systematically deprived of the mathematics that provides access to better paying jobs, and we want to eliminate that injustice. Thus, we set out to include all children in the mathematics once reserved for a few. We say, "All children can learn,"[7] and "Children *can* succeed in mathematics. If more is expected, more will be achieved."[8] With good will and a sense of justice, we set out to remove grievous inequalities.

But, perhaps, we should think more deeply on the problem. As we academics travel to conferences, lectures, and consulting engagements, we are served by many of the workers I mentioned earlier and a large number of others: hotel maids, airline attendants and ticket counter clerks, hairdressers, cooks, waitresses, truck drivers who transport our food, and farm workers who do the backbreaking work of harvesting it. Those jobs will not disappear if everyone studies algebra and geometry. It may be that all jobs—lower and higher—will be better distributed over racial and gender groups with equitable participation in school mathematics, but the jobs that do not require mathematics will still have to be filled. The work these people do is essential to our society, and it should be recognized as essential. No one who works conscientiously at an honest job should live in poverty, and yet many of these people do. These people *should count;* that is, in a moral sense, the well-being of these workers should matter to all of us.

In today's schools, we often add insult to injury. We suggest that students can escape the sort of labor their parents do by studying mathematics and, to a degree, this is true. It is true if not too many people take us up on it and succeed at it. The social problem remains; over 14 percent of our population now live in poverty, and that figure will in all likelihood grow as companies downsize and employ more part-time and temporary workers. The solution to poverty cannot be found in teaching everyone algebra and geometry. The solution lies more obviously in moral education than mathematical education, and I'll say more about this in a bit.

Everybody Counts, despite its generous spirit, is a seriously misleading document. The authors write, "Unless corrected, innumeracy and illiteracy will drive America apart."[9] They add, "Inadequate preparation in mathematics imposes a special economic hardship on minorities."[10] Educators should reflect deeply on such claims. The truth might well be almost the opposite of such statements. Innumeracy and illiteracy are almost certainly the products of divisions long present and maintained by practices largely outside the control of school. It is not illiteracy and innumeracy that doom people to an impoverished state; it is poverty that induces illiteracy and innumeracy. Further, as I have already pointed out, there is no morally or practically persuasive reason why lack of mathematical preparation should impose a debilitating economic hardship on minorities or on any of the individuals who contribute significant work to our society. Our culture *chooses* to pay such workers a poverty wage.

Many policy makers argue not only that mathematics is necessary for individual success but, also, that our national economy depends on a mathematically well-educated work force. Often the school system is blamed for the drop in national productivity and the loss of jobs. But, in fact, there is little or no evidence that American workers are less productive than their foreign counterparts. The relocation of manufacturing in other, usually third-world, countries is motivated by the desire for higher profits. It is true that we shamefully neglect the education of our noncollege bound students,[11] and this should change. But unless industry leaders pledge themselves to provide jobs here, there may be little incentive to increase the vocational sophistication of noncollege curricula. There are still compelling reasons to improve the education of this group along other lines, and I will discuss some of them in the next section.

If what I have said so far rings at all true, why do we educators endorse the party line so heartily? Many educators have undoubtedly accepted the prevailing arguments about the central importance of mathematics because they are concerned with equality. Others have thought through the issues in a critical manner and will offer rigorous arguments counter to the one I have presented here. But many are just caught up in the flow of events. Herbert Mehrtens has described convincingly how mathematicians in Germany were pressed by the social events leading to Nazism; self-preservation seemed to demand compromise.[12] Even before National Socialism, however, it was clear that self-interest governed much of what was decided in mathematical organizations. To maintain their productivity, mathematicians must have positions. Because most positions for mathematicians exist in universities, mathematicians must teach. Therefore, students of mathematics are required. The majority of math majors become teachers, and, so, if the supply of university and college students is to be maintained, there must be a need for pre-college teachers of mathematics and, thus, for hosts of high school students to take mathematics. Surely, the same conditions apply here and now. Many Ph.D.s in math and physics cannot find positions in which to use their highly developed skills, but there are positions in mathematics education, and the more teachers are required, the more numerous and secure those positions will be.

It is hard to accept the possibility that the arguments we are now making for more math for everyone are elaborate rationalizations, and I am not advancing such a hypothesis as a conspiracy theory. Rather, I am suggesting that we take seriously the ideas on power put forth by Foucault and others. We may indeed be constituted subjects—not wholly autonomous agents. But we can at least exercise our critical intelligence to examine the possibility and to consider what we might do if we become convinced that many current arguments for reform are largely artifacts of the organizational drive for self-preservation. If we believe something like this, or even suspect that we have been influenced a bit along such lines, we might ask ourselves what alternatives might be feasible.

Before considering what might be done differently as a result of honest reflection on our own motivation and the forces that work on us, I should say that, if I were once again teaching high school mathematics, I too would encourage students to take as much college-preparatory mathematics as they need to gain college entrance. Like other conscientious educators, I would want to do my part in enhancing the life-chances of as many students as possible. However, I would proceed with a somewhat heavy heart. What talents will go unnoticed and under-developed while I cram algebra and geometry into unwilling minds? What attitudes will my students develop toward work? What sense will they make of their world as a result of my teaching? Rejecting the role of Don Quixote, I would teach algebra and geometry, but I would also consider different forms of mathematics for different students, and I would add topics in the sociology and psychology of mathematics for all students.

Is There Something About Mathematics that Everyone Should Know?

Mathematics educators have rightly recommended that students today should learn at least some basic material on statistics, computers, and calculators in addition to the fundamental knowledge traditionally associated with elementary mathematics. They are also deeply and properly concerned with the development of pedagogical methods that will engage students and give them some sense of their own power as thinkers and problem solvers. These concerns seem reasonable.

But methods and ideas that are entirely reasonable at the elementary level may not be so at the high school level and beyond. Here, it seems to me, we are overly reluctant to face the fact that human interests vary widely and that many highly intelligent people are just not attracted to mathematics. Others, a smaller number, are fascinated by mathematics and will adopt it as a lifetime occupation and/or recreation. In between, there are those who will need mathematics for further study and those who will actually use it in eventual careers. Should all of these students be compelled to take the same courses?

In other places, I have argued that students should not be *required* to take any mathematics courses in high school.[13] By the time students reach high school age, the mathematics they study should actually be real-world; that is, they should use mathematics and learn new mathematics in the context of work they are considering or have already chosen. Vocational programs should be designed in partnership with local companies, and they should be exciting and rigorous. Colleges should demand college-preparatory mathematics only for courses of study that actually require it, and even those courses that are taught as college-preparatory should vary with the interests and aims of students.

The objection usually thrown up against such a plan is that high school students are too young to know how to choose wisely and that they may change their minds.

Some readers may even draw on personal experience and argue, "If I hadn't been forced to take algebra, I wouldn't be where I am today." It is indeed possible that young people will make choices that are unstable. They may in fact change their minds. Lots of people today change their careers even in their forties and fifties. The important thing is that, while they are working energetically on a line of study they have chosen, they will learn; if the courses are exciting and well-taught, they will learn how to learn, gain confidence in carrying out their own plans, feel a part of a significant community, and, with participation in a community, develop civic consciousness and fellow feeling. If, after a few months or years, they want to try something different, a society that talks about life-long learning should make it feasible for them to continue study and preparation for new lines of work.

But, you may protest, mathematics prepares students for so many opportunities. Does it really harm kids to force them to take a couple years of mathematics? I do not know the answer to that, but it is a question we should study seriously. I don't know what talents and interests are lost under such coercion, what levels of confidence are eroded, what nervous habits develop, what rationalizations are concocted, or what evils are visited on the next generation as a result of our benevolent insistence. Alice Miller's work is relevant in this connection.[14] Her description of "poisonous pedagogy" includes all those things we do to children for their "own good" against their own wills and interests and, then, forbid them to complain about. To be effective, poisonous pedagogy must be successful in convincing children that what their teachers and parents did was somehow good for them. Is the coerced study of mathematics poisonous in this sense? Maybe nothing really bad happens and the forced study of math is as healthful as, and no more painful than, forced immunizations or trips to the dentist. But taking mathematics is not like taking a shot or getting one's teeth repaired. "Taking" mathematics does not guarantee learning mathematics. When we force students to take mathematics, we can ensure only that they will have certain credentials to present; we cannot ensure that they have learned the mathematics required for the next level. They may or may not learn skills, concepts, and ways of thinking. As John Dewey argued so persuasively, people are far more likely to learn when they are thoroughly occupied and engaged in what they are doing and when they have participated in the construction of their own learning objectives.[15]

What many of us fear, I suspect, is that, if we allow teenagers to make significant choices, our own child may choose an "inferior" course of study. We want *our* children to go to college and get good jobs—perhaps even more important, to have high status. As fair people, then, we also want other children to have a similar opportunity. What I am arguing, of course, is that there should be no "inferior" course of study, that "tracks" should not be lower and higher but different. Every course of study offered should be enticing to those with relevant interests, and the community should grant all its students and workers the respect and dignity they earn in doing honest work.

At this point, I will insert a paragraph that would not have appeared ten years ago in a policy analysis—certainly not in a scholarly paper. I am going to answer (briefly) the question, "Who is speaking?" Postmodern thinkers, feminist epistemologists, and black feminists especially have argued strongly that this is an epistemologically relevant question.[16] Indeed, when I present my argument for differentiated courses of study in public lectures, members of the audience often ask, "And what about your children? Did *they* go to college?" The answer is that some did and some did not. One boy became a diesel mechanic and now holds a civil service job at considerably higher than average pay. He will be eligible for retirement at a very early age and plans to open a repair shop or sales agency of his own, but he may change his mind on this. Another son studied at a well known culinary academy and hopes, after a lengthy apprenticeship, to be a chef. In fact, my experience in raising a large, diverse family is as important in motivating my recommendations as my experience in mathematics teaching and philosophical analysis.

Whether my disclosure adds anything to the argument I've been trying to make depends on one's view of epistemology. The argument might well stand even if all my children went to college. (It might be, for example, that all of them really wanted to go; it might even be that all were interested in math, etc.) And the argument might hold even if I had had no children of my own. What such disclosure often accomplishes is the creation of trust. Listeners or readers feel that the speaker "has been there" and that her or his words carry the authority of lived experience.[17] But personal experience has many aspects. Our family had the knowledge, will, and means to support children in a wide variety of endeavors. We could help them select training programs that had excellent reputations. As an academic and as a citizen, that is what I am arguing for: excellent programs for all our children. Let's differentiate by interests and try to reduce differentiation by traditional status hierarchies.

To accomplish such a program, teachers would have to assume a counseling function. The psychology of learning mathematics would become part of the mathematics curriculum. Instead of using psychology *on* students to motivate and manipulate them, teachers would use psychology *with* students to help them understand their own motives, working styles, fears, hopes for the future, and how to capitalize on their strengths. With students who are considering (or are already in) strong vocational tracks, teachers could discuss options within the vocation and how an interest in mathematics might bear on those options. With students taking math simply because they must to get into college, teachers could work on test anxiety and teach students all the tricks they know about tests. We should not hesitate, with such students, to concentrate on helping them get respectable grades and high test scores. That does not mean that we should never share challenging problems with them or give them opportunities to achieve a deep understanding of certain topics. We might even joke with them occasionally and say, "Aha! I caught you. You *are* interested in math!" But, on the whole, our attitude should be one of respect for their choices, of understanding and sympathy for the trials our culture visits on them, and of steady commitment to helping them achieve their goals.

With students genuinely interested in math, we might share Poincaré's wonderful account of mathematical creation[18] and Hadamard's study of mathematical invention.[19] We might discuss intuition and elegance. With these students, too, we would work for deeper self-understanding, discuss the loneliness that sometimes accompanies extended intellectual work and the joy that emerges from successful encounters with mathematics. We would help them to understand, also, that their gifts are not "higher" than others—just wonderfully different. Nor, we would assure them, are they odd because they would rather do math than something else.

Sharing the psychology of mathematics learning with students is at least hinted at in several important approaches to mathematics today. Alan Schoenfeld, for example, wants students to adopt the mathematician's world view and learn to understand and monitor their own cognition. He wants them to attend to metacognition.[20] My suggestions are to some degree compatible with his. I would help students who are deeply interested in math to learn something about the way mathematicians look at the world. But I would not push all students to "think like a mathematician." They should learn to use math for their own purposes.

Similarly, the cognitive apprenticeship model recommended by John Seely Brown and his colleagues is not generous enough in its thinking.[21] Many of the techniques they suggest—for example, demonstrating, fading, coaching—are fine pedagogical practices, but the word apprenticeship is misleading. Apprentices lived with their masters; they learned not just skills but a whole way of life. With good masters, they acquired manners appropriate to their occupation and both excellences and moral virtues. In contrast, today's mathematics students typically spend less than an hour a day for less than a year with a given mathematics teacher, and the teacher, faced with more than one hundred students, rarely takes responsibility for the intellectual, emotional, and moral growth of particular students. Further, it is the special task of teachers, in contrast to masters, to encourage students to develop their own talents and styles directed toward their own ends—not to produce people who think and act in the mode of the master. Of course, there should be modeling, and there will be emulation, and teachers must be conscious of what they model and help students to reflect on patterns they emulate, but teachers should not suppose that the thinking and techniques they share must necessarily be adopted. Teaching—at least until graduate school and maybe even then—is properly more like the parent-child relationship than that of master-apprentice. The parenting metaphor has its risks and limits too. By using it, I do not mean to suggest a relationship of control and dependency, but, rather, one in which the parent is committed to the growth and growing autonomy of the child.

Both the Schoenfeld program and the cognitive apprenticeship model are aimed at providing something of value for all students. My argument is that mathematical thinking and activity cannot and should not be the same for all students. A third movement that attempts to improve the curriculum for all students concentrates on "real-world" problems. This program, like the others, has attractive features.[22] But a particular problem that is "real-world" in the sense that adult human beings actually grapple with it may not be "real" at all in the school setting. Some students may be interested in traffic patterns, models of finance, or actuarial calculations, but many will not be. A problem is real for actual people when they need to or want to solve it. Problems that are real enough in their original or regular settings become strange and unreal in the school setting. Conversely, school problems can be very real to students who identify themselves with the school culture. I am not arguing against problems that are real in the sense that they require formulation, gathering and sorting information, decisions with respect to both means and ends, and attention to alternative solutions. But if students are asked to spend extended periods of time on complex problems, then they ought to have some choice among topics. Slaving away at someone else's real-life problem can be as deadly as doing a set of routine exercises and a lot more difficult.

My argument so far has been that, at least by high school, we should provide different mathematics courses for students with different interests. This recommendation, I said, suggests attention to the psychology of creating and learning mathematics. But we should not use psychological strategies on our students to get them to do things they do not want to do. Rather, it requires us to do psychology (as well as mathematics) *with* them. The object is to educate persons who can make well-informed choices and take increasing responsibility for the direction of their own lives.

In addition to the psychology of mathematics, students need to learn something about the sociology and politics of math. Philip Davis writes:

> It is of vital importance to give some account of mathematics as a human institution, to arrive at an understanding of its operation and at a philosophy consonant

with our experience with it and, on this basis, to make recommendations for future mathematical education.[23]

Davis wants to take this thinking in two directions: toward a new philosophy of mathematics and into new approaches to math education. Here we are interested in the latter. What does Davis have in mind? He is concerned with both the benefits and dangers of mathematicization. Remarking on oppressive and constraining features of mathematics, he writes:

> The subconscious modalities of mathematics and of its applications must be made clear, must be taught, watched, argued. Since we are all consumers of mathematics, and since we are both beneficiaries as well as victims, all mathematicizations ought to be opened up in public forums where ideas are debated. These debates ought to begin in the secondary school.[24]

I agree. Students should know what it means socially and politically to live in a mathematicized world: how their futures are partly determined by models of testing, how their insurance rates are affected by mathematicizations of where they live—not how well they drive, how their tastes are shaped by consumer preference models. They may be amazed to learn that their desire for a particular brand of shoe or jeans is not entirely a product of either rational choice or genuine personal desire.

Some years ago, when I was serving as a public school administrator, an insurance investigator called at our office one day and asked to see the records of a boy who had recently died in an accident. At first I thought he might be trying to find out whether the boy was a reckless or irresponsible sort and thus perhaps culpable in the accident. But the truth was simpler and more horrifying. His company wanted to put a "fair price" on the boy's life. From the boy's grades and the courses he took, the company would project how much he might have earned and, therefore, what his life was worth. Students should also learn about the benefits of mathematicization—how air and automobile travel have been made more safe and comfortable, how agricultural output has been increased, and a host of other benefits.

In addition to topics in the psychology and sociology of mathematics, historical and biographical material should be made available. Students should learn that mathematicians have interests beyond mathematics. Many students have spiritual or religious interests, and they may find the theological interests of mathematicians quite fascinating: Descartes' well known proof of God's existence (can students find a flaw in it?), Pascal's criticism of Descartes and his own "wager" on God's existence, Leibniz's attempt to exonerate God from complicity in evil (his *Theodicy* and its discussion of possible worlds), Newton's belief that theology is more important than mathematics, Euler's use of a nonsense proof of God's existence to humiliate Diderot, Bertrand Russell's scathing denunciations of all religions—especially Christianity—and the exploration of contemporary mathematicians into the connections between God and the infinite.[25] Throughout all of these discussions, opportunities will arise to move in a variety of directions. Some students will want to know more about the social customs and politics of particular times, some may want to explore topics in logic and philosophy more deeply, some may engage in personal spiritual quests, and some may not be interested at all.

None of the material discussed so far on the psychology, sociology, history, and biographies of mathematics should become a tightly specified, required part of the curriculum. There is no guarantee that a given student will necessarily be more interested in these topics than in any others. But texts should include such material, and teachers should be prepared to lead discussions when the topics arouse interest. The more connections that teachers can make with other subjects and with the personal lives of their students, the more likely that each student will find something of interest.

So far I have said nothing about the conventional topics of mathematics and which ones are essential for all students to know. Beyond basic arithmetic I would hesitate to name anything as essential, but this is an area in which continued research might be very useful. How *do* people use mathematics in their jobs and everyday lives? Are their mathematical intuitions and skills increased or decreased by school knowledge? This last is not a foolish question. Nunes has shown how relatively unschooled young people can figure things out informally but become horribly confused when asked to use the standard algorithms taught in schools.[26] Similarly, I have seen many intelligent students draw the following invalid conclusion after elementary instruction in logic:

1. All fish can swim.
2. I can swim.
3. *I am a fish.*

Before instruction in logic, these students would not have announced to the world that they were fish! There is much to learn about both the harms and the benefits of our teaching.

Before concluding this section, I want to make it clear that I am *not* saying, "Math is unnecessary for most people. Throw it out!" Rather, I am urging open-minded skepticism and criticism of current recommendations for reform. We should not allow ourselves to be pushed into politically correct nonsense about uniform and universal capabilities and, from there, into well-meaning recommendations that coerce students into studies that waste their real talents and demean their genuine interests. Clearly, we are often pressed into such positions by a legitimate concern for poor and minority students, but we might respond to this concern in more healthy ways than to exercise more universal coercion. Robert Davis and Carolyn Maher have raised excellent questions concerning the problems minority children experience with school mathematics.[27] They, too, urge that we look beyond the drills, skills, and concepts of ordinary school mathematics to ask: Who has fun with mathematics and where (in school or outside?)? Do these young people envision a future for themselves? What sort? How do these students look at work? at play? How do they evaluate their own work? How do they look at errors? Do they help one another? Questions of this sort are more fundamental than those that proceed from abstract models drawn from the mathematical experience of a few and hastily proclaimed as mathematics for everyone.

However, some students *are* interested in mathematics for its own sake. These are the kids who enjoy the unfolding patterns of hard factoring problems and trigonometric identifies, do logic puzzles for fun, and appreciate the beauty of mathematical proof. Here I agree with Professor Wu (this issue) when he expresses concern about the effects of our current de-emphasis on proof and the lack of depth in some exploratory exercises. Surely some students should have mathematical experience that includes proof and depth. Students need not be separated into classes explicitly or implicitly labeled poor, fair, good, and excellent in order to provide appropriate mathematical experiences for all of them. As I said earlier, some students may need no formal mathematics in high school, although I think they should be exposed to psychological, sociological, and cultural aspects of mathematics somewhere. Many others should learn the mathematics they need in real contexts, not in formal math classes. Still others can profit from considerable formal study without great emphasis on proof or, even, deep mathematical understanding. And there are those who are passionately interested in mathematics. Instead of calling classes for these students "honors classes," we might call them "classes for the passionately interested" and allow any students to enter who are willing to devote the required time and energy.

As I read Professor Wu's papers, I fell to thinking about the difficult and powerful work some of my geometry students were able to do years ago. In a unit on altitudes, medians, and bisectors, many of them were able to complete three kinds of proofs for several of the theorems: a traditional demonstrative proof, one using analytic geometry, and one using vectors. The purpose of working in such depth was to help students appreciate freedom and choice in mathematics. Placement of the coordinate grid could make the solution easy or difficult, clumsy or elegant. Similarly, the notation used for a vector proof could facilitate or impede progress toward a proof. Further, even when students could not complete a proof using a particular method, they often said, "Thank goodness there's another way." It seems a shame to deprive interested students of such encounters just because the majority of students neither want or need them.

I will express one final note of skepticism on the current reform movement. Teachers all over the country are being urged to use forms of cooperative learning in mathematics classes. Some states even mandate the use of such methods. By and large, working together makes great sense. Reasonable teachers twenty and thirty years ago encouraged their students to work together. The present emphasis on a community of mathematical thought is also laudable. But there are two issues that should induce critical thinking. One is the proliferation of competing approaches to cooperative learning, each presenting more and more sophisticated and precise methods requiring considerable training. To define cooperative learning too narrowly and precisely is to risk implementation failures and the eventual loss of the entire movement. Teachers, like students, need to be encouraged to create and adapt, not just follow instructions and implement. Second, we should not get carried away with cooperative learning. Much of the hardest and most lasting mathematical learning is done in solitary concentration, and there is a certain joy, or at least satisfaction, that comes from working a problem through on one's own.

Perhaps the guiding principle is that we should care for and respect all our students and that we do this best by working with them closely enough to know what their interests are and the sorts of futures they envision. Of course, we should guide and shape those visions and interests, but we should not force them into one model, nor should we suppose that a mathematics program, however good it may be for some, can meet the purposes of all.

A Postscript on Teacher Education

Every curriculum project or framework engenders teaching training programs, and the failure of such projects is often blamed on faulty implementation. Teachers, for whatever reasons, just cannot or will not do things according to the new prescriptions. What chance has any reform if teachers are incompetent or, at least, recalcitrant?

Surely, if high school math curricula are to include psychological, historical, political, and sociological explorations, teachers will need a different kind of preparation from the one they receive now. They will need mathematical preparation especially designed for teachers.

On this topic, too, we have to exercise some postmodern skepticism. Why, for example, do so many of us buy into current recommendations for professionalization? Why do many of us insist that preparation for teaching should be conducted at the graduate level?[28] What we would like, of course, is for teaching to be a "real" profession, one like law and medicine. But it is obvious that most would-be teachers are not going to invest in three or four years of graduate school to enter a "profession" in which they have little autonomy, poor pay, and low status. Not so obvious is the possibility that medicine and law are not the examples we should emulate. Neither rates very high today in public credibility. A careful analysis of the contemporary movement toward professionalization culminates in the unsettling possibility that it is only about status, that it has little if anything to do with the actual improvement of teaching.[29]

If we were to take seriously the ideas I have sketched here, we might think of designing programs for teachers that more nearly resemble those of engineers instead of physicians and lawyers. College students would select education and their teaching major in their sophomore year. A math major would then study mathematics from the perspective outlined above. All or nearly all of the courses would treat psychological, historical, biographical, sociological, theological, and political aspects of mathematics. There would be references to music, art, and architecture, to war, insurance, taxes, and medical care. Would there be time for "real" mathematics, if all this must be done? Of course there would, but it would be real mathematics for teaching. Those preparing to teach need to know the high school mathematics curriculum very well, but they do not need the standard courses taken by those planning to do graduate mathematics, theoretical science, actuarial work, or engineering. They need broad and rigorous courses *designed for teachers.*

The present emphasis on subject matter majors for all teachers (even elementary school teachers) is, on one level, a highly conservative recommendation. It assumes that the problems of teaching boil down to status and that, if we can show that our people are education in exactly the same way as those who enter more prestigious fields, we will at one and the same time improve the status of teachers and gain respect for our own professional programs. After all, graduates would enter these programs from the same undergraduate base as other prospective professionals and, presumably, their choice would be a real choice, not one for "something easy." This thinking, as I said, is conservative because it bolsters a system that has little to commend it. Undergraduate liberal education needs massive transformation, not acceptance and emphasis.

On another level, educators' recommendations that all teaching candidates present a standard undergraduate major is somewhat insulting. It demeans what could be a proud and distinctly knowledgeable profession. If teachers had the sort of preparation we've been discussing here, there would be no question whether teachers know something that others do not know, and we would not have to discuss teacher knowledge merely in terms of classroom management, modes of evaluation, and alternative methods of presenting a topic. None of these is unimportant, but the full knowledge of mathematics as a social enterprise is more important, and that cannot be achieved in a single intensive year—especially not when that year follows four impoverished undergraduate years.

Now, of course, the objection we encountered earlier to differentiated high school programs arises in full force. Suppose young people, forced to choose teaching early in their college careers, change their minds? Won't all that preparation be wasted? The answer has to be two-fold: First, even if they change their minds, the education they will have undergone will be a fine one, and they will have had the wonderful experience of working on material of vital interest—material central to the interests they had at the time of choice. Second, we should *not* use the fact that people change their minds to excuse our failure to prepare adequately those who do not change their minds. Surely, it is better to be thoroughly prepared for a field one plans to enter (even if one's mind changes) than to be ill-prepared in the name of a nebulous "general" preparation. The traditional response to this line of thinking is that a broadly defined general ("liberal") education can prepare a wide variety of students for a multitude of varying occupations or further studies. I think it is time to question this assumption.

Could a program of the sort I envision be established in our colleges and universities? Asked this question, we come full circle to the concerns with which we started. Why do we make the recommendations we hear ourselves utter? Why do we not stand back and criticize our own enterprise? Who would teach the courses I have suggested? Why would university mathematics teachers resist such courses? Why have university teachers generally resisted designing courses for teachers, referring to them as "watered-down" math courses?

Turning the postmodern critical eye on myself and my own recommendations, I have to admit that my views, like all others, spring from a set of situations and conditions: from parenting that saw some of my children thrive and more of them suffer under irrelevant school experience, from a fairly good theoretical mathematical training, from academic experience that emphasized philosophy, from teaching experience that allowed me time and again to teach the same students for several years, from a habit of omnivorous reading, from an unfulfilled and yet oddly enriching fascination with religion, from sources I have not even identified. But the recommendations and arguments, whatever their source, now take their place beside other recommendations and arguments. If they ring true for others—students, teachers, parents, policymakers—then the voice of dissent from the current reform movement will grow. At least, perhaps, more of us will ask deeper and harder questions about what we are doing and why.

Notes

1. See, for example, Richard Bernstein, *The New Constellation* (Cambridge: MIT Press, 1992); Louise M. Antony and Charlotte Witt, Eds., *A Mind of One's Own: Feminist Essays on Reason and Objectivity* (Boulder, CO: Westview Press, 1993).

2. Michel Foucault is the prime-mover on the subject of power. See David Hoy, Ed., *Foucault: A Critical Reader* (Oxford: Basil Blackwell, 1986); also Michel Foucault, *Discipline and Punish: The Birth of the Prison*: trans. Alan Sheridan (New York: Vintage, 1979).

3. Jean-Paul Sartre, *Essays in Existentialism,* ed. Wade Baskin (Secaucus, NJ: Citadel Press, 1977).

4. For some essays that take the new epistemologies seriously, see Sal Restivo, Jean Paul Van Bendegem, and Roland Fischer, Eds., *Math Worlds* (Albany: State University of New York Press, 1993); Paul Ernest, too, at least raises the question whether the traditional cognizing subject should be accepted as unproblematic. See Ernest, "Constructivism, The Psychology of Learning and the Nature of Mathematics: Some Critical Issues," *Science and Education,* 1993, 2(1): 87–93.

5. See National Research Council, *Everybody Counts: A Report to the Nation on the Future of Mathematics Education* (Washington, D.C.: National Academy Press, 1989).

6. *Ibid.*, p. 4.

7. For criticisms of this slogan, see Nel Noddings, "Excellence as a Guide to Educational Conversation," in *Philosophy of Education* 1992, ed. Henry Alexander (Urbana, IL: Philosophy of Education Society, 1992), pp. 5–16; also *Teachers College Record,* 1993 94(4): 730–743.

8. *Everybody Counts,* p. 2.

9. *Ibid.*, p. 14.

10. *Ibid.*, p. 21.

11. William Brock, former secretary of labor, pointed out forcefully how shamefully we neglect our noncollege bound in an interview, July 23, 1990, with *Time,* pp. 12, 14.

12. See Herbert Mehrtens, "The Social System of Mathematics and National Socialism: A Survey," in *Math Worlds,* ed. Sal Restivo, Jean Paul Van Bendegem, and Roland Fischer (Albany: SUNY, 1993), pp. 219–246.

13. See Nel Noddings, *The Challenge to Care in Schools* (New York: Teachers College Press, 1992).

14. For an analysis and documentation of the unhappy results of coercion and rigidity in parenting, see Alice Miller, *For Your Own Good,* trans. Hildegarde and Hunter Hannun (New York: Farrar,Strauss,Giroux, 1983).

15. See John Dewey, *Experience and Education* (New York: Collier Books, 1963; original published 1938).

16. See the discussion in Patricia Hill Collins, "The Social Construction of Black Feminist Thought," SIGNS, 1989, 14(4): 745–773; see also Collins, *Black Feminist Thought: Knowledge, Consciousness, and the Politics of Empowerment* (Boston: Unwin Hyman, 1990).

17. See *ibid.*

18. Henri Poincaré, "Mathematical Creation," in *The World of Mathematics,* ed. James R. Newman (New York: Simon & Schuster, 1956), pp. 2041–2050.

19. Jacques Hadamard, *The Psychology of Invention in the Mathematical Field* (New York: Dover, 1954).

20. See Alan Schoenfeld, "Learning to Think Mathematically: Problem Solving, Metacognition, and Sense making in Mathematics," in *Handbook of Research on Mathematics Teaching and Learning,* ed. Douglas A. Grouws (New York: Macmillan, 1992), pp. 334–370.

21. See John S. Brown, A. Collins, & P. Duguid, "Situated Cognition and the Culture of Learning," *Educational Researcher,* 1989, 18(1): 32–42.

22. See the essays in Robert B. Davis and Carolyn A. Maher, Eds., *Schools, Mathematics, and the World of Reality* (Boston: Allyn and Bacon, 1993).

23. Philip J. Davis, "Applied Mathematics as Social Contract," in *Math Worlds,* p. 182.

24. *Ibid.*, p. 189.

25. See Nel Noddings, *Educating for Intelligent Belief or Unbelief* (New York: Teachers College Press, 1993).

26. Terezinha Nunes, "Learning Mathematics: Perspectives from Everyday Life," in *School, Mathematics, and Reality,* pp. 61–78; see, also, Geoffrey B. Saxe, "Candy Selling and Math Learning," *Educational Researcher,* 1988, 17(6): 14–21.

27. Robert B. Davis and Carolyn A. Maher, "What are the Issues?" in *Schools, Mathematics, and Reality,* pp. 9–34.

28. See Holmes Group, *Tomorrow's Teachers* (East Lansing: Holmes Group, 1986).

29. See Nel Noddings, "Professionalization and Mathematics Teaching," in *Handbook of Research on Mathematics Teaching and Learning,* pp. 197–208.

28

Who Decides What Schools Teach?

Elliot W. Eisner

It irks those of us who have devoted our professional lives to the study of curriculum to find that, when efforts are made to improve the schools, we are the least likely to be consulted. Why doesn't the public appreciate our expertise? Why aren't we pursued by the national commissions that shape education policy, by state boards of education, by foundations eager to make U.S. schools "competitive" with those in other nations? Why are we left on the sidelines, commenting on the recommendations others make, rather than making recommendations ourselves?

In some ways the answers to the foregoing questions are not particularly subtle or complex, and I have no intention of making them so. In the first place, curriculum scholars—by which I mean those educationists whose specialty is the *broad aims and content* of schooling (as contrasted with subject-matter specialists in math, fine arts, science, and other such fields)—have not had much appetite for addressing the content of school programs. When they have had something to say, it has tended to be an attack on the way capitalism exploits students and teachers, or it has been addressed to those who already occupy the choir: namely, other educationists rather than the American public. Those Marxist and Neo-Marxist critics who have lambasted American schools can cite chapter and verse concerning what they think is wrong with our schools. But they have comparatively little to say about what is right with them or about how to go about making them better. They are adept at pulling weeds, but rather inept at planting flowers.

For those of a more centrist bent, the overall mission of schools—and of what should be taught in them—has been largely absent from the intellectual agenda. The symposium from which the articles in this special section of the *Kappan* have been adapted was put together in desperation by an astute program chair who recognized that curriculum scholars in the American Educational Research Association were addressing everything except the most central of educational questions: What should be taught in schools? The papers delivered at that symposium and now published in the *Kappan* were created because of her initiative, not that of the writers.

One might reasonably ask, Why this neglect? How is it that broad, central questions pertaining to the aims and content of schooling should be marginalized in discourse on the curriculum? One reason is that such questions are not simply broad, they are unabashedly normative in character. In an age when discourse analysis, hermeneutics, feminism, and Foucault bombard us from one direction and a view of specialized scientific inquiry that regards only value-neutral description as cognitively

From *Phi Delta Kappan*, Vol. 71, March 1990: pp. 523–526. Reprinted by permission.

respectable assails us from the other, the appetite for broad, "messy," normative questions that hark back to Herbert Spencer's "What knowledge is of most worth?" seems a touch too romantic. Intellectual respectability leads us in other directions. The result is that in academic circles we find a preponderance of papers that offer interpretations of interpretations or present highly specialized studies of individual disciplines that neglect central issues entirely. Both approaches avoid the broader question of what is worth learning anyway.

Furthermore, many curriculum scholars have, in this day of research on teaching, shifted their focus from curriculum to matters of teaching and teacher education. Both are no doubt important areas of research, but they cannot replace attention to curricular matters. No matter how well something is taught, if it is not worth teaching, it's not worth teaching well.

Thus within the academy there is (1) a neglect of the broad aims and overall content of school programs, because of the growing interest in social criticism writ large and because of the difficulty of doing scientifically respectable work on issues that are scientifically intractable, and (2) a growing interest in teaching and teacher education that has shifted attention away from what should be taught. We appear to want better messengers more than better messages.

There are some exceptions to the picture I have just painted. For example, John Goodlad, a curriculum scholar par excellence, has not been quiet about what schools should teach. In *A Place Called School*, Goodlad not only identifies the strengths and weaknesses of schooling, but also identifies and justifies what should be taught there.[1] Similarly, within the academy, Theodore Sizer has offered Americans a view of curricula and a conception of the proper mission of schools that is built on a "less is more" principle.[2] Sizer argues that the compromises that teachers make in order to survive could be ameliorated if schools attempted less but did it better.

From outside the academy, Ernest Boyer's *High School* provides an articulate conception of what is worth students' attention and what schools would be well-advised to address.[3] And there is Mortimer Adler who, in his eighties, has much to say about curriculum and the forms of teaching that really count.[4] It is interesting to note that Goodlad, Sizer, and Adler have not only written books that are widely read and say something about what should be taught in schools, but they have also created organizations to build the kinds of schools they envision.

As noteworthy as these efforts to improve schooling in America have been, they are, alas, but minor themes within the larger score that is American education; more factors are at work to stabilize schools than to change them. What confers such stability on schools? Why do they appear so intractable? What will be necessary to change them? And what role, if any, can those who have studied schooling and curriculum best play in reforming the schools? It is to these questions that I now turn.

Stability and Change in Schools

When I was a student at John Marshall High School in Chicago some 40 years ago, I was enrolled in a curriculum that consisted of four years of English, two years of math, three years of social studies, two years of science, two years of foreign language (Spanish), one year of music, four years of physical education, and four years of art.

The school day was divided into nine 45-minute periods. We had about five minutes to move from one class to another. There were between 30 and 35 students in each of my classes, except in choral music and in gym, in which there were about 75. The school year lasted 40 weeks, beginning after Labor Day and ending in mid-

June. Teachers usually sat at a desk situated in the front of the room, while we sat at desks that were screwed to the floor and arranged in rows. We were graded four times each semester, largely on the basis of our performance on teacher-made tests and on homework assignments.

Aside from the fixed seating, I submit that the 4,000-student high school I attended 40 years ago is not fundamentally different, structurally and organizationally, from the high schools operating today. Furthermore, I believe that the school I attended is much like the ones that most *Kappan* readers attended, at least those who attended urban schools.

In the past decade or so, much of the literature on schooling has emphasized the influence of school structure on what students learn in school.[5] The content of a student's experience is shaped not only by the explicit curriculum, but by the kind of place any particular school is. And that is influenced by the way the school is organized, by the way teachers' roles are defined, by the way students are rewarded, and by the priorities that the school sets. From a structural perspective, American schools, particularly secondary schools, have been extremely stable.

Another source of stability derives from the content of the curriculum. In broad terms, the content areas that are emphasized in schools have been extremely stable: English, social studies, math, science, foreign language, art, music, and physical education. Today computer literacy has replaced typing, but where is anthropology or law or child development or political science or feminist studies? I am well aware that each of these subjects is taught in some schools somewhere. But these subjects are not among the mainstream subjects that have been staples in American schools for more than six decades. Why?

Part of the reason is tradition. We do what we know how to do. Furthermore, our professional associations of subject-matter specialists also stabilize the curriculum. When the American Anthropological Association developed an anthropology curriculum for American secondary schools in the 1960s, it had to disguise it as a social studies course rather than as a course in anthropology. We protect our turf.

Another stabilizing factor is our textbooks. They are designed to take no risks, and they strive to alienate no one. They are usually models of the dull, the routine, and the intellectually feckless. Typically, they are dense collections of facts that read much like the Los Angeles telephone book: a great many players, but not much plot. The recent efforts in California to create a framework for history and social science that *does* look interesting may motivate publishers to be a bit more courageous. Generally speaking, however, since textbooks define the content and shape the form in which students encounter that content, their conservative character serves to resist change.

Teachers with limited time for planning and little intellectual contact with their professional colleagues are unlikely to redefine curriculum content radically. In any case, the changes teachers make are almost always within the confines of the courses they teach, and these courses operate within the constraints of the traditional school. The 50-minute hour is as much a sacred cow in the school as it is on the psychiatrist's couch. In a conservative educational climate, such as we have today, the difficulty of substantially altering curriculum content is even greater.

Yet another stabilizing agent is standardized testing, which neither teachers nor school administrators can afford to ignore. As long as teachers are held accountable by tests other than the ones they design, testing programs are likely to foster conservative educational practices. Standardized tests are intended to measure the achievement of large groups of students for whom there are common expectations. Deviation from the content to be covered constitutes a political and professional hazard for teachers. Indeed, if the virtue of test scores is their ability to predict future grades or future test scores, a conservative function is built into the test: stability, not variability, of conditions is likely to increase the predictive validity of the tests.

But educational innovation is predicated on change—not only in the *form* of educational method used, but also in the *content* and *goals* of education. Innovation is also predicated, I believe, on the desire to cultivate productive idiosyncrasy among students. While some common educational fare is reasonable and appropriate for all students, standardized tests that make invisible the unique and productively idiosyncratic in students perform a conservative function in school programs. *A Dictionary of Cultural Literacy* is a testament to such a conservative function.[6]

Moreover, such conservatism in education is attractive, particularly when schools are receiving bad press. The past always seems to exude a rosy glow, and Americans seem to require an absence of ambiguity. Thus it is reassuring to have a cultural dictionary that identifies, once and for all, "what every American should know." This need for stability—more than the educationally trivial but publicly visible drop in scores on the Scholastic Aptitude Test (SAT)—is what Americans should really be concerned about. Why do we need such security? Why do we require a blueprint to follow on matters that beg for interpretation, for consideration of context, for flexibility, and most of all for judgment? If American educators have something to worry about, it is the national fear of exercising judgment, coupled with our political apathy, that must rank highest.

Methods of evaluation that are operationalized through standardized tests are given even more significance in the American university than in the public schools. With a few exceptions, American universities are not notable for adopting an adventurous—or even liberal—attitude toward defining admissions criteria. Universities protect tradition. They take SAT scores more seriously than they are willing to admit, and many now consider enrollment in Advanced Placement courses as admissions criteria. What were once "options" for students have become prescriptions for university admission. Not to have such courses on your transcript is tantamount to an admission of intellectual sloth, at least for those seeking entrance to our most prestigious universities.

Such expectations exert a chilling effect on innovative course development and on students' enrollment patterns. When students have the opportunity to take really innovative courses during that blue-sky period in high school known as the eighth semester, what are academically oriented students doing? They are taking courses in high school that they will have available to them in college six months later. Is faster always better?

Such practices and norms are essentially conservative. Collectively, tradition, textbooks, and evaluation systems work to stabilize the curricular status quo. As a result, when calls for change are made, they almost always focus on the least significant aspects of schooling: more days in school, higher standards, more years of math and science, more of the same.

Despite these stabilizing factors, what effects might curriculum scholars have if we reclaimed our voice in the public conversation about the schools? What would we have to say about what should be taught in schools? What if we were given a platform from which to address the public? The results, I think, would be as follows.

It would quickly become clear that there is a profound lack of consensus about what schools should teach among those whose line of work is curriculum. The Neo-Marxists would continue to complain. The feminists would want attention paid to gender issues in schools. Curriculum analysts would continue to analyze, to avoid commitment, and to advocate the need for more data and more deliberation. Curricular conservatives would advance (or is it retreat?) to a reemphasis on the disciplines. The developmentally oriented among us would begin with the needs of the individual child as a foundation for what should be taught in schools. Those still interested in the power of process would claim that what is taught is less important than how it is taught. Cognitive skills, they would argue, can be developed by repairing a Mazda as well as by studying *Macbeth*. The re-conceptualists would continue to remind us that it is personal experience that really counts and that other starting points for curriculum are essentially coercive or irrelevant. In short, we would have not a symphony, but a cacophony.

Would this be bad? I think not. What *is* bad is a false sense of certainty, and that has characterized too many of the recent recommendations for education reform. President Bush is going to improve American education the old-fashioned way: he's going to reward good schools with more money. Chrysler Corporation is going to improve American schools by frightening the American public with a Japanese boogieman. William Bennett's approach was to create a James Madison High School curriculum that would be good medicine for everyone.

The debate could use more voices and deeper, more penetrating analyses of what schools should teach and the kinds of places schools should be. America desperately needs serious discussion of the condition of our schools and of the content and form of school programs. If curriculum scholars, having once reclaimed their voices, could significantly deepen the dialogue by exploring the options, we would have made an extremely important contribution to the culture.

Does anybody hear any voices?

Notes

1. John I. Goodlad, *A Place Called School* (New York: McGraw-Hill, 1984).
2. Theodore R. Sizer, *Horace's Compromise* (Boston: Houghton Mifflin, 1984).
3. Ernest Boyer, *High School* (New York: Harper & Row, 1983).
4. Mortimer J. Adler, *The Paideia Proposal* (New York: Macmillan, 1982).
5. Robert Dreeben, *On What Is Learned in School* (Reading, Mass.: Addison-Wesley, 1968).
6. E. D. Hirsch, Jr., *A Dictionary of Cultural Literacy* (Boston: Houghton Mifflin, 1988).

29

Is There a Curriculum Voice to Reclaim?

MICHAEL W. APPLE

Herbert Spencer was not wrong when he reminded educators that one of the fundamental questions we should ask about schooling is, "What knowledge is of most worth?" The question is a deceptively simple one, however, since the conflicts over what should be taught have been sharp and deep. The issue is not only an educational one, but also an inherently ideological and political one. Whether we recognize it or not, curriculum and more general educational issues in the U.S. have always been caught up in the history of class, race, gender, and religious relations.[1]

A better way of phrasing the question—a way that highlights the profoundly political nature of educational debate—is, "*Whose* knowledge is of most worth?"[2] That this question is not simply academic is strikingly clear from the fact that calls for censorship and controversies over the values that the schools teach (or don't teach) have made the curriculum a political football in school districts throughout the country.

The public debate on education and on all social issues has shifted profoundly to the right in the past decade. The effects of this shift can be seen in a number of trends now gaining momentum nationally: proposals for voucher plans and tax credits to make school systems more like the thoroughly idealized free market economy; the movement in state legislatures and state departments of education to "raise standards" and to mandate teacher and student "competencies," thereby increasing the centralization of control of teaching and curricula; the often-effective assault on the school curriculum for its supposed biases against the family and free enterprise, for its "secular humanism," for its lack of patriotism, and for its failure to teach the content, values, and character traits that have made the "western tradition" what it is; and the consistent pressure to make the needs of business and industry the primary concerns of the education system.[3]

The rightist and neoconservative movements have entered education as the social democratic goal of expanding equality of opportunity has lost much of its political potency and appeal. The prevailing concerns today—panic over falling standards and rising rates of illiteracy, the fear of violence in the schools, and the perceived destruction of family and religious values—have allowed culturally and economically dominant groups to move the arguments about education into their own arena by emphasizing standardization, productivity, and a romanticized past when all children

From *Phi Delta Kappan*, Vol. 71, March 1990: pp. 526–530. Reprinted by permission.

sat still with their hands folded and learned a common curriculum. Parents are justifiably concerned about their children's future in an economy that is increasingly conditioned by lower wages, the threat of unemployment, and cultural and economic insecurity—and the neoconservative and rightist positions address these fears.[4]

One of the conservative movement's major successes has been to marginalize a number of voices in education. The voices of the economically disadvantaged, of many women, of people of color, and of many other groups are hard to hear over the din of the attacks on schools for inefficiency, lack of connection to the economy, and failure to teach "real knowledge." One group of people who have supposedly been silenced are the curriculum scholars. For them, the "wrong people" have captured the debate about what should be taught in schools. Individuals such as E. D. Hirsch, Jr.—whose *Cultural Literacy* owed much of its popularity to the propensity of many educators and others to play an intellectual version of Trivial Pursuit—now provide answers to Spencer's question.[5]

I agree in part with the judgment that the "wrong people" may have too much power in the debate about the curriculum, but the situation is considerably more complicated than this scenario of "good" versus "bad" would have it. And the problem certainly will not be solved by simply giving back to curriculum scholars the determining voice they once supposedly had.

What some people define as a crisis of loss of voice, others of course see as progress. In the view of former Secretary of Education William Bennett, for example, we are not involved in a deepening crisis but are emerging from one in which "we neglected and denied much of the best in American education." In the process "we simply stopped doing the right things [and] allowed an assault on intellectual and moral standards." This assault has supposedly led schools to fall away from "the principles of our tradition."[6] Moreover, it has been led by liberal intellectuals, not by "the people."

In Bennett's view, "the people" have now risen up. "The 1980s gave birth to a grass-roots movement for educational reform that has generated a renewed commitment to excellence, character, and fundamentals." Because of this, we have "reason for optimism." Why?

> [Because] the national debate on education is now focused on truly important matters: mastering the basics—math, history, science, and English; insisting on high standards and expectations; ensuring discipline in the classroom; conveying a grasp of our moral and political principles; and nurturing the character of our young.[7]

Part of the solution for Bennett and others is to take authority *away* from many of those professional educators who have supposedly had it. This attitude bespeaks a profound mistrust of teachers, administrators, and curriculum scholars. They are decidedly not part of the solution; they are part of the problem.

As all these developments have been taking place, most people in the field of curriculum have largely stood by, watching from the sidelines as if this were a fascinating game that had to do with politics but not with education. Others bemoaned their fate but fled to the relative calm of increasingly technical and procedural matters, thereby confirming the artificial separation between "how to" curriculum questions and those involving the real relations of culture and power in the world.

This situation is not a new phenomenon by any means. Curriculum workers have witnessed a slow but very significant change in the way their work has been defined over the past decades. Professional discourse about the curriculum has shifted from a focus on *what* we should teach to a focus on *how* the curriculum should be organized, built, and evaluated. The difficult and—as any examination of the reality of schooling would show—contentious ethical and political questions of content, of whose knowledge is of most worth, have been pushed into the background in our attempt to define technical methods that will "solve" all our problems. For years, professional debate about the curriculum has been over procedures, not over what counts as legitimate knowledge.

Although the process did not start in the late 1950s and early 1960s, it was certainly exacerbated during those years, which saw a resurgence of the discipline-centered curriculum. Government, industry, and academe formed an alliance that attempted to shift the curriculum radically in the direction of "real knowledge," that knowledge housed in the discipline-based departments at major universities. Since most teachers and curriculum workers were perceived to be incapable of dealing with such "real knowledge," it became clear that—to be effective—this alliance had to select the knowledge and organize it in particular ways. The National Defense Education Act, the massive curriculum development efforts that produced so much teacher-proof material, and the boxes upon boxes of standardized kits that still line the walls of many schools and classrooms bear witness to these attempts.

There are few better examples of the de-skilling of a field than this. If curricula are *purchased* (and remember that 80% of the cost of most of these new curriculum materials was repaid by the federal government) and if all curricula come ready-made, largely teacher-proof, and already linked to pretests and posttests, why would teachers need the skills to deliberate about the curriculum?[8] Of what use are those increasingly isolated curriculum scholars, unattached to "real disciplines" and housed primarily in schools of education, when what counts as legitimate knowledge is already largely predetermined by its disciplinary matrix?

At this point we need to remember a simple but telling fact. Most teachers, especially at the elementary level, are *women*. By disempowering them, by using governmental intervention to put curriculum deliberation, debate, and control into the hands of academics in the disciplines, we undercut the skills of curriculum design and teaching for which women teachers had long struggled in an attempt to gain respect.[9] The issue of the relative power of teachers bears directly on the question of who has really made decisions about curriculum in the past.

Yet it was not only teachers who lost power during the period of the discipline-based curriculum movement. A good deal of the scholarly literature in curriculum at this time was devoted to the declining power of curriculum "experts" in determining what should be taught.[10] Power was seen to have shifted from those people who were closely attached to a long tradition of curriculum debate to those who—like Jerome Bruner and his coterie of discipline-based experts—may have had interesting things to say about what should be taught in schools but whose primary affiliations were to their academic disciplines, not to teachers and schools. And while many curriculum scholars raised serious objections to what they believed to be an unwise move to a subject-based and perhaps elitist curriculum, they were by and large ignored outside of the limited professional audiences for whom they wrote.

The parallels between then and now are more than a little interesting. Powerful groups and alliances in the larger society, in government, and in the academy had more to do with determining curricular debate than those individuals whose special purchase on educational reality was supposed to be expertise in curriculum.

This problem was exacerbated by the propensities of the curriculum field it-self—by the increasing dominance of procedural models of curriculum deliberation and design. The model that became, in essence, the paradigm of the field was articulated by Ralph Tyler in *Basic Principles of Curriculum and Instruction*.[11] Even with its avowed purpose of synthesizing nearly all that had gone before, it was largely a behaviorally oriented, procedural model. It was of almost no help whatsoever in determining the difficult issues of whose knowledge should be taught and *who* should decide. It focused instead on the methodological steps one should go through in selecting, organizing, and evaluating the curriculum.[12] One of the ultimate effects of Tyler's model, though perhaps not intentional, was the elimination of political and cultural conflict from the center of curriculum debate.[13] Today, in confrontations with resurgent conservative movements that have thoroughly politicized the curriculum and the entire schooling experience, the curriculum field finds that it has lost any substantive ways of justifying why *x* should be taught rather than *y*.[14]

While it may be too harsh an assessment, it seems that curriculum specialists have become increasingly irrelevant. They are often transformed into "experts for hire"—people who know the procedures for writing documents based on what other people have decided is important for students to know, who have expertise in quantitative or qualitative evaluation, in methods of goal-setting and assessment, and in techniques of writing behavioral objectives. What they are decidedly not experts in is the immensely more difficult and contentious issue of what specifically we should teach. And because of the ahistorical nature of the field and the increasingly technical and specialized quality of graduate education, the knowledge of the different traditions for dealing with that issue is dwindling. Many people are simply unequipped to deal with the issue of what a society's "collective memory" should be.[15]

This state of affairs has its democratic side, to be sure. By not centralizing curriculum decisions in the hands of a few experts, we are trying to insure that more power will reside at a local level. This is a meritorious goal. Yet, as we know, the notion of local control is often a fiction, since, like it or not, we do have a national curriculum. Today, however, that curriculum is determined not by academics and the government but by the market for *textbooks*. And this market in turn is shaped by what is seen as important in the Sun Belt states that have textbook adoption policies. Curriculum scholars have very limited influence at this level. By ignoring the actual processes that establish the most important elements of the curriculum—what I have called "the culture and commerce of the textbooks"[16]—they have little to say about the political, economic, and ideological conditions that make the curriculum look the way it does.

Instead of focusing on the social realities that underlie the curriculum and on the way in which the curriculum has once again become an arena where different groups fight for their distinct social agendas, we look back nostalgically to a time when teachers, administrators, parents, business leaders, government officials, and others all sat up and paid attention to our "words of wisdom." In many ways, this picture of the past is just as romanticized as the one the conservatives paint of a time when we all shared the same values and had perfect schools, families, and communities.

I want to focus on this mythic past a bit more since I believe it is very much a part of the problem we face. We need to be very cautious about assuming that there once was a golden age in which curriculum scholars had an immense amount of independent power over the content of the curriculum. As I have stressed here and elsewhere, controversies over the content and form of the curriculum are most often informed by larger conflicts between and within groups that have or wish to have power.[17]

If we took an honest look at the historical record, we would see that the school curriculum has always been created by the conflicts and compromises that are themselves products of wider social movements and pressures that extend well beyond the school. More often than not, curriculum people have been carried along by these movements. Rather than being leaders, they have quite often been followers. Indeed, it is difficult to find more than a few instances in the last 30 years in which scholars *specifically within the curriculum field* have had any appreciable impact on debates over the content of the curriculum.

If curriculum scholars have not been primarily responsible for shaping the curriculum, what are some of the major forces that have? As I have argued in considerable detail in *Teachers and Texts*, among the least talked about but most significant factors are the gendered nature of teaching and the dominance of the standardized textbook.

For example, it is not simply an accident that the curriculum of the elementary school has been tightly controlled and subject to continued rationalization. Women's paid work in a number of fields has historically been dealt with in the same way. Yet the fact that elementary teaching has largely been women's paid work also means that women teachers have been activists. Indeed, the prominence of the standardized textbook was the result not only of rationalizing influences imposed from above or of the lure of a lucrative market for textbook publishers, but also of collective pressure from elementary teachers to change the awful conditions in which many of them worked. Overcrowded classrooms and the difficulties of planning for multi-age groups and for teaching a variety of subjects led teachers to argue for textbooks to help them.[18] The result was a curriculum increasingly dominated by standardized—and finally, grade-specific—texts. This development meant that the authors and publishers of textbooks had a significant amount of power in determining the form and content of the curriculum.

Thus the fact that the textbook became the *major* organizing element of the curriculum had little to do with curriculum scholars but was the complicated result of social policies and attitudes regarding gender, the politics of rationalization and bureaucratization in the schools and the teachers' responses to it, and the economics of profit and loss in the field of publishing. To look for the determining impact of a few specialized curriculum scholars in this situation is to look for what never was.

Among the other "external" forces that shaped curriculum was the rise of what has been called a "technocratic" belief system—both in education and in the larger society—which seemed to assume that if something moved, it should be measured. Of great importance as well was the steady growth of federal and state intervention in the shaping of curriculum policy, which was stimulated by cold war ideologies and the pressures of international economic competition.[19] As the conservative restoration gained power during the 1980s, this intervention became even more visible.

Of course, much more could be said about the influence of state intervention or economic crises on the national reform reports, on who has the power to speak and to be listened to on educational matters, and on where the money goes. We should consider, as well, how a conservative government has masterfully used the media to control the public debate on education. On a more positive note, we should also devote attention to the story of how African-Americans, women, Hispanics, and others have brought about major shifts in curricular content and authority. And we could focus on many other areas.

Yet my point is really a simple one. Almost none of these developments can be traced to the efforts—no matter how well-intentioned—of curriculum scholars. The nostalgic gaze into a golden age is largely a misreading of the historical record. It is actually a flight from acknowledging where power often lies and an even more dangerous flight from seeing the real depth of the problem.

Oddly, however, the feeling that curriculum scholars have lost their voice in the debate over the curriculum might be the first step in the right direction. Perhaps that feeling means that curriculum scholars do recognize the objective conditions that surround not only their own lives but the lives of so many talented and committed educators. The process of determining the curriculum for the classroom and for teacher education is increasingly politicized and increasingly subject to legislative mandates, mandates from state departments of education, and so on. Test-driven curricula, hyperrationalized and bureaucratized school experiences and planning models, atomized and reductive curricula—all of these *are* realities. There *has* been a de-skilling of teachers and of curriculum workers, a separation of conception from execution as planning is removed from the local level, and a severe intensification of educators' work as more and more has to be done in less and less time.[20] Power over curricula is being centralized and taken out of the hands of front-line educators, and this process is occurring at a much faster rate than are the experiments with school-based governance models.

Yet why should all this surprise us? Tendencies toward de-skilling jobs and disempowering workers, toward the elimination of reflection and thoughtfulness from work, and toward technically oriented and amoral centralized management are unfortunately part and parcel of our society. Many millions of people in the United States have already experienced a loss of power and control in their own daily lives.[21] Why should we assume that this won't happen to people involved in curriculum and education in general? The real issue is not what is happening, but why it has taken us so long to realize that we, like most other educators, do not stand above the centralizing and disempowering impulses and the political and economic forces that affect so many other individuals in this society. Perhaps the way that people in the field of curriculum are themselves educated—to believe that education is unconnected to economic, political, and ideological conflicts and that we can solve our problems by looking only within the school—is part of the reason for our reluctance to acknowledge these problems.

What can we do about this state of affairs? It should be obvious that I am not optimistic that curriculum scholars can make their solitary voices heard above those of the conservatives and neoconservatives, the centralizers, and the bureaucrats who now hold center stage. I am not arguing that curriculum scholars are powerless puppets controlled by large-scale social forces beyond their control. But I am suggesting that we be realistic. If social, political, and economic forces and movements have played such a large role in determining the shape and content of the curriculum in the past, then individual action by curriculum scholars will not be enough. We can and must join forces with other groups that stand in need of the knowledge of curricular debates and traditions and that wish to make schools more progressive in intent and outcome.

Numerous groups throughout the country are fighting to build a curriculum that reflects the knowledge and beliefs of all of us and not just those of one political and cultural group. Among them are the teachers in the Rethinking Schools group in Milwaukee, those involved in Substance in Chicago, and those involved in Chalkdust in New York City. Community-based advocacy groups, such as the Southern Coalition for Educational Equity, which has done important work in New Orleans; Chicago Schoolwatch; Parents United for Full Public School Funding in Washington, D.C.; the Citizens Education Center in Seattle; and People United for Better Schools in Newark are engaged in defending and building on many of the gains made over the past two decades in democratizing curriculum and teaching.[22] Curriculum scholars can join with these groups, contribute something of value to them, and—perhaps just as important—learn from them. Only by forming coalitions to restore a democratic vision in education will we be able to restore the voice of curriculum scholars to the public debates over whose knowledge should be taught. If we continue to stand above the fray, perhaps we don't deserve to have our voice restored.

The Right has done a good job of showing that decisions about the curriculum, about whose knowledge is to be made "official," are *inherently* matters of political and cultural power. And unless we learn to live in the real world and to find a *collective* voice that speaks for the long progressive educational tradition that lives in so many of us, the knowledge taught our children will reflect the fact that power is not shared equally. The sidelines may be comfortable places to sit. But sitting there will give us little influence on the lives of real children and teachers.

Notes

1. See, for example, William Reese, *Power and the Promise of School Reform* (New York: Routledge & Kegan Paul, 1986).

2. For further discussion of this point, see Michael W. Apple, *Ideology and Curriculum*, 2nd ed. (New York: Routledge, 1990).

3. Michael W. Apple, *Teachers and Texts* (New York: Routledge & Kegan Paul, 1986).

4. This is treated in considerably more detail in Michael W. Apple, "Redefining Equality," *Teachers College Record*, Winter 1988, pp. 167–84.

5. For interesting criticisms of Hirsch's proposals for "cultural literacy," see Herbert M. Kliebard, "Cultural Literacy or the Curate's Egg," *Journal of Curriculum Studies*, vol. 21, 1989, pp. 61–70; and Stanley Aronowitz and Henry Giroux, "Schooling, Culture, and Literacy in an Age of Broken Dreams," *Harvard Educational Review*, May 1988, pp. 172–94.

6. William J. Bennett, *Our Children and Our Country* (New York: Simon & Schuster, 1988), pp. 9–10.

7. *Ibid.*, p. 10.

8. Michael W. Apple, *Education and Power* (New York: Routledge & Kegan Paul, 1985), Ch. 5.

9. Apple, *Teachers and Texts*, Ch. 3.

10. See, for example, some of the reflections on the previous decade of curriculum work in Elliot W. Eisner, ed., *Confronting Curriculum Reform* (Boston: Little, Brown, 1971); A. Harry Passow, ed., *Curriculum Crossroads* (New York: Teachers College Press, 1962); and Glenys Unruh and Robert Leeper, eds., *Influences in Curriculum Change* (Washington, D.C.: Association for Supervision and Curriculum Development, 1968).

11. Ralph Tyler, *Basic Principles of Curriculum and Instruction* (Chicago: University of Chicago Press, 1949).

12. Herbert M. Kliebard, "The Tyler Rationale," *School Review*, February 1970, pp. 259–72.

13. Apple, *Ideology and Curriculum*. Ch. 6.

14. Michael W. Apple, "Curriculum in the Year 2000: Tensions and Possibilities," *Phi Delta Kappan*, January 1983, pp. 321–26.

15. See Herbert M. Kliebard, *The Struggle for the American Curriculum* (New York: Routledge & Kegan Paul, 1986); and Kenneth Teitelbaum, "Contestation and Curriculum: The Efforts of American Socialists, 1900–1920," in Landon E. Beyer and Michael W. Apple, eds., *The Curriculum: Problems, Politics, and Possibilities* (Albany: State University of New York Press, 1988), pp. 32–55.

16. Apple, *Teachers and Texts*, Ch. 4; and Michael W. Apple, "Regulating the Text: The Socio/Historical Roots of State Control," *Educational Policy*, vol. 3, 1989, pp. 107–24.

17. See Apple, *Ideology and Curriculum, Education and Power,* and *Teachers and Texts*.

18. Apple, *Teachers and Texts*, Ch. 3.

19. See Apple, *Ideology and Curriculum*; and Aronowitz and Giroux, op. cit.

20. Apple, *Teachers and Texts*, Ch. 2; and idem, *Education and Power*, Ch. 5.

21. Marcus Raskin, *The Common Good* (New York: Routledge & Kegan Paul, 1986).

22. Ann Bastian et al., *Choosing Equality: The Case for Democratic Schooling* (Philadelphia: Temple University Press, 1986).

30

Navigating the Four C's: Building a Bridge over Troubled Waters

Ann Lieberman

A crucial element has been missing from our debate about curriculum. No one has discussed the *interrelationships* of what I call the four C's: the process of change, the *culture* of schools, the context of classrooms, and the *content* of the curriculum.

In the past we dealt with these four C's individually. Reform movements typically focused on curriculum change without regard for such complicating factors as the people who were to make the changes or the institutions in which they were to occur. In the Seventies, during the period of "options, alternatives, and electives," large-scale research on the effects of federal initiatives for school reform revealed for the first time the complexity of the implementation process.[1] The focus on implementation was a powerful breakthrough because it shifted the discussion of school reform to the local site and to the means by which content actually made its way into the social system of the school. This was the first time that content, culture, and change were discussed within the specific contexts of school districts throughout the country.

Content

The conservative critique pays lip service to the complexity of the changing U.S. culture (poverty, homelessness, a deteriorating urban environment, a growing multicultural population) and the stresses it is putting on the society and the schools. However, when considering how the curriculum should respond to this new set of societal problems, conservatives tend to isolate a single factor: content. Certainly we must struggle with the essential curricular questions: What knowledge is of most worth, and what should the schools teach? But considering content in isolation is not enough. (Maxine Greene has long reminded us that our multiple perspectives will yield multiple meanings even if everyone is given the same core curriculum.)

Restructuring and the Culture of the School

One way to understand how the four C's interact is to look at the movement to restructure the schools, because it is here that we face head-on such factors as differences among students, changing curriculum demands, and the engagement of teachers. It is the intent of the school restructuring movement to change the roles and rela-

From *Phi Delta Kappan*, Vol. 71, March 1990: pp. 531–533. Reprinted by permission.

tionships of principals, parents, teachers, students, and, in some cases, businesses and community agencies. Issues of structure and governance—such as school-site decision making and the granting of greater authority at the local level—are paramount in this effort, but attempts to rethink the curriculum, to humanize and personalize instruction, to integrate subject areas, and to shift the focus from "teaching" to helping students learn are all part of the movement as well.

Teacher development is a vital part of restructuring, and it is a far more complicated process than previously thought. A study of staff development in California reported that, despite a tremendous amount of money being spent, most staff development made little difference in the way teachers actually worked with students. This large-scale study revealed long-standing differences between the kinds of staff development that teachers said they needed and what was planned by others *for* them.[2]

Teacher Unions and the Culture of the School

Teacher unions have often been involved in bargaining for such professional improvements as greater participation in decision making and the adoption of programs using mentor teachers, lead teachers, and teacher leaders. Nevertheless, many teachers feel that they have been victims of the reform movements rather than participants in them. In the words of a 20-year veteran who taught at a school actively engaged in reform, "We do not fear change, but we feel emotionally ripped off." Thus it is not enough to make decisions *for* teachers, even when this is done with the best of intentions; teachers themselves must be involved in the decision-making process.

When teachers participate authentically in making decisions about school governance, the culture of the school begins to change. Teachers come to feel that they have a significant stake in decisions concerning the curriculum as well. This attitude energizes teachers' participation in the school as a whole and commits them to greater involvement in issues of curriculum and instruction. Union contracts are important, but strategies to change curriculum content and the nature of the teacher/student relationship must come from within the culture itself, often with help from sensitive outsiders.[3] Teachers must be involved as willing partners in changing their own organizational culture. When the unions are part of school restructuring efforts, they too must work to locate greater authority for decision making at the local level.

But changing the culture of a school is hardly a simple process. Indeed, changing anything in schools is difficult. Those involved in the restructuring movement have found it to be time-consuming, labor-intensive, and fraught with conflict. And these difficulties are not just matters of reallocating resources. Restructuring involves trying to change human relationships that have been the same for decades. And every school differs from every other school in so many ways that standardized formulas make no sense.

Teacher Development and the Four C's

Our understanding of teacher development has grown and changed in recent years. Today we are more aware of issues related to the professionalization of teaching— teacher leadership, increased teacher participation, changes in the career structure, shared decision making, the growth of colleagueship, and so on. As teachers take on the new roles, they participate more actively in the reshaping of schools.

This kind of experience differs significantly from what teachers have known before. As one teacher leader told me, "On the one hand, this has been one of my most exciting years because of my involvement in this kind of thinking and work—but, on the other hand, the changing student population leaves me so depressed." This combination of exhilaration and discouragement has been documented by others as well. Teachers gain newfound strength and excitement from their participation in the restructuring of roles and relationships, but they become exhausted by the struggle with curricular and instructional issues.[4] For example, it is increasingly difficult to deal with such complex issues as equity for all students when the student population is increasingly poor and at risk.

While some curricular efforts have encountered difficulties, others have succeeded in engaging and exciting teachers, sparking their participation in changing curriculum and pedagogy. When we look at these successful efforts to change the nature of student/teacher relationships, we see that they all tend to combine in some way teachers' experiential learning with learning related to the classroom culture. They rely on networking to provide the kind of support and nonjudgmental help that teachers need as they develop new norms and expectations and take the risks involved in changing their own roles in order to improve student engagement and learning.

A number of programs and curricular innovations—e.g., the process approach to teaching writing, whole-language learning, cooperative learning, and the Foxfire experience—have given us the means to break teacher isolation, to build a sense of community, to look differently at the curriculum, to model experiences for teachers, to support them as they are learning, to celebrate their successes and, in some cases, to provide them with opportunities for leadership. Whether consciously or not, these programs have linked content and pedagogy, sensitivity to the classroom context, teachers' experiential learning, and the necessity for organizational supports to initiate and maintain the process of change. In the best of these programs, a unifying philosophy and a strong set of values underlie the activities and guide the teachers' interactions with their students. These programs and practices are based not on gimmicks or strategies but on a way of thinking about teaching, learning, and professionalism. This way of thinking sees content, context, and culture as integral to teachers' involvement in new ways of using curriculum and pedagogy and to their participation in making the organizational decisions that most affect their students and themselves.

Tensions and Tradeoffs in School Restructuring

Changing pedagogy and curriculum and involving teachers in restructuring efforts are very complicated matters. These two strands of teacher development are not always clearly linked, and the process of change brings tensions and tradeoffs that we are just beginning to understand.

The form that restructuring takes depends on many factors, including who initiates the change, how the restructuring efforts are actually played out, the histories of the particular districts and schools, and the values held by the state and local governments. Decisions about the place of administrative leadership and of teacher leadership, about process and content, about whether to start with students or to start with teachers, and about whether to do something first and analyze it later or to reflect before taking action—all these issues create tensions in the process of restructuring schools. Such tensions and tradeoffs do indeed make the waters of school restructuring treacherous, but they also point out how much we need to build bridges across these troubled waters.

We know more about school change than we knew 20 years ago. We know that we have to attach content to people and institutions, and we know that we have to consider the differences in the cultures of schools. But we cannot hope to influence the restructuring movement unless some of us work more closely with the schools. This means climbing down from our proverbial ivory towers and working with schoolpeople. There are thousands of researchable problems and hundreds of ways to engage in productive work in the schools. If we see ourselves working *with* schoolpeople—not *on* them—we can indeed exert an influence. However, if we continue to distance ourselves from the schools by acting only as critics rather than as participants, we will have little influence.

I once brought a student of mine to the annual meeting of the American Educational Research Association. She dutifully took notes at the many sessions she attended. On the last day I asked her, "So, what do you think of the AERA?" She answered, "You know, if all the schools sank into the Pacific Ocean, I don't think anyone here would blink."

David Cohen has reminded us that we researchers have created a language whose primary users seem to be ourselves. We study one thing at a time, oversimplify it for research purposes, and then become wedded to our conception. Not only are we isolated from the rest of the world, but our own house needs more teamwork, more efforts at developing colleagueship, and more opportunities for cooperation. This cooperation, in turn, might lead us to work more closely with the schools—a development that might help our research, our institutions, and the schools as well. Some few institutions are already involved in such efforts.

Murray Schwartz, dean of the College Arts and Sciences at the University of Massachusetts at Amherst, describes the "boundary anxiety" that exists today in the subject areas. We need to take account of that anxiety in our own work as well. There are exciting changes going on. We need to join in and make our voices heard, but that means that we must think of ourselves as learners as well as teachers. As Seymour Sarason and his co-authors have written, "You have to know and experience in the most intimate and tangible ways the situations which your actions purport to affect."[5]

To affect the current debate about curriculum, we will need to examine our behaviors—both as individuals and as institutions—and to find ways to participate. This means, for example, that we will have to struggle with a larger view of scholarship. There are a variety of ways of knowing and a variety of means to express that knowledge. *Educational Leadership* has as much meaning to its readers as *Educational Researcher* has for us. Can't we contribute to both publications? Instead of mourning our lack of influence, we need to join coalitions with schoolpeople. We can engage in collaborative inquiry and in a collective struggle over tough issues of content, which—in context—will help us to probe the limits and possibilities of change in both schools and universities.

Mechanisms such as school/university collaborations, which help establish networks and coalitions of all kinds, should be created—not for cosmetic reasons ("everybody is doing it") but because they offer us a unique opportunity to become involved with the schools in authentic ways. Establishing professional development schools, working to professionalize teaching, or restructuring schools will force us to deal with the construction of knowledge in its organic relationship to context.

We must shift our thinking about the knowledge base of teaching and learning. It in no way denigrates the university to admit that we have much to learn from the people who work in the schools. We are hampered from doing so because we typically adopt a paternalistic attitude toward schoolpeople and because there is a lack of institutional recognition and support for those professors who are actively working in the schools. The university must change its view of scholarship so that it recognizes and rewards active participation in schools (and the research and writing that it generates) as valuable—and time-consuming—scholarly activity.

We must struggle with these issues seriously, so that the university can become the important influence in education policies and practices that it should be. We must not allow ourselves to become increasingly irrelevant to the schools when the opportunity exists to become partners with them in the difficult—but incredibly rewarding—task of reshaping education in our country. To that end, let us navigate the four C's together.

Notes

1. Milbrey McLaughlin and David Marsh, "Staff Development and School Change," in Ann Lieberman and Lynne Miller, eds., *Staff Development: New Demands, New Realities, New Perspectives* (New York: Teachers College Press, 1978).

2. Judith Warren Little et al., *Staff Development in California: Public and Personal Investments, Program Patterns, and Policy Choices* (San Francisco: Policy Analysis for California Education and Far West Laboratory for Educational Research and Development, 1987).

3. Myrna Cooper, "Whose Culture Is It Anyhow?," in Ann Lieberman, ed., *Building a Professional Culture in Schools* (New York: Teachers College Press, 1988), pp. 45–54.

4. Marilyn Cohn et al., *Teachers' Perspectives on the Problems in Their Profession: Implications for Policymakers and Practitioners* (Washington, D.C.: U.S. Department of Education, Office of Educational Research and Improvement, 1987).

5. Seymour Sarason, Kenneth S. Davidson, and Burton Blatt, *The Preparation of Teachers: An Unstudied Problem in Education*, rev. ed. (Cambridge, Mass: Brookline Books, 1986), p. xix.

Index